Let's

Ecua

& the Galápagos Islands

"Refreshingly honest."
—The Los Angeles Times on
Let's Go: Ecuador & the Galápagos Islands

"Lighthearted and sophisticated, informative and fun to read. *[Let's Go]* helps the novice traveler navigate like a knowledgeable old hand."
—Atlanta Journal-Constitution

"The guides are aimed not only at young budget travelers but at the independent traveler, a sort of streetwise cookbook for traveling alone."
—The New York Times

▦ Let's Go writers travel on your budget.

"Retains the spirit of the student-written publication it is: candid, opinionated, resourceful, amusing info for the traveler of limited means but broad curiosity." **—Mademoiselle**

"The writers seem to have experienced every rooster-packed bus and lunar-surfaced mattress about which they write." **—The New York Times**

"All the dirt, dirt cheap." **—People**

▦ Great for independent travelers.

"A world-wise traveling companion—always ready with friendly advice and helpful hints, all sprinkled with a bit of wit." **—The Philadelphia Inquirer**

"Lots of valuable information for any independent traveler."
—The Chicago Tribune

▦ Let's Go is completely revised each year.

"Unbeatable: good sight-seeing advice; up-to-date info on restaurants, hotels, and inns; a commitment to money-saving travel; and a wry style that brightens nearly every page." **—The Washington Post**

"Its yearly revision by a new crop of Harvard students makes it as valuable as ever." **—The New York Times**

▦ All the important information you need.

"Enough information to satisfy even the most demanding of budget travelers... *Let's Go* follows the creed that you don't have to toss your life's savings to the wind to travel—unless you want to."
—The Salt Lake Tribune

"Value-packed, unbeatable, accurate, and comprehensive."
—The Los Angeles Times

Let's Go Publications

Let's Go: Alaska & the Pacific Northwest 1998
Let's Go: Australia 1998 **New title!**
Let's Go: Austria & Switzerland 1998
Let's Go: Britain & Ireland 1998
Let's Go: California 1998
Let's Go: Central America 1998
Let's Go: Eastern Europe 1998
Let's Go: Ecuador & the Galápagos Islands 1998
Let's Go: Europe 1998
Let's Go: France 1998
Let's Go: Germany 1998
Let's Go: Greece & Turkey 1998
Let's Go: India & Nepal 1998
Let's Go: Ireland 1998
Let's Go: Israel & Egypt 1998
Let's Go: Italy 1998
Let's Go: London 1998
Let's Go: Mexico 1998
Let's Go: New York City 1998
Let's Go: New Zealand 1998 **New title!**
Let's Go: Paris 1998
Let's Go: Rome 1998
Let's Go: Southeast Asia 1998
Let's Go: Spain & Portugal 1998
Let's Go: USA 1998
Let's Go: Washington, D.C. 1998

Let's Go Map Guides

Berlin	New Orleans
Boston	New York City
Chicago	Paris
London	Rome
Los Angeles	San Francisco
Madrid	Washington, D.C.

Coming Soon: Amsterdam, Florence

**Let's Go
Publications**

LET'S GO
Ecuador
& the Galápagos Islands
1998

Joanna R. Veltri
Editor

Marnie E. Davidoff
Assistant Editor

Macmillan

HELPING LET'S GO

If you want to share your discoveries, suggestions, or corrections, please drop us a line. We read every piece of correspondence, whether a postcard, a 10-page email, or a coconut. Please note that mail received after May 1998 may be too late for the 1999 book, but will be kept for future editions. **Address mail to:**

Let's Go: Ecuador & the Galápagos Islands
67 Mount Auburn Street
Cambridge, MA 02138
USA

Visit Let's Go at **http://www.letsgo.com,** or send email to:

fanmail@letsgo.com
Subject: "Let's Go: Ecuador & the Galápagos Islands"

In addition to the invaluable travel advice our readers share with us, many are kind enough to offer their services as researchers or editors. Unfortunately, our charter enables us to employ only currently enrolled Harvard-Radcliffe students.

Published in Great Britain 1998 by Macmillan, an imprint of Macmillan General Books, 25 Eccleston Place, London SW1W 9NF and Basingstoke.

Maps by David Lindroth copyright © 1998, 1997 by St. Martin's Press, Inc.

Map revisions pp. 2, 3, 4, 5, 61, 63, 87, 89, 105, 107, 109, 137, 139, 149, 163, 164, 165, 179, 193, 217, 247, 276, 277, 291 by Let's Go, Inc.

Published in the United States of America by St. Martin's Press, Inc.

ISBN: 0 333 71188 2

First edition
10 9 8 7 6 5 4 3 2 1

Let's Go: Ecuador & the Galápagos Islands is written by Let's Go Publications, 67 Mount Auburn Street, Cambridge, MA 02138, USA.

Contents

Maps

About Let's Go

THIRTY-EIGHT YEARS OF WISDOM

Back in 1960, a few students at Harvard University banded together to produce a 20-page pamphlet offering a collection of tips on budget travel in Europe. This modest, mimeographed packet, offered as an extra to passengers on student charter flights to Europe, met with instant popularity. The following year, students traveling to Europe researched the first, full-fledged edition of *Let's Go: Europe*, a pocket-sized book featuring honest, irreverent writing and a decidedly youthful outlook on the world. Throughout the 60s, our guides reflected the times; the 1969 guide to America led off by inviting travelers to "dig the scene" at San Francisco's Haight-Ashbury. During the 70s and 80s, we gradually added regional guides and expanded coverage into the Middle East and Central America. With the addition of our in-depth city guides, handy map guides, and extensive coverage of Asia and Australia, the 90s are also proving to be a time of explosive growth for Let's Go, and there's certainly no end in sight. The first editions of *Let's Go: Australia* and *Let's Go: New Zealand* hit the shelves this year, expanding our coverage to six continents, and research for next year's series has already begun.

We've seen a lot in 38 years. *Let's Go: Europe* is now the world's bestselling international guide, translated into seven languages. And our new guides bring Let's Go's total number of titles, with their spirit of adventure and their reputation for honesty, accuracy, and editorial integrity, to 40. But some things never change: our guides are still researched, written, and produced entirely by students who know first-hand how to see the world on the cheap.

HOW WE DO IT

Each guide is completely revised and thoroughly updated every year by a well-traveled set of over 200 students. Every winter, we recruit over 140 researchers and 60 editors to write the books anew. After several months of training, Researcher-Writers hit the road for seven weeks of exploration, from Anchorage to Adelaide, Estonia to El Salvador, Iceland to Indonesia. Hired for their rare combination of budget travel sense, writing ability, stamina, and courage, these adventurous travelers know that train strikes, stolen luggage, food poisoning, and marriage proposals are all part of a day's work. Back at our offices, editors work from spring to fall, massaging copy written on Himalayan bus rides into witty yet informative prose. A student staff of typesetters, cartographers, publicists, and managers keeps our lively team together. In September, the collected efforts of the summer are delivered to our printer, who turns them into books in record time, so that you have the most up-to-date information available for your vacation. And even as you read this, work on next year's editions is well underway.

WHY WE DO IT

We don't think of budget travel as the last recourse of the destitute; we believe that it's the only way to travel. Living cheaply and simply brings you closer to the people and places you've been saving up to visit. Our books will ease your anxieties and answer your questions about the basics—so you can get off the beaten track and explore. Once you learn the ropes, we encourage you to put *Let's Go* down now and then to strike out on your own. As any seasoned traveler will tell you, the best discoveries are often those you make yourself. When you find something worth sharing, drop us a line. We're Let's Go Publications, 67 Mount Auburn St., Cambridge, MA 02138, USA (email: fanmail@letsgo.com).

HAPPY TRAVELS!

Researcher-Writers

Karin Akre   *Quito, Near Quito, North of Quito,*
Northern Pacific Coast

Karin charmed Quito and the coast with her winning smile; she charmed us with her gorgeous prose and dead-on insights. Though she was relieved of her wallet on a train to San Lorenzo, she refused to let go of her steadfast enthusiasm. Pressing on, she braved Esmeraldas, and quite possibly every form of transportation imaginable, to send us copy as wonderful as ever (then it was our turn to be relieved). A bargain-*artesanía*-hunter by day, and a dancing daredevil by night, Karin wove her way in and out of Otavalo and the surrounding villages, and doubled the Nightlife section for all you *salsa*-philes. We'll miss her, but her devoted fans needn't worry—with luck, Karin will be back for another season.

Raymond Fisman   *Northern Oriente, Central Corridor,*
Cuenca, Southern Highlands

Fisman fought hard in the face of some of the worst luck ever known to humankind. Bouncing back from theft (twice), sickness (also twice), and road-erasing, itinerary-blocking mudslides (once, thank God), Ray "psycho-mountain-climbing" Fisman kept us on the edge of our seats with stories of Cotopaxi climbs, local legends, and mini bus-bandits. Without a second to lose, Ray descended from Chimborazo's peak to the heart of the Oriente, extensive copy in tow, discovering the secrets everyone should know about exploring both places—and did it all at light-speed. Indeed, there lies a wildman under that calm, placid exterior, ready to convert whatever fastball the fates pitch into grand-slammin' prose.

Ryan Hackney   *The Galápagos Islands, Guayaquil,*
Southern Pacific Coast

Not just any Galápagos tourist, Ryan applied his flora and fauna expertise to create that oh-so-special island experience for all you readers. His unceasing wit kept the pirates at bay (Aaarrgh!), but unfortunately not the finger-biting *tortugas*...Ryan's keen investigative eye uncovered lost legends, kept the cool company of all them frisky sea lions, and of course Lonesome George. What would we have done without his Ed expertise?? Back on the mainland, Ryan kept the tradition of battling with EME-TEL alive as he worked his way up the coast, putting in more than one cheek when necessary. With cool head and Darwinian passion, Ryan left no stone unturned; his evolution at Let's Go has far surpassed any sort of natural selection.

Jessica Seddon   *Lima, Tumbes, Border Area Lowlands,*
Western Lowlands, Southern Oriente

A die-hard fan of one of the world's most difficult cities, Jessica scoured Lima for its best and most beautiful. Back in Ecuador, with luck on her side, she escaped the perils of manic tourist agents, successfully fled from stark raving pigs (what's a little mud among friends?), evaded swarms of old ladies full of late-night warnings, and taught them what it was all about at EMETEL (blue eye-shadow and all). A lauded veteran R-W, our seasoned urbanite discovered her wilder side as she tackled the Oriente and won. With a knack for finding the real story amidst rumors, Jessica brought us the scoop on banana wars, gold mining disputes, Johnny Lovewisdom, the removal of the *ambulantes*, Claudia Schiffer's favorite Lima hangout, and much, much more.

Acknowledgments

Yo, Marn. What would I have done without you? From copy, to Clav, to the emergency room…thanks for dealing with all of it. My stellar R-Ws, you make me proud—thanks for going all those extra miles. 'Kia, Hoggs, Kushishtof, Cito and Cito—it's all about who wears the panties. Thanks for all the strategizing—I love you guys. MR, thanks for supporting all of my crazy ideas while consistently guiding me in the right direction. ACP, LMT, and TIM—hey, you survived all the random changes of heart—it's been great living with you guys. Anne Chisholm, you're the best. Meera and Alice, who could ask for cooler or more talented interns? Laurie, Emily, and Chuck—you rock. Thanks to all you incredibly fast typists for keeping the ship afloat. *Muchísimas gracias a* Paola Uccelli for that extra Lima help, and, of course, for teaching me Spanish in the first place. And a huge thanks to the best MEs ever, especially to production gurus Mel and Dave—I love you, Ma Let's Go. DJE, my Ed, you were the inspiration. And to the freaks I love so much: AEA, JMF, BPB, MBS, and DJE, your calls kept me sane. Thanks for the postcards. Finally, Mom, Dad, Tine, and John—oh, how I can't wait to come home…again. I love you. *Viva Let's Go, y Viva Ecuador!* **—JRV**

To Joanna, with whom it all starts and ends. Thanks for shrimp ecuatoriana (goes great with tequila!), salsa and meringue at Ryles, and for so thoughtfully and generously making me a part of Team Ecuador. Thanks also to Melissa for showing me how to care for my appendix, to the typists who did in minutes what would have taken me hours, and to the proofers, receptionists, and our awesome interns, Meera and Alice, for their invaluable support. To DM who turned my attitude on its head, to IC who has proven there *is* love after graduation, to Southeast Asia for giving me a home, and to the Latin America room for drawing me into theirs whenever I needed it most. To Mom, Dad, and Stu for long-distance phone calls, relief trips to NY, and, as always, lots of love. Finally, to the Coöp for showing me another side, and to Let's Go for all the insight. It's been a privilege. **—MED**

Editor	Joanna R. Veltri
Assistant Editor	Marnie E. Davidoff
Managing Editor	Melissa M. Reyen
Publishing Director	John R. Brooks
Production Manager	Melanie Quintana Kansil
Associate Production Manager	David Collins
Cartography Manager	Sara K. Smith
Editorial Manager	Melissa M. Reyen
Editorial Manager	Emily J. Stebbins
Financial Manager	Krzysztof Owerkowicz
Personnel Manager	Andrew E. Nieland
Publicity Manager	Nicholas Corman
Publicity Manager	Kate Galbraith
New Media Manager	Daniel O. Williams
Associate Cartographer	Joseph E. Reagan
Associate Cartographer	Luke Z. Fenchel
Office Coordinators	Emily Bowen, Charles Kapelke
	Laurie Santos
Director of Advertising Sales	Todd L. Glaskin
Senior Sales Executives	Matthew R. Hillery, Joseph W. Lind
	Peter J. Zakowich, Jr.
President	Amit Tiwari
General Manager	Richard Olken
Assistant General Manager	Anne E. Chisholm

Let's Go Picks

We wandered and wondered through the width and depth of this small South American country, loving it and loathing it. Here's what we found:

Best Artesanía: Otavalo (see p. 86), 'cuz it's got it *all*. And more. **Cotacachi** (see p. 93), with its loads and loads of lovin' leatherwork. **Agato** (see p. 93), for its weavings at the Tahuantinsuyo weaving workshop. Witness the weavers' acrobatic feats with the *telaros de español*. **Montecristi** (see p. 196), to find out where Panama hats are *really* made. **San Antonio de Ibarra** (see p. 99), home of the whittlers who aspire to the *artesanía* elite.

Best Mud Baths: Vilcabamba (see p. 157), a.k.a. Hostel Madre Tierra, for its hammocks, mud baths, and colon therapy...what more could a traveler's intestine ask for? **Baños de San Vicente** (see p. 212), for filthy good massages using all-natural *savila*. **Roads in Coca** (see p. 224); when you see them, you'll know why. Remember your knee-high rubber boots.

Best Surfing: Montañita (see p. 206), means bare feet, bronzed skin, unclad torsos, rolling barrels, and killer swells, especially from December to June. **Alandaluz** (see p. 205), one of Ecuador's premier surfing locales, with 10 to 12 ft. waves in winter.

Best Mountain Climbing: Volcán Cotopaxi (see p. 111), because you've got to respect the tallest active volcano in the world. Plus, it's got an awesome *refugio*. **Volcán Chimborazo** (see p. 131), whose summit is the farthest point from the earth's center, due to the equatorial bulge. As they can tell you at Mitad del Mundo, that means weight loss.

Best Nightlife: Guayaquil (see p. 170), because who wants to go to sleep when there are *chivas* roaming loose? **Montañita** (see p. 206), whose beachside bars open around 6pm and don't close until everyone's lying face-down in the sand.

Best Tree-Top Lodging: Cabaña del Arbol (see p. 206), the Alandaluz honeymoon suite that sways with love (and private bath). **La Casa del Ceiba** (see p. 302), at El Progreso in the Galápagos, in a gigantic ceiba tree 40 ft. off the ground, furnished with two beds, a bathroom, hot water, music, television, a refrigerator, and a bar.

Best Roof-top Rides: Train-top, surf up or down the Andes from Alausí to Bucay, and even pick the Devil's Nose (see p. 133). **Bus-top,** soak up the jungle mountain views from Papallacta to Quito (see p. 233). **Boat-top,** lather up for a shower and a half on the wet and wild waves between Cojimíes and Muisne (see p. 188).

Best Ceviche: Salinas (see p. 210), gateway to Cevichelandia, a magical world of raw seafood and *more* raw seafood. **Puerto Bolívar** (see p. 248), the best Machala has to offer. **Puerto López** (see p. 202), and the *ceviche de spondyllus* at Spondyllus Bar and Restaurant, if only for the name.

Best "Galápagos Experience": The Galápagos Islands (see p. 275), the genuine article, the real McCoy, the cream of the crop, the bee's knees, the enchanted isles. **Isla de la Plata** (see p. 204), in Parque Nacional Machalilla: the "Poor Person's Galápagos" for nature-lovers lacking the *plata*. **Guayaquil's Parque Bolívar** (see p. 170), with iguanas nearly as numerous as on the islands, and as much fun as the sea lions!

Best All-Around Resource: The South American Explorer's Club (see p. 1), friendly and knowledgeable to boot.

How to Use This Book

Let's Go: Ecuador and the Galápagos Islands 1998 is not a manual; it's an adventure companion. Read it, revel in it, but don't let it confine you in your journey to one of the most exhilarating, eye-popping, exciting, engaging countries in South America... nay, the world. Ecuador is the kind of spontaneous, rough and tumble place that doesn't follow the rules—so neither should you. Here, nobody can guarantee that the buses will run on time or that the volcano looming overhead won't spew its stuff tomorrow. While little can be taken for granted here, Ecuador does guarantee one thing—amazing diversity, both ecologically and culturally, from the summit of Chimborazo to the shores of Isla Santa Cruz, from Montañita's monster waves to Otavalo's markets. Ecuador's charisma comes from all that is pristine and un-gringo-fied about it. National parks and reserves preserve flora and fauna species found nowhere else in the world, traditional *indígenas* live in relative isolation in the Oriente, and some Pacific beaches go for days without a single footprint disturbing their sands. It's possible to experience the best Ecuador has to offer and leave it just as spectacular as it was when you arrived. Hopefully this book will help you do that.

The book begins with the **Essentials** section, information on all those things it's not so easy to figure out in a developing nation. How to get there, safety precautions, health information—it's all there. Ecuador is rich in history, culture, and wildlife, and all that's laid out for you in **Ecuador: An Introduction,** so you know exactly what treasures you're experiencing when you see them. We've explored every region of the country too, starting with **Quito,** the country's civil, cultural, and cosmopolitan capital, as well as some killer sights nearby, like Mitad del Mundo. Then we head up **North of Quito** to the slow-paced, misty villages of many *artesanía*-making *indígenas*. Jumping back over the capital, the **Central Corridor** between Quito and Cuenca soars between some of the tallest (and sometimes active) volcanoes in Ecuador. After a mountain climb and a soaking session in the hot springs, it's on to colonial **Cuenca and the Southern Highlands** that surround it. Ecuador's nitty-gritty commercial capital, **Guayaquil...and the Western Lowlands** to its north, run the length of the country just east of the coast. From there it's a hop, skip, and a jump to a sunny surfing scene on the country's **Pacific Coast.** We explore the country's jungle provinces of the **Oriente** next, which offer off-the-beaten-track Amazon adventures at every turn. For a brief saunter out of Ecuador, we trek through the **Border Area Lowlands** on the way to **Lima, Perú,** where a complex urban history and a raging nightlife await exploration. With our mainland odyssey at its end, we finally jump ship for the enchanting **Galápagos Islands,** 600 miles west off the country's coast. Along with the addition of **Lima,** our **Appendix** (especially the **Glossary**), is new and improved; the **Galápagos Islands** includes a special section on how to manage those rather non-budget islands without spending too much—it *is* possible; and finally, this year's book is endowed with all sorts of extra information for all of you **mountain-climbing, jungle-exploring types.** Have fun, and *¡buena suerte!*

A NOTE TO OUR READERS

The information for this book is gathered by *Let's Go*'s researchers from late May through August. Each listing is derived from the assigned researcher's opinion based upon his or her visit at a particular time. The opinions are expressed in a candid and forthright manner. Other travelers might disagree. Those traveling at a different time may have different experiences since prices, dates, hours, and conditions are always subject to change. You are urged to check beforehand to avoid inconvenience and surprises. Travel always involves a certain degree of risk, especially in low-cost areas. When traveling, especially on a budget, always take particular care to ensure your safety.

South America

Gulf of Mexico

Caribbean Sea

ATLANTIC OCEAN

PANAMÁ

VENEZUELA

GUYANA

SURINAME

FRENCH GUIANA

COLOMBIA

Galápagos Islands

Quito

Guayaquil

Amazon River

ECUADOR

B R A Z I L

P E R Ú

Lima

BOLIVIA

PARAGUAY

CHILE

PACIFIC OCEAN

URUGUAY

A R G E N T I N A

ATLANTIC OCEAN

N

0   600 miles

0   600 kilometers

A N T A R C T I C A

Learn Spanish in Cuenca

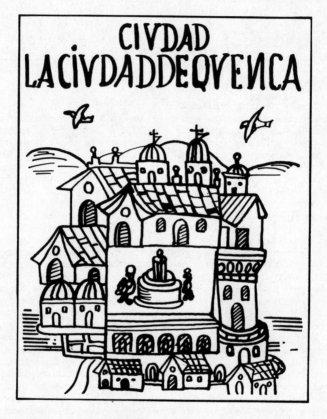

FUNDACION CENTRO DE ESTUDIOS INTERAMERICANOS

CEDEI offers individual tutorials and university accredited courses in Spanish, Quichua, or Latin American literature and culture, as well as field trips, family stays and E-mail access.

GRAN COLOMBIA 11-02, CUENCA   PHONE 839-003

(in the U.S., call 319-848-3159)

interpro@cedei.org.ec   http://www.netins.net/showcase/cedei/

CEDEI is a not-for-profit cultural foundation, licensed by Ecuador's Ministry of Education and Culture

Essentials

PLANNING YOUR TRIP

▓ When to Go

Despite Ecuador's location at zero degrees latitude, the climate varies greatly across the country's three geographical regions. On the Pacific coast and in the Oriente region you'll find sweltering heat typical of the tropics, but in the Sierra (highlands), the higher you get, the cooler you'll be. Ecuador's seasons do not cycle from summer to winter as in temperate regions, but instead from wet to dry. **Coastal** and **lowland** weather is affected by the currents of the Pacific. Warm waters bathe Ecuador's shores from January to April, bringing torrential downpours and daytime temperatures around 88°F (31°C). In May, cooler currents from the Antarctic mean less heat and less rainfall for the rest of the year (see **Appendix: Climate,** p. 318).

Sun worshippers and beach crawlers come and go with the seasons. Expect crowds during the *temporada* from December to April, especially on weekends and holidays. Despite the rains, many locals swarm to the beaches to find solace from the higher temperatures. The rest of the year you'll most likely have the beach to yourself; skies are cloudy and temperatures are cooler. In the **Sierra,** temperatures remain more or less constant all year, averaging 70°F (21°C) during the day and 47°F (8°C) at night. The driest time of year in the highlands is from June to September, but precipitation variation is not extreme. Variation in rainfall in the **Oriente** is not extreme either; you can count on rain year-round, with especially heavy rains from June to August. As long as you come prepared with adequate rain gear, a shower or two won't ruin your trip—rain makes your jungle tour more authentic. Year-round temperature and humidity approximates that of the coast during the wet season.

In short, there is no perfect time to visit all three regions of the country. Seasonal variation is less marked in the highlands and the Oriente, while the coast has the *temporada* from December to April. Also keep local festivals and holidays in mind when planning your trip. The most important nationwide holidays are Christmas, *Semana Santa* (Easter week), and Ecuadorian Independence Day, May 24. While these times of year are very festive, holiday destinations tend to be quite crowded. For info on other festivals and holidays see the **Appendix,** p. 317.

▓ Useful Organizations

TRAVEL ORGANIZATIONS

South American Explorer's Club (SAEC), 126 Indian Creek Rd., Ithaca, NY 14850 (tel. (607) 277-0488; fax 277-6122; http://www.samexplo.org; email explorer@samexplo.org), and Jorge Washington 311 y L. Plaza, Quito, Ecuador (Apartado 17-21-431, Eloy Alfaro, Quito, Ecuador; tel./fax (593) 2-225-228; email explorer@saec.org.ec). A nonprofit organization with extensive info about traveling, working, volunteering, and researching in Latin America. Clubhouses in Ithaca, New York; Quito, Ecuador; and Lima, Perú have trip reports and compiled info packets. They also have an extensive library with books on all Latin American topics and a catalog of travel gear. Their knowledgeable staff and endless resources are at your disposal for the U.S. tax-deductible membership fee of US$40 a year.

Council on International Educational Exchange (CIEE), 205 East 42nd St., New York, NY 10017-5706 (tel. (888)-COUNCIL/268-6245; fax (212) 822-2699; http://www.ciee.org). A private, non-profit organization, Council administers work, volunteer, academic, internship, and professional programs around the world. They

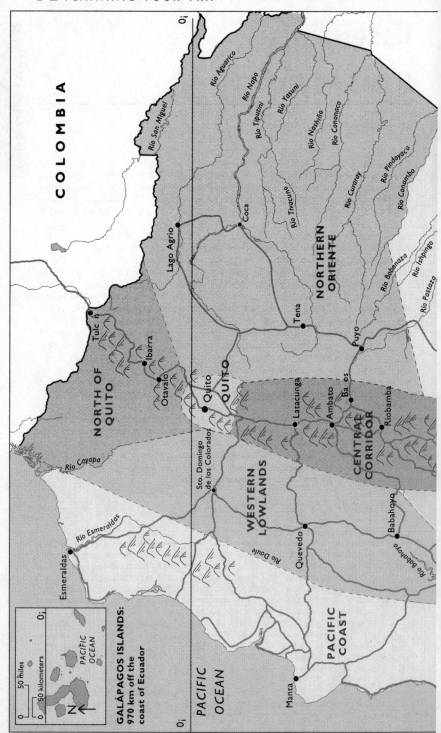

COLOMBIA

Río San Miguel

Río Aguarico

Río Napo

Río Tiputini

Río Yasuni

Río Nashiño

Río Cononaco

Río Pindoyacu

Río Curaray

Río Canambo

Río Tiwacuno

Río Bobonaza

Río Ishpingo

Río Pastaza

Coca

Lago Agrio

NORTHERN
ORIENTE

Tena

Puyo

Tulcán

Ibarra

NORTH OF
QUITO

Otavalo

Quito

QUITO

Latacunga

Ambato

Baños

Riobamba

CENTRAL
CORRIDOR

Río Cayapa

Sto. Domingo
de los Colorados

WESTERN
LOWLANDS

Babahoyo

Río Esmeraldas

Quevedo

Río Daule

Río Babahoyo

Esmeraldas

PACIFIC
COAST

Manta

PACIFIC
OCEAN

GALÁPAGOS ISLANDS:
970 km off the
coast of Ecuador

PACIFIC
OCEAN

50 miles

50 kilometers

N

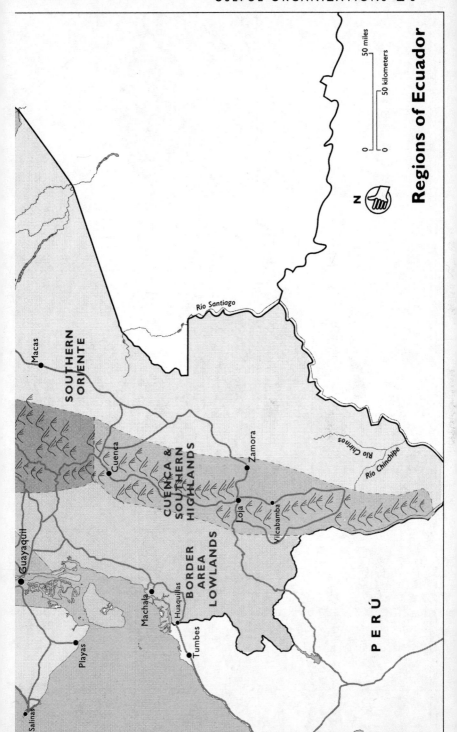

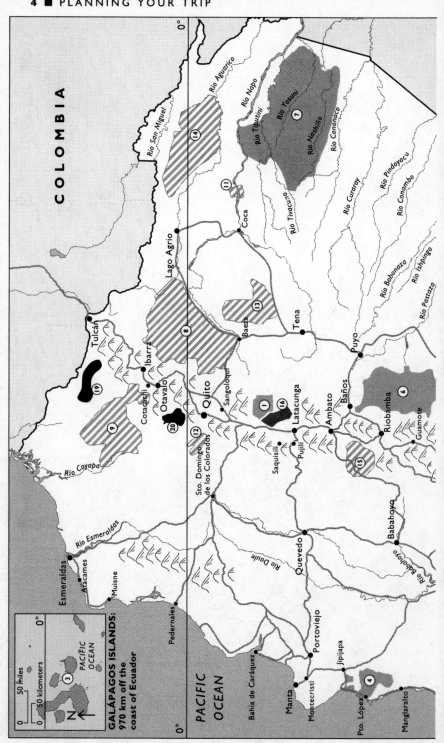

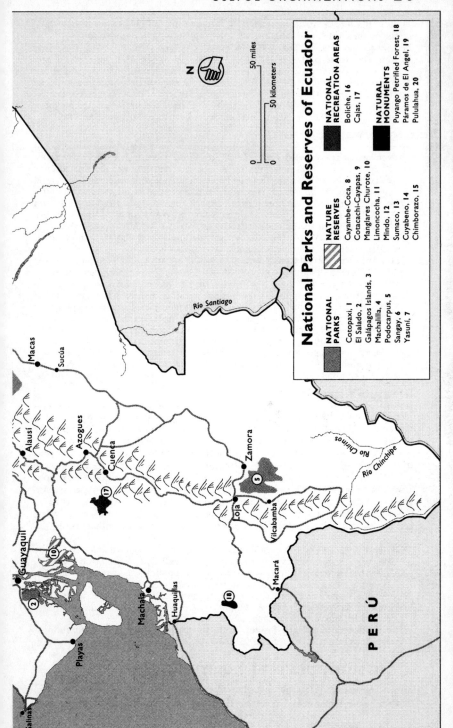

National Parks and Reserves of Ecuador

NATIONAL PARKS
Cotopaxi, 1
El Salado, 2
Galápagos Islands, 3
Machalilla, 4
Podocarpus, 5
Sangay, 6
Yasuní, 7

NATURE RESERVES
Cayambe-Coca, 8
Cotacachi-Cayapas, 9
Manglares Churote, 10
Limoncocha, 11
Mindo, 12
Sumaco, 13
Cuyabeno, 14
Chimborazo, 15

NATIONAL RECREATION AREAS
Boliche, 16
Cajas, 17

NATURAL MONUMENTS
Puyango Petrified Forest, 18
Páramos de El Angel, 19
Pululahua, 20

50 miles
50 kilometers

also offer identity cards (including the ISIC and the GO25) and publications, like the useful magazine *Student Travels* (free). Call or write for more info.

International Student Travel Confederation, Herengracht 479, 1017 BS Amsterdam, The Netherlands (tel. (31) 20 421 2800; fax 20 421 2810; http://www.istc. org; email istcinfo@istc.org). A nonprofit confederation of student organizations whose focus is to develop and facilitate travel among young people and students. Member organizations include International Student Surface Travel Association (ISSA), Student Air Travel Association (SATA), IASIS Travel Insurance, and the International Association for Educational and Work Exchange Programs (IAEWEP).

USEFUL PUBLICATIONS

Adventurous Traveler Bookstore, P.O. Box 1468, Williston, VT 05495 (tel. (800) 282-3963; fax 677-1821; email books@atbook.com; http://www.AdventurousTraveler.com). Free 40pp. catalogue upon request. Outdoor adventure travel books and maps for the U.S. and abroad. Their web site offers extensive browsing capabilities.

Blue Guides, published in Britain by A&C Black Limited, 35 Bedford Row, London WC1R 4JH, in the U.S. by W.W. Norton & Co. Inc., 500 Fifth Ave., New York, NY 10110, and in Canada by Penguin Books Canada Ltd., 10 Alcorn Ave., #300, Toronto, Ontario N4V 3B2. Blue Guides provide unmatched historical and cultural info, sightseeing routes, maps, and listings of pricey hotels.

Latin American Travel Consultants, P.O. Box 17-17-908, Quito, Ecuador (fax (593) 2-562-566; email latc@pi.pro.ec; http://www.amerispan.com/latc). Publishes quarterly newsletter on 17 countries in Latin America *(Latin American Travel Advisor)*, focusing on the public safety, health, weather, natural phenomena, travel costs, politics, and economy of each country. Offers Spanish immersion programs in 25 cities in 12 Latin American countries. US$39 for 1yr. newsletter subscription.

Superintendent of Documents, P.O. Box 371954, Pittsburgh, PA 15250-7954 (tel. (202) 512-1800; fax 512-2250; email gpoaccess@gpo.gov; http:// www.access.gpo.gov/su_docs). Open Mon.-Fri. 7:30am-4:30pm. Publishes *Your Trip Abroad* (US$1.25), *Health Information for International Travel* (US$14), and "Background Notes" on all countries ($1 each). Postage included in the prices.

INTERNET RESOURCES

Along with everything else in the 90s, budget travel is moving rapidly into the information age. The Internet can be used in many different ways, but the **World Wide Web** is the most useful to 'net-surfing budget travelers. **Search engines** (services that search for web pages under specific subjects) can greatly aid the process; **Lycos** (http://a2z.lycos.com) and **Infoseek** (http://guide.infoseek.com) are popular. **Yahoo!** is slightly more organized; check out its links at http://www.yahoo.com/Recreation/ Travel. **NetTravel: How Travelers Use the Internet,** by Michael Shapiro, is an informative guide to this process (US$25). Check out Let's Go's own page (http:// www.letsgo.com) for a current list of links, or try some of our favorites directly (we also list relevant web sites throughout different sections of the **Essentials** chapter):

City.Net (http://www.city.net). Impressive collection of regional and city-specific web pages. Select a geographic area and it provides links to related web pages.

CIA World Factbook (http://www.odci.gov/cia/publications/nsolo/wfb-all.htm), has tons of vital statistics on the country you want to visit. Check it out for an overview of Ecuador's economy, or an explanation of their system of government.

Shoestring Travel (http://www.stratpub.com), is a budget travel e-zine, with feature articles, links, user exchange, and accommodations info.

The Student and Budget Travel Guide (http://asa.ugl.lib.umich.edu/chdocs/ travel/travel-guide.html). Info on accommodations, transportation, packing, etc.

■ Documents and Formalities

All applications should be filed several weeks or months in advance of your planned departure date. Remember that you are relying on government agencies to complete these transactions. Demand for passports is highest between January and August, so apply as early as possible. A backlog in processing can spoil your plans.

When you travel, always carry on your person two or more forms of identification, including at least one photo ID. A passport combined with a driver's license or birth certificate usually serves as adequate proof of identity and citizenship. Many establishments, especially banks, require several IDs before cashing traveler's checks. Never carry all your forms of ID together; you risk being left entirely without ID or funds in case of theft or loss. If you plan an extended stay, register your passport with the nearest embassy or consulate. U.S. citizens seeking info about documents, formalities, and travel abroad should request the booklet *Your Trip Abroad* (US$1.25) from the Superintendent of Documents (see **Useful Publications,** p. 6).

EMBASSIES AND CONSULATES

For most matters you will want to contact the nearest consulate. Embassies can provide you with the address and phone number of the consulate nearest you.

Australia: The nearest embassy is in Tokyo, but the consulate is in **Melbourne:** 2nd fl., 405 Burk St., Melbourne, Victoria 3000 (tel. (03) 9600 0116; fax 9600 0414).
Canada: Embassy of Ecuador, 50 O'Connor St., Suite 1311, Ottawa, Ontario K1P 6L2 (tel. (613) 563 8206; fax 235 5776).
Ireland: The nearest embassy is in London, but there is a consulate in **Dublin:** 27 Library Road, Dun Laoghaire, CO, Dublin (tel. (01) 280 5917).
New Zealand: The embassy is in Tokyo, but there is a consulate in **Auckland:** 2 Akaroa Street, Parnell (P.O. Box 3), Auckland (tel. (09) 309 0229; fax 303 2931).
United Kingdom: Embassy of Ecuador, Flat 3B, 3 Hans Crescent, Knightsbridge, London, SW1X OLS, United Kingdom (tel. (0171) 584 1367; fax 823 9701).
United States: Embassy of Ecuador, 2535 15th St. N.W., Washington, D.C. 20009 (tel. (202) 234-7200; fax 667-3482).

PASSPORTS

Before you leave, photocopy the page of your passport that contains your photograph and identifying info, especially your passport number. Carry this photocopy in a safe place apart from your passport, and leave another copy at home. These measures will help prove your citizenship and facilitate the issuing of a new passport if you lose the original document. Consulates also recommend you carry an expired passport or an official copy of your birth certificate in a part of your baggage separate from other documents. You can request a duplicate birth certificate from the Bureau of Vital Records and Statistics in your state or province of birth. If you do lose your passport, it may take weeks to process a replacement, and your new one may be valid only for a limited time. In addition, any visas stamped in your old passport will be irretrievably lost. If this happens, immediately notify the local police and the nearest embassy or consulate of your home government (see **Embassies and Consulates,** p. 7). To expedite its replacement, you will need to know all info previously recorded and show identification and proof of citizenship. In an emergency, ask for immediate temporary traveling papers that will permit you to re-enter your home country.

Australia: Citizens must apply for a passport in person at a post office, a passport office, or an Australian diplomatic mission overseas. An appointment may be necessary. Passport offices are located in Adelaide, Brisbane, Canberra City, Darwin, Hobart, Melbourne, Newcastle, Perth, and Sydney. A parent may file an application for a child who is under 18 and unmarried. Adult passports cost AUS$126 (for a 32-page passport) or AUS$188 (64-page), and a child's is AUS$63 (32-page) or AUS$94 (64-page). For more info, call toll-free (in Australia) 13 12 32.
Canada: Application forms in English and French are available at all passport offices, Canadian missions, many travel agencies, and Northern Stores. Citizens may apply in person at any of 28 regional passport offices. Travel agents can direct you to the nearest location. Citizens residing abroad should contact the nearest

embassy or consulate. Children under 16 may be included on a parent's passport. Passports cost CDN$60, valid for 5 years. Approx. 5 business days needed to process in-person; 10 days by mail. For additional info, contact the Canadian Passport Office, Dept. of Foreign Affairs and International Trade, Ottawa, ON, K1A 0G3 (tel. (613) 994-3500; http://www.dfait-maeci.gc.ca/passport). Travelers may also call (800) 567-6868 (24hr.); in Toronto (416) 973-3251; in Vancouver (604) 775-6250; in Montréal (514) 283-2152. Refer to the booklet *Bon Voyage, But...*, free at any passport office or by calling InfoCentre at (800) 267-8376, for further help and a list of embassies and consulates abroad. You may also find entry and background info for various countries by contacting the Consular Affairs Bureau in Ottawa (tel. (800) 267-6788 (24hr.) or (613) 944-6788).

Ireland: Citizens can apply for a passport by mail to either the Department of Foreign Affairs, Passport Office, Setanta Centre, Molesworth St., Dublin 2 (tel. (01) 671 1633), or the Passport Office, Irish Life Building, 1A South Mall, Cork (tel. (021) 272 525). Obtain an application at a local Garda station or a passport office. The new Passport Express Service, available through post offices, allows citizens to get a passport in 2 weeks for an extra IR£3. Passports cost IR£45 and are valid for 10 years. Citizens under 18 or over 65 can request a 3-year passport that costs IR£10.

New Zealand: Application forms for passports are available in New Zealand from travel agents and Department of Internal Affairs Link Centres in the main cities and towns. Overseas, forms and passport services are provided by New Zealand embassies, high commissions, and consulates. Applications may also be forwarded to the Passport Office, P.O. Box 10526, Wellington, New Zealand. Standard processing time is 10 working days. The fees are NZ$80, child NZ$40. An urgent passport service is also available for an extra NZ$80. Different fees apply at overseas post: nine posts including London, Sydney, and Los Angeles offer both standard and urgent services (adult NZ$130, child NZ$65, plus NZ$130 if urgent). The fee at other posts is adult NZ$260, child NZ$195, and a passport will be issued within three working days. Children's names can no longer be endorsed on a parent's passport—they must apply for their own, which are valid for up to 5 years. An adult's passport is valid for 10 years.

South Africa: Citizens can apply for a passport at any Home Affairs Office or South African Mission. Tourist passports, valid for 10 years, cost SAR80. Children under 16 must be issued their own passports, valid for 5 years, which cost SAR60. An emergency passport may be issued for SAR50. An application for a permanent passport must accompany the emergency passport application. Time for the completion of an application is 3 months or more from the time of submission. Current passports less than 10 years old (from date of issuance) may be renewed until December 31, 1999; every citizen whose passport's validity does not extend far beyond this date is urged to renew as soon as possible. Renewal is free, and usually takes 2 weeks. For further info, contact the nearest Dept. of Home Affairs Office.

United Kingdom: British citizens, British Dependent Territories citizens, British Nationals (overseas), and British Overseas citizens may apply for a full passport, valid for 10 years (5 years if under 16). Application forms are available at passport offices, main post offices, many travel agents, and branches of Lloyds Bank and Artac World Choice. Apply in person or by mail to one of the passport offices, located in London, Liverpool, Newport, Peterborough, Glasgow, or Belfast. The fee is UK£18. Children under 16 may be included on a parent's passport. By mail, it usually takes 4-6 weeks. The London office offers same-day, walk-in rush service; arrive early. The former British Visitor's Passport (valid in some European countries and Bermuda only) has been abolished; every traveler over 16 now needs a 10 year standard passport. The U.K. Passport Agency can be reached by phone at (0990) 21 04 10; info available on the Internet at http://www.open.gov.uk/ukpass.

United States: Citizens may apply for a passport at any federal or state courthouse or post office authorized to accept passport applications, or at a U.S. Passport Agency, located in Boston, Chicago, Honolulu, Houston, Los Angeles, Miami, New Orleans, New York, Philadelphia, San Francisco, Seattle, Stamford, and Washington, D.C. Refer to the "U.S. Government, State Department" section of the phone directory or the local post office for addresses. Parents must apply in person for children under age 13. You must apply in person if this is your first passport, if you're under age 18, or if current passport is more than 12 years old or was issued before your 18th birthday. Passports are valid for 10 years (if under 18, 5 years) and cost US$65 (under 18 US$40). May be renewed by mail or in person for US$55. Processing takes 3-4 weeks. Rush service available for a surcharge of US$30 with proof of departure within 10 working days, or for travelers leaving in 2-3 weeks who require visas. Given proof of citizenship, a U.S. embassy or consulate abroad can usually issue a new passport. Report a passport lost or stolen in the U.S. in writing to Passport Services, 1425 K St., N.W., U.S. Department of State, Washington, D.C., 20524 or to the nearest passport agency. For more info, contact the U.S. Passport Information's 24hr. recorded message (tel. (202) 647-0518). Citizens may receive consular info sheets, travel warnings, and public announcements at any passport agency, U.S. embassy, or consulate, or by sending a self-addressed stamped envelope to: Overseas Citizens Services, Room 4811, Dept. of State, Washington, D.C. 20520-4818 (tel. (202) 647-5225; fax 647-3000). More info about documents, formalities, and travel abroad is available on the Bureau of Consular Affairs homepage at http://travel.state.gov, or through the State Dept. site at http://www.state.gov.

ENTRANCE REQUIREMENTS

For most nationalities, all that is required for entrance into Ecuador is a **passport** valid through the duration of the planned visit, and **proof of financial independence.** This can be in the form of a plane ticket to leave Ecuador, or evidence that you have sufficient funds (US$20 per day) to support yourself in the form of travelers checks, cash, or a credit card. Tourists are allowed to stay for a total of **90 days** in a one-year period.

Depending on your nationality, the duration of your stay, and what you will be doing in Ecuador, you may need an additional **visa.** Citizens of China, Costa Rica, Cuba, France, Guatemala, Honduras, India, North and South Korea, and Vietnam must acquire a 12-X visa from an Ecuadorian embassy or consulate before they will be allowed to enter Ecuador. Tourists who wish to stay longer than 90 days must acquire a 12-IX visa, good for up to **six months** in a one-year period, from an Ecuadorian embassy or consulate before they arrive. Those planning to work or study for longer than 90 days in Ecuador must also acquire a visa. To obtain a **study visa,** you must provide a letter of acceptance from the institution at which you are planning to study; for a **work visa** you must provide an employment contract.

For more info, consult the nearest Ecuadorian consulate or embassy. You may also consult *Foreign Entry Requirements* (US$0.50) published by the **Consumer Information Center,** Department 363D, Pueblo, CO 81009 (tel. (719) 948-3334), or contact the **Center for International Business and Travel (CIBT),** 25 West 43rd St. #1420, New York, NY 10036 (tel. (800) 925-2428 or (212) 575-2811 from NYC). This organization secures visas for travel to and from all countries.

When entering Ecuador, customs is generally a pretty laid-back process. Officials are more likely to stop Ecuadorian nationals returning with loads of foreign merchandise than a backpacking gringo. Nevertheless, they do sometimes search bags and you don't want to be busted: you may not enter or leave the country with firearms, ammunition, narcotics, fresh meat, or live plants or animals. You may bring in 300 cigarettes, 50 cigars, and a bottle of liquor tax-free.

CUSTOMS: GOING HOME

Upon returning home, you must declare all articles you acquired abroad and pay a **duty** on the value of those articles that exceed the allowance established by your country's customs service. Goods and gifts purchased at **duty-free** shops abroad are not exempt from duty or sales tax at your point of return; you must declare these items as well. "Duty-free" means that you don't pay a tax in the country of purchase.

Australia: Citizens may import AUS$400 (under 18 AUS$200) of goods duty-free, in addition to 1.125L alcohol and 250 cigarettes or 250g tobacco. You must be over 18 to import alcohol or tobacco. There is no limit to the amount of Australian and/ or foreign cash that may be brought into or taken out of the country, but amounts of AUS$10,000 or more must be reported. All foodstuffs and animal products must be declared on arrival. For info, contact the Regional Director, Australian Customs Service, GPO Box 8, Sydney NSW 2001 (tel. (02) 9213 2000; fax 9213 4000).

Canada: Citizens who remain abroad for at least 1 week may bring back CDN$500 worth of goods duty-free any time. Citizens or residents who travel for a period between 48 hours and 6 days can bring back up to CDN$200. Both of these exemptions may include tobacco and alcohol. You are permitted to ship goods except tobacco and alcohol home under the CDN$500 exemption as long as you declare them when you arrive. Goods under the CDN$200 exemption, and all alcohol and tobacco, must be in your hand or checked luggage. Citizens of legal age (varies by province) may import in person 200 cigarettes, 50 cigars or cigarillos, 400g loose tobacco, 400 tobacco sticks, 1.14L wine or alcohol, and 24 355mL cans/bottles of beer; the value of these products is included in the CDN$200 or CDN$500. For more info, write to Canadian Customs, 2265 St. Laurent Blvd., Ottawa, Ontario K1G 4K3 (tel. (613) 993-0534), call the 24hr. Automated Customs Information Service ((800) 461-9999), or visit Revenue Canada at http://www.revcan.ca.

Ireland: Citizens must declare everything in excess of IR£142 (IR£73 under 15) obtained outside the EU or duty- and tax-free in the EU above the following allowances: 200 cigarettes, 100 cigarillos, 50 cigars, or 250g tobacco; 1L liquor or 2L wine; 2L still wine; 50g perfume; and 250mL toilet water. Goods obtained duty and tax paid in another EU country up to a value of IR£460 (IR£115 under 15) will not be subject to additional customs duties. Travelers under 17 may not import tobacco or alcohol. For more info, contact The Revenue Commissioners, Dublin Castle (tel. (01) 679 27 77; fax 671 20 21; email taxes@iol.ie; http://www.revenue.ie) or The Collector of Customs and Excise, The Custom House, Dublin 1.

New Zealand: Citizens may import NZ$700 worth of goods duty-free if they are intended for personal use or are unsolicited gifts. The concession is 200 cigarettes (1 carton) or 250g tobacco or 50 cigars or a combination of all 3 not to exceed 250g. You may also bring in 4.5L of beer or wine and 1.125L of liquor. Only travelers over 17 may import tobacco or alcohol. For more info, contact New Zealand Customs, 50 Anzac Ave., Box 29, Auckland (tel. (09) 377 35 20; fax 309 29 78).

South Africa: Citizens may import duty-free: 400 cigarettes, 50 cigars, 250g tobacco, 2L wine, 1L of spirits, 250mL toilet water, 50mL perfume, and other consumable items up to a value of SAR500. Goods up to SAR10,000 above this duty-free allowance are dutiable at 20%; such goods are also exempted from payment of VAT. Items acquired abroad and sent to the Republic as unaccompanied baggage do not qualify for allowances. You may not export or import South African bank notes in excess of SAR2000. For more info, see the free pamphlet *South African Customs Information*, in airports or from the Commissioner for Customs and Excise, Private Bag X47, Pretoria 0001 (tel. (12) 314 99 11; fax 328 64 78).

United Kingdom: Citizens or visitors arriving in the U.K. from outside the EU must declare goods in excess of the following allowances: 200 cigarettes, 100 cigarillos, 50 cigars, or 250g tobacco; still table wine (2L); strong liqueurs over 22% volume (1L), or fortified or sparkling wine, other liqueurs (2L); perfume (60 cc/mL); toilet water (250 cc/mL); and UK£136 of other goods (incl. gifts/souvenirs). You must be over 17 to import liquor or tobacco. These also apply to duty-free purchases within the EU, except for the last category, other goods, which has an allowance of UK£71. Goods obtained duty and tax paid for personal use (regulated according to set guide levels) within the EU do not require further customs duty. For more info, contact Her Majesty's Customs and Excise, Custom House, Nettleton Road, Heathrow Airport, Hounslow, Middlesex TW6 2LA (tel. (0181) 910-3744; fax 910-3765).

United States: Citizens may import US$400 of accompanying goods duty-free and must pay 10% tax on the next US$1000. You must declare all purchases; have sales slips ready. The US$400 exemption covers goods purchased for personal or household use (includes gifts), not more than 100 cigars, 200 cigarettes (1 carton), and 1L of wine or liquor. You must be over 21 to bring liquor into the U.S. If you mail home personal goods of U.S. origin, you can avoid duty charges by marking the package "American goods returned." For more info, consult the brochure *Know Before You Go,* from the U.S. Customs Service, Box 7407, Washington, D.C. 20044 (tel. (202) 927-6724), or visit the web site (http://www.customs.ustreas.gov).

YOUTH, STUDENT, AND TEACHER IDENTIFICATION

Though international student discounts are not as common in Ecuador as in the U.S. or European countries, it is still worth your while to flash your student I.D. whenever you get the opportunity, even if no discount is advertised. Aside from your school's ID card, consider carrying the **International Student Identity Card (ISIC),** one of the most widely accepted forms of student identification. It provides insurance benefits, including US$100 per day of in-hospital sickness (maximum 60 days), and US$3000 accident-related medical reimbursement for each accident. Also, cardholders have access to a toll-free 24-hour ISIC helpline whose multilingual staff can provide assistance in medical, legal, and financial emergencies overseas.

Many travel agencies issue ISICs, including STA Travel in Australia and New Zealand; Travel CUTS in Canada; USIT in Ireland and Northern Ireland; SASTS in South Africa; Campus Travel and STA Travel in the U.K.; Council Travel, Let's Go Travel, and STA Travel in the U.S.; and any other organization under the auspices of the International Student Travel Confederation (ISTC). When you apply for the card, request a copy of the *International Student Identity Card Handbook,* which lists by country some of the available discounts. You can also write to Council for a copy. The card is valid from September to December of the following year and costs US$19. Applicants must be at least 12 years old and degree-seeking students of a secondary or post-secondary school. Because of the proliferation of phony ISICs, many airlines and other services require other proof of student identity, such as a signed letter from the registrar attesting to your status and stamped with the school seal or your school ID card. The US$20 **International Teacher Identity Card (ITIC)** offers the same insurance coverage, and similar but limited discounts. For more info on these cards, consult their web site (http://www.istc.org; email isicinfo@istc.org).

Federation of International Youth Travel Organizations (FIYTO) issues a discount card to non-student travelers under 26. Known as the **GO25 Card,** this one-year card offers many of the same benefits as the ISIC, and can be found where the ISIC is sold. A list of available discounts is free when you buy the card. You will need a passport, valid driver's license, or copy of a birth certificate, and a passport-sized photo with your name printed on the back. The fee is US$19, CDN$15, or UK£5. Info is available on the web at http://www.fiyto.org or http://www.go25.org, or by contacting STA Travel in the U.K., or Council Travel in the U.S. (see **Useful Organizations,** p. 1).

■ Money Matters

> All prices in this book are listed in sucres, except where payment is expected in US dollars. Prices were accurate in the summer of 1997, but due to the high inflation rates and frequent devaluation of the sucre they may have risen since. A useful currency converter website can be found at www.oanda.com/cgi-bin/ncc.

US$1 = 4068 sucres	**1000 sucres = US$0.25**
CDN$1 = 2932 sucres	**1000 sucres= CDN$0.34**
UK£1 = 6488 sucres	**1000 sucres = UK£0.15**
IR£1 = 5824 sucres	**1000 sucres = IR£0.17**
AUS$1 = 2992 sucres	**1000 sucres = AUS$0.33**
NZ$1 = 2596 sucres	**1000 sucres = NZ$0.39**
SARand = 867 sucres	**1000 sucres = SARand$1.15**

CURRENCY AND EXCHANGE

The cost of living in Ecuador is far lower than that in most western countries. Meals can cost from US$1-4, a night's lodging from US$2-7, and transportation is on the whole dirt cheap. Don't sacrifice your health or safety for a cheaper tab. No matter how low your budget, if you plan to travel for more than a couple of days, you will need to keep handy a larger amount of cash than usual. Carrying it around with you, even in a money belt, is risky but necessary; personal checks from home will probably not be acceptable no matter how many forms of identification you have, and even traveler's checks may not be acceptable in some locations.

In Ecuador, as in most Latin American countries, U.S. currency is widely accepted, and in many cases even preferred over the local currency of sucres. Other foreign currency, such as New Zealand or Australian dollars, is difficult or impossible to change. Upon arrival it is a good idea to have U.S. dollars until you can convert to sucres. Despite the versatility of U.S. dollars, it is good to avoid using them when you can. Throwing dollars around to gain preferential treatment is offensive and can attract theft. Also, it labels you as a foreigner and invites many locals to jack up prices.

When changing money, observe commission rates closely and check newspapers to get the standard rate of exchange. Banks generally have the best rates, but this is by no means a hard and fast rule; sometimes tourist offices or exchange kiosks are more competitive. In any case, shop around first. Since you lose money with every transaction, convert in large sums (unless the currency is depreciating rapidly), but don't convert more than you need, because it may be difficult to change it back to your home currency. If you are using traveler's checks or bills, be sure to carry some in small denominations (US$50 or less) for times when you are forced to exchange money at disadvantageous rates. However, it is a good idea to carry a range of denominations, since charges are sometimes levied per check or bill used.

TRAVELER'S CHECKS

Traveler's checks are one of the safest ways to carry funds since they can be refunded in case of loss or theft. When using them in Ecuador, remember that in small towns, traveler's checks are less readily accepted than in cities with large tourist industries. Also, it will be far easier to cash your traveler's checks in Ecuador if you purchase them in U.S. currency. Even if the banks in a town will not cash your checks, you may find a hotel or store that will. American Express and Visa are the most widely recognized. If you're ordering your checks, do so well in advance, especially if large sums are being requested. Each agency provides refunds if your checks are lost or stolen, and many provide additional services. (Note that you may need a police report verifying the loss or theft.) Inquire about toll-free refund hotlines, emergency message relay services, and stolen credit card assistance when you purchase your checks.

Keep your check receipts separate from your checks and store them in a safe place or with a traveling companion; record check numbers when you cash them and leave a list of check numbers with someone at home; ask for a list of refund centers when you buy your checks. American Express and Bank of America have over 40,000 centers worldwide. Never countersign your checks until you're prepared to cash them. Also, bring your passport with you when you plan to use the checks.

American Express: Call (800) 25 19 02 in Australia; in New Zealand (0800) 44 10 68; in the U.K. (0800) 52 13 13; in the U.S. and Canada (800) 221-7282. Elsewhere, call U.S. collect (801) 964-6665. American Express traveler's checks are now available in 10 currencies. They are the most widely recognized worldwide and the easiest to replace if lost or stolen. Checks can be purchased for a small fee (1-4%) at American Express Travel Service Offices, banks, and American Automobile Association offices (AAA members can buy the checks commission-free). Card members can also purchase checks at American Express Dispensers at Travel Service Offices at airports and by ordering them via phone (tel. (800) ORDER-TC/673-3782). American Express offices cash their checks commission-free (except where prohibited by national governments), although they often offer slightly worse rates than banks. You can also buy *Cheques for Two* which can be signed by either of two people traveling together. Request the American Express booklet "Traveler's Companion," which lists travel office addresses and stolen check hotlines for each European country. Visit their online travel offices (http://www.aexp.com).

Citicorp: Call (800) 645-6556 in the U.S. and Canada; in Europe, the Middle East, or Africa (44) 171 508 7007; elsewhere call U.S. collect (813) 623-1709. Sells Citicorp and Citicorp Visa traveler's checks. Commission (1-2%) on purchases. Checkholders automatically enrolled for 45 days in the Travel Assist Program (hotline (800) 250-4377; collect (202) 296-8728) which provides travelers with English-speaking doctor, lawyer, and interpreter referrals; also check refund assistance and general travel info. Citicorp's World Courier Service guarantees hand-delivery of traveler's checks when a refund location is not convenient. Call 24hr., 7 days per week.

Thomas Cook MasterCard: For 24hr. cashing or refund assistance, call (800) 223-9920 in the U.S. and Canada; from the U.K. call (0800) 622 101 free; (1733) 502 995 or (1733) 318 950 collect; elsewhere call U.S. collect (609) 987-7300. Commission (1-2%) on purchases. Thomas Cook offices may sell checks for lower commissions and cash checks commission-free. Thomas Cook Traveler's Checks are also available from **Capital Foreign Exchange** (see **Currency and Exchange,** p. 11).

Visa: Call (800) 227-6811 in the U.S.; in the U.K. (0800) 895 492; from anywhere else call (01733) 318 949) and reverse the charges. Any of the above numbers can tell you the location of their nearest office or can be used to report lost checks.

CREDIT CARDS

Credit cards are relatively widely accepted in Ecuador. Fancier hotels, restaurants, and shops in cities and bigger towns will accept major credit cards. While this is not much use to the budget traveler, many banks in cities and large towns allow cash advances on **MasterCard** and **Visa** credit cards. You can withdraw money from certain ATMs in some cities if you have your credit card's Personal Identification Number (PIN). Ask your credit card company to assign you a PIN before you leave or you will be unable to withdraw cash outside the U.S. Cash advances can be a bargain since credit card companies get the wholesale exchange rate, which is generally 5% better than the retail rate used by banks, and other currency exchange establishments. You will be charged ruinous interest rates if you don't pay off the bill quickly, so be careful when using this service. Credit cards are also invaluable in an emergency—an unexpected hospital bill, ticket home, or loss of traveler's checks—which may leave you temporarily without other resources. Furthermore, credit cards offer an array of other services, from insurance to emergency assistance—these depend completely, however, on the issuer. Some even cover car rental collision insurance.

American Express (tel. (800) 843-2273), has a hefty annual fee (US$55) but offers a number of services. AmEx cardholders can cash personal checks at AmEx offices outside the U.S., and U.S. Assist (24hr. hotline offering emergency medical and legal assist.) is also available from abroad; call the U.S. collect (301) 214-8228. Cardholders can also use the American Express Travel Service; benefits include assistance in changing airline, hotel, and car rental reservations, baggage loss and flight insurance, sending mailgrams and international cables, and holding your mail at one of the more than 1700 AmEx offices around the world. **MasterCard** (tel. (800) 999-0454), and **Visa** (tel. (800) 336-8472), are issued in cooperation with individual banks and some other organizations; ask the issuer about services which come with the cards.

CASH CARDS

ATM machines—known as *cajeros automáticos*—can be found in major Ecuadorian cities. Depending on the system that your bank at home uses, you may be able to access your own personal bank account whenever you're in need of funds. Happily, ATMs get the same wholesale exchange rate as credit cards. Despite these perks, do some research before relying too heavily on automation. There is often a limit on the amount of money you can withdraw per day (usually about US$500), and computer network failures are not uncommon. Be sure to memorize your PIN code in numeral form since machines often don't have letters on the keys. Also, if your PIN is longer than four digits, ask your bank whether the first four digits will work, or whether you need a new number. Many ATMs are outdoors; be cautious and aware of your surroundings.

GETTING MONEY FROM HOME

One of the easiest ways to get money from home is to bring an **American Express** card. AmEx allows green-card holders to draw up to US$1000 every 21 days from their checking accounts at any of its major offices and many of its representatives' offices (no service charge, no interest). AmEx offers Express Cash, with over 100,000 ATMs located in airports, hotels, banks, office complexes, and shopping areas globally. Express Cash withdrawals are automatically debited from the Cardmember's checking account or line of credit and may reach US$1000 in a seven day period. There is a 2% transaction fee for each cash withdrawal, with a US$2.50 minimum/$20 maximum. To enroll in Express Cash, Cardmembers may call (800) CASH NOW/227-4669. From Ecuador, call collect (904) 565-7875. Unless using the AmEx service, avoid cashing checks in sucres; they usually take weeks and a US$30 fee to clear.

Money can also be wired to **Western Union** (tel. (800) 325-6000) offices in Quito and Guayaquil. The rates for sending cash from a local U.S. office is US$10 cheaper than charging your credit card over the phone. The money is usually available for the recipient within an hour, although this may vary.

In emergencies, U.S. citizens can have money sent via the State Department's **Overseas Citizens Service, American Citizens Services,** Consular Affairs, Room 4811, U.S. Department of State, Washington, D.C. 20520 (tel. (202) 647-5225; nights, Sun., and holidays (202) 647-4000; fax (on demand only) (202) 647-3000; http://travel.state.gov). For a fee of US$15, the State Department will forward money within hours to the nearest consular office, which will then disburse it according to instructions. The office serves only Americans in the direst of straits abroad; non-American travelers should contact their embassies or info on wiring cash. The quickest way to have the money sent is to cable the State Department through Western Union.

BARGAINING, TIPPING, AND TAXES

In some places it's okay to **bargain,** and a little practice at playing "the game" can make it well worth the effort. Bargaining for rooms works best in the low season, and it's not hard to get prices lowered at markets or from street vendors (though vendors at markets are most certainly going to be better at bargaining than you are). The basic technique is to expect the first offered price to be higher than what the seller actually wants, pick a lower price, and marvel at the magic of compromise.

As far as **tipping** goes, relatively affluent foreigners are generally expected to tip. At fancier restaurants a 10% tip is included on the bill. When it is not included, consider leaving that much anyway. Tips may also be expected for other services, such as guided tours or maid service; in many cases, these people count on a small bonus.

It will come as no surprise that the Ecuadorian government takes its share of tourist dollars as well. Ecuador's more upscale restaurants, hotels, and shops charge a **10% sales tax,** which you should expect to appear on the bill. The real whammy hits you when you try to leave the country (they don't want you to be bitter until you're on your way out); there is a US$25 **airport/departure tax.**

■ Safety and Security

PERSONAL SAFETY

Tourists are particularly vulnerable to crime for two reasons: they often carry large amounts of cash and they are not as street savvy as locals. To avoid unwanted attention, try to **blend in** as much as possible. Respecting local customs (in many cases, dressing more conservatively) may placate would-be hecklers. The gawking cameratoter is a more obvious target than the low-profile traveler. Walking directly into a cafe or shop to check a map beats checking it on a street corner. Better yet, look over your map before setting out. Muggings are more often impromptu than planned; nervous, over-the-shoulder glances can be a tip that you have something valuable to protect. An obviously bewildered bodybuilder is more likely to be harassed than a stern and confident 98-pound weakling.

When exploring a new city, extra vigilance is wise, but no city should force you to turn precautions into panic. Find out about unsafe areas from tourist info, the manager of your hotel or hostel, or from a local whom you trust. Be sure that someone at home knows your itinerary and never say that you're traveling alone. You may want to carry a small **whistle** to scare off attackers or attract attention; memorize the emergency/police number of the city or area.

When walking at **night,** you should turn daytime precautions into mandates. Stick to busy, well-lit streets and avoid dark alleyways. Do not attempt to cross through parks, parking lots, or any other large and deserted areas. A blissfully isolated beach can become a treacherous nightmare as soon as night falls. Whenever possible, *Let's Go* warns of unsafe neighborhoods and areas, but you should exercise your own judgment about the safety of your environs; buildings in disrepair, vacant lots, and unpopulated areas are all bad signs. A district can change character drastically between blocks. Awareness of the flow of people can reveal a great deal about the relative safety of the area; look for children playing, women walking in the open, and other signs of an active community. If you feel uncomfortable, leave as quickly as you can, but don't allow fear of the unknown to turn you into a hermit. Careful, persistent exploration will build confidence and make your stay much more rewarding.

There is no sure-fire set of precautions that will protect you from all of the situations you might encounter when you travel. A good self-defense course will give you more concrete ways to react to different types of aggression. **Impact, Prepare,** and **Model Mugging** can refer both men and women to local self-defense courses in the United States (tel. (800) 345-KICK/5425). Course prices vary from US$50-400. Community colleges frequently offer less expensive self-defense courses.

If you are using a **car,** learn local driving signals. Motor vehicle crashes are a leading cause of travel deaths in many parts of the world. Be sure to park your vehicle in a garage or well-traveled area. Study route maps before you hit the road; some roads have poor (or nonexistent) shoulders, few gas stations, and roaming animals. In many regions, road conditions necessitate driving more slowly and more cautiously than you would at home. *Let's Go* does not recommend **hitchhiking,** particularly for women—see **Getting Around,** p. 31, for more information.

Exercise extreme caution when using pools or beaches without lifeguards. Hidden rocks and shallow depths may cause serious injury or even death. Heed warning signs about dangerous undertows. If you rent scuba-diving equipment, make sure that it is up to par before taking the plunge.

For official **United States Department of State** travel advisories, call their 24-hour hotline at (202) 647-5225 or check their web site (http://travel.state.gov), which provides travel info and publications. Alternatively, try the Superintendent of Documents (see **Useful Publications,** p. 6). Official warnings from the **United Kingdom Foreign and Commonwealth Office** are on-line at http://www.fco.gov.uk; you can also call the office at (0171) 238-4503. The **Canadian Department of Foreign Affairs and International Trade** (DFAIT) offers advisories and travel warnings (tel. (613) 944-6788 in Ottawa, (800) 267-6788 elsewhere in Canada; http://www.dfait-maeci.gc.ca). Their free publication, *Bon Voyage, But...,* offers travel tips to Canadian citizens; you can receive a copy by calling (613) 944-6788 from Ottawa or abroad, (800) 267-6788 from Canada.

FINANCIAL SECURITY

Ecuadorian cities have more than their fair share of hustlers. Those who speak some English will try to use this to their advantage. Fast-talking men frequently confront tourists, strike up a conversation, and soon begin demanding money. Con artists and hustlers often work in groups as well, and children, unfortunately, are among the most effective at the game. Be aware of certain classics: sob stories that require money, rolls of bills "found" on the street, mustard spilled (or saliva spit) onto your shoulder distracting you long enough to snatch your bag. You should give strangers a cold reception if they seem overly effusive or if they offer to accompany you. It's not unusual for tourists to be called racist if they refuse to give money, or if they are cool to advances. Ignore the epithets and head into a bank or restaurant for safety. Contact the police if a hustler is particularly insistent or aggressive.

Don't put money in a wallet in your back pocket. Never count your money in public and carry as little as possible. If you carry a purse, buy a sturdy one with a secure clasp, and carry it crosswise on the side, away from the street with the clasp against you. Secure packs with small combination padlocks which slip through the two zippers. (Even these precautions do not always suffice: moped riders who snatch purses and backpacks sometimes tote knives to cut the straps.) A **money belt** is the best way to carry cash; you can buy one at most camping supply stores or through the Forsyth Travel Library (see **Useful Publications,** p. 6). A nylon, zippered pouch with belt that sits inside the waist of your pants or skirt combines convenience and security. A **neck pouch** is equally safe, although far less accessible. Refrain from pulling out your neck pouch in public; if you must, be very discreet. Avoid keeping anything precious in a fanny-pack: your valuables will be highly visible and easy to steal.

In city crowds and on public transportation, pick-pockets are quite deft at their craft. Also, be alert in public phone booths. If you must say your calling-card number, do so quietly; if you punch it in, make sure no one can look over your shoulder. Making **photocopies** of important documents will allow you to recover them in case they are lost or filched. Carry one copy separate from the documents and leave another copy at home. Keeping some money separate from the rest is also a good idea.

Label every piece of luggage both inside and out. Be particularly vigilant on **buses** (carry your backpack in front of you where you can see it), don't check baggage on buses or trains if you can help it, and don't trust anyone to "watch your bag for a second." Thieves thrive on **trains;** professionals wait for tourists to fall asleep and then carry off all they can. **Never leave your belongings unattended;** even the most demure-looking hostel may be a den of thieves. If you feel unsafe, look for places with either a curfew or a night attendant. When possible, keep expensive jewelry, valuables, and anything you couldn't bear to part with at home. Keep valuables and important documents on you if you're staying in low-budget hotels or dormitory-style surroundings, and try to sleep on top bunks with your luggage stored above you.

DRUGS AND ALCOHOL

Drinking in any part of Latin America is not for amateurs; non-gringo bars are often strongholds of *machismo*. When someone calls you *amigo* and orders you a beer, bow out quickly unless you want to match him glass for glass in a challenge. If you carry **prescription drugs** while you travel, have a copy of the prescriptions readily accessible at country borders. Despite the prevalence of marijuana, cocaine, and hallucinogens, **illegal drugs** should not be touched. Drug users and carriers are never treated leniently and Ecuadorian jails are worse than your worst hostel nightmare. Similarly, don't bring drugs back into the U.S.; customs agents and their perceptive K-9s are not to be taken lightly. For the free pamphlet *Travel Warning on Drugs Abroad,* send a self-addressed, stamped envelope to the Bureau of Consular Affairs, Public Affairs #6831, Dept. of State, Washington, D.C. 20520-4818.

■ Health

Common sense is the simplest prescription for good health while you travel: eat well, drink and sleep enough, and don't overexert yourself. Travelers complain most often about their feet and their gut, so take precautionary measures. Drinking lots of fluids can often prevent dehydration and constipation, and wearing sturdy shoes with clean socks and talcum powder can help keep your feet dry.

BEFORE YOU GO

Though no amount of planning can guarantee an accident-free trip, preparation can help minimize the likelihood of illness and maximize the chances of receiving effective health-care. For minor health problems, bring a compact **first-aid kit.** It should include bandages, aspirin or another type of pain killer, antibiotic cream, thermometer, Swiss Army knife with tweezers, moleskin, decongestant for colds, motion sickness remedy, medicine for diarrhea or stomach problems, sunscreen, insect repellent, and burn ointment.

In your passport, write the names of any people you wish to be contacted in case of a medical emergency, and also list any allergies or medical conditions you would want doctors to be aware of. Those with medical conditions (e.g. diabetes, allergies to antibiotics, epilepsy, etc.) may want to obtain a **Medic Alert** identification tag (US$35 the first year, and US$15 annually thereafter), which identifies the disease and gives a 24-hour collect-call info number. Contact Medic Alert at (800) 825-3785 or 432-5378, or write to Medic Alert Foundation, 2323 Colorado Ave., Turlock, CA 95382. Diabetics can contact the **American Diabetes Association,** 1660 Duke St., Alexandria, VA 22314 (tel. (800) 232-3472), to receive copies of the article "Travel and Diabetes" and a diabetic ID card, which carries messages in 18 languages explaining the carrier's diabetic status. If you wear glasses or contact lenses, carry the prescription and an extra set or arrange to have your doctor or a family member send a replacement pair in case of emergency. Allergy sufferers should find out if their conditions are likely to be aggravated in the regions they plan to visit, and obtain a full supply of any necessary medication before the trip, since matching a prescription to a foreign equivalent is not always easy, safe, or possible. Carry up-to-date, legible prescriptions or a statement from your doctor, especially if you use insulin, a syringe, or a narcotic. While traveling, keep all medication in carry-on luggage.

If you are concerned about being able to access medical support while traveling, **Global Emergency Medical Services (GEMS)** offers 24-hour international medical assistance and support coordinated through registered nurses who have on-line access to your medical info, primary physician, and a worldwide network of screened, credentialed English-speaking doctors and hospitals. For more info call (800) 860-1111; fax (770) 475-0058, or write: 2001 Westside Drive, #120, Alpharetta, GA 30201. The **International Association for Medical Assistance to Travelers (IAMAT)** offers a membership ID card, a directory of English-speaking doctors around the world who treat members for a set fee schedule, and detailed charts on immunization requirements, various tropical diseases, climate, and sanitation. Membership is free, though donations are appreciated and used for further research. Contact chapters in the **U.S.,** 417 Center St., Lewiston, NY 14092 (tel. (716) 754-4883; fax (519) 836-3412; email iamat@sentex.net; http://www.sentex.net/~iamat), **Canada,** 40 Regal Road, Guelph, Ontario, N1K 1B5 (tel. (519) 836-0102) or 1287 St. Clair Avenue West, Toronto, M6E 1B8 (tel. (416) 652-0137; fax (519) 836-3412), or **New Zealand,** P.O. Box 5049, Christchurch 5.

VACCINATIONS AND OTHER DISEASE PREVENTION

When it comes to health, a few preventive steps go a long way. Take a look at your **immunization** records before you go to make sure your "childhood" vaccines (e.g. measles, mumps, tetanus) are up to date. Hepatitis A vaccine and/or an Immune Globulin injection (IG) is recommended for travelers to Ecuador. If you will be spending more than four weeks there, you should consider the typhoid vaccine as well. Check with a doctor for advice on immunization, and try to remember that no matter how bad the needles are, they're better than the diseases they prevent.

It is wise to avoid contact with animals. Dogs' vaccinations are frequently overlooked, so that sweet-faced pooch at your feet might very well be disease-ridden. **Rabies** is a concern in Ecuador, so if you are bitten be sure to clean your wound thoroughly and seek medical help immediately.

Many diseases are transmitted by **insects**—mainly mosquitoes, fleas, ticks, and lice. Insect bites are always annoying, but they can also be dangerous and sometimes life-threatening. Protect yourself in wet or forested areas, while hiking, and especially while camping. **Mosquitoes** are most active from dusk to dawn. Wear long pants and long sleeves (fabric need not be thick or warm; tropic-weight cottons can keep you comfortable in the heat), and buy a bednet for camping. Never go barefoot, and always tuck long pants into socks. Use insect repellents; DEET can be bought in spray or liquid form, but use it sparingly, especially on children. Soak or spray your gear with permethrin, which is licensed in the U.S. for use on clothing. Natural repellents can also be useful: taking vitamin B-12 or garlic pills regularly can eventually make you smelly to insects. Still, be sure to supplement your vitamins with repellent. Calamine lotion or topical cortisones (like Cortaid©) may stop insect bites from itching, as can a bath with a half-cup of baking soda or oatmeal.

Malaria is transmitted by Anopheles mosquitoes, which bite during the night. These pesky bloodsuckers are present in the coastal and Oriente regions of Ecuador. Preliminary symptoms include fever, chills, aches, and fatigue. Since early stages resemble the flu, you should see a doctor for any flu-like sickness that occurs after travel in a high-risk area. Left untreated, malaria can cause anemia, kidney failure, coma, and death. The disease poses an especially serious threat to pregnant women and their fetuses. Anti-malarial drugs are available but depend on the region in which you will be traveling, so consult your doctor for a prescription. **Other insect diseases** are less common but just as serious. **Filariasis** is a round worm infestation transmitted by mosquitoes which causes enlargement (elephantiasis) of extremities; there is no vaccine. **Leishmaniasis** is a parasite transmitted by sand flies. Common symptoms are fever, weakness, and a swollen spleen. There is a treatment, but no vaccine.

The **United States Centers for Disease Control and Prevention** (based in Atlanta, Georgia), an excellent source of info for travelers around the world, maintains an international travelers' hotline (tel. (404) 332-4559; fax 332-4565; http://www.cdc.gov). The CDC publishes the booklet "Health Information for International

The Rise, Fall, and Spiritual Renaissance of Dengue Fever

Dengue fever, also called "breakbone fever," is painful, relatively easy to catch, and spreading fast. It is present wherever its carriers swarm—the dread diurnal mosquitoes *Aedes aegypti* and *Aedes albopictus*—and these little guys give it a potential range of over two billion human targets. Breakbone can provoke a wide range of symptoms, and its early stages are easily confused with influenza, measles, typhoid, and a slew of other fever-inducing illnesses. "Classic" dengue is characterized by an abrupt onset of high fever after an incubation period of three to 15 days. Victims often experience one of more of the following: lower back pain, headaches, malaise, severe pain in the bones or joints, nausea, vomiting, diarrhea, blurred vision, and bleeding of the gums—classic! In severe cases of dengue hemorrhagic fever (DHF), patients can also suffer a large, painful rash, circulatory failure, and system-wide bleeding: these advanced cases can be fatal.

Although dengue has been breaking out and busting ass since at least the late 18th century, DHF did not emerge until the 1950s, in Southeast Asia. It was first spotted in the New World in 1975, and it has since spread to at least 12 countries in South and Central America, including Ecuador. Attempts to create a vaccine have not yet been successful and epidemiologists expect the disease to spread. DHF seems ripe to rip through Ecuador sometime soon.

If you have been in possible contact with mosquitoes anywhere in the Americas and experience dengue-like symptoms, seek medical assistance as soon as possible. Because of the lengthy incubation period, it is possible to develop symptoms up to two weeks after your travels. Until you can get to a hospital, treat the dengue like an ordinary fever, but be sure to use acetaminophen and not aspirin. However, it is best to get yourself to a hospital and avoid mosquitoes in the first place—it is discourteous to spread dengue to your hometown.

Travelers" (US$20), an annual global rundown of disease, immunization, and health advice, including risks in particular countries. This book may be purchased by sending a check or money order to the Superintendent of Documents, U.S. Government Printing Office, P.O. Box 371954, Pittsburgh, PA, 15250-7954. Orders can be made by phone with a credit card (tel. (202) 512-1800; Visa, Mastercard, or Discover).

FOOD- AND WATER-BORNE DISEASES

To ensure that your food is safe, make sure everything is cooked properly (deep-fried is good, the fresher the grease the better), and be sure water you drink is clean. Don't order meat "rare," and eggs should be thoroughly cooked, not served sunny-side up.

Cholera is an intestinal disease caused by a bacteria found in contaminated food; the disease has recently reached epidemic proportions in parts of South America, including Ecuador. The first severe symptoms of cholera are lots of watery diarrhea, dehydration, vomiting, and muscle cramps. Untreated, cholera can be fatal. Antibiotics are available, but the most important treatment is rehydration. Consider getting a vaccine (50% effective) if you have stomach problems (e.g. ulcers), will be camping a good deal, or are living where water is not always reliable.

Typhoid Fever is more of a concern to those visiting villages and rural areas of Ecuador. While mostly transmitted through contaminated food and water, it may also be acquired by direct contact with another person. Symptoms include fever, headaches, fatigue, loss of appetite, constipation, and a rash on the abdomen or chest; antibiotics treat typhoid fever. The Center for Disease Control and Prevention recommends vaccinations (70-90% effective) for those going off the "usual tourist itineraries," that is, those hiking, camping, and staying in small cities or rural areas.

Parasites (tapeworms, etc.) also hide in unsafe water and food. Giardia, for example, can be acquired by drinking untreated water from streams or lakes all over the world. It can stay with you for years. Symptoms of parasitic infections in general include swollen glands or lymph nodes, fever, rashes or itchiness, digestive problems, eye problems, and anemia. Boil your water, wear shoes, avoid bugs, and eat only cooked food.

Hepatitis A (distinct from B and C) is a risk to all travelers, including those visiting Ecuador. It is a viral infection of the liver acquired primarily through contaminated water, ice, shellfish, or unpeeled fruits, and vegetables (as well as from sexual contact). Symptoms include fatigue, fever, loss of appetite, nausea, dark urine, jaundice, vomiting, aches and pains, and light stools. Ask your doctor about a new vaccine called "Havrix," or ask to get an injection of immune globulin (IG; formerly called Gamma Globulin). Risk is highest in rural areas and the countryside.

Hepatitis B is a viral infection of the liver transmitted by sharing needles, having unprotected sex, or coming into direct contact with an infected person's lesioned skin. If you think you may be sexually active while traveling or if you are working or living in rural areas, you are typically advised to get the vaccination for Hepatitis B. Vaccination should begin six months before traveling.

Hepatitis C is like Hepatitis B, but the methods of transmission are different. At risk are intravenous drug users, those with occupational exposure to blood, hemodialysis patients, or recipients of a blood transfusion; doctors aren't sure if you can get it through sexual contact.

TRAVELER'S DIARRHEA

Traveler's diarrhea, also known as *turista*, is the most common health risk for visitors to Ecuador. It is the dastardly consequence of consuming contaminated food and water. It often lasts three to seven days; symptoms include diarrhea, nausea, bloating, vomiting, chills, and a fever as high as 103°F (39°C). If the nasties hit you, have quick-energy, non-sugary foods with protein and carbohydrates to keep your strength up. Over-the-counter remedies (such as Pepto-Bismol© or Immodium©) may counteract the symptoms, but they can complicate serious infections; avoid anti-diarrheals if you suspect you have been exposed to contaminated food or water; they put you at risk for other diseases. The most dangerous side effect of diarrhea is dehydration; the simplest and most effective anti-dehydration formula is eight oz. of (clean) water with ½ tsp. of sugar or honey and a pinch of salt. Down several of these mixtures each day, rest, and wait for the disease to run its course. If you develop a fever, or your symptoms don't go away after four or five days, consult a doctor. Also consult a doctor if children develop traveler's diarrhea, since treatment is different.

To avoid *turista,* **never drink unbottled water;** ask for *agua purificada* in restaurants and hotels. To purify your own water, bring it to a rolling boil (simmering isn't enough), or treat it with iodine drops or tablets. Don't be fooled by the clever disguise of impure water—the ice cube. Stay away from salads—uncooked vegetables (including lettuce and coleslaw) are a great way to get *turista.* Other culprits are raw shellfish, unpasteurized milk, and sauces containing raw eggs. Peel all fruits and vegetables, and beware of watermelon, which is often injected with impure water. Watch out for food from markets or street vendors that may have been washed in dirty water or fried in rancid cooking oil. Always wash your hands before eating. A golden rule in Latin America: boil it, peel it, cook it, or forget it, but don't get so paranoid about the water that you get dehydrated.

HOT, COLD, AND ALTITUDE

Equatorial heat is no small concern. Common sense goes a long way toward preventing **heat exhaustion:** relax in hot weather, drink lots of nonalcoholic fluids, and lie down inside if you feel awful. Continuous heat stress can eventually lead to **heatstroke,** characterized by rising body temperature, severe headache, and cessation of sweating. Wear a hat, sunglasses, and a lightweight long-sleeved shirt to avoid heatstroke. Victims must be cooled off with wet towels and quickly taken to a doctor.

Always drink enough liquids to keep your urine clear. Alcoholic beverages are dehydrating, as are coffee, strong tea, and caffeinated sodas. If you'll be sweating a lot, be sure to eat enough salty food to prevent electrolyte depletion, which causes severe headaches. Less debilitating, but still dangerous, is **sunburn.** If you're prone to sunburn, bring sunscreen with you (it's often more expensive and hard to find when traveling in Ecuador), and apply it liberally and often to avoid burns and risk of skin cancer. If you get sunburned, drink more fluids than usual.

Despite the fact that the country is named for the equator, temperatures can get quite cold high in the Andes. Extreme cold is just as dangerous as heat—overexposure to cold brings the risk of **hypothermia.** Warning signs are easy to detect: body temperature drops rapidly, resulting in the failure to produce body heat. You may shiver, have poor coordination, feel exhausted, have slurred speech, feel sleepy, hallucinate, or suffer amnesia. **Do not let hypothermia victims fall asleep**—their body temperature will drop more, and if they lose consciousness they may die. Seek medical help as soon as possible. To avoid hypothermia, keep dry and stay out of the wind. In wet weather, wool and most synthetics, such as pile, will keep you warm, but most other fabric, especially cotton, will make you colder. Dress in layers, and watch for **frostbite** when the temperature is below freezing. Look for skin that has turned white, waxy, and cold. If you find frostbite, do not rub the skin. Drink warm beverages, get dry, and slowly warm the area with dry fabric or steady body contact. Take serious cases to a doctor as soon as possible.

The extreme variation in altitude in Ecuador means that **altitude sickness** is a risk as well. Travelers to the highlands should avoid exertion during their first day or two, until their bodies have adjusted to the lower level of oxygen in the air. Ignoring this advice can result in symptoms such as headache, nausea, sleeplessness, and shortness of breath, even while resting. It is best treated with rest, deep breathing, and moving to a lower altitude. If the symptoms persist or worsen, or if the victim begins to turn blue, *immediately descend to a lower altitude and proceed to a hospital if necessary.* Those planning to climb some of Ecuador's taller peaks should take a week in the Sierra to adjust to the altitude before attempting the climb, and should remember to climb slowly. You should also be careful about alcohol, especially if you're used to

U.S. standards for beer—many Ecuadorian brews and liquors pack more punch, and at high altitudes, any alcohol will do you in quickly.

WOMEN'S HEALTH

Women traveling in unsanitary conditions are vulnerable to urinary tract and bladder infections, common and severely uncomfortable bacterial diseases which cause a burning sensation and painful and sometimes frequent urination. Drink tons of vitamin-C-rich juice, plenty of clean water, and urinate frequently, especially right after intercourse. Untreated, these infections can lead to kidney infections, sterility, and even death. If symptoms persist, see a doctor. If you often develop vaginal yeast infections, take along an over-the-counter medicine, as treatments may not be readily available in Ecuador. Women may also be more susceptible to vaginal thrush and cystitis, two treatable but uncomfortable illnesses that are likely to flare up in hot and humid climates. Wearing loosely fitting trousers or a skirt and cotton underwear may help. Tampons and pads are sometimes hard to find when traveling; certainly your preferred brands may not be available, so it may be advisable to take supplies along. Refer to the *Handbook for Women Travellers* by Maggie and Gemma Moss (published by Piatkus Books) or to the women's health guide *Our Bodies, Our Selves* (published by the Boston Women's Health Collective) for more extensive info specific to women's health on the road.

BIRTH CONTROL

Reliable contraceptive devices may be difficult to find while traveling. Women on the pill should bring enough to allow for possible loss or extended stays and should bring a prescription, since forms of the pill vary a good deal. The sponge is probably too bulky to be worthwhile on the road. If you use a diaphragm, be sure that you have enough contraceptive jelly on hand. Though condoms are available, you might want to bring your favorite national brand with you; availability and quality vary. **Abortion** is illegal in Ecuador, except in cases in which a woman's physical health is threatened by the pregnancy, cases of fetal defects, and cases of rape or incest.

AIDS, HIV, AND STDS

Acquired Immune Deficiency Syndrome (AIDS) is a growing problem around the world. The World Health Organization estimates that there are around 13 million people infected with the HIV virus. Well over 90% of adults newly infected with HIV acquired their infection through heterosexual sex; women now represent 50% of all new HIV infections. The easiest mode of HIV transmission is through direct blood-to-blood contact with an HIV+ person; *never* share intravenous drug, tattooing, or other needles. The most common mode of transmission is sexual intercourse. Health professionals recommend the use of latex condoms; follow the instructions on the packet. Since it isn't always easy to buy condoms when traveling, take a supply with you before you depart for your trip. Casual contact (including drinking from the same glass or using the same eating utensils) is not believed to pose a risk.

For more info on AIDS, call the **U.S. Center for Disease Control's** 24-hour hotline at (800) 342-2437. In Europe, write to the **World Health Organization,** attn: Global Program on AIDS, 20 Avenue Appia, 1211 Geneva 27, Switzerland (tel. (22) 791-2111). Or, write to the **Bureau of Consular Affairs,** #6831, Department of State, Washington, D.C. 20520 (http://travel.state.gov). The brochure, *Travel Safe: AIDS and International Travel,* is available at all Council Travel offices.

Sexually transmitted diseases (STDs) such as gonorrhea, chlamydia, genital warts, syphilis, and herpes are a lot easier to catch than HIV, and can be just as deadly. It's wise to *look* at your partner's genitals before you have sex. If anything looks amiss, that should be a warning signal. The warning signals for STDs include: swelling, sores, bumps, or blisters on sex organs, rectum, or mouth; burning and pain during urination and bowel movements; itching around sex organs; swelling or redness in the throat; flu-like symptoms with fever, chills, and aches. If these symptoms develop, see a doctor immediately. During sex, condoms may protect from certain STDs, but oral and even manual contact can lead to transmission.

■ Alternatives to Tourism

STUDY

Many students come to Ecuador to learn Spanish from one of the language schools around the country. Prices and programs vary, but they usually cost around US$200 a week and often include 4-7 hours of daily instruction, a homestay with a local family, and weekly excursions to surrounding cultural and ecological sites. In Quito, these schools are as abundant as shoeshiners, and sifting through the available opportunities can be a daunting task. The South American Explorer's Club can help narrow down the options, as can the resources listed below. Arrangements can be made before leaving your home country or after you arrive in Ecuador. In addition to these schools, American universities and other more global organizations have different academic programs in Ecuador. Local libraries and bookstores can be useful sources for current info on study abroad. The Internet has a study abroad web site at **http:// www.studyabroad.com/liteimage.html.**

American Field Service (AFS), 198 Madison Ave., 8th fl., New York, NY 10016 (tel. students (800) AFS-INFO/237-4636, administration (800) 876-2376; fax (503) 241-1653; email afsinfo@afs.org; http://www.afs.org/usa). AFS offers summer, semester, and year-long homestay international exchange programs for high school students, recent high school graduates and short-term service projects for adults in Ecuador (as well as other countries). Financial aid available.

College Semester Abroad, School for International Training, Kipling Rd., P.O. Box 676, Brattleboro, VT 05302 (tel. (800) 336-1616; fax (802) 258-3500). Offers semester-long programs in Ecuador, as well as other countries. Programs cost

US$9300-11,500, including tuition, room, board, and airfare. Scholarships are available and federal financial aid is usually transferable from your college or university.

Council on International Education Exchange, 205 E. 42nd St., New York, NY 10017 (tel. (888) COUNCIL/268-6245; fax (212) 822-2699; email info@ciee.org; http://www.ciee.org), sponsors over 40 study abroad programs worldwide.

Institute of International Education (IIE), 809 United Nations Plaza, New York, NY 10017-3580 (tel. (212) 984-5413; fax 984-5358). For book orders: IIE Books, Institute of International Education, P.O. Box 371, Annapolis Junction, MD 20701 (tel. (800) 445-0443; fax (301) 206-9789; email iiebooks@pmds.com). A nonprofit, international and cultural exchange agency, IIE's library of study abroad resources is open to the public Tues.-Thurs. 11am-3:45pm. Publishes *Academic Year Abroad* (US$43, US$5 postage) and *Vacation Study Abroad* (US$37, US$5 postage).

The Experiment in International Living, P.O. Box 676, Brattleboro, VT 05302 (tel. (800) 345-2929 or (802) 257-7751; http://www.worldlearning.org). A division of World Learning, Inc., it offers summer ecology programs in Ecuador for high school students, Programs are 3-5 weeks long. Positions as group leaders are available worldwide if you are over 24, have previous in-country experience, are fluent in the language, and have worked with high school students.

Youth For Understanding International Exchange (YFU), 3501 Newark St. NW, Washington, D.C. 20016 (tel. (800) TEENAGE/833-6243 or (202) 966-6800; fax 895-1104; http://www.yfu.org). Places U.S. high school students worldwide for year, semester, summer, and sport homestays.

VOLUNTEER AND WORK

Volunteering is an excellent way to immerse yourself in Ecuadorian culture and the Spanish language while giving back to the place you are visiting. The good news is that it's very easy to find volunteer positions, especially if you are willing to shell out a few bucks; the bad news is that paid work can be exceedingly difficult to find. Countries are reluctant to give up precious jobs to traveling gringos when many of their citizens are unemployed. It's not impossible, though, as some businesses are eager to hire English-speaking personnel for prestige or for the convenience of their patrons. The following is a list of useful publications and organizations.

Addison-Wesley, Jacob Way, Reading, MA 01867 (tel. (800) 822-6339). Published *International Jobs: Where They Are, How to Get Them* in 1993-1994 (US$16). Jobs in Ecuador are included, but they are listed by job, not country.

Council has a Voluntary Services Dept., 205 E. 42nd St., New York, NY 10017 (tel. (888) COUNCIL/268-6245; fax (212) 822-2699; email info@ciee.org; http://www.ciee.org), which offers 2- to 4-week environmental or community service projects in over 30 countries. Participants must be at least 18 years old. Minimum US$295 placement fee; additional fees may also apply for various countries.

Global Volunteers, 375 E. Little Canada Rd., St. Paul, MN 55117-1628 (tel. (800) 487-1074 or (612) 482-1074; fax 482-0915). The organization sends groups of volunteers all over the world. The programs in Ecuador are with Camp Hope, a local organization in Quito that works with orphaned and abandoned children, 50% of whom have disabilities. Programs last for 2 weeks and include day care, health care, teaching, and construction. The cost is US$1795 without airfare.

Transitions Abroad, 18 Hulst Rd., P.O. Box 1300, Amherst, MA 01004-1300 (tel. (800) 293-0373; fax (413) 256-0373; email trabroad@aol.com). This magazine lists publications and resources for overseas study, work, and volunteering (US$24.95 for a 1-year subscription). Also publishes *The Alternative Travel Directory,* a comprehensive guide to living, learning, and working overseas (US$20; postage US$4).

WorldTeach, Harvard Institute for International Development, 1 Eliot St., Cambridge, MA 02138-5705 (tel. (617) 495-5527; fax 495-1599; email info@worldteach.org; http://www.igc.org/worldteach). Volunteers teach English, math, science, and environmental education to students of all ages in developing countries, including Ecuador. Bachelor's degree required for most programs.

■ Specific Concerns

WOMEN TRAVELERS

> Note: The northwest region of Ecuador, particularly the province of Esmeraldas, is reported to be unsafe for lone women travelers. *Let's Go* does not recommend that women travel alone there. Excepting Esmeraldas, the following suggestions are not meant to discourage solo travel, but to encourage women to travel safely.

Women exploring on their own inevitably face additional safety concerns, but these warnings and suggestions should not dissuade women from venturing solo. Trust your instincts: if you'd feel better somewhere else, move on. Always carry extra money for a phone call, bus, or taxi. Consider staying in hostels which offer single rooms that lock from the inside. Communal showers in some hostels are safer than others; check them before settling in. Stick to centrally-located accommodations and avoid solitary late-night treks or metro rides. **Hitching** is never safe for lone women, or even for two women traveling together.

The less you look like a tourist, the better off you'll be. Look as if you know where you're going (even when you don't) and consider approaching women or couples for directions if you're lost or feel uncomfortable. In general, dress conservatively, especially in rural areas. Avoid shorts and short skirts. If you spend time in cities, you may be harassed no matter how you're dressed. Your best answer to verbal harassment is no answer at all (a reaction is what the harasser wants). In crowds, you may be pinched or squeezed; wearing a wedding band may help prevent such incidents. Don't worry about compromising your independence by referring to your (fictional) "husband." Even mentioning a spouse waiting at the hotel may be enough to deter a would-be suitor. Women traveling alone and in another country should not attempt to challenge custom or assert strong feminist beliefs. You won't change anything but may endanger yourself. The bottom line: don't take unnecessary risks, but don't lose your spirit of adventure either. For additional info, consult the resources below:

National Organization for Women (NOW), boasts branches across the country that can refer women travelers to rape crisis centers and counseling services, and provide lists of feminist events. Main offices include 22 W. 21st St., 7th Fl., **New York,** NY 10010 (tel. (212) 260-4422); 1000 16th St. NW, 7th Fl., **Washington, D.C.** 20004 (tel. (202) 331-0066); and 3543 18th St., **San Francisco,** CA 94110 (tel. (415) 861-8960; fax 861-8969; email sfnow@sirius.com; http://www.sirius.com/~sfnow/now.html).

A Foxy Old Woman's Guide to Traveling Alone, by Jay Ben-Lesser (Crossing Press, US $11). Info, informal advice, and a resource list on solo travel on a budget.

A Journey of One's Own, by Thalia Zepatos, (US$17). Interesting and full of good advice, with a bibliography of books and resources. *Adventures in Good Company,* on group travel by the same author, costs US$17. Available from The Eighth Mountain Press, 624 Southeast 29th Ave., Portland, OR 97214 (tel. (503) 233-3936; fax 233-0774; email eightmt@aol.com).

Women Travel: Adventures, Advice & Experience, by Miranda Davies and Natania Jansz (Penguin, US$13). Info on several foreign countries plus a decent bibliography and resource index. The sequel, *More Women Travel,* costs US$15. Both from Rough Guides, 375 Hudson St. 3rd fl., New York, NY 10014.

Handbook For Women Travellers, by Maggie and Gemma Moss (UK£9). Encyclopedic and well-written. Available from Piatkus Books, 5 Windmill St., London W1P 1HF (tel. (0171) 631 07 10).

BISEXUAL, GAY, AND LESBIAN TRAVELERS

Not the most liberal country, Ecuador punishes homosexual acts by up to 8 months in prison. Bars and meeting points are reportedly raided by the police from time to time. The existence of a few gay bars and clubs in Quito and Guayaquil proves that there is a small homosexual community in Ecuador, but gay and lesbian travelers should be aware that being "out" here is a drastic statement, and may not be a good idea. Many Ecuadorians tend to think of homosexuality as a sickness or a lower-class phenomenon. For more info, consult the organizations and publications listed below:

Ferrari Guides, P.O. Box 37887, Phoenix, AZ 85069 (tel. (602) 863-2408; fax 439-3952; email ferrari@q-net.com; http://www.q-net.com). Gay and lesbian travel guides: *Ferrari Guides' Gay Travel A to Z* (US$16), *Ferrari Guides' Men's Travel in Your Pocket* (US$16), *Ferrari Guides' Women's Travel in Your Pocket* (US$14), *Ferrari Guides' Inn Places* (US$16). In bookstores or by mail order (postage/handling US$4.50 first item, US$1 each additional item mailed within the U.S.).

International Gay and LesbianTravel Association, P.O. Box 4974, Key West, FL 33041 (tel. (800) 448-8550; fax (305) 296-6633; email IGTA@aol.com; http://www.rainbow-mall.com/igta). An organization of over 1300 companies serving gay and lesbian travelers worldwide. Call for lists of travel agents, accommodations, and events.

International Lesbian and Gay Association (ILGA), 81, rue Marché-au-Charbon, B-1000 Bruxelles, Belgium (tel./fax 32-2-502-24 71; email ilga@ilga.org). Not a travel service. Has political info like homosexuality laws of individual countries.

Spartacus International Gay Guides, published by Bruno Gmunder (US$33), Postfach 61 01 04, D-10921 Berlin, Germany (tel. (30) 615 00 3-42; fax (30) 615 91 34). Lists bars, restaurants, hotels, and bookstores around the world catering to gays. Also lists hotlines for gays in various countries and homosexuality laws for each country. Available in bookstores and in the U.S. by mail from Lambda Rising, 1625 Connecticut Ave. NW, Washington D.C., 20009-1013 (tel. (202) 462-6969).

DIETARY CONCERNS

Vegetarians should have no problem finding suitable cuisine. Most restaurants will have vegetarian selections on their menus (rice, beans, fresh fruits, and vegetables are always an option), and if they don't you can ask for it. In addition, many crunchy expatriates have made a place for themselves in Ecuador. As a result, there are quite a few restaurants that cater specifically to vegetarians. For more info, contact the **North American Vegetarian Society,** P.O. Box 72, Dolgeville, NY 13329 (tel. (518) 568-7970), which stocks numerous helpful publications.

There is a Jewish community in Quito; the **Asociación Israelita de Quito** synagogue, 18 de Septiembre y Versalles (tel. 502-734), has services Fridays at 7pm and Saturdays at 9am. As far as keeping **kosher,** most meat in Ecuador is probably not, so stick to vegetarian dishes. If you are strict in your observance, consider bringing your own disposable plates and utensils, or preparing your own food on the road. **The Jewish Travel Guide** lists synagogues, kosher restaurants, and Jewish institutions in over 80 countries, and is available from Ballantine-Mitchell Publishers, Newbury House 890-900, Eastern Ave., Newbury Park, Ilford, Essex, U.K. IG2 7HH (tel. (0181) 599 88 66; fax 599 09 84). It is available in the U.S. from Sepher-Hermon Press, 1265 46th St., Brooklyn, NY 11219 (tel. (718) 972-9010; US$15 plus US$2.50 shipping).

OLDER TRAVELERS

Senior travelers should bring a medical record that includes up-to-date info on conditions and prescriptions; the name, phone number, and address of a regular doctor; and a summary of recent medical history. The following organizations and publications can be helpful:

Elderhostel, 75 Federal St., 3rd Fl., Boston, MA 02110-1941 (tel. (617) 426-7788; fax 426-8351; email Cadyg@elderhostel.org; http://www.elderhostel.org). For those 55 or over (spouse of any age). 1- to 4-week programs at colleges, universities, and learning centers in over 70 countries, including Ecuador, on varied subjects.

National Council of Senior Citizens, 8403 Colesville Rd., Silver Spring, MD 20910-31200 (tel. (301) 578-8800; fax 578-8999). Memberships cost US$13 per year,

US$33 for 3 years, or US$175 for a lifetime and include hotel and auto rental discounts, a senior citizen newspaper, and use of a discount travel agency.

DISABLED TRAVELERS

Ecuador is not very well-prepared to meet the needs of disabled travelers. Rainforests, volcanoes, and beaches rarely have smooth paths, and wheelchair-accessible buildings are rare. Still, there are exceptions, and the region is not off-limits to disabled tourists. Those with disabilities should inform airlines and hotels of their disabilities when making arrangements for travel; some time may be needed to prepare special accommodations. Travelers with seeing-eye dogs need to inquire as to the specific quarantine policies of Ecuador. At the very least, they will need a certificate of immunization against rabies. The following organizations provide helpful info and publications, or help to organize trips for the disabled:

Directions Unlimited, 720 N. Bedford Rd., Bedford Hills, NY 10507 (tel. (800) 533-5343; in NY (914) 241-1700; fax 241-0243). Specializes in arranging individual and group vacations, tours, and cruises for the disabled. Group tours for blind travelers.

Mobility International, USA (MIUSA), P.O. Box 10767, Eugene, OR 97440 (tel. (514) 343-1284 voice and TDD; fax 343-6812; email info@miusa.org; http://miusa.org). International Headquarters in Brussels, rue de Manchester 25 Brussels, Belgium, B-1070 (tel. (322) 410-6297; fax 410 6874). Contacts in 30 countries. Info on travel programs, international volunteer sites, accommodations, access guides, and organized tours for those with physical disabilities. Membership US$30 per year. Sells the 3rd Edition of *A World of Options: A Guide to International Educational Exchange, Community Service, and Travel for Persons with Disabilities* (US$30, nonmembers US$35, organizations US$40).

Society for the Advancement of Travel for the Handicapped (SATH), 347 Fifth Ave., #610, New York, NY 10016 (tel. (212) 447-1928; fax 725-8253; email sathtravel@aol.com; http://www.sath.org). Publishes a quarterly color travel magazine *Open World* (free for members or by subscription US$13 for nonmembers). Also publishes a wide range of info sheets on disability travel facilitation and accessible destinations. Annual membership US$45, students and seniors US$30.

■ Packing

If you don't **pack lightly,** your back and wallet will suffer. The more you have, the more you have to lose. Before you leave, pack your bag, strap it on, and imagine yourself walking uphill on hot asphalt for the next three hours. A good guideline is to lay out only what you absolutely need, then take half the clothes and twice the money.

If you plan to cover most of your itinerary by foot, the unbeatable piece of luggage is a sturdy **backpack.** Many are designed specifically for travelers, while others are for hikers; consider how you will use the pack before purchasing one or the other. Get a pack with a strong, padded hip belt to transfer weight from your shoulders to your hips. When purchasing, avoid excessively low-end prices—you get what you pay for. High-quality packs cost anywhere from US$150 to US$420. Bringing a smaller **daypack** in addition to the mother-pack allows you to leave your big bag in the hotel while you go sight-seeing. It can also be used as an airplane carry-on. Guard your money, passport, and other important articles in **moneybelt** or **neck pouch,** and keep it with you *at all times.* They are available at any good travel or camping store.

As far as **clothing** is concerned, packing lightly does not mean dressing badly. Aim for versatility and comfort, and avoid fabrics that wrinkle easily (to test a fabric, hold it tightly in your fist for 20 seconds). Remember that solid colors mix best. For dressier occasions, remember that simple is elegant, not boring. Black is ideal because it is always in fashion and you can't tell if it's been worn five times. Women should bring a simple, solid-colored dress made of cotton or another versatile fabric. Men should bring a pair of khakis, which can be both dressy and casual, and the essential white button-up shirt. Be sure to bring enough warm clothing, especially if you plan to visit the Sierra. **Good shoes** are essential, not a place to cut corners. Well-cushioned sneakers are good for walking, but if you plan to do any hiking, a water-proofed pair of hiking boots is better. Whatever kind of shoes you choose, break them in before you leave. **Rain gear** is also essential. A waterproof jacket and a back-pack cover will take care of you and your stuff at a moment's notice. Gore-Tex® is a miracle fabric that's both waterproof and breathable.

. If you plan on doing any camping, a sturdy, compact, lightweight **sleeping bag** will serve you well. Otherwise, a **bedsheet** can come in handy; you may have to crash somewhere that does not have sheets. In terms of **washing clothes,** *Let's Go* attempts to provide info on laundromats, but in case you have to use a sink, bring detergent soap, and a rubber squash ball to stop up the drain. Ecuador uses the same **electric current** as North America (110 volts, 60 cycles). Your preferred brand of contact lens supplies are sometimes rare or expensive. Bring enough saline and cleaner for your entire vacation, or wear glasses. In any case, bring a backup pair of glasses. Consider bringing a disposable **camera** rather than an expensive, permanent one. **Film** is pricey; bring lots from home. Also, airport security X-rays *can* fog film; always pack it in your carry-on luggage, and either pack it in a lead-lined pouch (sold at cam-era stores) or ask the security to hand inspect it. **Additional essential items** are: resealable plastic bags (for damp clothes, and spillables, like shampoo), alarm clock, hat, needle and thread, safety pins, pocketknife, water bottle, compass, towel, pad-lock, flashlight, insect repellant, sunscreen, and vitamins. Items not readily available on the road include: deodorant, razors, condoms, and tampons. For other important packing tips see **Health: Before You Go,** p. 16.

GETTING THERE

■ Flying to Ecuador

The airline industry attempts to squeeze every dollar from customers; finding a cheap airfare in their deliberately mysterious and confusing jungle will be easier if you understand the airlines' systems. Call every toll-free number and don't be afraid to ask about discounts. Have a knowledgeable **travel agent** guide you.

Students and people under 26 with proper ID qualify for enticing reduced airfares. These are available from student travel agencies (listed below) which negotiate spe-cial reduced-rate bulk purchase with airlines, then resell them to the youth market. Return-date change fees also tend to be low (around US$35 per segment through Council or Let's Go Travel). Most flights are on major airlines, though in peak season some agencies may sell seats on less reliable chartered aircraft. Sunday newspapers often have travel sections that list bargain fares from local airports. Michael McColl's *The Worldwide Guide to Cheap Airfare* (US$15) is an incredibly useful guide for finding cheap airfare. On the web, try the **Air Traveler's Handbook** (http://www.cis.ohio-state.edu/hypertext/faq/usenet/travel/air/handbook/top.html).

Most airfares peak between mid-June and early September. During midweek (Mon.-Thurs. morning), round-trip flights run about US$40-50 cheaper than on weekends; weekend flights, however, are generally less crowded. Traveling from hubs such as Miami, Houston, and Los Angeles is usually cheaper than flying from smaller cities. The two Ecuadorian cities with international airports are Quito and Guayaquil. Return-date flexibility is usually not an option for budget travelers; "open-return" tick-ets can be pricier than paying to change a set return date. Pick up tickets well in advance of the departure date, have the flight confirmed within 72 hours of depar-ture, and arrive at the airport at least three hours before your flight departs.

COMMERCIAL AIRLINES

Both U.S. and Latin American commercial airlines fly to Ecuador. While the U.S. air-lines are typically more expensive, they allow you to fly from anywhere in the United

States. The Latin American airlines, on the other hand, fly only to and from Miami, Houston, Los Angeles, and sometimes New York. U.S. airlines that fly to Ecuador are **American** (tel. (800) 433-7300) and **Continental** (tel. (800) 231-0856); the Latin American ones are **LACSA** (tel. (800) 225-2272) and **SAETA** (tel. (800) 827-2382). Round-trip fares normally run around US$700 (give or take US$100), but may drop closer to US$500, depending on the season and other more mysterious factors.

The commercial airlines' lowest regular offer is the **Advance Purchase Excursion Fare (APEX);** specials advertised in newspapers may be cheaper, but have more restrictions and fewer available seats. APEX fares provide you with confirmed reservations and allow "open-jaw" tickets (landing in and returning from different cities). Generally, reservations must be made seven to 21 days in advance, with seven- to 14-day minimum and up to 90-day maximum stay limits, and hefty cancellation and change penalties (fees rise in summer). Book APEX fares early during peak season; by May you will have a hard time getting the departure date you want. Even if you pay an airline's lowest published fare, you may waste hundreds of dollars. For the bargain-hungry, there are other, perhaps more inconvenient or time-consuming options, but before shopping around it is a good idea to find out the average commercial price in order to measure just how great a "bargain" you are being offered.

CONSOLIDATORS AND COURIER COMPANIES

Ticket consolidators resell unsold tickets on commercial and charter airlines at unpublished fares. The consolidator market is by and large international. Consolidator flights are the best deals if you are traveling: on short notice, (you bypass advance purchase requirements since you aren't tangled in airline bureaucracy); on a high-priced trip; to an offbeat destination; or in the peak season, when published fares are jacked way up. Fares sold by consolidators are generally much cheaper; a 30-40% price reduction is not uncommon. There are rarely age constraints or stay limitations, but unlike tickets bought through an airline, you won't be able to use your tickets on another flight if you miss yours, and you will have to go back to the consolidator to get a refund, rather than the airline. Keep in mind that these tickets are often for coach seats on connecting (not direct) flights on foreign airlines, and that frequent-flyer miles may not be credited. Decide what you can live with before shopping.

Not all consolidators deal with the general public; many only sell tickets through travel agents. **Bucket shops** are retail agencies that specialize in getting cheap tickets. Although ticket prices are marked up slightly, bucket shops generally have access to a larger market than would be available to the public and can also get tickets from wholesale consolidators. Look for bucket shops' tiny ads in the travel section of weekend papers; in the U.S., the *Sunday New York Times* is a good source. In London, a call to the **Air Travel Advisory Bureau** (tel. (0171) 636 50 00), can provide names of reliable consolidators and discount flight specialists.

Be a smart shopper; check out the competition. Among the many reputable and trustworthy companies are, unfortunately, some shady wheeler-dealers. Contact the local Better Business Bureau to find out how long the company has been in business and its track record. Although not necessary, it is preferable to deal with consolidators close to home so you can visit in person, if necessary. Ask to receive your tickets as quickly as possible so you have time to fix any problems. Get the company's policy in writing: insist on a **receipt** that gives full details about the tickets, refunds, and restrictions, and record who you talked to and when. It may be worth paying with a credit card (despite the 2-5% fee) so you can stop payment if you never receive your tickets. Beware the "bait and switch" gag: shyster firms will advertise a super-low fare and then tell a caller that it has been sold. Although this is a viable excuse, if they can't offer you a price near the advertised fare on *any* date, it is a scam to lure in customers—report them to the Better Business Bureau. Also ask about accommodations and car rental discounts; some consolidators have fingers in many pies.

For destinations **worldwide**, try **Airfare Busters,** (offices in Washington, D.C. (tel. (202) 776-0478), Boca Raton, FL (tel. (561) 994-9590), and Houston, TX (tel. (800) 232-8783); **Pennsylvania Travel,** Paoli, PA (tel. (800) 331-0947); **Cheap Tickets,** offices in Los Angeles, CA, San Francisco, CA, Honolulu, HI, Seattle, WA, and New York, NY, (tel. (800) 377-1000); or **Moment's Notice,** in New York, NY (tel. (718) 234-6295; fax 234-6450; http://www.moments-notice.com), which offers air tickets, tours, and hotels; US$25 annual fee. **NOW Voyager,** 74 Varick St. #307, New York, NY 10013 (tel. (212) 431-1616; fax (212) 334-5243; email info@nowvoyager-travel.com; http://www.nowvoyagertravel.com), acts as a consolidator and books discounted international flights, mostly from New York, as well as courier flights (see **Courier Companies and Freighters** below), for a registration fee of US$50. For a processing fee, depending on the number of travelers and the itinerary, **Travel Avenue,** Chicago, IL (tel. (800) 333-3335; fax (312) 876-1254; http://www.travelavenue.com), will search for the lowest international airfare available, including consolidated prices, and will even give you a rebate on fares over US$300. Kelly Monaghan's *Consolidators: Air Travel's Bargain Basement* (US$7 plus US$2 shipping) from the Intrepid Traveler, P.O. Box 438, New York, NY 10034 (email intreptrav@aol.com), is an invaluable source of info and lists consolidators by location and destination.

Traveling as a **courier** can get you some of the cheapest flights around, but there are many restrictions. Courier flights to Ecuador leave only from Miami, and you have to travel light. Fares are between US$300-400, and maximum length of stay ranges from 14 to 60 days. The company hiring you will use your checked luggage for freight; you're only allowed to bring carry-ons. You are responsible for the safe delivery of the baggage claim slips (given to you by a courier company representative) to the representative waiting when you arrive—don't screw up or you will be blacklisted as a courier. You will probably never see the cargo you are transporting—the company handles it all—and airport officials know that couriers are not responsible for the baggage checked for them. Restrictions to watch for: you must be over 21 (18 in some cases), have a valid passport, and procure your own visa (if necessary); most flights are round-trip only with short fixed-length stays (usually one week); only single tickets are issued (but a companion may be able to get a next-day flight); and most flights are from New York. The following companies handle courier flight to Ecuador: **Discount Travel International** (tel. (212) 362-3636; fax 362-3236), **Line Haul Services** (tel. (305) 477-0651), and **Trans-Air Systems, Inc.** (tel. (305) 592-1771).

■ Budget Travel Agencies

Council Travel (http://www.ciee.org/travel/index.htm), the travel division of Council, is a full-service travel agency specializing in youth and budget travel. They offer discount airfares on scheduled airlines, hosteling cards, low-cost accommodations, guidebooks, budget tours, travel gear, and international student (ISIC), youth (GO25), and teacher (ITIC) identity cards. For the U.S. office nearest you: (tel. (800) 2-COUNCIL/226-8624). Also 28A Poland St. (Oxford Circus), **London,** W1V 3DB (tel. (0171) 287 3337), **Paris** (146 55 55 65), and **Munich** (089 39 50 22).

STA Travel, 6560 Scottsdale Rd. #F100, Scottsdale, AZ 85253. A student and youth organization with over 150 offices worldwide. Discount airfares for young travelers, railpasses, accommodations, tours, insurance, and ISICs. 16 offices in the U.S; for the nearest office: tel. (800) 777-0112 nationwide; fax (602) 922-0793; http://sta-travel.com. In the U.K., 6 Wrights Ln., **London** W8 6TA (tel. (0171) 938 47 11 for North American travel). In New Zealand, 10 High St., **Auckland** (tel. (09) 309 97 23). In Australia, 222 Faraday St., **Melbourne** VIC 3050 (tel. (03) 349 69 11).

Let's Go Travel, Harvard Student Agencies, 17 Holyoke St., Cambridge, MA 02138 (tel. (617) 495-9649; fax 495-7956; email travel@hsa.net; http://hsa.net/travel). Railpasses, HI-AYH memberships, ISICs, ITICs, FIYTO cards, guidebooks (including every *Let's Go* at a substantial discount), maps, bargain flights, and a line of budget travel gear. Items available by mail (or see catalogue in center of this publication).

Campus Travel, 52 Grosvenor Gardens, London SW1W 0AG (http://www.campus-travel.co.uk). 46 branches in the U.K. Student and youth fares on plane, train, boat, and bus travel. Skytrekker, flexible airline tickets. Maps and guides, discount and ID cards for students and youths, travel insurance for students and those under 35. Puts out travel suggestion booklets. Telephone booking service: in Europe (0171) 730 34 02; in North America (0171) 730 21 01; in Manchester (0161) 273 17 21; in Scotland (0131) 668 33 03; worldwide (0171) 730 81 11.

ONCE THERE

■ Embassies and Consulates

IN QUITO

Canada, Av. Corea 126 and Amazonas, Edificio Belmonte, 6th fl. (tel. (2) 506-163; fax 503-108).

Colombia, Colón 133 and Amazonas (tel. (2) 228-926 or 222-486; fax 567-766).

France, Leonides Plaza 107 and Patria (tel. 560-789).

Rep. of Ireland, Montes 577 and Las Casas (tel. (2) 462-521; fax 501-444).

Israel, Eloy Alfaro 969 and Amazonas (tel. (2) 565-509 or 565-512; fax 504-635).

Perú, Amazonas 1429 and Colón, Edificio España (tel. (2) 468-410; fax 468-411).

U.K., Av. Gonzáles Suárez 111, Casilla 314 (tel. (2) 560-670 or -671; fax 560-730).

U.S., Patria 120 and Av. 12 de Octubre (tel. (2) 562-890, emergency/weekend 234-126; fax 502-052).

IN GUAYAQUIL

Australia, San Roque and Av. Orellana (tel. (4) 298-800 or 298-700; fax 298-822).

Canada, Córdova 810 and Víctor Manuel Rendón, 21st fl., office 4 (tel. (4) 566-747 or 563-580; fax 314-562).

Colombia, Córdova 812 and V.M. Rendón, 2nd fl. (tel. (4) 563-308; fax 563-854).

Israel, Av. 9 de Octubre 729 and García Aviles (tel. (4) 322-000; fax 328-196).

Perú, Av. 9 de Octubre 411 and Chile, 6th fl. (tel. (4) 322-738; fax 325-679).

U.K., Córdova 623 and Padre Solano (tel. (4) 560-400; fax 562-641).

U.S., Av. 9 de Octubre and García Moreno (tel. (4) 321-152; fax 325-286).

■ Getting Around

BY BUS

Only the most fatalistic can enjoy Ecuador's buses. If you are among the many budget travelers who actually care about their well-being, you will know fear on Ecuadorian roads. Bus travel in Ecuador means whipping around hairpin turns through thick clouds on cliffs, dropping into oblivion as you pass another bus on a one-lane dirt highway. One technique for coping with the constant feeling of impending doom is to give in to the experience. Consider it a ride at an amusement park and make believe that no matter how scary it gets, the car is still attached to the tracks (even though it's not). Whether or not this strategy works, every budget traveler in Ecuador will eventually have to come to grips with the realities of bus travel, as it is by far Ecuador's cheapest and most ubiquitous means of transportation.

Buses of some kind or another travel to practically every part of Ecuador. They leave town from the *terminal terrestre* (bus station), or from a particular street with a high density of *cooperativos* (bus companies). The bus fare is usually paid upon entering the bus, or collected en route by an *ayudante* (helper). Occasionally, tickets must be purchased in advance at the *cooperativo* office. Departure times are usually approximate, and buses run between most destinations frequently enough that it is practical just to show up at the *terminal terrestre* and board the next bus headed your way. The destination is usually indicated on the bus itself, as well as advertised by a man yelling the town's name over and over again. The vehicles themselves vary greatly in quality, from open-air converted trucks *(camionetas)* to second-hand school buses to sparkling new Mercedez-Benz mega-buses. A general guideline: the longer the route, the nicer the bus will be, so it may be worthwhile to board a long-distance bus even if you plan to get off before the final destination.

A particularly peculiar aspect of Ecuadorian bus travel is that the buses rarely get "full;" drivers are often happy to pack as many passengers as they can into the aisles or even hanging out the door. If the buses get *really* full, drivers will let passengers ride on the roof, an especially amazing (and potentially dangerous) experience in the Sierra. It is a good idea to keep your belongings with you if at all possible.

BY CAR

Taxis can be a convenient way to get around, especially when you are in a hurry or traveling to places where buses don't venture. They are commonly used for travel between towns or to outlying destinations, and they are not outrageously expensive. It is usually cheaper to arrange for a taxi to drop you off and pick you up at an out-of-the-way spot it is to rent a car and drive there yourself. If you do decide to take a taxi, try to find out a fair price for the trip before hailing a cab. Once you do stop one, be sure to settle on a price before entering; if you don't, the driver might try to take advantage of you and charge more than the ride is worth. You can also travel by **colectivo;** these Volkswagon vans travel regular routes and pick up numerous passengers, falling in-between taxis and buses in price, speed, and size.

Car rental in Ecuador can be a real nightmare, but the convenience of having you own wheels can be truly liberating. However, it will cost between US$30-80 a day (Budget has the best deals), the roads and drivers in Ecuador can be quite scary, and a car is one more thing to worry about getting stolen. To rent a car you need a passport, a valid driver's license from your home country, and a credit card. Most credit cards cover standard insurance, but you may also have to purchase additional insurance from the rental company. Info on particular companies is found in **Practical Information** of Quito, Guayaquil, and Cuenca. Budget, Avis, and Hertz are all represented in Ecuador; you may want to make arrangements before you leave home.

BY TRAIN

Railroad travel within Ecuador is not the most convenient, cheapest, nor quickest way to get around. Some are willing to make these kinds of sacrifices for the strangely soothing sensation of traveling by train. Not only do Ecuadorian trains travel through some of the most spectacular terrain in the world, but roof-riding is also permitted. While the tracks run the length of the country, much of this distance is in disrepair due to mudslides and other natural damage. Nevertheless, there are several stretches that have been repaired and maintained. The most well-traveled stretches lie between Guayaquil and Alausí in the south (see **The Riobamba-Alausí-Bucay-Durán Railway,** p. 133), and Ibarra and San Lorenzo in the north (see **Ibarra: Practical Information,** p. 97). Especially in the case of the train between Ibarra and Lorenzo, do not count on a regular schedule. The train runs roughly every other day, but weather often causes the tracks to be inoperable for a day or two. Both of these routes travel from the coast into the Sierra and give passengers the opportunity to see the land change with the altitude. Another train also runs between Quito and Riobamba. For info on prices and travel times, check the **Practical Information** sections of these towns.

BY PLANE

Air travel within Ecuador is definitely more expensive than traveling by bus or train, but much quicker. If time really *were* money, flying might actually be worth it. Flights within Ecuador are relatively cheap excursions, except to the Galápagos. Ecuador's two main airlines, **SAN/SAETA** and **TAME,** have daily flights between Quito and Guayaquil (s/150,000); TAME flies to Cuenca (s/190,000), Loja (s/160,000), Macas (s/128,000), and Lago Agrio (s/165,000). All prices are one-way and roughly double for round-trip. These airlines are listed in **Practical Information** of each of these towns. For flights to the Galápagos, see **Galápagos, Getting There and Back,** p. 279.

BY BOAT

In the **Oriente,** motorized dugout canoes travel the murky, winding rivers that connect many towns. While this may seem like a glamorous way to travel, hours under the hot equatorial sun and the constant threat of torrential downpours add up. Also, since the riverbanks are the most accessible parts of the jungle, hopes of seeing more isolated and untouched areas by river are rarely realized. On top of these minor inconveniences, traveling by river is more expensive than going by bus on roads that now connect Oriente towns. If you still want to travel by river, ask about regular boat schedules and prices at a local marina. Public transportation boats regularly run up and down the **Río Napo** between Tena and Coca. You can also charter a canoe and customize your itinerary, but this is only economically feasible for larger groups.

Roads run along most of **Pacific Coast,** making boat travel unnecessary and thus quite rare. One exception is the stretch between the undeveloped northern coast towns of Muisne and Cojimíes; the only way to travel between these is a cheap and frequent, one-and-a-half-hour, wet-and-wild boat trip. Lastly, though it is not commonly done, it is possible to travel to the **Galápagos Islands** by boat. For more info, see **Galápagos, Travel by Boat,** p. 280.

BY THUMB

Let's Go urges you to use common sense if you decide to hitch, and to seriously consider all possible risks before you make that decision. The information listed below and throughout the book is not intended to recommend hitchhiking; *Let's Go* does not recommend hitchhiking as a means of transportation.

Buses travel almost everywhere in Ecuador and cost very little, so it is rarely necessary to hitchhike. However, there are more remote places where buses don't travel, and hitchhiking is a common way of getting around. Trucks will often pick up passengers to make a little extra money. Usually they cost about the same as taxis, but don't be surprised if the truck driver charges a little more; settle on a price before getting in.

Suspicion is often warranted. Hitchhikers should find out where the driver is headed before getting in. Think twice if the driver opens the door quickly and offers to drive anywhere. If any cause for concern arises, make an excuse and wait for another ride. Women should never hitchhike alone. Never accept a ride without sizing up the driver. Before getting in, make sure the passenger window or door opens from inside, perhaps by stalling so the driver opens the door for you. If there are several people in the car, do not sit in the middle. Assume a quick-exit position, which rules out the back seat of a two-door car. Keep backpacks and other baggage where they are easily accessible—don't let the driver store them in the trunk. If trouble arises for any reason, affecting the pose of someone about to vomit works wonders.

■ Accommodations

Most budget accommodations in Ecuador are in the form of basic **hotels.** Rooms are small and simple, bathrooms may be private or communal, and there is often a lounge area, be it a plant-filled courtyard, sparsely-decorated TV-room, or dining area. These places may offer laundry service for a fee, they may have a place where guests can do their own laundry, or there may be no laundry facilities at all. It is expected everywhere that after you've finished your business, you throw your toilet paper into the waste basket—*not* the toilet. Otherwise, the rules vary. There is a generally a lockout time before which you must return to the hotel. If you get locked out, you can try to wake the owner or receptionist, but don't expect their usual cheery selves.

There are also numerous **hostels** in Ecuador; much like hostels elsewhere in the world, they may be more like dormitories. Multiple guests may have to sleep in the same room, perhaps on bunkbeds. Some of these hostels are part of **Hostelling International (HI),** a worldwide hostel organization that guarantees a certain level of quality in terms of cleanliness, comfort, and friendliness. A HI membership (1yr. membership US$25, under 18 US$10, over 54 US$15, family cards US$35) will get you discounts at the 21 HI hostels in Ecuador. Many travel agencies sell HI memberships. Contact HI in the U.S. at 733 15th St. NW, Suite 840, Washington, D.C. 20005 (tel. (202) 783-6161; fax 783-6171; email hiayhserv@hiayh.org; http://www.hiayh.org) or in Quito, Ecuador at the *Asociación Ecuatoriana de Albergues,* Pinto 325 and Reina Victoria (tel. 543-995; fax 508-221).

Camping is definitely possible in Ecuador, even though it is neither terribly common nor very well organized. Some parks and reserves have designated camping areas, and some more frequently climbed mountains have *refugios* (rustic shelters) at various altitudes. Some landowners may allow camping on their property, but be sure to ask. Be cautious camping in non-designated spots, especially in isolated areas. It's best to bring equipment with you, since buying it in Ecuador will be much more expensive. There are shops in Quito should you lose equipment or need repairs.

Long-term accommodations should not be difficult to find in Ecuador. Many organizations can arrange for you to stay with an Ecuadorian family (see **Alternatives to Tourism,** p. 22). Classified ads in local newspapers (*El Comercio* in Quito) contain the most complete info on apartment rentals. Also consult the bulletin boards of any prime gringo hangouts, (in Quito: the Magic Bean, Cafecito, Super Papa, and SAEC). Otherwise, housing advertisements may be found in or around university campuses.

■ Outdoor Activities

Ecuador is one of the most geographically and ecologically diverse countries in the world, which makes for excellent outdoor adventure opportunities. The Pacific coast and the Galápagos Islands are good for saltwater fun, from surfing to snorkeling with seals. The Andes provide mountains of possibilities for outdoor recreation, from refreshing scenic walks to hardcore mountain climbing. And in the Oriente, there's the Amazon experience, with more species of plants and animals than you can count on all the fingers and toes of a small army. Whatever your particular interests may be, from ocean shores to jungle tours, Ecuador's out-of-doors have something in store.

MOUNTAIN CLIMBING

With 10 peaks standing over 5000m tall, Ecuador has long been considered one of the premier mountain-climbing destinations in the world. A French expedition of the *Académie des Sciences* visited Ecuador in 1736, and after calculating the distance from the equator to the North Pole (the calculation that forms the basis of the metric system of measurement), they determined that Ecuador's 6310m Mt. Chimborazo (20,703ft.) was the highest mountain in the world, a misconception that was not challenged until the 1820s.

In 1880, the famous English climber, Edward Whymper (the first man to climb Matterhorn), conquered five of Ecuador's most formidable virgin peaks, including the mighty Chimborazo. His expedition put Ecuador on the map; since then, more and more adventurers have been scrambling up and down her bodacious peaks. As a result, refuges *(refugios)* have been built on many of the mountain trails to shelter climbers, and numerous national parks and reserves have been created to protect the mountains and surrounding areas. There are routes for climbers of all abilities, and numerous organizations can help arrange and lead trips. Should you decide to attempt any of the more challenging climbs, finding a competent guide is very important, especially since many who call themselves guides are actually quite inexperienced. There is an Ecuadorian Guide Association, the *Asociación Ecuatoriana de Guías de Montaña* (ASEGUIM), that certifies guides. Another good place to look for a guide is at one of the climbing shops in Quito. These shops can put you in touch with a guide and often rent gear as well. SAEC can provide useful info about climbing and guides (see **Useful Organizations,** p. 1). The book *Climbing and Hiking in Ecuador* (Bradt Publications, US$15.95), is an excellent resource, offering everything from advice on equipment to trail specifics, as well as details about some of the more mellow hikes through the mountains.

JUNGLE TOURING

Tourists mainly visit Ecuador's Oriente to take a jungle tour through the Amazon basin. While the different tours vary greatly, they typically include treks through dripping rainforests, canoe rides down muddy Oriente rivers, visits to remote indigenous communities, and overnight stays in jungle *cabaña* outposts. Some regions of the jungle have less primary growth and smaller wildlife populations, mainly because oil companies have built roads opening the jungle up to colonization, deforestation, and the destruction of native habitats. Other sections are still more or less intact, but this is precisely because they are more isolated and harder to reach.

Tours operate out of just about every town in and around the Oriente, but to reach the most remote parts, you'll want to head out of either **Coca** or **Lago Agrio.** These northern Oriente towns sit just west of Ecuador's most undeveloped rainforests and provide access to the country's most impressive protected jungle areas, including the prominent **Cuyabeno Reserve** and the enormous, remote **Parque Nacional Yasuní.** To the south and west of Coca, the pleasant town of **Tena** and the tourist village of **Misahuallí** send trips into the less pristine but still impressive jungle wilderness that stretches out just to the east of them. The undisputed base for southern Oriente jungle tours is **Macas,** which offers access to remote Shuar villages, the nearby Cueva de los Tayos, and the rugged expanse of the *zona baja* of **Parque Nacional Sangay.**

After deciding which area you want to explore, you must make the equally important decision of who will guide you through it. You might end up having an excellent time with a tour guide who knows what he's doing, points out interesting wildlife, and respects the land and the people, or you could go along silently as your guide mentally counts his profits and stares out into a jungle he doesn't know much about. SAEC can be helpful, providing trip reports that offer recommendations and warnings about various companies. The companies listed in this guide are generally quite reliable, but don't come guaranteed. In general, it pays to ask a lot of questions and follow your gut feeling; after all, there are plenty of companies. If you plan on visiting any nationally protected areas, make sure the company you choose is approved by the National Park Administration (INEFAN) to lead tours through the areas you want to visit. Check the list of INEFAN-approved companies in the **Appendix** (p. 320).

RAFTING AND KAYAKING

Wherever you've got a wet climate with geography as extreme as Ecuador's, you're going to get some killer whitewater rafting. Aside from the adrenaline rush provided by crashing down a raging river, the views from the river are often spectacular, since river-running enables you to get to places that cannot be reached otherwise. Ecuador's recently discovered whitewater pours down from the jungle mountains west of Tena in the country's Oriente region. With a higher density of whitewater than nearly anywhere else in the world, the rivers here run year-round, beckoning tourists to enjoy their frothy fun. With sections ranging from class II (easy/mild) all the way up to class VI (virtually impassable), these waters were discovered so recently that only one company has risen up to make them accessible to the masses: **Ríos Ecuador.** This outfit offers rafting and kayaking trips as well as a week-long kayaking course. For more info, see **Tena, Sights,** p. 220.

TOUR COMPANIES

Ecuador overflows with tour companies eager to show you the wonders of their extraordinary country. Most companies are fairly small, based in towns near the sights they visit. Below are some bigger-scale companies based in Quito that lead all-inclusive tours to destinations throughout the country.

Safari Tours (tel. (02) 552-505 or 234-799; fax 223-381; email Admin@Safariec.ecxec), at Calama 380 and J. L. Mera and also Roca 630 and Amazonas, is reputedly the biggest climbing agency in the city of Quito. This famously dependable company conquers Cotopaxi, Cayambe, Chimborazo, Pichincha, and the Ilinias (to mention a few), and organizes a huge list of other trips to Ecuadorian destinations (open daily 9am-7pm).

Etnotur, Luis Cordero 1313 and J. L. Mera (tel. 564-565; fax 502-682), has a team of guides decked out with the latest gear that leads trips to most of Ecuador's national parks and protected areas, including climbs up Cotopaxi, treks in the Oriente with overnight stays at their camp in Cuyabeno, and boat tours in the Galápagos Islands. Prices depend on the trip and number of people.

■ Environmentally Responsible Tourism

Visitors inevitably affect a country's ecology, especially in poor nations where rapid development has taken place in order to encourage tourism. Nevertheless, there is not a cut-and-dried list of activities that do or do not make you an environmentally responsible tourist, and no objective criteria exist that can be used to judge your fellow traveler's guilt or innocence. Being responsible does not mean never going on a jungle tour or only using biodegradable shampoo. Rather, being responsible means understanding the short- and long-term effects of your actions on the environment and allowing these effects to guide your behavior. This is especially true with spending your money. When purchasing a good or service, a sucre does much more than simply provide for you—it influences the growth of industries and the lives of those who work in them. Responsible tourism means being aware of these factors and weighing them in such a way as to make an informed decision.

As a traveler, there are certain measures you can take to minimize your impact on the countries you visit. Always turn off the lights and the air-conditioning when you leave a room, and make sure that the doors and windows are shut when the air-conditioning is on. Better yet, stay in a place without air-conditioning; most Ecuadorians do this their entire lives. Don't accept excess packaging, particularly non-biodegradable styrofoam boxes. Women can buy feminine hygiene products with minimal packaging; O.B. brand tampons have no applicators. Choose glass soda bottles over drinking boxes or marginally recyclable aluminum cans. Reuse plastic bags. It's hard to convince Ecuadorian market vendors not to give you three bags where one would suffice, but with a little extra effort, you'll succeed. To be water-friendly, carry a refillable water bottle. While the water in Ecuador can present a credible health hazard, purifying tablets or iodine drops from home can treat it. This method will save you from buying countless plastic water bottles which will probably end up floating down Rio Napo or decomposing next to the railroad tracks. Not a pretty sight.

One of the best ways to undo some of the effects of environmental destruction in Ecuador and to minimize your own impact is to volunteer for one of many environmental organizations (see **Alternatives to Tourism,** p. 22). For websites offering listings of ecotour operators and environmental advocacy groups, try http://www2.planeta.com/mader/ecotravel/resources/southdex.html, http://www2.planeta.com/mader/ecotravel/south/ecuador.html, or http://www.podi.com/ecosource/tour.htm#rest. Should you happen to uncover a great "ecotourism" operator or have further ideas on how to be a low-impact tourist, we at *Let's Go* would love to hear of them. Please call or write to us.

Earthwatch, 680 Mt. Auburn St., Box 9104, Watertown, MA 02272 (tel. (617) 926-8200; fax 926-8532; email info@earthwatch.org; http//www.earthwatch.org), is a non-profit organization that matches volunteers with scientific field research projects around the world. Programs last 1-3 weeks and range in cost from US$595-3000. Minimum age of participation is 16.

Traveler's Earth Repair Network, PO Box 4469, Bellingham, WA 98227 (tel./fax (360) 738-4972), is a service offered by the Friends of the Trees Society which provides travelers with a list of projects where they can volunteer. Tell them where you are going and they will send you at least 20 references in your area of destination. The service costs US$50, free for people from developing countries who could not otherwise afford it. Also publishes the *Third World Resource Guide* (US$5), which has addresses and brief descriptions of organizations working in forestry, sustainable agriculture, and conservation.

▓ Keeping in Touch

MAIL

The Ecuadorian postal service is functional, but not always reliable. Airmail usually reaches the U.S. in around two weeks, but can easily take a month or more. Mail to Europe and other destinations takes even longer. If you choose to send something via surface mail, be prepared to give it time. Official estimates average 40 days by boat, but in reality, it may take months. Important documents should be sent via certified mail, or else duplicates should be sent.

You can have letters sent to you in Ecuador through **Lista de Correos,** a letter-holding service similar to the General Delivery service in the U.S. and Canada, *Entrega General* or *Poste Restante* in other countries. Address letters as follows:

> David <u>EILENBERG</u>
> Lista de Correos
> Quito
> Ecuador

The letter should also be marked *Favor de retener hasta la llegada* (Please hold until arrival). The mail will go to the central post office unless you specify a post office by street address. When picking up mail sent to you via Lista de Correos, give your name and explain that you are expecting mail. Try to keep names as simple as possible on the envelopes. Because Latin American *apellidos* (paternal last names) fall in the middle of the written name, confusion arises for foreigners with more than a simple first and last name. A letter could be filed under any misspelled permutation of the recipient's names. To avoid confusion, the last name should be capitalized and underlined. Check for mail under both your first and your last name, just to make sure. Bring a passport or other ID to pick up mail through the Lista de Correos. Letters and packages will be held for varying lengths of time, usually around two weeks.

It's wise to use the Spanish abbreviations or names for countries (EEUU or EUA for the U.S.). Write *Por Avión* (airmail) on postcards and letters not otherwise marked, unless you don't mind it arriving sometime in the next millennium. While it is possible to send packages from smaller towns, larger cities provide more reliable service.

If you have friends or family in the area, using their address may be preferable. You may be able to receive mail at a hotel where you expect to stay, but call ahead to arrange it in advance. **American Express offices** will also hold mail for 30 days for cardholders before returning it; just write "Client's Mail" on the envelope. There are two AmEx offices in Ecuador, in Quito and Guayaquil. You don't need to be a cardholder to receive this service as long as you purchase traveler's checks from AmEx. Call American Express customer service for more info (tel. (800) 528-4800). Ask for the free directory of traveler service offices. The **South American Explorer's Club** (SAEC) in Quito will also receive and hold mail for its members.

TELEPHONES, FAXES, AND EMAIL

Calling home is a hard nut to crack in Ecuador. The national phone company goes by two names, EMETEL and IETEL, and has offices in most cities and towns. These offices are usually open daily 8am-10pm for local and national calls, though times may vary slightly from town to town. However, their policies on **international calls** vary widely. Some offices can't do them at all, some only do them for exorbitant rates, others allow collect and calling-card calls for a fee or with the use of tokens *(fichas)*, and the nicest ones allow collect and calling-card calls for free. In cases where collect and calling-cards calls are not allowed, try making a short call and arrange to be called back at a number in Ecuador.

Collect and calling-card calls are by far the cheapest ways to call home. Many phone companies have toll-free access numbers that you can dial from Ecuador to get an operator from your home country. These can be dialed from some EMETEL/IETEL offices, from pay phones, and from fancy hotels for a fee. Some companies will be able to connect you to numbers only in your home country; others can provide other worldwide connections. If calling the U.S., there are several options: the **AT&T USA Direct** access number from Ecuador is 999-119, the **MCI World Phone** access number is 999-170, and **Sprint** has a U.S. toll free number that can be used to make a collect or calling-card call (tel. (800) 877-4646); from abroad, dial the country access number (999-171) but be forewarned that it is not always operable. If you are not from the U.S., call your phone company in your home country; they may offer similar services. Phone rates tend to be highest in the morning, lower in the evening, and lowest on Sundays and at night (AT&T's and MCI's phone rates remain constant).

To call Ecuador, you must first dial your country's international access code (011 in the U.S.), followed by Ecuador's country code (593), followed by the two-digit area code for the part of Ecuador you are trying to reach (listed in the **Appendix** and in individual towns' **Practical Information**), followed by the six-digit phone number.

Faxes are not uncommon in Ecuador, especially in larger towns and cities, though the fee for sending or receiving an international fax may be outrageously high. Some EMETEL/IETEL offices offer fax service, and hotels and businesses may also allow you to use their fax machines for a fee. **Electronic mail** (email) is also possible, for a fee, from a few select locations, such as SAEC and the British Council in Quito (see **Quito, Practical Information,** p. 60).

Ecuador: An Introduction

■ History

THE EARLIEST ECUADORIANS

While the Incas may have left the biggest mark on Ecuadorian indigenous life today, **pre-Columbian civilizations** actually thrived in the region long before the Inca's 1463 arrival. Archeological evidence shows that the earliest cultures in Ecuador lived on the southern coast, in the Loja area, and near Quito, over 12,000 years ago. Auspicious ocean currents and winds made the coast especially ideal for agriculture, and for 8000 years an industrious settlement thrived there. The oldest extensive archeological findings are remnants of the **Valdivia culture,** a people who lived along the coast of the Santa Elena Peninsula roughly between 3500-2000 BC. Early Valdivians were hunter-gatherers; later they developed farming techniques. Villages consisted of wood and straw huts arranged in a semi-circle around a central plaza, paved with shells for ceremonial purposes. Valdivian culture foreshadowed a major schism in later Ecuador; when some moved to nearby river floodplains to farm, a differentiation between urban and rural lifestyles arose for the first time.

By about AD 1, various tribes dotted the Andes and settled on the northern coast, in what are now known as the Manabí and Esmeraldas provinces. Little is known about the different pre-Inca tribes, except that each had its own language and all frequently declared war on each other. Groups in the coastal lowlands—the Esmeralda, Manta, Huancavilca, and Puná tribes—were hunters, fisherman, agriculturalists, and extensive traders. The sedentary and mainly agricultural Sierra tribes—the Pasto, Cara, Panzaleo, Puruhá, Cañari, and Palta—used irrigation to cultivate corn, quinoa, beans, many varieties of potatoes and squash, and fruits, like pineapples and avocados. Local chieftains raised armies, distributed communal lands, and united different villages in political confederations headed by single monarchs.

THE INCA EMPIRE

Based in their capital in Cuzco (in modern-day Perú), the Incas had an itching to expand their empire, moving north into Ecuador in the late 15th century. The Inca conquest began in 1463 under the leadership of the warrior **Pachacuti Inca Yupanqui.** Several Ecuadorian tribes met the Inca troops with fierce resistance, and it took nearly four decades before both the Sierra and coastal populations surrendered. **Huayna Cápac,** grandson of Pachacuti Inca Yupanqui and son of a Cañari princess, became ruler of the entire extended Inca empire.

Though the Incas only controlled Ecuador for about a half-century before the Spanish conquest, they left a tremendous mark. Some aspects of life among the native Ecuadorian tribes, such as their traditional religious beliefs, did not change much, but nearly every other area of society was greatly influenced. The new dominators introduced crops from Perú, such as yucca, sweet potatoes, cocoa, and peanuts; the use of llamas and irrigation also increased greatly. The biggest change involved the possession of land. Instead of the previous system of private ownership, land became property of the Inca emperor, held collectively by the **ayllu,** a kinship-based clan. Each *ayllu* allotted individual families a piece of land to cultivate for its own consumption, as long as it gave tribute payments to the **kuraka,** or chieftain.

Huayna Cápac grew up in Ecuador, and throughout his rule he adored his childhood homeland, naming Quito the second capital of the Inca empire. Fearful of unrest in his ever-expanding kingdom, he spent many years traveling all over the empire, putting down uprisings and strengthening unions whenever he could—sometimes by marriage, other times by replacing troublesome populations with colonists from more peaceful parts of the empire. These colonizations helped spread the traditionally Peruvian language of Quechua (known as Quichua in Ecuador) north of the border, which is still used today by *indígenas* in the Ecuadorian Andes.

Huayna Cápac's sudden death in 1526 brought on a bitter power struggle. Rather than leaving the empire to one heir, he split the kingdom between two sons. Cuzco and the southern empire were left to Huáscar, a son by Huayna Cápac's sister and therefore the legitimate heir. Ecuador and the northern empire went to **Atahualpa**, borne by a lesser wife, but his father's favorite. In 1532, Atahualpa decisively defeated Huáscar near Riobamba in central Ecuador, a victory that still remains a source of great national pride as one of the rare occasions when Ecuador defeated a hostile neighboring power. The Inca empire was left weakened and divided, unprepared for the arrival of the Spanish conquistadors a few months later.

THE SPANISH CONQUEST

The Spaniards landed near Esmeraldas in northern Ecuador on September 21, 1526, but the first conquering mission, led by **Francisco Pizarro,** did not get underway until 1532. Spain's King Carlos I granted Pizarro the titles of governor and captain-general of Perú, so Pizarro set out determined to conquer the troublesome Incas, whose independence kept him from his fame and fortune. At a pre-arranged meeting between Atahualpa and Pizarro in the town of **Cajamarca** in northern Perú, the Inca emperor disdainfully rejected both the Spanish crown and the Christian god, and was promptly attacked. Thousands of Incas were killed and Atahualpa was taken captive by the Spaniards and held for ransom. Although Atahualpa's loyal followers poured enough riches into Cajamarca to completely fill his cell once with gold and twice with silver, Pizarro had no intention of setting the Inca emperor free. Instead, he set him up in a corrupt trial at which Atahualpa was convicted of numerous accusations, including polygamy, worship of false gods, and crimes against the king. The punishment: Atahualpa was executed on August 29, 1533. Yet despite the loss of their leader, some Inca warriors continued to defend their empire. The general **Rumiñahui,** with the help of Cañari tribesmen, continued the struggle against the Spanish conquistadors. **Sebastián de Benalcázar,** one of Pizarro's lieutenants, defeated Rumiñahui near Mount Chimborazo and began pushing the Incas north. In mid-1534, when Rumiñahui realized that the Spaniards would soon conquer Quito, he set it ablaze, preferring to destroy this secondary Inca capital rather than surrender it to the conquistadors. The defeat of Rumiñahui marked the final victory in the Spanish conquest. Quito was refounded by the Spaniards on December 6, 1534 (a day that is still celebrated with parades, bullfights, and dances in the modern city).

> In mid-1534 Rumiñahui set Quito ablaze, preferring to destroy this secondary Inca capital rather than surrender it to the conquistadors.

THE COLONIAL ERA

Initially part of the **Viceroyalty of Perú,** Ecuador was tightly controlled by the Spanish crown, subject to the king's administrative agencies: the **viceroy,** the **audiencia** (court), and the **cabildo** (municipal council). In 1563, Ecuador gained separate status from Perú, attaining its own **Audiencia of Quito,** meaning it could deal more directly with Madrid on certain matters, especially those of jurisdiction. In 1720, in an attempt to tighten Spanish control over the colonies, Ecuador became part of the **Viceroyalty of Nueva Granada,** and central authority shifted from Lima to Bogotá.

Spanish **encomenderos** created huge plantations for themselves and depended on indigenous agricultural labor, which they obtained peacefully by making deals with the *kurakas.* The *kurakas* really had no choice but to acquiesce to the more powerful Spaniards, and agreed to hand over their *ayllu*'s tribute payments, supposedly in exchange for the order that Spanish Christianity brought to them. During the 1570s, however, Spanish officials began tightening their control over the Incas, abolishing the *encomiendas* and establishing a social system known as the **repartamiento de indios,** which made the entire indigenous population vassals of the Spanish crown. It also introduced the **mita,** a system of forced labor that required all men between the ages of 18-50 to work for the Spanish crown for at least two months each year. Overseen by **corregidores,** new Spanish officials in charge of administering the *mita,* Ecuadorian **mitayos** (workers) labored on huge agricultural **haciendas** or in **obrajes** (primitive textile sweatshops). As treacherous as the *mita* was for Ecuadorians, they were fortunate relative to their Peruvian counterparts; in Perú, where there were much heftier deposits of valuable minerals, miner *mitayos* experienced even more brutal conditions. Disease hit the indigenous population severely. **Smallpox and measles** virtually wiped out the coastal population and drastically reduced the Sierra population, especially during an epidemic in the 1690s.

THE INDEPENDENCE MOVEMENT

Ecuador's struggle for independence was part of a larger independence movement sweeping Spanish America. During the 18th century, tensions escalated as the **criollos** (people of European descent born in the New World) resented their limited access to indigenous labor, high taxes of the Spanish crown, trade restrictions, and the privileges the Spanish-born **peninsulares** had in gaining political office. Tensions heightened further after Europe's **Seven Years War** (1756-63), when the defeated and bankrupt Spanish kingdom passed the **Bourbon Reforms,** increasing their control of and taxes in the colonies. Ironically, the first revolts against colonial rule were actually expressions of support for the Spanish king. The independence movement gained steam when Napoleon Bonaparte invaded Spain in 1808 and deposed **King Ferdinand VII** to assume control of the New World colonies. The general consensus among the colonists advocated support for Ferdinand, and many conservatives formed **cabildos abiertos** (town councils) organized to pledge their support for the king. In some areas, these councils even seized authority. One of the first patriot uprisings in all of Latin America is believed to have occurred when a group of leading citizens took control of Quito in August 1809. However, as troops threatened the city, the rebels returned power to the *audiencia* authorities.

But after Ferdinand VII returned to the throne in 1814, his severe and absolutist restriction of colonial autonomy caused even the conservatives of the New World to turn against him. In Guayaquil, a patriotic junta under the leadership of poet **José Joaquín Olmedo** proclaimed the city's independence in October 1820. Troops from both the independence movements of the Argentine **José de San Martín** in the south and the Venezuelan **Simón Bolívar** in the north helped fight for Ecuador's independence in the struggle against the royalist forces. Led by Lieutenant **Antonio José de Sucre,** a string of patriotic victories culminated in the decisive victory at the **Battle of Pichincha,** just outside of Quito, on May 24, 1822. Yet independence did not mean an end to the struggle. For the next eight years, Ecuador was part of the **Confederation of Gran Colombia,** along with the modern-day nations of Colombia and Venezuela, part of Bolívar's grand plan to unite Latin America. Yet this tumultuous confederation was plagued by regional rivalries, and split up in 1830, with a small section of its southwest finally becoming the independent Republic of Ecuador.

THE EARLY REPUBLIC (1830-60)

> *America is ungovernable. Those who have served the revolution have plowed the sea.*
>
> —Simón Bolívar

Ecuador suggested this to be true during its early, tormented years; various rivalries plagued the country, causing divisive hostilities between politicians, ideologues, and even regions. Quito and the Sierra region emerged as conservative and clerical, dominated by semi-feudal estates that still relied upon indigenous labor. The cosmopolitan, commercial port of Guayaquil, on the other hand, had more exposure to the ideas of 19th-century liberalism. These coastal bourgeoisie favored free enterprise and anticlericalism. A common division in 19th-century Latin America, the liberal-conservative split made it impossible for the people of Ecuador to peacefully agree on a national leader.

The most natural leader seemed to be **General Juan José Flores,** whom Bolívar appointed governor of Ecuador when it was part of Gran Colombia. As part of the *criollo* elite, Flores found his support among the conservative *quiteños* while **José Vicente Rocafuerte** rose as his rival in liberal Guayaquil. For the next 15 years, the two politicians struggled for power, taking turns in the presidency. While Rocafuerte considered himself an enlightened despot, promoting civil liberties and developing the nation's public school system, Flores put more effort into commanding the military and securing his hold on power. Starting with an overthrow of Flores's regime in 1845, Ecuador experienced another 15 years of chaos. A series of coup d'états made for increasingly weak leadership and an increasingly strengthened military. One of the more powerful and influential leaders, **General José María Urbina,** ruled from 1851-56. As soon as he came into office, Urbina emancipated the nation's slaves, and later played a large role in ending the indigenous population's required tribute payments. But by 1859, a year known in Ecuadorian infamy as the **Terrible Year,** the country again stood in a state of near-anarchy after one local *caudillo* stirred up anger by trying to cede some Ecuadorian territory to Perú.

THE CONSERVATIVE REGIMES (1860-95)

A strong leader was exactly what Ecuador needed, and a strong leader is what it got. Gaining power in 1860, **Gabriel García Moreno** is known as the father of Ecuadorian conservatism, and is both hailed as the country's greatest nation-builder and condemned as its worst tyrant. During the 1840s and 50s, he watched as his country fell deeper into a pit of chaos. García Moreno's diagnosis: the nation needed more cohesion. At first he believed that incorporation into the French empire could provide this solidarity, but when the French appeared more interested in Mexico, he decided that the Roman Catholic Church could unite Ecuador.

From that point on, Catholicism was the magic ingredient in García Moreno's social cement; he believed that the order, hierarchy, and discipline cultivated by the Church could unify the nation's population. After coming to power in 1860, García Moreno based his 15-year regime on two things: personal authoritarian rule and a strict adherence to Roman Catholic orthodoxy—education, welfare, and other matters of government were put in the hands of the Church. An 1861 charter declared Catholicism the state religion, ties to the Vatican strengthened in 1863, and a decade later the republic was officially dedicated to the Sacred Heart of Jesus. Ecuador deviated from the path of most other Latin American nations at the time, which had military rather than Church-based dictatorships and passed many anticlerical measures. Yet despite the conservative nature of García Moreno's ties to the Church, his accomplishments were actually quite progressive— he constructed a railroad from Guayaquil to Quito, ending the isolation of the Sierra; built many new roads, schools, and hospitals; planted Australian eucalyptus trees in the highlands to combat erosion; and infused a greater sense of nationalism to the cities. In 1875, while standing on the steps of the presidential palace, García Moreno was hacked to death with a machete by disgruntled peasants. García Moreno's conservatism continued weakly for the next 20 years. By 1895, however, the progressive conservative leaders were plagued with scandal, and the liberals finally saw the chance to make their move. Led by **General José Eloy Alfaro Delgado,** the **Partido Liberal Radical (PRL)** stormed Quito, emerging victorious after a brief civil war.

> **Catholicism was the magic ingredient in García Moreno's social cement; he believed that the order and discipline could unify the population.**

THE ERA OF LIBERALISM (1895-1925)

While García Moreno was the leader who best personified the conservative years, Alfaro (president from 1897-1901 and 1906-11) exemplified the next 30 years of liberal rule. Attempting to erase anything vaguely associated with the right, one of his first moves as president was the creation of a new secular constitution removing the Church's privilege of censorship, exiling prominent clergy members, secularizing education, instituting civil marriage and divorce, seizing church lands for the state, breaking the concordat with the Vatican, and ending the nation's dedication to the Sacred Heart of Jesus. Later, Alfaro created stronger connections between Ecuador and the rest of the world by constructing ports and roads, and completing the Guayaquil-Quito railroad. Because of his close ties with the United States, Alfaro's plan for development was condemned by some to be "delivering the Republic to the Yankees." Yet Alfaro's accomplishments—the roads, ports, and railroads—served little purpose without a profitable export to transport. In addition, oppression of the *indígenas* did not change, and his attempts to hold onto power were just as ruthless as those of his predecessors. When he refused to step down after his second term ended in 1911, Alfaro was forced into exile in Panamá. The new president died only four months later; when Alfaro returned, a lynch mob killed him.

In the next 13 years, government changed hands four times among liberal leaders and their respective constitutions. After Alfaro, the president held little power in Ecuador; rather, a plutocracy of coastal agricultural and banking interests known as **la argolla** (the ring) called the shots from Guayaquil. During World War I and the short economic boom following, cocoa became Ecuador's dominant export, and the country's economy thrived briefly. Disaster struck in the early 1920s when a fungal disease ravaged Ecuador's cacao trees and the British colonies in Africa became a major cocoa-growing competitor. The resulting inflation and unemployment hit the poor and working classes especially hard. In the **July Revolution** of 1925, a group of young military officers overthrew the government in a bloodless coup, believing they could start a new program of national regeneration and unity.

THE TURBULENT YEARS (1925-48)

Although many of the leaders of the July Revolution preached socialist ideology, they soon discovered that most army officers envisioned a new regime based more on Mussolini than Marx. The 1926-31 military dictatorship of **Isidro Ayora** seized the nation with an iron fist. Attempting economic reform, Ayora created the Central Bank of Ecuador, which took the power to issue currency away from private banks. Other reforms included the devaluation of the sucre to help highland exporters, labor legislation regulating hours and conditions of work, and the establishment of a pension program for state workers. Still, the living conditions of the poor did not improve; one critic claimed that Ayora's "public cleansing" reforms put "prohibitions on entering markets, public buildings, schools, parks, and theaters without wearing shoes—but no reforms which gave the unshod means to buy them." With the **stock market crash** of 1929, nearly every Latin American government came crashing down with it—including Ayora's. Overthrown in 1931, Ayora was the first of 14 presidents of the turbulent 1930s. In fact, between 1931 and 1948, none of Ecuador's 21 presidents succeeded in completing a full term in office. Ecuador fared no better than the rest of the world during the **Great Depression;** global demand of cocoa dropped drastically, the price fell by 58%, and Ecuador's exports decreased nearly 50%. To add to the strife and instability, a four-day bloody civil war broke out in Quito in August 1932.

The scene was perfectly set for a charismatic leader like **José María Velasco Ibarra,** who took on his first of five presidential stints in 1934-35 (also president 1944-47, 1952-56, 1960-61, and 1968-72). A master of 20th-century populist politics, Velasco later went on to create his own personal movement, **Velasquismo,** centered around a combination of his charisma, a carefully cultivated image of honesty and sincerity, and fiery orations. Yet during Velasco's first term in office, his strong personality was apparently not well received, and the military overthrew him after less than a year for trying to assume dictatorial powers. The nine years before Velasco returned to office were marked by fiscal crisis, political coups, and fraudulent elections. The transitory regimes represented the struggle for power between the elites, the middle class, and the military. **Carlos Alberto Arroyo del Río** claimed victory in the disputed 1940 presidential election (it was popularly believed that Velasco had actually been the victor). Arroyo del Río's government fell apart when a border dispute with Perú became a disastrous 1941 military defeat. Perú's occupation of Ecuador continued until January 1942, when both countries signed a treaty known as the **Rio Protocol,** ceding about 200,000 sq. km of Ecuadorian territory in the Oriente to Perú. The Rio Protocol ignited national pride, completely discredited the Arroyo del Río government in the eyes of the Ecuadorians, and is still a cause of dispute between Ecuador and Perú.

Velasco returned to power in 1944 with whopping bipartisan demonstrations of support. Fine-tuning his populist rhetoric, Velasco managed to enchant the masses, regardless of individual ideology. Yet instead of dealing with the country's pressing economic problems, Velasco obsessed over restoring Ecuador's morality and social justice. Inflation and the standard of living worsened, and when he was ousted in 1947, Velasco had alienated so many of his supporters that nobody rose to defend him.

Overstepping Their Boundaries

Wondering why this book's map of Ecuador doesn't look like the same one you see in CETUR offices? That's because of a pesky little dispute over some land in the Oriente that has soured relations between Ecuador and Perú for nearly 150 years. Ecuador insists on its rightful claim to over 200,000 sq. km of Amazon basin because of its initial exploration of the great river, but most of the controversy has focused on a stretch of border in the Cordillera del Cóndor. Nobody really cared who technically owned these 78 sq. km of pure jungle until 1854, when Ecuador made an agreement with private creditors to use this stretch of the border. Sporadic mini-wars ensued for decades—and each time Perú emerged as the victor. But Ecuador refused to give in. In 1941, the issue's worldwide attention backfired for Ecuador; the 1942 **Rio Protocol Treaty,** designed to end the tiff once and for all, forced the world to recognize the land as Perú's. Ever since, the border issue has aroused Ecuadorian national pride and fury, the stuff presidential campaigns are made of. Leader after patriotic leader promises to get the land back, and every January (the month the Rio Protocol was signed), the inevitable border shootings occur. On a few occasions, the catfight has erupted into full-scale war—for a few days in 1981, and for an entire month in January to February 1995. The last time, it cost Ecuador 10 lives, US$680 million, and a lot of pride—President Sixto Duran-Ballen vowed early on, "Ecuador will not withdraw"... but two months later, the land was back in Perú's hands.

THE RISE OF THE MILITARY (1960-79)

Between 1948 and 1960, Ecuador experienced something with which it had little familiarity—a period of political stability. This calm was mostly due to the onset of another atypical event—economic prosperity, due to a **banana boom.** Ecuador became the U.S.'s main banana supplier when disease ravaged the Central American crop in the late 40s. Prosperity led the people back to Velasco, re-elected in 1952, who became so popular that he got away with referring to himself as "the National Personification." By the time Velasco began his fourth term in 1960, however, lower export prices initiated a rise in unemployment and general social discontent.

The 1959 **Cuban Revolution** had profound reverberations throughout Latin America. Suddenly, the presence of Communism was very real, as a threat or an attraction, and Latin American nations had to decide where their loyalties fell. Steering towards Communism, Velasco began including more leftists in his government and consciously antagonizing the U.S. The National Congress's debate over Ecuador's ideological future became so heated that gunshots were fired in the Chamber of Deputies. In 1961, Vice-president **Carlos Julio Arosemena Monroy** ousted his superior and immediately sent a goodwill mission to Washington, eager to renew favorable terms with the U.S. But Ecuador grew dangerously tumultuous, and with every terrorist act Arosemena was accused of weakness or Communist sympathy.

ECUADOR

In July 1963, a four-man military junta seized power, vowing to implement basic socio-economic reforms and to take a hard-line against Communism. However, the military junta was unable to gain much popular support; its land reforms actually accomplished very little, and the economy worsened with the continuing decline in banana exports. In 1966, after a bloody attack on the students of the Central University in Quito, the military reformers stepped down.

When in doubt, Ecuadorians could always vote for Velasco, and in 1968 this master of charisma began an unprecedented fifth term. Disillusioned with the gridlock caused by an uncooperative Congress, Velasco assumed dictatorial powers in June 1970 with a self-seizure of power, known as an **autogolpe.** Until his overthrow in 1972, he held onto these dictatorial powers primarily with the support of the military. The military coup in 1972 was not due to the army's lack of support for Velasco; rather, it was provoked by the army's fear that **Asaad Bucaram Elmhalim** might be elected after Velasco's term ran out a few months later. The leader of the populist Concentration of Popular Forces (CFP) and extremely popular two-time governor of Guayaquil, Bucaram was considered by both the military and the business community to be dangerous, unpredictable, and unfit for the presidency. For the next seven years, Ecuador was ruled by military leaders determined to make structural changes in the country and encourage development. Yet they were not prepared for the **1970s oil boom.** After joining the Organization of Petroleum Exporting Countries (OPEC), the minister of natural resources tried pricing Ecuadorian oil well above the world market price. Exports fell and combined with a lack of infrastructure reforms, the country's economic problems simply worsened.

The creation of a new constitution and the democratic election of a president was supposed to happen in 1976, but the process was delayed due to disagreements, and to ensure that Bucaram would not be elected. Bucaram was eventually barred from running, but the second-in-command of the CFP, **Jaime Roldós Aguilera,** with his reformist platform, won a run-off election in 1979 with 68.5% of the vote with **Osvaldo Hurtado Larrea,** leader of the Christian Democratic Party (PDC), as his running mate.

A RETURN TO DEMOCRACY (1979-PRESENT)

The Roldós-Hurtado regime began under auspicious circumstances. With the country's preferential treatment as part of the Andean Common Market, the oil boom was finally having positive repercussions for Ecuador. Unfortunately, this new wealth only increased the domestic gap in income distribution. To make things worse, a rivalry developed between Roldós and Bucaram, and the president became at odds with his own party. In 1981, Roldós died in a plane crash near Loja.

Ecuador's economic luck didn't last long. Oil reserves ran dry, and massive foreign borrowing led to a debt of almost US$7 billion by 1983. The warm ocean currents from **El Niño** in 1982-83 brought drastic climate changes, resulting in nearly US$1 billion in infrastructure damage. Hurtado's regime responded to the -3.3% GDP change and record-high 52% inflation in 1983 with austerity measures. Steps such as ending government food subsidies helped devalue the sucre but hurt the poor terribly. Unemployment skyrocketed to 13.5%, and the **United Workers Front (FUT)** launched three riotous strikes during Hurtado's term in office.

Elected in 1984, **León Febres Cordero Ribadeneyra** believed in free-market economics and a pro-U.S. policy, attempting to emulate and ingratiate his government to Reagan's. Understandably, Febres Cordero was not popular in Ecuador. Oil prices continued to fall, and Febres Cordero continued to have troubles with the National Congress and the military. A March 1987 earthquake left 20,000 homeless and destroyed a stretch of the country's main oil pipeline, forcing the president to suspend interest payments on Ecuador's US$8.3 billion foreign debt.

In late 1988, Ecuador's inflation grew so much and the government's austerity measures were so painful, that large-scale protests ensued. The recently-elected president, **Rodrigo Borja Cevallos,** made agreements with various paramilitary protest organizations, guaranteeing their civil rights in exchange for demilitarization of his

"Y este hombre quiere ser presidente?!"

"No puede ser," cried the television commercials of the Social Cristiano candidate Jaime Nebot before his narrow defeat at the hands of *"El Loco,"* Abdala Bucaram. With an uncanny resemblance to Adolf Hitler—mini-mustache, arm sweeps, and all—Abdala marched on the campaign path, with *"una sola ideología: derrotar a la oligarquía"* (one ideology: tear down the oligarchy). His resemblance to Hitler may not have been merely incidental: Abdala (he is known by his first name) once cited *Mein Kampf* as his favorite book. However, his antics put him in his own class entirely; in his unsuccessful 1988 campaign, Abdala once showed up in a helicopter in a Batman costume. Traveling with an Uruguayan rock band on the trail, Abdala would pack the working class into squares and sing *boleros* on demand. But when it came to speaking, Bucaram was all business: his charismatic content matched his throaty shouts, and he somehow motivated almost all of Ecuador's poorer areas to vote for him (in the provinces of Zamora and Morona-Santiago, he won by approximately three to one). One reason may have been the female vote: Rosalía Ortega, his running mate, was the first female vice-president of Ecuador, but once elected, she seemed to have little place in the actual running of the country. Abdala's brothers also received attention: one, who was rumored to be Abdala's new Minister of Finance, has studied to be a witch doctor; and an Abdala brother was detained in Guayaquil the day after the election for driving a stolen vehicle. Scared members of Ecuador's upper classes fled the country the day after the results were announced (one hour late, because exit polls revealed a difference below the margin of error). Perhaps they fled for good reason; it is revealing that the man actually lost by two to one in the city he was mayor of—Guayaquil.

government. One guerilla organization, **Montoneros Patria Libre (MPL),** refused and continued violent action. Cevallos not only faced opposition from outside the government, but from within it as well. In 1989, the vice-president's plans to organize a coup were exposed. Another overthrow attempt came to the public light in 1990, when the President of Congress unsuccessfully tried to stage a legislative coup that resulted in the impeachment of multiple members of Congress. The year 1990 also saw a rise in indigenous protests. The **National Confederation of the Indigenous Population of Ecuador (CONAIE)** planned a seven-province uprising, seizing oil wells and taking military hostages. Their demands included the return of various traditional community lands, recognition of Quechua as an official language, and compensation for the environmental damage caused by petroleum companies. Though the protests ended when the government agreed to consider CONAIE's demands, tensions heightened again in April 1992, when thousands of *indígenas* from the Oriente marched to Quito, demanding that their territorial rights be recognized.

During his 1992-96 presidency, **Sixto Durán Ballén** dealt with many of these same problems on a larger scale. Austerity measures designed to cut inflation continued to cause widespread protest and general strikes, especially with 70% price increase of fuel in 1994. CONAIE and other indigenous movements caused an even bigger stir with widespread demonstrations in June 1994, when they protested the **Land Development Law,** which allowed commercialization of indigenous lands for farming and resource extraction. The next month, the law was modified to protect the rights of landowners. Disaster hit when many top government officials, including the vice-president, were indicted in financial scandals. So many top authorities were impeached that demands even arose for Ballén to resign, voiced through student demonstrations throughout 1995 and early 1996. Plans to privatize the petroleum industry also caused strikes in the energy sector in late 1995.

Abdala Bucaram of the Partido Roldolista Ecuatoriano (PRE) defeated **Jaime Nebot** of the Partido Social Cristiano (PSC) in the presidential run-off election of July 7, 1996. Bucaram, the former mayor of Guayaquil, lost to Nebot in Ecuador's two biggest cities—Guayaquil (63% to 37%) and Quito (52% to 48%)—but overwhelmingly defeated him in the tiny towns and the Oriente. The conservative Nebot did not inspire enough confidence with his slogan, *"Primero La Gente"* (People First), while Bucaram used the motto, *"Primero Los Pobres"* (The Poor First), and advocated mass nationalization, insisting that the country's poor would come first when rebuilding the gubernatorial structure. After Bucaram's final 54-46% victory was confirmed, revelers from poor neighborhoods caroused all night on the city streets while disgruntled members of the bourgeoisie packed their bags.

LAST YEAR'S NEWS

Bucaram took the office from Sixto Durán Ballén amid much hoopla on August 10, 1996, and took his first presidential measure by devaluing the sucre a few weeks later. From then on, his popularity entered a state of rapid decline. Hikes in gas, telephone, and electricity taxes resulted in a 300% rise in the price of utilities, a proposal to make the sucre fully convertible against the dollar met strong resistance in Congress, and labor market reforms allowing easier dismissal of public sector employees infuriated trade unions. Rumors of the leader's corrupt and authoritarian tendencies also ruffled the feathers of the masses. By early January 1997, public discontent began bubbling up into pockets of often violent protest, and the man of *los pobres* found himself steadily abandoned by the very constituency that had put him into office. Tensions culminated on February 5-6, 1997 when the public sector unions, the left-wing political group Movimiento Popular Democrático (MPD), and the indigenous group CONAIE launched a united strike against the government.

Congress' response was swift and unprecedented. On February 6, 1997, the legislative branch ousted Abdala Bucaram from the presidency on grounds that he was mentally unfit. Bucaram replied by barricading himself in the presidential palace, but was forced to resign when even the military withdrew its support from the hapless leader. Bucaram fled the country insisting that a "civilian dictatorship" had been imposed and was granted political asylum in Panamá, where he awaits charges of misappropriation of funds. The second claim on the presidency was made by Vice President Rosalía Arteaga, who was temporarily handed the reigns while Congress decided who would lead next. When it was decided by a vote of 57-2 that **Fabián Alarcón,** and not Arteaga, would serve as the country's new president, the Vice President insisted that the act was unconstitutional and that the position was rightfully hers. Accusing Congress of staging a "coup against the constitution," Arteaga held out for several days before acknowledging Alarcón as Bucaram's heir.

Since assuming the presidency, Alarcón has proposed a seven-step plan to reduce the deficit, which includes an increase in import tariffs and electricity rates, reinstatement of an 8% income tax, a 10% across-the-board budget cut, and a task force to reduce corruption in both customs and tax collection. He has also put Bucaram's privatization efforts on hold and reinstated all teachers and public servants fired during the deposed president's six-month term. Calling his plan *el paquetito* (the little shock), he hopes to jolt economic growth to 4% by 1998, curb the deficit (currently 6.6% of the country's GDP) to a mere 2.5%, and calm fears of instability in the wake of Bucaram's departure. A May 1997 referendum showed approval for the Alarcón administration to hover at 65-75%. Alarcón's term is to end in August 1998, at which time the Ecuadorian presidency will, once again, be up for grabs.

■ The People

The ethnicity of the people of Ecuador is the result of a process of continuous biological and cultural infusion, beginning with the arrival of the first *indígenas* in the country's coastal region over 12,000 years ago. Since then, many other groups have mixed in their genes and cultures. First the Quechua-speaking Incas conquered and assimilated the natives, and then the Spanish did the same. Other groups have also intermingled themselves in along the way—African slaves came to work plantations on the coast, and small but thriving communities of Chinese and Lebanese immigrants live in Ecuador today.

The majority of today's diverse racial, ethnic, and cultural population of 11 million lives in the highland and coastal regions; the urban centers of Quito and Guayaquil each hold between 2 and 2.5 million. The Amazon is still sparsely populated, but more colonists move there every day. Issues of race and ethnicity are closely intertwined; an individual's identity as white, black, *mestizo* (mixed white and indigenous), or indigenous is a combination of biological and social factors. Since the elite has always been predominantly white, and the working class mainly *mestizo* and indigenous, a biological *mestizo* of high social rank may be called white, while a biological white with a low social rank may be called *mestizo*. This kind of ambiguity makes it impossible to know exactly how the population breaks down racially; however, the estimate is 5% black, 15% white, 40% *mestizo,* and 40% indigenous.

The small **black population** lives mostly in the northern coastal province of Esmeraldas and in the Chota Valley of the northwest. A slave ship supposedly wrecked on the coast of Esmeraldas in the 17th century, and the survivors lived in this remote region, independent from the rest of Ecuador for many years. The residents of the Chota Valley are the descendants of slaves brought during the 1600s to work the sugar plantations of the coastal region. Today, both of these regions and their inhabitants clearly maintain a distinct culture and ethnicity. The country's **white population** is predominantly made up of the descendants of Spanish conquistadors and colonists. Just like their ancestors, they make up the majority of the country's elite, concentrated primarily in urban centers such as Quito, Guayaquil, and Cuenca. **Mestizos** or *cholos,* with mixed white and indigenous heritage, are members of a kind of catch-all group that includes all Ecuadorians who are not black, white, nor affiliated with any particular indigenous ethnicity. They make up the bulk of Ecuador's urban population, and also inhabit rural areas that sometimes overlap with indigenous communities. But the *mestizos* of Ecuador are far from a homogenous group. Their cultures and lifestyles are the complex result of many different influences, and they vary greatly from coastal lowland, to highland, to Oriente.

> An individual's identity as white, black, mestizo, or indigenous expresses an intertwining of social as well as biological factors.

The ancestors of the **indigenous peoples,** or *indígenas,* lived on the land that became Ecuador when the Spaniards arrived. The largest indigenous group (numbering over 2 million) are the highland **Quichua,** collectively referred to with this name because they speak dialects of the Inca Quechua language. There are many regional distinctions among the Quichua people. Some of the better known groups are the **Otavalos** who live in and around the town of Otavalo (north of Quito), the **Salasacas** who live south of Ambato, and the **Saraguros** who live north of Loja in southern Ecuador. In the coastal lowlands, only a few small groups remain: the **Awa,** the **Cayapas,** and the **Colorados.** These groups are dwindling in number and they regularly put their dress and customs on display simply to earn a few tourist dollars. The Amazon also has its share of autochthonous groups. The largest of these are the **Jívaro,** who live in the central and Southern Oriente and number over 70,000. Within the Jívaro are the **Achuar** and the **Shuar.** Other smaller Oriente groups, some of which continue to live in relative isolation, are the **Cofán,** the **Siona,** and the **Secoya** in the Northern Oriente, and the **Huaorani** (or Auca), who live primarily in and around Yasuní National Park.

INDIGENOUS IDENTITY

Each of Ecuador's indigenous groups has a distinct ethnic identity, and all of their members identify more strongly with their ethnicity than with the Ecuadorian state. It's no wonder—until the middle of this century, the government of Ecuador paid little attention to the needs of the indigenous and *mestizo* majority of its population, mainly catering to its white, mostly urban, elite. As in most of Latin America, this unbalanced socio-political order is the legacy of colonial times, when indigenous peoples were made to labor in the *haciendas,* mines, and factories of the Spanish and

Creole elites. This exploitation continued even after independence. With the beginning of the 20th century, there was a move by a more liberal government to try to incorporate the *indígenas* into the national community, mainly because the ruling class saw them as an obstacle to development. Under the guise of fighting for equality, the liberals attempted to pass legislation that would free *indígenas* from ties to the church or private land-holders by dissolving their communal lands. The ulterior motive of these liberals was to gain access to indigenous land and labor for themselves. Indigenous groups resisted the division of their lands, and in 1937, two laws were enacted to reinforce indigenous rights to own land communally.

Beginning in the 60s, various indigenous and human rights organizations began to demand changes that would alleviate the subordinate status of *indígenas* in Ecuadorian society. A demonstration in Quito in 1961 by 12,000 indigenous peasants demanded social change, and in 1964 an agrarian reform bill was passed. Though the reform was more developmentalist than redistributive, it still effectively weakened the political power of the land-holding elite.

Around this time, one of Ecuador's most successful and well-known indigenous groups, the **Shuar Federation,** was founded in response to new pressures from outside forces, including missionaries, colonists from the highlands, and later, oil companies. The Shuar organized themselves into groups of about 30 families called *centros,* who hold land communally in order to prevent the break-up and loss of indigenous land. They have also instituted a health-care program and radio schooling system independent from the government. A move from traditional subsistence farming to cattle ranching has been criticized as dangerous to the environment and incompatible with their traditional way of life. While their new practices deviate from tradition, they allow the Shuar to preserve their ethnic identity, rather than lose it to the more heterogenous national one. This has happened in other indigenous communities of Ecuador as well. The northern highland town of **Otavalo** is world-renowned for its weaving industry, and people come to its Saturday market from all around. Some would argue that such commercialism is contrary to traditional ways, but the weaving industry is the only thing that has allowed *otavaleños* to maintain their ethnic identity. Like the Shuar, they have adapted and thus kept an indigenous identity in the face of nationalist domination.

> Many indigenous people value the attention given to their dance and music; others recognize the state's agenda behind such events.

More recently, the Ecuadorian government has attempted to incorporate aspects of indigenous experience and tradition into collective national identity. The Roldós-Hurtado administration (1979-84), concerned with winning the approval of the *indígenas,* expressed a desire to include formerly marginalized groups in national political life. They created the **Fund for Rural Development for Marginalized Groups (FODERUMA),** which was intended to integrate peasant labor and products into the national market. However, outsider administrators disagreed with the *indígenas* on how funds should be used, and the organization received the nickname JODERUMA (*jodear* being the verb "to screw someone over"). Such resistance to integration attempts is common and understandable, given the people's history of subordination, oppression, and manipulation by the state. A report from 1975 found that 60% of an indigenous community only 100km from Quito did not know the colors of the Ecuadorian flag. Polls from 1980 revealed that the majority of highland *indígenas* did not know who Ecuador's president was, and thought the term *la patria* (the country) referred not to the state, but to a local bus company.

In other cases, populations have shown more active resistance to the integration of a local, ethnic identity into a national one. A number of state-sponsored celebrations of popular culture, aimed at fostering national identity, have received mixed responses. Many indigenous people value the attention being given to their dance and music, however, more radical groups recognize the state's agenda behind such events and criticize them as fictionalized versions of indigenous culture. Some new celebrations are grounded in local tradition but lose their original meaning through celebration in a national context. One such celebration, Otavalo's festival of Yamor, was boycotted by a group of *indígenas* in 1983 and 1984. The festival was originally a celebration of the corn harvest but today is promoted by the tourism industry and includes parades and fireworks. The offended indigenous group objected that this traditional ritual must not be manipulated by outside interests. Otavalo's economic success allows locals to protest high-profile nationalist projects, but less-affluent communities often accept them for lack of a better option. In another instance, the government issued a series of stamps celebrating Ecuador's indigenous heritage, a move clearly intended to link the *indígenas* with the nation. The town of Quimsa, whose culture was shown on one of the stamps, denounced the stamps because their traditions had been wrongly depicted. Such tactics angered *indígenas* by implying that their culture can function like a collectible item. Inaccurate depictions have done more to alienate native peoples than to embrace them.

Irritated that the government has never wanted indigenous support, only indigenous assimilation, the *indígenas* have developed a number of organizations to voice their desires and complaints. In 1986, these organizations came together under an umbrella organization called the **Confederation of Indigenous Nationalities of Ecuador (CONAIE).** In 1990, CONAIE organized the largest indigenous uprising in Ecuador's history, paralyzing the country for a week. Their rallying cry, "500 years of resistance and survival," was a protest against the upcoming 1992 quincentenary celebration of Columbus's landing in the Americas. Their agenda included 16 demands to help create a satisfactory relationship between indigenous people and the state, including more indigenous autonomy and a proposed constitutional amendment making Ecuador a multi-nation state. These demands run contrary to the state's national vision; granting indigenous people the lands that they claim would obstruct the government's plans for oil development in the region and would threaten the socio-political status quo. In the December 1996 CONAIE elections, when the candidate from the less radical Amazonian and coastal regions claimed the organization's presidency, highlanders accused the government of vote-tampering. It remains to be seen whether CONAIE and the indigenous people of Ecuador will achieve their goals.

▓ Religion

An enormous result of the influence of the Spanish on indigenous life was the conversion of the *indígenas* to **Catholicism.** The earliest colonists were granted the labor of indigenous groups by the Spanish monarchy on the condition that they convert them before working them to death. The Spanish justified this cruelty by reasoning that they had at least saved the *indígenas'* souls before they took their lives. As indigenous labor became slightly more scarce, missionaries headed into the wilderness and established missions there. Often this resulted in peaceful conversion, but as soon as the missionaries had done their work, others used the trails they had blazed to enslave and exploit the native populations (as depicted in the movie *The Mission*). Today in Ecuador, as in the rest of Latin America, the population is mostly Roman Catholic. As a result of missionary activities during this century, a small percentage of the population is also **Protestant.** Even these modern-day missions can be quite coercive, offering medical services or other aid only to those who visit their churches.

In many cases the indigenous populations have not given up their own traditions, but have simply incorpo-

> **Diagnostic techniques include rubbing a guinea pig over the sick person and then reading the pattern of the pig's entrails.**

rated Catholicism into their belief systems. The resulting **hybrid religion** intertwines identities of indigenous gods and spirits with those of Christian saints. Indigenous celebrations are now often held on Saints' Days; for instance, the June 24 festival of Saint John the Baptist is thought to have replaced the Inca festival of *Inti Raymi*, held on the summer solstice. In other cases, a given situation (e.g. an illness) requires an offering to a certain saint instead of to an indigenous spirit. Still other traditions have remained completely distinct from Catholicism. The indigenous people of the Andes have always worshipped the mountains, which they believe are the homes of mighty spirits that control fertility and the rain. In addition, **shamans** (*curanderos* in Spanish) are often called upon to cure the sick. Many techniques are used to diagnose and treat illnesses, including rubbing a guinea pig all over the sick person's body and then using the convoluted pattern of its entrails to learn something about the ailment. Another process involves rubbing the person with a raw egg and then interpreting the noise the egg makes when shaken. Alcohol and tobacco are often consumed in bulk in shamanic practices.

■ Festivals and Holidays

Semana Santa, the Holy Week just before Easter, occasions the most parties in Ecuador. Quito is the biggest party-mecca on Good Friday, but its processions are rivaled by those in some Chimborazo province towns, like Chambo, Chunchi, Tixán, and Yaruquíes. Plan well in advance for accommodations at more popular destinations. The festivities aren't confined to the hotspots, though; you're bound to find something going on during this week wherever you are.

Keep your eyes peeled for local *fiestas*, which can be fascinating and exceptionally fun. Most towns celebrate a different **Independence Day,** the day they were liberated from Spain. Quito, Guayaquil, and Cuenca's independence days are national holidays, but many of the lesser-known celebrations take on more of a local flavor—Esmeraldas's August 3-5 festivities include African music and *marimba* dancing. Even familiar holidays are given a new twist; unlike the hyper-commercialized **Father's** and **Mother's Day** celebrations common to the United States, there is no gift-giving or flower-sending in Ecuador. Instead, mothers and fathers simply get to take the day off from work to relax or party with other mothers or fathers.

Regional festivals, such as those dedicated to patron saints of local communities, are another common reason to cut loose; usually they're celebrated by drinking, dancing to local music, and sometimes a beauty pageant or two. Don't worry if you think you hear some gun shots; most of the time, it's just some celebratory firecrackers. Men doll up in drag and blackface for Latacunga's **La Virgen de las Mercedes** holiday on September 24, in honor of the city's dark-skinned statue of the Virgin Mary, known as La Mama Negra. For more information on other local holidays, as well as a list of Ecuadorian National Holidays, see the **Appendix,** p. 317.

■ Customs and Manners

As a traveler, it doesn't take long to figure out that local customs and manners aren't always what you're used to. No one bats an eye when an elderly woman hawks a loogie on a public bus, but a traveler might be frowned upon for having a stubbly beard. You'll be more likely to earn the respect of the people you encounter if you take a moment to familiarize yourself with their social norms.

Foreign visitors are often shocked by the overwhelming *machismo* in some parts of Ecuador. Women in bars—and foreign women in general—are often believed to be lascivious. If you are female, drinking, and becoming raucous, even expressing your opinions may shock men who believe women should be quiet and meek. Whether you're a man or woman, be sensitive to rising testosterone levels. Never say anything about another man's mother, sister, grandma, daughter, wife, or girlfriend.

Personal hygiene and appearance are often difficult to maintain while traveling, but your appearance definitely affects how you are treated by locals. Clean-shaven men with short hair and women who don't show much skin are more likely to be well-received than scruffies and smellies or women without bras. Men should remove hats when entering a building.

Punctuality isn't as important as it is in Europe and the United States (as you'll quickly confirm), but there are limits, of course. A different perspective on time is also apparent during meals, which are rarely hurried in Ecuador. Enjoy the ingenious tradition of *siesta*, a time in the afternoon when it's just too hot to do anything but relax, have a drink, and maybe nap. Don't expect much to happen during the mid-

When in 172-1011, do as the 172-1011's do.

All you need for the clearest connections home.

Every country has its own AT&T Access Number which makes calling from overseas really easy. Just dial the AT&T Access Number for the country you're calling from and we'll take it from there. And be sure to charge your calls on your AT&T Calling Card. It'll help you avoid outrageous phone charges on your hotel bill and save you up to 60%.* For a free wallet card listing AT&T Access Numbers, call 1 800 446-8399.

http://www.att.com/traveler

Photo: R. Olken

Greetings from Let's Go Publications

The book in your hand is the work of hundreds of student researcher-writers, editors, cartographers, and designers. Each summer we brave monsoons, revolutions, and marriage proposals to bring you a fully updated, completely revised travel guide series, as we've done every year for the past 38 years.

This is a collection of our best finds, our cheapest deals, our most evocative description, and, as always, our wit, humor, and irreverence. Let's Go is filled with all the information on anything you could possibly need to know to have a successful trip, and we try to make it as much a companion as a guide.

We believe that budget travel is not the last recourse of the destitute, but rather the only way to travel; living simply and cheaply brings you closer to the people and places you've been saving up to visit. We also believe that the best adventures and discoveries are the ones you find yourself. So put us down every once in while and head out on your own. And when you find something to share, drop us a line. We're **Let's Go Publications,** 67 Mount Auburn St., Cambridge, MA 02138, USA (email: fanmail@letsgo.com; http://www.letsgo.com). And let us know if you want a free subscription to *The Yellowjacket,* the new Let's Go Newsletter.

afternoon, as banks and businesses often shut their doors. While eating at a table with Ecuadorians, keep your hands on the table and not in your lap.

Ecuadorians hold politeness in high esteem, both to acquaintances and strangers. Jaded foreign travelers, ingrained in cultures that consider urban indifference the highest virtue, need to adjust if they expect to be treated with respect. When meeting someone for the first time, shake hands firmly, look the person in the eye, and say *"Mucho gusto de conocerle,"* (pleased to meet you). When entering a room, greet everybody, not just the person you came to see. Females often greet each other with a peck on the cheek or a quick hug. Sometimes men shake hands with women in a business situation, but the standard greeting between a man and a woman—even if they are meeting for the first time—is a quick kiss on the cheek.

Salutations in passing are considered common courtesy in smaller towns, particularly in the Oriente. *"Buenos días"* in the morning, *"Buenas tardes"* after noon, and *"Buenas noches"* after nightfall should be said to almost anyone with whom you come in contact. This charming Latin American custom epitomizes a general feeling of *amistad* on the streets, even between strangers. A similar custom is saying *"buen provecho"* ("bon appetit") to everyone in a restaurant upon entering or leaving.

Finally, be sensitive when taking photographs. Devotees at a shrine might be interesting to look at, but their religiosity is no novelty. If you must take pictures of locals, ask first if they mind. Indigenous peoples tend to object strongly to being photographed, so just preserve the moment mentally.

■ Food

From conventional stand-bys to exotic local dishes, Ecuador's got something to satisfy people of all tastes. The fruits encountered here are as succulent and varied as those grown anywhere in the world. Distinctive grains and tubers abound, and a plethora of vegetables are cultivated and cooked. As for meat, just about anything is considered fair game, and every part of that game is used somehow, from hoof to heart and tentacle to testicle. Despite this variety, certain things are encountered more often than others. For the most part your culinary experience will be determined by the region you're in and type of restaurant you choose to visit.

There are a number of dishes that are particular to Ecuador. Perhaps the most shocking to westerners is the mouth-watering delicacy known as **cuy** (guinea pig). A specialty dating back to Inca times, the dish gets its name from the sound the animal makes just before it's getting skewered and roasted, *"Cuy, cuy, cuy…"* The more vegetarian-friendly **llapingachos** (Andean potato and cheese pancakes) also date back to ancient times, and get their name from the sound the potatoes make when being boiled and mashed, *"Llapingacho, llapingacho, llapingacho…"* Andean natives really know their potatoes; they were first cultivated in the Andes before becoming a starchy staple the world over. Another Andean starch favorite is the **yucca root** (also called *manioc*). As a vegetable dish it is served boiled, but fermented it becomes the alcoholic beverage know as *chicha*.

> **Llapingachos date back to ancient times, and get their name from the sound the potatoes make when being boiled and mashed….**

Ecuador also boasts **bananas** and **plantains** (*plátanos*) in every size, shape, color, and flavor. There are also truckloads of other **tropical fruit;** papayas, passion fruit, avocados, tangerines, pineapples, melons, and tamarinds are all found here, mostly in the fruit-friendly lowland, coast, and jungle regions. If things seems fishy, you're probably on the coast or Oriente, where seafood is served *frito* (fried), *empanado* (breaded), and *a la plancha* (grilled). Fish is often referred to as *corvina* (sea bass), or *trucha* (trout) instead of the generic *pescado* (fish). In the Oriente you may find yourself dining on Amazonian gill-breathers, such as *balgre* (catfish) or piranha. Another fruit of the sea is **ceviche,** a dish made from raw seafood marinated in lemon and lime juice with cilantro and onions. While you may enjoy these delicacies at a marketplace or back in your hotel, chances are you'll do most of your eating in small, local diners known as **comedores,** or in pricier Ecuadorian restaurants.

The most commonly served meal at the *comedores* is the **almuerzo,** with similar meal deals commonly referred to as the **merienda** or **menú del día** (meal of the day). This is a set two-course plate with various extras, which has been prepared in advance and is served at a special price (usually s/3,000-6,000). The first course is **soup** (*sopa* or *caldo*); you may luck into a creamy potato and cheese soup, a catfish soup (*caldo de balgre),* or a hearty beef stew (*caldo de res).* Vegetables from spinach and asparagus to corn and carrots are all possible ingredients, as are various cuts of meat, like *higado* (liver) and *tripa* (tripe). The second, main course (**segundo** or **plato fuerte**) is based on some kind of meat (usually chicken, beef, or pork), often smothered in some kind of savory sauce. Along with the *carne* comes rice, a vegetable, and perhaps a salad or french fries. In every town there is a *comedor* or two known and loved by the locals, the perfect place to get an *almuerzo.* Fancier restaurants serve *almuerzos* as well, often at a higher price with extras like coffee, dessert, cloth napkins, and tuxedod waiters.

If the *menú del día* doesn't do the trick, check out the menu for *a la carta* selections. These will almost always cost more and provide less food than the *almuerzo,* but sometimes it's worth the extra sucres to be able to choose your own meal. The food is often the same kind of thing you will find in the *almuerzo:* creamy soups, potato pancakes, chicken, fish, and *lomo* (a plain cut of meat, *not* a real steak). The fancier restaurants may serve veal (*ternera),* or more quality cuts of steak (*lomo fino*) with fancy wine or mushroom sauces. Good **steakhouses** in bigger cities will serve choice Argentinian beef in all its various forms (a satisfying splurge for meat-lovers). You may choose to try the **parilla** or **parillada,** a sizzling grill heaped full of 10 or more different kinds of meat: steak, pork chop (*chuleta de chanco),* liver, kidney (*riñon),* sausage (*chorizo),* and more unusual cuts such as intestine, udder, heart, or blood sausage (mmmmmm).

But blood sausage just doesn't cut it first thing in the morning. Luckily, breakfast food abounds in Ecuador. Most common are eggs (*huevos),* which can be prepared just about any which way, from *frito* (fried) to *revuelto* (scrambled). Breakfast is commonly served with toast (*pan tostado),* juice, coffee, and sometimes rice and beans. For a lighter (and cheaper) breakfast just visit the local *panadería* (bakery). *Empanadas* (bread stuffed with cheese), *cachos* (croissants), *pan dulce* (sugar coated rolls), and *pan de sal* (salted rolls) all go unbelievably cheaply. Meatier, *almuerzo*-like breakfasts can also be had. Well-touristed areas may offer a *Desayuno Americano,* which includes a bit more food for the voracious American appetite.

> While traditional Ecuadorian cuisine does vary some, travelers staying more than a fortnight should prepare for gustatory monotony.

While traditional Ecuadorian cuisine does vary some, travelers staying more than a couple of weeks should prepare for **gustatory monotony.** The same things tend to turn up on every menu. However, with a little searching more international cuisine can be found in the form of burgers, pizza, or Ecuador's own version of chinese food, served at *chifas* (Chinese restaurants) throughout the country. In addition, most well-touristed areas have a few gringo-oriented establishments that cater more to foreign tastes. These can be a refreshing break from traditional Ecuadorian fare.

DRINK

If urgent visits to the toilets of Ecuador is not your idea of fun, try to avoid drinking the tap water. Water advertised as *purificada* (purified) may have just been passed through a filter. While this may be comforting, these filters do not necessarily catch all of those diarrhea-causing demons. Water that's been boiled or treated with iodine is safe to drink; otherwise, stick to the bottled water that can be found everywhere. Make sure the cap is the original, and that you're not just buying well water.

Sweeter, more effervescent options are Ecuador's soft drinks, always referred to as **colas.** Flavors include the worldwide Coke, Sprite, and Fanta, as well as various types of *fiorivanti* (including strawberry, apple, and pineapple), and the occasional Pepsi.

Another option is the uniquely fruity Inca Kola, made from an ancient recipe that was deciphered from the hieroglyphics of the Macchu Picchu ruins in Perú.

Juices made from Ecuador's abundance of exotic fruits are common and delicious, but almost always made with water. Before consuming, make sure the water used to make the juice has been purified. **Coffee** is not as good as it should be, considering the fact that Ecuador is a coffee-producing country. It is usually served as *esencia* (boiled down concentrated coffee that is mixed with water or milk). Otherwise, you may just be served Nescafé instant coffee. **Milk** is also readily available but is much creamier than the skim milk many foreigners may be accustomed to. Before downing a tall, cold glass of the white stuff, make sure it's been pasteurized.

If you're looking for something a little more intoxicating than milk, try one of Ecuador's beers, **Pilsener** or **Club,** both of which are light lagers. Club has a little bit of an edge, while Pilsener is smoother. One of these beers will set you back a mere s/1,500-3,000 (a little more in fancier places). At these prices, why hold back? Most **wine** is Chilean and tends to be quite expensive, not really a budget beverage. If you really want drown your sorrows, liquor is readily available at almost every corner store at absurdly cheap prices (s/3,000-6,000 for a liter of decent rum). But beware, prices rise dramatically if you wish to consume your beverage in a nice bar or restaurant. Ecuador's local firewater is **aguardiente,** a sweet, tangy, and delicious sugar cane alcohol. Many a tasty drink is made from *aguardiente*. The *caneliza,* made from boiling water, *aguardiente,* cinnamon, and lemon juice, is guaranteed to warm your insides on those cool, misty highland evenings (just make sure that the water came to a boil). Another local liquor, **chicha,** is popular in the Oriente. Made from fermented yucca plant, the recipe also includes a special treat—human saliva.

▓ The Arts

Ecuadorian art is a complex blend of influences—indigenous and European, ancient and modern. The legacy was laid down by the Incas and other pre-Columbian groups, with their *artesanía* (arts and crafts) and distinctive Andean music. When the Spanish arrived, they mixed the artistic influences and technology of the Old World with the indigenous art. *Artesanía* was modernized, colonial buildings went up, and cobblestones were laid down. The religious art so well-known in the Old World began being produced in a distinct new style by the Quito School. With time, the art of Ecuador followed modern trends more and more. Indigenous artisans, combining ancient and modern techniques, began making products for an international market. A number of talented painters, in touch with worldwide artistic currents, began producing modern art with Ecuadorian subject matter. Today's art scene in Ecuador is as active as ever, and numerous museums, festivals, and markets continue to celebrate the country's artistic tradition. Whether you seek the holy splendor of a colonial cathedral, or the mellifluous notes of the Andean *zampoñas,* Ecuador's got the cultural color to further decorate your cerebral canvas.

ARTESANÍA

Crafts of all kinds are produced in Ecuador, but the country is best known for its large variety of **textiles,** almost all of which are produced by various indigenous groups. The most prolific and well-known center of textile production is **Otavalo,** an indigenous community 96km north of Quito. *Otavaleños* have been in the textile business for centuries; when the Incas conquered the area in the late 15th century, they forced the inhabitants to pay tribute with their textiles. A few decades later, the Spanish brought new technology in the form of the treadle loom, hand carders, and new materials, like silk and wool. Under one guise or another, they forced the *indígenas* to work under horrible conditions in *obrajes* (textile workshops) well into the 19th century. In the early 1900s, the *otavaleños* got their start in the modern textile industry by producing imitations of British tweeds (called *casimires*). Since then, the region has continued to put out quality textiles, with almost all production taking place in indigenous households. Most weaving is done with the treadle loom, but some families still use the backstrap loom, a pre-Columbian design, with one end attached to the weaver's back. All kinds of their products, from ponchos to belts and to tapestries, are exported to markets around the world. The **Saturday market** in Otavalo is one of the most popular attractions in all of Ecuador. Some regions of northern Ecuador have taken to **embroidery** and ply their wares at the Otavalo and Ibarra markets. Most striking are their blouses, along with exquisite napkins, dresses, and tablecloths.

Other regions of the country are also known for their weavings. **Cuenca** and the nearby region make **ikat** textiles. This technique involves dying the threads, usually with indigo, before weaving takes place. *Paños* (elaborate shawls) are common *ikat* items, as are *macanas* (carrying cloths), commonly made in the town of Salcedo. Ponchos and wool blankets are also made using the *ikat* technique. **Salasaca** is the country's other main tapestry producer. Along with **Cañar,** it is known for its fine wool **belts** *(chumbis),* which are decorated in various indigenous motifs. **Hand-knitted** sweaters, socks, gloves, and hats are made throughout the highlands and are sure to keep you roasty-toasty. Before buying, make sure the size is right. Most foreigners are quite large compared to the average highlander.

The leatherwork capital of Ecuador is **Cotacachi,** just north of Otavalo. Wallets, purses, belts, whips, and leather underwear can all be found in the many shops lining the town's main street. The handiwork of the Cotacachicans can also be found in less abundance at the market in Otavalo. Ecuador's highest-quality **woodwork** is made in **San Antonio de Ibarra.** Locals carve wood products of all kinds, from intricate wooden boxes and sculptures to furniture. Many artisans work and sell goods right out of their homes. Listen for the sounds of saws and chisels and look out for the trails of sawdust.

> **Crafts of all kinds are produced, but Ecuador is best known for its large variety of indigenous textiles.**

Pre-Hispanic metal work is amazing and in some places the tradition of hand-crafting **jewelry** lives on. Elaborate **shawl pins** (called *tupus*) are made and worn by the *indígenas* of **Saraguro.** These pieces are often family heirlooms passed from one generation to the next. **Chordeleg** is also well known for its contemporary jewelry stores. Much Ecuadorian jewelry incorporates beads into the design, a tradition that began before the Spanish conquest. Beads made of red Spondylus shell were traded throughout the Andes, and to this day red is the favored bead color.

Ceramics are made throughout Ecuador. The Quichua *Sacha Runa* (jungle people) who inhabit the Oriente between the Pastaza and Napo rivers produce fine hand-coiled pots with paintings of Quichua life and mythology on the sides. Other well-respected ceramics are made in the area around **Latacunga.** The small town of **Pujilí** is known for its **painted ceramic figurines.** Shops in Quito and the market at Otavalo also have reputable ceramics for sale.

MODERN ART

The unifying theme of 20th-century Ecuadorian art is its indigenous subject matter, and this common thread lends the movement the name **indigenísmo.** Ecuador's most famous member of this school is **Oswaldo Guayasamín.** The son of an *indígena,* his paintings are strongly pro-indigenous, carrying social and political messages with blatant symbolism—typically abstract depictions of down-trodden, suffering *indígenas.* He worked for a time with the Mexican muralist José Clemente Orozco, and was also influenced by cubism, as evidenced by the choppy style of *La Edad de la Ira (The Age of Anger), Los Turturados (The Tortured Ones),* and *Cabezas (Heads).* In 1988, Guayasamín painted a 23-panel mural in the meeting hall of the Ecuadorian Congress, depicting episodes from Ecuador's history in his trademark anti-establishmentarian manner. Most shocking was a black-and-white panel of a skeletal face wearing a Nazi helmet, with the letters CIA marked across the front. The U.S. Ambassador demanded that the letters be painted over, and members of the U.S. Congress even considered cutting off economic aid to Ecuador. The best place to see Oswaldo's work today is at his museum in Quito (p. 75).

Eduardo Kingman, another indigenist, is considered by some to be the trail-blazer of the movement. The figures in Kingman's paintings are stylized and sorrowful, often depicting scenes of oppression. His 1985 work, *Jugetería (Toy Store),* shows a young indigenous girl painted in dark, shadowy colors peering into a brightly-colored toy store. **Camilo Egas** was part of the early indigenous movement, though his style was much more varied and also influenced by French surrealist currents. In the 50s, he started painting indigenous subjects in a very different realist style. His figures conveyed a feeling of strength and dignity instead of the sadness and abuse depicted by other indigenists. Egas has his own museum in Quito as well. **Manuel Rendón,** another well-known Ecuadorian painter, was not especially indigenist, but is still considered part of the movement. He grew up in Paris, the son of the Ecuadorian Ambassador, and like Egas, was influenced by the modern art there. His works use various modernist styles, such as cubism and pointillism.

Of the more recent generation of painters, **Ramiro Jácome** is the most famous. Not a part of the indigenist movement, he instead prefers to paint abstract human figures using deep colors. Paintings by Jácome and other modern Ecuadorian artists are on display at the Casa de la Cultura in Quito (p. 75).

MUSIC

The music of Ecuador is the result of the confluence of two distinct musical streams: Spanish and pre-Columbian. This tranquil hybrid music of the Andes, rife with fife, strings, and other things, has been popularized around the world by traveling musicians from Ecuador, Perú, and Bolivia. Often the music is just instrumental, but when there's singing, it is usually in Quichua. Bands frequently play at festivals, and recently, people have begun holding music competitions. Get into the groove at one of the many folk music clubs (called **peñas**), where locals get together to celebrate and have a good time.

Indigenous contributions to the typical Andean band include wind instruments, drums, and rattles. The first instrument that pops into most people's minds when thinking of Andean music is the **panpipe** or **rondador.** This ancient instrument is believed to be over 2000-years-old, and where would **Zamfir** be without it? A relative of the *rondador,* originating from the southern Andes but commonly played in Ecuador, is the *zampona,* with two rows of pipes instead of just one. This instrument, along with the five-note scale on which the tunes are based, gives the Andean music its distinctively haunting sound. Two **flutes** of different sizes are also used quite often—the larger *quena* and the smaller *pingullu.* The flutes and the panpipes are both carved from Ecuadorian bamboo. **Bells, drums,** and **rattles** made from gourds *(maracas)* comprise the rest of the indigenous contributions to the modern Andean band.

When the Spanish arrived, they brought with them **stringed instruments** of all shapes, sounds, and sizes, including the *guitarra* (guitar), *violín, bandolín* (mandolin), *charango* (a ukulele-type instrument commonly made from an armadillo shell), and *arpa* (harp). These have added even more variety and texture to the already rich local music.

ARCHITECTURE

The oldest architecture around is, of course, what the Incas left behind. The ruins of **Ingapirca,** just north of Cuenca, are Ecuador's best. Located on an old Inca road, the complex is believed to have served as an inn, a fortress, a temple, or some combination of the three. The ruins exhibit the fine stonework and carving for which the Incas are famous (see **Ingapirca,** p. 134). Little else of Inca origin remains, primarily because the Spanish either destroyed or co-opted their buildings. A number of important Ecuadorian towns are built on the rubble of the Inca civilization; in many cases, the Spaniards even used the very same stones. Many colonial churches are perched on hilltops because they were built over foundations of Inca temples.

Colonial architecture is a blend of the Old and New Worlds; the style of religious art and architecture that resulted from the mix is called the **Quito School.** The Spaniards commissioned the works to be in the popular baroque style, but the indigenous peoples who executed them added their own distinctive touches. Churches and convents in the older towns of Quito and Cuenca are decorated with intricately carved facades and statuaries. The ornate interiors sparkle with gilt; leafy stone vines wrap around classically styled columns as archangels peer down from vaulted ceilings. Municipal buildings and private residences are usually more modest. Large wooden doors open onto rather blocky two-story buildings with high ceilings, interior courtyards, and covered verandas. Simple stonework and elegant wrought-iron decorates whitewashed interiors, while ancient wooden beams and weathered red tiles make up the roofs above. While Riobamba and Latacunga are old cities, they have been destroyed by earthquakes and volcanos, so few (or no) colonial structures remain. Much of Ecuador has been built in the 20th century, when building costs have assumed a primary position in the architectural mind; blocky cement and rebar buildings crowd each other on the more modern streets of New Quito and Guayaquil.

LITERATURE

Ecuador's earliest literature, its **pre-Columbian oral tradition,** was mainly indigenous stories, songs, poetry, and theater intimately linked with religious practices. With the arrival of the Spanish and the forceful conversion of the indigenous peoples to Catholicism, much of this tradition was lost. One notable exception is the preserved story of the war between Atahualpa and his brother Huascar for control of the Inca Empire just before the Spanish Conquest.

The first textual works were the writings of various clergymen during the 17th century, including poetry and discourse on social and political issues in the Spanish colony. The most well-preserved authors of the following century were three Jesuit clergymen, **Antonio Bastidas** (1615-81), **Xacinto de Evia** (1620-?) and **Gaspar de Villarroel** (1590-1665). In the 18th century, bourgeois professionals began to express discontent with the state of affairs that eventually led up to the independence movement. Called "the literature that did not yet have a country," these writings were the first to explicitly focus on what was to become Ecuadorian society. **Juan de Velasco** (1727-92), a historian and narrator, is considered by many to be the most talented writer of his time. A journalist, physician, and philosopher, **Eugenio Espejo** (1747-95) advocated sweeping societal reform and wrote on a vast array of topics including education, theology, politics, health, and the economy. He also started Quito's first newspaper, though it lasted only three months. **Juan Bautista Aguirre** (1725-86), is best known for his *Brief Design of the Cities of Guayaquil and Quito,* which examines the still-present rivalry between the two cities.

The 19th century brought Ecuador its independence from Spain, and with that a distinctive national literature established by the founding fathers, **Juan León Mera** (1832-94) and **Juan Montalvo** (1832-89). Though their Romantic style was influenced by Spanish literature, the content was very anti-monarchy and attempted to create a uniquely Ecuadorian national identity. The most important work is Mera's *Cumandá,* the first Ecuadorian novel. Mera also published other short novels, articles, poetry, and collections of Ecuadorian folklore. Known as the favorite novelist of Ecuador's liberal movement, Montalvo was more political in his writing. His fictional *Chapters that Cervantes Forgot* narrates Don Quixote's adventures through the Americas, dotted with criticism of intellectual and political enemies.

Since the 19th century, Ecuadorian literature has taken on a life of its own, dealing with uniquely Ecuadorian social, political, cultural, and historical topics. One of the most marked differences between the writings of the 19th and 20th centuries is the

> Called "the literature that did not yet have a country," these writings were the first to focus on what was to become Ecuador.

move away from a romanticization of indigenous traditions toward a more realistic portrayal of the indigenous struggle. One of the first works to mark the movement known as **Indigenism** is the 1934 *Huasipungo,* by **Jorge Incaza** (1906-78), a story of the indigenous resistance to their exploitation. Another important work of the 1930s is the collection of short stories by different authors, *Los que se van (Those Who Leave)*. Subtitled "Tales of Halfbreeds and Hillbillies," the stories use crude language and themes that deviated from traditional literary norms and shocked the readers of that time. **Pablo Palacio** (1906-47) was active during 20s and 30s, laying the foundations of a writing style that would become more widespread in the 60s and 70s. His writing is filled with irony and a questioning of reality; subjective descriptions, existentialism, and psychic trauma run throughout. Two authors of the 60s, **Miguel Donoso Pareja** and **Pedro Jorge Vera,**, wrote anti-imperialist works reflecting Ecuador's frustration with its dependency on foreign powers. In 1978, the first Meeting on Ecuadorian Literature lent legitimacy to the growing literary movement, which has since continued to flourish.

■ The Land

Ecuador lies on the western coast of South America, north of Perú and south of Colombia. Its topography is dominated by the volcanic Andes, which span the country lengthwise. The earth's surface is made up of a number of **tectonic plates,** each of which is constantly being pushed and pulled by the plates around it. The Andes were formed as an **uplift** that resulted from a brutal collision of two of these plates several million years ago. Because the mountains are so young, geographically speaking, wind and water have had little time to work their erosive magic on the rugged peaks. The country's geology is far from static; the entire South American coast lies on the edge of a **continental plate** that is being subducted by the **oceanic plate** of the Pacific, providing some heavy-duty geologic action. The interaction of the two plates causes Ecuador's volcanic activity and frequent earthquakes.

> Only the size of Oregon, just bigger than Great Britain, Ecuador is as diverse a country as you'll find anywhere in the world.

This dramatic geology makes for some pretty intense geography. Only the size of the state of Oregon (just bigger than Great Britain), Ecuador is as diverse a country as you'll find anywhere in the world. In the west is the **Pacific coast,** characterized by sparsely populated sandy beaches, swampy areas, and fishing and shrimp farming industries. Just east of the coast are the **lowlands.** Fertile and humid, this land was once completely forested, but now most of it is cleared and cultivated with cacao and bananas. In fact, Ecuador was one of the first banana republics and remains the world's largest banana exporter. East of banana country stretches the highlands, or the **Sierra.** Here, two mountain ridges run from north to south with a high, fertile valley between them. All of the land that can sustain it is cultivated with cereal crops such as barley, wheat, and corn. This results in a typically Andean landscape of patchwork fields dominated by snowcapped volcanoes, with an occasional lake thrown in for good measure. Finally, to the far east is the western Amazon basin and **Oriente.** Sparsely populated for most of Ecuador's history, this region is presently booming because of the oil discovered there in the 70s. Like the rest of the Amazon, flora and fauna are diverse and mind boggling, but threatened by development.

■ Flora and Fauna

Ecuador hosts an unbelievably diverse range of plants and animals, especially given the region's relatively compact size. This variety is packed into less than a 400km span, from palm-lined beaches, to the lowland banana plantations, to the low-growing vegetation of the Andean highlands, to the wet rainforest of the Amazon basin. The rainforest has by far the greatest biodiversity; of the two million plant and animal species known to exist in the world today, half live exclusively in rainforests. Activists around the world have recently stepped up efforts to protect the biodiversity of these forests, where tall, enveloping trees form a several-story-high canopy under which smaller ferns, palms, and other plants grow. Thousands of animal species thrive in the Oriente, from the familiar deer, squirrels, and bats, to the powerful tapirs and jaguars, to the comically exotic guatusa, capybaras, and three-toed sloths. The high-altitude cloudforests of the Sierra are remarkable for their strange combinations of cool, moist air and fairy-tale flora. Wizened trees are covered in bright moss and colorful mushrooms, and one can't help thinking that area must be home to at least a few gnomes or pixies. The spectacled bear, the only species of bear found in South America, resides in the highland region, as do the domesticated alpacas. The palm-lined coasts, meanwhile, are a dream come true for fishermen and divers alike, and bird-watchers will delight at the tropical species found in the western lowlands, where banana, coffee, and cacao crops thrive.

■ Ecotourism

As recently as a decade ago, tourism to Ecuador and the Galápagos Islands destroyed natural resources as quickly as any other industry. Cruise ships brought littering foreigners to beaches, where they bought ornaments fashioned from the shells of endangered tortoises. Developers paved roads through the jungle, and scuba resorts encouraged divers to feed the fish and fondle the coral. Since then, countries around the world have faced strong demands for more responsible, sustainable tourism—"ecotourism" is the pop-name for this trend. The fastest-growing sector of the tourist industry, ecotourism is intended to encourage enjoyment and appreciation of nature while contributing to its continued existence. While few can object to the goal of encouraging respect for the environment, ecotourism has still garnered its share of criticism. Some say "eco" has come to represent the interests of economics rather than ecology, pointing to greedy entrepreneurs who lead ecotours with little or no concern for nature; others warn that increased traffic in natural settings, no matter how "low-impact" it is, can only harm the ecology in the long run.

Since the early days of the movement, ecotourists have flocked to Ecuador and the Galápagos for their bevy of natural beauties. In 1991, 364,585 foreign visitors to Ecuador handed over nearly US$200 million in revenues. The **Jatún Sacha Biological Station** was founded in 1986 with the intent to conserve the incredible biodiversity of the land and to provide a window for researchers. Located on the Río Napo, this wet tropical rainforest has 70% primary growth. It has been such a conservation success that in 1993, it was named the second International Children's Rainforest (the first was the groundbreaking Monteverde Cloudforest in Costa Rica). While Jatún Sacha limits its number of human visitors, the hundreds who cannot enter look elsewhere for some other sort of environmental experience. Such numbers tantalize entrepreneurs and experienced tour leaders alike, who readily grasp that tagging their services as "eco" could yield huge profits. The most legit tour companies have government-issued licenses (see **INEFAN-Approved Tour Companies,** p. 320). But no certification is required to simply call oneself an "environmental" tour guide. True eco-devotees should seek out organizations that actively support conservation efforts and strive to minimize their impact on the environment (see also **Environmentally Responsible Tourism,** p. 35).

> **Visitor numbers tantalize entrepreneurs and experienced tour leaders alike, who readily grasp that the "eco" tag could yield huge profits.**

The recent discovery of oil in the Oriente region puts the rainforest at risk. For the first time, water and air pollution are serious threats *outside* of the cities. The effects of oil drilling have been more destructive, as they ravage the regional wildlife and environment. Indigenous peoples such as the Huaorani and the Cofan, who live in the rainforest, have turned out to be allies of the environmentalists, as their lands and lifestyles have been pillaged by the multi-national oil companies. Political protests have been enough to save some areas—the **Limoncocha Biological Reserve,** downriver from Coca, was founded with the help of angry birdwatchers determined to push oil companies away from their haven. **"Debt-for-nature swaps,"** in which foreign creditors allow lending nations to pay off their debts by protecting areas of the rainforest, has also helped save parts of the environment. But the **Parque Nacional Yasuní** has been the source of the most controversy; while it houses hundreds of bird, animal, and fish species, it is also potentially one of the most valuable oil-drilling areas—a serious consideration in a country with a dwindling economy.

Though progress may occur slowly, environmental awareness is on the rise. Overall, environmental consciousness has been immensely rewarding for Ecuador's economy, to tourists with a thirst for adventure and immersion in nature, and most importantly, to the environment itself, which will only continue to serve visitors if Ecuador continues to pursue its commitment to minimum-impact ecotourism.

Quito

Though Ecuador's capital is home to over 1.25 million people, it's hard to call Quito immense. Nature overshadows what man has created, even though man first created it over 1400 years ago. Carved into a narrow plateau towering 9405 feet (2850m) above deep Andean valleys, Quito is still dwarfed by the cloud-topped peaks above and the looming Volcán Pichincha to the west.

Even Quito's own long and varied history makes the modern city seem small. The peaceful Quitu, Cara, Shyri, and Puruhá tribes inhabited the valley since the sixth century. Conquered by the expansionist Incas from the south, Quito became part of their gargantuan empire around 1500, just as the Spanish began their own binge of ruthless exploitation to the northeast. Wars between the Incas and the long-standing residents of the northern Sierra continued until Francisco Pizarro's 1532 invasion, when he captured the Quito-born Inca emperor Atahualpa. *Quiteños* today celebrate Sebastián de Benalcázar's 1534 arrival as the "founding" of their city, but it was in fact the third or fourth resettling of the short-lived Inca capital. Rumiñuahi, a general of Atahualpa, had torched the city a few months earlier as Spanish troops approached, preferring to bury the Incan architectural achievements under ashes than have them used in the conquistadors' exploitation of the natives.

Little remains of the pre-Columbian people today other than their blood, flowing through the veins of 80% of Quito's population, and the subsequent social stratification reflected in the city's geography. Separated into two sections—tattered Old Town *(La Parte Colonial)* and opulent New Town *(Quito Moderno)*—the divided capital aptly reflects the economic split of most of modern South America. Predictably, the old/new dichotomy has also developed along ethnic lines.

Old Quito has changed little since colonial days, maintaining the classic narrow cobblestone streets, steep inclines, and bustling traditional markets. But as the Ecuadorian economy continues to divide the population into more distinct classes, this home to Quito's poor becomes increasingly decrepit. The wrought-iron balconies of its traditional Spanish dwellings are slowly losing their luster while struggling to maintain their character. As the sunset sends the market vendors home, it invites out the city's underbelly—its drunkards and prostitutes. But Old Quito retains its charisma; the United Nations declared it a "World Cultural Heritage" site in 1978, prohibiting skyscrapers and thus protecting the grand churches and government palaces from being overshadowed. Though pollution-ridden, Colonial Quito's sloping alleyways and plazas, as well as the Río Machángara flowing south of town, remain quite charming by day and elegantly haunting by night.

A busy commercial and social center, Quito's New Town is not beautiful by any architectural standard—though one need only look past the modern mini-skyscrapers to the misty peaks of the wooded Andes for aesthetic enjoyment. Despite its relative lack of architectural beauty, New Town is brought to life by the universities located here. Quito has had more than its share of radical student uprisings—another mark of the vitality of its people and the importance of its place in Ecuador's diverse landscape and population. New Town offers most of what there is to do in this densely-populated mecca, giving a small taste of everything. Wealthy businessmen step over toothless beggars, antique colonial palaces and gaudy ultramodern constructions line the same streets, and all are surrounded above and below by green peaks and valleys. It is as if all of humanity and nature are captured here in one honest glimpse.

■ Practical Information

USEFUL ORGANIZATIONS

Tourist Office: CETUR, Venezuela and Chile (tel. 514-044), in Old Town, can provide a map of Quito, basic tourist information, and some friendly advice (in Span-

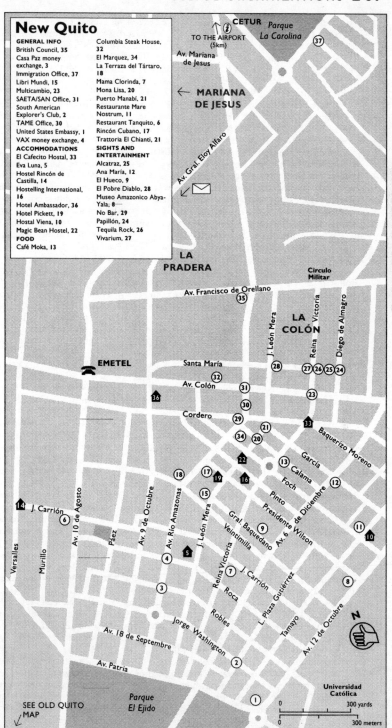

New Quito

GENERAL INFO
British Council, 35
Casa Paz money exchange, 3
Immigration Office, 37
Libri Mundi, 15
Multicambio, 23
SAETA/SAN Office, 31
South American Explorer's Club, 2
TAME Office, 30
United States Embassy, 1
VAX money exchange, 4
ACCOMMODATIONS
El Cafecito Hostal, 33
Eva Luna, 5
Hostel Rincón de Castilla, 14
Hostelling International, 16
Hotel Ambassador, 36
Hotel Pickett, 19
Hostal Viena, 10
Magic Bean Hostel, 22
FOOD
Café Moka, 13

Columbia Steak House, 32
El Marquez, 34
La Terraza del Tártaro, 18
Mama Clorinda, 7
Mona Lisa, 20
Puerto Manabí, 21
Restaurante Mare Nostrum, 11
Restaurant Tanquito, 6
Rincón Cubano, 17
Trattoria El Chianti, 21
SIGHTS AND ENTERTAINMENT
Alcatraz, 25
Ana María, 12
El Hueco, 9
El Pobre Diablo, 28
Museo Amazonico Abya-Yala; 8—
No Bar, 29
Papillón, 24
Tequila Rock, 26
Vivarium, 27

CETUR
TO THE AIRPORT (5km)
Parque La Carolina
Av. Mariana de Jesus

← MARIANA DE JESUS

Av. Gral. Eloy Alfaro

LA PRADERA

Círculo Militar

Av. Francisco de Orellano
35

LA COLÓN

J. León Mera
Reina Victoria
Diego de Almagro

EMETEL

Santa María
32
Av. Colón
31
36
30
Cordero
29
34 20
21
33 Baquerizo Moreno
22
13 García
Calama
17 19
18 16
15
Foch
12
9 Pinto
Presidente Wilson
Av. 6 de Diciembre
11
10

14 J. Carrión
6
Versalles
Murillo
Páez
Av. 10 de Agosto
Av. 9 de Octubre
Av. Río Amazonas
J. León Mera
5
4
Gral. Baquedano
Veintimilla
9
Reina Victoria
7
J. Carrión
Roca
3
L. Plaza Gutiérrez
Tamayo
Av. 12 de Octubre
8

Robles
Jorge Washington
Av. 18 de Septembre
2

N

Av. Patria

SEE OLD QUITO MAP ↙

Parque El Ejido

1

Universidad Católica

0 ____ 300 yards
0 ____ 300 meters

QUITO

ish, French, or English). The New Town CETUR, at Alfaro and Carlos Tobar (tel. 507-555), in a slightly out-of-the-way business area across the street from Parque La Carolina, is not quite as accessible but just as friendly (both offices open Mon.-Fri. 8:30am-5pm). To get to the New Town office, take a bus north on Av. 6 de Diciembre and get off at Alfaro; walk west on Alfaro. CETUR is on the left. The South American Explorer's Club (see below), however, is a far better resource.

Tourist Resource: The **South American Explorer's Club** (SAEC), Jorge Washington 311 and Leonidas Plaza (tel./fax 225-228; email explorer@saec.org.ec for club information), is an absolutely indispensable resource for the traveler visiting any part of Ecuador. A friendly, helpful English-speaking staff will help you make the most of your vacation with trip reports, a guidebook with up-to-date information, a place to store your gear, a safebox for important things like tickets, listings of current cultural events, volunteer opportunities, a large selection of maps, a lending library, and much, much more. Membership isn't cheap (US$40 for one, US$20 for each additional member), but it's certainly worth it if you're spending some time in Quito. Membership services include free tea, nice restroom facilities, a message board, a book exchange, lounge and chat rooms (with a fireplace that really gets used!), consultation on just about any Ecuadorian matter, fax, email, and reliable mail service. Non-members are welcome to stop by once to hear about the club, and also pick up some information. Open Mon.-Fri. 9:30am-5:00pm.

British Council: Amazonas 1646 and Niña (tel. 508-282; fax 223-396), a 5min. walk from downtown. The council offers a vegetarian restaurant and tea room (open Mon.-Fri. 7am-7pm), a language school for Ecuadorian students, a photocopier (s/ 100 per page), and rare email service with telnet (US$0.17/min.). English-language newspapers, like the *London Times,* and *Times Higher Education Supplement,* are available up at the well-stocked library. Non-members can browse, but loans are made only to members. Free movies shown on large screen, and they have a good video library as well (membership s/100,000 per year). Both libraries are open Mon.-Fri. 7am-noon and 2-8pm.

Tour Company and Tourist Information: Safari, Calama 380 and J.L. Mera, and Roca 630 and Amazonas (tel. 552-505 or 234-799; fax 223-381; email Admin@Safariec.ecx.ec). Reputedly the biggest climbing agency in Quito, this incredibly helpful, English-speaking company has books of hotels and tours from all over Ecuador and offers full service itinerary planning or just some friendly advice. Tours are a bit expensive (US$180 for a 2 day guided Cotopaxi climb) but less pricey adventures come up periodically—like US$35 to spend a day at Andean Condor nesting sites—and discount trips are sometimes available to SAEC members. Stopping in for ideas, advice, or brochures is welcome and costs nothing. Open daily 9am-7pm.

Immigration Office: The **Oficina de Migración,** Amazonas 2639 and Republica (tel. 454-122). This is where you get a tourist card extension (for a length of stay) or a (rarely needed) "Certificate of Exit." Open Mon.-Fri. 8am-12:30pm.

Embassies: Canada, Avenida Corea 126 and Amazonas, Edificio Belmonte, 6th fl. (tel. 506-163; fax 503-108). Open Mon.-Fri. 9:30am-12:30pm. **Colombia,** Colón 133 and Amazonas, 7th floor (tel. 228-926 or 222-486; fax 567-766). Open Mon.-Fri. 8:30am-1pm and 2:30-6pm. **France,** Leonides Plaza 107 and Patria (tel. 560-789). Open Mon.-Fri. 8:30am-1pm and 3-5:30pm. **Ireland,** Montes 577 and Las Casas (tel. 462-521; fax 501-444). Open Mon.-Fri. 9:30am-12:30pm. **Israel,** Eloy Alfaro 969 and Amazonas (tel. 565-509; fax 504-635). Open Mon.-Fri. 8:30am-4:30pm. **Peru,** Amazonas 1429 and Colón, Edificio España, penthouse (tel. 468-410; fax 468-411). Open Mon.-Fri. 8:30am-1:30pm. **United Kingdom,** Av. Gonzáles Suárez 111, Casilla 314 (tel. 560-670; fax 560-730). Open Mon.-Fri. 8:30am-12:30pm and 1:30-5pm. Weekend emergencies at tel. 09-723-021. **United States,** Patria 120 and Av. 12 de Octubre (tel. 562-890; fax 502-052). Open Mon.-Fri. 8am-noon and 1:45-5pm. For emergencies, call tel. 234-126 for help 24hr.

Currency Exchange: *Casas de cambios* all over town, as well as banks, will exchange cash. **VAX,** on New Town's main thoroughfare, Amazonas and Roca, exchanges traveler's checks and cash at good rates, and offers student discounts. Open Mon.-Fri. 8:30am-6pm, Sat. 9am-1pm. **Multicambio** has four offices—Colón 919 and Reina Victoria, Roca 720, Venezuela 689, and the airport (tel. 567-347;

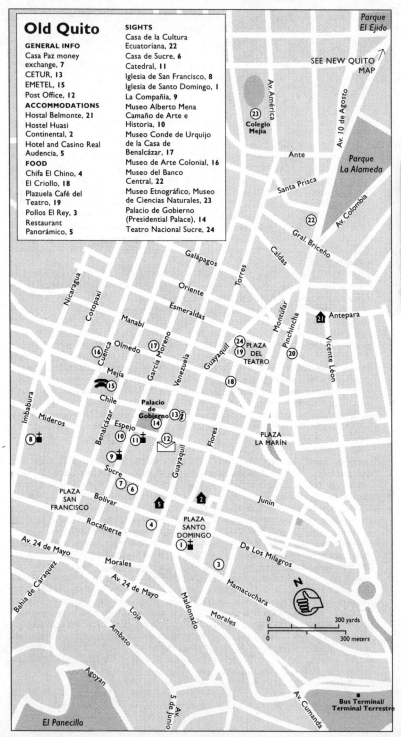

Old Quito

GENERAL INFO
Casa Paz money exchange, 7
CETUR, 13
EMETEL, 15
Post Office, 12

ACCOMMODATIONS
Hostal Belmonte, 21
Hostel Huasi Continental, 2
Hotel and Casino Real Audencia, 5

FOOD
Chifa El Chino, 4
El Criollo, 18
Plazuela Café del Teatro, 19
Pollos El Rey, 3
Restaurant Panorámico, 5

SIGHTS
Casa de la Cultura Ecuatoriana, 22
Casa de Sucre, 6
Catedral, 11
Iglesia de San Francisco, 8
Iglesia de Santo Domingo, 1
La Compañía, 9
Museo Alberto Mena Camaño de Arte e Historia, 10
Museo Conde de Urquijo de la Casa de Benalcázar, 17
Museo de Arte Colonial, 16
Museo del Banco Central, 22
Museo Etnográfico, Museo de Ciencias Naturales, 23
Palacio de Gobierno (Presidential Palace), 14
Teatro Nacional Sucre, 24

QUITO

open Mon.-Fri. 8:30am-2pm and 3-5:30pm). **Casa Paz,** Amazonas 370 and Robles (tel. 563-900; open Mon.-Sat. 9am-6:15pm).

Banks: Av. Río Amazonas is filled to the brim with banks. Hours vary slightly, but most will only exchange for cash on Mon.-Fri. from 9am-1:30pm. Reliable banks include: **Banco Guayaquil,** Colón and Reina Victoria (tel. 566-800; open Mon.-Fri. 9am-4pm and Sat. 9am-1:30pm); **Banco Pichincha,** Amazonas and Colón (tel. 547-006; open Mon.-Fri. 8am-8pm); **Banco Popular,** Amazonas 3535 (tel. 444-700; open Mon.-Fri. 9am-4pm, Sat. 9am-2pm); and **Banco del Pacífico,** Amazonas and Veintimilla (tel. 437-537; open Mon.-Fri. 9am-6pm, Sat. 9am-2pm). Cash **traveler's checks** at any bank, and buy them at **Lloyd's Bank,** Amazonas 580 and Carrión (tel. 564-177; open Mon.-Fri. 9am-4pm).

ATMs: Plentiful in New Town and non-existent in the Old, but most will only take Visas or MasterCards that have been PIN-enabled. Normal ATM cards (Cirrus, Plus, etc.) only work at **BanRED** machines, located many places—especially Amazonas. Specifically, machines can be found at **Banco de Prestamos,** Amazonas at Veintimilla, **Hotel Oro Verde,** Av. 12 de Octubre and Cordero, and **Filanbanco,** smack in the middle of Amazonas at Robles, but there are tons out there.

Credit Card Offices: MasterCard, Av. Nac. Unidas 825 and Shyris (tel. 462-770; open Mon.-Fri. 8am-5pm). **Visa,** Banco de Guayaquil, Colón and R. Victoria (tel. 566-800; open Mon.-Fri. 9am-4pm). **American Express,** Amazonas 339 and J. Washington, Ecuadorian Tours, 5th fl. (tel. 560-488; open Mon.-Fri. 8:30am-5pm).

Emergency: tel. 111.

Police: The **Criminal Investigation Office** is in Old Town at the intersection of Cuenca and Maderas. Open daily 9am-midnight. Police can be reached at tel. 101.

Internet Access: See **SAEC** and **British Council** above.

Post Offices: In the **Old Town,** Espejo between Guayaquil and Venezuela, ½ block towards Guayaquil from the Palacio de Gobierno. Open Mon.-Fri. 7:30am-7pm, Sat. 8am-2pm. Stamps sold inside. Mark mail "Correo Central" underneath Lista de Correos to have it sent to this post office. In the **New Town,** Eloy Alfaro 354 and 9 de Octubre. If you want mail sent to this branch, mark it "Correo Central, Eloy Alfaro" otherwise it will be sent to the Old Town office. Stamps are sold on the seventh floor. Open Mon.-Fri. 8am-7:30pm, Sat. 7:30am-2pm. **Packages** should be sent via **Correo Maritimo Aduana,** Ulloa 273 and Ramirez Dávalos, located next to the Santa Clara market. Open Mon.-Fri. 7:30am-3:30pm. **EMS** (Express Mail Service) is centrally located on Reina Victoria 1325 between Cordero and Lizardo García (tel. 569-741), Mon.-Fri. 7:30am-7pm. **FedEx,** Amazonas 5340 between Tomás de Berlanga and Isla Floreana (tel. 448-371 or 253-552). The best place to receive mail—if you're a member—is **SAEC** (see **Tourist Resource,** p. 62).

Faxes: You can send faxes from **EMETEL,** but they charge by the page. They have cheaper rates on weekends and after 7pm on weekdays. **Luiwan Co. Ltd.,** Veintimilla 910 and J.L.Mera (tel. 221-869), has good fax services, open Mon.-Fri. 10am-1pm and 2-6pm. It's easiest to receive faxes at the **South American Explorer's Club,** J. Washington and Leonidas Plaza (tel. 225-228; can't *send* from there). Many copy places offer fax services, such as **Compucopies,** Tamayo and Roca (tel./fax 227-420), at s/2000 for Quito faxes, and varying prices internationally.

Telephone Service: Quito is probably the easiest place in the country from which to make international calls. Nearly everything can be done from **EMETEL,** which has four locations: Av. 10 de Agosto and Colón, the airport (Mariscal Sucre), Benalcázar and Mejía, and the Terminal Terrestre. EMETEL lets you make free calling-card calls from private booths, but you may have to wait in quite a line. Local calls s/600 per minute, national calls s/1,800 to s/2,800 for three minutes. Open daily 8am-9:30pm. **Pay phones** do not exist, at least not those of the coin variety—small-phone operators working out of stands on the street offer sometimes-overpriced local service (don't even think about making international calls there), and many stores will let you use their phones if you offer to pay (s/1000-2000). In general, **AT&T** (toll-free tel. 999-119) and **MCI** (toll-free tel. 999-170) calling-card calls can be made from any direct-dial phone, including those in the lobbies of most expensive hotels. Be careful they don't charge you by the minute—there is no need for this—ask first. It should cost s/1,000-3,000 for the service. These include the **Hotel Amaranta,** across from SAEC at J. Washington and Leonidas (tel. 238-385), and the

Hotel Oro Verde, Av. 12 de Octubre and Cordero (tel. 566-479). Collect calls and local calls (for around s/1,500-3,000 per 3min.) can also be made at these posh hotels. **Telephone Code:** 02.

TRANSPORTATION

Airport: Aeropuerto Mariscal Sucre is on Amazonas to the far north of town, near Av. La Florida. You may be a bit disoriented walking off the plane and right onto the runway, Air Force One-style; simply follow the crowd inside, and be sure to get your tourist card and passport stamped. Save yourself some cash by hailing a cab a few blocks away from the airport, instead of getting one right out front. Taxis shouldn't charge more than s/20,000 to or from the airport, but late at night they can get away with a lot more. To get to the airport on public transportation, take the "Aeropuerto" or #1 bus heading north from New or Old Town, or grab the trolley and change to Rumiñuahi at Estación Norte. On the trolley, get on the Rumiñuahi route at Estación Norte at the end of the New Town.

Airlines: SAETA/SAN, Colón and Amazonas in the Edificio España (tel. 565-005; open Mon.-Fri. 8:30am-6pm); **TAME,** Amazonas 13-54 and Colón (tel. 509-375; open Mon.-Fri. 8:30am-5pm, Sat. 9am-noon); **Aerogal,** Amazonas 7797 and Juan Holguín (tel. 257-202; fax 430-487).

Trains: A trolley heading south will take you to the station on Maldonado (get off at the Machangara stop), past Old Town. Trains are not a prominent mode of transportation in Ecuador, but the weekly departure to Riobamba offers fantastic mountain views (every Sat. 8am, 8hr., US$7 to Latacunga, US$11 to Ambato, US$14 to Riobamba). Tickets on sale Fri. 8am at the station (tel. 656-142; open Mon.-Fri. 8am-4:30pm). For the best views, some ride the roof (though it may be chilly). Another route runs from Quito to Cotopaxi (every Sun. 8am, US$27), and a train goes on to Duran from Riobamba (Mon., Wed., and Fri.-Sun., US$19). Tickets on sale Mon.-Fri. 8am-4:30pm, Bolívar 443 and Benalcázar (tel. 582-921), in Old Town.

Local Buses: Local buses are ubiquitous and confusing. Perhaps the most daunting initial hurdle to local bus-riding is the fact that the buses don't actually stop—they merely slow down to around 5mph, at which point passengers must jump onto the moving bus. Once you're prepared both mentally and physically for this task, you'll have to decide which class to take. All buses are cheap, but some buses are cheaper than others. The cheapest are the ridiculous, but ridable, schoolbus-style **"Servicio Popular,"** at s/400; next are the over-crowded but more comfortable **"Servicio Ejecutivo,"** at s/600; and finally the **"Selectivo,"** slightly less crowded and a bit quieter, at s/800. Usually there is someone who will give you change if you can't pay the exact amount. Buses always have names of streets and/or landmarks on their front windows, and sometimes numbers as well. A common route is the **Old Town-New Town pathway,** traversed by the Colón-Camal (#2) on 10 de Agosto, the San Bartolo-Miraflores (#10) on 10 de Agosto, the El Tejar-El Inca (#11) on Av. 6 de Diciembre, and other buses on Av. 12 de Octubre. Buses to the **airport** can be caught on Amazonas, marked "aeropuerto" (#1), and buses to the Parque La Carolina section of New Town can be caught on Av. 6 de Diciembre—these are often marked "Estadio" and continue on to the Olympic Stadium on Av. 6 de Diciembre and Naciones Unidas. Getting off the bus is easier than getting on—just move to the door and say "Gracias" and the bus will stop (or slow down at least). If you have luggage, you're better off with a taxi—it's not expensive, it's safer, and most public buses don't allow big backpacks or suitcases.

Long-Distance Buses: The *terminal terrestre* lies next to a highway at the end of **Av. 24 de Mayo** in Old Town. Take the trolley to the Cumandá stop, then descend the stairs on the north side of the highway and keep walking. Inside the several-story *terminal* are a police station, an EMETEL office, many small restaurants, and an excessive number of bus company windows offering frequent departures to wherever you want to go. Buses to destinations that are high in demand often leave as soon as they are full; otherwise, they leave somewhat regularly as listed below. **Transportes Ecuador** runs to **Guayaquil** (every hr., 5:30am-12:20am, 7½hr., s/27,000), with buses leaving 40min. earlier from New Town office at Mera 330 and Washington. **Cooperativa Chimborazo** (tel. 570-601), is one of many that constantly go to **Riobamba** (5:30am-7pm, 3½hr., s/11,000), via **Ambato** (2hr., s/

7,000). **Transportes Latacunga** (tel. 583-316), strangely enough, serves **Latacunga** (every 10min., 6am-8pm, 1¾hr., s/5,000). **Transportes Putumayo** goes to **Lago Agrio** (every hr., 9:30am-9:30pm, 8hr., s/25,000). **Transportes Amazonas** (tel. 571-747) travels to **Baños** (every hr., 2:35pm-7:25pm, 3hr., s/10,000). **Transportes Esmeraldas** (tel. 572-985), heads to **Esmeraldas** (at least every 1½hr., 7:30am-11pm, 6hr., s/22,000) via **Santo Domingo** (3hr., s/12,000). **Cooperativa Sucre** (tel. 612-826), hits **Cuenca** (13 per day, 7:30am-midnight, 8hr., s/25,000). **Cooperativa Reina del Camino** (tel. 572-673), makes a beach run to **Manta** (16 per day, 6:30am-11pm, 10hr., s/22,000) and many other places en route. Buses to **Ibarra** leave every 20min. starting at 6am (s/7,500).

Trolleys: The spanking-new **trole (trolley)** system in Quito (runs Mon.-Fri. 5am-midnight, Sat.-Sun. and holidays 6am-10pm) is easy to understand, fast, efficient, sparklingly modern, and crowded. You can't miss the glass-walled, arched *trole* stops— at s/1000 (s/500 for children under 18, seniors, or handicapped people) it costs slightly more than a bus, but the *trole* stops! The *trole* runs along one street in New Town (10 de Agosto) and two in Old Town (Guayaquil and Montufar), so it's hard to get lost as long as you know which direction you want to go. The *trole* zips way out to Quito's outskirts, branching out into several routes, but unless you're going to the airport or a suburb, you won't need to go that far. Cards sold for 7 or 35 rides at the amazing deal of s/7,000 or s/35,000.

Taxis: With **TeleTaxi** (tel. 411-119 or 411-120; open 24hr.), s/150,000 buys a driver for an entire day. Other recommended services are: **Transportes y Turismo,** Patria and Amazonas, in the Hotel Colón (tel. 520-100). Call tel. 222-999 to get a taxi anytime (not terribly necessary since taxis are everywhere in Quito).

Car Rental: Horozontes Ecuatorianos, Pinto 560 and Amazonas (tel. 230-463), rents cars and minibuses with or without drivers. **Budget Rent-a-Car,** Colón 1140 and J. Luis Mera (tel. 237-236 or 548-237; airport 459-052 or 240-763). **Avis Rent-a-Car,** Aeropuerto Mariscal Sucre (tel. 440-270 or 255-890).

OTHER PRACTICAL INFORMATION

Lost-and-Found Center: On Montufar between Olmedo and Manabí. Bring your police statement to see if your lost item is there. The Second Coming is more likely.

English Bookstore: Confederate Books and Cafe, Calama 410 and León Mera (tel. 257-890), has a great selection of used books—from a Stephen King collection to old Ecuadorian guidebooks, in the s/15,000 to s/30,000 range. Open Mon.-Sat. 10am-7pm. **SAEC** (see **Tourist Resource,** p. 62) has Quito's best selection of English guidebooks to peruse while at the club, with a variety of books available for borrowing (US$30 deposit), and some used books for exchange. Often hostels will have small book exchange shelves, too.

Spanish Bookstores: Libri Mundi is a stellar chain, though not bargain-basement priced, with a large store at León Mera 851 and Veintimilla (tel. 234-791), one in Quicentro Shopping at Av. Naciones Unidas and Av. Los Shyris (tel. 464-473), and another in the Hotel Colón, Amazonas and Patria (tel. 464-473). Books in Spanish, German, French, and English. Open Mon.-Fri. 8:30am-7pm, Sat.-Sun. 9am-1:30pm and 3:30-6:30pm. **Atenea Librería,** Alfaro 2013 and Suiza (tel. 456-795), offers an elegant, extensive selection of Spanish books. Open Mon.-Sat. 9:30am-7:30pm.

Shopping: The major shopping district is on and around **Avenida Río Amazonas,** the main thoroughfare of New Town. Buy anything from Panama hats to cheesy tourist souvenirs, and electronics to clothing. Half the fun is just looking. If you want, however, you can sit in one place on Amazonas and buy nearly anything from street vendors, who will approach you with gum, shirts, jewelry, sculptures, sunglasses, cellular phones, office chairs (!), and much, much more.

Computer Rental: Old clones can be used for s/3,000 per hour (printers cost s/500) at Luis Cordero and 9 de Octubre (tel. 540-677). Copying shops sometimes have computer services available—just ask.

Photocopies: Copies can be made at practically 2 places on every block, reflecting the curious infestation of photocopy services in all of Latin America. Among the choices are **Copifull,** Av. 6 de Diciembre 1045 and J. Washington (tel. 228-473), s/150 per copy, and **Comucopies,** Tamayo and Roca (tel. 227-420), s/100 per copy.

Supermarkets: Lark, Dávalos and Versalles, offers a huge selection of clean meats and cheeses, as well as liquor and other standard supermarket fare. Open Mon.-Sat. 8am-8pm, Sun. 9am-1:30pm. The high-quality, all-purpose **Supermaxi** chain has branches at the airport Centro Comercial, Centro Comercial El Bosque on Occidental, and Multicentro on Av. 6 de Diciembre and La Niña, among other locations. Open Mon.-Sat. 9:30am-8pm, Sun. 9:30am-2pm.

Laundry: Most hotels offer some sort of laundry service, from complete machine service to a wash-basin and clothesline (beware daily afternoon rainfall, however). Another option is the laundromat route—*lavanderías* are available every couple of blocks. Options include: **Lavanderías Lavalimpio,** Tamayo 420 and Roca, s/2,500 per pound (open Mon.-Fri. 8am-6pm, Sat. 8am-3pm); **Lavandería Lavanda Calama,** Calama 244 and Reina Victoria (tel. 237-510), s/1,800 per pound, also offers dry cleaning (s/6,000 for pants; open Mon.-Sat. 8am-8pm, Sun. 8am-noon); **One Hour Martinizing,** Av. 12 de Octubre 1486 (tel. 225-223), among other locations. Dry cleaning only (s/8250 for pants; open Mon.-Fri. 8am-7pm, Sat. 8am-1pm). Prices at laundromats tend to be higher than hotel prices.

Hospitals: Hospital Vozandes, Villalengua 267 and 10 de Agosto (tel. 252-142), on the "Iñaquito" bus line, is English-speaking and highly recommended. This is the best place to come for a rabies vaccination (5 shots over 1 month, US$185). Visiting fee s/40,000. **Hospital Metropolitano,** Av. Mariana de Jesus and Occidental (tel. 431-520 or 431-457). Get there on a "Quito Sur-San Gabriel" bus from El Tejar downtown. Also English-speaking; high-quality, but expensive.

Clinics: Private medical practitioner **Dr. John Rosenberg,** Foch 476 and Almagro (tel. 521-104, pager 223-333), at the medical center bearing his name. Fluent in English, German, French, and Hebrew. Fee US$20 for a consultation; also offers vaccinations for Hepatitis A and B, and Yellow Fever. **Dr. Wallace Swanson** (tel. 252-142), an American doctor at the Hospital Vozandes. **Clínica Pichincha,** Veintimilla 1259 and Paez (tel. 560-820), is recommended for emergency care (tel. 562-408). **Laboratorio Clínico Ecoamerican** (tel. 456-610 or 443-155). Dra. Sarita Espinosa de los Monteros in charge, high quality service, English speaking.

▓ Accommodations

NEW TOWN

Hotels and hostels abound in New Town, but because a place calls itself a hostel does not necessarily mean that it meets any particular standards. The main distinction between the two types of accommodations is this: in hotels, single rooms are guaranteed, while in hostels, rooms are usually shared between two to 10 people. Many of the hostels are gringo-run, or at least gringo-populated, and tend to congregate in prime locations—either right in the middle of New Town activity near Amazonas, or in the posh-hotel district near Av. 12 de Octubre and the grand Hotel Oro Verde. Budget *hotels,* on the other hand, tend to lie slightly outside the main strips. Watch out for the definite price-location correlation among hotels.

La Casona de Mario, Andalucía 213 and Galicia (tel. 544-036 or 230-129). Comfort couldn't come from a nicer guy. Mario, the Argentinean owner, sets guests up in his delightful house, a bit out of the way in a usually safe, quiet residential area. Nobody interior decorates quite like Mario; he has decked out rooms with aesthetic wonders such as indigenous weavings and cloth parrots. Very social atmosphere—rooms are shared: the bedrooms (some with balconies!), hot-water bath, living room, dining room, kitchen, and patio. Laundry and barbeque facilities round out amenities. US$6 per person; 10% discount on stays of 15 days or longer.

Hostal Viena, Tamayó 879 and Foch (tel. 235-418). An unmistakable aura of cleanliness is found at this centrally-located hostal. The white-tiled floor of the lobby and the extra-tiny but spotless private bathrooms might result in a feeling of sterility were it not for the bright bedspreads, holy shrines, and perks like TVs, telephones, and hot water in every room (s/22,000 per person).

El Cafecito, Luis Cordero 11-24 and Reina Victoria (tel. 234-862). A paradise for anyone in love with the hip coffeehouse scene, this hostel has comfortable rooms upstairs from a popular vegetarian cafe. Colorful wall hangings of Matísse prints and Ecuadorian crafts add to the flavor, and the deep blue- or green-tiled shared bathrooms (cleaned every day—along with the rooms) are almost inviting. A youthful, largely European crowd populates this Canadian-owned lodging, where English is spoken better than Spanish. Hot water is always available, and there is a luggage storage area and a safe for extra important stuff. One double-bed room available for long-term stays; other rooms with four or five beds. Rooms s/23,000 per person.

Hostal Eva Luna, Pasaje Roca 630 (tel. 234-799), a side street between Mera and Amazonas, is Quito's only women's hostal. The purply-pink door, rickety old steps, and painted flowers spilling down the walls add to the comfortable appeal. Common room with wide movie selection, homey kitchen, and boxy cement balcony for barbecues and fresh mid-city air. Prices go down with longer stays; 1-10 nights s/19,800 per person, per night; 10-19 nights s/17,600 per person, per night.

La Familia Sanchez, Gerona and Madrid (tel. 235-439). Follow Madrid from 12 de Octubre to the very end, turn left on Gerona and walk to the second house on the left. The view of mountains outside your door beyond the sun roofed deck area is enough to make the distance outside of town seem unimportant. Clean single rooms, friendly people, usable kitchen and living room, hot water, washing machine, TV, private baths, and Graciela's stories make this a relaxing, pleasant place to be. Prices vary depending on length of stay; generally around US$5 per person, some meals available upon request (not included in price given here).

Hostal Rincón de Castilla, Versalles 1127 and Carrión (tel. 548-097; fax 224-312). Stay here if you're visiting Ecuador to explore, not to lounge. Very basic rooms—with beds, table, window, and little else—are clean enough and cost next to nothing (s/15,000). They offer help in getting tickets for further travels or a guide to show you Quito (US$15 per day), so there's no need to feel trapped. Communal table, laundry services, luggage safety spot, hot water, and usable kitchen. Under 10min. from most New Town activity.

Centro del Mundo, García 569 and Reina Victoria (tel. 229-050). This bustling hostel calls itself "the backpacker's hang-out," and lives up to its motto. Mostly twentysomethings pour into the Canadian-Ecuadorian owned establishment, whose loose, liberal, international atmosphere has gained a reputation as a big party house. Dim, futon-strewn living room has a homey fireplace, cable TV, tables, and cheap gourmet meals cooked-to-order. Showers steam, refreshingly hip music plays, and sun deck simmers on sunny days. Lower ("party") room, decked out with tapestries and wood chests for locking up backpacks, 10 bunks for only US$4 apiece. More tranquil rooms upstairs go for US$5 a bed.

The Magic Bean Hostel, Foch 681 and León Mera (tel. 566-181). The best known of Quito's gringo hostelling hotbeds, the Magic Bean enchants with an absolutely *prime* location—amidst the New Town's activity and popular nightspots. The friendly management has conjured up well-maintained, inviting wood-paneled rooms, shared among three or more. Communal bathroom has hot water. The slightly expensive restaurant and coffeehouse downstairs have a relaxed feel, with a straw-thatched roof for outdoor seating. US$7 per person. Private rooms also available at steeper rates: singles US$20; doubles US$24.

Hotel Pickett, Wilson 712 and León Mera (tel. 551-205 or 541-453). These spacious rooms with large beds are relatively safe and centrally located, however bare. The communal bathrooms are not places in which you will want to spend much time, but nothing dangerous is growing in there. Rooms with double beds s/20,000, with bath, TV, and phone s/40,000.

Hostelling International (HI), Pinto 3-25 and Reina Victoria (tel. 543-995). Part of the huge HI chain, this branch dutifully provides what you've come to expect: meticulous cleanliness, virtually identical rooms with familiar melon colored bedspreads and thin mattresses, immaculately tiled bathrooms, and that classic standardized institutional, er, hostel feel. Usually a safe choice, though it lacks the character of some other centrally located New Town accommodations, and the management can be harried. HI members $9 with TV and bath shared within one room of three to four people, $8 with fully communal bath. Non-members $10 and $9. Includes continental breakfast.

Hotel Ambassador, Av. 9 de Octubre 1052 and Colón (tel. 561-777, 562-054, or 561-993), is a 10min. walk to the bustling center of everything, as well as the best deal among the better-than-budget hotels. Beautifully kept, voluminous double rooms (s/90,000). Some center around a central garden; all have sparkling spotless and roomy bathrooms, color cable TV, and direct-dial phones. Services include a travel agency, private parking, and a bar/restaurant.

OLD TOWN

Hotels in Old Town tend to be lower in both price and quality than their New Town counterparts. Price is generally the biggest reason why tourists stay here, but as budget spots open in New Town, the benefits of staying in Old Town are dwindling. Little of interest goes on in Old Town after about 9pm, and safety is a concern in Old Town's budget hotel districts at night. If you choose to stay here, you'll either be confined to your room shortly after the sun sets, or else face a wee-hour cab ride back to the neighborhood (trolleys stop at 10pm or midnight, and buses vary in how late they run). However, not all Old Town accommodations are as decrepit as one might imagine, and most are cheaper.

Hostel Huasi Continental, Flores 332 and Sucre (tel. 517-327 or 518-441). Usually lighting this poor is a bad omen, conjuring images of skeletons in the shadows. But the spotless Huasi Continental has nothing to hide, with its immaculate stucco-walled rooms, comfortable beds, and tidy private bathrooms. Squint a little and note the narrow mahogany desks, mirrors, and thumbtack-sized wastebaskets in each room. Restaurant 8:30am-8:30pm, private parking for small cars (s/4,000). Ask for a back room if you mind noise (singles s/15,000, with bath s/20,000, with TV s/25,000; doubles s/24,000, with bath and TV s/36,000).

Hostal Residencial Marsella, Los Ríos 2035 and Castro (tel. 515-884), in a quiet section near the New Town. Basic, small rooms cost next to nothing. Marsella boasts a cafeteria open for breakfast (s/4,000) and dinner (s/6,000-7,000), a small garden area with an old swingset, and a communal balcony with a great view of the city. Duos should ask for the topmost room for an exciting and precarious look at Quito (s/16,000 per person, with private bath s/35,000).

Hotel & Casino Real Audencia, Bolívar 220 and Guayaquil (tel. 512-711; email realaudi@hoy.net), at the corner of Plaza Santo Domingo. Although the fanciest hotel in the Old Town, the Real Audencia actually offers some rooms at amazing bargains. Enjoy the same comfort, cleanliness, cold air, and breathtaking view as guests paying twice as much. Ask for a third floor room to fully appreciate the sweeping panorama of Old Quito, El Panecillo, and the surrounding residential highland hills. "Budget rooms" equipped with telephones, large closets, wooden dressers, and private bath cost s/40,000 per night. Only about five of these cheap rooms exist, but if you show a student ID or belong to a club, the staff may make more available. Services also include free luggage storage, low-priced phone calls, laundry, money exchange, free information, and US$8 airport transportation. Blow the money you saved at the casino downstairs, or splurge with a gourmet meal at the scenic restaurant on the third floor.

Hotel Viena Internacional, Flores and Mejía (tel. 514-860 or 519-611). Though a bit more expensive than other Old Quito rooms, the style and comfort here make s/38,000 a good price. A central fountain area is surrounded by ferns, tables and chairs, little religious shrines, and Ecuador travel information boards. A beautiful wooden staircase leads to rooms with jazzy bedspreads, telephones, TV, and private (hot-water) bathrooms. Some have balconies as well. A restaurant downstairs has a continental breakfast for s/5,000.

QUITO

> ### When in Quito...
>
> McDonald's, Chicago Bulls baseball caps, cell-phones—signs of Westernization in Ecuador are everywhere. Many differences remain, and learning some of the differences in customs and conventions can save a lot of embarrassment, humiliation, and confusion. Here are a few things to keep in mind:
>
> The American 'OK' symbol is considered to be vulgar and offensive—move your hand rapidly back and forth, and you'll understand why.
>
> When indicating a person's height, hold your hand perpendicular to the ground—the horizontal positioning most of us are accustomed to is used for animals and inanimate objects only.
>
> *Always* use a person's official title when addressing him or her; this is taken quite seriously in Latin America.
>
> To get a bus to stop, point at the ground. This signals that you want them to stop *and* that you are willing to pay. If you just stick your hand out, the driver may think you're just pointing at something.
>
> Proper salutations are important—make sure to always greet people appropriately, even in stores and restaurants. Failing to do so can be taken as an affront, and goes a long way in explaining the seemingly mysterious poor service that a lot of foreigners receive.

■ Food

NEW TOWN

Predictably, New Town restaurants tend to be pricier and more upscale than their Old Town counterparts, but it's still possible to eat on a reasonable budget here. The low value of the sucre means that even the ritziest joints are practically budget spots by first-world standards. Travelers can "splurge" and get a classy gourmet meal for the price of average grub meal back home. Be aware that much of most of the extra cost at the ritziest New Town restaurants simply covers the frills around the edges: tuxedos on waiters, chandeliers—the food is not necessarily better than that in the *comedor* around the corner. Don't forget that in Ecuador, meals are not rushed—there are few "fast food" joints and it is rare to find even a slightly quick food establishment. Don't worry, you will be served. Just ask for the bill when you are ready to leave—it is considered rude to rush one's customers, so you may wait a while if you don't ask.

For cheap eats, hit the *almuerzo* (lunch) spots, mostly on the side streets off of **Av. Río Amazonas.** Restaurant Row, the informal name for another strip of eateries, is between León Mera and Reina Victoria, around **Calamá.** Fancy restaurants tend to cluster here, but there are some less expensive options as well. On Amazonas itself, **sidewalk cafes** are good for people-watching and a moderately-priced drink or two.

Cheap Eats

Restaurante Tanguito, Carrión (tel. 543-565), between 10 de Agosto and Murillo. The locals know where to go, and this is where the hungry flock. Worth the stray off the beaten path—just follow the army of loyal lunchtime regulars. Tanquito serves up an absolutely mouthwatering *almuerzo* with soup, rice, meat, and vegetables (s/3,800). The atmosphere aims to please: a congenial staff, attractive green tablecloths downstairs, and mini-sofas at the tables upstairs. Lively music, piles of fruit at the front counter, and even fake red flowers at each table add a special spice to this inexpensive find. Open daily 7am-8pm.

Mini Bar Francisco, 526 Wilson and Diego de Almagro, a typical *almuerzo* spot with clean blue and white table cloths and an intimate atmosphere. Set *desayunos* and *almuerzos* (s/4,500; natural juices s/3,000). Open Mon.-Sat. 8am-4pm.

Munch Café and Bar, Calama 336 and León Mera (tel. 244-248), is a bizarrely elegant yet inexpensive Brazilian spot. Mostly tourists come for the *almuerzo* of soup, fish, rice, salad, juice, and fruit for s/5,000. Live music on weekend nights, groups can request Brazilian, Colombian, Ecuadorian, Arabian, or Italian meals ahead of time. Open daily noon-1am.

Cevichería Viejo José, on Calama and Reina Victoria (tel. 520-931). Friendly music encourages high spirits, which are heightened even more by meals like *camarones y arroz* (s/8,000) or delicious *sopa de mariscos* (seafood soup with all sorts of marine creatures, s/8,000). Everyone starts out with a bowl of popcorn and fried plantain chips. Open daily 9am-9pm.

Restaurant Row

Mama Clorinda, Reina Victoria 1144 and Calamá (tel. 544-362). She's the Ecuadorian *mamacita* you never had, serving traditional dishes in a room as lively, bustling, and warm as a maternal kitchen. You haven't lived until you've tried Ecuadorian specialties like cattle tongue (s/8,500), cattle legs broth (s/7,500), and figs with cheese (s/3,500) for dessert. But don't worry, Mama Clorinda also serves less adventurous meat and seafood dishes for the not-so-Ecuadorian at heart, such as rice with beans, lentils, and beef steak (s/14,000). Chilean wine (s/7,000) and beer (s/2,500-3,500) flow freely. Open daily noon-8pm.

El Maple, Paez 485 and Roca (tel. 520-994). A vegetarian restaurant with an atmosphere as fresh and healthy as the food. Veggie burgers (s/3,500), Chinese rice with tofu and vegetables (s/8,500), and Mexican tacos (s/9,900) are all made with organically grown vegetables washed in purified water. A health-conscious crowd keeps this place hopping. Open daily 11:30am-9:30pm.

Super Papa, León Mera 741 and Veintimilla (tel. 239-955). Potato lovers of all ages celebrate this alternative to greasy french fries or potato chips. Potatos here come as Super (s/8,000) or Guagua (s/6,400; for the not-quite-so-hungry) doused in vegetables. Also available with meat (chicken s/9,500 and s/11,400). Seating both inside and out, but if you sit outside, be prepared for endless street vendors to offer their wares. Open daily 7am-9:30pm.

El Cafecito, Cordero and Reina Victoria (tel. 234-862). This coffeeshop and vegetarian restaurant serves as proof that the trendy alternative scene has hit Ecuador— the dimly candlelit room has dried flowers hanging on mustard, orange, and green walls. Fruit and yogurt salad (s/6,500), potatoes with spinach (s/5,000), full bar, less-than-stellar coffee drinks, and a variety of excellent desserts tempt hip travelers from all over the world. Open daily for breakfast (8am-noon), lunch (noon-3pm), and dinner (Sun.-Thurs. until 10pm, Fri.-Sat. until midnight).

The Magic Bean Restaurant and Coffeehouse, Foch 681 and León Mera (tel. 566-181). Like the hostel upstairs, the Magic Bean eatery is an absolute gringo stronghold in Quito. Eager to please, it's just as its patrons would have it: a homey, two-room dining area, wood-paneled and dimly-lit (with outside seating under straw-thatched roofs), housing an almost entirely English-speaking bohemian crowd. Coffee drinks start at s/2,000. Huge salad entrees s/11,500-s/16,000—you pay for the safe lettuce. Dinner specialities include numerous kabobs; veggie (s/15,000), steak (s/18,000), and so on. But really, the Magic Bean is best known for its inexpensive breakfast selection, featuring eight varieties of pancakes, like pineapple (s/6,000) and chocolate chip (s/7,500). Open for breakfast Mon.-Fri. 7-11:30am, Sat.-Sun. 7am-1pm; dinner daily 6:30-10pm.

Restaurante El Holandés, Reina Victoria 600 and Carrión (tel. 522-167). The real toucan head sticking out from a spread of its own green, red, and black feathers on an Amazonian wall-hanging at first makes one question the seriousness of the Holandés's claim to be vegetarian, but the concern is quickly forgotten with a glance at the menu. Pineapple grilled cheese sandwiches with guacamole (s/4,900), banana crepes (s/6,000). Dutch, Indonesian, Hindu, and Greek platters range from s/11,500 to s/13,500. The relaxed staff and wicker furniture allow you to fully enjoy this sensory experience

On the Expensive Side

Restaurante Mare Nostrum, Tamayó 172 and Foch (tel. 237-236). This outstanding seafood restaurant inhabits a beautifully-restored 1930s mansion, with stunning hardwood floors and castellar ceiling beams. Solid pewter plates, a suit of armor by the fireplace, some stained glass windows, and a small collection of canons on the wall add to the awe. *Paella de mariscos* (s/20,500), crab crepes (s/20,900), or a fish platter (s/17,900-s/27,900) will cost you, but order some Chilean, Spanish, or French wine and the bill will seem less painful. Open daily 12:30-11pm.

Trattoria El Chianti, L. García 668 and León Mera (tel. 544-683). The best pizza west of Naples, or was that the Río Napo? Either way, a native Florentine cooks up authentic, gustatorily satisfying pizzas (s/14,000-s/16,000) at this inexpensive but upscale Italian spot. Pastas and other entrees ranging from s/13,000-s/19,000. A special includes spaghetti or pizza, beverage, and dessert for s/15,000. All food served on quaint coffee tables. Bourgeois locals and gringos populate the trattoria most heavily. Open Mon.-Sat. 12:30-3:30pm.

La Choza, Av. 12 de Octubre 1821 and Cordero (tel. 507-901), across the street from the Hotel Oro Verde. High ceilings and an open stairway leading down to the restaurant floor let you make a dramatic entrance into this somehow pastorally elegant room—with farm equipment on the walls and colored wands of wheat on the tables. Try *llapingachos* (potato and cheese croquettes served with rice, beef, and eggs, s/16,000-s/18,000) without worrying about the quality of the street vendor's oil. Ecuadorian meat and fish entrees (s/18,000-27,000), along with traditional *caldos* (broths) with every part of the pig but the squeal, are also whipped up in style. Open Mon.-Fri. noon-3pm and 7-10pm, Sat.-Sun. noon-3:30pm.

Colombia Steak House, Colón 1262 (tel. 541-920 or 551-857), just past Amazonas. Behind a faded orange and brown exterior, a dark and serious meat-eating atmosphere, complete with stuffed bull head, constitutes a steak heaven. Argentinean cuts of beef fill the kitchen landscape. T-bones the size of Andorra (s/19,000) and an exciting alcoholic beverage of choice (s/7,000-s/14,000) will satisfy any meateater. Eleven types of enticing salads for the herbivores (s/6,000; but remember the risks of eating raw vegetables). The entryway doubles as a fast-food stop. Hamburgers and sandwiches s/4,000- s/9,000. Open daily 11am-11pm.

Sidewalk Cafes and Coffeeshops

Usually small, crowded, and overflowing with trendy drinks like espresso and cappuccino, coffeeshops can't be beat in terms of atmosphere and a good place to chat. But don't come hoping for any deals—coffeehouses are notoriously overpriced, and the same finger food can be easily be found elsewhere for less. After all, you're paying for the ambience here as well.

Grain de Café, Baquedano 332 (tel. 565-975 x14), between Reina Victoria and León Mera, offers a huge selection of imported coffees and teas. Espresso is s/2,000, and the bar has many offerings (tequila shots s/8,000-s/13,000, coffee with Brandy s/9,500). Comic strips in English and Spanish decorate the menu, which has both vegetarian and meaty meals. Quiche with a salad (s/8,500), New York Cheesecake (s/4,000), and Walnut Pie (s/5,000) come in huge slices. Open daily noon-11pm.

Manolo's, Amazonas 426 and Robles (tel. 550-449), typifies the sidewalk cafes lining Amazonas. Yuppify your life—sip a tasty cafe espresso (s/2,000) and watch the cellular-phone-toting bourgeois *licenciados* (educated elites) saunter by. Savor *churros rellenos* (pastries stuffed with chocolate or vanilla cream, s/2,200), but beware of the overpriced pizza (s/10,300-35,000). Waiters in snazzy vests aggressively recruit passers-by to come sit in the sea of plaid tables. Open daily 7am-11pm.

El Escocés, Amazonas 410 and Robles (tel. 554-704). Another sidewalk cafe right in the thick of things, this one with a corner location. Seemingly the female counterpart to Manolo's, waitresses in glittering vests try to draw in customers by flashing menus at them as they walk by. Cappuccino s/2,400, *pescados* and *mariscos* s/9,500-s/19,000, *churros* s/2,500.

Café Cultura, Robles 513 and Reina Victoria (tel. 504-078). Vines of flowers painted with curling tendrils along the walls, a mix of Latin and American music, and a large number of English speakers soothe the homesick gringos. Trendy meals, like Veggie Quiche with bread and a purple/orange salad (s/11,500), are offered along with many teas (s/2,000), coffee (a mammoth mug is s/6,000), and desserts (carrot cake s/6,000; open Mon.-Fri. 7:30am-6pm, Sat.-Sun. 7:30-11:30am and 3-6pm).

Café Moka Bar, Calama 247 (tel. 520-931), between Reina Victoria and Almagro. Look carefully for this tiny cafe, sandwiched by more prominent upscale restaurants. The perfect intimate atmosphere for chatting; good luck getting a seat at one of the three tables. Serves coffee starting at s/2,000, 10 types of juices (s/3,000), some sandwiches (s/5,000), and French crepes (s/10,000). Open daily 9am-11pm.

Café Bangalô, Carrion 185 and Tamayo (tel. 520-499). Upstairs, a laid-back three-room Brazilian teahouse offers standard cafe fare—tea, coffee, pastries, scones, and cakes—as well as some expensive meals. Lose yourself in cups of gourmet imported teas (s/2,900) and romantic Brazilian beats, and admire the tasteful art on the walls for hours from your flowery seat. A great spot for avoiding afternoon downpours. Pastries aren't cheap (s/6,000 and up). Open Mon.-Sat. 4-8pm.

OLD TOWN

The Old Town's plethora of small *almuerzo* and *merienda* (afternoon snack) restaurants makes it the perfect place to explore for that tasty, local s/4,000 three-course lunch. These restaurants are plentiful, similar, and change hands often. Look around for a clean lunch spot filled with locals and no flies, and more often than not you'll come away satisfied. Otherwise, just try one of the dependable favorites below.

El Criollo, Flores 825 and Olmedo (tel. 219-811). A traditional Old Town restaurant with a classy touch: silverware served in a black with shiny gold basket, red and white cloths on tables illuminated by red lanterns, surrounded by copper-plate wall ornaments complementing the full bar in back. Gringos aplenty congregate here—sometimes the management tries to take advantage of it by raising prices on the weekends. Three styles of beef tongue (s/10,500-s/11,000), *tortillas* (omelettes s/7,900-s/9,900), sandwiches (s/2,700-s/6,700). Also add extra 20% to bill for taxes and service charge. Open daily 8am-10pm.

Restaurant Panorámico, Bolívar 220 and Guayaquil (tel. 512-711), in the Hotel Real Audiencia, on the corner of Plaza Santa Domingo. The name says it all—nowhere else in Quito will you find such an amazing view of the colonial city to entertain you as you eat. Feast your eyes on *El Panecillo* watching over the bustle of Santo Domingo square, while feasting your palate on avocado stuffed with chicken (s/10,000) or vegetarian steak with rice and salad (s/10,000). Prices are surprisingly cheap, considering the high quality of the crystal, the tasty food, the pleasant staff, and the incredible view. 10% tax will be added to bill. Open Mon.-Sat. 7:30am-2:30pm and 4-10pm, Sun. 7:30-9:30am.

Chifa El Chino, Bolívar 256 (tel. 513-435), between Venezuela and Guayaquil. This bustling *chifa* (Chinese restaurant) actually serves only a few Chinese entrees; mostly it dishes out local specialties and seafood. Soups from s/2,800-s/6,500. Omelette with tomato s/3,900, rice or spaghetti with vegetables and juice s/4,200, or for the Ecuadorians-at-heart, beef tongue s/7,800. Open daily 9am-11pm.

Pollo Dorado El Rey, Montufar 1234 and Rocafuerte (tel. 516-373), near the Plaza Santo Domingo. One of many Old Town *pollo* spots, this place fixes chicken so many ways it'll leave you dumbfounded. It is particularly popular with the locals due to its cheap, quality food. *Almuerzo* (s/3,800 for *simple*, s/5,000 for *especial*) and rotisserie-roasted chicken (¼ chicken s/8,000) are served up on faux-wood tables and benches beneath truly tasteless wall decorations such as the painting of a cooked chicken resting on a fancy bed. Open daily 7am-10pm.

Restaurant Costa y Sierra Marisquería, Flores 332 and Sucre (tel. 517-327). This restaurant to the Hotel Huasi Continental has nice dark redwood banisters connecting its two levels and some painted wooden tropical fish sparsely distributed on the wall to set the tone for *almuerzos* of seafood (s/4,000-s/15,000) or rice with chicken (s/7,000). Never mind the plastic table coverings. Conveniently located and nicely priced. Open daily 8:30am-8:30pm.

Bakeries

Panaderías and *pastelerías* line the streets of Quito, both in Old and New Town, with amazing abundance. It is virtually impossible to walk two blocks without coming to one. All are of approximately equal quality (the bigger ones tend to be fresher and more reliable; bakeries inside supermarkets are sometimes overpriced and slightly stale). But if you are overwhelmed and at a complete loss as to where to begin, **Productos de la Real** is a good *panadería/pastelería*—there are many of them and in some there is even outdoor seating (6 de Dic. and Colón). Also good are **Panificador—El Gran Pan,** on Andalucia and Madrid, and the **El Pan Especial** shops. Filling breads and pastries can be had for less than pocket change—bakeries are one place where Ecuador will seem inconceivably inexpensive. Try *cachos* or *cachitos* (croissants, s/200-s/400), or *empanadas* (sugar-topped bread filled with either cheese or marmalade, s/500). Rolls of various varieties are good but vary in freshness (s/100-s/500), and French loaves and *baguettes* are amazingly cheap (s/750-s/2,500).

■ Sights

Throughout its long and varied past as an Incan, Spanish, and Ecuadorian capital, Quito has always taken the role as jet-setter of the country's culture. The city has an abundance of museums, with collections ranging from ancient artifacts to cutting-edge modern art. Anything but monotonous, much of Quito's Old Town architecture is a unique mix of indigenous and Spanish baroque styles, and it creates a striking juxtaposition against the contemporary highrises of Quito Moderno.

LA PARTE COLONIAL (OLD TOWN)

When the United Nations declared Old Quito a "World Cultural Heritage" site in 1978, scores of 300-year-old plazas, churches, and government palaces were guaranteed both longevity and a high profile. Strict zoning and construction laws have kept much of the architecture in the well-preserved Old Town more or less the way it looked in the days of Spanish colonization. Most of Quito's interesting plazas and cathedrals are found on Old Town streets, but so are many of the city's dirtier neighborhoods and poorer inhabitants. Exercise caution in Old Quito, even by day. Pickpockets roam the streets, particularly around the market area and the *terminal terrestre.* By night the streets are even more dangerous, and tourists should retreat to the New Town, as the economically-able Ecuadorians do.

The centerpiece of colonial Quito, the **Plaza de la Independencia,** or the **Plaza Grande,** wows with its stunning **Palacio Presidencial** (presidential palace) with men in blue and gold holding flags, the orange historical Hotel Magestic (Quito colonial's first hotel), and the colossal **catedral,** flashing green and bronze domes and a high white turret. However, the plaza is best-loved by *quiteños* as a relaxing retreat with shady palm trees and meticulously-maintained gardens. Few realize the true historical significance of this favorite rest stop. Built in 1667, the plaza's cathedral contains the grave of Independence hero Antonio José de Sucre, the namesake of the country's currency. A statue commemorating Quito's August 10th Independence Day dynamizes the plaza's center, but old men engaged in the art of people-watching make sure the plaza's energy level remains low. Sitting counts as a fulfilling pass-time among the Spanish wrought-iron balconies and majestic stone pillars here; weary wanderers often stay awhile to take in the air of Quito's colonial days before moving on.

A few blocks away, the gorgeous and gigantic **Monastery of San Francisco,** constructed from 1535 to 1605 featuring statues of San Pedro and San Pablo, flanks **Plaza San Francisco.** The bare concrete area known as **Plaza Santo Domingo** serves as an important *trole* stop near the *terminal terrestre,* but not much else. The benches and green painted plant holders are a weak attempt at decoration or atmosphere, and though it houses an attractive gilt statue, the accompanying **Church of Santo Domingo** has seen better days as well. The **Plaza del Teatro,** at Guayaquil and Manabí, is the backdrop for the grand **Teatro Nacional Sucre,** constructed in 1878 and under reconstruction in 1997. Though the landmark theater no longer stages many plays, a free symphony plays here from time to time.

Visible from the Plaza del Teatro, as well as most other locations on the outskirts of the Old Town, the majestic statue of **La Virgen de Quito** surveys her domain from the summit of **El Panecillo.** From the top of the hill, the views of Quito and its surrounding mountains are as fantastic as the elaborate iconography that decorates the virgin. The trip up El Panecillo involves a long and dangerous walk up the stairs at the end of García Moreno. Even groups get robbed frequently; to be safe, have a taxi take you up and wait at the top to bring you back down (round-trip around s/15,000).

One of Quito's narrowest and most colonial streets, **Calle La Ronda,** also called Juan de Dios Morales, forks off of Av. 24 de Mayo at Benalcázar. Though it has become a bit destitute and stinky, it still exudes some of the charm from way back when the street was known for its many serenaders.

The abundance of **churches** that clutter the streets of Old Quito is astonishing: one stands tall on practically every other block. **La Compañía,** at Benalcázar and Sucre, is perhaps the most beautiful. Its stone exterior features exquisite carving and gargoyles, and the ornate gold-leaf walls and facades inside consumed over seven tons of gold during their 163-year construction (1605-1768). Other churches of note are the simple **La Merced,** on Cuenca between Chile and Mejía, **La Concepción,** on Moreno between Chile and Mejía, melon colored **Santa Catalina,** on Flores and Mijía, **El Sagrario,** on Moreno between Sucre and Espejo, **Carmen Alto,** at Moreno and Rocafuerte, and **San Agustín,** at Chile and Guayaquil, where Ecuador declared her independence. The **Basillica,** Moreno and Carchi, is hard to miss; big, beautiful, and gothic—get anywhere close and you'll find it.

MUSEUMS

Quito has such a plethora of museums that anyone who ever took the time to visit them all would end up a bona fide Ecuadorian, satiated with loads of information about archeology, history, indigenous groups, flora and fauna, and colonial and modern art. If you really are a student, be sure to show your ID at every opportunity, and you may gain entrance for the national rate despite your lowly foreign status.

New Town

The New Town is where the money is, and not so coincidentally it boasts the best museums. **Museo Nacional del Banco Central,** in the huge circular, metallic building at Av. Patria and Av. 6 de Diciembre (tel. 223-258), is a recent consolidation of several separate Banco Central museums in the city, and by far the most extensive and high-class museum in Quito. Enormous winding rooms, many dim and glass-partitioned, contain exhibits of archaeology (like pots with faces from the Panzaleo), pre-Independence paintings, religious portraits by colonial Ecuadorians, modern art (Guayasamín, Kingman, etc.), pre-Columbian gold works, and indigenous *artesanía.* The museum also offers a cafeteria and gift shop (open Tues.-Fri. 9am-5pm, Sat. and Sun. 10am-3pm; admission for foreigners s/10,000, with student ID s/5,000).

As part of the same building, the **Casa de la Cultura Ecuatoriana** (tel. 223-392), presents a collection of 19th- and 20th-century art and musical instruments you can be sure you've never seen before, like the *Charango,* made from an armadillo shell, and the *Pifono,* a flute made from an armadillo tail. An Amazonian shrunken head (!) and indigenous regional garb are mixed in with the sculptures and paintings (open Tues.-Fri. 10am-6pm, Sat.-Sun. 10am-2pm; admission s/5,000, weekends free). A hangout for college students and Quito's cultural elite, movies and plays are shown here from time to time. There is also a library open to the public (Mon.-Fri. 9am-6:30pm, Sat. 9am-5:30pm). Recently a new building opened as part of Casa de la Cultura, 6 de Diciembre 794, to have expositions like the Japanese flower show that happens once a year (open Mon.-Fri. 9am-6pm, Sat. 9am-1pm).

Another fine museum in an entirely different part of town, the **Fundación Guayasamín,** José Bosmediano 543 (tel. 446-455), is in the Bellavista neighborhood. Take Av. 6 de Diciembre north to Eloy Alfaro, where Bosmediano begins, and start climbing—the museum is way up the hill (they don't call it Bellavista for nothing). The entrance opens into a spacious garden with metal statues and several white *casas.* The collection includes an extensive exhibit of pre-Incan artifacts, all found in Ecuador, and some 18th-century colonial religious art from the *Quiteña* and *Cuzqueña* schools. The rest of the museum is dedicated to the riveting, magnificent paintings of the foundation's namesake, Oswaldo Guayasamín. Part of the indigenist movement, his images capture the problems and pains of racism, poverty, and class stratification in South America, with plenty of references to the original Spanish conquest of the *indígenas* (see **Modern Art,** p. 54, and **Indigenous Identity,** p. 47). The 78-year-old artist was president of the Organization for Human Rights in Latin America in 1980. Includes a library, cafeteria with an incredible view of Quito, and jewelry store (open Mon.-Fri. 9:30am-1pm and 3-6:30pm, Sat. 9:30am-1pm; admission s/3,000).

The **Vivarium,** Reina Victoria 1576 and Santa María (tel. 230-988), is not the place for people who fear snakes. These, as well as iguanas, a small alligator, several turtles, and some tiny poisonous frogs, are all that's on display in this miniature zoo. Pythons, cobras, snapping turtles, and other scaly friends are caged and color-coded with information cards so that you can tell who is venomous, where they live, and what they eat. Ask nicely to hold the boa (open Tues.-Sat. 9am-1pm and 2:30-6pm, Sun. 11am-6pm; admission s/4,000, children s/2,000).

Relatively close to each other on Av. 12 de Octubre are two other museums, both of a more or less ethnographic nature. The **Museo Amazonico Abya-Yala,** Av. 12 de Octubre 1430 and Wilson (tel. 562-633), is a one-room exhibit on Oriente life, but the room's a big one. Exhibits about indigenous culture, wildlife, musical instruments, and photos of oil exploitation are all on display. Downstairs in the bookstore, a huge variety of publications are available on the foundation's main interest, indigenous anthropology (open Mon.-Fri. 9am-1pm and 2-6pm; admission for foreigners s/2,000, nationals s/1,500). A few blocks north, **Museo Centro Exposiciones y Ferias Artesanales,** Av. 12 de Octubre 1738 and Liz. García (tel. 503-873), has interesting Ecuadorian handicrafts, including strange metal sculptures like a mesh of flowers, faces, a 3 ft. long key, and birds in the front yard (open Tues.-Sat. 9am-5pm; free).

Instituto Geográfico Militar, Calles Paz and Miño (tel. 502-090 or 502-091), is on a hill overlooking Quito, southeast of the city center. Getting there is a taxing uphill walk or a s/5,000 taxi ride. The Instituto boasts the best maps for every region of Ecuador. Political, topographical, Sierra, Oriente…you name it. Many are for sale or to copy, starting at around s/6,000, but be prepared to wait around a long time—there is a long procedure to make copies. There is also a planetarium (shows Mon.-Fri. 9, 11am and 3pm, Sat. 11am; admission s/4,000) and a geographical museum. Great photos of Ecuador's volcanic craters are on display in the main room. Spanish is helpful for getting past the military guards at the entrance. You might have to leave your passport with them (open Mon.-Fri. 8am-4pm).

Old Town

Not surprisingly, many of the museums in Old Town are of a historical nature. Colonial Quito comes alive at these exhibitions, housed at times in buildings as old as the artifacts themselves. One of the highlights is the **Museo del Convento San Diego,** Calicuchima 117 (tel. 512-516), overlooking the city from the south, next to the cemetery west of El Panecillo. Follow Calle Imbabura south from Old Quito until it dead-ends in the plaza in front of the convent. The religious institution was established 400 years ago by Spanish colonists, and the 45-minute guided tour through the complex (given in Spanish, and necessary to enter museum) reveals many intimate windows into the distant past, including original murals, cooking facilities, and a chamber where bones are buried deep in the earth. The walls are decked out with religious artwork: one painting shows a rendition of the Last Supper, with the indigenous delicacy *cuy* (guinea pig) substituted for Christ's main course (open Tues.-Sun. 9:30am-12:30pm and 2:30-5pm; admission for foreigners s/5,000, nationals s/1,000).

Farther down in the traffic-heavy blocks of Old Quito, the Casa de la Cultura lives up to its cosmopolitan name with the **Museo de Arte Colonial,** Cuenca 915 and Mejía (tel. 212-297). The impressive artwork dates back to the 16th-18th centuries and includes a collection of miniature sculptures and carvings. Christ, monks, saints, and other religious figures abound; don't miss the 17th-century Christ figure whose heart (seen through a tear in the skin) moves when you lightly stamp your foot (open Tues.-Sat. 10am-6pm; admission for foreigners s/5,000, nationals s/2,000). The **Museo Alberto Mena Camaño de Arte e Historia,** is found at Calle P. Espejo 1147 and García Moreno (tel. 510-272). Follow Espejo about 10m west of Moreno where it is a footpath; the entrance is on the left. The museum's permanent exhibit is an historical journey that descends into the maze-like basement where wax figures lie in murdered positions, and surfaces in a courtyard near the entrance. There's also a ground-level room for temporary art exhibits (open Tues.-Sat. 9am-4:45pm; free, supposedly closed until September 1998 for renovations).

The **Museo Casa de Sucre,** Venezuela 573 and Sucre (tel. 512-860), celebrates Ecuador's battle for independence (The Battle of Pichincha) in the house of one of its key participants, Mariscal Antonio José de Sucre. Weapons, painting, and fighting uniforms emphasize the military influence. The museum includes a library and free tour of the house, giving a glimpse into Sucre's personal life—his chapel, bedroom, and a picture of his skull after his assassination by a shot through the head (open Tues.-Fri. 8am-noon and 1:30-4pm, Sat. 8am-1:30pm; admission s/6,000). The continuation of this museum, **Museo Templo de la Patria,** is located up the hill of Pichincha, under the monument to the Independence fighters of Ecuador: Mariscal Sucre triumphed here and independence was won on May 24, 1822. A monument to the event, the museum contains an eternal flame, among other things. Definitely a hike (open Tues.-Fri. 9am-4pm, Sat.-Sun. 10am-2pm).

The **Colegio Nacional Mejía,** on Ante between Varga and Venezuela, has two separate museums behind the school's high walls. The **Museo Etnográfico** (tel. 583-412), on Venezuela, presents a series of life-size dioramas of different indigenous peoples throughout Ecuador, as well as a taxidermy exhibit of animals that were once found throughout the country but have since been killed, cut open, and stuffed with dry material. Check out the two live tortoises in the yard. Guided tours required (open Mon.-Fri. 8am-noon, and 2-6pm; free). **Museo de Ciencias Naturales,** Vargas 989 (tel. 583-412), accessible via the school's main entrance, contains a thorough collection of brightly colored birds, turtles, sharks, and other animals, including several bats captured in a Quevedo movie theater (open Mon.-Fri. 7am-3pm and 5-8pm; free). As is often the case, these hours are somewhat flexible, and if you are traveling a long way specifically to see something, call ahead to be sure of hours that day.

The **Museo Conde de Urquijo de la Casa de Benalcázar,** Olmedo 968 and Benalcázar (tel. 218-102), resides in the historical home the founder of Quito, but doesn't devote itself to the glorification of Sebastián de Benalcázar. Instead, through the Ecuadorian Hispanic Culture Institute, it houses an extensively decorated chapel, paintings, and a collection of sculptures from the 16th to 18th centuries, donated in 1966 by the Conde de Urquijo, then the Spanish ambassador. The art is devoutly religious, the public library devoutly intellectual (open Mon.-Fri. 9am-1pm and 2-6pm; free).

■ Entertainment

SPORTS AND RECREATION

In Quito, as in all of Latin America, **fútbol** (American soccer) is king. Giant crowds flock to the weekend *fútbol* games at the enormous **Estadio Atahualpa,** Av. 6 de Diciembre and Naciones Varidas, near Parque La Carolina. Take a bus marked "Estadio" on Av. 6 de Diciembre. Teams from the intra-Ecuador *liga* compete on this field; matches between Quito and its vicious rivals from Guayaquil or Cuenca are the norm. Tickets run about s/15,000 and are readily available the day of the game if you arrive a bit early. If you're lucky, you might get to see the **Selección Nacional** (Ecuadorian national squad) play another South American country in hopes of qualifying for a coveted spot in the 1998 World Cup in France. While Ecuador has never qualified, a 1996 victory over Argentina has raised hopes for '98. Ecuador isn't known for its **corridas de toros** (bullfights), but those hungry for some real bloodsport can contact **La Plaza de Toros** (tel. 246-037 or 247-850; tickets around s/20,000).

Ready for an afternoon of frisbee and pickup soccer? **Parque La Carolina,** north of the city center on Amazonas, is Quito's answer to all recreational desires. A Sunday afternoon at the park is perfect for kids, athletes, and dawdlers; it may not be *Grande Jette,* but Seurat would nevertheless be charmed by the roller-blading park, the carousels, benches, fields, trees, and pond with pedal boats. The central **Parque El Ejido,** sandwiched between the Old and New Towns, has similar greenery, but not as much tranquil charm. **Parque Alameda** in Old Town has an old observatory, some monuments to science, a pond for rowing in, and a small restaurant (open daily 8:30am-5pm), but lacks the relaxed atmosphere of La Carolina. If you are really hot and have extra *dinero* to spend, go **swimming** at the beautiful pool in **Hotel Quito** (tel. 544-600), on Gonzalez Suárez outside the city. Non-guests pay a large fee of s/50,000.

Ecuador Strikes Gold

July 26, 1996. It was a mild summer morning. More than 80,000 people watched with bated breath as 22-year-old Jefferson Perez, decked out in slinky shorts and honest-to-God professional walking shoes, wobbled into the Olympic Stadium in Atlanta, Georgia to claim the first gold medal of the '96 Track and Field competition, **Ecuador's first Olympic medal ever.** Walking 20km in one hour, 20 minutes, and seven seconds, he beat his best time by 14 seconds, and the rest of the field by 25m. The closest Ecuador came to medaling before this was in 1972, when Jorge Delgado Panchama came in 4th in the 200m butterfly. In interviews, Perez reminisced, "When I took the lead, I felt very tired, as if I was asleep. It felt like a dream. Then I thought that *this* is my dream. I have to go for it, even if I died." Back in Quito, patriots filled the streets, celebrating the momentous occasion into the wee hours of the morning. Then president-elect Abdalá Bucaram announced, "This triumph has to help the country!" and declared that a special postage stamp be issued in Perez's honor.

SHOPPING

Quito's most cosmopolitan thoroughfare, New Town's **Avenida Río Amazonas** is the most popular (but not necessarily the cheapest) place to buy souvenirs and Ecuadorian handicrafts. If you plan to buy a lot, keep in mind that markets in neighboring towns like Otavalo offer both lower prices and a more cultural shopping experience. Even so, it's a good idea to check out some of the shops on Amazonas, if only to browse, check out prices, and get an idea of the *artesanía* Ecuador has to offer in a more comfortable, aestheticized setting than the hectic local markets. Directed at tourists, these Río Amazonas shops aim to please, stocked with the most popular handmade crafts Ecuador has to offer: Panama hats, tagua-nut carvings, hand-painted pottery, and *lots* of handwoven rugs, shawls, wall hangings, and bags. **El Ejido** has a craft market every Sunday from around 10:30am to 5pm, and here, too, is a good place to get an idea of what's out there. Unless prices are marked or it is explicitly stated that prices are fixed, bargaining is expected. If you don't bargain, you will most likely be ripped off. At the same time, squabbling over sucres that mean much more to the poor vendor can be petty. Every shopper must strike a comfortable balance. But remember—the best bargaining is done by the person who's perfectly ready to walk away if the price isn't right.

MOVIES

The many movie theaters in Quito generally screen American movies in English, with Spanish subtitles. The best movie listings are in the newspaper **El Comercio; Hoy** also lists the movies playing in town. Some theaters have matinees, but most screen twice during the evenings, around 6:30 and 8:15pm. Tickets range from s/2,000 to s/ 10,000, with a definite correlation between price and movie quality or age. (Sometimes new releases in Ecuador came out in the U.S. six months to one year earlier.) Incredibly cheap, s/2,000-3,000 shows are usually pornos or chintzy action flicks. Some of the highest-quality theaters in New Town Quito are **Universitario,** Av. Américas and Verez Guerrero at the Universidad Central (tel. 230-280); **Colón,** Av. 10 de Agosto and Colón (tel. 224-081); **Benalcázar,** Av. 6 de Diciembre and Portugal; **24 de Mayo,** Grunaderos and Av. 6 de Diciembre; and the **Casa de la Cultura,** which sometimes has film festivals (see p. 75). In the Old Town, **Bolivar,** (tel. 210-960), on Espejo, is decent, though New Town films are generally of a much higher caliber.

THEATER

Although **Teatro Nacional Sucre** (p. 74) was built to satisfy cultural Quito's dramatic desires, more people visit it today to see the ornate exterior than the performances inside. Though music, dance concerts, and plays are still performed on Sucre's stage, **Teatro San Gabriel** (call Colegio San Gabriel at 230-060 or 230-061 to reach the theatre), on Av. América at Mariana de Jesus, has taken over as the place to see theater in Quito. North of the city center, San Gabriel has **ballet folklórico** (traditional ballet) twice weekly. The **Casa de la Cultura** (see p. 75) also offers occasional theater performances. Check *El Comercio* for all listings.

NIGHTLIFE

Compared to Guayaquil, after dark Quito yawns and then goes to sleep. The law sets a bedtime curfew at 2:30am, so the city closes up relatively early even on popular Thursday, Friday, and Saturday nights. Despite this setback, Quito still gushes with bars and dance clubs *(discotecas)*, catering to the city's flocks of young people and tourists who just wanna have fun. One block north of Colón, Calle Santa María claims some of Quito's most jammin', traveler-friendly nightclubs, including **Tequila Rock, Papillón,** and **Cafecito.** Lesbian and gay travelers have options in Quito as well… two of them. Ecuadorian law makes homosexuality a crime (see **Bisexual, Gay, and Lesbian Travelers,** p. 24); gay hang-outs are a quiet, cautious phenomenon. A confusing number of club names makes it hard to keep track of any of these silent legacies.

Stick to nightlife in the New Town; not only is the scene hipper, but Old Town's streets are too dangerous for night wandering, especially if you're a bit *borracho*. But New Town's not such a safe haven either; recent reports of robberies and assaults have put the revelers of the night on guard. Follow their example, especially around Reina Victoria, and take a taxi back to your hotel.

No Bar, Calama 442 and Av. Amazonas (tel. 546-955), on Calama's Restaurant Row. The blue-and-red sign atop the roof shouts "NO," but by all means come on in to one of the trendiest night spots in Quito. A mixed crowd of locals and travelers pack the narrow, compact floor; revelers often stand on the tables, and the bartenders dance amongst themselves. Beer s/6,000. Open daily 6pm-3am; no cover.

El Pobre Diablo, Mera and Santa María (tel. 224-982). For a more relaxed evening, head to this 6-room cafe/bar. Sounds of happy chatter and a crackling fire mix with jazz music to make this a cheerful, mellow bar. Good coffee (s/2,500), Pilsener beer s/5,000. Open Thurs.-Sat. 4:30pm-1am, Tues.-Wed. 4:30pm-midnight.

Seseribó, Veintimilla and 12 de Oct., downstairs in el Edificio El Girón. Latin music lovers will find a lot to dance to here—salsa, merengue, or some other Latin beat. Plenty of tables and room to rest or down a *chupa* (shot) or two in this trendy club. Cover s/10,000, open Thurs.-Sat. 9pm-3am.

Ramón Antigua, Isla de Católica and Veintimilla. The excellent live music that starts at 11:30pm is enough to convince lots of locals to pay the s/25,000 drink minimum and commit to an entire night of dancing and fun in this one spot. As long as you have to spend s/25,000 on drinks, try something exotic like a Pink Lady with banana liquor. Open Thurs.-Sat. 8pm-2am.

Tropicana, Whimper 330 and Orellano (tel. 507-339 or 527-353). There are 2 dance floors in this multi-level club, and music changes from Latin salsa to rock techno at the drop of a hat. Trendy 20-somethings and up fill the dance floors with all kinds of moves. Cover s/10,000, open Thurs.-Sat. 8pm, until the crowd goes home.

Tequila Rock, Reina Victoria and Santa María. This club has a long bar along a sort of runway to the dance floor, or as a dance floor. Balloons and ribbons hanging from the ceiling give a festive look, and it's quite probable you'll get a few looks yourself in this traveler friendly bar. No cover, open Thurs.-Sat. 7pm-2am.

Papillón, Diego de Almagro and Santa María. Already hopping with techno by 10pm, this club is an excellent place for beginner bar dancers—the ceilings have low, large pipes to grab if you lose your balance, and you will blend into an entire crowd of bar dancers, tourists and locals alike. Even behind the bar there is dancing amongst the bartenders as drinks are made. No cover, open daily 5pm-2am.

Varadero (Bodega Cubana), Reina Victoria and Pinta (tel. 542-476). The music at this coverless bar is live and really fun. You can't help but dance! A crowd of locals fills the scene, but as long as you appreciate rhythm and style, you should fit in okay. A warm yellow glow fills the room to add to the cheer. Open Wed.-Sun. noon-4pm and 7pm-2am.

Alcatraz, Santa María near Reina Victoria (tel. 715-996). Though the theme of prison life may not add so much to your club experience, it does make this place stand out in your memory. The plastic man dressed in black and white prison striped garb hanging from the ceiling adds an element of excitement—apparently there used to be two and one fell from the vibrations of so much dancing! Other than the remaining plastic man and a few pictures on the wall, though, the metaphor doesn't go too far, and you can definitely enjoy yourself at this friendly club. No cover, open daily 6pm-2am.

Bohemia Bar Discoteca, Baquedano 188 (tel. 505-017), a little east of Reina Victoria. This gay club is "members only," which means you'll have to meet an Ecuadorian member beforehand and enter together. The white-and-pastel interior doesn't dazzle, but the dance floor is bigger than most in Quito. Fits crowds up to 300, mostly male but with some lesbian and heterosexual women. Grinds techno tracks straight out of a NYC palace. Cover US$5, open Fri.-Sat. 9:30pm-2:30am.

Ana María, Liz. García 356 and Av. 6 de Diciembre (tel. 226-714), hiding past a restaurant sign that says, *"Menestras."* A more intimate gay bar that goes by a number of other names, this boys' club has a tiny square dance floor nestled amidst cushiony benches and tables, and a variety of danceable music. Bright, red lit, and festive. No cover, open Tues.-Sat. 8pm-3am.

NEAR QUITO

■ Mitad del Mundo

Latitude 0°0'0". Yes, you're on the Equator, the namesake of the entire country and arguably the most famous thing about Ecuador. Since the equatorial monument known as Mitad del Mundo (Middle of the World) was erected 15km north of Quito, Equator-mania has transformed this spot into an amusement park of Ecuadorian culture, history, and capitalist ventures. Perhaps more than any other location in the country, Mitad del Mundo has become a bona fide, First-World-style tourist attraction, emitting a kind of Disney World feel. A sprawling complex of museums, restaurants, gift shops, banks, and various other tourist facilities form a self-contained, overpriced tourist "village" with bleach-white sidewalks, smooth stone pathways, and a landscape that clearly gets constant upkeep. In the center of it all, the main attraction is the 30m-high monument, a wide obelisk perfectly aligned with the cardinal points of the compass. The Equator itself is denoted by a red stripe on the ground, extending from the eastern face of this structure, host to armies of straddling tourists enchanted by the idea of simultaneously standing in both hemispheres.

Ironically enough in this land of overpriced souvenirs, visiting the site itself is free. The pathway past the parking lot (s/2,000 to park) leads through two rows of busts, pointing directly toward the obelisk. As multiple inscriptions explain, the structure was built in commemoration of a French-Spanish scientific expedition that measured the equator's location here between 1736 and 1744. You can buy tickets from the *boletería* below EMETEL in the main info building (s/3,000) which will get you into the monument for the elevator ride up and the **Ethnographic Museum** (tel. 394-806), on the way down (surrounding the winding staircase). This consists of bits of Ecuadorian culture like clothing, foods, shelters, *guaguas de pan,* etc. to which you can get really close. Free guides in Spanish or English. The same ticket will get you into the **French Museum,** located southeast of the Obelisk, to learn a bit about the history of science in France. (Ethnographic and French museums open Mon.-Fri. 10am-5pm, Sat.-Sun. 9am-6pm.) The centerpiece is simply the high-profile start of the sightseeing experience. The Mitad del Mundo complex contains several more discreet museums;

most impressive is the outdoor, thatched-roof **Museo de Sitio Intiñan,** to the northeast of the obelisk. This tribute to the sun includes a carefully-positioned model of the sun's path, sundials, replicas of indigenous culture, shrunken heads, bottled snakes, and some live birds, cuy, and Galápagos tortoises with no obvious solar connections (open daily 9am-6pm; admission s/3,000, children or students with ID s/1,000). On the other side of the complex, a spiffy modern **planetarium** (tel. 395-795), waits for at least 15 tourists to arrive before beginning its shows (open Tues.-Fri. 9:30am-5pm, Sat.-Sun. 9am-6pm; admission s/3,000, children s/2,000). Nearby, **Fundación Quito Colonial** houses **miniature city models** of colonial Quito, downtown Guayaquil, and Cuenca (open daily 9:30am-5 or 6pm; admission s/3,000, children s/2,000). A recent addition to the complex, the monument dedicated to the **Heroes del Cenepa,** near the entrance, honors soldiers who died in the recent battles with Perú. A **scale** across from the post office lures weight-watching tourists to marvel at the pounds they seem to lose on the equator. They haven't really trimmed any inches; the equatorial bulge causes them to be farther from the center of the earth, so gravity has a weaker pull and they consequently weigh less, a bit of trivia restaurants in the area love to use to their advantage. The **plaza de toros** hosts bullfights and killer roosters compete in savage cockfights at the **gallera** on weekends and holidays. Predictably, the major festival days in these parts are March 21 and September 23, the **equinoxes.**

Straight Flush

When 18th-century French explorers came to Ecuador in search of the "middle of the Earth," they (or rather their huffing lackeys) hauled along the finest compasses and astrolabes that the king's court could provide. Their find wasn't worth all the fuss, though—the Frenchmen could have done the job with a bidet. Among the odd phenomena that occur at the Earth's equator, which include feeling lighter than at any other spot on Earth, is the strange fact that toilets don't know which way to flush. A toilet in a house to the north will flush counterclockwise, while a porcelain pal to the south will flush as the clock flies. The query: what is a poor potty to do when it's set squarely in the middle? Scientists claim that something called the **"Coriolis effect"** causes the swirly switcharoo, but even they can't predict which way an equatorial whirlpool will turn. Rumor has it that, in order to dispel the mystery, a group of experts has set up a make-shift laboratory of 10 toilets, one bathtub, and a lava lamp in the basement of Mitad del Mundo's obelisk. These gurus of bowl mechanics follow a strict daily regimen (reposition toilet, pull cord, reposition, pull cord) all in search of one thing—the mythical straight flush. No one knows if they've seen it, some believe they never will, but if you want to see for yourself, grab a toilet on wheels, head towards Mitad del Mundo, and keep on flushin'.

Upstairs in Mitad del Mundo's main information building resides **CETUR,** ready to hand out brochures and answer equatorial questions (open Wed.-Sun. 9:30am-4pm). Make phone calls from **EMETEL** (tel. 394-032), also above the main information building (open Tues.-Sun. 10am-5pm). **Banco del Pacífico** is on the eastern side of the village, adjacent to the bullfighting stadium (open Mon.-Fri. 10am-5pm). **Buses** leave Quito for Mitad del Mundo from the **El Tejar** bus area in the northern part of Old Town, around J. López and El Tejar (every 5min. daily, 5am-8pm, 45min., s/1,300). You can also flag down buses along Av. de las Américas; try the intersection of Colón and Américas. Returning buses leave from the base of Equinoccial near Av. 13 de Junio in San Antonio de Pichincha (every 5min. until 6pm). The post office, **Correos del Ecuador,** is in the main information building on the plaza, first floor, directly in front of the monument (open Mon.-Thurs. 9am-1pm and 2-5pm, Sun. 11am-4pm).

If you plan to stay the night, don't count on luxury hotels; most tourists return to Quito for the night. **Hostal Residencial La Mitad del Mundo,** Av. Equinoccial, is 10m down the cross-street Shrigua, on the right. Second-floor rooms have private baths; rooftop rooms share a communal one. A private home with plenty of rooms, the hostel has a warm, domestic atmosphere (s/25,000 per person, with bath s/30,000).

Next to Mitad del Mundo, the cleverly-named **Complejo Dos Hemisferios** (tel. 394-299; coming from Mitad del Mundo turn right on Consejo Provincial from Manuel Cordiva G.), lies in the southern hemisphere. This resort comes complete with a bar, restaurant, sauna, heated pool, and conference room (s/60,000). Catering to international tastebuds, Mitad del Mundo's restaurants, cafeterías, and ice cream stores consistently overcharge in true tourist-mecca form. **Restaurante Rincón Manabita,** Av. Equinoccial and Shrigua, serves heaping helpings of moderately-priced munchies. At s/5,000, the *almuerzo* is the best deal on the menu; other entrees cost about twice as much (open daily 9am-8pm). As the fanciest, priciest eatery in town, the **Restaurante Equinoccio** (tel. 394-128), occupies its own chunk of the village near the entrance to town. Veal with mushrooms, rice, and extras s/23,000, *llapingachos* (potato and cheese pancakes) with tomato, avocado, and peanut sauce s/17,000. Vegetarian-friendly dishes too (open daily 10am-5pm). For cheaper eats, follow the distinguished budget path down Av. Equinoccio to San Antonio and scout out a *comedor*.

■ Pululahua and Rumicucho

Visits to nearby Pululahua or Rumicucho are sometimes combined with the almost obligatory Mitad del Mundo visit. A trip to the volcanic crater **Pululahua,** whose rising ridge is visible from the equatorial extravaganza nearby, offers great views of mist and clouds rolling through the patchy green farmland depths of the crater (no smoking fumaroles; it has been inactive for 4,000 years). After the hike into the crater and back again, you can relax for the night at **Pululahua's Hostal,** or enjoy dinner at the hostel's **restaurant** (tel. 890-360 or 538-848), on the main road. The hostel has shared bathrooms with hot showers and rooms with bamboo covered walls (s/30,000 per person—a good price considering the location; meals cost around s/12,000). The hostel rents horses for rides around the crater or beyond (s/10,000 for 3hr. if you are a hostel guest, 1hr. if not), and the owners can recommend routes to find flora and fauna spectaculars such as orchids, rabbits, and armadillos. There is an info center for the **Reserva Geobotanica Pululahua** along the same road as the hostel. **El Crater Restaurant** (tel. 439-254), high up on the ridge, is expensive but may be worth the treat. Overlooking the crater to one side and the mountains around Quito to the other, the well-groomed lawns, cobblestone path, and high white walls provide adequate atmosphere for high-priced food (pasta s/24,000-28,000, meaty meals s/28,000-36,000; open Wed.-Fri. 12:30-5pm, Sat.-Sun. 12:30-6pm). For quick eats you're better off at **Mr. Willy,** at the first turn to the crater from Mitad del Mundo, for *empanadas*, sandwiches, and specialty sangria (s/3,000 per glass; open daily 7am-8pm).

From Mitad del Mundo, the crater is about 5km away. There are two paths that reach it, both of which continue as trails to the crater floor. The paths turn off the highway between San Antonio de Pichincha and the town of Calacalí, 8km to the west. Both trailheads are marked with signs; the first leads 2km up to a lookout point and to a foot trail (fork left to go down inside or right to El Crater Restaurant). The second trail, 3km past the first along the highway, is a 15km road into the crater. The foot trail into the crater is steeper and takes half an hour to hike in (tough on the knees) and one hour to hike out (tough on everything). There are several ways to get to the trailheads; the cheapest is the steep hike from Mitad del Mundo. But why do that when you can catch one of the **buses** that pass through Mitad del Mundo's traffic circle (every 45min., 6am-7pm, 20min., s/1,300) headed for Calacalí? Buses run back to Mitad del Mundo, often continuing to Quito, with the same frequency (daily 5am-5pm). **Taxis** and **camionetas** also run tourists to the first trailhead for s/5,000-10,000; it's three times that price if you want the driver to wait and drive you back.

The other jaunt from Mitad del Mundo is to **Rumicucho,** a set of Incan ruins atop a hill to the northeast. The roughly rectangular arrangement of rocks is barely visible from the equator lookout; locals took stones from the site to build their own homes, so there is not much more to see. Free guides, usually available in English or Spanish, will lead you through the ruins and tell you where the Incas ate, slept, and sacrificed. The easiest way to get there is with a *camioneta* from Mitad del Mundo (s/5,000 each way). Walking leads you through hot and dusty not-so-picturesque neighborhoods for over an hour. If you do choose to walk, take Av. Equinoccial to Av. 13 de Junio, the principal strip of San Antonio de Pichincha that runs north-south. Head north for 30 to 45 minutes; when you see a sign that says "Rumicucho" pointing to the right, the ruins are close (open daily 10am-6pm; admission s/3,000).

■ Volcán Pichincha

One of the most awe-inspiring aspects of Quito—from wherever you may be within the city—is the surrounding terrain. The dramatic volcanoes and mountains give Quito a majestic dignity—especially those to the West, which come right up to the edges of the city. These volcanoes, **Rucu** and **Gua Gua,** with **Padre Encantado** (a mere rock formation, no eruptive history here) between them, share the surname **Pichincha** along with the entire region surrounding Quito. Rucu is the old, craggly one with antenna peaks; easy to see and hard to ignore. Back when he was a young volcano, Rucu shook loud and active, but the time has come when his lava just doesn't flow anymore. Now he rests, covered in hardened souvenirs from his glory days. West of Rucu sits Padre Encantado, while 15km farther west restless Gua Gua steams and groans. Rising above its relatives at 4794m, Gua Gua's eruptive orifice continues to inspire the twinge of fear that goes with the name: Pichincha.

The double-cratered Volcán Pichincha achieves most of its fame simply due to its proximity to Ecuador's distinguished capital city. The younger, energetic Gua Gua Pichincha erupted in 1660, 1881, 1931, and 1981, to name a few fiery occasions. While the volcano rumbles alarmingly close to Quito, it does not pose an enormous threat; the closer crater, Rucu, is utterly inactive, and Gua Gua fires off in a western direction, foreshadowing doom for the tiny town Mindo but greatly relieving the distraught *quiteños.* As history has shown, the most severe threat to Quito itself is ash. The October 27, 1660, eruption piled more than a foot of volcanic soot atop the city, causing rooftops to collapse.

Despite its disastrous reputation, Pichincha's proximity to Quito makes it one of the most popular climbs in Ecuador. Less strenuous than some of Ecuador's other choice peaks, Pichincha serves as a convenient acclimatization trek before visitors venture on to higher peaks further south. Also worthwhile in and of itself, Pichincha provides amazing views of Quito, the valley, and a slew of other mountains.

The closer crater, **Rucu,** tempts tourists simply to start scrambling straight up the hillside from the city. Theoretically this is possible, but quite dangerous—not for mountain-climbing reasons, but because of thieves from shady neighborhoods that lie at the foot of the mountain. Dogs can usually be fended off or frightened away by bending over and picking up a rock or brandishing some sort of stick, but thieves are a serious danger as sometimes they are armed. Check with Safari or the South American Explorer's Club to hear the present state of affairs before attempting this climb. If you get the OK, there are a few choices in how to begin. One route heads west from **Avenida La Gasca** and turns south on **Occidental** into the Miraflores neighborhood. Before the tunnels, look for a road that turns off to the right and heads up the mountain. This is the trail to the antenna peak, **Cruz Loma,** where a ridge leads west to the peak of Rucu (2-3hr.). Climbers warn that the path has loose vegetation at times, and that the hike is a full and exhausting day, up and back. Start early and time the trek so that nightfall doesn't catch you on the way down. Alternatively, take a taxi up **24 de Mayo** to Cruz Loma (s/25,000) and begin hiking from there. Again, it is a good idea to strike out early to avoid nightfall, and be sure to find out the most current, reliable information from other climbers' reports.

The baby **Gua Gua** outdoes the elder Rucu in terms of altitude, scenery, and safety, though one should still be wary of dogs. From its peak, vistas stretch to the uninhabited west and south, and when clouds don't get in the way, climbers can see down into its plummeting crater. The summit is accessed from the village of **Lloa** (Yo-a), an hour drive away from Quito at the southern base of the volcano. There are two roads to Lloa; the first route heads out **Avenida Venidores de Pichincha** to the military batallion, where the greatly damaged and almost impassable **Avenida Chilibulo** begins its bumpy way up. The other route continues farther down Venidores to the neighborhood of **Mena Dos,** where a street named **Angamarca** (also called "Via Lloa") begins to ascend. To reach Lloa through public transportation, take a Mena #2 bus south from Universidad Central (every 5min., 30min., s/600) and get off at Via Lloa. **Camionetas** or **taxis** can be found to take you to Lloa from there for a hefty charge (s/30,000), though you may hear talk of a seemingly mythical **buseta** that would bring you there for a few thousand sucres. Also a possibility, at the junction of Venidores and Angamarca, **volquetas** (yellow dump trucks) run toward Lloa daily from about 7am to 5pm, and the drivers will often give climbers a lift for a minimal fee. In the town of Lloa, signs point the way to the road that winds up to the **refuge,** which sits just shy of the crater's edge. The refuge can be reached by 4WD vehicles in one and a half hours or by foot in six to eight. The refuge provides a bathroom, some rainwater barrels, and several mattresses (s/5,000 per person). The sometimes snow-covered summit towers close by, a one- to two-hour round-trip hike. It's cold up there, so warm clothing is a must. It is possible, but generally discouraged and officially prohibited, to hike down into the crater, as some climbers were asphyxiated by gaseous emissions several years ago while camping down there. A memorial has been erected at the edge of the crater. Check with Quito resources to see if the crater is fuming before considering the trek inside. While the hike up Gua Gua is not difficult, transportation can be quite difficult to coordinate and taxi fares may start to add up. Without a 4WD vehicle to take you to the refuge from Lloa, you'll be hard-pressed to complete the climb up and back in a day. It might be worth the bucks to hire a guide to worry about the transportation and food (see **Tour Companies,** p. 35).

■ Sangolquí

Two hours to the north, the town of Otavalo hosts Ecuador's most famous outdoor market, full of sensational Saturday steals. If you just can't get enough of all the bargains, head out to Sangolquí the next day for its smaller, but still bustling, **Sunday market.** The village itself is more modern than most places of its size, mostly because it's less than 20km southeast of the capital. The outdoor market spills over several blocks in the middle of Sangolquí, starting next to the principal avenue **Enriquez,** where the buses drop their loads. The majority of shoppers are local, so the market is not aimed at travelers. Vendors wait under tarps next to piles of their goods: banana bread, rubber gloves, chicken heads, jello, jeans, bras, razor blades, and chocolate bears. The selection is eclectic, the tourists rare, and Quito nearby, so there's no reason to stay the night. The Sunday market offers its first cow intestine at 4am and persists relentlessly until about 8pm. **Buses** leave Quito from the south end of **Plaza La Marín,** on the west side of a traffic circle (every 5min., 4am-11pm, 45min., s/800). The same buses return to Quito until about 9pm, leaving from Enriquez.

■ Bosque Protector Pasochoa

Long, long ago, before man arrived to ravage this land and then set aside tiny fragments of it to protect from himself, the volcano Pasochoa violently erupted. The explosion was so powerful that the mountain collapsed, tearing the crater inward and downward, leaving a slanted, lava-steaming remnant for a peak. In the 100,000 years that followed, the ash-enriched ground sprung to life with a dark green forest. The relative inaccessibility of the crater's interior kept human interference to a minimum for many a millennia. Nevertheless, somehow man pushed in, and it took the destruction of part of the area's primary growth before Ecuador's Ministry of Agriculture proclaimed the area a protected forest in 1982. Today the area is managed by the **Fundación Natura,** Av. América 5653 and Vozandes (tel. 447-341 through 344), in Quito. Well-groomed and marked trails offer routes ranging from an easy half-hour at about 2700m to a taxing eight-hour climb to the peak at 4200m. Branches arching over the trail make tunnels hiding some 120 different species of birds that sing exotic melodies as you search for a puma, orchid, or butterfly. Rare plant species like the *podocarpus,* the only conifer native to the Andes, fill the dense, rich forest. The area receives most rain in April, and is especially dry and dusty from July to September.

Facilities are basic. No restaurant, no food stores, but **Hostelling International**-affiliated lodgings provide a roof over your head. The accommodations consist of stark cots in two attic-like lofts. Clean bathrooms have showers and hot water, and a kitchen is at your disposal, complete with fridge and stove (foreigners US$5, nationals s/8,000). You can also pitch a tent in the campground, which has bathrooms and charcoal grills (foreigners US$3, nationals s/4,000). Entrance fees are steep: foreigners US$7 (s/25,000), children US$3 (s/13,000) covers access to Education Center, gift shop, and conference room (lectures given Sat. and Sun.). The forest is a popular Quito getaway for the jeep-endowed. Reservations for groups over 15, at least eight days ahead of time; contact Fundación Natura through SAEC. Without a car, the best way to get here is by bus; take it to **Amaguaña** (every 7min., 5am-8:30pm, 45min., s/1,000) from the south end of Plaza La Marin, past the buses to Sangolquí. To **La Marin,** take a bus or the *trole* to Plaza Grande and walk down Chile to the east. If you're in Sangolquí, intercept the buses to Amaguaña on Av. Enriquez (about 25min. out of town), away from Quito, a block past the giant statue of Rumiñahui. You could ask the bus driver to let you off at the road past Amaguaña leading to Pasochoa (there's a sign on your left) but it is a long 6km hike following signs mostly uphill to the reserve's entrance. Otherwise, take a *camioneta* from Amaguaña. They cost about s/15,000-20,000, but bargain. The way back to the highway goes through beautiful eucalyptus groves, but is still long, so some beg a departing party in the parking lot to take them to Quito, or at least to Amaguaña. From there, buses return to Quito.

■ Reserva Maquipucuna

In the northwestern region of the Andes, just a 40km from Quito, the Reserva Maquipucuna protects an ecological gem. Its borders contain 4546 hectares of land, with altitudes rising from 1200m to 2800m, 80 percent of which is primary cloud forest. Inaugurated in 1988 with a total of 3000 hectares, the reserve has since taken over much of the abandoned surrounding farmland. Researchers have swarmed into the reserve in its short decade of existence, and their work has produced numbers to brag about: in Maquipucuna's boundaries, next to the Choco bioregion, one of the world's top-ten "biodiversity hotspots," they have found 1160 species of plants, 45 mammals, 320 birds, and 250 butterflies. The warm-blooded creatures include pumas, spectacled bears, bats, agoutis, peccaries, tapir, and deer. In addition to wildlife, Maquipucuna shelters a number of archaeological sites left by the **Yumbo,** a people who inhabited this forest 1000 years before the Incas arrived.

Maquipucuna is one of the strictest reserves. The **Thomas H. Davis Ecotourist Center** has an open-aired, thatched-roof ecotourist oasis that can accommodate 18 people. It features dining and living areas, swimming in the waterfall, three meals per day, and bathrooms with hot water (foreigners US$45, children US$36; nationals US$26, children US$21). For daily entrance, 7am-6pm (foreigners US$5, nationals US$2; not possible from Quito without private transportation; check with the SAEC).

Transportation to and from Maquipucuna is the hardest part. The roundabout route from Quito goes through the towns of **Calacalí, Nanegalito, Nanegal,** and **Marianitas,** 4km from the reserve's entrance. **Buses** run to Nanegal (Mon.-Wed. and Fri., 1pm; Thurs., 2pm; Sat., 10am and 2pm; Sun., 9am and 2pm, 2½hr., s/5,000) from the **San José de las Minas** terminal near Parque Alameda on José Antepara, passing through Plaza Cotocollao in north Quito 45 minutes after departure. Get off the bus 2km short of Nanegal at the big green and yellow house at **La Delicia** crossing. From here, it's a 2km hike to Marianitas, and another 4km to Maquipucuna (walking time 1¼hr.). From December to May, when it's excessively muddy, walking is not recommended. Truck drivers Octavio, Alejandro, Diogenes, and Norton can be hired in Marianitas to go the remaining 4km (US$10). To get back, a milk truck leaves Marianitas each morning between 7:15 and 7:45am (catch in front of the white store), and will give you a lift to Nanegalito (30min., s/1,500). In Nanegalito buses pass by on the way to Quito (every 30min., s/4,000). For more information, contact **Fundación Maquipucuna** in Quito at Baquerizo 238 and Tamayo, P.O. Box 17-12-167 (tel. 507-200; fax 507-201; email root@maqui.ecx.ec).

North of Quito

North of the hustle and bustle of Quito, sit back and enjoy life. Placid lakes like the mystical Lagunas de Mojanda, neatly tucked in the highlands of the Andes, enchant with their serene charm. The pace slows down as you head north, where indigenous villages maintain their traditional lifestyles (see **Indigenous Identity,** p. 47). Locals speak Quechua on the streets, wear traditional indigenous clothing, and often specialize in handcrafted *artesanía,* much of which is sold in the famous Saturday markets at Otavalo. Packed with tapestries and leather, wood carvings and hand paintings, the hopping market draws crowds not just from all over Ecuador, but from all over the world. But in the midst of the highland cloud forests, even the larger communities like Otavalo are merely specks on the steep mountain cliffs. Though the cloud forest appears to flourish and thrive, in reality it is severely endangered; protected areas like the Intag Cloud Forest are the last remaining havens for the threatened flora and fauna of the northern Sierra.

▓ Otavalo

Otavalo is one of the most prosperous and respected indigenous communities in Latin America, but its success hasn't come easily. Restrained by a history of oppression and racism, the local *indígenas* have been persecuted since the Incan invasion of 1496. The Spanish took the brutality to grim new heights, forcing *otavaleños* to work 15-hour days under dangerous conditions in textile sweatshops called *obrajes.* This form of tyranny gradually dissipated and, eventually, in 1964, an agrarian reform law returned much of the Otavalan land back to its indigenous residents. Most *mestizos,* however, still treated the *indígenas* like second-class citizens until *otavaleños* became recognized worldwide for the beauty of their weavings and music in the early 1980s. Now *otavaleño* products are sold internationally, and foreigners flock to Otavalo's **Saturday market** specifically to buy locally-made goods. A feast of sights, sounds, and smells, this frenzied fanfare overflows with Ecuador's largest selection of handmade indigenous handicrafts (see **Artesanía,** p. 53).

As the *indígenas* became more and more prosperous, they came to dominate Otavalo life. Today the city of Otavalo is a testament to the strength, determination, and talent of the indigenous *otavaleños.* No longer solely weavers, many *indígenas* are now leaders in the community as lawyers, doctors, and politicians. As the indigenous youth grows in this now prosperous culture, they promise to build off the success around them and to surpass even the great accomplishments of their parents. Perhaps most impressive is the fact that despite economic success, the *otavaleños* remain grounded in their traditions. Local women staunchly wear their traditional outfits of embroidered white blouses, blue skirts, blue shawls, and elegant gold necklaces, while men sport calf-length white pants, dark ponchos, felt hats, and rope sandals. Some accuse the *otavaleños* of selling out to tourism, but it is precisely their adaptability that has allowed them to maintain their distinct indigenous identity (see **Indigenous Identity,** p. 47).

ORIENTATION

Buses usually drop visitors off in the southeast corner of town, in front of the **Plaza Copacabana,** on the corner of **Atahualpa** and **Calderón.** If you get a bus that only drives by the city, not through it, you should be dropped off at Atahualpa and make the easy walk into town from the Panamerican Highway. Every bus company uses the east-west Calderón as a runway for its daily departures and arrivals, making it the most chaotic street in this relatively peaceful market town. The town's major north-south artery is **Sucre,** which runs past both **Parque Rumiñahui** and **Poncho Plaza,** the site of the famous Saturday market.

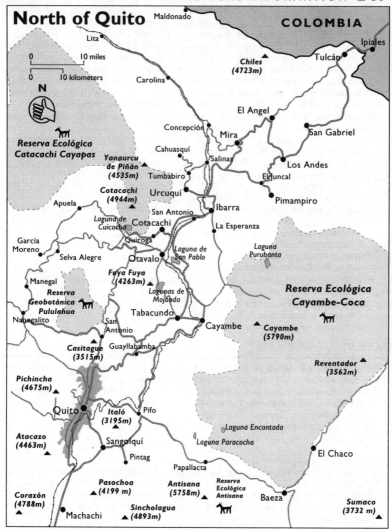

North of Quito

PRACTICAL INFORMATION

Travel Agencies: A number of travel agencies offer tours to neighboring towns and ecological reserves. Several are situated on Sucre between Calderón and Salinas, including **Inty Express,** Sucre 11-10 (tel. 921-436; fax 920-737; open Mon.-Sat. 8:30am-7pm, Sun. 8:30am-1pm), and **Diceny Viajes Zulay,** Sucre 10-14 and Colón (tel./fax 921-217; open Mon.-Sat. 8am-6:30pm, Sun. 8:30-10am and 4-6pm).

Banks: Banco del Pichincha, Bolívar 6-14 (tel. 920-214), exchanges money and traveler's checks and has a 24hr. ATM. Open Mon.-Fri. 8am-6pm, Sat.-Sun. 8am-2pm. **Banco Previsora,** Sucre 10-07 (tel. 921-213), has a 24hr. ATM but does not change cash or traveler's checks. Open Mon.-Fri. 9am-4pm. Some hotels and travel agencies will also change cash or traveler's checks, including **Hotel Otavalo,** Roca 504, and **Diceny Viajes Zulay** (above), which changes cash and **Inty Express** (above), which changes cash or traveler's checks.

Buses: There are 3 major bus lines based at the Terminal north of Av. Quiroga. **Trans Otavalo,** and **Cooperativa Los Lagos** go to: **Quito** (every 20min., 3:50am-7:10pm, 2½hr., s/6,000); **Ibarra** (every 5min., 4:50am-7:30pm, 30min., s/1,100); and smaller towns. **8 de Septiembre,** Atahualpa at Plaza Copacabana, goes to: **Peguche** (every 20min., 10min., s/400); **Agato** (every 20min., 15min., s/600).

Taxis: Taxis congregate around the parks and plazas. Otavalo's companies include **Cooperativo de Taxis Copacabana** (tel. 920-438), **Taxi 31 de Oct. Otavalo** (tel. 926-485), and **Cooperativo de Taxis el Jordan Otavalo** (tel. 920-298).

Laundromat: New Laundry Lavandería, Roca 9-42. Open Mon.-Sat. 8am-1pm and 3-6pm. Many hotels also have laundry service.

Pharmacies: La Dolorosa, Calderón 3-05 and Bolívar (tel. 921-817). Open Mon.-Sun. 8am-10pm. **Farmacía Modesna** (tel. 920-395), Moreno and Bolívar, to the left of the main entrance of the municipal building. Open Mon.-Sat. 7am-9pm.

Medical Services: Hospital San Luis de Otavalo (tel. 920-444, 920-600, 920-700, or 922-461), on Sucre at the northern edge of town. Emergency medical care can also be handled in the municipal building. All emergency treatment is free.

Police: Policía Nacional (emergency tel. 920-101), on the northern outskirts of town. Though they normally don't handle inner-Otavalo problems, they have the only emergency telephone. The **Policía Municipal,** at Sucre and García Moreno, in the municipal building, serve Otavalo (daily hours 8am-12:30pm and 2-5:30pm). No telephone, but can be seen on motorcycle and on foot in town, or reached through the Comisera Municipal (tel. 920-460).

Post Office: Sucre and Salinas, the corner of Poncho Plaza. Open Mon.-Fri. 8am-7pm, Sat. 8am-2pm.

Telephone: EMETEL, Calderón between Sucre and Jaramillo, offers phone and telegram service. Open Mon.-Sun. 8am-9:45pm.

Phone Code: 06.

ACCOMMODATIONS

Hostal Valle del Almanecer, Roca and Quiroga (tel. 920-990; fax 920-216). Constructed of sturdy avocado trees and bamboo ceilings, El Valle is a refreshing switch from the conventional plaster and cement. Quichua-named rooms are big enough to be comfortable, but small enough to make mingling in the courtyard more pleasurable. Rooms s/13,000 per person.

Samay Inn, Calderón 0-05 and Sucre (tel./fax 922-871), 2 blocks from the bus stop. All 14 rooms have 24hr. hot water and private baths. At the snap of a finger you can have a color TV in your room for no charge. Plain as vanilla, but beds are big and rooms are cleaned daily. Rooms s/20,000 per person.

Residencial Santa Martha, Colón 7-04 and Av. 31 de Octubre (tel. 920-147). Pennypinchers need not look farther for all basics. Thick walls mute the outside world, and sagging mattresses make for soft slumber. Common bath and shower shared between every 4 of the 16 rooms. Sleep tight and save your money for Sat. Singles s/8,000, doubles s/12,000, triples s/18,000.

Hotel Otavalo, Roca 5-04 (tel. 920-416), between García Moreno and Montalvo. Spacious rooms have 15ft. ceilings and giant beds, some of the softest in Otavalo—just ignore the obnoxious blue tint of the walls. Spigots struggle to supply hot water, bathrooms are outdoor stalls. Rooms s/12,000 per person, with bath s/25,000.

El Hotel Indio, Sucre 12-14 and Morales (tel./fax 920-060). Don't confuse it with the bigger Hotel Indio on Bolívar. This one can be a bit pricey too, but the location, just a jump from the market, helps justify the fee. Disparate rooms either overlook Av. Sucre or Mt. Imbabura. Remove your shoes and enjoy the carpet, a rare pleasure. Private bath (hot water 24hr.) and TV. Rooms s/26,000 per person.

FOOD

Cafe Restaurant Vegetariano, on Salinas on the south side of Poncho Plaza. Typical indigenous food with a twist. All ingredients grown organically, all water purified. Many meals come with fun garnishing like fried banana bits and green sauces. Stuffed avocado s/6,000, fruit salad s/6,300, daily special s/8,000. Perpetual Andean music, live on Sat. 12:30-7:30pm (cover s/2,000). Open daily 7am-9:30pm.

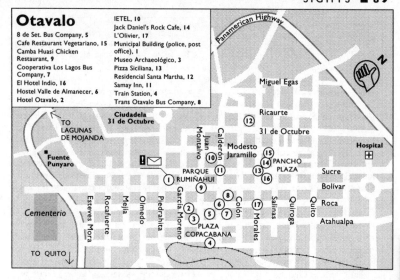

Otavalo

8 de Set. Bus Company, 5
Cafe Restaurant Vegetariano, 15
Camba Huasi Chicken
Restaurant, 9
Cooperativa Los Lagos Bus
Company, 7
El Hotel Indio, 16
Hostel Valle de Almanecer, 6
Hotel Otavalo, 2

IETEL, 10
Jack Daniel's Rock Cafe, 14
L'Olivier, 17
Municipal Building (police, post office), 1
Museo Archaeológico, 3
Pizza Siciliana, 13
Residencial Santa Martha, 12
Samay Inn, 11
Train Station, 4
Trans Otavalo Bus Company, 8

Shanandoa, The PieShop/Cafeteria, Salinas 515 and Jaramillo (tel. 921-465). It really is incredible pie, filled with blackberries, apples, pineapple, or whatever else is available. With ice cream, you will say "mmmm..." in that savory don't-want-to-swallow-cuz-it-tastes-so-good kind of way (pie s/3,000, with ice cream s/3,000 more). Also offers large sandwiches and drinks. Open Mon.-Sun. 7:30am-10pm.

Pizza Siciliana, Morales 15-01 and Sucre (tel. 926-439). Huge pasta servings (s/12,000-15,000) and extra large pizzas (s/10,000-40,000). The usually dim and mellow restaurant comes alive with lights and live Andean music from 7:30-9:30pm on Fri. and Sat. nights. Open daily noon-midnight.

Camba Huasy Chicken Restaurant, Bolívar and Montalvo (tel. 920-359). Meets all moods with its 2 dining rooms. One's dandified with Daffy Duck paintings, the other embellished with stained glass. Set *desayuno* s/5,000, or be more adventurous and get the *lengua a la española* (tongue) s/7,500. Open daily 8am-8:30pm.

Restaurant/Pizzería Rincon de Suecia, Salinas 316 and Bolívar. A comfortable and friendly place to get a quick *almuerzo* (s/5,000) or specialized pizza at more reasonable prices than other spots in town (s/6,000-s/25,000). Open daily 8am-10pm.

Ali Micuy Restaurant, Jaramillo 907 and Quiroga (tel. 921-744). A big selection of vegetarian food as well as meaty, Veggie burgers (s/6,000) and seafood spaghetti (s/12,000). Moderately priced, mellow music and decor, breakfast too (pancakes s/4,000). Open daily 8am-approx. 9pm.

SIGHTS

Market day is a sight to behold in Otavalo. The uncontainable fanfare of the **Saturday market** starts in Poncho Plaza, but overflows onto the surrounding streets, stretching blocks away. **Local weavings** are concentrated in the plaza and all along Sucre, where many *indígenas* simply set up booths in front of their shops. **Wood carvings** and **leather goods** are found all over, but some of the best are sold on Sucre and in the southeast end of the market. The fried egg, pork, and potato aroma that permeates the entire market originates on Quiroga where streetside stands cook up **market munchies** for all. Av. Jaramillo is the most eclectic area, selling American goods like Air Jordans and Levi's jeans, as well as purely South American stock, such as Incan jewelry and hand carved pipes. Although this advice holds true everywhere in the market, be especially careful with valuables along Jaramillo. It is by far the most crowded street on market day, and thieves position themselves here deviously.

Sheep's Clothing

Remember some basic facts when examining textile pieces in the Otavalo market. There are three types of wool: **lana borrego** (lamb), **lana alpaca,** and **lana sintética** (synthetic). *Lana borrego* is generally considered the highest quality wool, and goods made from it tend to be more expensive. *Lana alpaca* is used solely on tapestries *(tapices)* and creates an entirely different-looking tapestry than those made of synthetic or lamb's wool. *Tapices* of *lana alpaca* resemble paintings, with rich colors depicting local scenery or indigenous peoples. Pieces constructed of *lana borrego* have duller colors, but the best way to determine the type of wool is to examine the back side of woven goods. If you pull on the wool and a thick fluffy strand emerges, it is *lana borrego;* if the strand that emerges is thin and stringy, it is *sintética.* Both are durable, but if you're a perfectionist, go with the real stuff. Most market vendors are extremely ethical and will answer questions concerning wool type and quality honestly, but a little knowledge of the materials goes a long way toward enriching the market experience.

Vendors usually begin selling as early as 6:30am and pack up around 5pm. An intriguing phenomenon occurs about an hour before the market starts. The **animal auction,** located just outside of town (follow Colón or some parallel street west away from town; you will hear, see, or smell the market to your left) is possibly the most peculiar event in Otavalo. Pigs of all sizes, cows, sheep, goats, and who knows what else squeal and moo, making noises and smells to jump start your day. An added benefit to the early-morning auction is that you'll beat the crowds to the main market.

Most tourists begin to arrive around 10am, but it is a good idea to purchase goods earlier, as bargains *(gangas)* and discounts *(discuentas)* are more readily available before demand escalates. Another good bargaining time is just before 5pm, when most vendors close up shop and eagerly try to dispose of their inventory. If you're really bargain-hungry, try shopping in the Friday market. In most cases, the starting price offered on Friday is lower than that on Saturday, but of course, then you miss out on the spectacular carnival that is Otavalo's main market.

For such a popular tourist draw, Otavalo has relatively few sites of interest aside from the market. The **Museo Arqueológico,** Montalvo and Roca, on the second floor of Hostería Los Andes, has over 9,000 pieces, including flutes made from condor leg bones, skulls shaped and manipulated at birth, astrological chart photographs, and much more. César Vázquez Fuller has a huge wealth of knowledge about everything there; museum open when César is there (tel. 921-290; admission s/5,000). The **Museum of Anthropology,** on the northern outskirts of town across the Panamerican Highway, has English and Spanish info on the history and culture of Otavalo *indígenas* (open Tues.-Fri. 8am-noon and 2-6pm, Sat. 8am-noon; free). The **Parque Rumiñahui,** in front of the municipal building, is a great place to rest your legs under shady trees and admire **Volcán Imbabura** (4609m; see **La Esperanza,** p. 100) towering over the town's rooftops to the east. Across the street, at Sucre and Montalvo, locals play volleyball on a dusty **playground.** You can sip a drink and just watch, or test your spiking skills and join the match. On Saturday afternoons, the corner of 31 de Octubre and Montalvo sometimes offers **cockfighting.** Across the Panamerican Highway from the Coliseum is a small dirt **soccer field** where local teams often compete on Sundays. They won't let you play, but you're welcome to stay and watch.

The indigenous villages and Andean landscape surrounding Otavalo also offer a multitude of diversions. Daytrips to Peguche, Agato, and Lagunas de Mojanda, to name a few, are well worth the time. They can be visited independently (see below), but tourist agencies also offer tours to these and other destinations. **Zulay Tour Agency** arranges a two-day excursion to Apuela, which also visits Nalgumbi natural springs, an ecological reserve, and local pyramids in Gualiman. Horseback riding, lodging, and meals are included (US$85 per person). They also offer an indigenous village tour that visits local homes in La Compañía, Agato, Peguche, Cotacachi, and finishes at Laguna de Cuicocha (8:30am-4:30pm; US$10). **Inty Express** offers hiking tours with English-speaking guides to Lagunas de Mojanda or Lake Cuicocha, jeep ride included (US$20). Their indigenous village tour costs US$15.

ENTERTAINMENT

Though Otavalo's nightlife is not wild and crazy by any standard, there are a few quality *peñas* that can make any weekend night a memorable one. **Pizza Siciliana** has weekend live music from 7:30-9:30pm to start off an evening of fun, but the real dancing clubs don't get going until later. **The Peña Tucano,** Morales 8-10 and Sucre, heats up on Friday and Saturday nights when local Andean groups play. The dancing never stops; in between bands, a DJ thumps salsa and reggae. Bands are so close you can reach out and touch their authenticity (open daily 9pm-2am; cover s/3,000). The one and only bamboo palace in Otavalo goes by the name **Peña Tuparina,** Morales and Av. 31 de Octubre. Speakers are so big they threaten to shake the hut to the ground. Local Andean bands play on Friday and Saturday from 9:30pm-2am (cover s/ 3,000). **Peña Amauta,** Jaramillo and Salinas (tel. 922-435), has the most atmosphere: an underground cellar with dim lighting, massive *tapices,* and a fireplace. It has a small dance floor and plenty of tables with good views of the local groups. This is the home of a mysterious, potent brew known as *guayusa* (s/15,000 for 1 liter). Sip it slowly and float away into the forests of the Andes (open Fri.-Sat. 8pm-2am; cover s/ 4,000).

■ Near Otavalo: Lagunas de Mojanda

17km south of Otavalo, the Lagunas de Mojanda are three peaceful lakes tucked between the extinct volcano **Fuya Fuya** and a range of smaller rolling mountains. If you get there before the clouds roll in or on a rare clear day, the views are astounding. Camping and fishing are popular but not as common as day hiking. The trail begins to the right of **Laguna Grande,** the only lake immediately visible. There is a dirt trail and a less well-used trail through the grass; the latter is on a steep bank and leads to another dirt trail. If you choose the path more traveled, admire the spectacular scenery, but also watch the ground, as many horses travel this path. Campers should avoid the *refugio* (refuge) like the plague, as there literally may be one brewing in the depths of its muddy, littered floors. Careless guests have left heaps of trash here, and enough graffiti mars the walls to embarrass even the most ardent vandal. The path diverges near the far end of the lake, but be calm, Anxious Traveler, both paths lead to enlightenment. The trail that cuts to the left winds around the back of **Montaña Pequeña,** leading to an amazing view of **Laguna Negra,** so named because it is tightly surrounded by cliffs that keep the waters eternally shadowed. The other path leads to a view of the less spectacular **Laguna Chiquita,** providing glimpses of the misty mountaintops of Fuya Fuya and Montaña Pequeña. Check in Otavalo before doing this hike alone, as loners occasionally have had problems with thieves.

Taxis to Mojanda charge about s/50,000 round-trip, but this price increases rapidly the longer you make the driver wait. A cheaper option is to take a cab up to the lakes and hike back, a three-and-a-half-hour walk. You could walk the whole way, but the trip there is uphill and so steep that buses can't even cut it. *Camionetas,* found in Otavalo's Poncho Plaza, will generally charge the same fare as a taxi, but will probably be more reasonable concerning the wait at the lakes. Hitching is possible, but *Let's Go* does not recommend hitchhiking. If this is your only option, walk south on the Panamerican Highway just outside of Otavalo for a few hundred yards. A dirt road, the only route to Mojanda, heads up to the right. When the road ends, you'll be face-to-face with the immense Laguna Grande. Often, a *camioneta* or vehicle of some sort can be flagged down as you walk down the road on your way back to Otavalo; don't spend much time waiting for one at the *lagunas*—it gets *cold* up there.

■ Peguche

An indigenous community known for the quality of its vibrant tapestries, Peguche is regarded as the most prosperous of Otavalo's satellite towns. Its affluence is not seen so much as it is heard. Strange rumblings emanate from Peguche's tiny homes; electric weaving machines, which are unheard of in poorer communities, are commonplace here. While the people are prosperous, the success has not gone to their heads. Aside from the *borachos* during holidays, everyone in town radiates friendliness.

Orientation and Practical Information Peguche is situated roughly 4km northeast of Otavalo, between the Panamerican Highway and the community of Agato. The quiet central plaza, **Centro Pachacutic,** is home to the Santa Lucia Church. There are no real street names in town, so don't look for signs. With your back to the church, the road running from right to left in front of you is **Calle Cascada.** The cross street heading directly away from you is **Calle Principal.** On the left side of the corner of Principal and Cascada, **José Cotacachi's folklore shop** sells tapestries and bags made by various locals. An unofficial, one-man tourist office, José will answer questions regarding the history and culture of Peguche, provided you speak decent Spanish. Ask nicely and he'll escort you to a house to observe weaving in progress. If you don't have the courage to ask, or if your Spanish isn't strong enough, the best way to experience backstage weaving excitement is to visit Peguche with a tour group from Otavalo. The bus line **8 de Septiembre** routinely travels between Plaza Copacabana in **Otavalo** and the central plaza of Peguche (every 20min., 10min., s/400). Some buses from Otavalo continue on to **Agato** (s/600). The local **dispensario,** the next best thing to Otavalo's hospital, is found by following Calle Principal down from the *centro* and turning left at the signs for Aya Huma. It will be on your right side, next to a greenish building (open daily 8am-12pm and 2-4pm). Peguche's **police station,** Calle Cascada (tel. 922-234), just before the train tracks, also serves and protects neighboring *pueblos,* such as Agato (open daily 8am-2pm).

Accommodations and Food Although there are no restaurants in Peguche, the two hostels in town more than pick up the slack. **Hostal and Cafetería Aya Huma** (tel. 922-663; fax 922-664), is on the train tracks where the road splits near Loma Pucará, or can be reached from the central plaza by walking down Calle Principal and turning left at the sign. The soothing sound of the trickling stream below and the enormous jugs of purified water in each room make this a refreshing place to catch your breath. The wool comforters are straight off the sheep's back, and the blankets are the finest woven in Peguche. Phone/fax, storage of valuables, laundry, mini-library, Spanish lessons, and hiking maps available. Singles US$7, with bath US$12; doubles US$10, with bath US$18; triples US$15, with bath US$27. Restaurant has delectable treats daily, live music on Saturday (open Mon.-Sat. 7am-8:30pm, Sun. 8am-8:30pm, bar Sun.-Fri. until 10pm, Sat. 11pm). **Peguche Tio Hostería** (tel. 922-619; fax 922-619), is across the tracks near the police station. Take a left when the road ends; the *hostería* is around the corner on the right. Built in November 1995, it still looks spankin' new. Fireplaces and locally-woven blankets ensure your feet won't get cold. Overflowing with cultural flair, the enthusiastic Muenala Vega family bombards visitors with classes and workshops on indigenous heritage. Monstrous Mt. Imbabura can be seen from the high wooden *mirador* or from the volleyball courts out back. Private hot-water bath in all rooms. (Mon.-Thurs. s/20,000 per person, Fri.-Sun. s/30,000 per person. Restaurant open Sun.-Fri. 8am-8pm, Sat. 8am-10pm.)

Sights The well-shrouded waterfalls **Las Cascadas de Peguche** provide a nice pit stop near the entrance to town. *¡Qué refrescante!* Tell the bus driver to drop you off at Loma Pucará. Here women wash clothes in the river below the road and corn fields grow slowly on the steep hill across the way. The waterfall is straight up the hill; walk up the path/road through the corn. When you come to the ruins of Bohio at the top of the hill, take a right through the archway and follow signs for the waterfalls through a dense forest of blackberry bushes, pines, and trees. From the forest entrance, it's a five-minute walk until the waterfall emerges through the misty air, but there are beautiful trails through much of the woods. Thieves have been known to lurk in the forest; check to see if other hikers are around in the woods.

■ Near Peguche: Agato

At first glance, Agato seems to be a ghost town. The dusty streets of this village, 3km southeast of Peguche and 8km northeast of Otavalo, are often empty except for the usual scattering of young children, roosters, and pigs. A barrage of questions may enter your mind. Where is everybody? Whose children are these? And why is this dog sniffing my leg? The answers are quite simple. The parents of these children, along with the rest of the town, are either hard at work on the looms within their homes or out in the fields tending crops of wheat, barley, corn, and potatoes.

Near the center of town, the **Tahuantinsuyo weaving workshop,** Rumiñahui 9 and Atahualpa (tel. 921-547), is run by the jovial Miguel Andrango. He's usually happy to demonstrate Agato's unique hand-weaving process. Locals of Agato, unlike their high-tech neighbors in Peguche, use old-fashioned looms. These are either of the sit-down, backstrap variety, or they're **telaros de español,** larger looms that require the use of both feet and hands at once. The tapestries, blankets, and sweaters produced in Agato are generally considered to be more carefully crafted than those of other towns, but are also more expensive. Miguel can also be persuaded to show how vegetables are used to dye wool yellow and orange, and how chemicals imported from Germany are used to create a red, pink, or blue hue. Wool that is off-white, black, or brown is usually natural. Miguel doesn't sell his goods in Otavalo, so if you're interested in making a purchase, you'll have to pay him a visit in his workshop.

The bus lines **8 de Septiembre** and **Coop Imbaburapaq** both go to Agato (s/600), but Imbaburapaq is faster because it doesn't always stop in Peguche. Walking is the slowest way of all, but it can be fantastic. Remember that the hike is mostly uphill and can take up to one and a half hours from Otavalo. If you're up for the exercise (see **Otavalo: Sights,** above), head northeast out of town and up the same hill that leads to Las Cascadas de Peguche from Loma Pucará. At the ruins of Bohia, keep going straight up the hill. A simple rule when hiking to Agato: if a fork in the path appears, always go right. Alternatively, walk from Peguche's central plaza; go up the road to the left of the church until you reach Rumiñahui, then turn right. If you take a bus, consider walking back into town. The stroll past the ruins of Bohia provides glimpses of glistening **Laguna San Pablo** and other picture-perfect views of the countryside.

■ Cotacachi

Endowed with more leather than a sadomasochist's dream, Cotacachi is Ecuador's leatherwork capital. Planted 15km northwest of Otavalo under the watchful eye of **Mount Cotacachi** (4939m), the town is made up of indigenous and **mestizo** peoples and their leather shops. The serene atmosphere of Cotacachi can be misleading; there is an underlying spice of life that can be sensed, especially on **festival days**.

Orientation and Practical Information There is only one road into Cotacachi, cleverly named **Av. Cotacachi.** Once in town, it's impossible to get lost—**Av. 10 de Agosto** is always in view, no matter where you roam. **Buses** to **Otavalo** can be picked up at the west end of Av. 10 de Agosto, or on Peñaherrera near the park (every 20min., 20min., s/800). A **taxi** ride from Otavalo is only five minutes faster, but much more expensive (15min., s/8,000). There are few phones in town, but there is an **EMETEL** office on Calle Sucre 1427 to the north of town (open Mon.-Fri. 9-11am and 3-6pm, Sat. 9-11am). **Farmacía Familiar,** Bolívar 14-14, is open daily 7:30am-9:30pm. There is a small emergency **hospital** with the scary name *El Servicio de Laboratorio,* Bolívar 12-34 (emergency tel. 915-342 or 915-932; open Mon.-Sat. 8am-6pm). The Cotacachi **police,** Rocafuerte 10-36 and Imbabura (tel. 915-101), are always open. The **post office,** Modesto Peñaherrera and Bolívar, is in the black doors on the right side of the old church (open Mon.-Fri. 8am-noon and 2-6pm). The **Casa de Cambio,** 10 de Agosto and Bolívar (tel. 915-995), is eager to exchange cash or traveler's checks for leather hunting tourists daily 8am-6pm.

Accommodations and Food Cotacachi has few true budget accommodations. The **Hostal Bachita,** Sucre 1674 (tel. 915-063), just past Peñaherrera, has a colorless exterior, but rooms with private bath and hot water are s/20,000 per person. **The Hostal Plaza Bolívar,** Bolívar 12-26 and Av. 10 de Agosto (tel. 915-327), is nicer but more expensive at s/30,000 per person. Private baths with hot water and towels, washing machines, luggage storage, and use of kitchen round out the amenities.

Dining options in Cotacachi are scarce as well. For a quick and affordable filler-up, try the **Delicia Casera,** Sucre 11-23 (tel. 915-161). Entertain yourself with fake fruit and ponder the juxtaposition of a Last Supper reproduction with a poster of a woman in a g-string. Rejuvenate with a mammoth soda for s/2,500 or a typical *almuerzo* for s/5,000. For a slower-paced, more indigenous meal, you'll have to pay a bit more. The **Restaurante Inty Huasi,** Bolívar and Av. 10 de Agosto (tel. 915-789), next to Hostal Cotacachi, has an appearance that implies reservations, but they're not actually needed. *Inty Huasi* means "house of the sun" in Quechua, but this shady dining room houses *from* the sun. Specialties include river trout prepared in several flavors, *trucha* marinera is s/12,000, sandwiches s/3,500 (open daily 9am-10pm).

Sights and Entertainment The grand happening in Cotacachi is **shopping.** The leather products here are of sublime quality and, even though they are more expensive than the local weavings, they're a steal as far as leather goods go. Much of the *cuero* found elsewhere in Ecuador is made from sheep, but the leather in Cotacachi comes only from the finest steers. There are almost too many different leather shops in this small town, selling everything from briefcases to women's heels. Most places accept credit cards, but give discounts of up to 10% for customers with cold, hard cash. One of the largest shops in town, **El Palacio del Cuero** (tel. 915-490; fax 915-286), along Av. 10 de Agosto, has gregarious employees who speak a fair amount of English. None of the Cotacachi leather goods are sold in Otavalo. There is a Sunday market with fruit and trinkets along Av. Cotacachi, but if you've just been to Otavalo, then Cotacachi's market will be only mildly amusing.

The well-timed can visit Cotacachi during its festival celebrating the sun at the end of June. Locals dance for hours in the park, dressed in camouflage, gorilla masks, or cardboard wizard hats. Use caution, though, because traditionally the dancing erupts into fights, and police wait ready with cans of tear gas in case things get really rough.

■ Near Cotacachi: Laguna de Cuicocha

Strange stories surround the Laguna de Cuicocha, 18km west of Cotacachi. Perhaps part of the mystique comes from its curious location inside the mouth of a live volcano crater. A common fear among locals is that the volcano will soon erupt and flood the town with lava and water. The name Cuicocha comes from the story that tons of *cuy* (guinea pigs) live on the island in the lake. More mysterious, according to local lore, an enormous condor makes a sweeping flight to the two islands in the middle of the lake between 4-5pm every day. You can try to catch the Loch Cuicocha Monster on film, but locals say this colossal condor somehow avoids being captured by usually dependable cameras. Another legend claims that at midnight the corpses within the lake begin to howl and make ghoulish noises. While it might be romantic if the lake were an ancient burial ground, supposedly the only dead people in its depths are two suicides. When a multi-millionaire and his mistress drove off a cliff into the lake, millions in gold sank with them. Unfortunately, scuba diving lessons aren't offered, but a boat service does take visitors around the lake (30min., s/5,000).

You can walk to the lake from Cotacachi, but it's all uphill and can take up to two and a half hours; a *camioneta* is the only other option. From Cotacachi, a round-trip should be about s/20,000, though if you want to spend much time at the lake you'll have to pay the driver to wait. Brush up on your bargaining skills. The hike all the way around the lake is picturesque, but can take up to six hours. Who knows—if you stay long enough, perhaps you'll glimpse the elusive condor of Cotacachi.

■ Apuela

Apuela's attractions begin with the bus ride there. As the bumpy road approaches town, the scenery becomes more and more staggering, with jaw-dropping views of the western Andean cloud forests. Vehicles tread inches from the steep mountain cliffs as they pass the occasional waterfall or mountain stream. Depending on the time of day and the season, you may even find yourself looking down through the epiphytes at clouds below you. Don't fall asleep on the bus to Apuela; a five-minute nap would be enough to miss it entirely. Nested 2000m high in the lush, green mountains to the west of Otavalo, Apuela supports itself with agricultural activity. Visitors come to this mellow mountain town for its hiking and its piping hot springs.

Orientation and Practical Information Apuela is laid out symmetrically. Two similarly-sized *montes* (small mountains) lie on either side, and two parallel rivers run along their bases, forming Apuela's natural boundaries. The town follows suit, with two parallel roads running its length. The road entering town is referred to as **Avenida 20 de Julio** by some locals (others simply shrug and comment that it's never needed a name). The **bus stop**, as well as all places to sleep and eat, are on this street. The dusty **central plaza** behind the bus stop has a volleyball court and a small, dilapidated church. Apuela's other street, **García Moreno** (about this name most Apuelans are confident), runs across the plaza. Get here from Otavalo by bus (8, 10am, and 2pm). From here, buses run to **Otavalo** (7, 8, 9:30, 10, 11:15am, and 2pm, 2½hr., s/ 6,000) and the scenic, elevated village of **García Moreno** (10:30am, 12:30, and 4:30pm, 1hr., s/3,500). **Gualiman** can be reached by foot in one hour. Along García Moreno, across from the bus stop, is the **police station** (open 24hr.). The only phone is at the **EMETEL** (tel. 957-657), next door, which functions as the town's **emergency line**. The **Tenencia Política** room contains the **post office** next door to **EMETEL** (both open Mon.-Sat. 8am-noon and 2-6pm). The **hospital**, or *centro de salud,* is on Av. 20 de Julio, 30m up the road from the bus stop (open Sun.-Fri. 8am-5pm).

Accommodations and Food The accommodations in Apuela are so unimpressive that it's better to stay at the *cabañas* just outside of town. If the sun's setting and you're still in the *centro,* **Residencial Don Luis** provides a cheap night's stay and a smile. Beds are stiff and rooms are protected by the world's smallest locks, which would be a problem anywhere but in Apuela. If you want a cold shower, go outside to the communal bathroom (rooms s/10,000). A bit of a change of pace, the **Cabañas Río Grande** (Otavalo tel. 920-442 or 920-548, Quito tel. 534-196), are a 45-minute walk away, next to the hot springs. To get here, head out of town. After crossing the second bridge, take a left; this road leads to the *cabañas* and pools. Surrounded by papaya, avocado, banana, and lime trees, the *cabañas* are a fruit-lover's paradise. The spotless wood cabins are built for three people and have electricity and meticulously-maintained private baths (24hr. hot water). Watch out for the fumigating—you might ask to have yours left alone (s/20,000 per person, rates vary by season).

There are a couple of places to get a quick bite to eat before heading out for the day. The **Restaurant La Estancia,** Av. 20 de Julio across from the bus stop, serves an *almuerzo* (s/4,000) that comes with San Gacho soup, filled with bananas, potatoes, and meat (open daily 7am-8pm). Just up the road, **El Rincon del Buen Sabor** offers another setting for inexpensive meals (*merienda* s/3,500). The restaurant at **Cabañas Río Grande** offers deals for breakfast, brunch, or dinner. The servings are adequate and food is excellent. Giant trout freshly caught from the nearby river, with fries and salad costs s/8,000. The selection is minimal when few guests are staying there.

Sights There is not much to see in town, but there are many amazing spots outside. The hills that surround Apuela are criss-crossed with paths that make for good **hiking,** and the rivers on either side of town are known for their **trout fishing.** A one-hour walk leads to a **museum of archaeology** (s/10,000) and some minor **ruins** in Guali-mar. A set of natural **hot springs,** 7km from Apuela next to the Cabañas, make for an easy-going day of sun and relaxation. Locals pipe hot water from a nearby volcanic crater into three jacuzzi-like wading areas and a 15m pool. An even bigger pool is kept cold, to provide a refreshing plunge when the hot tub gets too hot. The pools are kept in decent shape; it costs only s/1,000 to lounge in the mineral water all day.

■ Near Apuela: Intag Cloud Forest

Situated on the verdant western slopes of the Andes mountains, this reserve protects a portion of Ecuador's endangered cloud forests. Less than 15% of the original forests remain; much has been lost to deforestation, agriculture has suffered due to desertifi-cation, rivers have become contaminated, and animals have lost their habitat. How-ever, amidst all the tension and controversy surrounding forest conservation, especially with recent copper mining plans, taking a walk through Carlos and Sandy Zorilla's majestic reserve is the ideal experience for anyone who either doubts or fanatically appreciates the cloud forest's value and importance.

With elevations of 1850-2000m and temperatures ranging from 12-27°C (55-80°F), Intag Cloud Forest is a far-from-static place. Particular combinations of clouds, fog, and constant humidity produce an incredible variety of flora and fauna. The plethora of epiphytes (plants that grow on other plants and trees) includes orchids, bromeli-ads, and araceas. Medicinal plants like **sangre de drago,** only recently discovered by modern medicine to cure child respiratory problems, grow here amongst the ferns and mosses. The mammals that live in the region—spectacled bears, pumas, spider monkeys, and mountain tapirs—tend to elude observation, as most are nocturnal and afraid of humans. All are threatened by deforestation and in danger of extinction. While mammals are a rare sight, the forest is a birdwatcher's paradise; its 22 species of hummingbird outnumber North America's mere 16.

A stay on the reserve costs US$40 per person and includes lodging, food, and a bilingual guide. The purely vegetarian fare is almost as raved over as the scenery. The rooms are all-organic as well—simple wood cabins have sturdy roofs and straw mats for the floors. All beds come equipped with thick blankets for those chilly mountain nights. No electricity, solar heated water for rustic outside showers. Carlos and Sandy only accept groups of six or more. The minimum stay is two nights, and while there is no maximum length of stay, keep in mind that this is a family-run farm and these people have lives of their own. If you don't have a group to go with, contact them a few weeks in advance so that they can place you in a group. Reservations required; write to them a couple of months in advance at Casilla 18, Otavalo, Imbabura, Ecua-dor, and they will send you more info. If you are not interested in staying at the farm, but still want to help save the Intag Cloud Forest, write to the above address to receive more info about Intag preservation projects.

■ Ibarra

A peculiar balance between past and present exists in Ibarra. Much bigger than nearby Otavalo, Ibarra manages to have more of a small town atmosphere. After an earthquake destroyed much of the city in 1868, the survivors were left with the mon-umental task of piecing the rubble back together. Whether by chance or premedita-tion, they built many of the public buildings and business centers in the southern half of the city, and most of the colonial-style, white-with-red-tile homes in the northern half. This balance persists today; as the people of Ibarra race into modernity in taxis, buses, and Mercedes Benzes, the city gently pulls them back with the clatter of horse-drawn buggies on cobblestone avenues. Even this provincial capital's culture has reached a balanced equilibrium. Ibarra is one of the few Ecuadorian cities where all three major ethnicities are successfully integrated—black, indigenous, and *mestizo*.

ORIENTATION

Buses from Quito and Otavalo drop visitors off along Borja and Enrique Vacas, on the western outskirts of town. To get to town, walk a short distance south toward Mt. Imbabura and take a left on **Mariano Acosta.** The immense **obelisk,** visible from a distance, serves as a good landmark. Three blocks north of the obelisk, east-west **Flores** passes both major parks in Ibarra, **Parque La Merced** and, two blocks to the east, **Parque Pedro Moncayo.** One block north of the obelisk, east-west **Pedro Moncayo** runs the width of the city, splitting Ibarra into two manageable halves. North of Moncayo, the city is a bit slower and you're more likely to find interesting architecture and historical monuments. To the south, buildings tend to be gray and menacing, the people move at a more frantic pace, and establishments go in and out of business in the time it takes to stop for a drink.

PRACTICAL INFORMATION

Tourist Information: CETUR, Olmedo 956 (tel. 958-759; fax 958-547), between Moncayo and Velasquez. Open Mon.-Fri. 8:30am-1pm and 2-5pm.

Banks: Banco La Previsora, Oviedo 8-13 and Olmedo (tel. 955-900 or 957-294; fax 957-295), has 24hr. ATM, Visa cash advances, and cash exchange, but doesn't accept traveler's checks. Open Mon.-Fri. 9am-4pm. **Banco Continental,** Olmedo 11-87 and Guerrero, has a 24hr. ATM and cash exchange. Open Mon.-Fri. 9am-2pm; *cajero* 2-7pm. **Banco del Pacífico,** Olmedo and Moncayo (tel. 957-728 or 957-714), changes cash and traveler's checks, MasterCard cash advances, Cirrus ATM 24hr. Open Mon.-Sat. 9:30am-2:30pm.

Trains: The **train station** (tel. 915-390), is just southwest of the obelisk as you enter town. The train goes to **San Lorenzo** usually every other day (supposedly at 7am, 8hr., US$20). It is often full, so get there early to buy a ticket; they are only sold the day of departure, starting at 6:30am. Most people get there around 6am to wait in line (or to find out the train isn't running that day). Check the night before, after 5pm, and you should get a semi-final answer as to whether or not the train will be going to San Lorenzo the next day. The 8hr. trip can sometimes turn into a 12hr. one, depending on the number of stops, the weather, and the farm animals on the tracks. If possible, **sit on the roof** of the train; the view is incredible and it's especially fun going through tunnels and over skinny bridges. Don't worry about falling off—the train is moving pretty slowly—but do hold on and look out for low-hanging branches. You may be handed a machete and asked to chop away at trees that have fallen too close to the tracks. Make sure your passport is available, because occasionally there are routine checks along the way. And keep a close eye on your bags. It's a good idea to have a hotel in mind before getting off the train, or ask the driver for a recommendation and directions. Locals will offer to find you a hotel and bring you there for a small fee in the form of a tip (from you or from the hotel); rumors exist that this might be a plan to lead you to a den of thieves.

Buses: Andina Bus Lines, Acosta and Borja (tel. 950-833), serves **Quito** (every 15min., 6am-8:45pm, 2½hr., s/7,000). **Trans Otavalo,** E. Vacas and M. Acosta (tel. 920-405), goes to **Otavalo** (every 15min., 4:15am-10pm, s/1,100). **Cooperativo Espejo** (tel. 952-190), at the train station, goes to **San Lorenzo** (6:30, 8:30, 11:30am, and 2:30pm, 6hr., s/16,000). **Valle del Chota,** at the train station, also goes to **San Lorenzo** (9am, 6hr., s/16,000). **Expreso Turismo,** Pedro Moncayo and Carvajal (tel. 980-492), goes to **Tulcán** (every hr., 5am-6pm, 2hr., s/7,000).

Taxis: In parks and near bus stations. **Cooperativo Pasquel Monge** (tel. 915-415), at train station, goes to **Otavalo** (around s/25,000) and **Quito** (around s/100,000).

Library: Bolívar and Flores, 1st fl. of municipal building. Open Mon.-Fri. 8am-noon and 3-6pm.

Pharmacies: Farmacía Ross, Velasco 8-108 and Narváez (tel. 952-220). Open Mon.-Sat. 7:30am-10:30pm, Sun. 7:30am-12:30pm. **Farmacía Estrada,** Cifuentes 11-43 (tel. 955-691). Open daily 8am-10pm.

Medical Services: Hospital San Vicente de Paul, Luis Vargas Torres 1-156 (emergency tel. 131 or 950-666, tel. 957-272 through -275). Emergency treatment, consultations, lab work, and X-rays free. Open 24hr. **Clínica Mariano Acosta,** M. Acosta 11-20 (tel. 950-924; emergency tel. 642-211), is a 24hr. emergency clinic.
Emergency: tel. 101.
Police: 120 Villamar and Roldos, tel. 101.
Post Office: Salinas 6-62 and Oviedo (tel. 950-412; fax 958-038). Lista de Correos. Open Mon.-Sat. 8am-7pm.
Telephone: EMETEL, Sucre 4-48 and Moreno. Open daily 8am-10pm. Public phones throughout the city for local calls only.
Telephone Code: 06.

ACCOMMODATIONS

While there is certainly no shortage of rooms in Ibarra, quality rooms at moderate prices can be hard to come by. If you have no qualms about roughing it (i.e. cold water, cracked ceilings, and rusted bathrooms), you'll be like a kid in a candy store here. Most low-rent-type places congregate near the train station and provide pole position for the race to the morning train; just make sure they don't rent by the hour.

Hotel Imbabura, Oviedo 9-33 (tel. 950-155), between Narváez and Cifuentes, ½ block west of Parque La Merced. Wood-paneled floors and cot beds decorate barren but immaculate rooms, some with small sofas. Flair found elsewhere, like in the courtyard with an old fountain or in the lounge with invaluable info on tours and trips. Meticulously-maintained common baths. Rooms s/10,000 per person.
Residencial San Andrecito, Cifuentes and Oviedo (tel. 958-644). Sunshine fills most rooms here—and there is plenty of space for it to fill. Simple beds and surreal-blue shared bathroom cost s/8,000 per person.
Hotel Nueva Colonia, Olmedo 5-19 and Grijalva (tel. 952-918; fax 955-543), just north of the Parque La Merced. Sacrificing aesthetic appeal for technology and comfort, rooms are not much to look at but they do have wall-to-wall carpeting and color TVs. Same goes for the bathrooms, which could be cleaner, but have 24hr. hot showers. Singles s/27,000; doubles s/44,000; triples s/55,000.
Hotel Magestic (tel. 950-052), between Oviedo and Flores. Though hallways are dim and a musky smell lingers in the rooms, s/9,000 for a room with a private (hot water) bath makes this overlookable. Rooms with shared bath s/8,000 per person.

FOOD

Ibarra's dining options are severely limited, a sad state of affairs for a busy provincial capital. Ask Ibarrans where to find a good restaurant, and they'll be as stumped as you are, but the town is inundated with sidewalk vendors, tiny bakeries, and snack food establishments, and it's easy to find a typical *almuerzo* spot around the parks. A few establishments endeavor to redeem the culinary failures of this colonial town.

El Cedrón, Olmedo and Flores (tel. 958-562). Incredibly low priced *merienda* (s/3,000) makes this spot popular among locals; it comes with a macaroni and cheese type pasta, so vegetarians can get a decent amount of food as well. Eat and be entertained by the latest *telenovela*. Open daily 7am-8pm.
Café Coffee Kaffee, Moreno 404 and Rocafuerte (tel. 640-438 or 951-848). Filled with an aura of romance, the red velvet seats and slow mellow music complement an incredible cappuccino (s/4,000) sprinkled with chocolate dust. *Desayunos* s/5,000, hamburgers s/4,000, fruit salad s/5,000. Open Mon.-Thurs. 9:30am-1pm and 4-10pm, Fri. 9:30am-1pm and 4pm-1am, Sat. 6pm-1am.
El Horno Pizzeria, Rocafuerte 6-38 (tel. 959-019 or 958-508). Tasty pizzas, though still lacking on tomato sauce, an endless source of frustration in all of Ecuador. El Horno comes with peppers, meats, onions, cheese, and tomatoes (small s/12,000, large s/22,000). The Vegetarian has cheese, carrots, cucumbers, peppers, mushrooms, and onions. Open Tues.-Sun. 6pm-midnight.
Restaurant Ajari, Mariano Acosta 16-38 (tel. 955-221 or 955-555), 6 blocks from the obelisk in Hotel Ajari. Since it's so inconvenient (unless you're going out of town),

the fact that Ajari is still in business is a testament to its food and service. Fancy setting and prices: salad s/9,500, pasta from s/14,500-s/17,500, menu of the day s/25,000. Weekend piano player and seafood specials. Open daily 7am-midnight.

SIGHTS AND ENTERTAINMENT

For its size, Ibarra is a bit lacking in entertainment. However, it is home to many incredible historical and architectural structures. Rising more than 100 ft. high, the stunning white **obelisk** at Narváez and Velasco couldn't be a sorer thumb in its surroundings. The landmark looks more like a monument to Cleopatra than a dedication to Miguel de Ibarra, who founded this Spanish colony in 1606. Ibarra has two remarkable parks, both surrounded by outstanding architecture. **Parque La Merced,** on the corner of Flores and Cifuentes, exhibits a statue of Dr. Victor Manuel Peñaherrera looking awfully bookish and distinguished. Peñaherrera (1865-1930) was a judge on the Ecuadorian Supreme Court and Deacon of the Faculty of Law in the Universidad Central. On the west side of the park, the **Basílica La Merced** supports a portrayal of the Virgin Mary adorned with a crown of silver. Within the *basílica* is an elaborate altar of gold, which reaches up to the 70 ft. high arched ceilings, but be prepared to view it through barred windows; it's only sporadically open to the public. The **Parque Moncayo,** at Flores and Bolívar, is a magnificent place for mundane activities; lying around on the shady grass tops the list. The surrounding architecture is exceptional, especially the **cathedral** and the municipal building. While the golden altar outshines most everything else in the cathedral, the church also houses huge portraits of all 12 apostles, painted by a local artist Rafael Troya. Again, though, entrance may not be possible—be prepared to gaze upon the artistry from the outside. If you follow Moncayo to its easternmost point, you'll run right into the **Iglesia de San Francisco,** home of Ibarra's Franciscan fathers.

On weekends, the **Cine Grand Columbia,** on Moreno between Sucre and Rocafuerte, sometimes shows cultural films; stop by to check a schedule. **D'club,** Bolívar 10-39 and Colón (tel. 956-907), offers billiards, video games, concerts, art exhibits, theatre, and drinks daily from 5pm until the crowds go home. Ask for a calendar of events. **Café Coffee Kaffee** (see above) sometimes hosts live music on weekends.

■ Near Ibarra

SAN ANTONIO DE IBARRA

With its economy firmly rooted in exquisite woodcarving, San Antonio de Ibarra caters to tourists who have a hankering for a carved chess set, Ecuadorian sun, or wooden unicorn with wings. The town has little to offer outside of its woodwork, but the work is of such quality that it has carved a place for itself among the South American *artesanía* elite. People from across the Americas migrate to San Antonio to witness the town's handiwork and buy a piece or two. Only recently has San Antonio become known for its craft worldwide, but already many shops sell pieces overseas, and the influx of foreign visitors keeps increasing.

San Antonio is located west of Ibarra along the Panamerican Highway. The layout is simple—**Avenida 27 de Noviembre** is the main street and runs from the town center, **Parque Francisco Calderón,** to the Panamerican Highway. Most of the woodcarving galleries are either around the park or along Av. 27 de Noviembre. **EMETEL** (tel. 932-110) is on Cevallos just left of the park if facing the highway (open Mon.-Fri. 9am-noon and 3-6pm). **Trans Otavalo buses** drop off on the Panamerican Highway, at the edge of town (every 15min., 10min., s/400). From here, **taxis** go directly to the heart of San Antonio for around s/3,500, but the uphill walk from the Panamerican Highway to the town center only takes about 10 minutes. Some buses go all the way to the park; catch these on the corner of Acosta and Narvaez (every 20min., 10min., s/500; they should say "San Antonio"). A taxi from Ibarra should cost about s/7,000.

The **Hosteria Nogales,** Sucre 11-85 (tel. 932-000), is the only place to stay in San Antonio. The lack of market competition reveals itself in their extremely basic rooms.

Plan on an intimate evening with your daily grime accumulation, because bathrooms only have hot water in the morning (s/10,000 per person, s/15,000 with bath). The **restaurant** downstairs is decorated with local woodcarvings and a tiny fish tank, definitely the decorative highlight of the Nogales experience. *Almuerzo* runs around s/5,000, a la carte dishes around s/8,000 (open daily 7am-9pm). Only one other place in town serves food, the **Restaurante Fogon del Chief,** along Cevallos on the north side of Parque Calderón, second floor. Though not much to look at, it is a great place to look from, offering a wonderful view of the Park and Imbabura. It serves huge, reasonably-priced portions of Creole and Peruvian cuisine; the management is amicable and gregarious; and the food is a refreshing break from typical indigenous fare (menu of the day s/6,000, full meal with chicken s/7,000).

San Antonio's woodwork stands out because of its meticulous, stunning precision. The **Unión Artesanal de San Antonio de Ibarra,** at the south end of the Parque Calderón, is a set of 10 woodcarving workshops that sell pieces straight from the tables they're made on. This is the best place to watch the work in progress, and workshop #1 even offers classes in woodshaping. Many shops carry very similar carvings, but there are a few unique pieces waiting to be found. All the shops in the Unión accept Visa, but better discounts go to those who carry cash. To the east side of the park, the **Galería de Arte Luis Potosí** (tel. 932-056) has several rooms and two floors of work that's a little finer and more detailed than in other shops (open daily 8am-6pm). More shops line Av. 27 de Noviembre towards the Panamerican Highway. Some of these galleries, including the **Galería de Arte Ruben Potosí** (tel. 932-302), produce larger works, some as tall as six feet, and carry a multitude of abstract, modernist carvings. The furniture shops are farther down Av. 27 de Noviembre.

LA ESPERANZA

Strange things start happening as you head south out of Ibarra. Life slows down dramatically, hearts beat at a healthier pace, and buses will sometimes even decelerate as they attempt the rocky incline that is the road to La Esperanza. At first glance, it seems only idyllic and picturesque, with Volcán Imbabura and other mountains nearby. But then a truck filled with military men rumbles by and you realize what that noise you've been hearing is—military training groups shouting exercise responses in synch. Then you notice graffitti-painted mushrooms, signs of past problems the tiny pueblo had with this hallucinogenic drug. Despite its troubled past, serenity reigns over the little town situated 7km from Ibarra. Its economic life is rooted in agriculture but, as a supplement, many of its inhabitants hand-embroider goods to sell in Otavalo. Although La Esperanza does not glitter with excitement, the views of Imbabura and the scenic countryside make it an ideal getaway from Ibarra's hustle and bustle. La Esperanza's one road, which locals call **Gallo Plaza,** runs north-south past the two or three establishments in town, towards Imbabura.

Esperanza is great for outdoors-lovers—nearly everything to see and do is out in the fresh air. The walk down to the **Río Tajuando,** which leads to Ibarra, is painless and pleasurable. Head down Gallo Plaza from Casa Aida, take a right at the first cross street, and continue for a half-hour. Watch out for men with very big guns at the nearby military base; they don't like tourists getting in their way. For a more serious trek, try getting to the top of **Loma Cubilche** (3836m). Facing Imbabura, Cubilche is the smaller mountain to the left. To get there, head up Gallo Plaza, cross the dry-river bridge, and turn right immediately. Follow this road all the way to the top. Expect a three-hour hike up and a two-hour return. Die-hard climbers can make a go at **Volcán Imbabura** (4609m). Leave early in the morning, as the climb takes over 10 hours. Directions to Imbabura are similar to those to Cubilche, but turn right on the street just before the bridge. This road goes most of the way up, and various paths lead to the very top. A small store on Gallo Plaza before the dry bridge sells bottled water, a necessity before attacking either Cubilche or Imbabura. Esperanza has a few resident guides available for this hike—check with Casa Aida about contacting them. Embroidered goods can be bought at Casa Aida or at **Don Eugenio's Cuero Shop,** which also sells leather goods like homemade pants. This shop is past Hostería Mania from Casa Aida, and is open as long as the family is at home.

A unique accommodation, the **Casa Aida** is located in the middle of town. It consists of a four-person straw hut with two beds in a tree-fort loft, accessible only by a step ladder, and several less exciting grounded rooms. Thick brick walls and blankets provide plenty of warmth on frigid nights, and the kitchen and baths are impeccably clean. Two of the four common bathrooms have 24-hour hot water (s/10,000 per person). Casa Aida also has one of the only restaurants in La Esperanza. Outdoor dining in the vegetable garden provides a view of the grand Imbabura in its entirety, as well as of a smaller volcanic chunk that was blown off in an eruption 120 years ago before landing in the hostel's backyard (pancakes with berry sauce s/3,000, fresh river trout s/10,000; open daily 6am-9pm).

Buses from Ibarra to Esperanza (every 20min., 20min., s/650) can be picked up at the Parque Grijalva on the corner of Sánchez and Cifuentes and Toro Moreno, or at the southernmost end of Ibarra, on the corner of Torre and Retorno (Montalvo). **Taxis** from anywhere in Ibarra charge about s/20,000 for the trip to Esperanza. If your boots are made for walking, the two-hour hike to La Esperanza is along Retorno, the same road the buses use. Exhaust fumes prove unpleasant from time to time, but if you bring your gas mask the scenic walk can be rewarding.

▒ Tulcán

In Tulcán, everyone is always going somewhere. Whether it's travelers crossing the border into Colombia or those who have recently arrived, Tulcán's importance lies in its ability to transport visitors to their desired destinations. A large percentage of Tulcán's population is employed as taxi and *camioneta* drivers, and four or five different bus companies compete for travelers' sucres and Colombian pesos. People often rush to get in and out of Tulcán, but if your bus doesn't leave for another hour, catch your breath at Tulcán's only tourist sight, the **topiary garden** within the cemetery at Av. 10 de Agosto and Esmeraldas. Filled with bushes and trees pruned into arches, faces, birds, and elephants, the garden is a magical respite from the rat-race to the border.

ORIENTATION

The two most happening streets in Tulcán, **Bolívar** and **Sucre,** run the length of town. Right in the center of things, the **Parque Principal** (sometimes called the **Plaza Central**) lies between Sucre and Olmedo, Ayacucho and Av. 10 de Agosto. The bigger **Parque Isidro Ayora** is northeast along Bolívar, two blocks southeast of the enormous **cemetery.** Head uphill along Bolívar, about 1.5km southwest of *el centro,* for the **terminal terrestre.** Counterintuitively, the **Colombian border** is south and east of town, about 6km down Av. Brazil, which leaves from the northeast end of town.

PRACTICAL INFORMATION

Tourist Information: CETUR, Pichincha 467 and Sucre, 2nd fl. (tel. 983-892). Open Sun.-Fri. 8:30am-noon and 2-5pm.

Travel Agency: EccoTur, Sucre 51029 (tel. 980-468; fax 980-368), at Parque Principal. National and international tours and packages. Open Mon.-Fri. 8:30am-1pm and 2:30-6pm, Sat. 8:30am-1pm.

Banks: Filanbanco, Sucre 5086 and Av. 10 de Agosto, has a 24hr. ATM and gives Visa cash advances. Open Mon.-Fri. 8:30am-7pm, Sat. 9am-2pm. **Banco Pichincha,** Sucre and Av. 10 de Agosto (tel. 980-529), next door to Filanbanco, changes cash and traveler's checks. Open Mon.-Fri. 8am-7pm, Sat.-Sun. 8am-2pm.

Currency Exchange: Casa de Cambio, Bolívar 52006 and Ayacucho (tel. 980-910). Open Mon.-Fri. 8am-noon and 4-7pm, and **Casa Paz S.A.,** Ayacucho 373 and Bolívar (tel. 950-058). Open Mon.-Fri. 8:30am-12:30pm and 2:30-5:30pm. Both exchange Colombian pesos and U.S. dollars.

Buses: Only taxis and *camionetas* go to the border from Tulcán (see below). All buses leave from the *terminal terrestre.* Bus companies go to: **Quito** (every hr.

1:30am-10:30pm, 4½hr., s/14,500); and **Ibarra** (every 5min. 1:30am-10:30pm, 2hr., s/7,000). **Cooperativo de Transportes Expreso Tulcán** (tel. 980-480), sends the most buses throughout the day.

Local Buses: Trans Popular buses can be picked up across the street from the *terminal terrestre.* The 5min. ride to the **Parque Principal** costs s/500.

Camionetas: Coop Carchi, on Venezuela along the north side of Parque Ayora, goes to and from the border for only s/1,500. They leave whenever vans fill up.

Taxis: The older-looking the taxi, the less expensive the ride. Some drivers try to pack people going in similar directions in the same cab, thus decreasing fares. Taxis can be picked up anywhere in town, but especially at the bus terminal and the Parque Principal. From the *terminal terrestre* to the border is around s/10,000.

Library: Olmedo and Av. 10 de Agosto (tel. 980-487, ext. 34), 4th floor of municipal building, entrance on 10 de Agosto. Open Mon.-Fri. 8am-12:30pm and 2:30-6pm.

Pharmacies: Farmacía Moderna, Sucre and Ayacucho (tel. 980-825), in Parque Principal. Open Mon.-Sat. 8am-9pm, Sun. 7am-6pm.

Hospital: Hospital Luis G. Davilla de Tulcán, Av. 10 de Agosto 12051 and Lojan (tel. 980-316 or 980-315). 24hr. emergency treatment is free.

Emergency: tel. 101.

Police: Manabí and Coral (tel. 981-321 or 980-345), on the northern outskirts of town. Open 24hr.

Post Office: Bolívar 53027 and Junín (tel. 980-552). Open Mon.-Fri. 8am-7pm, Sat. 9am-noon.

Telephones: There are 3 **EMETEL** offices, with national and international calling service: at the *terminal terrestre* (open Mon.-Sat. 8am-10pm, Sun. 8am-8pm), at the border (tel. 982-012; open Mon.-Sat. 8am-6pm, Sun. 8am-1pm), and on Olmedo and Ayacucho (open daily 8am-10pm). A public phone for national calls is at Sucre and Pichincha, in Parque Concordia behind the bust of Simon Bolívar.

Phone Code: 06.

ACCOMMODATIONS

Unless you want to spend more than s/30,000 per person, the *habitaciones* in Tulcán are far from elegant. The constant influx of sucre-laden Colombians, exploiting the beneficial exchange rate, has upped the prices of the more refined hotels considerably. There are still plenty of affordable places to rest your head; just don't expect them to glow with ambience. Calle Sucre, just west of the Parque Principal, hops with lodgings—some ritzy, some reasonable.

Residencial Oasis, Av. 10 de Agosto and Sucre (tel. 980-342). Footsteps away from Parque Principal and convenient for dining expeditions. Thick brick walls and windows facing inside rather than toward the street create silent sleeping shelters. Doors made for munchkins, dark and spooky common baths (24hr. hot water), but once lit they're grimeless. Rooms s/12,000 per person, with bath s/15,000.

Hotel Internacional Azteca, Bolívar and Atahualpa (tel. 981-447; fax 980-481), a block west of Parque Ayora, above the *discoteca.* The extra sucres go a long way; these are the cleanest rooms in town. Fluffy beds and pillows make for plush slumber. Invest in earplugs; the weekend *discoteca* music blares until 2am. Private bath, hot water, A/C, phone, TV. Singles s/32,400; doubles s/45,000; 2 beds s/52,800.

Residencial Sucre, Junín and Bolívar, in a cuisine-friendly locale. Windows face walls, when there are windows at all, making rooms pitch-black. Creaky beds and old-style coat racks round out the furnishings. Perk up in the lobby with the friendly staff, fuzzy TV, and comfy red leather chairs. Large baths (24hr. hot water). Rooms cost the same with or without bath. Singles s/8,000; doubles s/16,000.

FOOD

Colombian cuisine knows no boundaries, and a number of Colombian restaurants have made a place for themselves alongside the Ecuadorian establishments of Tulcán. To sample this international culinary excitement, visit eateries along Sucre and Bolívar, west of Av. 10 de Agosto.

Euro Palace, Olmedo 50071 and Av. 10 de Agosto (tel. 983-950), on the central plaza, 2nd fl. European posters and a wall-sized painting of the Swiss Alps bring the Old World to the New. Enchanting view of Parque Principal and fresh flowers at every table. Russian and Italian salads (s/4,000), goulash (s/10,000), veggie pasta with peas, carrots, peppers, and mushrooms (s/8,000). Open daily 9am-9pm.

Restaurante El Patio, Bolívar (tel. 984-872), between Pichincha and Av. 10 de Agosto. Monstrous plates of Colombian cuisine, like the *Bandeja Paisa* (s/10,000), loaded with eggs, vegetables, rice, and meat, at reasonable prices. Antique grama-phones, sewing machines, and black-and-white photos provide glimpses of the Tul-cán of old. Open Mon.-Sat. 8am-9pm, Sun. 9am-3pm.

Wimpy La Verdadera Hamburguesa, Sucre and Boyacá, around the corner from Hotel Azteca. This streetside cheapie cures late-night munchies and afternoon hun-ger pains alike. Far from wimpy, the jumbo burger comes with fries and the works (s/4,000). Open daily 9am-midnight.

CROSSING THE BORDER

Crossing the *frontera* between Ecuador and Colombia at the Rumichaca Bridge is usually fairly straightforward. Tourists are required to present a **passport** for stamping at the immigration office of each country, and to turn in and/or receive a 90-day tour-ist card. Very few nationalities need a visa to enter Colombia. Those that need a visa to enter Ecuador are listed under **Entrance Requirements** (p. 9). Copies of passports, driver's licenses, birth certificates, and doctor's notes are not acceptable identifica-tion, and officials are fanatically strict about this. A **provisional passport** may be acceptable. Problems can sometimes occur on the Colombian side of the road. If crossing from Colombia into Ecuador, be sure to get your passport stamped inside the Colombian immigration office. There are plenty of thieves pretending to be bor-der officers, offering to stamp passports and escort people across the border, but instead running off with travelers' bags and money. Just look for an authentic uni-form. Occasionally, especially scruffy-looking tourists will be asked to prove that they have **sufficient funds** (US$20) for each day they plan to stay in the country (US$10 for poor traveling students). Officials may also ask to see a **round-trip ticket** proving that visitors intend to leave the country within **90 days,** the maximum amount of time a traveler can spend in either country in a one-year period. If you want to stay longer, you'll need to obtain a visa (see **Entrance Requirements,** p. 9). Tulcán's border is open daily 6am-10pm, and the **Ecuadorian Immigration Office** (tel./fax 980-704), is open daily 24 hours. There are no taxes or fees at the border except for Ecuadorian residents, who have to pay a s/3,000 charge.

The Central Corridor

Dubbed the "Avenue of the Volcanoes" by German explorer Alexander van Humboldt in 1802, the strip of Andean highlands between Quito and Cuenca is Ecuador at its most geologically extreme. Some prominent snow-capped peaks assert their fire-spitting authority here—the towering cone of Volcán Cotopaxi (the tallest active volcano in the world), the angry spew of Sangay, and the sheer majesty of Chimborazo. But as intimidating as the volcanos may seem, the jaw-droppingly beautiful views from the misty Andean ridges somehow soften the sharp peaks. Natives in Andean dress move in and out of the fog and clouds, over rolling patchwork-quilt farmlands, often meeting at local weekly markets to sell handmade crafts. The natural hot springs at Baños relieve weary travelers—especially at sunrise, when the stunning dawn sky illuminates the lush valleys thousands of meters below. The 6310m Volcán Chimborazo offers an adrenaline rush for the citied-out through its sheer altitude, and is easily accessible from the typically tranquil central highland city of Riobamba.

■ Latacunga

Between 1534 and 1949 the gigantic Volcán Cotopaxi, the tallest active volcano in the world, spewed its stuff nine times. Each time, the fire-spitter devastated and sometimes entirely destroyed the neighboring city of Latacunga. The citizens of Latacunga, which means "land of my choice" in an indigenous tongue, always dutifully chose to return to their ruined home and rebuild virtually everything. This leads to one of the classic Ecuadorian mysteries—why the *hell* did they keep going back? Maybe it was the incredible panorama, with a crown of Andean peaks surrounding the 2700m-high town, and the proximity to natural wonders that has made it a popular tourist base today. Maybe it was all the gold and silver discovered and mined here, especially after the conquistadors arrived. It could have been the fruit, coffee, sugar, cacao, rubber, and herds of cattle that are sustained on soil made rich by millennia of volcanic ash. And then again, in some hypnotically masochistic way, perhaps it was Cotopaxi itself—its surreal, tranquil, white cone in the northeast horizon—that drew the Latacungans to this spot, and like a spell cast by Pele himself, held them here for more than 450 years.

ORIENTATION

The most heavily traveled part of Latacunga is along the Panamerican Highway. This strip has its selection of solid hotels and restaurants, but as the mechanic shops and Castrol Oil center suggest, its main concern is the vehicular traffic passing through. On the other side of the **Río Cutuchi** lies the main part of the city, sloping up the mountainside in a grid-like fashion. Although hotels and restaurants are sprinkled throughout the streets, the main municipal and tourist section is on and near the **Parque Vicente León,** roughly along Quito and Quevedo. The market starts above the river and covers several blocks, including the **Plaza Chile,** between Av. 5 de Junio and Valencia. Most buses will take you across the river into the main part of the town; if one doesn't, it's only a short walk anyway.

PRACTICAL INFORMATION

Tourist Office: Latacunga doesn't really have a tourist office, but the proprietors of the **Hotels Cotopaxi, Estambul,** and **Tilipulo** happily provide maps of and information on the town.
Currency Exchange: The **Banco Popular,** Sanchez de Orellana and Salcedo (tel. 810-179), will exchange cash or traveler's checks from dollars to sucres.
Trains: The **train station,** M.A. Subia and J. Andrade (tel. 800-700), is on the far side of the Panamerican Highway. Hardly running anymore, trains travel only to

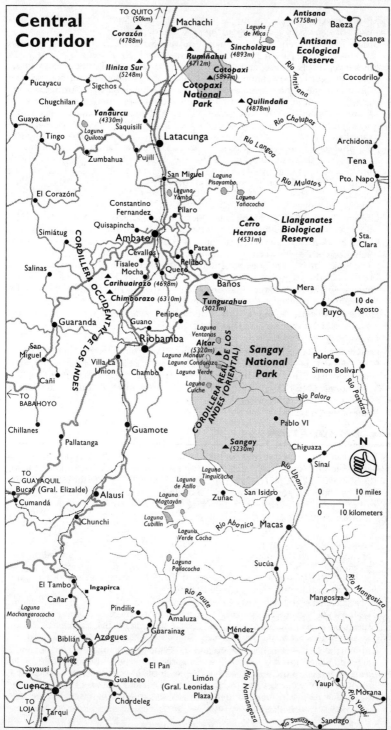

Central Corridor

Riobamba (Sat., 11:30am, 4hr., s/10,000) and **Quito** (Fri., 3½hr., s/5,000). Schedule varies, so check at the station. Buy tickets at departure.

Buses: The most useful bus company is **Transportes Cotopaxi** (tel. 800-752). Main offices are on the Panamerican Highway across from Calle J. Andrade, but nearly all buses depart elsewhere, and only tickets to Quevedo need to be bought there. Buses to **Quito** (every 10min., 3:30am-7:10pm, 2hr., s/4,000) leave from a parking lot next to the market at Amazonas and Av. 5 de Junio. Buses to **Ambato** (every 10min., 5am-6pm, 1hr., s/2,000) and **Baños** (Sun., 6:30am, 2hr., s/3,500) leave from the Panamerican Highway at Av. 5 de Junio. Buses to **Quevedo** (every 1½hr., 5am-7pm, 5hr., s/8,500) leave from Av. 5 de Junio, 1 block west of the Panamerican Highway. On its way to Quevedo, the bus stops in **Pujilí** (10min., s/500) and **Zumbahua** (1½hr., s/3,000). Buses to **Santo Domingo** (7am and 2:30pm, 3hr., s/8,000) leave from the Panamerican Highway at Jones. Buses to the loop of small **pueblos** surrounding Latacunga line up along Benavidez, next to the river, starting at Simón Bolívar: **Saquisilí** (every 10min., 5:30am-6:30pm, 20min., s/800), **Sigchos** (9, 11am, and 1pm, 3hr., s/4,000), and **Chugchilán** (11am, 4hr., s/5,500). If you're heading to Saquisilí on Thurs., expect a wait.

Library: The **Biblioteca Municipal,** Quevedo and Salcedo (tel. 800-849), reflects the town's healthy reading appetite. Open Mon.-Fri. 8am-noon and 2-6pm.

Public Market: A required ingredient in the Latacunga experience, the *mercado* falls more or less between Av. 5 de Junio and Valencia, bordered on the east by Amazonas. Open daily 7am-6pm, but Sat. is the big day. Anything you might need to feed, clothe, or groom yourself at low, low prices.

Pharmacy: Farmacía Santa Marianita, 2 de Mayo and Hmas. Paez (tel. 800-728), across from the hospital. Open daily 7am-8pm.

Hospital: Hospital General, Hmas. Paez and Av. 2 de Mayo (tel. 800-331 or 800-332), has ambulance service. Open 24hr.

Emergency: 101.

Police: (tel. 612-666), on General Proaño about 1km from the center of town.

Post Office: Quevedo and Maldonado (tel. 800-500), a block from the Parque Vicente León, has a Lista de Correos. Open Mon.-Fri. 8am-7pm, Sat. 8am-2pm.

Telephones: EMETEL, Quevedo and Maldonado (tel. 810-128), calling card calls s/1500. Open daily 8am-9:45pm.

Telephone Code: 03.

ACCOMMODATIONS

While Latacunga is not tourist-swamped, it does have its fair share of hotels. Several lie conveniently along the Panamerican Highway; others are in the midst of town across the river. All are pretty cheap, though some stretch down to the deepest, darkest realms of the budget world in terms of quality. Be sure to make reservations well ahead of time if you're coming to Latacunga on Wednesday—tourists always flock here for the Saquisilí market the next morning.

Hotel Tilipulo, Guayaquil and Quevedo (tel. 820-130), 1 block north and then west of the Parque León. A brand-spankin' new place, its wood floors and furniture still gleam proudly. Not just rooms but actual suites—complete with bedroom, private bath, and a charming little living room with TV. Ask at the front desk for hot water when you want to shower. Singles s/20,000; doubles s/40,000.

Hotel Cotopaxi (tel. 801-310), on Salcedo next to the Parque León. Some rooms with excellent views of the park. As majestic as its namesake, comfort abounds; spacious rooms have restful beds and private hot water baths, as well as a helpful though somewhat erratic staff. Singles s/20,000; doubles s/40,000.

Residencial Los Andes, Eloy Alfaro and the Panamerican Highway (tel. 800-983); enter on Alfaro side, it is 1 block down from the bus station. The view of the Andes may be limited to the wallpaper, but the comfortable beds and low price make it the best bet if you must stay by the highway. Quieter rooms are in the back; the buses start rolling by long before the sun comes up. Rooms are s/12,000 per person, with private bath s/15,000. Curfew 10pm.

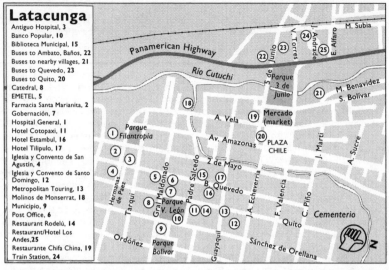

Latacunga

Antiguo Hospital, 3
Banco Popular, 10
Biblioteca Municipal, 15
Buses to Ambato, Baños, 22
Buses to nearby villages, 21
Buses to Quevedo, 23
Buses to Quito, 20
Catedral, 8
EMETEL, 5
Farmacia Santa Marianita, 2
Gobernación, 7
Hospital General, 1
Hotel Cotopaxi, 11
Hotel Estambul, 16
Hotel Tilipulo, 17
Iglesia y Convento de San Agustín, 4
Iglesia y Convento de Santo Domingo, 12
Metropolitan Touring, 13
Molinos de Monserrat, 18
Municipio, 9
Post Office, 6
Restaurant Rodelú, 14
Restaurant/Hotel Los Andes, 25
Restaurante Chifa China, 19
Train Station, 24

Hotel Estambul, Quevedo 73-40 (tel. 800-354), between Salcedo and Guayaquil. A favorite, but unpredictable in availability. Rooms can get cold at night, but private baths have continuous hot water. Secure luggage-storage room for guests heading up to Cotopaxi and a TV in the *sala* (living room). Rooms are s/15,000 per person.

FOOD

Latacunga's narrow streets are crammed with scores of *restaurantes típicos* that are virtually identical. Sit down at any one for a meal, and you're unlikely to be surprised by what appears on your plate (*almuerzos* go for about s/5,000). Alternatively, even cheaper meals can be found in the *mercado*, but eat at your own risk, and don't even consider any prepared food that hasn't been (literally) cooked to death. There is a decent selection of fruit stalls clustered near the east end. *Panaderías*, like the identical little breads they sell, are a dime a dozen. A major cut above is the **Panadería Centeno** (open daily 6:30am-8:30pm), at the corner of Amazonas and C. Piño, which sells quality baguettes for s/1,500. For general supplies (cheese, peanut butter, etc.) try the *supermercado* next to **Restaurante Rodelú.**

Restaurant Rodelú (tel. 800-956), Av. Quito between Salcedo and Guayaquil. A little pricey, but food this good is hard to come by. Lonely for some English? This gringo spot will fill that void, popular for its warm, cozy atmosphere and hot-out-of-the-brick-oven pizza (medium s/12,500-18,000). Meat and chicken dishes s/11,000 and up. Open daily 7:30am-2:30pm and 5:30-9:30pm.

Restaurant Hostal Quilotoa (tel. 800-099), on the Panamerican Highway underneath the hotel of the same name. The eatery stays warm with the heat and scent of the fire, as the chickens do their slow methodical dance, each on its own spit. Filling portions of *arroz con pollo* (s/6,000), or *almuerzo* (s/5,000). Especially convenient if you're on the far side of the river. Open daily 8am-11pm.

Restaurante Chifa China, Av. 5 de Junio and Vela, a block from the market. One of several similar reasonably tasty Chinese places in Latacunga. Copious quantities of chow in the *mein* dishes (chicken with vegetable s/8,000, beef with pineapple s/10,000), but the soups (wonton s/5,000) and rice dishes (*arroz chop suey* s/10,000) are meals in themselves. Open daily noon-11pm.

El Coyote Loco, Av. Roosevelt and C. Marquez de Muenza (tel. 812-246), about 15min. outside of town. Ask in town for directions. The restaurant of choice for Latacungans, who flock to this upscale Mexican restaurant for a break from the usual *típicos.* Burritos, tacos, and everything else Mexican s/12,000-20,000. Open daily 5:30pm-10pm, though rumor has it that they may soon be open for lunch.

SIGHTS AND ENTERTAINMENT

Admittedly, most tourists coming to Latacunga are here to see sights outside of town—Volcán Cotopaxi, Laguna Quilotoa, and various other highland destinations. However, if you're here for the night, there are a few things to keep you busy. The **Molinos de Monserrant,** next to the waterfall at Vela near Maldonado, is the center of the province's **Casa de la Cultura** organization. Built by Jesuits way back in 1736 and remodeled in 1967, it now houses (among other things) a museum of ethnology. Unsure of what that entails? Well, if you're interested in dolls and antiquated stone mills, this is your heaven (admission s/1,000; open Tues.-Sat. 9am-noon and 2-5:30pm). The city also has its fill of parks, the coolest of which is **Parque Vicente León,** in the tourist area at Maldonado and Quito. Bordering this clean, green, blooming machine are several buildings of note. The **Municipal Building** is the worn brown structure that looks like it has seen its share of volcanic eruptions, the rather unspectacular **Government Building** is across the way on Quito, and the city's Cathedral is kitty-corner to the **Gubernación,** on Quito and Maldonado. The **Catedral** was first put up in the 17th century. After being slammed by many earthquakes and volcanic eruptions, it was restored in 1973. There are other impressive churches in Latacunga, such as the **Iglesia y Convento de Santo Domingo,** near Quito and Guayaquil. While you're there, you can check out the selection of colorful jackets and sweaters on sale at the artisan fair next door.

The **mercado** is by far the most noticeable sight in Latacunga; its mammoth offerings take up several blocks from the river to Av. Amazonas with bananas, super glue, Calvin Klein jeans, cow hooves, cow buttocks, cow heart, and (sorry, but there's no other way to describe it) yanked-open, spread-out, sledgehammered cow heads. The big day is Saturday, but this place is busy daily from about 7am-6pm.

Visitors here November 3-5th will have lots of stories to tell about the **Mama Negra** festival. The city's principal holiday, it's marked by the *macho* Latacunga men roaming the streets dressed up as black women. While you're at it, you could stick around for **Latacunga's Independence Day,** on November 11, commemorating the day Latacunga patriots defeated the Spanish royalists in 1820. This date is celebrated each year with parades, fairs, and bullfights. The Ecuadorian partying tradition can also be witnessed during the fiesta of **La Virgen de las Mercedes,** held September 23-24th.

■ Near Latacunga: The Latacunga Loop

To the west of Latacunga, this loop of less-touristed towns are a postcard maker's fantasy come true. The small villages are hidden away among the patchwork farms and vast, undeveloped jagged-rock faces of the Andean peaks. Hidden is the operative word—populated almost entirely by indigenous people, these towns aren't exactly well-trod tourist destinations. Visiting them is an excellent way to take a trip off-road and submerge yourself in a foreign world, but expect to be a pioneer of sorts in figuring your way. Hiking will probably be required on more distant trips, as the bus service to these out-of-the-way places is inconvenient and inadequate. However, buses are plentiful to the two closest towns, Saquisilí and Pujilí, popular for their indigenous markets on Thursday and Sunday respectively.

PUJILÍ AND ZUMBAHUA

The first step in the loop, **Pujilí,** is effectively a suburb of Latacunga. The town has recently been flattened by a major earthquake, so the town has one attraction: the **market,** which appears every Sunday at Rocafuerte and Pinchincha. There is frequent bus service to Pujilí from the corner of Av. 5 de Junia and M.A. Subia, one block from the Panamerican Highway (every 5min., 6:30am-8pm, 15min., s/800). There is nowhere to stay in Pujilí; you'd better head back to Latacunga for the night.

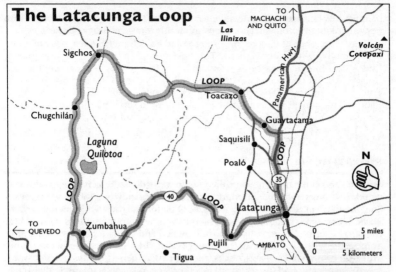

The Latacunga Loop

TO MACHACHI AND QUITO

Las Ilinizas

Volcán Cotopaxi

Sigchos

LOOP

Toacazo

Chugchilán

Guaytacama

Laguna Quilotoa

Saquisilí

Poaló

35

N

40

LOOP

LOOP

Latacunga

TO QUEVEDO

Zumbahua

Pujilí

TO AMBATO

Tigua

0   5 miles
0   5 kilometers

Alternatively, hop on a bus towards Quevedo that stops in **Zumbahua.** As Latacunga and Pujilí fade slowly into the distance (nothing changes quickly when the road is this bad), the scenery becomes increasingly barren and mountainous. Few communities interrupt the ride's natural splendor, until Zumbahua appears 90 minutes later. Travelers generally spend little time in Zumbahua; the only excitement that the town ever sees is the **Saturday market,** which some find dangerous and disturbing. Market festivities include alcohol, bullfighting, alcohol, colorful clothing, more alcohol, thoroughly blasted Quichuas, and villagers being carried off because their legs no longer hold them up. What they do not include is a significant, or even visible, tourist contingent. The town is poor and when the people are drunk, the outsider is at serious risk of being harassed. A group may provide some protection, but always be on guard. There is one "hotel": the **Residencial Oro Verde,** above a restaurant near the plaza, that only has two rooms and a common bathroom leaving some cleanliness to be desired (s/8,000 per person).

Get to and from Zumbahua on Transportes Cotopaxi's Latacunga-Quevedo bus (every 1½hr. until 8pm, 1½hr., s/4,000 back to Latacunga). Adventurous trekkers moving north along the loop to the lake of Quilotoa can catch the bus to Chugchilán.

LAGUNA QUILOTOA

Somebody could point out Laguna Quilotoa from the road and you still wouldn't notice the concealed lake. A closer look reveals a 360-degree ridge that towers over giant mountain slopes that plummet into a green-blue lagoon. Welcome to Quilotoa, the crater lake that remains where a colossal volcano once stood. A glance into this crater will probably justify whatever hardships you endured to get here, and then some. Hikes down to the lake take a half hour or less, but the hike back up is quite steep and may take more than double that time. A walk around the edge of the crater reputedly lasts about five hours—halfway around, you're already well on your way to Chugchilán. "Halfway around" assumes you start at the access road at the top of the crater, where three "hotels" in a little settlement compete for the scanty overnight crowd. Each place is run by a family that has its home adjacent to its guest rooms. The hosts rely on guests, tours, and art sales for their livelihood. Both **Cabañas Quilotoa** and **El Refugio de La Laguna** charge s/5,000 for a bed, and food prices are negotiable, depending on the meal size (s/3,000 for dinner is a good ballpark figure). The major consideration in choosing a place is *warmth,* since the temperature plummets at night; good clues are healthy fires and heavy blankets.

There are a range of options for getting to and away from Quilotoa, none of which is especially easy or convenient. The best option is to catch the Zumbahua-Chugchilán bus that passes right by Quilotoa. Failing that, a *camioneta* to Quilapungo will get you within a steep 3km walk of Quilotoa for a reasonable s/3,000. Trucks from nearby towns will take tourists to Quilotoa, but rates start at s/30,000. Hiking all the way from Zumbahua takes about five to seven hours. The hike crosses through the **Río Toachi Canyon** and cuts the 22km road trip between Chugchilán and Quilotoa significantly. Water and warm clothes are key on these walks—it gets cold up there and the weather can change quickly.

CHUGCHILÁN

At the far end of the highland loop, the *pueblo pequeño* of Chugchilán explodes with quirkiness. Quiet and far from tourist-oriented, it has only one tourist accommodation, but what an accommodation it is! Like Quilotoa and the wild Sierra scenery, the **Black Sheep Inn** is another prime reason to venture into the villages west of Latacunga. This up-and-coming hotel/hostel, owned and operated by a young couple from Seattle who have ingratiated themselves with the locals, is more an experience than an accommodation. Dogs, ducks, and the mascot herself, an *oveja negra* (black sheep), wander around the courtyard together. The indigenous townspeople stop to chat with the owners while alternative tunes play in the background, and the view—whoa, the view. Resting on a crop-green hillside, the Inn looks out at the canyon, Quilotoa, and a huge panorama of the mountains in the distance. The price of a room includes two delicious home-cooked vegetarian meals. To round out the Inn's organic features, the shared bathroom doubles as a compost pile. Follow the road through Chugchilán, about 0.5km past the plaza towards Sigchos; the sign and steep driveway are on the left. There is no phone and reservations are unnecessary; the owners promise they'll never turn people away (US$15 per person for a bed in a dorm room; doubles US$36; triples US$51; quads US$64).

The owners of the Black Sheep Inn can suggest some eccentric yet excellent excursions in the vicinity. Quilotoa is not far off, and the **Río Toachi Canyon** is even closer. Following your nose in the other direction will lead to a **European cheese factory,** established decades ago by a Swiss entrepreneur, and now run by local Ecuadorians. Some mysterious **Inca ruins** of the "circle in the ground" UFO variety lie three hours away by foot. For avid hikers, a one- or two-day trek leads into the **cloud forest** on the western slopes of the Andes, an amazing descent from about 12,000 to 2000 ft.

Chugchilán's location on the loop means that numerous buses pass through town and almost all of them stop. Several buses leave Latacunga for Chugchilán; the **La Iliniza** line has a bus leaving from Benavidez that goes via Sigchos (Sun.-Wed. and Fri., 11:30am, Sat. 10:30am; 4hr.; s/6,000). These buses pass through Saquisilí and can be caught there about one half hour after leaving Latacunga. On Thursday the bus departs directly from Saquisilí on account of the market (11am, 4½hr.). The **14 de Octubre** line goes to Chugchilán via Zumbahua and Quilotoa (Fri.-Sat., 10:30am, 4hr.). **Reina de Sigchos** also has another bus from Sigchos (every Wed. and Fri., 5am, 1hr.). To leave Chugchilán, simply hop on one of these buses as they pass through, or catch one of the painful early-bird buses (3am, plus Sun. at 6am, 3½hr., s/6,000). Check at the Black Sheep Inn for current bus info.

SIGCHOS AND SAQUISILÍ

Very few travelers see any more of Sigchos than what is visible from the windows of the buses that pass through. While there isn't really anything to do in town, it provides an alternative to Chugchilán for exploring the *páramo.* Perhaps because of the near complete absence of tourists, the people in town are quite hospitable to those that stop here. There are a couple of places to stay—the best is **Residencia Sigchos,** which provides comfortable mattresses and clean, shared baths for s/10,000 per person. There are a few restaurants in town that are run out of some local homes. The food is decent and cheap, but be prepared to share your table with kids doing homework, grandmothers darning socks, and other domestic types. Aside from the bus routes to Chugchilán, most of which pass through Sigchos, the village has its own bus schedule (9, 11am, and 1pm, s/4,000), leaving from Benavidez in Latacunga.

The reason hordes of people come to Latacunga in the first place is the acclaimed Thursday morning market of Saquisilí. Visit any other day of the week and find a quiet, ordinary village with no frills or bright hues. But come Thursday, Saquisilí explodes in living color, splashing its goods out among the various town plazas. Buses leave daily from Latacunga at Benavidez (every 10min., 5:30am-6:30pm, 20min., s/800), and on Thursday mornings they fill to capacity. So do Latacunga's hotels each Wednesday night, not to mention the **Salón Pichincha,** Av. Pichincha and Bolívar (tel. 721-247), in Saquisilí, which is even higher in demand. This cozy hotel has conscientious owners as well as hot water for its guests (singles s/10,000, doubles s/20,000). Unexpected guests probably have a chance at a room any night but Wednesday. For the big night, it's probably more fruitful to concentrate efforts on securing a place near Latacunga. **Buses** arrive and depart in the area of Pl. La Concordia and the principal avenue, Bolívar. The **police** (tel. 721-101), **hospital** (tel. 721-015), and **EMETEL** office (tel. 721-105) are off Bolívar near the buses.

■ Parque Nacional Cotopaxi

Situated only 14km to the northeast of Latacunga and 60km southeast of Quito, Cotopaxi National Park is dominated by the snow-capped monster, **Volcán Cotopaxi** (5897m), the tallest active volcano in the world. While many visitors come only to scale this mammoth chunk of now-hardened lava rock, the park offers more subtle pleasures as well. The *páramo* (highland plain) surrounding the peak is home to many of Ecuador's most unique species of animal life.

The park was established in 1975 after a startling study concluded that there were fewer than 10,000 **llamas** left in Ecuador. Since that time, the park has struggled to nurture and preserve the llama population, along with the rest of the Ecuadorian *páramo*. The park is hopping with **white-tailed deer,** who have made an impressive comeback under the watchful eyes of park management. Hot on their tails, literally, are the **Andean pumas,** whose numbers have slowly but steadily climbed since a low point in the mid-1970s. Other mammal species, seldom seen but still alive and well in the park, are the **Andean fox,** the **Andean spectacled bear,** and the **knee-high red brocket deer.** Though well-recognized by ornithologists the world over, the winged population of Cotopaxi fights for the attention of visitors. The park has received much attention as the last refuge of the endangered **Andean condor** (less than 100 remaining), but also nests such rarities as the **Andean hillstar,** the **Andean lapwing,** the **Andean gull,** the **great thrush,** and the tongue-twisting **carunculated caracara.**

Also a sanctuary for a certain two-legged mammal, Cotopaxi satisfies adventure-seekers who yawn at Quito's fast-paced life and bright lights. Without a doubt, the major adrenaline-inducing attraction of the park is the immense Volcán Cotopaxi. The first climber to reach Cotopaxi's rim was the energetic German Wilhelm Reiss in 1872. Since then, thousands of world-class mountaineers and adventurers have made the icy ascent to the snow-capped summit. The climb itself is not considered technically difficult—with a properly-qualified guide. Even inexperienced climbers can reach the summit, provided they are strong-willed and in good shape. Despite the technical facility of the climb, experienced climbers can also benefit from a guide's knowledge of the particularities and peculiarities of the ascent.

Expeditions to the 5900m summit begin from the **José Ribas refuge** (4800m) at around midnight or 1am, to insure hard-packed snow and safer conditions. It usually takes six to seven hours to reach the top, but only about two to three hours to return to the refuge. Due to the necessity of an early start, it is imperative to stay in the refuge the night before. Though basic, the 70-person shelter has bunk beds, clean water, and a gas oven. Visitors must bring their own heavy sleeping bags and nourishment. For the climb, bring plenty of water and fruit for energy. The absolute necessities for the ascent are plastic boots, crampons, an ice axe, a harness, gaiters, windpants, a head lamp, a heavy waterproof jacket, gloves, and a wool hat. A good general rule for clothing: three layers of clothing for the legs, four layers for the torso. Acclimatization, another vital prerequisite, should be taken seriously (see **Hot, Cold, and Altitude,** p. 20). A good acclimatization for Cotopaxi is a week in Quito, but an even better preparation is a couple days of hiking around the national park or an ascent up one of the smaller peaks.

For more information on climbing Cotopaxi, check out one of the travel agencies in Quito, which are especially abundant along Av. J. León Mera. Make sure your guide is certified by the **Ecuadorian Association of Mountain Guides** (ASEGUIM), the most respected association around. **Compañía de Guias,** Av. 6 de Diciembre 425 and Jorge Washington (tel./fax 504-773), in Quito, offers a two-day summit climb for around US$160 per person, complete with food, shelter, transportation, equipment, and an ASEGUIM-certified guide who speaks English, German, Italian, or French (open 9:30am-1pm and 3-6:30pm). **Safari Travel,** Calama 380 and León Mera (tel. 552-505; fax 223-381; email admin@safariec.ecx.ec), also provides experienced, ASEGUIM-approved mountain guides equipped with more languages than the Tower of Babel. Their two-day summit package averages around US$145 per person and includes everything but the US$6.50 admission into the park. Safari is open daily 9am-7pm.

Vertigo sufferers and those sane enough not to climb a 19,000 ft. ice cube can safely enjoy the park's lesser-known hiking and camping opportunities. The two campgrounds within the park are both good four-hour hikes from the entrance gate. Just follow the main road as it winds through the imported Monterrey Pine forest for about half an hour. A sign for campgrounds will be on the left, and a short jaunt leads to a campsite fit for a king. Most people stay in tents, but there is a standing structure with four walls and a concrete floor that could, by some standards, be considered a cabin (a mere s/2,000 per night). At least it has running water. This campground is close to the shore of the immense **Lake Limpiopungo,** but don't get out the fishing rods—it's against the rules to fish in the park. Up the road another 15 minutes is a second sign for campgrounds on the right. This campground is about as big as the other, and provides a neck-bending, awe-inspiring view of Mt. Cotopaxi. There is a s/2,000 cabin here also, but it lacks running water.

A tiny museum on the path up to the campgrounds is a tribute to the National Park, and is furnished with stuffed wildlife, a 3-D representation of the park, and wall-to-wall info on the history of Cotopaxi. Outside the museum, there is a helpful map of the park, which you can use to locate the park's other, lesser-known volcano, **Volcán Rumañahui** (4712m). There is a strenuous but rewarding four-hour hike from the museum to the base of Rumañahui. If you head back up the road toward Limpiopungo, you will reach the lake on your left, and you should see a stream running from the lake towards Rumañahui. Follow the hiking trail running along this stream until it becomes a heap of rocks—the top of the great Rumañahui. If you want to go further, you'll need a portable phone to call Safari or Compañía de Guias, because the rest of the way is treacherous. Although a shorter climb than Cotopaxi (only four to five hours), it is more technical and involves some rock climbing.

The best way to reach Cotopaxi is by bus from Quito. The *terminal terrestre* has various bus lines going past Cotopaxi, including **Transportes Latacunga Asofficiale** (every 10min., 6am-8pm, 1½hr., s/4,000). The buses will drop you off at the second, more southern entrance to the park, where there is a huge Cotopaxi sign. Those who risk hitchhiking say that it is fairly easy to catch a ride into the park from this point. If you plan on walking in, expect a two-hour trek to the entrance along a dusty, lonely road. Or you can take the bus 10 minutes farther to Lasso, or 25 minutes farther to Latacunga. In Lasso, taxis and trucks take passengers into the park. If you want to go all the way to the refuge, it'll cost around US$30, and you'll still need to hike about 30 minutes up from the parking lot. From Latacunga, trucks go to the refuge for around US$35; pick one up at Hotel Estambul. (Admission to the park s/20,000, under 13 s/10,000, residents s/2,000. Park open daily 7am-6pm.)

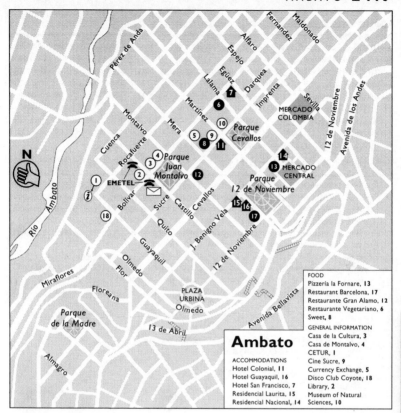

FOOD
Pizzería la Fornare, 13
Restaurant Barcelona, 17
Restaurante Gran Alamo, 12
Restaurante Vegetariano, 6
Sweet, 8

GENERAL INFORMATION
Casa de la Cultura, 3
Casa de Montalvo, 4
CETUR, 1
Cine Sucre, 9
Currency Exchange, 5
Disco Club Coyote, 18
Library, 2
Museum of Natural
Sciences, 10

Ambato

ACCOMMODATIONS
Hotel Colonial, 11
Hotel Guayaquil, 16
Hotel San Francisco, 7
Residencial Laurita, 15
Residencial Nacional, 14

■ Ambato

Nearly every Ecuadorian city claims to have miraculously survived some sort of natural catastrophe. Fires, earthquakes, volcanos—you name it, some town has lived through it. Ambato is no exception. In 1949, a serious earthquake shook the city into a pile of rubble. Instead of simply bouncing back to its previous glory, the new city far surpassed what it had been before. Many *ambateños* view the destruction of the old Ambato as the spark that fired up the spirit of the people. Half a century later, the modern mountain metropolis, resting at 2577m below the nearby peaks of Tungurahua and Chimborazo, still vibrates with this impassioned fresh start. *Ambateños* pride themselves on being productive, hard-working people who have continued the centuries-old tradition of farming the region's rich land, growing sugar cane, tobacco, coffee, and an extensive catalog of fruits and vegetables. Ambato's fertility has also broken ground in South American literature. Novelists **Juan Montalvo** and **Juan León Mera** hailed from here, as well as several other intellectual figures whose names now meet at the city's street corners and in its impressive museums. The development of tourism is evidenced by the recent proliferation of hotels in Ambato, along with a sprawling yet surprisingly sparkling spectacle of offices, apartments, and highways. Fiestas every November 12 commemorate Ambato's independence. In the month of February, the week before Carnival, the city celebrates the Festival of Fruit and Flowers, a holiday that only dates back to 1951. Like the city itself, the event is spirited, bountiful, and has yet to celebrate its Silver Anniversary.

ORIENTATION

Ambato extends far beyond any visitor's interest or immediate comprehension. The **terminal terrestre** and **train station** are both in the northern end of the city, about 2km from the *centro*. Ambato's more congested downtown area is linked to the transportation hub via **Avenida 12 de Noviembre,** which begins up the hill from the train tracks and runs south. A handful of hotels border the **Parque 12 de Noviembre.** Two other important parks are found in the downtown area: **Parque Juan Montalvo** (the center of the city's government offices and agencies) and **Parque Cevallos** (the departure spot for many local buses), bordered by a bustling commercial area. The entire downtown area is clustered within a five-by-five block area.

PRACTICAL INFORMATION

Tourist Information: The city is blessed with a **CETUR,** Guayaquil and Rocafuerte (tel. 821-800), in front of the Hotel Ambato. Located in an uphill, somewhat out-of-the way western corner, this office provides information on Ambato in a patient, light-hearted manner—but only in Spanish. Open Mon.-Fri. 8:30am-5pm.

English-Speaking Language Association: Centro Ecuatoriano Norteamericano de Ambato, Egüez 383 and Vela, 4th floor (tel. 822-137).

Travel Office: There is a wide choice of travel agencies, but a popular and convenient one is **Metropolitan Touring,** Rocafuerte and Montalvo (tel. 824-084), across the street from the post office. Open Mon.-Fri. 9am-1pm and 3-7pm.

Currency Exchange: Produbanco, Vela and Sucre (tel. 846-615). Open Mon.-Fri. 9am-6pm.

Trains: Terminal Ferroviaria, next to the bus station, has 2 trips every week: to **Quito** (Fri., 12:30pm, s/3,000) or **Riobamba** (Sat., 1:30pm, s/3,000).

Long Distance Buses: The **terminal terrestre** is to the north of downtown up Av. 12 de Noviembre. To: **Guayaquil** (every 30min., 7:15am-10:45pm, 5½hr., s/12,000); **Quito** (every 5min., 2hr., s/6,000); **Santo Domingo** (every 30min., 6:30am-6:30pm, 4hr., s/8,000); **Babahoyo** (every hr., 4am-4:15pm, 5hr., s/10,000); **Riobamba** (every 15min., 5:30am-7pm, 1hr., s/3,000); **Baños** (every 10min., 3am-9pm, 1hr., s/1,800); **Tena** (2pm, 8hr., s/17,000); **Puyo** (Tues.-Sat., 2pm, 10hr., s/22,000). Sun.-Mon., when the Baños road is open to Puyo, a cheaper, faster bus runs from Baños to the Oriente.

Local Buses: Buses to towns in the vicinity of Ambato depart from several places in the downtown area. From **Parque Cevallos,** buses depart every 15min. to **Ficoa, Atocha, Ingahurro,** and **Pinllo** (s/250). From **Parque La Merced,** at Av. Unidad Nacional and Colón a bit north of the *centro,* buses depart for **Píllaro** (every 15min., 6am-8pm, 30min., s/1,500). Buses to **Picaigua** leave from Av. Los Andes and Tomás Sevilla on the other side of Av. 12 de Noviembre (every 15min., 6:30am-6:30pm, 30min., s/400). The most popular nearby tourist destinations, Salasaca and Pelileo, are served from a "mini-terminal" on Carihuarazo in the suburb of Ferroviaria, farther up the hill from Av. 12 de Noviembre. To **Pelileo** (every 10min., 6:10am-6:10pm, 30min., s/1,000) via **Salasaca** (20min., s/800). Long-distance buses bound for Baños will also stop at these destinations en route.

Taxis: A trip across town costs about s/4,000. One taxi dispatch is **Cooperativa de Taxis Bolívar** (tel. 822-111).

Library: Biblioteca Municipal, Bolívar and Castillo, in the Municipal Building. Open Mon.-Fri. 9am-noon and 2:30-6pm, Sat. 9am-noon.

Public Market: One of the biggest in Ecuador, held on Mon. Partly indoors on Av. 12 de Noviembre between Martínez and Egüez; also spread along Cevallos and into other nearby areas. Active all other days as well, especially Fri.

Laundromat: Química Automática, Vela 432 and Quito (tel. 822-888). Open Mon.-Sat. 8am-6:30pm.

Pharmacy: Botica Bristol, Martínez 307 and Cevallos (tel. 822-015). Part of the *de turno* system (listed in that day's *Herald*).

Hospital: There are 2 options, the **Hospital de IESS,** Av. Los Capulies (tel. 821-805 or 844-719 through 723), and **Hospital Regional Ambato,** Av. Pasteur and Nacional (tel. 821-059).

Police: Atahualpa 568 (tel. 843-656 or 846-400).
Post Office: Correos Ecuador, Castillo and Bolívar (tel. 823-332). Has a Lista de Correos. Open Mon.-Sat. 7:30am-7:30pm.
Telephones: Two **EMETEL** (tel. 822-122) offices: next to post office, and a block away along Castillo towards Rocafuerte. Open daily 8am-12:30pm and 1-10pm.
Telephone Code: 03.

ACCOMMODATIONS

Hotel San Francisco, Egüez and Bolívar (tel. 821-739). Spacious rooms with private or shared bath, both with periodic spurts of hot water. Friendly, accommodating owners treat guests like family. Check beds when choosing rooms—all mattresses are not created equal. Rooms are s/15,000 per person, with bath, TV s/15,000.

Hotel Guayaquil, Mera (tel. 823-886), near Av. 12 de Noviembre, bordering on Parque 12 de Noviembre but hard to see from the sidewalk. Unlike the city of Guayaquil, the hotel is centrally located, friendly, and conscientiously cared for, providing stark substance and comfort instead of flash. But similar to the coastal beaches, water is hot. Rooms are s/10,000 per person, with bath s/20,000.

Residencial Laurita (tel. 821-377), on Mera between Vela and Av. 12 de Noviembre, truly screams of simplicity. Arranged around a courtyard with a scenic vista of clothes hanging out to dry, these stripped-down rooms contain walls and, yes, beds. The cost is bare-bones, too, with rooms s/8,000 per person.

Residencial Nacional, Lalama and Vela (tel. 843-820), near the indoor market. Separated from the more touristy part of the city, the Nacional is, quite simply, cheap. Padlocked doors open like castle entrances into less-than-royal rooms. Common bath with hot water, central lounge with TV. Rooms s/10,000 per person.

Residencia America, Av. Vela, near Mera. Run by yet another friendly *ambateño* family, rooms are simple but clean. The only furniture is your bed, but you're welcome to join the family watching TV in their living room. Common baths, hot water. Rooms are s/12,000 per person.

FOOD

Restaurant Barcelona, Mera and Av. 12 de Noviembre, next to Hotel Guayaquil. Complete with posters of the Eiffel Tower, either for the cosmopolitan European name or because the decorator never learned geography. The most costly dish at this late-night *comedor* is the *arroz con menestra* (s/6,000). Open daily until 4am.

Comida Familiar: Carmita de Taco (tel. 828-178), beside Hotel San Francisco. If this cozy restaurant looks like someone's living room, that's because it is. Carmita serves excellent *almuerzos* to the lucky few that find her home. She only cooks one dish each day; s/6,000 buys *sopa, arroz,* and *jugo.* Open daily noon-2pm.

Cafe de Cultura, on Castillo, is a haven for Ambato's young intellectuals. By day, they serve *almuerzos típicos* (s/5,000); at night, they shift to coffeehouse mode, with sandwiches involving ham and cheese in any combination (s/4,000), *tortas* (s/3,000-4,000), drinks (s/2,000-4,000). Poetry readings on Thurs. nights if your Spanish is up for it. Open Mon.-Wed. 9am-9pm, Thurs.-Fri. 9am-late, Sat. 9am-2pm.

Pizzería La Fornare, Lalama and Vela, near the central market area. A blast of heat from the brick oven greets guests to this economical Italian diner. Serves a selection of mini-pizzas (about s/5,000), and a good range of pasta, including spaghetti (s/5,500) and lasagna (s/5,000). Takeout available. Open daily noon-10pm.

Restaurante Faraon (tel. 821-252), on Bolívar, between Egüez and Lalama. Locals are drawn by the *comida ecuatoriana,* served in a cavernous dining room covered with Panamanian tourism posters. So where does the Egyptian theme fit in? "We liked the name," says the owner with a shrug. *Desayunos* s/6,000, *almuerzos* s/12,000, *cenas* s/7,000. Open daily 8-9am, noon-3pm, and 6-10pm.

SIGHTS

By far the most arresting sight in Ambato is the **Museum of Natural Science** in the **Instituto Técnico Superior Bolívar** (ITSB), Sucre 839 (tel. 827-395), on the Parque Cevallos, between Lalama and Martínez. Though the museum's admission is a bit steep, the quality of the extensive exhibits rises to the occasion. It starts slow, with black-and-white photos of the Sierra at the beginning of the century (including a Cotopaxi eruption), a truly solid geology display, and some indigenous musical instruments and clothes. The highlight of the museum, however, is its seemingly endless collection of preserved animals, all but two of which were found in Ecuador. Jaguars, birds, tarantulas, and snakes all preserve their final contorted poses, some from inside the murky confines of a glass jar. This excellent exhibit climaxes in the back with the stuff bad dreams are made of—unfortunate **freak animals** such as a two-headed goat and cyclops dog, whose frozen forms are definite nightmare material (open Mon.-Fri. 8am-noon and 2-6pm; admission s/5,000).

The city also provides plenty of opportunities to pay homage to its literary hero, **Juan Montalvo** (see **Literature**, p. 56). First there's the park that bears his name, well-groomed with bushes carved into topiary shapes. Next to the park, on the corner of Bolívar and Montalvo, is our hero's birthplace and lifelong home, the **Casa de Montalvo.** The various rooms of this open-air museum/mausoleum astound with the pure repetition of Montalvo renderings. On most walls is a painting of the man, next to it another, and next to that yet another. Interwoven with these images are long articles and captions with tons of interesting information about both Ambato's and Ecuador's past. The spacious room with the coffin raised up on an altar-stage marks the final resting place of the man, the myth, and the legend (open Mon.-Fri. 9am-noon and 2-6pm; admission s/1,000).

The Trash Mouth

So you're finally starting to settle in. You've reluctantly accepted that three vehicles can fit across most any highway when necessary, and so you've relieved yourself of that vigilant, terrified gaze each time the bus driver moves to pass. But as a stranger in a strange land, the most violent culture shock probably still agonizes you: What is the *deal* with all those **clown trashcans?** In front of ice-cream shops, restaurants, and food stores, their eyes follow like a sinister painting, their gaping mouths hungry for more garbage. The original mastermind behind this ubiquitous shape lives just 7km south of Ambato in the suburb of Huachi Chico. A self-proclaimed artist, 80-year-old **Victoria Pasmiño,** the creator of the *basurero de payaso,* came up with the colorful trashcan some 25 years ago. Though her name is far from familiar, her art is arguably the most recognized in the country. Why has she chosen garbage cans as her medium of expression? Simple: to try and teach the children of Ecuador to put their trash where it belongs. A great idea that has yet to fully penetrate the Ecuadorian mindset 25 years later. Interested in starting a trend back home? Señora Pasmiño sells the clowns, as well as alligator and Mickey Mouse heads, for s/65,000 apiece. But make sure you're getting the real thing. By now, imitations of Basmino's genius are everywhere.

Don't worry—the Montalvo-fest isn't over yet. A couple of kilometers from the *centro* lies the **Quinta de Montalvo,** Juan's country residence. Located in the suburb of Ficoa, it can be reached by taking the bus marked with that destination, leaving from the Parque Cevallos every 15 minutes. This is only one of three homes of dead *ambateño* celebs outside the downtown area. There are also the **Quinta de Mera** (home of **Juan León Mera**) and **Quinta de La Liria** (home of **Nicolas Martínez,** renowned mountain climber), located near each other in the suburb of Atocha (both open Mon.-Fri. 9am-4:30pm). For both, take the Atocha bus from Parque Cevallos.

Ambato's headquarters for the arts, the **Casa de la Cultura,** Bolívar between Montalvo and Castillo (tel. 820-338), is next to the Casa de Montalvo. The third floor houses free exhibits that change every other month (open Mon.-Fri. 9am-1pm and 3-6pm). It also organizes entertaining events, such as musical concerts, which are listed in the *Herald.* Across the way on Montalvo looms Ambato's **cathedral,** the eyesore of the city's skyline with a worn, dirty modern dome and jungle-gym spire.

ENTERTAINMENT

Once upon a time there were six movie theaters in Ambato. Then VHS took over, and slowly the theaters struck bottom and were converted into *iglesias evangélicas*. Listen to numerous *ambateños* recount this story, or go to the **Cine Sucre,** at Martínez and Mera, to witness the sad fate of the Ambato movie palaces. The city's only remaining theater, Sucre screens XXX films to a loyal clientele of middle-aged *ambateño* men every Saturday and Sunday.

Fortunately, Ambato's clubs haven't followed the same path. One popular nightclub is the **Disco Club Coyote,** Bolívar 2057 and Guayaquil (tel. 827-886), in the city's western corner. Usually a restaurant and bar, on weekends the Coyote powers up the disco ball and blasts everything from salsa to rap to techno for a young, somewhat wealthy crowd. Beers are s/5,000 (open Fri.-Sat. 10pm-2am). The rest of Ambato's nightlife sits along Av. Olmedo, just above Parque 12 de Noviembre. A popular spot is the **Bufalo Cervecero,** Olmedo 681 and Mera (tel. 841-685), which opens its doors to an 18-and-over crowd. Plays all kinds of music, but leans toward techno. Fridays and Saturdays are most crowded (open Mon.-Sat.; cover s/12,000).

■ Near Ambato

The road to Baños is so well traveled that nothing remains untouched. Because of the tourist-magnet status of that hot springs hang-out, the innocent bystanding towns southeast of Ambato have also felt tourism's heavy hand. **Salasaca** is little more than a plaza along the road with an artisan fair (daily 8am-6pm), that is busiest on Sundays. The Quechua *indígenas* who live here specialize in making woven ponchos and tapestries, with designs rich, attractive, and inexpensive enough to tempt the budget browser. The town has its own fiesta in January and a well-known Corpus Cristi celebration in early summer. **Pelileo,** a significantly larger town with a rather turbulent history, is 10 minutes farther east of Salasaca. Destroyed by earthquakes in 1698, 1797, 1840, 1859, and 1949, it now rests several kilometers from its original spot. After Ambato, it has the most important market in the province of Tungurahua, held every Saturday. Buses to Pelileo (every 10min., 6:10am-6:10pm, 30min., s/1,200) via Salasaca (20min., s/800) leave from the Ambato suburb of Ferroviaria. Baños-bound buses, leaving Ambato's *terminal terrestre,* also stop at these towns en route.

The smaller towns farther from Baños are less visited and more traditional. **Picaigua,** only a 15-minute bus ride southeast of Ambato, demands respect for the jackets that the locals sew and sell. The second half of January is a continuous party here, marking the festival of patron saint San Isidro. The town of **Patate,** 5km northeast of Pelileo, was founded in 1570, later destroyed by the 1797 earthquake, and finally canonized in 1973. Set in a fertile valley, the town is a fruit-producing marvel, chugging out grapes, peaches, and oranges, among other juicy fruits. Both villages can be reached via the Salasaca/Pelileo buses.

North of Ambato, the 2803m-high **Píllaro** looks down on its neighboring metropolis without any envy. This village of abundance bursts with agriculture, apples, and cattle galore. There's a big market on Sunday, but unlike other traditional villages, that's not even the most intriguing draw. Píllaro is the gateway to the Llanganates mountain chain, where the emperor Atahualpa supposedly buried his treasure. Nobody has found it—yet. Less materialistic travelers can simply enjoy the value of the landscape and wait for the brand-new **Parque Nacional Llanganates** to become more accessible to visitors.

▨ Baños

The undisputed draw of this tiny highland town, and the reason people flock here from all over the world, is the prospect of a leisurely soak in the legendary **baños.** These pools of water, some steaming and others just relaxingly warm, are geothermally heated by the same fiery god that created nearby **Volcán Tungurahua.** The baths have worked wonders for the town. Many locals and tourists sport the demeanor of a recently emerged springs-soaker—loose and relaxed. Other aspects of the town only add to the already utopian ambience. A wall of neighboring green mountains, including Tungurahua, seems to shelter the town from the turmoil beyond. The mountains loom so high and so close that, at night, the lights on top could easily be mistaken for planes flying overhead. As word spreads about Baños's stunning natural beauty, this quintessential Ecuadorian dazzler has adapted to harvest as many as possible of the tourist dollars that flow through its streets. American and European restaurants with multilingual menus are the norm. On every block, not only hotels but tour companies eagerly vie for attention, with postcard-perfect photos of past expeditions. Resting in the eastern flank of the Andes, the town's popularity comes not just from its own attractions, but from its status as a jumping-off point for jungle tours and other exotic excursions. The conveniences are here because the gringos are here, bearing witness to the industry that over decades has risen up to greet them and has blossomed so fully that at times it is difficult to envision local life here. But there *is* a "normal" Ecuadorian town under the tourist Baños—it's just hard to see. Children head off to school in uniform, worshippers fill the *basílica* at mass, and in this land of traveler's checks, people still beg in the streets.

ORIENTATION

Baños is a simple town to get the hang of. The main highway between Ambato and Puyo runs east-west across the northern end of town. From the bus station on the highway, it is about three blocks south along **Maldonado** to the **Parque Central,** which lies between the consecutive east-west streets **Rocafuerte** and **Ambato** (the principal street in Baños). These parallel ways also form the sides of the **Parque Basílica,** marked by the Lego-looking church on Ambato, and the **market area.** Lots of the town's action is along **Ambato** between the two parks, though plenty of stores, restaurants, and hotels can be found several blocks away as well.

PRACTICAL INFORMATION

Tourist Office: There is no official CETUR in Baños, but numerous tourist businesses (hotels, restaurants, drug stores, etc.) offer reliable info.

Currency Exchange: Banco del Pacífico, Montalvo (tel. 740-162), between Av. 16 de Diciembre and Alfaro. Open Mon.-Fri. 9am-5pm, Sat. 9am-1:30pm. **Banco del Tungurahua,** Ambato and Maldonado (tel. 740-414), on Parque Central. Open Mon.-Fri. 9am-2pm, Sat. 9am-1pm. Both change cash and traveler's checks.

Buses: The **terminal terrestre** takes up a block between Maldonado and the main road to Ambato. Buses sally forth to several key destinations from the parking lot in front and from the station's border streets. To: **Quito** (every 30min., 3am-7:30pm, 3½hr., s/4,000); **Ambato** (every 10min., 3am-7:30pm, 1hr., s/2,500); **Riobamba** (every hr., 6am-5pm, 1hr., s/3,000). The scenic road to **Puyo** has been under construction for a while; the official date of completion came and went in February 1997, so locals aren't holding their breath. Currently, the road is open to buses on Sun. and Mon. only (every hr., 5am-9pm, 2hr., s/7,000).

Taxis: Baños is quite walkable, but one dispatch is **16 de Diciembre** (tel. 740-416).

Rental Info: Every hotel, cafe, drug store, and tour agency in Baños seems to rent some mode of transport for the tourist traffic. **Sierra Selva Adventures,** Maldonado and Oriente (tel. 740-298), charges the going rates in town (bikes s/15,000 per day; horses s/60,000 for 4hr., including a guide). Be aware that much of what is for rent is of lesser quality—shop around.

English Bookstore: Used books in English at **Café Hood,** Av. 16 de Diciembre (tel. 740-516), between Rocafuerte and Martínez. Open Wed.-Mon. 8am-9pm.

Library: Biblioteca Municipal (tel. 740-458), in the **Municipio,** on Rocafuerte at Halflants. Open Mon.-Fri. 8am-noon and 2-6pm.

Public Market: Mostly in a building boxed in by Rocafuerte and Ambato, Alfaro and Halflants. Open daily 8am-6pm. **Sunday** is the biggest day.

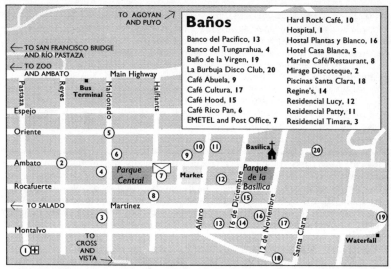

Banco del Pacifico, 13
Banco del Tungarahua, 4
Baño de la Virgen, 19
La Burbuja Disco Club, 20
Café Abuela, 9
Café Cultura, 17
Café Hood, 15
Café Rico Pan, 6
EMETEL and Post Office, 7

Hard Rock Café, 10
Hospital, 1
Hostal Plantas y Blanco, 16
Hotel Casa Blanca, 5
Marine Café/Restaurant, 8
Mirage Discoteque, 2
Piscinas Santa Clara, 18
Regine's, 14
Residencial Lucy, 12
Residencial Patty, 11
Residencial Timara, 3

Laundromat: One of the benefits of a town that caters to travelers is that laundry services are prevalent, especially in hotels. **Hostal Plantas y Blanco** charges s/ 9,900 for a medium load and has next-day service.

Public Toilets: At the Parque Central on Halflants, across from the post office.

Pharmacy: Farmacia Baños (tel. 740-237), on Ambato between Alfaro and Halflants. Open daily 8:30am-12:30pm and 1-9pm. Part of *de turno* rotation.

Hospital: Pastaza and Montalvo (tel. 740-443).

Police: (tel. 740-443), on Oriente, 3½ blocks west of the Parque Central.

Post Office: Correos Central (tel. 740-901), on Halflants between Ambato and Rocafuerte, bordering the Parque Central. Has Lista de Correos. Open Mon.-Fri. 8am-noon and 1-6pm, Sat. 8am-2pm.

Telephone: EMETEL, Rocafuerte and Halflants (tel. 740-104), on Parque Central. Open Mon.-Fri. 9am-8:45pm, Sat.-Sun. 9am-1:45pm.

Telephone Code: 03.

ACCOMMODATIONS

Thanks to the high demand for lodging, Baños offers great budget accommodations. The lowest-end places have comfortable beds with clean, shared baths. The tier above includes private bath and several other spiffy services, like a complimentary breakfast. Hotels virtually pile on top of each other along Av. Ambato, and there are also dense patches on Montalvo in the direction of the pools.

Hostal Plantas y Blanco, Martínez and Av. 12 de Noviembre (tel. 740-044), a block off the Parque Basílica. The French owner holds the secret behind this popular choice, and its name as well. Simply calling it a lodging would be a severe understatement. Aside from the good location, daily cleaning, and private hot water baths, there's a slew of other services. Laundry service, phones, fax, storage, and most importantly, early morning "purifying" steam baths. Rooftop terrace bar/restaurant (open 7:30am-10:30pm). Loads of American movies, with TV and headphones (s/3,000). Dollars exchanged from cash or traveler's checks at rates promised to be better than the bank's. US$4 per person; with bath US$5.

Residencial Tímara, Maldonado and Martínez (tel. 740-599), 2 blocks south of Parque Central along Maldonado. A reliable hotel on the budget level, it includes plain rooms, a clean communal bath blessed with hot water, a sink for washing clothes, and a kitchen at your money-saving disposal. Owners are conscientious about maintaining their positive reputation. Rooms are s/10,000 per person.

Hostal Los Nevados (tel. 740-673), right near Parque Basílica; from Ambato, take the first left past Av. 12 de Noviembre. Los Nevados seems to have sprung up in the hopes of competing with Plantas y Blanco, and is doing a good job at that. Clean rooms with private baths (with hot water), travelers' message board, friendly atmosphere, and laundry services, all for the absurdly low price of s/12,000 per person.

Residencial Lucy, Rocafuerte and Av. 16 de Diciembre (tel. 740-466), just west of Parque Basílica. Do you want to pet my monkey? That's the operative question at Lucy, where clean rooms come with or without private bath, hot water either way. A restaurant runs out front, and in the courtyard Pepe the monkey yanks his chain every which way but loose. Rooms are s/10,000 per person, with bath s/15,000.

FOOD

Like the hotels and just about everything else in Baños, the restaurants have been molded especially for the tourist. There are *comedores, chifas, restaurantes típicos,* and they're all cheap! Even better, a lot of travelers with incredible culinary skills have liked the town so much that they've stayed and set up superb restaurants. Avoid the temptation to stick to the few tourist-packed cafes—while they are certainly good, travelers looking a little further will be justly rewarded.

Restorante Scaligeri, Calle E. Alfaro near Ambato. Run by 3 Italians—to make pasta this good, you'd have to be. Homemade *tagliatelle,* just like Mama used to make, with peas and tomato sauce (s/11,000); *Penne all'arrabiata* (s/8,000) is also wonderful; the list just goes on. Open daily noon-midnight.

Café Hood, Av. 16 de Diciembre (tel. 740-516), between Martinez and Montalvo, will be moving 2 blocks down the street to Martinez and Alfaro in early 1998, to a location that might even be big enough to handle all its customers. The only ones actually speaking Spanish here are the waitresses. An international selection of tourists happily consume quality vegetarian incarnations of international cuisine. 'Hindu plate' (s/7,000) seems particularly popular. Open Wed.-Mon. 8am-9pm.

Café Rico Pan, Ambato and Maldonado (tel. 740-387), on Parque Central. The *pan* is definitely *rico*—selection of fresh breads baked daily, starting at s/500 for a whole wheat roll. Breakfast, Italian lunches, and dinners available. *Penne* with bacon, mushrooms, and tomato s/10,000.

Mariane Café/Restaurant, Halflants and Rocafuerte (tel. 740-911). Another entry in the 'authentic cuisine of the world' category. Mariane sits and eats while her French husband cooks superb *provençal* cuisine. You might be tempted to have seconds, if the servings weren't so damn big. Locally grown trout with tons of vegetables s/15,000; beef stew s/15,000. Open Mon. and Wed.-Sat. noon-10:30pm.

Café 'El Artesano,' next to Hostal Plantas y Blanco. Possibly Baños' most sophisticated cafe, packed with the requisite *artesanía*. Not so great after a long day of hiking—it will take several 'large falafel plates' (s/10,800) to fill you up. 7-course menu for the culinarily sophisticated (s/15,800). Open Mon.-Sat. 5:30-9:30pm.

SIGHTS

Baños is one big sight. The tourist magnets begin at the hot spring pools and radiate outwards to the volcanoes, the Oriente, and beyond. There are three **baños** in town. The locals have the right idea—they soak themselves in the salubrious springs at sunrise. Tourists who take a dip later miss the splendor of daybreak over the Andes. The pools are quietest early in the week, busiest on Fridays and Saturdays.

The most heavily touristed *baño* is the **Baño de la Virgen** (tel. 740-462), at the eastern end of Montalvo. A waterfall cascades down the mountainside into this pool, but it's really the crowds and taxis that make it a bit conspicuous. Several murky brown pools, reputedly cleaned daily, are filled with the legendary hot healing waters (open daily 4:30am-5pm, must leave by 6pm; admission s/3,000, children s/1,500). A block away, at Montalvo and Santa Clara, the **Piscinas Santa Clara** (tel. 740-915), are much more a local thing than their not-so-pure virgin neighbor. In addition to the warm or cool volcanic water, the complex also includes a gym, sauna, and a disco for dancing (all services s/10,000, pool only s/5,000). The third pool, **El Salado** (tel. 740-493), is a

On the Trail of Don Sergio

It seems that almost every visitor to Ecuador comes home with at least a few stories of the miracles performed by Ecuadorian auto mechanics. Following in this grand tradition of tinkerers, an old man named Don Sergio decided in the late 1970s to build his own car. Seventeen years later, it was finished, and in it, a 68-year-old Don Sergio set out to travel the countryside. Constructed mostly of scrap metal and old pieces of wood, Sergio's car resembles an old corrugated shack, and with a top speed of 5 km per hour, it isn't much faster. But that's OK, he's not in any hurry; he simply enjoys the freedom of traveling the road and seeing the world at his own pace. When the car breaks down, as it frequently does, Don Sergio simply parks on the side of the road for however long it takes for him to fix the problem. With his toothless grin and wild, white beard, the man is as conspicuously strange as his mechanical creation, and has attracted national and even international attention. Some people consider him to be a genius; others think he's crazy...he's probably at least a little of both.

15-minute walk or a 5-minute bus ride from the *centro*. Head west up the hill on Martínez, then cross a creek and follow the road until hotel signs beckon you to take a left (there is no sign for El Salado itself). That's El Salado, and the pools with the same name are at the end of the road. Cleaned each day, the six pools include one cold, three hot, and two scalding (open daily 4:30am-5pm, must leave by 5:40pm).

If your skin has pruned beyond a healthy level, Baños has many other worthwhile sights. The **basílica,** Ambato and Av. 12 de Noviembre, imposes its strange zebra-like form upon the backdrop of the city. The church was built in honor of the great Virgen de Aguas Santos, displayed in all her neon-lighted glory inside the church. There are many stories of exactly how this plaster sculpture began working her miracles. The official version is depicted in one of the church's many murals. Apparently, in 1773, during a religious procession, Volcan Tungurahua suddenly threatened to blow its top yet again. The people of Baños, in a fit of religious fervor, prostrated themselves before the image of the virgin that they had been parading around the plaza. The eruption came to a sudden halt, and the rest, as they say, is history. The murals of the church illustrate the many miracles that the virgin has since performed to assist those that incite her name in moments of crisis. She has saved *Bañeros* from every type of natural disaster, even a foreign tourist whose driver drove off a cliff after a visit to Baños. Seems to make the words *'Salvami Virgen de agua santo!'* worth remembering for those long bus rides through the Andes.

The **San Martín Zoo,** a 20-minute walk on the road west to Ambato, detains its animal residents on the mountainside above the **Cascada Ines María.** The magnificent entranceway is a short bridge under which canyon walls plummet. With a professed mission to conserve, educate, and rehabilitate (though the key word seems to be 'confine') the private **Ecozoológico** houses condors, jaguars, roaming tapirs, and rock-like tortoises, among other animals (open 7am-6pm; admission s/3,000, children s/1,500). Buses to the zoo leave from Alfaro at the market (s/400).

There is more to Baños's art scene than the rows of identical *artesanía* shops lining every street. For the real thing, visit Carlos Moreta's **Taller de Arte,** on Montalvo, just past the Hotel Palace. He's usually working on something interesting (masks, painting, sculpture) with an *artesanía* bent. If he's not around, you can talk to his brother and apprentice, who is also the bartender at the Bamboo Salsateca (see **Entertainment** below). A slightly more off-beat artform is practiced by a couple of women in town. At **El Arte con Natura,** on the corner of Martinez and 16 de Diciembre, amateur entomologists may browse among the extensive collection of **mounted insects,** ranging from the bizarre to the beautiful.

The steep, green hills surrounding Baños are visible from anywhere in town and beg to be hiked in. To do the standard first hike, follow Calle Maldonado toward the mountainside. Where the road ends, a path leads to the illuminated **cross** on top of the hill. From here you can count the number of gringos per block as the city appears beneath you. To get away from the tourist scene in Baños, you need not go far. A wonderful walk begins at the dirt road on your right just before you enter El Salado (see above). Follow the path beside the river, which has views of the forest and the patchwork of farms across the valley. Continue until you get tired, then turn around and walk back (there is no real endpoint—the hill you're climbing ends at the summit of Tungurahua). A more relaxing stroll heads to the **Granja Ecológica** (organic farm) of Agosto Muñoz, about 20 minutes outside of town. Just follow Av. 12 de Noviembre past the Basílica, and continue until you see the *Granja*'s smiling chicken waving on your left. Sr. Muñoz sincerely loves visitors and will be happy to show you around.

For excursions to places both nearby and not-so-near, the rental possibilities are comprehensive and ubiquitous (see **Practical Information,** p. 118). Transportation to specific destinations? Guides for a day, a week, or a month? No problem—everyone is eager and willing to take your money. Dozens of tour agencies pack the streets of Baños; just keep in mind that relatively few of these are legitimately registered agencies and serious problems have been reported with a number of them. Longer, more distant excursions can be a sizeable investment, and justifiably so, since they may be the highlight of an Ecuadorian experience. One reputable business is **Rainforestur** (tel. 740-743; fax 740-743), right off the Parque Central. General manager Santiago Herrera sets up trips to the mountains (Tungurahua, Cotopaxi, or Chimborazo), the Galápagos, and the Oriente. Jungle packages come in many shapes and sizes (US$45 per person per day for a minimum of 4 days). All tours are led by guides with specific experience on that particular river or mountain. Rainforestur also rents bikes and horses (open daily 8am-8pm).

ENTERTAINMENT

In spite of Baños's 2am closing law, the town has some of the wildest nightlife in Ecuador. After dinner, tourists wander across the street from Café Hood to **Bamboo Salsateca.** Not much *salsa* going on here—mainly a lot of foreigners getting drunk. When the new **Café Hood** is finished, its spacious patio will no doubt dominate the night life scene as well. If your evening plans include the search for a disco ball, try the **Mirage Discotheque** (tel. 740-381) or **La Burbuja Disco Club** (tel. 740-520), but you may be dancing alone (both open Tues.-Sat. around 8pm).

Plenty of bars provide the opportunity to meet other travelers or hang out with friendly Ecuadorians, minus the disco ball. One is **Tequila,** on Ambato between Alfaro and Av. 16 de Diciembre. Another, the **Hard Rock Café,** on Alfaro between Ambato and Oriente, probably awaits a lawsuit for trademark infringement. *Peñas,* like the one at the restaurant **El Marquez,** are excellent places to settle back and take in the authentic sounds of *música folklórica.*

While the **cine** is currently next to the Basílica, it will be moving to the lower level of the new Café Hood entertainment complex in 1998. It will continue to show the same high quality 'art' films, and possibly house performing arts of all kinds.

■ Parque Nacional Sangay

Come to Parque Nacional Sangay, where lava streams and the tapir run side-by-side. This unwieldy 517,765-hectare (over 5000 sq. km) park sprawls south from Baños through five Ecuadorian provinces, falling from jagged Andean ridges in the west to the Amazon River basin in the east. The mountainous portion of the park boasts three of Ecuador's 10 highest peaks, including two active volcanoes. Excursions to Sangay's snow-capped summits and virgin forests are less commercialized than those to Chimborazo or Cotopaxi, and are virtual pioneering expeditions through relatively undiscovered and resplendent lands. With altitudes ranging from 5319m (17,446ft.) on the peak of Volcán Altar, to 900m (3000ft.) in the Amazon basin, much of the amazing landscape is simply impossible to traverse. This inaccessibility, combined with the park's main objective (to protect and conserve), bars visitors from reaching some of Sangay's more remote areas. First founded as a reserve in 1979, the park shelters a selection of flora and fauna almost as diverse as the geography, and includes such rare and strange specimens as the endangered **Andean tapir** *(Tapirus pinchaque),* also known as the *canta de monte.*

INEFAN, the Parque Nacional's administration, is a tremendous resource for those planning to explore the park. In addition to providing info, the staff offers advice for finding guides. They also give free rides from the Riobamba office to the three park entrances at **Alao, Pondoa,** and **Candelaria.** For more info, contact them at the Riobamba office, listed in **Riobamba Practical Information,** p. 124.

The park's unreachable areas may fascinate, but the accessible ones are nothing to scoff at. Sangay is divided into two sections—the *zona alta,* in the Sierra (1500-5319m), and the *zona baja,* in the Oriente (900-1500m). The *zona alta* contains the Parque Nacional's main attractions, and its entrance points are easily accessible from Baños or Riobamba. The four main sites in Parque Sangay's *zona alta* are the relaxing **El Placer** and the towering fire-spewers, **Volcán Tungurahua** (5016m), **Volcán Altar** (5319m), and the namesake itself, **Volcán Sangay** (5230m).

One of least difficult snow climbs in Ecuador, the young **Volcán Tungurahua** is technically easy but physically arduous. This 10th-highest peak in Ecuador was most recently volcanically active from 1916 to 1925. The two-day excursion begins at **Pondoa,** at the base of the mountain, from where it is about a four-hour hike to the **Santos Ocaña refugio** (3800m). The shelter (about s/15,000 per person) is equipped with a gas stove and straw mats, but you should bring your own food, toilet paper, and matches. Staying in the *refugio* is imperative, as the four-hour ascent to Tungurahua's summit must begin at 2am, when snow is hardest. Trails can be muddy, especially during the June-August rainy season. Crampons, ice axes, ropes, and experience are necessary for the climb. Non-climbers can make Tungurahua into a daytrip and simply hike to the *refugio* and back. From Riobamba, INEFAN has a one-hour free shuttle to Pondoa. From Baños, various tour agencies offer rides to the climb's starting point (s/5,000).

One of the most active volcanoes in the world, **Volcán Sangay** constantly spews ash and smoke to make sure the world doesn't forget it. This lava-dripping peak has three deep craters way up top. The park's mammoth namesake requires a six-day trip at minimum: two and a half days hiking each way, and one day for the climb. Begin the hike up Sangay from the entrance at **Alao,** on the western side of the park. Hiring a guide is a must, at least for the start of the climb. In Alao, you can find a guide (about s/20,000 per day) and a mule for your luggage and equipment (about s/20,000-25,000 per day). You'll also need all the proper hiking and mountain-climbing equipment, plus clothing and six to eight days worth of food and water. Stock up in a Baños or Riobamba supermarket; there's not much in Alao. It is dangerous to climb all the way up to Sangay's crater, as you might get in the fiery path of all that spewed ash and lava. Experience is a must, and visitors should only climb as far as guides recommend. INEFAN rides from Riobamba to Alao leave as early as 4am—call to check definite times. INEFAN officials can give advice on equipment and help you find a guide.

El Altar (Los Altares), the highest mountain in the park, collapsed in 1460 and is now partially covered by glaciers. Accessible from yet another park entrance at **Candelaria** (a 45min. free ride from INEFAN in Riobamba), this eight-hour climb to the crater is similar to the two-day Tungurahua ascent, though there is no worthwhile daytrip to a *refugio*. Prices are similar to those of other trips, and guides are readily available in Candelaria (INEFAN officials will assist you). Again, equipment is needed for the climb to the crater. Camping is possible in a cave near the crater (ask guides for help); you can also stay overnight at the park entrance near Candelaria.

El Placer is a relatively low, swampy area with *aguas termales* for bathing. There is a *refugio* with amenities for staying overnight, but most just make this into a long daytrip, departing for Alao at daybreak (INEFAN leaves at 4am) and returning at dusk. **Atillo,** a picturesque lagoon, is a two-hour drive (free from INEFAN, 8am), and also the head of a path crossing the park from the Andes to **Macas** in the Oriente, the best means for discovering the true diversity of the park's terrain. Some amazing species populate the park; the Andean tapir, visible from the Atillo and El Placer areas, is found nowhere else in the world. Plant and animal stalkers in the know head to **Playa**

THE CENTRAL CORRIDOR

de **Sangay** and **El Palmar** for their observational kicks. Others take a walk on the wild side of the Oriente by heading to **Culebrillas** and the **Lagunas de Sardmayacu** (*zona baja*) in the never-ending quest for still more jaguar and bear sightings. Both places are accessible from Palora and Macas (see **Jungle Tours from Macas,** p. 243).

The admission fee at any entrance to the park is s/20,000 for tourists, s/2,000 for locals. The Riobamba INEFAN offers friendly and extremely useful assistance (as usual) in finding a guide, as does SAEC in Quito, with trip reports and info on recommended guides (see **Useful Organizations,** p. 1).

■ Riobamba

Known as the "Sultan of the Andes," Riobamba (pop. 120,000) needs no orchidaceous show of regalia to prove that it is master of its domain. Tranquil and relatively tourist-free, this quintessential Andean city will allow you to immerse yourself in Ecuadorian life without the fast pace and possible dangers of a major metropolis. Cobblestone streets weave in and out of three plazas and five parks, including the **Parque 21 de Abril,** with its awe-inspiring views of snow-capped Volcán Chimborazo and neighboring El Altar and Tungurahua. These towering volcanoes keep watch over a city that bears the scars of its tremulous past. After an earthquake in 1797, the entire city, then the capital of Ecuador, was moved to its present site on a highland valley plain. As a result, the city's oldest architecture is neoclassical with one notable exception; the **catedral** on Velez and Av. 5 de Junio was transported stone-by-stone from its pre-quake location. The past 200 years have taken their toll on the grand old buildings that frame the streets and parks of Riobamba. Crumbling reminders of the town's former glory, many of the buildings have been taken over by *ferreterías* (hardware stores) and fast-food restaurants. The majestic **Colegio Nacional Maldonado** at Plaza Sucre is one of the few buildings that has managed to stay grease-free. It still serves its original purpose—as a local high school.

Most visitors, however, don't come for the parks, plazas, and architecture. The city is known primarily as a departure point for some of Ecuador's most thrilling sights and expeditions. You can try a daytrip up Chimborazo, Ecuador's tallest peak, or experience the jaw-dropping train ride to Guayaquil, which travels through every tropical habitat from highland *páramo* to coastal lowland. Alternatively, you can visit nearby indigenous villages, or explore Parque Nacional Sangay, home of one of the world's most active volcanoes. Seated high on his Andean throne, the Sultan offers an array of experiences you won't find anywhere else.

ORIENTATION

Riobamba's straightforward grid layout and clear, consistent street signs make it one of the most navigable cities in Ecuador. Activity centers around the area squared off by **Argentinos** and **Olmedo** to the north and south, and **Avenida 5 de Junio** and **Angel León** to the east and west. **Primera Constituyente** and **Avenida 10 de Agosto** are the city's main thoroughfares. From the bus station, head east for 1km on León Borja, which turns into Av. 10 de Agosto. The train station is in the center of town at Av. 10 de Agosto and Carabobo. Out of the city limits and above the clouds, Chimborazo lies to the northwest, El Altar to the east, and Tungurahua to the northeast.

PRACTICAL INFORMATION

Tourist Information: CETUR, Av. 5 de Junio and Av. 10 de Agosto (tel. 960-217, 941-213), will amiably distribute city maps and brochures, as well as help any lost or querying souls. English spoken. Open Mon.-Fri. 8:30am-5pm.

Immigration Office: España 10-50 and Guayaquil (tel. 969-844). For affairs relating to visas and tourist cards. Open Mon.-Fri. 8am-noon and 2-6pm.

INEFAN: (tel. 963-779), at the **Ministerio del Cultura Agrícola (MAC),** Av. 9 de Octubre near Duchicela. Super-helpful staff has info about Sangay and free rides to all 3 park entrances, leaving at 8am. Open Mon.-Fri. 8am-4:30pm.

THE CENTRAL CORRIDOR

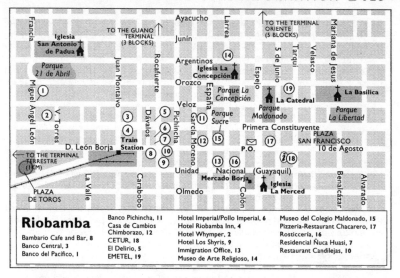

Riobamba

Bambario Cafe and Bar, 8
Banco Central, 3
Banco del Pacífico, 1

Banco Pichincha, 11
Casa de Cambios
Chimborazo, 12
CETUR, 1
El Delirio, 5
EMETEL, 19

Hotel Imperial/Pollo Imperial, 6
Hotel Riobamba Inn, 4
Hotel Whymper, 2
Hotel Los Shyris, 9
Immigration Office, 13
Museo de Arte Religioso, 14

Museo del Colegio Maldonado, 15
Pizzeria-Restaurant Chacarero, 17
Rosticcería, 16
Residencial Ñuca Huasi, 7
Restaurant Candilejas, 10

THE CENTRAL CORRIDOR

Currency Exchange: Casa de Cambios Chimborazo, Av. 10 de Agosto (tel. 967-427 or 940-545), between García Moreno and España, near the Parque Sucre. The only place in town, so lines move slowly. Dollars and traveler's checks exchanged. Open Mon.-Fri. 9:30am-1:30pm and 3-6pm, Sat. 9:30am-1pm.

Banks: Abundant in the main section of town—look up and you'll see one. Large banks include the **Banco del Pacífico,** Veloz and Angel León, and **Banco Pichincha,** Primera Constituyente and García Moreno. Both open Mon.-Fri. 9am-6pm. **BanRed** ATM machines, found at many banks, take Cirrus/Plus cards, open 24hr.

Trains: The **train station,** Av. 10 de Agosto and Carabobo (tel. 961-909). Open daily 8am-noon and 2-5pm. The magnificent **Riobamba-Guayaquil** route was recently reopened after over 10 years of repair to tracks, which had been destroyed by the catastrophic El Niño of 1982-83. Loads of tourists catch this train just for the scenery; ride the roof for the best views. The track runs south from Riobamba to Alausí, then cuts west to the town of Bucay. The small **Alausí-Bucay** section is the most scenic, and some tourists only hop on for this portion of the ride. The last stretch from Bucay to the Guayaquil suburb of Durán is uneventful, and the train may arrive after dark. The train leaves from Riobamba quasi-daily (Fri.-Mon. and Wed., 6am, 12hr., s/40,000 depending on how far and long you travel). Check the schedule, however, as it often changes. A **Riobamba-Quito** route (Fri., 9am, s/45,000) offers fantastic yet frigid volcano views from the train roof. Make sure to arrive at the station by 5:30am on the morning you plan to take the train, to ensure that you get a ticket (see also the **Riobamba-Alausí-Bucay-Durán Railway,** p. 133).

Buses: The main **terminal terrestre** is on León Borja (the western part of Av. 10 de Agosto) and Daniela, about 1km to the northwest of the center of town. From there, buses head to: **Quito** (18 per day, 3:15am-7pm, 3½hr., s/9,000); **Guayaquil** (6 per day, 5:30am-6:30pm, 4½hr., s/9,000); **Cuenca** (6 per day, 5½hr., s/25,000); **Huaquillas** (2 per day, 9hr., s/25,000); and **Machala** (9pm, 12hr., s/40,000). All buses except those marked "express" stop at all towns along the way, so take the Quito line for towns like **Ambato** (1½hr., s/4,500) and the Cuenca line for **Alausí** (1½hr., s/9,000). The **Terminal Oriental,** on Espejo and León Borja (tel. 960-766), north of town, sends buses eastward and on to the Oriente daily. Like most Ecuadorian buses, these generally do not run on strict schedules; rather, they either leave roughly every 30min. or simply depart when they're full. To **Baños** (every 30min., 5am-7pm, 1hr., s/4,000), **Puyo** (every 30min., 5am-7pm, 3½hr., s/14,000), **Tena,** and locations further east (every hr., 5am-7pm). The **Guano Terminal,** Rocafuerte and Nueva York (north of town) sends buses to **Guano** (every 15min., 30min., s/2,000) and **Santa Teresita** (every 15min., 30min., s/2,500). Buses for **Cajabamba, Laguna de Colta,** and **Guamote** leave from the area around Av. Unidad Nacional, Angel León, and Bolivia (every 30min., 30min., s/2,500). Additional buses leave on Thurs. for the Guamote market. Buses to **San Juan,** the closest town to Chimborazo, leave from Av. Unidad Nacional and Av. Prensa (6 per day, s/2,000). Note that many more buses traveling the Quito-Loja route stop in Riobamba. To catch one of these, wait *outside* the station.

Local Buses: Unless you're in a big hurry, local buses are unnecessary; Riobamba is eminently walkable. There are two routes—"Control Norte," along León Borja and Av. 10 de Agosto, and "Control Sur," running through Orozco between Carabobo and Unidad Nacional on the other end of town. The fare is a paltry s/400.

Taxis: These ubiquitous nightcrawlers—they're everywhere, all night long—charge a reasonable s/4,000 to go between any two points in the city.

Pharmacy: Farmacia Perpetuo Socorro, next to the Hotel Zeus on León Borja toward the *terminal terrestre.* This perpetually helpful place is open 24hr. In the *centro,* there's a pharmacy on almost every block.

Hospital: The **Policlínico,** Olmedo and Cuba (tel. 965-725), is the most modern and highly recommended medical facility in town. Open 24hr. The **Hospital del Seguro Social,** Av. Unidad Nacional and Carlos Zambrano (tel. 961-811), is another option, as are the numerous private clinics.

Emergency: tel. 101.

Police: Av. de la Policía and La Paz (tel. 969-300), on the Vía al Chembo. Open 24hr.

Post Office: Av. 10 de Agosto and Espejo (tel. 966-066). Postcards and envelopes sold. Don't count on incoming mail. Open Mon.-Fri. 8am-6pm, Sat. 8am-2pm.

Information: 104.

Telephone: EMETEL, Tarqui and Velos (tel. 969-816 or 962-001), offers local, long-distance, and international calling services, s/1,500 for an AT&T or MCI calling card. EMETEL also sends and receives faxes for a fee. Use a calling card, make a collect call, or receive calls at local upscale hotels such as the **Hotel El Galpón,** Argentinos and Zanibrano (tel. 960-981); or **Hotel Whymper,** Angel León 23-10 and Primera Constituyente (tel. 964-575). Guests can receive international calls at virtually all hotels, usually a cheaper option than dialing home from Ecuador.

Telephone Code: 03.

ACCOMMODATIONS

Hotel Imperial, Av. 10 de Agosto and Rocafuerte (tel. 960-429), is right in the heart of Riobamba. Relax in spacious, airy rooms or lounge on the balcony. Large beds with holey sheets are reasonably clean; bathrooms are puny but bearable. Singles and doubles have shared bathrooms; private bathrooms for triples and quads. Management arranges Chimborazo excursions. Rooms s/15,000 per person.

Hotel Los Shyris, Av. 10 de Agosto and Rocafuerte (tel. 960-323), is a step above the Imperial in both sheet and overall room quality, but doesn't quite have the same warm, fuzzy atmosphere. The clean, telephone-equipped rooms (local calls s/1500 per 3min.) seem all the larger in comparison with the smallness of the bathrooms, which are tidy with so-so showers. Rooms s/15,000 per person.

Hotel Riobamba Inn, Carabobo 12-20 and Primera Constituyente (tel. 961-696 or 940-958), across from the Banco Central. It may have a redundant name, but that is because day after day it keeps repeating the same meticulous cleanliness. Sparkling private bathrooms and spotless rug-bearing bedrooms. Though the TVs in each room are black-and-white, the glare from the colorful phones and hot pink bedspreads more than make up for it. Hot water 24hr. At s/33,000 per person, it's a step up in price (though not necessarily in taste).

Hotel Whymper, Angel León 23-10 and Primera Constituyente (tel. 964-575), is a bit outside the center of town. Whimper with delight at the sight of the king-sized beds. With its green bedspreads and linoleum floors, it rivals Hotel Riobamba Inn for the "Best Decor from a Past Decade" award. Telephones and private bathrooms give each room an added bonus. Rooms s/30,000 per person.

Residencial Ñuca Huasi, Av. 10 de Agosto between Rocafuerte and Dávalo (tel. 966-669). A block away from the Hotel Imperial, it offers a reasonable fall-back position—and a sexy palindromic phone number. Try to imagine this decaying mansion as it once was, and perhaps watching the paint peel won't seem so bad (rooms s/8,000; with bath s/12,000—though this also includes a cleaner room and a more comfortable mattress).

Hotel Humboldt, León Borja 35-48 and Uruguay (tel. 961-788 or 940-814). More expensive than its in-town counterparts, but what you get for the extra money could keep you amused for days. Bright, airy rooms with color TV, telephone, cheery color schemes, and knick-knacks galore—including candy bars and bags of chips on the bedside table. No, they're not complimentary. Private baths, but not quite the utmost in bathroom quality. Cafeteria downstairs (open 7:30am-8:30pm). Singles s/44,000; doubles, far larger, s/60,000.

FOOD

Riobamba, because it's the classic Ecuadorian city, has plenty of budget *almuerzo* stops with meals for around s/4,000, but very little to excite the palates of travelers passing through. Most eateries serve seemingly identical meals though their kitchens vary in cleanliness—choose carefully, or you may find yourself hopping off the Riobamba-Bucay train to "take care of business." Come dinner time, locals crowd around outdoor stands that scoop various traditional stews and meat dishes out of steaming bowls lit up by little floodlights. The food can be good, but eat at your own risk—look for flies, and remember, no raw veggies. These stands cluster around Carabobo and Guayaquil, selling their goods for around s/1,500-3,000. The cheapest filler-uppers are the bakeries *(panaderías)*, which sell bread for s/210 and up.

Ristorante Pizzeria Il Paladiuo, Garcia Moreno 24-42 between Veloz and Orozco. César, yet another Italian-trained Ecuadorian pizza man, creates easily the best pizzas in town in his brick oven (personal pizza s/5,000-s/9,000). He must have learned something about pasta as well—his spaghetti with tomato sauce (s/6,000) is superb. The salads are big, tasty, and have no reported negative side effects (s/5,000-s/7,000). Open daily noon-10pm.

Restaurant Candilejas, Av. 10 de Agosto (tel. 960-220), between Pichincha and Rocafuerte, is secluded from the street with yellow curtains and a covered door. The elegant setting—tablecloths, flowers, and chandeliers—is misleading given the budget prices. The menu includes Kodachrome pictures that preview your meal in living color—perhaps just a tad too vividly. Pizza s/8,000 and up. Plenty of meat entrees *(bistek* s/7,000). Open Mon.-Sat. 7:30am-8:30pm, Sun. 7:30am-1:30pm.

Chifa Joy Sing, Unidad Nacional 29-33 and Carabobo (tel. 961-285). The huge portions of savory cuisine at this typical Ecuadorian *chifa* will have you singing with joy. Creative dishes as well as old favorites. Fried "wantans" s/6,000. Tasty *tallarin especial* (angel hair noodles with Chinese vegetables, chicory pork, beef, and shrimp) s/8,200. The large dining room is rather nondescript, but draws in crowds of Ecuadorians and Chinese. Open Mon.-Sat. noon-10pm.

Pizzeria-Restaurant Chacarero, Av. 5 de Junio 21-46 and Av. 10 de Agosto (tel. 969-292). An inexpensive Italian joint that serves with a smile. Chefs go above and beyond with abundant toppings; pasta dishes like the *putanesca* overflow with olives, garlic, onions, peppers, tomatoes, and more (s/9,000). Meat entrees s/8,000. Pizzas with your choice of toppings ("individual" s/10,000, medium s/20,000, large s/30,000). Open Mon.-Sat. 3-10pm.

El Delirio, Primera Constituyente and Rocafuerte (tel. 967-502), beautifully situated in Simón Bolívar's old house, a historical landmark. Outdoor tables in a charming patio garden under blossoming trees. If it was nice enough for the liberator of South America, it's probably nice enough for you. A slight splurge, but entrees like the *lomo al jugo* (tenderloin, s/13,000) aren't costly by foreign standards, and the hamburgers (s/6,000) are downright cheap. Riobamba's best *almuerzo* for s/12,000. Pleasant indoor dining as well, with historic pictures decking the wooden walls and woven hanging lanterns. Open Mon.-Sat. noon-10pm, Sun. noon-3pm.

Pollo Imperial, Av. 10 de Agosto and Rocafuerte beneath the Hotel Imperial, serves chicken in *all* its various forms. The prices may seem steep for food from a fast food joint (¼ chicken s/6,000, chicken soup s/4,000), but these are pretty succulent birds. Perhaps not surprising for a place called *The Imperial Chicken,* walls are a vibrant orange and a large-screen TV shows English-language subtitled movies until late into the night. Open daily noon-midnight.

SIGHTS

Riobamba's scenic parks just cry out to be strolled in. One of the most compelling pleas comes from **Parque 21 de Abril,** also known as **La Loma de Quito,** perched above the rest of Riobamba. Head to the northern part of town; the park is boxed in by Orozco, Argentinos, Grancia, and Juan Montalvo. Due to its auspicious position, Parque 21 de Abril monopolizes the best panoramic views and photo opportunities in the city. On a clear day, the vista captures not only Riobamba, but the surrounding peaks as well, with Volcán Chimborazo reigning as king of them all. Romantic and beautiful at sunset, the park also holds a church, **San Antonio de Padua,** which has stone steps leading up to its picturesque patio gardens from every direction.

The **Parque Sucre,** in the center of town at España and Primera Constituyente, graces the inland city with the next best thing to the sea—a beautiful bronze **fountain** and **statue of Neptune.** Local old men gather on the palm-tree-shaded benches, socializing and people-watching. Within the park, the regal schoolhouse **Colegio Nacional Maldonado** takes up an entire block along Primera Constituyente. The engaging **Parque Maldonado,** Primera Constituyente and Espejo, next to the CETUR office, displays a monument to its namesake, Pedro Vicente Maldonado. This *riobam-beño* historian and cartographer drew up the first political map of Ecuador. Big and bustling with weekend activity on its swings and play structures, **Parque Guayaquil,** Unidad Nacional and León Borja, provides the perfect opportunity to let your inner child roam free. There's no end to Riobamba's peaceful parks and strolling spots; other halcyon hangouts include **Parque La Libertad,** across from the Basílica at Veloz and Benalcazar; and **Parque de la Concepción,** Orozco and Larrea.

The city's **churches** reveal the Riobamban penchant for atypical architecture. **La Basílica,** Veloz and Benalcazar, constructed from 1883-1915, gained fame as the only round church in Ecuador. The main **Catedral,** Veloz and Av. 5 de Junio by Parque Maldanado, is the oldest building in town. The sole remnant of Riobamba's pre-earth-quake site, it was transported, one stone at a time, in 1797. **La Concepción** (La Loma de Quito), Orosco and Larrea, and **La Merced,** Olmedo and Espejo, don't have fasci-nating histories, but do open for mass Mon.-Fri. 6-8am and 6-8pm, Sat.-Sun. 6am-8pm.

Two museums of note grace Riobamba. **La Concepción,** or the **Museo de Arte Religioso,** Argentinos and Larrea (tel. 965-212), has a collection of religious art and artifacts (open Tues.-Sun. 8:30am-12:30pm and 2:30-6pm; admission s/8,000, chil-dren s/4,000). The **Museo del Colegio Maldonado,** also known as the *Museo de Cien-cias Naturales,* is a tiny natural history and science exhibit inside the monumental schoolhouse at Parque Sucre (open Mon.-Fri. 8am-1pm and 3-6pm; admission s/400).

ENTERTAINMENT

The **Saturday market** is literally a *huge* affair. The entire length of every street boxed in by España, Av. 5 de Junio, Guayaquil, and Argentinos—as well as all the space in-between—fills up with vendors, shoppers, and good old Ecuadorian energy. People from all the small surrounding villages come to join in the spectacle. Nearly *every-thing* imaginable is sold somewhere, from live chicks to toothbrushes, traditional Indian weaving to entire cow legs. More touristy items center around Parque La Con-cepción between Orosco, Veloz, España, and Colón.

Even on the weekdays, the shopping scene stays strong. Riobamba is famous for its carved **tagua nuts,** ivory-white, rock-hard palm tree nuts from the rain forest. Local craftsmen carve them into various gadgets and souvenirs; look for a super selection at **The Tagua Shop/Alta Montaña,** León Borja 35-17 and Uruguay (tel. 963-694 or 942-215). Tagua nuts and their various reincarnations are far from cheap by Ecuadorian standards (the smallest souvenirs start at s/4,000; chess sets go for s/50,000 and up), but that's not so surprising given that the store is an actual artisan's workshop where you can see the nuts being carved (open Mon.-Sat. 9am-1pm and 3-7pm). Those with a strong artistic bent can purchase uncarved nuts for s/2,000. Another well-known form of local *artesanía* are the woven bags known as **shigras.** Market spots include Colón and Veloz, Junín and Av. 5 de Junio, and the area around the post office at Primera Constituyente and Espejo.

For the testosterone-abundant, **cockfights** can be seen Saturdays and Sundays in a house at Almagro and Chimborazo, or at the *Colizeo de Balles* at Ciudadela in the Barrio Tapi (ask at CETUR for details). After all, what could be more *macho* than a bunch of men watching roosters peck each other to death? Riobamba's biggest *fiesta,* **La Loma de Quito,** commemorates the city's founding. The actual holiday falls on April 21, but *riobambeños* know how to party—the celebration lasts from April 18-22, when fairs, bullfights, and parades swamp the streets.

By night, **The Bluff,** Av. 10 de Agosto and Carabobo, is the hangout of choice for locals. This bar/*discoteca* features an indoor slide—just make sure you don't slip up and drink too much before you start slidin'. *Peñas* are ubiquitous in Riobamba; some of the best are **El Faraon,** León Borja 43-40 and 44 (tel. 963-488 or 968-161), near the *terminal terrestre;* **Ureja Guardea,** Manuel E. Flor and Zambrano; and **Media Luna,** Zambrano and Veloz. Most *discotecas* cluster around the same area—on León Borja between the *terminal terrestre* and Hotel Zeus at Duchicela—making a night of club-hopping all too easy. Some of the most dance-friendly *discotecas* are **Casablanca** and **Gems Chop,** which has a large dance floor and UFO-style flying colored lights. At the *terminal* itself, **La Casa del Billar** entertains with pool, ping-pong, and a disco. It all gets going around 9-10pm and keeps on rollin' usually until 2-5am.

The high *párama* around Riobamba is littered with lakes, villages, and picturesque vistas of the surrounding mountains. For those with well-acclimatized legs and lungs (and plenty of cash), perhaps the best way of seeing this area is from the seat of a **bicycle. Pro-Bicí,** Primera Constituyente 23-51 and Larrea (tel. 960-189), run by cyclist and mechanic Galo Bríto, runs trips into the surrounding countryside for US$25-30 per day. While this does not include food or lodging, it does cover the use of a Cannondale M900 mountain bike with Deore XT components (i.e. a really good bicycle). Galo, a native Riobamban educated in the U.S., knows enough of the history of Chimborazo province to keep you interested for days. He and his assistant Freddy (who speaks only Spanish) keep you on quiet backroads for most of your ride.

■ Near Riobamba

GUANO AND SANTA TERESITA

Only a 30-minute bus ride from Riobamba, this tiny village offers a close-up glimpse into a different sort of Ecuador, a rural Andean lifestyle that makes even tranquil Riobamba seem bustling. **Guano** specializes in rug-making and slow living, with a picturesque plaza in the hilly shadow of the Volcán El Altar. Numerous *artesanía* shops vend monstrous rugs, leather goods, and hemp items; many will custom make any design that you can communicate to them with pictures or broken spanish. The simple pleasures of all Ecuadorian towns can be found here as well—only in a smaller, quieter version. The central square houses a lovely **park** with a garden in its center, and a small **church** stands at Colón and García Moreno. One of the only restaurants in town, **Los Fuentes** dishes out chow at Hidalgo and García Moreno, near the main plaza (hours erratic). *Panaderías* and small stands throughout town offer bread, soda, chips, and other snacks. It's hard to imagine an emergency happening in so placid a place, but in case of any sort of disaster, there's a **bank** across the street from Los Fuentes, and a **pharmacy** and **medical center** at García Moreno and Ramirez. To get here from Riobamba, catch the bus from Rocafuerte and Nueva York (every 30min., 5am-7pm, 30min., s/1,500).

The five to six km walk down García Moreno to the town of **Santa Teresita** lasts about an hour. You won't see another tourist for miles as you walk through the rural valley, down dusty cobblestone streets, past shacks and sweatshops, and by small gardens and suspicious dogs. Except for Sunday market days, the towns are eerily silent, so expect stares. If you don't want to walk the whole way, buses rumble along García Moreno every few minutes, kicking up clouds of dust that linger in the silence. There's no way to get lost heading to Santa Teresita—absolutely nothing else is around. A **bus station** next to a 24-hour liquor store and another of those churches welcomes visitors to some of Ecuador's more remote **natural springs.** Take a right down the highway and walk for about 20 minutes to get to the *aguas termales.* The setting of these swimming pools, in a pasture against a mountainside, framed by Andean hills and Volcán El Altar, is better than the quality of the actual pools, but it's a refreshing plunge nonetheless. An s/200 entrance fee grants free rein to wander between two lower cool-water pools, and the warmer, larger upper pool. Located in a spooky, run-down building reminiscent of a suburban high school gym, the whole complex appears to be a mere shadow of its former self; you'll likely have a pool to yourself, so you can take a swim alone.

CAJABAMBA, LAGUNA DE COLTA, AND GUAMOTE

Aside from the Sunday Indian market a bit further down the highway, there's not much to see in **Cajabamba.** The village was devastated by a 1797 earthquake, but from the way this run-down industrial town sags, the trembler might have happened last week. As a matter of fact, Cajabamba is an excellent place to leave—that is, it makes a good starting point for the scenic one-hour hike to the **La Balbonera church** and the lovely **Laguna de Colta.** Start walking uphill just after the road peaks—the hills and fertile valley spread behind while Chimborazo looms above.

In 1959, the conductor of a derailed train prayed to the Divine Lady of La Balbonera, and by an apparent miracle the train was saved. A painting of this crash hangs on the wall of Cajabamba's tiny, no-frills church. Basic wooden benches serve as pews, and a thatched roof and adobe walls shelter the interior of La Balbonera in darkness. Beyond the church to the left sits the large Laguna de Colta. While the lagoon is visible from the highway, there's also a small dirt road that meanders through several beautifully-framed rural villages to the backside of the lake. The backwoods route reveals charming rural settlements with indigenous farmers working fields on the slopes of picturesque, clouded hills. The thousands of reeds growing out of the lagoon obscure the water from view; it's a surreal experience to watch the locals float through the reeds on their bamboo rafts. Eventually, after about a two and a half-hour walk around the lagoon, the road bends back around to the highway (turn right at the end of the lake). There's a small store on the road where you can wait for buses back to Riobamba or forward to Guamote, both of which run until dark.

Guamote, about 45 minutes down the road, is a very high (3056m), very pretty town, but it's probably only worthwhile for the bustling and non-touristy Thursday market. The Riobamba-Alausí-Durán railway goes right by the basic *pensión* (s/ 15,000 per night) and a couple of restaurants.

Buses bound for Cajabamba, Laguna de Colta, and Guamote leave Riobamba from the area around Unidad Nacional and Bolivia every half hour, or as often as they fill up. More buses leave on Thursdays for Guamote's market.

PALITAHUA

Halfway between Baños and Riobamba lies the humble village of **Palitahua,** surrounded on all sides by towering green mountains and volcanoes. The setting is much like that of Baños, Palitahua's more touristed neighbor to the east, and remains much as Baños probably once was. It has its very own hot spring, about an hour's hike above the town (ask for directions). High in the hills, in the middle of the jungle, the setting is as pristine as you might have hoped Baños's *baños* would be. Sadly, the same cannot be said of the baths themselves. In an attempt to earn itself a piece of the tourist pie, the town recently poured concrete into the spring to make it more accesible to a larger number of visitors. Those who visited the springs before the cement arrived find it depressing to see what has happened to the site. The rest of us can enjoy the springs for what they are today. To get to Palitahua, take any bus headed toward Baños (every 30min., s/2,000).

■ Volcán Chimborazo

> How fearful
> And dizzy 'tis, to cast one's eyes so low!
>
> —William Shakespeare, King Lear

Have you ever felt really, really tiny? Volcán Chimborazo (6310m) overwhelms even the most lordly with the powerful magnitude of nature and the relative helplessness of humanity. This dormant volcano is absolutely not to be missed if you're in the area. Topped by snow year-round, Chimborazo peeks above the clouds into the silence of space. The trip to the summit is breathtaking, due to both the unparalleled view and the lack of oxygen at these altitudes. Chimborazo's second refuge (5000m) offers stunning views as well, and can be reached in half a day, without any climbing experience, equipment, or extreme expense.

Superb scenery graces the ride to the rural *parrochia* of San Juan (s/2,500), the starting point for most trips up Chimborazo. *Comunas* and *caseríos*—tiny villages without any government administration—dot the fertile farmlands and the *cerros* (hills) in the shadow of Chimborazo. Tourists and local *indígenas* find each other equally foreign sights; schoolchildren in polychromatic shawls gape at visitors, and even the local cows stare. The rocky ascent passes through cloud forests lined with pines and tiny shrubs covering misty boulders, hills, and slopes. Suddenly, above the treeline, everything disappears—only rocks, clouds, and snow remain. Clouds are a mixed blessing; while they curb visibility, they also add to the mystical wonder. Not surprisingly, Chimborazo was once believed to be the highest mountain in the world. Look farther up than you imagine land could be, and there in the distance is the peak, enough to render anyone but an Everest-veteran speechless.

A relatively cheap way to reach the second refuge is through the **Hotel Imperial** (tel. 960-429), in Riobamba. Tell them the night before, and they'll set you up with a driver who can take you on the two-hour trip to the Edward Whymper refuge (4800m). While you hike up to the second refuge, the driver will wait for a few hours, then take you back. The round-trip runs about US$15 per person; trips generally leave at 7am and return between 1-2pm. Be careful climbing to the second refuge (5000m); though it's only an hour-long walk at most, it must be taken at a snail's pace. Frequent rest stops and water are a must, as your body will not be acclimatized to the altitude. Going alone isn't the best idea; try to find a companion for the walk up, since it's always good to have a partner in case of emergency. The drive to Chimborazo can also be done by any 4WD taxi that you find in Riobamba, or by guides arranged by any of the numerous but expensive travel agencies in town.

Most people stop at the second refuge, but experienced, adventurous climbers can take on the challenging ascent to Chimborazo's summit (9hr. ascent and 4hr. descent at best). Crampons, ropes, and other standard equipment are essential. Though the summit is not the highest in the world, it is the farthest point from the center of the earth due to the earth's bulge at the equator. Climbs leave at 1am from the second refuge; a guide is a necessity. For info on guides see **Mountain Climbing,** p. 34. **Alta Montaña** (tel. 963-964 or 942-215), in Riobamba, can provide qualified guides.

Both refuges on the mountain have basic food items, coffee, and tourist souvenirs (t-shirts s/28,000, postcards s/1,500). They also offer accommodations (US$10)—but bring your own sleeping bag, and stock up on plenty of extra water and food. If you stay overnight at a refuge, arrange for the 4WD taxi to pick you up the next day (round-trip around s/100,000). Sleeping under a full moon high above civilization comes at a price. Altitude sickness can be a serious problem for those not acclimatized to heights above 3000m. For more info, see **Hot, Cold, and Altitude,** p. 20.

■ Alausí

Alausí is a tranquil mountain stop in the central Sierra, where the general silence of the town's streets is disturbed only by the Sunday market and the regular chug-chugging of the train descending the "devil's nose" en route to Bucay. But with a towering, cloudy mountainside dominating everything, who has much to say anyway? At least the alpine overseer is a charismatic one, providing an amazing backdrop for Alausí's ancient buildings and sleepy streets. A beautiful setting and a slower pace of life make Alausí a worthy stop for weary travelers about to pick the devil's nose.

Orientation and Practical Information Plaza Bolívar and the **train station** are at the base of *el centro*, near Av. 5 de Junio and Sucre. It takes about five minutes to walk through the entire downtown area. The streets heading down the mountainside are Av. 9 de Octubre, De Loza, Ricaurti, and Sucre. Cross-streets are Bolívar, Villaluz, Av. 5 de Junio, and **García Moreno,** the main thoroughfare in town. **Buses** stop in the middle of Av. 5 de Junio between Av. 9 de Octubre and De Loza, and go to: **Riobamba** (every 30min., 6am-6pm, 2hr., s/6,000); **Quito** (2 per day, 5½hr., s/14,500); **Cuenca** (2 per day, 4hr., s/13,000); **Guayaquil** (3 per day, s/14,000); and **Ambato** (every hr., 3hr., s/8,000). Buses traveling the Quito-Cuenca route pass along the Panamerican highway at all hours of the day and night. For **train** info, see **The Riobamba-Alausí-Bucay-Durán Railway,** p. 133. The basic **Farmacía Americano** sits under the Hotel Americano. Phone calls (national only) can be made from the **EMETEL** office opposite the train station, service is slow—it may be quicker to catch a bus to Riobamba, and call from there. The **post office** is at the corner of Av. 9 de Octubre and García Moreno. Better to hold onto those postcards for another few days—the *correo* has a, let's say, relaxed atmosphere. **Banco de Guayaquil,** Av. 5 de Junio and Reaurti, provides remarkably good rates on dollars and traveler's checks (open Mon.-Fri. 9am-6pm). If you need **medical services,** you'd be better off heading up to Riobamba.

Accommodations and Food Hotel Americano, García Moreno 59 and Ricaurti (tel. 930-159), is located above the Farmacía Americano and run by the same management. In a town of unexciting hotel choices, this is probably the most appealing of the bunch. Clean, quiet, and cozy rooms with wooden floors, street views, and bathrooms with hot water (don't be misled by the electric shower heads—there's gas heating down below) cost only s/15,000 per person. The **Hotel Gampala,** Av. 5 de Junio (tel. 930-138), rents similar, though somewhat run-down rooms, for the same s/15,000. All other accommodations line Av. 5 de Junio, where the rooms have views of the mountains, but the buses below start rumbling by 4am. **Hotel Panamericano,** Av. 5 de Junio (tel.930-156), near the bus stop, may inspire a game of one-on-one with its parquet floors. Just be sure not to mess up the tidy rooms and well-washed sheets when dunking (s/10,000 per person with common bath, s/15,000 with private, though the extra sucres also buy you a better view, hotter water, and a better mattress). The most appealing culinary choices in town are the hotel restaurants. Like the lodgings, the **Hotel Gampala Restaurant,** Av. 5 de Junio (tel. 930-138), delivers the standard goods. *Corvina frita* s/7,500, *bistek* with fries, rice, and salad s/8,200 (open daily 7am-11pm). The **Hotel Panamericano Restaurant** has slightly cheaper meat entrees (s/4,500-8,000) and soups (s/3-5,000). *Almuerzos,* s/5,000 (open daily 7:30am-9pm). Or eat under the stars while the buses whiz by at the **Parador Vera del Camino** (tel. 930-055), on the highway just past town. Climb up the steps to the highway, turn right, and walk five minutes. Food has the taste and appearance that you would expect from a late-night Ecuadorian truck stop. Fuel up on *almuerzo* (s/5,000) or *carne a la plancha* (s/6,000), indoors or out (open daily 10am-4am).

■ The Riobamba-Alausí-Bucay-Durán Railway

The Riobamba-Alausí-Bucay-Durán Railway is one of the most exhilarating train rides in Ecuador, and the heart-racing stretch between Alausí and Bucay is the climax of the entire trip. A lengthy 464km, the line actually begins in Riobamba and snakes its way to the Guayaquil suburb of Durán. Some people go all the way; others, for lack of patience, only stick around for the quick thrills. From Riobamba, the train climbs along steep mountainsides and mounts the towering Andean cliffs, peaking at 3609m, then suddenly thrusting into the steamy jungle at Bucay. Many travelers ride on top of the train for the best views. As with the rest of the world, train travel in Ecuador is quickly becoming an anachronism. The Riobamba-Durán route is the last in Ecuador to maintain a consistent schedule, though its cargo these days consists almost entirely of sight-seeing gringos and field-tripping Ecuadorian school children.

The train was originally planned as the primary transportation link between Quito and Guayaquil, and construction began in 1899. Everything proceeded smoothly for the first year, until the tracks reached a rather difficult obstacle—an almost perpendicular kilometer-high wall climbing from Huigra to Alausí. Vaguely shaped like a nose, the rock earned the nickname **El Nariz del Diablo (the Devil's Nose)**. Ignore fellow travelers who claim to have inside info on Satan's facial features—the sinister aspect of this rock has to do with the number of lives that were lost during the construction of the track that zig-zags up its side.

The Quito-Riobamba route, though spectacular in its own right, is rarely traveled these days. Most tourists hop on at Ríobamba, though the first few hours to Alausí don't offer much in the way of spectacle (it often takes 2hr. of driving back and forth in the Ríobamba station to get all the cars connected in the "correct" order). The track opened in 1908, but a large section between Guayaquil and Alausí was washed out by El Niño in 1983 and took 10 years to rebuild. In the first 26km, the train does nothing but gain altitude. Just before the **Sibambe** station, the tracks run straight into the rocky roadblock, El Nariz del Diablo, where the train surmounts a perpendicular cliff by means of two amazing switchbacks—quite a feat of railroad acrobatics. In under 30km, it descends from 2347m to 1255m at the **Huigra** station. On each bend, heartstopping horseshoe twists and turns reveal magnificent views of the countryside. If you decide to get your adrenaline-rushing thrills on top of the train, be careful as there are no guard rails. Center your weight towards the middle of the train and hang on tight. Also try to get a car toward the rear to avoid the steam engine's constant spew of ash. Before you touch solid ground again, you'll have descended from snow-capped volcanoes and highland cloud forests to the sea-level, banana-growing tropics of the western lowlands. Those with little patience, or a tour bus waiting, get off at Huigra. However, those who stay on the train experience the whole package; watching the landscape gradually shift to tropical rainforest as the train descends to the Bucay station. Watch your bags, as there have been reports that young thieves have been known to grab a backpack, then hop off the moving train, assuming that their victim will not follow (a sensible assumption). Coming properly prepared will make your ride a lot more pleasant—you need clothing to protect you from weather ranging from a cold and rainy morning in the Andes, to a steamy midday ride under the tropical sun. Also nice is something soft to sit on—this is a *long* ride.

Catch this famous train in **Riobamba** (Fri.-Mon., Wed., 6am; see **Riobamba Practical Information: Trains**, p. 125) or **Alausí** (Fri.-Mon., Wed., 9:30am). Arrive at least half an hour early to buy tickets. The train is unreliable, and the schedule often changes; don't plan your trip around its transportation. The uphill return trip from Durán is less popular (Tues., Thurs., and Sat.-Sun., 6:25am). **Bucay** (also known as Gral. Elizalde) is not a pleasant place, and when the train arrives around 2-3pm, most catch the next bus to Riobamba, Guayaquil, or El Triunfo (for Cuenca). If you continue to Durán, you may arrive at night; ferries run to Guayaquil until 10pm. The total ride each way averages 12 hours, and depending on the length, costs US$10-16 for tourists. You don't want to know how much less the locals pay.

■ Ingapirca

Ingapirca, or "Wall of the Inca," located two hours north of Cuenca just off the Pan-american Highway, is Ecuador's most notable Inca ruin site. Constructed over 500 years ago, the ruins are neither as impressive nor as important as those in Perú. But, set on a highland plain in the rural hills of the south central Sierra, they still make for a worthwhile daytrip from Cuenca or the nearby town of Cañar.

The **central structure** of the ruins is called the "Adoratorio," "Castillo," or "Temple of the Sun." Scholars speculate that this elliptical *usnu* platform was originally used to worship the sun, but it may have had astronomical as well as religious uses. The impressively solid structure, 37.5m by 13.5m, is filled with small niches and windows. The **aposentos** (lodges) next to the Temple of the Sun were most likely used in the administration of Ingapirca's religious activity. Although the trapezoidal **plaza** is eroded almost to the ground, it still reveals a 20m by 10m building also believed to have been used for religious purposes. The **pilaloma** section, to the extreme south of the complex, has revealed the biggest collection of artifacts from the **Cañari Tribe,** who inhabited the area before the Incas. The **intihuayco collcas** (circular receptacles for food), **incahurgana** (ceremonial spot), **bodega** (market), and many **stairways** are also worth checking out (ruins open daily 9am-5pm; admission US$4). There are free but not overly well-informed government-funded guides at the site. To make a visit truly worthwhile, hire a guide in Cuenca (see below).

There are two ways to get to Ingapirca by bus. One **direct bus** runs to Ingapirca from Cuenca's *terminal terrestre* (9am, 2hr., s/4,000). Alternatively, Cuenca buses depart more frequently for the town of **El Tambo,** on the Panamerican Highway between Cuenca and Riobamba (every hr., 6am-5pm, 2hr., s/4,000). From there, *camionetas* go to Ingapirca (every 45min., 7am-5pm, 30min., s/5,000). To return, there is a direct bus to Cuenca at 1pm, or catch a *camioneta* back to El Tambo and flag down any bus traveling the Panamerican Highway. When visiting the ruins, it is a good idea to bring enough food and water for the day. Don't plan on staying the night. One restaurant, **Posada Ingapirca,** is right at the ruins (tel. 838-508), but it aims to seat the well-off tourists willing to pay exorbitant prices for grub. Just down the road from the ruins, the small town of Ingapirca is home to the **Hostal Into Huasi,** which offers accommodations and food, both very cheap and basic (rooms s/10,000 per person; *almuerzo* s/4,000; restaurant open daily 7am-8pm).

Some visitors spend the night in the nearby colonial town of **Cañar,** south of El Tambo on the Panamerican Highway. While it may make a nice rest stop on the way to or from the ruins, it is of little interest and only has a sparse selection of hotels. The **Hostal Ingapirca,** Av. Sucre (tel. 235-201), just below the main square, has the best beds in town, with pictures of its namesake covering every inch of wallspace (doubles s/25,000; triples s/30,000, with bath s/45,000). A number of *comedores* nearby serve the standard *platos* (*almuerzos* s/15,000). Only one bus per day travels the rugged direct route to the ruins from the town plaza (6am, 45min., s/3,000), and is both less comfortable and more expensive than the normal route via El Tambo. Guided tours from Cuenca generally cost US$35 per person.

■ Azogues

Set in the rolling mountains north of Cuenca, **Azogues** (pop. 30,000) pales in comparison to its more cosmopolitan neighbor to the south when it comes to tourist attractions, but still radiates charm. The humbly prosperous town and surrounding countryside are blessed with saintly mountaintop churches, most notably Azogues's **Iglesia San Francisco** and neighboring Biblián's **Santuario de la Virgen Del Rocío.** The capital of the Cañar province, Azogues also hosts a bustling Saturday morning market and is a center of Ecuador's Panama hat industry (see **Panama Hats Are Not from Panamá,** p. 197). So while it is not the shining star of southern Ecuador, Azogues provides a genuine glimpse of a busy but untouristed Ecuadorian city.

Orientation and Practical Information The **Panamerican Highway** doubles as **Avenida 24 de Mayo** and forms the western boundary of town. The bus station is on Av. 24 de Mayo, two blocks north and two blocks west of the **main plaza**. The **market** is one block south of the plaza on Matovalle. Most activity centers around the plaza area at **Bolívar** and **Serrano. Cambiara del Cañar** (tel. 241-925), on Bolívar between Sucre and Solano, offers decent rates for cash or traveler's checks (open Mon.-Fri. 8:30am-1pm and 2:30-4:30pm, Sat. 8:30am-2:30pm). **Filanbanco,** Bolívar and Sucre (tel. 240-332), will change traveler's checks but not cash (open Mon.-Fri. 9am-4pm). **EMETEL** (tel. 240-590 or 240-515), at the corner of Bolívar and Serrano on the main plaza, dials national and international calls (open daily 8am-10pm). **Buses** from the *terminal terrestre* go to: **Biblián** (every 15min. during daylight, 15min., s/400); **Santo Domingo** (5 per day, 7:45am-9:30pm); **Quito** (10 per day, 6:30am-11:30pm, 10hr., s/30,000); **Loja** and **Guayaquil** (9 per day, 7:30-12:30am, 6hr., s/20,000) via **Cuenca. Super Taxis** sends fancy buses to **Quito** (1:30 and 10pm, 10hr.) and **Guayaquil** (12 per day, 5:30am-7pm, 6hr.) via **Cuenca** (1hr.). **Cooperativa de Taxis Azogues** is found on the main plaza (tel. 240-450), as are numerous **pharmacies.** The **Hospital Crespo** (tel. 240-600 or 240-502), heals across the river. The **emergency** number is tel. 101, and the **police** are at tel. 240-289. The **post office** (tel. 240-380), is on Bolívar in the main plaza, across from the church (open Mon.-Fri. 8am-noon and 2:30-6pm, Sat. 8am-3pm). The **phone code** is 07.

Accommodations and Food The **Hotel Charles International,** Serrano (tel. 241-210), between Abad and Bolívar, is perhaps the best hotel in town. Slide into the slippery wood-floored rooms and shining bathrooms through an airy, plant-covered lobby (s/20,000 per person). At the plain **Hotel Charles** (tel. 241-364), at Solano and Rivera, you lose hot water, firm mattresses, and that "international" flavor and save s/10,000. Clean sheets are the selling point of the rooms (s/10,000 per person). If this is not a concern, save s/2,000 more at the **Pensión Tropical** (tel. 240-511), on Serrano at Sucre. They don't even claim to have hot water, but the price is right (s/8,000).

Restaurants in Azogues are cheap and basic. Next-door neighbors **El Padrino** (the Godfather) and **El Gran Padrino** (the Great Godfather), Bolívar 60-11 between Sucre and Av. 3 de Noviembre (tel. 240-534), suffer from the same mafia obsession as Hotel Chicago. But where's the pasta? Both offer the same old traditional Ecuadorian menu, like *pollo* with potatoes and rice (s/6,000) and *caldo* (s/3,000; open Mon.-Sat. 8am-9pm, Sun. 8am-10pm). Dripping with ferns, **Chifa Familiar** also specializes in standard *platos* (¼ chicken, s/9,000), but does offer some respite from Ecuadorian cuisine (*tallarin chop suey*, s/9,000; open daily 8am-11pm).

Sights and Entertainment The **San Francisco Church** sprawls out over a hill to the southeast, and is visible from various places in town. A 45-minute climb pays off with a socks-knocking view of the surrounding hills and the town below. The ornate church interior also delights the eyes. Down closer to sea level, Azogues's placid **main plaza** is a pleasant place to kick back with a cup of coffee. A huge 1994 monument to Ecuador's working classes, **"El Trabajador,"** poses with mallet in hand. Though market day is Saturday, the **main market,** Av. 3 de Noviembre and Rivera, is active throughout the week, with a peculiar concentration of hat salesman. Check out **Cine y Video Azogues,** on Azuay between Bolívar and Ayacucho just east of the bus station. Movies are shown daily at 4:30pm (s/3,000) and 8:30pm (s/5,000).

Other than its inherent rural attractiveness, the nearby town of **Biblián** has one significant sight: the **Santuario de la Virgen del Rocío.** Its white turrets evoke images of fairy tale castles, and its steep hillside setting overlooking idyllic Biblián is the stuff postcards are made of. Biblián is a quiet, lonely town with virtually no tourists, so look forward to your shadow's company during the 45-minute haul up to the Santuario. At the top, you'll be treated to a panoramic view of the town and countryside. Drawer-type graves and an interestingly-shaped main chamber may pique your interest. If the walk up is not your speed, wait for the local *cooperativo* bus or pickup truck that occasionally travels the rough, steep road to the church. To get back to

Azogues or Cuenca, flag down a bus along the Panamerican Highway; you may have to try awhile before one actually stops. Biblián is either a 10- to 15-minute bus ride from Azogues's *terminal terrestre* or a challenging, two-hour hilly walk. Lazy *and* impatient travelers can take a taxi (s/10,000 each way).

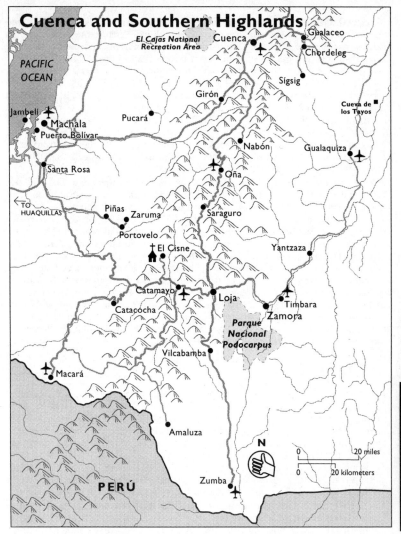

Cuenca and Southern Highlands

El Cajas National
Recreation Area

Cuenca

PACIFIC
OCEAN

Gualaceo

Chordeleg

Sígsig

Girón

Cueva de
los Tayos

Jambelí

Machala

Puerto Bolívar

Pucará

Nabón

Gualaquiza

Santa Rosa

Oña

← TO
HUAQUILLAS

Piñas

Zaruma

Saraguro

Portovelo

Yantzaza

El Cisne

Catamayo

Loja

Timbara

Catacocha

Zamora

Parque
Nacional
Podocarpus

Vilcabamba

Macará

Amaluza

N

0   20 miles

0   20 kilometers

PERÚ

Zumba

Cuenca and the Southern Highlands

The southern tip of Ecuador's Sierra may be out of sight of the snow-capped peaks of the central *Cordillera de los Andes,* but the southern highlands' natural and architectural wonders leave little to be desired. The mild climates of alpine elevations cool their equatorial warmth, and the cloud cover that results lends a distracting, mystical quality to each of the bumpy bus rides on unpaved cliff-hanging roads (and there are *plenty*). Cosmopolitan yet charmingly colonial, Cuenca, the most brilliantly shining star of the region, is one of Ecuador's most bucolic environs, the nation's only true *city* that carries out all of its important business in its historic colonial center—and this in the shadow of the most beautiful cathedral in the country. Only a few hours away, the rugged cloud forest and alpine lakes of windy El Cajas mark the territory just before the western ridge of the Andes. Even farther south, Loja, smaller and more *tranquilo* than its northern neighbor, sprawls over a highland plain carved into a narrow valley; the "gateway to the Oriente" (a breathtaking two-hour ride from Zamora) is also a gateway to Vilcabamba, the sacred valley of longevity, and to Parque Nacional Podocarpus's wondrous mountain cloud forests. The ruins at Ingapirca—Ecuador's largest Inca site—call the southern highlands home as well, though veterans of travel through Perú will be less than stunned.

More interesting are the living villages and market towns that are to be found not far from the southern highlands' urban centers; they have all the charm of the Ecuadorian Sierra yet greater *tranquilidad* than northern tourist hotspots like Otavalo. The rolling, clouded countryside provides a perfect backdrop for lonesome strolls through silent thatched-hut villages like Biblián. But the southwestern ridge of the Andes range—as seen from the routes that descend from Cuenca and Alausí to the coast (El Triunfo and Guayaquil)—is home to the most spectacular scenery in all Ecuador. Roads and train tracks alike descend almost 3000m, hugging cliffs and deep ravines as they pass through innumerable vegetation zones, from mountain *páramo* to coastal jungle wetlands, dipping into layer after layer of misty cloud cover en route to their muggy destinations. Gaping tourists scramble to keep their weight in the center of the passenger car as they strain to keep from falling off the top of the steam train that traverses *El Nariz del Diablo* from Alausí to Bucay. Thankfully, the view is too fantastic to worry seriously about matters mortal.

■ Cuenca

Ecuador's third-largest city, Cuenca (pop. 300,000) sits in the Guapondélig Valley (2530m), at the heart of southern highland culture and at the hub of several wonderfully scenic roads. Once a prosperous indigenous city worthy of its original Cañari name, *Tomebamba* (plain as big as heaven), the city was more plain than heavenly by the time the Spanish arrived. When Gil Ramirez Dávalos re-founded Cuenca in 1557, the mysteriously deserted Tomebamba already lay in ruins, saving the Spanish the trouble of doing it themselves. Today, cobblestone streets, wrought-iron balconies, and ornate buildings ooze colonial influence. Unlike Quito, Cuenca is not a city divided between old and new, but brings a temporal harmony central to its charm.

A lively locale bursting from the banks of the Río Tomebamba, cosmopolitan Cuenca offers travelers tasteful brown-roofed buildings, raging nightlife, and some of the finest international restaurants and museums in Ecuador. Life in this cultural mecca revolves around the old colonial center, Parque Calderón, where a blue-domed cathedral towers over tree-lined benches. Despite its relatively cool climate (average temperature of 15°C/59°F), Cuenca is an artistic hotbed, nurturing communities of artisans renowned for their baskets, shawls, and Panama hats. Cuenca's charisma is powerful enough to overcome even its terrible traffic, a sure sign that even the most devoutly anti-urban travelers run the risk of falling under its spell.

ORIENTATION

Most of Cuenca's activity transpires in the area framed by **Mariscal Lamar, Honorato Vasquez, Tarqui,** and **Mariano Cueva**. The **Río Tomebamba** flows through town south of *el centro*, parallel to Calle Larga, and its grassy banks look anything but citified. Another respite from everything urban, **Parque Calderón** lies at the heart of the colonial center. The **terminal terrestre** is a 30-minute walk, s/5,000 taxi, or s/400 bus ride northeast of *el centro*.

Cuenca

Cafecito, 22
Casa de Cambio
VAZ, 10
CETUR, 20
Chifa Pack How and La Cantina, 16
El Pedregal Azteca, 4
EMETEL, 15
Gran Hotel, 5
Heladeria Holanda, 8
Hospital, 27
Hostal Chordeleg, 6
Hotel Milan, 17
Hotel Pichincha, 2
Immigration Office, 18
Museo de Arte Moderno, 1
Museo de Artes Populares de America, 23
Museo de las Conceptas, 19
Museo del Banco Central, 26
Museo Remigio Crespo Toral, 21
New York Pizza Restaurant, 12
Pizzeria La Tuna, 9
Police, 14
Post Office, 11
Residencial Paris, 13
Restaurant Govindas, 3
Ruinas de Pumapungo, 25
Santo Domingo, 7
Todos los Santos, 24

PRACTICAL INFORMATION

Tourist Information: CETUR, Hemano Miguel 686 and Presidente Córdova (tel. 822-058 or 839-337), offers brochures, maps of the city, and a list of licensed guides. Open Mon.-Fri. 8am-5:30pm. **INEFAN,** on Hermano Miguel and Bolívar, is the administrative headquarters of Ecuador's 14 national nature reserves. Provides info on all of these areas and gives weak maps of El Cajas (p. 146). Open Mon.-Fri. 8am-4:30pm, at times sporadically.

Money Exchange: Casa Cambios Yaz, Cordero and Gran Colombia (tel. 833-434 or 832-795). Changes dollars and traveler's checks and has Western Union service. Open Mon.-Fri. 9am-1pm and 3-5:30pm, Sat. 9am-12:30pm.

Currency Exchange: Banks are abundant in the center of town. **Filanbanco** (tel. 813-322), on Sucre between G. Torres and Padre Aguirre, **Banco La Previsora,** Gran Colombia and Benigno Malo (tel. 831-444), and **Banco del Pacífico,** Benigno Malo 9-75, which gives MasterCard advances, are among the largest. All open Mon.-Fri. 9am-6pm, Sat. 9am-1pm. Most have Cirrus/Mastercard/Visa ATM machines.

Consulates: Colombia, L. Cordero 955 and Pasaje Hortencia Mata, 2nd fl. (tel. 830-185). Open Mon.-Fri. 9am-1pm and 3-6pm. **Chile,** Tomás Ordoñez 327 (tel. 831-383 or 830-529). Open Mon.-Fri. 8:30am-12:30pm and 2:30-6:30pm.

Immigration Office: (tel. 831-020), on Benigno Malo between Juan Jaramillo and Calle Largo. Open Mon.-Fri. 8am-noon and 2-6pm.

Airport: Av. España (tel. 862-203), 15min. north of the city by taxi (s/5,000) or bus (s/400). Open daily 6am-1pm and 3-6pm. For reservations, go to individual airline offices. **SAETA,** Benigno Malo 727 (tel. 839-090; fax 835-113), in Edificio El Galeón, next to the main cathedral. **TAME,** Gran Colombia and Hermano Miguel (tel. 827-609, airport tel. 862-193). **American Airlines,** Herman Miguel 8-67 (tel. 831-699 or 827-134). **LACSA,** Gran Colombia 12-18 and Tarqui (tel. 837-360). TAME flights head to **Quito** (1 per day, s/150,000), **Guayaquil** (Mon.-Fri., 1 per day, s/104,000), and smaller national destinations.

Buses: The **terminal terrestre,** España (tel. 842-023), is northwest of the center of town. It is a bit difficult to get to and from, and a taxi (s/4,000) may be preferable to the local buses (s/400), which are horribly overcrowded and don't go directly to the *terminal.* Many companies operate out of Cuenca, and most passengers arbitrarily gravitate towards whomever happens to be yelling out their destination. If comfort is important to you, get on one of the better buses (usually the long-distance ones), even if you're only going a short distance. **Turismo Oriental** goes to: **Guayaquil** (every 40min., 1am-11pm, 5hr., s/20,000); **Quito** (6 per day, 7:30am-8:45pm, 10hr., s/30,000); **Macas** (5 per day, 10am-9pm, 13hr., s/30,000); and **Zamora** (9am, 7hr.). **Transportes Loja** has brand-new Mercedes-Benz buses to **Loja** (noon, 5, and 10pm, 5hr., s/15,000) via **Saraguro** (3½hr., s/13,000). **Express Sucre** goes to: **Machala** (10 per day, 6am-6:45pm, 4hr., s/9,000); **Santo Domingo** (7:15am, 2:30, and 7:30pm); and **Milagro** (1 per day, 5pm). **Azuay** buses go to the Peruvian border at **Huaquillas** (5 per day, 5:45am-11:30pm, 7hr., s/23,000).

Car Rental: Cuenca Rent-a-Car, Pres. Cordova and Av. Huayna Capac (tel. 825-318), is affiliated with Budget. Expect to pay s/90,000-150,000 per day, including insurance, but excluding mileage. Open Mon.-Fri. 8am-noon and 2:30-6:30pm, Sat. 8am-noon. **Internacional Rent-a-Car,** Av. República 221 and Huayna Capac (tel. 801-892). **Oro-Rent** (tel. 831-200), on Av. Ordoñez Lazo at Hotel Oro Verde. **Localiza Rent-a-Car,** Av. España 14-85 (tel. 828-962).

Markets: Plaza Rotary, in the Machuca and Sangurima area northeast of *el centro,* hosts a market favored among locals, selling everything from animals to watches to clothing; come on Tues. or Fri. morning to watch the *curanderos* (healers) work their magic. A smaller, livestock-less market specializing in clothing and weaving dwells next to the Hotel Milan, at Pres. Córdova and Aguirre.

Laundromat: Lavahora, on Vasquez at Machuea (next to El Cafecito) offers self-service washers (s/5,000 per load) and dryers (s/5,000). Detergent is free. Open Mon.-Sat. 9am-8pm, Sun. 9am-1pm.

Pharmacy: Local pharmacies work on the rotating *de turno* schedule, so one of them is always open 24hr. The schedule is published in *El Mercurio,* the local newspaper. **Farmacía International,** on Gran Colombia between Luis Cordero and Pres. Borrero, is large and centrally located. Open Mon.-Fri. 8am-noon and 2:30-7pm, Sat. 8am-noon.

Hospital: Clínica Santa Ines, Av. Córboda Toral 2-113 and Av. Cueva (tel. 817-888), on the far side of the river, just south of Av. 12 de Abril. **Clínica Santa Ana,** Av. Manuel J. Calle 1-104 (tel. 814-068), southeast of the river, near Av. 12 de Abril and Calle Paucarbamba. Look for it behind the monument to José Peralta.

Emergency: tel. 101.

Police: The **Central Office** is on Pres. Córdova and Luis Cordero. Report crimes and stolen items to **OID** *(Organización de Investigación del Delito),* Benigno Malo and Torres (tel. 831-041), south of the river.

Post Office: Borrero and Colombia (tel. 840-271). **EMS** (Express Mail Service), for 3-day international mail, next door. Both open Mon.-Fri. 8am-6pm, Sat. 9am-1pm.

Telephones: EMETEL, Benigno Malo and Mariscal Sucre, ½ block from Parque Calderón, offers free MCI and AT&T calling-card calls and expensive domestic and international calls. Open daily 8am-10pm.

Phone Code: 07.

ACCOMMODATIONS

Hotel pricing in Cuenca is a tricky business. Though accommodations are on the expensive side, at least by Ecuadorian standards, don't just make a mad dash for the cheapest place around. For only a few more sucres, hotel quality shoots up drastically. Avoid ritzy hotels in town unless you absolutely need their amenities: they charge tourists twice as much as locals, and they're not that outstanding for the price.

Hostal Macando, Tarqui 11-64 and Lamar (tel. 840-697). Some claim the Macando is the best hostel in Ecuador; it has all the basics—clean, comfortable rooms, friendly, knowledgeable staff, access to clean, modern kitchen, beautiful gardens, and the welcoming community that American owners, Steve and Maren have created. Shared bathrooms. Singles US$8; doubles US$12; HIYA member discount.

Hotel Milan, Córdova 989 and Padre Aquirre (tel. 835-351), in the center of town. Live it up in commodious comfort with phone, color TV, and hot-water bath. Gaze lazily over your balcony into the chaotic local market. But ask to see your room first, as there's not a pot of gold in every one. A good bargain: singles s/15,000, with private bath s/25,000; doubles s/25,000, with private bath s/40,000.

Cafecito, Honorato Vasquez and Barrero (tel. 827-341). You won't find many Ecuadorians at this shared-room hostel, but you will find washed, warm, and well-decorated rooms. Bathrooms are as good as shared ones can get. Two leafy courtyards: one with a cafe, the other with Ecuador's most impressive climbing wall. US$4 for noisy shared rooms with thin mattresses; US$6 for nice, quiet rooms at the back.

Gran Hotel, Gral. Torres 9-20 and Bolívar (tel. 831-934 or 841-113). Rooms offer everything a weary traveler needs, like private baths, color TVs, and lots of space. The real excitement emanates from the indoor courtyard; festooned with bizarre, out-of-place trees and ferns. Singles s/18,000, with bath s/30,000; doubles s/ 32,000, with bath s/48,000. Breakfast included.

Hostal Chordeleg, Gran Colombia 1115 and Gral. Torres (tel. 824-611 or 822-536). Everything looks so perfect, you might not even want to touch the lacquered-wood railings, the fountained center courtyard, or your immaculate room with exhilaratingly comfortable beds, private bath, phone, and color TV. Choose between balconied street room or inner one. Rooms s/33,000 per person. Breakfast included.

Hotel Pichincha, Torres 8-82 and Bolívar (tel. 823-868). Dirt-cheap but dirt-free for strict penny-pinchers, right in the center of town. Only small sinks, mirrors, and large, clean-sheeted beds break up the whiteness of the walls. Sketchy (or absent) toilet seats make electric hot-water bathrooms less-than-inviting. Friendly common lounges on each floor have huge Trinitron TVs. Rooms s/15,000 per person.

Hostal Colonial, Gran Colombia 10-13 at Padre Aguirre (tel. 841-644). Another solid, if slightly upscale, choice. Situated in a restored colonial mansion. Singles s/ 35,000; doubles s/60,000; triples s/90,000; quad s/110,000. Includes breakfast.

FOOD

With its attractive and diverse array of delectable diners, Cuenca is a great place to cure some hunger pangs. From the ubiquitous *almuerzo* stops with their traditional budget lunches, to the costly world-class cuisine at **El Jardín,** Cuenca satisfies even the most selective stomach. For picnic supplies, start out at **Supermaxi** (Cardero and Lamar). You can buy bread from a standard **panadería** on just about any block, or make the pilgrimage to **Delicatessan D'Oro,** next to Hotel D'Oro, Borrero at Gran Colombia, for bread with European quality and prices. As usual, ubiquitous little *restaurantes* offer s/15,000 *almuerzos*.

De Película, Beniguo Malo 4-104 at Calle Larga (tel. 884-087). New American/Ecuadorian fusion cuisine. Try *un pescado llamado Wanda* (a fish called Wanda, s/6,500) or a Gandhi sandwich (strictly vegetarian, s/6,500). Old 16mm movies shown on Thurs.; live entertainment Wed. Open daily 10am-midnight.

Raymipampa Café-Restaurante, Benigno Malo 8-59 (tel. 827-435). This lively room, as bouncy as its name, absolutely hops with gringos and the local bourgeoisie. The view onto the Plaza Calderón complements the casual, coffee-shop feel. Enjoy scrumptious dinner *crepes* (chicken and mushroom s/9,000, vegetarian s/6,500) and delectable cream soups (s/2,500), along with the requisite 3-course *almuerzo* (s/8,000). Open Mon.-Fri. 8:30am-11pm, Sat.-Sun. 9:30am-11pm.

El Pedregal Azteca, Gran Colombia 10-29 and Padre Aguirre (tel. 823-652), dishes out some of the best Mexican food in Ecuador. No bargain basement, but authentic *tacos* (s/11,000) and *burritos* (s/11,000) accompanied by ice-cold Pilseners (s/4,000) are well worth the price (though portions can be small). Be prepared to dine in relative solitude—beyond the means of many locals, this dark, romantic setting can be sparsely populated. Open Mon. 6-11pm; Tues.-Sat. 12:30-3 and 6-11pm.

Bar-Restaurante Vegetariano, Benigno Malo and Av. Sucre (tel. 839-976). Not an original name; all the thought went into the food. Quality vegetarian *almuerzos* (s/7,000), and an a la carte menu. Open Mon.-Fri. 11am-6:30pm, Sat. 11am-2pm.

Chifa Pack How, Presidente Córdova 772 and Cordero. Popular with the wealthier local crowd for its tasty fare (entrees s/12,000-16,000) and late hours. Open daily 11am-3pm and 6pm-midnight.

Hostal Chordeleg Restaurant, Gran Colombia 1115 and General Torreo (tel. 824-611 or 822-536). Perfect for a cheap and convenient date, the hostel transforms into a romantic outdoor restaurant complete with courtyard tables, stone fountains, and a surprisingly reasonable menu. Filet mignon with mushrooms s/11,000, shrimp *al ajillo* s/11,000, *cordon bleu* s/11,000. Open daily 7am-11pm.

Café Austria, Benigno Malo and Jaranillo, (tel. 840-899). Their desserts are the real thing; the best cakes in Cuenca s/3,500, coffee s/2,500; also mediocre sandwiches, limited to all combinations of ham and cheese (s/14,500). Open daily 11am-7pm.

Heladería Helanda, Benigno Malo 9-51 and Bolívar (tel. 831-449). Widely acknowledged to serve the best ice cream in town. Single cone s/1,500; *Copa Los Enamarados* (s/12,000) reported to be deserving of its name. Open daily 8am-7:30pm.

Hostal Macando, Tarqui 11-64 and Lamar (tel. 840-697). Wonderful breakfasts, including the indulgent *desayuno Macando* (s/8,500); pancakes (s/2,500); fruit salad (s/3,500). For the *almuerzo*, stop by during the morning to get your name on the lunch list. Breakfast daily 7-11:30am; lunch Mon.-Fri. until 1:30pm.

SIGHTS

Though the area's most compelling sights are out of town—at Turi, Ingapirca, Baños, Biblián, and the nearby markets—Cuenca offers more diversions than simply fine dining. With a booming *artesanía* community and almost too many museums to count on your fingers, Cuenca serves up cultural offerings as well as culinary ones. Fun-lovers also flock to Cuenca's two preeminent annual festivals. During the **El Septenario** (Corpus Christi) celebration in early June, the main plaza explodes with fireworks and dancing. Drinks like the cinnamon- and *aguardiente*-filled *caneliza* help the Cuencans let loose for unusual games of chance and wild matches of the ever-popular foosball. The **Pase del Niño** festival on the Saturday before Christmas features surreal parades celebrating the upcoming holiday.

Museums

Cuenca puts its museums where its mouth is, with enough galleries to support the city's claim to cultural significance and prove its sophistication. Founded in 1947, **Museo Remigio Crespo Toral,** Calle Larga and Borrero (tel. 830-499), honors the eponymous Cuencan poet with unrhymed exhibits of miscellaneous historical items (open Mon.-Fri. 8am-4pm). **Museo del Banco Central,** Calle Larga and Huayna Cápac (tel. 831-255), outside of the center of town at the ruins of Pumapungo, houses Cuenca's most extensive collections of art and historical artifacts, in a style that only Central bankers could afford. The downstairs area includes an exhibit showing the development of art in Ecuador since 1600, more of interest for its illustrations of Ecuadorian people and places than artistic merit. Adjacent is an archeological display chronicling the Cañari civilization in the area. Upstairs is an ethnographic exhibit, and an impressive collection of indigenous musical instruments. The museum also organizes children's events and art shows (open Tues.-Fri. 9am-6pm, Sat.-Sun. 10am-1pm; admission s/4,000). Just as Cuenca has more than one set of ruins, it has multiple museums to honor them. The **Todos los Santos** ruins support the next-door **Museo de Sitio de la Casa de la Cultura "Manuel Agustín Landivar"** (tel. 832-639), on Calle Larga and Manuel Vega, and its archaeological exhibits. There's even a library to answer those more esoteric post-museum questions (open Mon.-Fri. 8am-noon and 2-6pm). For those who just can't get enough of those ancient *indígenas,* **Museo de las Culturas Aborígenes,** Av. 10 de Agosto 4-70 and J.M. Sánchez (tel. 811-706), sports an array of Cañari and Incan artifacts. Though the museum is a little out of the way in Ciudadela Santa Anita, it's accessible by a cheap taxi ride (open Mon.-Fri. 8:30am-12:30pm and 2:30-6:30pm, Sat. 8:30am-12:30pm; admission s/6,000).

Cuenca's claim to cultural fame doesn't rely exclusively on the remains of the dead. Several museums promote livelier local arts and crafts. Founded in 1982, the **Museo de Arte Moderno,** Calle Sucre and Col. Talbot, operating in the ancient House of Temperance, displays mainly Ecuadorian modern art, and hosts the *Biennial Internacional de Pintura* (open Mon.-Fri. 9am-1pm and 3-7pm, Sat.-Sun. 10am-1pm). **Instituto Azuayo de Folklore,** Cordero 7-22 and Presidente Córdova, third floor (open Mon.-Fri. 9am-6pm), and **Museo de Artes Populares de America,** Larga and Hermano Miguel (tel. 828-878; open Mon.-Fri. 9:30am-1pm and 2:30-6pm, Sat. 9am-1pm), exhibit fascinating arrays of local and regional *artesanía.* An upscale *artesanía* store next door sells high quality, high-priced goods. For art with religious sensibilities, there's **Museo de las Conceptas,** on Hermano Miguel between Pres. Córdova and Jaramillo (tel. 830-625), in the 400-year-old Monastery of the Immaculate Conception. Explore Catholic mysteries as you peruse pious art and Guayasamín lithographs (open Mon. 2:30-5:30pm, Tues.-Fri. 9am-5pm, Sat. 10am-1pm; admission s/5,000).

Churches

Cuenca's two most striking churches face each other across Parque Calderón in the heart of town. Built in 1557, the **Iglesia de Sagrario (Old Cathedral)** is rarely open, but back in the 18th century it was the toast of the town. In 1739, a French geodesic mission used the cathedral's spire to measure the curvature of the recently unflattened earth. But out with the old and in with the new—across the street, the massively exquisite **Catedral de la Immaculada Concepción (New Cathedral)** towers over Parque Calderón and glows spookily by night. Designed by Obispo Miguel León Garrido but actualized by the German Juan (Johannes) Stiehle in 1885, the cathedral is one of the most recognized churches in Ecuador. Its ornate domes and brick face cover a cavernous marble interior, where brilliant angles of sunlight enter through the various windows and radiate off a four-column, gold-leaf canopy. Another church, **Todos Los Santos,** on Larga and Machuca south of *el centro,* was the site of Cuenca's first outdoor mass. **Santo Domingo,** on Gran Colombia and Padre Aguirre, rose up along with the city in the 16th century.

ENTERTAINMENT

La Cantina, Borrero and Córdova, serves beers to Cuenca's bourgeoisie (in a glass of course, s/4,000). After catching a few mellifluous notes and sneaking a peek into the beautiful, wood-paneled room lined with musical instruments, Andean-music lovers might want to stay, but proletariat wallets will not. Piping-hot *caneliza* (made with *aguardiente,* a local-firewater) s/4,000. Open daily 5pm-1am. For a scene that's "too hip for Cuenca" (or anywhere else, for that matter), shoot some pool at **Kaos,** Vasquez 6-11 and Miguel, where Cuenca's alternative crowd goes to smoke cigarettes and act cool. Beer s/4,000 and good lasagna s/9,000 (open Mon.-Sat. 5:30-midnight).

A haven for the performing arts, **Teatro Casa de la Cultura,** Cordero and Sucre, shows movies and houses local events like *mariachi* concerts. **Cine 9 de Octubre,** Cuerva and Lamar, and **Teatro Cuenca,** at Padre Aguirre between Lamar and Gran Colombia, advertise their cinematic screenings in *El Mercurio,* the local paper available all over town. They often show quality American movies in English, but the sound is so bad that it's probably easier to read the Spanish subtitles (admission s/8,000, good for both halves of a double feature).

The area around Cuenca has long been a center of **artesanía** production for the rest of Ecuador, which makes the city itself a great place for souvenir shopping. A good starting point is the **Cooperativa Azuayana,** Malo 10-24 near Gran Colombia (don't look for a sign—they don't have one). An artisan's cooperative, their small showroom is crammed with the standard *artesanía*. The real treasures are hidden in the back, though, in the knitters' *bodega*, which houses one of Cuenca's best sweater collections (s/40,000 each). You can have a sweater custom-made if you can come back in 15 days to pick it up—the design is limited only by your ability to communicate through some combination of Spanish and pictures (open Mon.-Sat. 9am-1pm and 3-7pm; *bodega* open only in the morning). Cuenca's artistic traditions have continued to evolve, and the city is home to numerous *talleres de arte* (art studios). Wander the streets around Jaramillo and Bordero to see what's new. Those interested in the art of hat making can continue down Jaramillo to the workshop of **Alberto Pulla-Sombrero,** Tarqui 6-91 (tel. 829 399). Sr. Pulla's card claims that his are *Los Mejores Sombreros del Ecuador* (the best hats in Ecuador). A bold claim, but his scrapbook full of articles about him from around the world gives him some credibility. Panama hats cost s/50,000-250,000—a lot of money, but this is "Hat as Art."

■ Near Cuenca

MIRADOR TURI

Nobody navigates Cuenca better than the birds, and from Turi, a treacherously high lookout spot 4km south of the city center, you can experience that avian outlook as only the high-fliers do. A 15-minute bus ride up a steep, pothole-ridden road pays off at the top, with a breathtaking panoramic view of all of Cuenca and its surrounding mountains. It looks like a map of the city laid out in front of you: closest are more remote rivers, while farther north flows the Río Tomebamba. The stadium and the city center, with the Old Cathedral's blue-and-white domes, are both clearly visible. A cartographic tiled painting of the city matches the view and provides a guide to the scenery. Pay-binoculars let you look closer (s/1,000). Even El Cajas Recreation Area inches its way into the view, in a notch to your left looking down. Turi is actually a little town of its own; sharing the hill are a quiet blue church, an orphanage, a few small grocery stores, and stairs that lead even further up the hill, past Virgin statues, to a radio tower. Charmingly-painted city scenes of children curiously adorn many of the tiny town's outside adobe walls. Turi attracts both local and foreign visitors, and it seems that only tourists break its silence.

Getting up to Turi means taking either a bus or a cab. The buses leave from Av. 12 de Abril and Fray V. Solamo, south of the river (every 90min., 7:30am-4:30pm, s/400). Facing the river, wait on the right side of the wide Fray V. Solamo near the intersection. A taxi up is a more comfortable ride, but costs s/10,000. Getting down means waiting for the next bus (similar schedule) or catching one of the numerous cabs that drive by. Walking it one or both ways is also possible—allow about two hours for the climb and at least an hour for the descent.

BAÑOS

Five km east of Cuenca, *ecuatorianos* indulge in the national obsession of soaking in thermal baths. An impressive resort has been built around this particular *baño*. Day-trippers can enter the baths for s/13,000. Tennis, raquetball, volleyball, and a fitness center may be used for s/10,000 per hour (open daily 7:30am-7pm, Wed. and Sun. closed 1pm for cleaning). To get to the baths, take any bus for Baños passing along Calle Sangurina (s/400), and get off half an hour later at **Hostelería Duran.**

THE MARKETS OF GUALACEO AND CHORDELEG

Every Sunday, the center of activity in the Cuenca area shifts. The weekly markets in these two tiny villages east of Cuenca draw in bargain-hunters from neighboring mountain towns and even more rural settlements. *Indígenas* from highland farms come to town to make their living for the week. Despite the outsiders who frequently discover these villages, the markets manage to maintain their local flavor.

If Otavalo is the retail mall of Ecuador, **Gualaceo** is its factory outlet. In previous generations, family life in the town and surrounding area centered around the production of woolen *chumpas* (sweaters), *gorras* (hats), and *tapetes* (woven carpets). In a sad process that has been repeated around the country, many of the younger generation of Gualaceo have left their traditional lives for work in the city. Still, if you wander the *barrios* in the hills around the town, you will find old men working at their looms, and women knitting on their front porches. Every Sunday, production ceases, and the week's output is brought into town. Heaps of handmade sweaters are sold to middlemen in the plaza by the bus station for resale in Otavalo and elsewhere. On any other day, you can visit the artisans in their homes, see the process, and buy souvenirs with the satisfaction of no intermediary getting a piece of the action. One caveat—pressure to buy can be strong. The market at Gualaceo is the most tantalizing taste-bud temptation. The **main market** lies diagonally across from the town square. From the bus station, head down Cordero and turn right on Cuenca, or better yet, follow the herd. Only a couple of tourists can be spotted among the teeming masses of fruit- and vegetable-hawking vendors. Rows of outdoor eateries, selling every part of the pig but the squeal, make a meat-lover's paradise. Whole pigs on spits, skewered with their heads at attention and ears pricked up, get ripped apart by numerous hands. Vendors drip flavorful pig fat onto delicious *llapingachos* (potato and cheese cakes, s/200) and talented chefs whip even those hard-to-find pork parts into culinary wonders. Try grilled stomach *(guatita)* or hoof soup *(caldo de pata)*...if you dare. If the vendor has washed hands (look for rags and soap) and the victuals are boiled and aren't surrounded by flies, then the food's probably fit for consumption. Look for the *Hay Rosero* ("We have *rosero* today") signs in various *comedores* and ice cream stores around town. What is it? A beverage made from various fruits and fruit juices, then thickened with corn flour (that should make warning bells in your head go haywire). Its saving grace is that the mixture is boiled as part of its preparation. It's very tasty—make a risk-benefit assessment, and proceed with caution. The **indoor food market,** toward the bus station on Cuenca, might look cleaner. Remember not to partake of any water, ice, or raw fruits and veggies (unless peeled), as tempting as they may be. The prices don't do anything to detract from the allure. Everything is cheap; a multi-course *almuerzo* for over s/3,000 is unheard of. Non-food items lurk around the edges of the market. Practical goods from watches to toothbrushes to Panama hats abound, but don't look for baskets and shawls of the tourist variety—that's not what locals come for.

If you must eat outside the market (you're not scared, are you?), there are a number of cheap *restaurantes* near the *terminal* that seem marginally safer (*almuerzos* s/

4,000). Near the charming central park, **Bar-Restaurant Don "Q,"** Av. 9 de Octubre and Gran Colombia, aims for more ambience than other restaurants in town, with an indoor, skylit courtyard and hanging plants (entrees s/8,000; open daily 7am-7pm). **Residencial Gualaceo,** Gran Colombia (tel. 255-006), is one block from the main plaza (away from the market). Nondescript rooms have decent private baths, clean enough for a night's slumber. Lounge on a communal balcony out back (s/10,000 per person). Across the street, the **Residencial Carlos Andres** (tel. 255-379), defies economic theory by providing near identical rooms to those at the Gualaceo at higher prices (s/12,000 per person). The **Museo Artesanal de Gualaceo,** 1km south of Gualaceo off the highway toward Chordeleg, displays local artists' work (open Tues.-Sat. 9am-5pm, Sun. 8am-noon). For a splurge, continue past the *museo,* along the Beverly Hills-style palm-lined drive, to the **Gualaceo Parador Turistico** (tel. 255-010). Its white-washed stuccoed rooms serve the few well-healed *equatorianos* who can afford its luxuries. A popular resort among Ecuadorians, its facilities include a pool with glorious views of the surrounding hills, volleyball, soccer, satellite TV, an expensive restaurant, and the ubiquitous foosball machine (singles s/74,000; doubles s/88,000; triples s/108,000). **Buses** from Gualaceo go to **Cuenca** (every 15min., 5am-7pm) and continue on to **Azogues** or **El Triunfo** and **Machala.** Don't just get on a Cuenca bus; buy tickets at the window beforehand. To get to Gualaceo, catch the bus at Cuenca's *terminal terrestre* (every ½hr., 6am-6pm, 1hr., s/2,000).

While Gualaceo's market specializes in the daily necessities, the market at **Chordeleg** has a lock on the luxuries. The main plaza is absolutely studded with **jewelry stores,** sparkling with good deals thanks to all the competition (be wary of some of the great deals—all that glitters is not gold or silver). Some artisan goods are also sold on the main plaza, but the best pottery shops, including the large and upscale **Centro de Artesanías** (open daily 9am-6pm), are outside the center of town, toward Gualaceo on the main road. Everything in the smaller Chordeleg is quieter than in Gualaceo, including the market. While the plaza is generally silent, a little more activity goes on a few blocks down at the market, a small-scale version of Gualaceo. A modern **church** is on the main plaza. To the right, facing the church, three decent **comedores** of the local variety spoon out chow. The small but info-packed **Museo Communidad** is on the plaza diagonally across from the church (open Mon.-Sat. 8am-6pm, Sun. 8am-4pm). Most **buses** heading back to **Gualaceo** and on to **Cuenca** or **Sigsig** leave across from the market (every 10min.). Buses depart for Chordeleg from Gualaceo's *terminal terrestre* as soon as they fill up (about every 10min., 10min., s/500). Buses coming from Cuenca to Gualaceo also generally continue to Chordeleg (s/2,500). The **walk** between Gualaceo and Chordeleg is a beautiful saunter past picturesque rolling countryside and farmland. The downhill stretch from Chordeleg to Gualaceo takes about an hour; the return uphill can take one and a half hours. On blind curves, be careful of cars hugging the right side of the highway.

Other market villages in the area, including **Sigsig** and **Paute,** are accessible by one-hour bus rides from Gualaceo. Both are less touristy and more rural than either Gualaceo or Chordeleg. As with the other markets in the Cuenca area, the big activity is on Sundays. The **tour agencies** listed under Ingapirca and El Cajas offer daytrips for US$35-45 per person to all of these markets.

EL CAJAS NATIONAL RECREATION AREA

Taking the high road is easy on any trail through El Cajas National Recreation Area, a 28,808-hectare reserve that exemplifies the word "highlands" in its truest sense. Nowhere in the reserve does the altimeter dip below 3150m (10,330ft.), and the zenith, at Arquitectos, reaches a skyscraping 4450m (14,600ft.). Ancient glaciers carved boxlike, U-shaped valleys into the high rock ridges, lending the reserve its name (*cajas* means boxes in Spanish), while failing to explain its grammatical error. A geologically hip place for water to gather, the range hosts 232 lakes and over 750 ponds, distinguishing itself from its generally cold, rainy Sierra cousins with its aquatic take on alpine beauty. Not only does the water nestled in the barren mountains present a feast for the eyes, but it also provides life's sustenance for diverse flora and fauna. El Cajas is a haven to standard-issue wildlife like deer, foxes, and rabbits, as well as the more distinctive spectacled bear, llama, puma, *huagur*, and *tigrillo* (little tiger). Bird-watchers can feast their eyes on land, air, and lake as the Andean condor, highland toucan, and hummingbird are also regular tenants of "The Boxes." Those who prefer Flora to her sister Fauna will enjoy diminutive Quinua trees, the highest-altitude trees in the world, whose gnarled trunks sprout from the grassy humid *páramo* (highland plain) covering most of the park's area. El Cajas's unique climate makes it one of the few places where the rare *cubilán*, *chuquiragua*, and *tushig* plants flourish. Virgin humid mountain forests cover the east and west ends of the area. Offering more than just the wild plant and animal life of the present, though, the reserve also provides glimpses into the past. Pre-Columbian **indigenous ruins** lie scattered throughout, and the ancient Inca Road of **Ingañan** stretches for 4km between **Luspa Cave** and **Lake Mamamag** in the center of the park. The best preserved ruins are at **Paredonesñ**, but Lakes Luspa and Avilahuayco serve up similar slices of Inca history closer to the information center. In fact, El Cajas is lacking only one thing - a *really* big mountain. As a result, many of Ecuador's altitude-hungry tourists simply pass it by, leaving that much more solitude for those interested in taking advantage of the park's subtler charms.

A would-be mountain oasis, the **Information Center** at **Lake Toreadora** (3810m; 12,500ft.) offers basic shelter and a cafeteria, but you need to bring your own sleeping bag, and might as well bring your own food (the cafeteria is often closed). There are two more basic shelters along the shores of Lake Toreadora. Temperatures drop to -5°C at night, and despite the humidity, daytime mercury can sink to 8°C. Warm, waterproof gear is a must, as is powerful sunblock (high Ecuadorian altitudes mean you're that much closer to the sun). A solid supply of bottled water can help with thirst, altitude sickness, and avoiding those pesky mountain water bacteria. Take extreme care wherever you walk in the park and pace yourself slowly (see Hot, Cold, and Altitude, p. 20). The excellent hiking and mountaintop views are to die for, but not literally; deaths from overexertion in the harsh climate have been reported. Dense fog often arrives in the early afternoon, and visitors without maps, compass, and experience have been known to get seriously lost.

For a somewhat less strenuous outdoor activity, **sport fishing** on Lake Toreadora is permitted. Tour agencies in Cuenca can provide necessary equipment rentals. Admission to the park is s/21,000.

From the Information Center, the only immediate recreation is a beautiful three-hour stroll around Lake Toreadora, replete with views of Volcán Chimborazo in the distance. To see the park properly really requires a guide. **Santa Ana** (Quito tel. 832-340), right around the corner from CETUR in Quito, charges US$40 per person regardless of number, and transports people in a 4x4 Trooper with an English-speaking guide (open Mon.-Fri. 9am-1pm and 3-7pm, Sat. 11am-1pm). **Apullacta Tours,** most easily contacted through the Hostal Macondo, offers day trips for US$35 per person - make sure either Pedro or Pablo is your guide, as some of the others are less reliable. The best resource for El Cajas, hands down, is **INEFAN,** in Cuenca, which can provide a good map of the entire recreation area—a necessity, as it's easy to get lost. To contact INEFAN, see Cuenca Practical Information, p. 140.

Buses leave from San Sebastian Park at Talbot and Mariscal Sucre in Cuenca (Fri.-Wed., 1 per day, 6-7:30am, 1hr., s/8,000). Arrive well before 6am to assure a seat for the crowded and treacherous ride. The bus drops off and picks up at the Information Center. Return trip leaves from the Visitor's Center at 2-3pm.

SARAGURO

A tiny stop on the Panamerican Highway between Cuenca and Loja, the town of Saraguro offers little in the way of sights, other than typical small-town charm and untouristed solitude. Its main attraction is the *artesanía* of the Saraguro *indígenas*. While blankets, beaded shawls, sweaters and other crafts are not hawked on any corner, souvenir-hungry tourists will be able to find plenty on Sundays, when the market brings traditionally dressed, black-robed farmers into town from surrounding areas.

On other days, pigs, chickens, and horses are the most active things in the streets. This area of the country, with its splendid scenery, clear starry nights, and unhurried lifestyle is about as far from Guayaquil or Quito as you get without a guide.

Everything of importance is located within two blocks of the **main plaza,** a pleasant garden with benches and trees, typical for a small highland village. By night, there is little to do but look up at the **starry sky** or have a beer at one of the two bars: Saraguro Barta-Bar or Picaultería La Fogata (both erratically open). For a place with such a small-town feel, Saraguro has a large number of useful services. **EMETEL** (tel. 200-104 or 200-105; open daily 8am-10pm), a series of general stores (rubber boots, wooden saddles, mahogany furniture, anyone?), and **Farmacía La Salud** (open daily 8am-1pm and 2-10pm) are all located along the main plaza, across the street from the church. Buses pass by the **bus stop,** also on the main plaza across from the church, heading north (toward **Cuenca**) and south (toward **Loja**) every 30 minutes or so. **Pullman Viajeros** (tel. 200-165), runs north to **Cuenca** (10 per day, 6:30am-1am, 3½hr., s/10,000) and **Quito** (3 per day, 10:30am-8pm, 13hr.). **Transportes Sur Oriente, Transportes Union Carramanza,** and **Coop Loja** all go south to **Loja** (1½hr., s/5,000) and the **Oriente** (via **Zamora** and **Yantzaza**). The **post office** is on Av. 10 de Marzo on the main plaza (open Mon.-Fri. 8am-noon and 2-6pm). Next door reside more municipal facilities—the **police** (Policía Municipal) and the **public bathroom.**

There are two hotels and two restaurants in Saraguro—no more, no less. **Pensión Saraguro** might be a little hard to spot, since it's run out of a grocery store. From the plaza facing the church, head left one block toward the mountains and look for the Pensión sign diagonally across the street. Laundry facilities unsully guests' clothes and sheets. It has a courtyard with rampant flowering plant life, and simple rooms with shared baths (hot water 6am-6pm; s/6,000 per person). Its rival down the street, **Residencial Armijos** has more civilized furniture in its courtyard, but only cold water in the common bathrooms. Facing the church, head left one block, then turn right and walk half a block; it's on the left. The **Reina del Cisne** restaurant-bar, on the main plaza on Eloro, across from the post office and police, serves some of the tastiest victuals in town. Wolf down an *almuerzo* (s/3,000) or *merienda* (s/5,000) under the Virgin Mary's watchful eye (open daily 8am-10:30pm). Samantha Fox's buttocks replace the Virgin at the other dining choice, **Cristal.** Despite the contrast in decor, food and prices are nearly identical (open daily 7am-9pm).

▓ Loja

Always on the move, Loja (pop. 100,000) was relocated from the Catamayo area in 1548, rebuilt after earthquakes twice, and, as its first city to use electric energy, pioneered Ecuador into the Age of Electricity. A gateway to the Oriente, Loja sits only a stone's throw from the most seductive and secluded spots in the southern *cordillera*—Vilcabamba, Zamora, Saraguro, and the Parque Nacional Podocarpus. Beautiful and friendly, Loja boasts enough endowments to be a siren of the Sierra in its own right. Home to two universities, a law school, and a musical conservatory, Loja has developed a sense of modern culture that many other towns in the area lack, while retaining ties to its rustic origins. No buildings rise past the fourth story, and the local **Saraguro indígenas** in their traditional black dress are a strong presence throughout the city. No longer a mobile metropolis, Loja has comfortably settled into its mountain setting, offering visitors a rich combination of scholarly atmosphere, safe streets, traditional charm, and excellent restaurants.

ORIENTATION AND PRACTICAL INFORMATION

Loja lies along two rivers. The main one, **Río Malacatos,** runs between (and underneath) Av. Universitaria and Manuel Agustín Aguirre in town. **Río Zamora** parallels **Avenida 24 de Mayo,** marking the eastern boundary of the city. The **terminal terrestre** is about a 15-minute walk north of *el centro* along Universitaria.

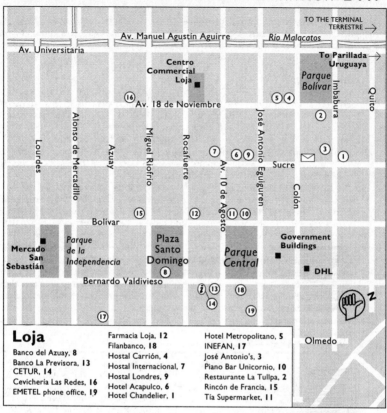

TO THE TERMINAL TERRESTRE →

Av. Manuel Agustín Aguirre   Río Malacatos

Av. Universitaria

To Parillada →
Uruguaya

Centro
Commercial
Loja

Parque
Bolívar

⑯ Av. 18 de Noviembre   ⑤④

②

③ ①

Alonso de Mercadillo

Azuay

Miguel Riofrio

Rocafuerte

Av. 10 de Agosto

José Antonio Eguiguren

Sucre

Colón

Quito

Imbabura

Lourdes

⑦   ⑥⑨

⑮   ⑫   ⑪⑩

Bolívar

Mercado
San
Sebastián

Parque
de la
Independencia

Plaza
Santo
Domingo
⑧

Parque
Central

Government
Buildings

■ DHL

Bernardo Valdivieso

ⓘ⑬   ⑱

⑭   ⑲

⑰

Loja

Banco del Azuay, 8
Banco La Previsora, 13
CETUR, 14
Cevichería Las Redes, 16
EMETEL phone office, 19

Farmacia Loja, 12
Filanbanco, 18
Hostal Carrión, 4
Hostal Internacional, 7
Hostal Londres, 9
Hotel Acapulco, 6
Hotel Chandelier, 1

Hotel Metropolitano, 5
INEFAN, 17
José Antonio's, 3
Piano Bar Unicornio, 10
Restaurante La Tullpa, 2
Rincón de Francia, 15
Tía Supermarket, 11

Olmedo

Tourist Information: CETUR, Valdivieso 8-22 and Av. 10 de Agosto (tel. 572-964), provides info and maps. Open Mon.-Fri. 8:30am-5pm. **INEFAN** (tel. 571-534 or 563-131), on Valdivieso, administers **Parque Nacional Podocarpus** southeast of town. Usually open Mon.-Fri. 9am-noon and 2-5pm. **Biotours Ecuador,** Colón 1496 (tel. 578-398), near Sucre, can customize tour packages for you. Open Mon.-Fri. 8am-1pm and 2-7pm. The **Carirera Provincial de Turismo,** Azuay and Bolívar, has info, but is mainly commercial. Open Mon.-Fri. 8:30am-5pm.

Immigration Office: Argentina and Bolivia (tel. 573-600), next to the police station. Open Mon.-Fri. 8am-noon and 2-6pm.

Peruvian Consulate: Sucre 10-56 (tel. 571-668 or 579-068). Open Mon.-Fri. 8:30am-1pm and 2-5pm.

Banks: If time is money, then you'll want to change your cash (no traveler's checks) at **Casa de Cambio Delgado,** 16-50 Eguiguven. Open Mon.-Fri. 9am-6pm. The lines there are nonexistant because the banks give better rates. **Banco del Azuay** (tel. 570-262), and **Banco La Previsora** (tel. 572-733), both at Av. 10 de Agosto and Valdivieso. Only **Filanbanco** (tel. 571-811), on Valdivieso between Av. 10 de Agosto and Eguiguren, changes traveler's checks. Open Mon.-Fri. 9am-2pm.

Airport: The **La Tola airport** is a 30km, s/15,000 taxi ride out of town in **Catamayo** (see p. 151). Loja's **TAME office** (tel. 570-248 or 573-030), is on the extension of Av. 24 de Mayo across the Río Zamora. Open Mon.-Fri. 9am-5pm. Some advise against taking afternoon flights into Loja/Catamayo, as fierce winds blow through town and the airstrip is precariously wedged between several mountains.

Buses: Transportes Nambija goes to Machala (5:30, 10am, 9:45, and 11pm, 8hr., s/15,000). **Transportes Viajeros** and **San Luis** go to **Cuenca** (12 per day, 5am-

12:30am, 8hr., s/16,000) via **Saraguro** (2½hr., s/5,000). **Pullman Viajeros** also goes to **Quito** via **Santo Domingo** (3:30 and 6:30pm, 14hr., s/35,000). **Transportes Catamayo** goes to **Catamayo** (every 30min., 6am-7pm, 1hr., s/2,800), and **El Cisne** (daily 4pm, also Sun. 7:30 and 8:30am, Fri. 9pm, 3hr., s/5,300). **Panamericana International** goes to **Guayaquil** (10:30pm, 8hr., s/30,000). **Transportes Loja** goes everywhere—literally—but prices tend to be higher.

Taxis: Standard fare between locations in Loja is s/3,000, s/4,000 to the *terminal terrestre.* **Taxi Ruta,** on Universitaria near the Gran Hotel Loja, crams 5-6 people into their cabs bound for **Vilcabamba** (1hr., s/4,000). The ride is about twice as fast as buses to Vilcabamba, and costs only s/1,000 more.

Supermarket: Tía, Av. 10 de Agosto and Bolívar (open daily 9am-8pm).

Pharmacy: Pharmacies are on the *de turno* schedule—check the local paper to see which one is open on any given night. **Farmacía Loja** (tel. 570-266), is on the corner of Bolívar and Rocafuerte (open daily 8am-9pm).

Hospital: Hospital General (emergency tel. 560-159 or 570-540), on Isidro Ayora and Kennedy. Far from *el centro,* so it's best to take a taxi. Free 24hr. emergency treatment. **Hospital Militar de Loja,** Colón 13-28 and Bolívar (tel. 570-254 or 573-941), charges for its medical services. Both have ambulance services.

Police: Argentina and Bolivia (tel. 115).

Post Office: Sucre 05-85 and Colón (tel. 571-600). Open Mon.-Fri. 8am-6pm. **DHL,** 14-23 Colón near Bolívar, in Metroplitan Tours. Open Mon.-Fri. 8am-6pm.

Telephone: EMETEL (tel. 573-050 or 573-990), has 2 branches in Loja: at Eguiguren and Valdivieso, and on Aguirre between Lourdes and Catacocha. Both allow collect and calling-card calls for the comparatively low price of s/2,800 per connection, s/1,000 per minute after. Open daily 8am-10pm.

Telephone Code: 07.

ACCOMMODATIONS

Hotel Acapulco (tel. 570-651), on Sucre between Av. 10 de Agosto and Eguiguren. Not quite Mexico's Pacific coast, but it does provide liveable rooms with color TV, lacquered desk set, and floors shiny enough to use as mirrors. Rooms on 2nd and 3rd floors escape noise from the indoor 1st floor corridor (strangely used as a driveway/parking lot). Many windows face the interior central hall; quieter back rooms have natural light. Singles s/24,000, with TV s/30,000; doubles with TV s/56,000.

Hotel Metropolitano, Av. 18 de Noviembre and Colón (tel. 526-000 or 570-007). Single-handedly keeping local lumberjacks in business, the Metropolitano outdoes itself with wood panelling: striped, zig-zagged, solid, on floors, walls, over the ceiling. Clean, yellow-tiled private baths have plentiful steaming water. Somewhat staticky color TVs and quiet surroundings. A good deal at s/18,000 per person.

Hostal International, Av. 10 de Agosto (tel. 570-433), between Av. 18 de Noviembre and Sucre. For the price, bathrooms are surprisingly decent, and rooms aren't too shabby either. Centrally located, with a courtyard in the absolute center of it all. Old wood floors support the feet, and strange furniture in the hallway holds the imagination captive. Rooms s/10,000 per person, with bath s/20,000.

Hostal Londres, Sucre and Av. 10 de Agosto (tel. 561-936), next to Hotel Acapulco. Less comfortable than its neighbor, but the price is hard to beat. You'll find the shower directly above the toilet in the common bathrooms—definitely a shower-shoe environment, but the water's hot. Padlocked rooms have that bare, hanging-lightbulb look, but they're very clean for the money. Rooms s/10,000 per person.

Hotel Chandelier, Imbabura 14-84 and Sucre (tel. 563-061 or 578-233). No chandeliers, but carved pillows and a tiled courtyard fulfill the slightly-run-down-grand-old-house requirement. Ask for an upper floor (much lighter) room and for showers with gas-heated (not electric) water. Some have TVs. Rooms s/12,000 per person, with bath s/18,000.

Hostal Carrión, Colón 16-36 and Av. 18 de Noviembre (tel. 561-127). Despite the evocative name there's no rotting flesh here. Basic shared-bath rooms satisfy fundamental living needs with a bed, table, and clean sheets (s/10,000 per person), while significantly snazzier private-bath rooms have color TVs. Hot water, rooftop terrace, and helpful owner to boot. Singles s/20,000; doubles s/30,000.

FOOD

Bread seems to be unusually good in Loja and *panaderías* diffuse warm bakery smells on every block. **Panadería La Europa,** 18 de Noviembre and Colón, sells coconut cakes (s/1,500), cheese-filled croissants (s/400), and sweet bread (s/300) for pennies.

Benvenuto, Valdivieso between Rocafuerte and Riofrío. Have your conversational Italian and appetite ready. Even though this lunch stop is Italian-run and named, its menu is typically Ecuadorian. Inexpensive, tasty, and filling *almuerzos* (s/4,000). A la carte dishes, like *lomo picante* (s/2,000) and *espaguetis de camarón* (s/6,500), are just as welcoming. Open Mon.-Sat. 8am-8pm.

Parillada Uruguaya, Salinas (tel. 570-260), near Universitaria. Flee yon vegetarian, hasten dear carnivore. It's hard to find a table and figure out the prices, but they serve some of the best grilled meat in the southern highlands. *Chuleta de chancho* (a huge pork chop, s/11,000), house specialty *lomo fino* (grilled beef, s/10,000), *parillada* (mixed grill, s/15,000 per person).

La Tullpa, on Av. 18 de Noviembre at Parque Bolívar. Fancy touches and a huge dinner put other *criollo* restaurants to shame. Dishes aren't dirt-cheap, but they don't taste like it either. *Chuleta de chancho* (pork chop, s/8,000), *lengua a la española* (Spanish-style tongue, s/7,000). Scrumptious *almuerzo* (s/4,000) is quite a deal.

Cevichería Las Redes, Av. 18 de Noviembre and Riofrio (tel. 578-787). This net-decorated seafood joint offers more than just your average *ceviche*. Breaded squid (s/7,800) and whole boiled crab (s/2,900) are among the specialties, but the *sopa de mariscos* (with octopus, squid, shrimp, crab, and more, s/9,000), is big enough for a meal, and swims above the rest. Open Mon.-Sat. 8am-10pm, Sun. 8am-3pm.

Rincón de Francia, Riofrio and Bolívar (tel. 578-686). For the cheap romantic in everyone. A dark room, candlelight, elegant French dining, soft music—the works. Filet mignon s/12,000, tongue s/10,000, crepes s/5,000. Open daily noon-10pm.

SIGHTS AND ENTERTAINMENT

The area surrounding Loja is so amazingly scenic that every visitor ends up outdoors, whether it's trekking in the nearby hills or admiring the view from the **Virgen de Loja** statue. Guarded by a terrified-looking stone lion below, the Virgin overlooks sprawling Loja from between the Andean hills. To get there, head east on Rocafuerte, go uphill past the river, head right then left on the dirt road to the base of the statue.

The **Parque Universitario La Argelia,** run by the **Universidad Nacional de Loja,** is another outstanding outdoor experience. Full of beautifully-maintained hiking trails, it covers the campus hills a couple miles south of the town center across the Río Malacatos from the campus (catch the "Argelia" or "Univ. Nacional" buses, or take a s/4,000 cab). Finding a good view is effortless: any way you go, you'll come to a *mirador* within 20 minutes. There is a small museum and info center at the base of the trail, and a wooden sign outside illustrates the various hikes. The trail that heads left provides a complete two-hour loop through a flowered pine forest, full of tranquil mountain streams, and (depending on the time of year) squadrons of butterflies. Across the road from the trail base, the **Jardín Botánico** boasts a wonderful collection of blossoms and buds (open daily during daylight hours; admission s/6,000).

Entertainment is a bit scarce in Loja, but the decor at the **Piano Bar Unicornio,** Bolívar 7-63 and Av. 10 de Agosto (tel. 574-083), is amusement enough. They don't serve cheese, but they might as well—the bar is decked out from head to toe in velvet and red and white stripes. Mirrors, a disco ball, and a piano/mike set-up threaten to add to the 70s lounge atmosphere. Beer s/3,000, daquiri s/6,000, ham sandwich s/2,500 (open Mon.-Sat. until 11pm).

■ Near Loja

CATAMAYO

Busy but uninspiring, Catamayo's main contribution to the traveler subculture is the **La Tola** airport (2.5km away), the nearest spot for flights in and out of Loja. Once the

CUENCA & S.HIGHLANDS

site for the city of Loja itself, Catamayo has been untroubled by major happenings ever since the better-known metropolis moved 30km east in 1548, two years after its founding. However, travelers with early-morning, late-evening, and standby flights can avoid complete boredom by staring at the cops in unusual straw cowboy hats striding along Catamayo's main street, **Isidro Ayora,** or finding shapes in the dust clouds that swirl through the surrounding roads. A sunny afternoon at the **Centro Recreacional Popular Eliseo Arias Carrión,** 5km away, is the perfect antidote to air-port claustrophobia (s/500 by bus from Catamayo, s/2,500 from Loja). A popular spot for families on the weekends, the center has sports facilities, a large pool, fresh air, and appropriately enough, an airplane smack in the middle of the grounds (open daily during daylight hours; s/1,500).

Activity centers around the **parque principal** between the east-west Isidro Ayora and Bolívar and the north-south Av. 24 de Mayo and Catamayo. Pay thousands of sucres (cash only) for calls from **EMETEL,** on Isidro Ayora across from the gas station (no credit card or collect calls allowed; open daily 8am-10pm). **Cooperativa Transportes,** on Catamayo near Isidro Ayora and the Parque Principal, has **buses** to **Loja** (every 30min., 45min., s/2,500). **Camionetas** to El Cisne leave from the corner of Catamayo and Mercadillo when full (1hr., s/3,000). **Farmacía Macará,** Bolívar and Av. 24 de Mayo (tel. 677-149), is on the *parque principal* (open Mon.-Sat. 7am-9pm, Sun. 7am-noon). Catamayo's equivalent of a hospital is the **Centro de Salud de Catamayo,** Av. 18 de Noviembre and Espejo (tel. 677-146; open Mon.-Fri. 8am-noon and 2-6pm). Call the **police** at tel. 677-101. The **phone code** is 07.

There's not much reason to spend the night in Catamayo unless you have an early-morning flight and want to sleep in a bit, rather than catching a sunrise bus from Loja. The **Hotel Granada,** Av. 24 de Mayo and Espejo (tel. 677-243), has snug, grayish rooms. Street-side windows and balconies provide a built-in sound system (s/12,000 per person with bath, groups of 3 or more s/10,000). **Hotel Turis,** Ayora and Av. 24 de Mayo (tel. 677-126), is conveniently close to the bus stop, has private baths, and is the most economical option around (s/10,000 per person). The sunny courtyard is compensation for the dark surrounding rooms. At **Hotel Rosarina** next door (tel. 677-006), the clean, shiny linoleum-floored rooms are a pleasant surprise after climbing the dingy cement staircase (with bath and color TV s/15,000 per person).

Restaurants in Catamayo are basic; choose a cheap *almuerzo* spot near the *parque principal* and hope it's clean. The **Embajador,** Isidro Ayora and Catamayo, is near the *parque principal* and next to the Hotel Reina el Cisne. Its staple Ecuadorian grub comes recommended from frequent fliers (entrees s/3,500-5,000). **Bachita,** on the corner of 18 de Noviembre and Ayora, is shadier and quieter (*merienda* s/5,000). Both the Embajador and Bachita are open daily 8am-10pm. **Hostería Bella Vista's restaurant** has the best mountain view and is the only restaurant with matching silverware and plates, but the food is unexciting: grilled meats and a few rice dishes (*pollo a la plancha* with all the trimmings, s/8,000; open daily 8am-10pm).

EL CISNE

For five days every summer (Aug. 16-20), a river of faith pours into Loja from El Cisne, led by a famous statue—**La Virgen del Cisne.** The local virgin, a common postcard image, floats on the shoulders of the hearty pilgrims who clog the 40km road to Loja. Not one to settle down, the Virgin stays in Loja for only a short while; on November 1, she begins her crowd-surfing return to El Cisne. A sign of die-hard Catholicism, the Chaucer-worthy pilgrims consider the trek almost enough to merit canonization. After all, for some of them, completing the one-way trip, sometimes on their knees, amounts to a minor miracle in itself. The easier, though less devout, route to El Cisne involves taking a three-hour bus ride from Loja's *terminal terrestre* (Catamayo Transports has one direct bus daily at 4pm, Fri. 9am, Sun. 7:30 and 8:30am). Take a bus to Catamayo to catch the erratic, unpredictable *camionetas* to El Cisne, or take the marathon trip from Loja to Catamayo to San Pedro to El Cisne, changing buses along the way. Make sure to ask about return times. Outside of the fascinating procession, the town's best offering is the sanctuary itself, a building gargantuan in both scale and

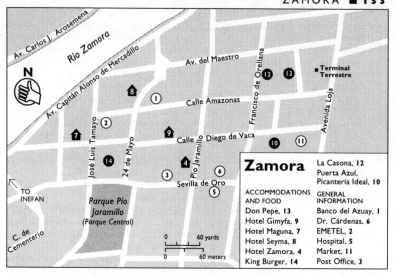

Zamora

Zamora	La Casona, 12 Puerta Azul, Picantería Ideal, 10
ACCOMMODATIONS AND FOOD	**GENERAL INFORMATION**
Don Pepe, 13	Banco del Azuay, 1
Hotel Gimyfa, 9	Dr. Cárdenas, 6
Hotel Maguna, 7	EMETEL, 2
Hotel Seyma, 8	Hospital, 5
Hotel Zamora, 4	Market, 11
King Burger, 14	Post Office, 3

reputation among Catholics. The statue of the Virgin (which is originally from Quito) and her sanctuary have conspicuously moved the locals—especially when it came time to name buildings and buses. Despite regional Catholic significance, generally only the truly fascinated, the well-timed, and the imminently papal take the long daytrip between El Cisne and Loja. Since El Cisne has no hotels, lesser pilgrims have to proceed at least 40km back out of town to Catamayo for a bed.

■ Zamora

Maybe Coronado was looking too far north when he searched the American southwest in vain for the mythical golden city of El Dorado. According to local legend, El Dorado glistened right around here in the Amazon Basin. Ecuador's modern city of gold, Zamora (pop. 9000) is a rustic jungle town that suddenly found itself in the center of things when the gold rush began in nearby **Nambija.** Situated just before the eastern Sierra becomes the southern Oriente, Zamora remains wonderfully untouristed and friendly, yet is home to a comfortable hotel, decent restaurants, and easy access to primary tropical rainforest and Amazon basin through the **Parque Nacional Podocarpus** and the **Yankuam** tour agency. Some come to Zamora just for the ride; the newly-finished highway winds along cliffs and roadside waterfalls on the side of the Río Zamora valley, descending from *páramo* highland cloud forests to the leafy, palm-laden habitats of the tropical Oriente. But all that's gold does not glisten. The industrial mining equipment and tin-roofed gold-boom houses haphazardly grip the sides of tropical river-valley hills, interrupting the jungle-town habitat.

Orientation and Practical Information Activity in Zamora centers around the town's main park and church, **Parque Pio Jaramillo,** at the junction of **Tamayo** and **Diego de Vaca.** Essential for Parque Nacional Podocarpus excursions, **INEFAN** is on the highway before you enter town coming from Loja, across from the cemetery (open Mon.-Fri. 9am-noon and 2-5pm). **Banco del Azuay** (tel. 605-235), next to EMETEL, will change dollars but not traveler's checks (open Mon.-Fri. 8am-4pm, Sat. 9am-1pm). Many stores will also change cash on weekends, but at lower rates. Make collect or calling-card calls from **EMETEL** (tel. 605-104 or 604-105), near Tamayo, one block from the main plaza away from the church (open daily 8am-10pm). **Yankuam,** 24 de Mayo and Diego de Vaca, has tourist info and can help find tours to the jungle (open Mon.-Fri. 8am-noon and 2-5pm, Sat. 9am-1pm). The **termi-**

CUENCA & S.HIGHLANDS

nal terrestre is at the end of town, one block from Diego de Vaca. **Cooperativa Loja** sends the best buses to: **Loja** (3, 5, 9, 11am, 1, and 6pm, 2 hr., s/6,000); **Gualaquiza** (6, 10am, and 2:30pm, 5hr., s/9,000) via **Yantzaza** (1½hr., s/3,000) and **El Pangui** (3hr., s/6,000); **Quito** (3pm, 18hr., s/46,000); **Machala** (8pm, s/22,000); and **Guayaquil** (5pm, s/30,000). **Transportes Pullman Viajeros** sends the most buses to **Cuenca** (9:45am, 6, and 10:30pm, 11hr., s/21,000); and **Saraguro** (6:25pm, s/11,000). **Samora-Chiuchipe** has the most comprehensie provincial bus schedule to: **Yantzaza** (every hr., 5am-6pm, 1½hr., s/3,000); **Romerillos** (6:30am, 2pm, s/3,000); and other nearby villages. **Farmacías Santa Fé** and **Santa Aria** are on Diego de Vaca toward the *terminal terrestre* (open Mon.-Sat. 8:30am-noon and 2-10pm). **Hospital Julius Deepfuer** (emergency tel. 605-149), is two blocks left from the church (open Mon.-Fri. 8am-noon and 2-6pm). Dr. Jorge Cardenás (tel. 606-123), makes emergency house (or hotel) calls 24 hours. The **phone code** is 07.

Accommodations and Food Hotel Maguna, Diego de Vaca (tel. 605-919), 1½ blocks from plaza towards the river. Wood-parquet floors are a polished work of art, while the beds are some of the softest and cleanest in town. All rooms have large windows and TV. The rooms are ready for hot nights: with refridgerators and cold water showers (singles s/27,000; doubles s/50,000). **Hotel Zamora**, Sevilla de Oro and Pio Jaramillo (tel. 605-253), near the plaza, offers simple but airy rooms. Unfortunately, cold water shared bathrooms are for shower-shoe wearers only (s/10,000 per person). **Hotel Seyma**, Av. 24 de Mayo and Amazonas (tel. 605-583), near the plaza, explores the fundamental essence of simplicity: bare wood floors, a hanging light bulb, and cold-water shared bathrooms. Windows and downstairs courtyard are small concessions to luxury (s/10,000 per person). The **Hotel Gimfa Internacional,** Diego de Vaca and Pío Jaramillo (tel. 605-024), is the only place you'll find hot water and carpeted floors. Color TVs and underpopulated downstairs disco launch it into executive-class (comparative) luxury (singles s/30,000; doubles s/50,000).

Puerta Azul and **Picantera Ideal,** Diego de la Vaca, near the market, grill, fry, and chop sea bass into locally popular *almuerzos* (s/5,000) and a la carte dishes (s/6,000-7,000). **La Casoria,** on Orellano downhill from Amazonas, serves *bistec,* chicken, and other non-swimming creatures next door to a laundry-filled courtyard. At **Don Pepe's,** near the *terminal terrestre,* order the *almuerzo* (s/4,000) or *merienda* (s/3,500) if you want to fit in—it's what everyone else does. Or assert your individuality and get an a la carte dish, such as the whole grilled *corvina* (sea bass, s/8,000). **King Burger,** across form the church on the corner of the plaza, grills beef for s/4,000. Restaurants are open daily roughly 8am-10pm, but don't always stick to those hours.

Sights and Entertainment Zamora is a sleepy town, particularly at night. You might check out the unusually-shaped **church** in the center of town, the pleasant park, or the **market** on Diego de Vaca across from the bus station. When it gets dark, you can admire the tropical stars. Otherwise, hit the sack early and save your energy for the town's main attraction: **Parque Nacional Podocarpus** (see below).

When the El Dorado myth died in the 16th century, **gold** fell out of the conquistadors' minds and the Ecuadorian limelight. Few suspected that a hard-to-access area of the Oriente offered more riches than its oil and biodiversity. When gold was unexpectedly discovered in the Zamora area about 15 years ago, a mining frontier culture sprouted up alongside the Oriente vegetation and the conservationist colonies of the rainforest (see **We Don't Need No Stinkin' Badges!,** p. 157).

The gold-rush town of **Nambija,** four hours from Zamora near the road to Gualaquiza, has been a mining spot for hundreds of years, yet was unknown outside of *indígena* communities until the 1980s. Ever since Ecuadorian miners struck upon a rich lode here, Nambija has attracted hopeful adventurers with a pick-axe in one hand and a hard-hat in the other. The traditional, isolated village was rapidly transformed into a cluster of tin-roofed shacks and clanking gold-sifting sluices perched on steep slopes surrounded by a Podocarpus-worthy cloud forest. The scruffy town is definitely daytrip material (hotels are rudimentary, and the slippery muddy paths that serve as streets can be unsafe), but it's a fascinating segment of rural Ecuador. The bus (s/4,000) from the Namirez stop on the Zamora-Yantzaza highway winds up through waterfall-infested cloud forest for three hours before leaving you at a clearing with a ramshackle wooden building. From there, follow the muddy path along the cave-dotted cliff until the town comes into sight. There are several small stores and *sandwicherías* interspersed with the houses across the river—but it's safest to bring your own food. The caves and small mines in the cliffs above town are tempting, but beware of the huge pigs, dogs, and occasional armed owners guarding them. When you've gawked (and been gawked at—this is not tourist country) enough, buses return to Namirez every hour until 6pm.

Over the past two years, the military has maintained a higher profile, trying to prevent and eradicate the growth of more Nambijans mining in restricted areas like the nearby Parque Nacional Podocarpus. Nevertheless, signs of mining culture line the Zamora-Macas highway, the southern Oriente's only road. **Gualaquiza, Yantzaza, Limón,** and similar villages play host to roving miners and oily mining trucks barreling through town. Machete-wielding prospectors venture deep into the untamed jungles in search of the next mother lode. The **Guadalupe** area, near La Paz and Av. 28 de Mayo, as well as areas to the north, are hotbeds of mining-development activity. Rifle stores, mining supply stores, and miners on vacation mingle with the small-town *tranquilidad* of these slopes on the main Zamora-Macas highway, but true lawless frontier towns require longer, harder trips over footbridges and mule paths. Use caution: gold-hungry, cave-protecting miners, the Perú-wary army, poisonous snakes and spiders, and poor sanitation create a very volatile atmosphere to wander in.

■ Parque Nacional Podocarpus

ZONA ALTA (LOJA ENTRANCE)

Layer upon layer of rolling cloud forests obscure the misty mountain scenery in the high-altitude section of Parque Nacional Podocarpus. Miles of cliffside paths traverse this *zona alta,* a hearty ecosystem which overcame the winds and rains to grow, flower, breed, and proliferate at 3,600m above sea level. Notorious and elusive highfliers—the toucan *de altura,* the quetzal, and the Andean cock-of-the-rock—hide in the fingers of fog that cloud the Podocarpan sky.

It takes three or four days to reach the interior part of Podocarpus, but dayhikers need not feel deprived. There are four main *senderos* (paths) through beautiful mountain terrain, all of which leave from the main *refugio* at the park entrance. Mainly for children or families, **Sendero Oso de Anteojos** (Spectacled Bear Path) is a short 400m loop near the entrance. Although this trail gives a taste of the park's natural nirvana, only the paths that go onward and upward provide climactic vistas. **Sendero Bosque Nublados** (Cloud Forest Path) climbs higher through the clouds and offers slightly larger servings of the scenic delights below. This 700m trail is more difficult and takes two hours to complete. **Sendero al Mirador** captures the essence of Podocarpus, revealing a veritable banquet of foggy soup vistas along the way. The view from the 3600m *mirador* astounds, and a post-peak picnic here is an excellent reward for a challenging uphill journey. Birdwatchers can observe a feathered cabaret, and lucky hikers who smell strongly of food might glimpse a spectacled bear, mountain tapir, fox, or puma. Don't get too comfortable, because half the hike is still to come. The 3.5km, medium-difficulty trail stammers along a precarious ridgewalk, obscured by mist in the summertime, but clear and dry in the winter. Less ambitious hikers, whether plagued by lethargy or a stone in the shoe, can opt out of the second part of the trail and do only the one-hour hike to the *mirador* and back.

If Sendero al Mirador is a banquet, **Sendero Las Lagunas del Compadre** is a culinary orgy worthy of the gods. The 14km trail leads to the jewel in the crown of Podocarpus—shimmering lakes buried deep in the mountain forest. The total excursion takes two or three days, and the absence of trail facilities makes proper camping equipment essential for this festival of scenery. With water everywhere, trails can be muddy during the summer and steep parts are often slippery. Huge, waterproof rubber boots are the intrepid hiker's only defense against mud-soaked footwear and pants. Animals scatter in the more well-hydrated climate, making the drier season best for fauna-watching. In January and February, grab the nearest pair of binoculars and follow the circling birds. Spectacled bears and *dantas* (tapirs) prefer to romp during November and December. The plants, however, are less particular about road conditions. The punk era never ends for the red-spiked bromeliads that line the trails; orchids and bamboo provide an off-setting floral chorus.

Staying in the park for more than a few hours? Drinking a lot of water? The *refugio* is the perfect refuge, with a bathroom, several beds, a kitchen, and an overnight staff. Cabañas near the *refugio,* farther into the forest, are an *au natural* alternative. The trails begin at the Cajanuma station, where a US$10 fee buys access to the entire Sierra section, including the camping cabañas and resource-laden *refugio.* The station lies about 15km from Loja, off the road to Vilcabamba. Unfortunately, buses and shared taxis heading to Vilcabamba will drop you off on the highway, leaving a grueling 8km uphill hike to the station itself. A hired taxi can handle the road all the way there on good days (about s/35,000 round-trip), but 4WD vehicles are ideal.

ZONA BAJA (ZAMORA ENTRANCE)

Tropical butterflies flutter across virtually every step of the trails in Parque Nacional Podocarpus *zona baja,* a primary tropical rainforest along the Río Bombuscara. Though lovers of the cloud forest might beg to differ, a consensus of INEFAN officials and butterfly aficionados hold that the jungle section of Podocarpus outshines its uphill counterpart. Beautifully kept trails wind past waterfalls and rainforest streams, creating an omnipresent chorus of rushing water to accompany the scenic symphonies of river views and jungle greenery. Budding botanists can explore the Universidad Nacional de Loja study area, home to a cacophonous diversity of plants. Highlights include over 40 varieties of orchids and the *cascarilla* tree, the source of quinine, a key ingredient in both malaria remedies and tonic water. Colorful wildlife accompanies you on your journey through the *zona baja:* yellow butterflies fluttering with each footstep, spectacled bears rustling nearby trees, and toucans croaking overhead. Wildlife is best in the heart of the park—farmers, miners, and other humans have shoved most of the creatures away from the park's edges.

The *zona baja's* entrance fee reflects its good standing with the locals—twice as nice for twice the price, admission runs US$20. Buy tickets from the INEFAN office in Zamora (tel. 605-315), a 10-minute walk from town on the highway (open Mon.-Fri. 8am-noon and 2-5pm). Those looking to save some sucres can buy tickets from the INEFAN office in Loja for half the price—admission tickets for either part of the park are honored at all entrances for a week after purchase date. Inside the park, the station at the trail entrance is staffed 24 hours. Get a taxi from Zamora's *terminal terrestre* for about s/35,000 round-trip (arrange a pickup time with the driver in advance). Even with a car, visitors must make a 2km uphill walk to the Bombuscara ranger station. INEFAN trucks also come and go periodically, but are often full.

Several *zona baja* trails start from the Bombuscara ranger station. A short trail from the station down a wooden staircase leads to the river itself, where you can **swim** in fresh water next to a **large waterfall.** Water clarity varies depending on recent rainfall, but take proper jungle-swimming precautions. **Los Helechos** is a trail so short that spending a half-hour on it requires self-control. INEFAN helps the time-killing process with a brochure, available in Zamora, offering 11 points of interest along the trail. Among the labeled botanical attractions are the orchids, *guarumo, helechos* (huge trees), palms, and *cascarilla.* The longest path, **Sendero Higuerones,** is a two-hour round-trip trek along the Río Bombuscara. Bushwhacking, backwoods camping, and general exploring away from trails are legal, allowing the more outgoing to explore the rainforest more intimately. Bring a mosquito net if you plan to camp in the heart of the jungle. The less-intrepid can explore the *cabañas,* near the station. There are also accommodations in the station itself for one or two people on research excursions. If interested, make arrangements with INEFAN in Zamora.

Another entrance to Podocarpus's *zona baja* is two hours south of Zamora at a tiny town called **Romerillos.** INEFAN officials staff a *refugio* similar to the one at Bombuscara, but much smaller. **Buses** head to Romerillos from Zamora each morning (see **Zamora, Practical Information,** p. 153); ask about return times. The Romerillos entrance is not only off the tourist trail, but it is also in one of the hot spots of miner-conservationist conflict.

We Don't Need No Stinkin' Badges!

Gold miners and conservationists have traditionally mixed about as well as mayonnaise and ice cream, and nowhere in Ecuador are the gold wars more heated than in Parque Nacional Podocarpus's primary tropical rainforest. In the years since the recent gold rushes in Nambija and the Zamora area, miners have viewed the government-protected national park as treasure just waiting to be dug up. Photos in Podocarpus's *refugios* show the San Luis, Cerro Toledo, and Río Numbala areas, defaced and devastated by illegal mining excavations. In the high *refugio,* some of the chairs have holes in the upholstery, marks left by miners' knives in the INEFAN-run shelter, vandalism of 1996. One conservationist was recently shot by miners in another scuffle.

As gunshots and illegal bulldozers echo through the leafy jungle grounds and drown out the gentle buzz of rainforest insects, INEFAN and other conservation groups' messages of ecological awareness, "Take only photos, leave only footsteps," have never been more pressing. While taking care to heed their warnings, try not to lose perspective of the miners' side of the battles. They deem conservationists rich kids with nothing better to do than impede the working class's honest attempts to support their starving families. Where conservationists see endangered species, miners see dinner for their children. A solution is not as simple as it might seem; the battle over mountains, valleys, and rivers is a symptom of class struggles that cut as deep as the Río Bombuscara itself.

GETTING THE MOST OUT OF PODOCARPUS

All of Podocarpus is impressive, but as usual, the best parts are the hardest to get to. The easy-access fringes of the park, overrun with tourists, miners, farmers, and the occasional grazing cow, will satisfy casual plant-lovers, but will disappoint hard-core botanists and animal seekers. **Tours**—to both parts of the park—are easy to find in Loja and Vilcabamba. The **Arco Iris Foundation** in Loja, Lauro Guerrero, and Mercadillo (tel. 572-926), one block from the river, is a local, non-profit conservation group that frequently jeeps up and down the hill and offers guided park tours (free if you have a "special" purpose; otherwise, negotiate a price). Talk to director Fausto López for details (open Mon.-Fri. 8am-5pm). **Biotours Ecuador,** Colón 14-96 and Sucre (tel./fax 578-398), Loja, has three- to six-day tours with all equipment and food included for approximately US$90 per person. Tour routes and guide style can be adjusted to suit your preferences and the office has a huge collection of slides and other info to help you choose your trip. **Vilcatur,** Colón and Bolívar (tel. 56-493), Loja, specializes in shorter, more docile tours to the park for curious but sedentary people. Prices range from US$20-$75 per person per day. The Vilcabamba guides **Orlando Falco** and **Gavin's Tours** tend to use their favorite little-known access trails and avoid the state-run INEFAN-dominated sections of the park.

■ Vilcabamba

Gently resting in a rolling valley at the southern tip of the highlands, the hot, sleepy town of Vilcabamba looks like any other small town: activity centers around a church-endowed main plaza, cars and burros mix on the streets, and roosters replace alarm clocks. But it only takes a second to realize that, from the neon-blue lights highlighting the church's cross to the tie-dye-era delicacies like banana bread and granola in the stores, Vilcabamba is in a gringo-infused world of its own. The town's fame has its origins in the legends of residents who lived to ridiculously old ages in the clean air, mild climate, and unpolluted surroundings of the *Valle de la Juventud Eterna* (Valley of Eternal Youth). But modern-day Vilcabamba owes its reputation as an unforgettable trip to its flora, like the remarkable San Pedro cactus, often used as a hallucinogenic drug. Religious cult leader Johnny Lovewisdom may have imported the original group of gringo invaders in the 60s, but today's group of young, friendly and somewhat *fiesta*-oriented foreigners are very different than their white-clad, sexually abstinent predecessors. Drawn by the desire for a psychadelic experience more than the promise of contegenarian life, Vilcabamba's gringo contingent is a mellow mix of merrymakers who ask nothing more than to lounge around and enjoy the countryside, perhaps on short hikes or longer "journeys" through the surrounding hills. Although travelers seeking exoticism will quickly move on, the gringo-driven expansion of tourist services—from horse rentals to swimming pools to vegetarian restaurants—makes Vilcabamba a natural paradise with all the comforts of home.

Orientation and Practical Information Every 15 minutes or so throughout the day, buses and shared "Taxi Ruta" cars cruise in from Loja along **Avenida de la Eterna Juventud.** Activity in Vilacamba's center crowds around a **main plaza,** overlooked by a **church** on one side. Most of the bars and cafes are on the lower edge of town on Diego Vaca de la Vega and Agua de Hierro. Street names are hard to come by—but don't worry, most of the restaurants, bars, and cafes have signs with detailed maps in the main plaza. The **EMETEL** office, on the corner of the main plaza, does not allow anything but ridiculously expensive toll calls—no collect or calling-card calls. Calls to the U.S. cost s/27,000 per minute (open daily 8am-9pm). The **Hostal Madre Tierra** (tel. 580-269), is slightly more reasonable. You can call someone for about US$6 if you keep it under a minute, then receive a call back from them at normal rates. National calls cost s/5,000 for five minutes. Most **buses** stop near the main plaza in town. All buses pass through **Loja,** but **Sur Oriente** has the most buses that go directly there (17 per day, every hr., 5:30am-7pm, 1½hr., s/3,000). **Transportes Loja** goes to: **Quito** (5 per day, 2:30-9pm, 14hr., s/40,000); **Cuenca** (4 per day, 4:30am-9pm, 6hr., s/16,500); **Ambato** (5 per day, 1-8pm, 10hr., s/25,000); **Macará** (7 per day, 7am-11pm, 8hr.); **Machala** (4 per day, 4:30am-11:30pm); **Huaquillas** (9:30pm and 11:15pm, 8hr., s/15,000). Other *cooperativos* heading north are **Transportes Santa** and **Transportes San Luis.** The luxurious **Panamericana** buses, with food, toilet, A/C, and bus attendants, go to: **Riobamba** (12hr., s/28,000); **Quito** (5 per day, 2:30-9pm, 12hr., s/38,000); and **Guayaquil** (10:30pm, 9hr., s/24,000). **Taxi Ruta Av. 24 de Mayo** cabs get to Loja in less than one hour, but cram up to six people in a small car (s/4,000). Taxis leave from the center of town. **Farmacía Reina del Cisne** (tel. 580-289), is one block from the plaza, near EMETEL on the corner. **Hospital Kokichi Otani** (tel. 673-128 or 673-188), is three blocks away from the plaza along the road to Loja (clinic hours Mon.-Fri. 8am-noon and 2-6pm; 24hr. emergency service with one local ambulance). The **police** are three blocks from the plaza in the direction opposite the church (open 24hr.). The **post office** is located one block from the plaza, two blocks opposite the church (open Mon.-Fri. 8:30am-6pm, Sat. 9am-1pm). Vilcabamba's **phone code** is 07.

Accommodations and Food Outside town on the road from Loja, a 350m walk from the turn-off with a wooden sign, sits **Hostal Madre Tierra.** An icon of the gringo culture that has sprung up in Ecuador and Perú, Madre Tierra is a social, international spot (especially popular with Israelis), with summer-camp style communal meals that make it easy to find friends even if you come alone. The rustic but well-kept cabins cover a large section of country farmland with wide-perspective views of the hills and *fincas,* while the main lodge has a restaurant, outdoor swimming pool, and garden with hammocks cradled between palms and psychedelically-colored tropical flowers. Some cabins are a 10-minute hike from the main building, but have better views of the Andean countryside. Somewhat like a health spa, Madre Tierra offers a huge variety of fee-based activities, from horseback riding (s/25,000 per 4hr.) to massages (US$25). The more daring can try "colon therapy" (US$5.50 per 30min.). Otherwise stick to a whirlpool bath (US$1.75 per 30min.), hot clay bath (US$4.25 per 30min.), steam bath (US$4.25), or facials with clay and herbs or corn and honey US$4.25 (rooms US$9-13.50 per person—depending on gas or solar heated shower—includes unlimited lemonade and chilled water, breakfast, and a 3-course dinner fit for kings). The **Hidden Garden Pension** (tel./fax 580-281), one block downhill from the main plaza on Sucre, has a well-foliated inner courtyard, a chilly swimming pool, and a very talkative English-speaking owner. The guest kitchen includes an honor system store (singles US$6; doubles US$11; triples US$14; quads US$17), all with common bath (very clean with gas-fired shower). Email service and Internet access available. **Hotel Valle Sagrado,** right on the plaza in town, is the cheapest lodging in Vilcabamba. Rooms are far from sacred; they're quite small, but clean enough to sleep in. Electric hot water flows from the showers in the communal bathrooms. Hammocks, ping pong, a kitchen, and a laundry basin in the dusty court-yard round out the amenities (s/5,000 per person). **Hostal Mandango,** across the street from the *terminal terrestre,* has clean, airy rooms and a pleasant inner court-yard with hammocks and chairs. Common bathrooms lack toilet seats, but do have electrically-heated hot water (s/8,000 per person, with bath s/12,000). Ivan's Tours operates from the reception desk. **Hostería Vilcabamba** (tel. 580-271 or 580-273), on the Loja-bound road downhill from town, offers a central pool surrounded by idyllic tropical gardens, sauna, jacuzzi, and exercise room as well as beautiful, if character-less, rooms. Prices are steep for one, but a good bargain for larger groups (singles s/58,000; doubles s/86,000; triples s/108,000). An excellent but pricey **restaurant-bar** (entrees s/12,000 and up) and **Spanish language school** (tel. 673-131; US$4 per hr.), are also on the grounds. The pool is available for use by non-guests for a small fee. Orlando Falio's **pole-house** (leave message at tel. 673-186), located just outside of town on the river, accommodates four people in unspoiled solitude. Full kitchen, porch with hammocks, river view, and access to banana and other tropical fruit plants in the garden (doubles US$14; triples US$15; quads US$16).

Vilcabamba, in keeping with its gringo subculture, offers a wider selection of gra-nola, vegetarian food, banana bread, and other tie-dyed delicacies than any other Ecuadorian village. The **Valle Sagrado** vegetarian restaurant on the *parque central* serves basil-laden pesto (s/5,000), fresh salads, and various veggie sandwiches (s/4,000) on whole wheat bread. *Almuerzos* s/5,000. *Desayuno* (with granola, scram-bled eggs, vegetables, and coffee) s/5,000. **Restaurant Katherine,** one block uphill from the main plaza on Sucre, serves above-average Ecuadorian favorites at below average prices. Chicken with garlic (s/5,000), *almuerzo* (s/4,000). **Restaurant Valle Eterna Juventud,** two blocks downhill form the plaza, is Canadian-run and gringo-infested, but the menu is still mostly Ecuadorian. You're guaranteed a clean and tasty meal, and it won't break the bank (entrees s/3,000-6,000; open Mon.-Fri. 11am-9pm, Sat.-Sun. 3-9pm). **Pizzería Pepito's** outdoes itself to satisfy any cravings you may have for vegetable and herb filled omelettes (s/4,000-6,000) or homemade crust pizza (s/4,000-6,000 per monstrous slice). The Italian parmesan salad dressing is also a rare treat in Ecuador (open Tues.-Sun. 11am-11pm).

Sights and Entertainment The countryside provides all the sights and enter-tainment most Vilcabamba-goers could ask for. The sunny days are easily filled with leisurely strolls, heartier hikes, and horseback rides through the land's forested ter-rain. A number of trails criss-cross the hills near the town; one runs up from a left turn in the road just past the pizzeria—follow the river here up the mountain for awesome views. Most hotels have ample tourist-oriented displays that suggest other hikes. Horse-renters line the streets and constant price wars keep the fees down to the US$4-6 range for a four-hour tour with guide. Gavilan's **Enchanted Excursions to the Edges of the Earth** (tel. 571-025), offers more structured three-day horseback tours into the nearby cloud forest. While many satisfied customers recommend the guide, his price is a bit steep, at US$75 per three-day trip. His bulletin board on the western side of the main plaza gives details on upcoming trips. **Orlando Falco,** a trained zool-

Vilcabamba: The Early Years

Forty years ago, Vilcabamba was much like the other villages that dot the mountainsides of southern Ecuador. Change was to come from an unlikely source: an American paraplegic hermit named **Johnny Lovewisdom**. Mr. Lovewisdom's life of isolation came to an end in the 1950s, when he appeared in a TIME magazine article, and was sought out by a flock of disciples. He subsequently formed a religious sect, and brought his followers down to Vilcabamba to live a spiritually pure existence—members wore only white, were sexually abstinent, and ate only fruit. Soon, however, their chaste existence was disturbed by the arrival of a new member. At first, she fitted in with the sect's way of life, but before too long, she and Johnny went into "moral decline"—soon, she had experienced moral decline with just about every male member of the group. After that, things fell apart pretty quickly. Some of the original members have stuck around, though, and some say that Señor Lovewisdom himself continues to live on in the Vilcabamban countryside.

ogist, offers one-day cloud forest walks for US$20 per person, for groups of four or more. Tours can be arranged from the **Artesanal Primavera** shop in town near the plaza. **Ivan,** based at the Hostal Mandango, offers cheaper, more flexible horseback and hiking tours without extras like English-speaking guides and naturalist experts.

When the sun finally sinks below the Vilcabamban hills, nocturnal life begins to stir around town. **Disco Rami Bamba,** located at the turn-off to Madre Tierra, recreates southern California beach culture with pounding bass and volleyball nets. The gringo crowds gravitate toward the equally loud Led Zeppelin, Rastafarian decor, and barbeque-equipped roof garden at **Max's.** The German-run bar offers all the comforts of home: 35 different cocktails (s/7,000), two-for-one happy hour from 6-7pm, a large screen Sony TV with ample video collection, pool table, and a kitchen that's yours for the asking (open Tues.-Sun. 5pm-midnight, later on the roof). **The Green Triangle,** downhill from Max's, replaces Bob Marley with (fine?) art on the walls, and substitutes quiet "world/folk" music for Max's metal. Occasional Latin dancing nights. Saturday night fever complete with psychedelic cocktails, disco music, and John Travolta on TV (open Tues.-Fri. 4:30pm-midnight or later). **J.J. Bar Café Peña,** one block from the plaza behind the church, and **Rumors,** near the river bridge off the main street, are other popular, though less rambunctious, nightspots filled with gringos and Ecuadorians alike (both open Tues.-Sun. 8-11pm).

If the gringos get to you, **Zumba** and **Malacatos** offer the same scenery, but fewer tourists. Zumba, three hours south via a bumpy highway through the mountains is tantalizingly close to Perú (5km), but you can't cross the guarded border here. The town caters to the military, but if you like heavily forested mountains, it's worth a daytrip. Malacatos, about 30 minutes to the north along the road to Loja, features a massive blue-domed church that seems out of place in the otherwise small-town.

Guayaquil and the Western Lowlands

The lowlands—fertile plains sitting at the western base of the Andes—have long played a pivotal role in Ecuador's history. It was here that the first banana and cacao crops were planted on plantations during the 17th century, crops that would later take over the majority of this low, flat, well-irrigated land. The endemic forests that once shaded the fertile soil here were pushed farther and farther towards the perimeter of the lowlands, and in many cases pushed all the way out of their habitat and into extinction. Today, Río Palenque Science Center, to the north, shelters a small patch of what was once an expansive forest.

Such is the price burgeoning Ecuador was willing to pay to develop its most prosperous industry. Coming into its own during the youthful era of independence, the liberal port of Guayaquil was the luckiest benefactor of the newly booming agricultural industry. The profits that poured into Guayaquil made it more and more of a commercial city, and in turn further fueled the agricultural development that had already given it so much. This self-perpetuating cycle of agricultural, commercial, and urban development continued well into the 20th century. The discovery of oil in the Oriente in the 1970s decreased the economic significance of this area's agriculture, but Guayaquil and the lowlands continue to develop on the same path—as a commercial capital and the agricultural machine that fuels it.

▓ Guayaquil

Once an indigenous settlement, this coastal city was conquered by the Spanish in the 16th century. Legend has it that before surrendering their pride and their beloved home, the native prince and princess committed suicide. His name was Guayas, her name Quil, and from their martyrdom was born the name of the most populous city in Ecuador, with a population of over two million.

Guayaquil bustles. If Quito is the heart of Ecuador, Guayaquil is the liver; it's not pretty, but it's essential to the welfare of the country. From the day Francisco de Orellana landed here in 1537, this crowded port has been bombarded by commerce from the sea. Industry exploded in the early part of this century, establishing the nitty-gritty disposition that dominates Guayaquil's character to this day. The result is that millions of people can make a living here, but you have to question why they'd want to.

Most *guayaquileños* are kind, proud, and eager to show you why their "Pearl of the Pacific" is worth visiting. Aside from being a convenient stop on the way to the coast or Perú, Guayaquil offers the dense, winding, 400-year-old **Las Peñas** neighborhood, as well as an assortment of museums and very old but restored churches. But that's just the downtown. A whole other world—Mercedes Benzes, *Beverly Hills 90210* billboards and all—is found in *el norte:* not the U.S., but the suburbs of **Urdesa** and **Alborada** to the north of the city. The insane crowds and numerous clubs in these areas have given Guayaquil's nightlife a reputation as the wildest, most memorable around.

ORIENTATION

Guayaquil sprawls far to the north and south, but the 2 sq. km gridlike downtown—or *centro*—next to the river is easy enough to navigate. **El Malecón Simón Bolívar,** called **Malecón** for short, is a busy thoroughfare with many hotels and offices that follows the waterfront. **Avenida 9 de Octubre,** the main east-west boulevard in the city, starts at Malecón where **La Rotonda** (see **Sights,** p.169) stands and passes through the central **Parque del Centenario.** The "T" formed by Av. 9 de Octubre

161

and Malecón outlines the most important parts of the city. In general, the farther north and south you head from Av. 9 de Octubre in *el centro,* the more dangerous the area will be. **Guayaquil is not a safe city:** watch where you walk and who's walking with you. Take caution if you find yourself on an abandoned street. Eyes will be on you, especially if you're carrying a lot of baggage. The most common tourist area is along **Pedro Carbo** near the **Hotel Doral** and **Parque Bolívar.** This municipal area is generally safe for walking, alone or in groups. Taxis are helpful, even though the downtown area is almost small enough to cover on foot.

To get to the nearby suburbs, taxis or buses are a must. **Urdesa** and **Alborada** are north of *el centro,* in the same direction as the airport and bus station. These bourgeois suburbs are cleaner, safer, and strikingly more healthy-looking. The main strip in Urdesa, **Victor Emilio Estrada,** is packed with restaurants and shops and is *the* place for nightlife in Guayaquil, and probably in Ecuador. The **Las Peñas** neighborhood is to the east, near the **Río Guayas.** This river, which runs east of *el centro,* is spanned by the largest bridge in the country, the **Bridge of National Unity.** On the other side of the river is the run-down suburb of **Durán,** home to the train station. A ferry from Malecón also goes to Durán.

PRACTICAL INFORMATION

Tourist Offices: CETUR, Malecón and Aguirre (tel. 328-312 or 531-794; fax 531-044 or 329-377), 3 blocks south of La Rotonda. Tucked next to a pharmacy on the corner, it's up the stairway entrance on the 2nd floor. Mediocre photocopied maps and other info provided. One employee speaks English. They don't offer any tourist services, but they'll help you with questions or problems if they can (open Mon.-Fri. 8:30am-5pm). **Airport Kiosk,** in the middle of the larger terminal room, near international departures. English is spoken, and they have more experience in offering assistance (open daily 7am-7pm).

Consulates: Australia Ciadadela Kennedy Norte, Calle San Roque and Av. Francisco de Orellana (tel. 298-800; fax 298-822; open Mon.-Fri. 9am-1pm). **Canada,** Cordova 810 and Víctor Manuel Rendón, 21st floor, office 4 (tel. 563-580, 566-747; fax 314-562; open Mon.-Fri. 9:30am-1:30pm). **Colombia,** Córdova 812 and V.M. Rendón, 2nd floor, office 11 (tel. 563-308; fax 563-854; open Mon.-Fri. 9am-12:30pm and 2:30-5pm). **Israel,** Av. 9 de Octubre 729 and García Aviles (tel. 322-000; fax 328-196). **Perú,** Av. 9 de Octubre 411 and Chile, 6th floor (tel. 322-738 or 327-639; fax 325-679; open Mon.-Fri. 8:30am-1:30pm). **U.K.,** Córdova 623 and Padre Solano (tel. 560-400 or 563-850; fax 562-641 or 322-062; open Mon.-Fri. 9am-noon and 2:30-5pm). **United States,** Av. 9 de Octubre and García Moreno (tel. 321-152; fax 325-286; open Mon.-Fri. 8am-noon and 1:30-5pm).

Currency Exchange: The first several blocks of Av. 9 de Octubre, starting from the waterfront, are loaded with banks and *casas de cambio.* Swapping cash or traveler's checks is no problem during business hours, but afterward the search becomes a challenge. **Cambiosa,** on the 1st block of Av. 9 de Octubre (tel. 325-199 or 325-284), has good dollar-to-sucre rates. If the lines are long at the official *casas de cambio,* a swarm of quasi-legal cash traders congregate on Pichincha just south of Av. 9 de Octubre. Dubious, but fast.

American Express: Av. 9 de Octubre 1900 and Esmeraldas, 2nd floor (tel. 394-984 or 286-900). Offers travel information and receives mail without charge for card members (Spanish only; open Mon.-Fri. 9am-1pm and 2-6pm). Send mail to: Ecuadorian Tours, American Express, Av. 9 de Octubre 1900, Guayaquil, Ecuador.

ATMs: Most are located on and around Av. 9 de Octubre, near the waterfront.

Western Union: Malecón and P. Icaza (tel. 561-364; fax 564-986).

Airport: Simón Bolívar International Airport, Av. de las Américas (tel. 282-1000; fax 290-018), about 5km north of the city. The airport has 2 terminals separated by less than 1km. The larger one houses national and international flights. The smaller is the place to catch one of the more frequently departing *avionetas* to a national destination. A *casa de cambio* changes money for arriving international flights.

National flights: To: **Quito** (s/150,000); **Cuenca** (s/104,000); **Loja** (s/89,000); **Machala** (s/83,000); **the Galápagos** (US$167, $334 round-trip for foreigners). **Taxis** wait out front, but prepare to be ripped off. From the airport to the city cen-

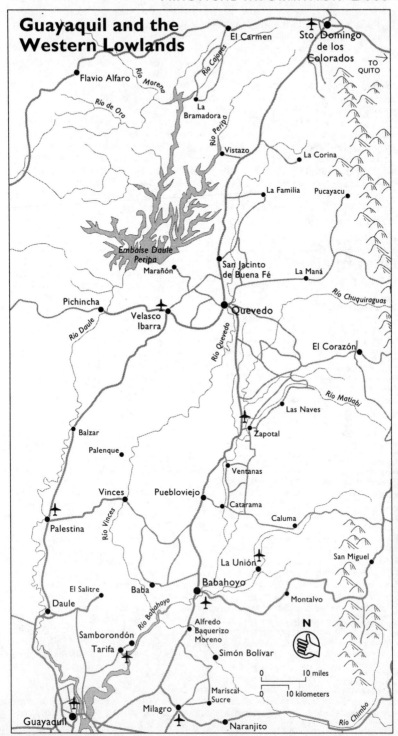

Guayaquil and the Western Lowlands

El Carmen
Sto. Domingo de los Colorados
TO QUITO
Flavio Alfaro
Río Morena
Río Coipres
Río de Oro
La Bramadora
Río Peripa
Vistazo
La Corina
La Familia
Pucayacu
Embalse Daule Peripa
Marañón
San Jacinto de Buena Fé
La Maná
Río Chuquiraguas
Pichincha
Velasco Ibarra
Río Daule
Quevedo
Río Quevedo
El Corazón
Río Matiabi
Las Naves
Balzar
Zapotal
Palenque
Ventanas
Vinces
Puebloviejo
Catarama
Caluma
Palestina
Río Vinces
San Miguel
La Unión
El Salitre
Baba
Babahoyo
Montalvo
Daule
Río Babahoyo
Samborondón
Alfredo Baquerizo Moreno
Tarifa
Simón Bolívar
N
0   10 miles
0   10 kilometers
Mariscal Sucre
Guayaquil
Milagro
Naranjito
Río Chimbo

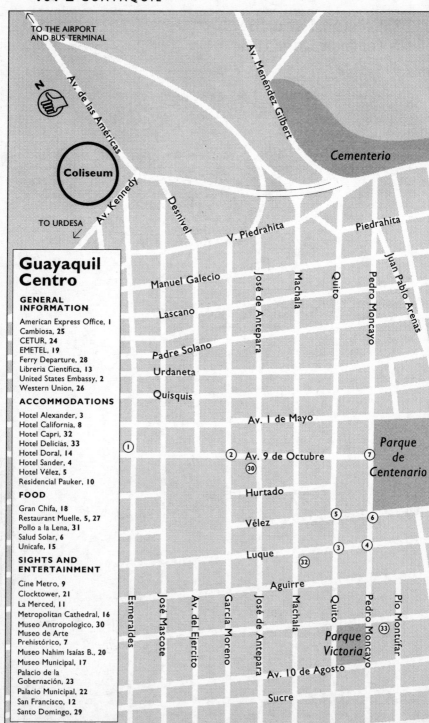

TO THE AIRPORT
AND BUS TERMINAL

Av. de las Américas

N

Av. Menéndez Gilbert

Cementerio

Coliseum

Av. Kennedy

TO URDESA

Desnivel

V. Piedrahita

Piedrahita

Juan Pablo Arenas

Guayaquil Centro

GENERAL INFORMATION

American Express Office, 1
Cambiosa, 25
CETUR, 24
EMETEL, 19
Ferry Departure, 28
Librería Científica, 13
United States Embassy, 2
Western Union, 26

ACCOMMODATIONS

Hotel Alexander, 3
Hotel California, 8
Hotel Capri, 32
Hotel Delicias, 33
Hotel Doral, 14
Hotel Sander, 4
Hotel Vélez, 5
Residencial Pauker, 10

FOOD

Gran Chifa, 18
Restaurant Muelle, 5, 27
Pollo a la Lena, 31
Salud Solar, 6
Unicafe, 15

SIGHTS AND ENTERTAINMENT

Cine Metro, 9
Clocktower, 21
La Merced, 11
Metropolitan Cathedral, 16
Museo Antropologico, 30
Museo de Arte Prehistórico, 7
Museo Nahim Isaías B., 20
Museo Municipal, 17
Palacio de la Gobernación, 23
Palacio Municipal, 22
San Francisco, 12
Santo Domingo, 29

Manuel Galecio

Lascano

Padre Solano

Urdaneta

Quisquis

José de Antepara

Machala

Quito

Pedro Moncayo

Av. 1 de Mayo

① ② Av. 9 de Octubre ⑦
③⓪

Parque de Centenario

Hurtado

⑤ ⑥

Vélez

③ ④

Luque
㉜

Aguirre

Esmeraldes

José Mascote

Av. del Ejercito

García Moreno

José de Antepara

Machala

Quito

Pedro Moncayo

Pío Montúfar

Parque Victoria

㉝

Av. 10 de Agosto

Sucre

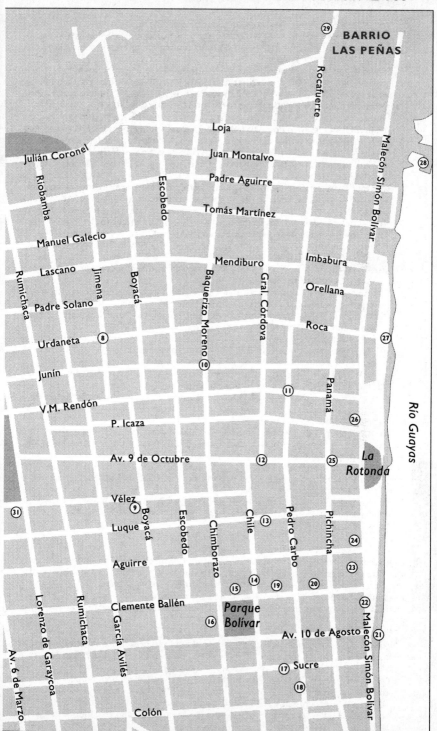

ter, a taxi ride should cost no more than s/8,000. If you are headed to the nearby outgoing bus station, argue the taxi driver down to around s/6,000. Avoid exorbitant prices by walking out to the highway and catching a taxi or bus there (the highway is not safe at night).

Travel Agencies: Guayaquil is bloated with travel agencies. Two which can help with inexpensive Galápagos trips are **Galasam,** Av. 9 de Octubre 424, Gran Pasaje (tel. 311-042; fax 313-351) and **Filantravel,** Bullén 212 and Pichincha (underneath Museo Nahim Isaís Barquet; tel. 324-080 or 325-529; fax 328-733).

Trains: The station is in **Durán,** about 2 blocks from the ferry landing. Head left from the landing, then down to the street that runs along the tracks. The train runs only to **Riobamba** and in-between locations, leaving daily at 6:25am (11hr., s/ 8,000 for Ecuadorians, US$14 for foreigners). Since the first ferry leaves Guayaquil at 7am, to get to the station before departure you'll either have to take a taxi or stay overnight in Durán.

Regional Buses: Jaime Roldos Aguila Terminal Terrestre, Av. de las Américas (tel. 297-574), a few km past the airport. A veritable food court of ticket counters and different *cooperativos,* the main room seems to go on forever, as do the departure times and destinations of the bus lines. Consistent prices to the same destinations spare you the task of shopping around. To: **Quito** (every 30min., 7hr., s/ 23,000); **Cuenca** (approx. every hr., 4½hr., s/17,000); **Salinas** (every 15min., 2¼hr., s/8,500); **Babahoyo** (every 10min., 5am-10:20pm, 1¼hr., s/3,000); **Ambato** (approx. every hr., 6hr., s/15,000); **Huaquillas** (approx. every 2hr., 4½hr., s/13,000); **Riobamba** (s/13,000).

City Buses: These ubiquitous vehicles are usually crammed with locals. Their cheapness is the key to their popularity. A bus ride is s/600-s/800, so if you have the time and skill to analyze the system, by all means wave one down. Be careful if you're carrying excessive luggage; crowded buses can be hotspots for thievery. Bus routes are occasionally printed in the newspaper; most people just know them by experience. Ask locals for help. Most routes run from the city center to outlying regions; the destination and cost of each bus is printed on the front window.

Ferries: To get to **Durán,** a boat leaves from the waterfront at Malecón and Juan Montalvo, 9 blocks north of La Rotonda. Departs for the other side of the Río Guayas every 30min. from 7am-6:30pm, except from 9am-noon and 2-4pm when departures are only on the hour. Returns to Guayaquil are equally frequent. The trip lasts 15min.

Taxis: Guayaquil drivers are notorious for taking advantage of "new arrivals" and tourists in general. It is best to decide on a fare before getting into a vehicle. Suggest a price and be willing to let a taxi go. Taxis between 2 places in *el centro* shouldn't cost more than s/2,000-3,000. Taxis between the airport or Urdesa and the city should run around s/7,000-8,000. Try the dispatch **Taxi Paraíso** (tel. 201-877 or 204-232).

Car Rental: Expensive and probably unnecessary. **Avis** (tel. 285-498), **Budget** (tel. 288-510 or 284-559), and **Hertz** (tel. 293-011, 511-316, or 327-895) all have offices in or near the airport.

Library: The **Guayaquil Municipal Library** is at Sucre and Pedro Carbo (tel. 515-738). Open Mon.-Fri. 9am-5pm, Sat. 10am-2pm.

Pharmacy: Street-level pharmacies are scattered throughout the downtown area. One popular chain is **Fybreca,** with a branch at V.E. Estrada 609 and Las Monjas (tel. 881-444 or 381-468), in the suburb of Urdesa (open 24hr.).

Medical Services: Two reputable hospitals are **Clínica Kennedy** (tel. 286-963) and **Clínica Guayaquil** (tel. 563-555). **Red Cross** ambulance service can be reached at 560-674.

Emergency: 199.

Police: Av. de las Américas (tel. 101), several km from center towards the airport.

Post Office: On the west side of Pedro Carbo between Aguirre and Ballén (tel. 514-713). Has a Lista de Correos (open Mon.-Fri. 8am-6pm, Sat 8am-2pm).

Telephones: EMETEL, at Pedro Carbo and Ballén, in the same building as the post office. The place to go to make international calls, but beware. Calls over longer distances are charged by the minute, so expect to pay for operator problems and dialing mistakes. Local and long-distance national calls and telegram service are

also available (open daily 8am-12:20pm, 1-6pm, and 7-9:30pm). There is another office on the corner of Boyacá and Urdaneta. For calls on public payphones, tokens are sold all over by street vendors. The number for **information** is 104.
Telephone Code: 04.

ACCOMMODATIONS

As you would expect with a commercial city of this size, Guayaquil has many fine hotels, offering all the amenities of the industrial world. Unfortunately, these come with prices that correspond. Affordable options exist, but they tend to be drab, shabby, and located at dangerously unfashionable addresses; be sure to see the room before you pay for it. Air conditioning costs extra, but in muggy Guayaquil many find that it's worth the extra sucres. Most hotels in *el centro* have armed guards out front—don't be alarmed, be thankful.

Ecuahogar, Av. Isidro Ayora (tel. 273-288 or 240-388; fax 248-341), across from the B.E.V. bank. About 10km north of *el centro*, near the airport and bus terminal. All 4 floors of this breezy, relaxed hacienda are open to the residential suburban air. A hammock and panoramic city view give the top floor rooms an especially lazy ambience. The multilingual *dueña* speaks Spanish, English, German, and French. Laundry (s/6,000) and phone services (s/2,000). Reservations suggested. US$9, HI/ISIC members US$8; with private bath US$11; US$10. Light breakfast included. Organizes tours to the city and surrounding area; helpful in finding cheap tours to the Galapagos. Books rooms in other HI hostels through internet connection.

Hotel Capri, Machala and Luque (tel. 326-341; fax 517-166), provides plain but very comfortable rooms; check out the marble bed frames. All rooms come with A/C, TV, private bath, and hot water. Singles s/50,000, doubles s/70,000.

Residencial Pauker, Baquerizo Moreno 902 and Junín (tel. 565-385). This dank establishment is at the top of the lower-end motels, so don't be too alarmed that most guests don't stay the night. Staff is eager to please. All rooms have beds, some even 3 or 4. Some private baths (but no hot water), and all except the cheapest rooms have A/C or fans for those sweaty nights. Can often be noisy. Mattresses and sheets look well-worn. Some rooms have balconies, reception/TV room in front. Singles s/15,000, with A/C s/20,000; doubles s/25,000.

Hotel Sander, Luque 1110 and Pedro Moncayo (tel. 320-030 or 320-944). The Hotel Sander is like a tuna fish sandwich: it's plain, it's not too expensive, and it gets the job done. The tuna is the A/C and television in every room; it's cold though—there's no hot water. The bread is the plain beds in single or double rooms, both s/36,000. No mayonnaise. Got any chips?

Hotel Alexander, Luque 1107 and Pedro Moncayo (tel. 532-000, 532-651, or 532-652; fax 328-474), between Quito and Moncayo. Almost attached to the Sander, the Alexander offers more for more. The multiple floors rise above a busy, generally safe part of Guayaquil. Some rooms have A/C and a hot-water private bath; a few even have eye-jolting fluorescent comforters covering soft, heavenly mattresses. Awesome staff stores guests' valuables in a safe in the main office. Elevators provide wheelchair access. Reservations suggested. Singles s/46,000; doubles s/64,000; add 10% service tax.

Hotel Vélez, Vélez 1021 and Quito (tel. 530-356, 530-311, 530-292, or 532-430; fax 328-864). So close to the Parque del Centenario you can almost hear the masses congregating. Functional, bland, no hot water, and staff is less than eager to help. No matter, though; for the price, this ascetic place does its job. Rooms begin at s/36,000, with A/C s/40,000.

Hotel California, Urdaneta 529 and Jimena (tel. 302-296, 302-376, 302-406, or 302-484; fax 562-548). The rifle-toting guard at the door is a good hint that the area is not a safe place to frolic with a bevy of luggage, but he also insures that the inside is plenty safe. It's also much more luxurious than other similarly-priced places in Guayaquil. All rooms have A/C, private bath, and cable TV. The ceilings are high, but have no mirrors; no pink champagne on ice, either. Full phone services, and cafeteria downstairs (open 7am-11:30pm). Choose *"moderada"* level rooms (singles s/40,000; doubles s/50,000), or *"superior"* rooms that include a carpet, refrigerator, phone, and hot water (singles s/50,000; doubles s/60,000).

Hotel Delicia, Bullén 1105 and Pedro Moncayo (tel. 324-925). Not the nicest neighborhood or hotel in town, but the rooms are decent and the simple rooms are cheap. There's a common area with TV on the first floor. Singles s/15,000; doubles s/30,000, with private bath s/40,000, with A/C, s/60,000.

FOOD

Along the sidewalks of Guayaquil, locals in the know frequent the anonymous one-room restaurants whose few tables spill out into the streets. These *comedores,* so similar to one another that it's difficult to tell them apart, serve cheap *almuerzos* and *meriendas* of the day. Often, though, the food quality reflects the roughly s/3,000 price tag attached to most meals. Fancier restaurants come complete with names, a bigger selection of food, and higher, but still reasonable, prices. The nicer hotels usually have dependable restaurants open for all three meals, though they won't provide the best deal in town. Beware: nicer places often charge the 10% tax and 10% service charge. Ask your server.

Salud Solar, Pedro Moncayo 1015 (tel. 519-955), between Luque and Velez, a few stores away from Parque Centenario. The bright yellow and red walls of this one-room sidewalk restaurant house creative and cheap vegetarian food (s/5,000-8,000). But wait—how can that *arroz con pollo* be vegetarian? Soy! A good option in a not-very-vegetarian-friendly city (open daily 7am-10pm).

Restaurant Muelle 5, on the waterfront at Malecón and Roca (tel. 561-128), at the site of the old Pier 5. Muelle 5's wooden planks are supported by pilings on the bank of the Río Guayas. Appropriately, the menu includes plenty of seafood dishes as well as other tasty Ecuadorian-style grub (s/10,000-17,000). Get a sunny table at the end of the deck and watch banana branches float toward the Gulf of Guayaquil (open daily 11am-11pm).

Restaurant Manantial, V.E. Estrada 520 and Monjosa (tel. 382-983), a lively, patioed place on the Urdesa strip. Loud, young, and often visited by travelers, this restaurant and bar is an escape from the humdrum of many Guayaquil eateries. Wood interior is packed with beer-guzzling *jóvenes* (youths) chatting above the general roar. Come for a drink or a meal (a mere s/8,000-14,000) and lounge out front on the covered deck. Wide selection of food, drink, and *cigarillos* (open Mon.-Sat. 9am-2am, Sun. 9am-1am).

Gran Chifa, Pedro Carbo 1018 (tel. 530-573 or 530-784), near Sucre. There are many *chifas* in Guayaquil, but none like the great one. Stroll in on a boardwalk, past trimmed bushes and genuine Chinese decor. Once your mind has entered the People's Republic, you can enjoy copious noodles and such (*menu del día:* shrimp, lo mein, fried rice, egg roll, and soup–s/15,000). English translations on the menu are a blessing, and the kitchen is spacious and clean (open Tue.-Sun. 11:30am-2:30pm and 6:30-10pm).

La Parrilla del Ñuto, V.E. Estrada 1219 (tel. 387-068). This Urdesa eatery pulls in scores of suburban *guayaquileños* for its grilled meat and pizza. Servings are big; the filet mignon is a bit of a splurge at s/30,000, but the hearty *porciones* of pizza are a bargain at s/5,000. (Don't order the *metro* unless you have five hungry friends.) The smell of the meat and chicken grilling on the open stove brings out the carnivore in all of us.

Unicafe, Ballén 406 (tel. 327-100, ext. 1420), between Carbo and Chimborazo, on the 1st floor of the Unihotel shopping mall, across from the Parque Bolívar. The zany pirates on the wall shout, "Ahoy, matey." Polite, helpful waitstaff serves Ecuadorian dishes (s/20,000 and up) as well as your standard sandwiches and killer cheeseburgers (s/12,000-18,000). A window to the kitchen assures that all is clean (open daily 6am-midnight).

La Nuestra, Estrada 903 and E. Higueras (tel. 386-398 or 882-168), on the Urdesa strip. Pressing the limits of budget dining, this suburban restaurant is well-known for its excellent offering of Ecuadorian edibles. The owners of the place present their own in an intimate, elegant, and carefully-created ambience. Wandering serenaders sometimes included in the s/15,000-25,000 prices (open Mon.-Thurs. noon-midnight, Fri.-Sun. 7am-3am).

Pollo a la Lena, Vélez and Garaycoa, on the corner of Parque del Centenario. The chainlink walls and high ceiling give the impression of a giant chicken coop, but all the birds in here are rotisseried. Order at the counter for plates of lip-smacking chicken and starch (¼ chicken, rice, potato, and cola s/8,000). Latin tunes boom on the radio to drown out the buses booming outside.

SIGHTS

Guayaquil has no stellar attractions, and the most impressive ones aren't very safe. Nonetheless, the city is sprinkled with parks, museums, and historically significant buildings that are good for a day of sightseeing. None of these really merit a detour in your travels, but if you're tired of jungles, mountains, beaches, and tortoises, here is your urban alternative. The **Las Peñas neighborhood,** climbing the hills that begin at Malecón's northern end, contains the oldest houses in the city. The product of over 460 years of development, this area shows its age with its almost complete lack of empty land or urban planning. Tin-roofed homes pile onto each other, some rising majestically at the water's edge. The higher up you go, the more spectacular the views of the city and the river become. Watch for cars as you ascend, and keep an eye out for the house of the musician who composed the Ecuadorian national anthem. Many artists live around here, as is reflected by the high concentration of art galleries. Before the road's end, a series of stairs towers up to the left. If you decide to climb them, expect an incredible view—but also get ready for lots of stares, and remember that these are people's homes all around you. It's a good idea to travel through Las Peñas in a group, various parts of the area are frequented by thieves. The veritable maze of houses closes in and if you run into trouble, you're effectively trapped.

Down at sea level, a **clocktower** rises at Malecón and Av. 10 de Agosto, on the waterfront. The Moorish-style tower traditionally called the population to prayer or to fend off attacks by scurvy pirates. A friendly woman who is sometimes there will let you climb to the top. The mayor of the city rules from the ornate, gray **Palacio Municipal,** across the street and up a bit from the clocktower. Next to this stands the smaller, peachier **Palacio de la Gobernación,** the headquarters of the provincial office. Visit the top-notch public relations staff on the second floor with your questions about this site or about Ecuador in general.

The **waterfront,** or Malecón, stretching roughly from Av. Olmedo to the foot of the Las Peñas neighborhood, makes for an interesting walk. The milky-brown Río Guayas flows serenely (muckily?) by your side, and various historical plaques, statues, and fountains decorate the nearly 20-block stroll. In between, though, a community of homeless people naps under trees, amid trash-strewn sidewalks and patches of grass. Watch your step. High points include a noteworthy monument to the UN, *CONU* in Spanish, the above-mentioned clocktower, a strange bronze statue of a boar, and the august **Rotonda** at Av. 9 de Octubre. It's hard to miss this last landmark—at the edge of the water, a row of columns rises from a curved marble base. In front of this, the great liberators Bolívar and San Martín shake hands, commemorating their secret 1822 Guayaquil meeting in a vaguely homoerotic pose.

Some of Guayaquil's most beautiful buildings are its old Catholic churches. Just past the end of Malecón near Las Peñas, **La Iglesia de Santo Domingo** rests comfortably at the end of Calle Rocafuerte, secure with its title as the oldest church in Guayaquil; it's been around since 1548. When younger, better-looking churches sprang up, it fought back with facelifts, the most recent of which was in 1938. This area of the city should be approached with caution. The church of **La Merced,** about 10 blocks farther south on Rocafuerte, dates back to 1787, but the present version was constructed during the flurry of church renovations in 1938. Today, in homage to Guayaquil's commercialization, it is glued to an office building. Where Rocafuerte becomes Pedro Carbo, at Av. 9 de Octubre, *el centro* opens up to a plaza dominated by the facade of the church of **San Francisco.** The **Metropolitan Cathedral** is even farther south on Chimborazo, between Ballén and Av. 10 de Agosto. The original wooden building, built in 1547, would have beat Santo Domingo out as the oldest *guayaquileño* church, but it burnt down. The current stained-glass splendor was built in 1948.

The Cathedral overlooks the **Parque Bolívar,** also called the **Parque Seminario.** Never fear, this parque provides that crazy iguana action you were looking for. You can feel the lizard love of approximately 200 iguanas in the trees, in the manicured gardens, and under those comfy benches. There's a fish pond, too. Not ready for the Galápagos splurge?

Several of the museums in Guayaquil are worth at least a cursory visit, especially the free ones. The **Museo Nahim Isaías Barquet,** Pichincha and Clemente Ballén (tel. 329-099), has 2 large square-shaped halls. The first displays an interesting exhibit of prehistoric regional artifacts. The second houses works from the Quito School of Art. Paintings range from religious Baroque to modern abstract. The kind staff goes out of its way to help the English-speaking (open Mon.-Fri. 10am-5pm; free). The **Museo Municipal,** Sucre between Chile and Pedro Carbo (tel. 531-691), is a slightly larger set of rooms attached to the library. Aside from the works of some modern Ecuadorian artists, it features paintings done in a special program for deaf-mute Guayaquil children (open daily 8:30am-12:30pm and 1-4:30pm; free). Across town, the **Museo de Arte Prehistórico,** Av. 9 de Octubre and Pedro Moncayo (tel. 300-500 or 300-586), is perched on the sixth floor on the western side of the Parque del Centenario. Unlike the other museums, this display of regional archaeological finds can only be seen at a cost (open Tues.-Fri. 10am-5:30pm, Sat. 9am-3pm; admission s/5,000). Larger and better displayed, however, is the **Museo Antropológico del Banco Central de Ecuador,** Av. 9 de Octubre and José de Autepara (tel. 329-784 or 327-402), which contains detailed exhibits, an interactive computer display in Spanish and English, and a knowledgeable staff (open Tues.-Fri. 10am-6pm, Sat. 10am-4pm; admission s/3,000).

Morbidly spectacular, Guayaquil's hillside **cemetery** faces the city from the north. Mausoleums and elaborate tombs crowd the slopes of this virtual city of the dead like mini high-rises, and pathways wind like streets through the resting sites. Because of the preponderance of white marble, it is sometimes called **La Ciudad Blanca** (White City). The cemetery is located on the far side of a highway, past a rough part of the city, so going in a group is a good idea. Inquire for more information at the gate.

ENTERTAINMENT

As the saying goes, spend your days in Quito and your nights in Guayaquil. Like the rainforests of the Oriente, this urban jungle goes wild after dark. Clubs and *discotecas* in *el centro* light the sky in shades of neon until sunrise, but the downtown area can be dangerous and considerably unpredictable. Instead, head to Urdesa, the wealthier suburb to the north. A parade of suped-up sports cars cruises the main strip here, each competing for the loudest stereo system (especially Thursday through Sunday). They're all heading to the scores of nightclubs. Some clubs let in anyone who pays the cover charge, while others admit *socios* (members) only, meaning you have to look good to get in. Don't expect any action until after 11pm. Women can often get in for free. In its quest to become an official South American party mecca, Guayaquil shocks visitors from even the most festive cities of the world with its **chivas.** These huge trucks carry at least 100 revelers, whose bodies hang out the windows, on the hood, and off the roof where the Latin band plays. The vehicles shuttle their passengers all night from hotspot to hotspot throughout the city, including downtown, for a price. Go to Infinity (see below) to find out how to be a part of the drunken caravans. As for the clubs themselves, they're nothing to complain about either. Guayaquil is tough during the day—enjoy it at night.

Bauhjaus, on Estrada near Guaycán, and **Falls,** Estrada 612 (tel. 881-352), spin the latest in techno and house. Young crowds swamp Bauhjaus, but not *that* young— the drinking age is 18 (open Thurs.-Fri. 10pm-5am; cover s/25,000, free before midnight). Down the street, Falls lures slightly older mobs (cover s/20,000).

Infinity, Estrada 505 and Ebamos (tel. 389-390), across the street from Falls, attracts an eclectic crowd of travelers, perhaps because of its equally eclectic musical offerings. Techno and house in the front room, more sultry Latin tunes in the back. Or come to hop onto one of Guayaquil's infamous party *chivas* (open Tues.-Sat. 9pm-4am; cover s/15,000, free before 11pm).

Metropolis, Estrada 302 (tel. 884-026), further down the strip near Cedros. Where Guayaquil's beautiful people flock. The bouncers at this elitist *socios* club ensure that only the most glamorous are admitted, but George the *dueño* will grant concessions to those who identify themselves as travelers. The interior could be straight out of a Madonna video (open Thurs.-Sat. 11pm-5am; cover s/40,000).

Amen, Av. Francisco de Orellana 7-96 (tel. 298-276; fax 298-963). A departure from the strip, Amen is the answer to your prayers—that is, if you pray for confetti-filled balloons, pool table downstairs, and gyrating butt cheeks. Mix of techno-merengue and Latin love songs (open Tues.-Wed. 9pm-3am, Thurs.-Sat. 9pm-7am; cover s/30,000).

Clubs are certainly the highlight, but not the entirety of the Guayaquil entertainment experience. While Guayaquil isn't known for its artistic and cultural achievements, it does have plenty of cinemas showing slightly dated Hollywood films. Check newspapers for showtimes. The most comfortable, and therefore most expensive, of these are **Alborines,** at the C.C. Plaza Mayor in Alborada (tel. 244-986; tickets s/15,000); the **Maya,** Avenue Las Lomas and Dátules in Urdesa (tel. 386-456; s/15,000); and **Multi-Cines,** in the acclaimed new Riocentro Shopping Plaza between the bridges to Durán (tel. 831-230). Avoid taxi fees at the **Cine Metro,** downtown at Boyacá and Vélez (tel. 322-301; s/10,000). Aside from movie theaters, the **Teatro del Angel,** Bálsamos 602 and Ficus (tel. 382-056), in Urdesa, presents a variety of live shows. If you're in town on a Sunday and in need of a workout, you can attend the open-air aerobics class in Parque Kennedy, in the suburbs north of the city.

Guayaquil has all the malls and specialty stores of a big city, so if you need to buy something it's probably here. There are plenty of stores in the area between Av. 9 de Octubre and Parque Bolívar. For a more American-style shopping experience, take a cab to the **PoliCentro Shopping Center** in the suburbs. An **artisan's market** provides indigenous crafts on Loja and Cordova near Las Peñas. For those very cheap, vaguely contraband items, there's a crowded, maze-like street market called the **Bahía** on Pedro Curbo and Villamil between Olmedo and Colón. The brands are mostly fake and pickpockets are common, but you can get a real bargain—they buy the goods tax-free in Panama and pass the savings on to you!

▓ Babahoyo

Today's Babahoyo began in a blaze. When the original city burnt down in the mid-19th century, then-president Jerónimo Carrión moved the public offices across the river and founded the new-and-improved Babahoyo on May 27, 1869. Today, that date is wildly celebrated in a not-so-new Babahoyo, which has since endured the extraordinary El Niño flooding of more than a decade ago (see **"The Watery Child"** below). About an hour northeast of Guayaquil by bus, this capital city of the Los Ríos province is surrounded by rice paddies and orderly rows of banana trees. The city itself is nothing to gawk at: several blocks of dusty, child- and dog-filled streets huddled next to a sluggish river. It's less commercial than Quevedo, and not as friendly as larger cities. Use caution in this less-than-touristy city, as some people may be interested in more than just your goofy foreignness.

Orientation and Practical Information Although Babahoyo spreads away from the river for at least 15 blocks, only the five closest to its bank are vital for navigation. These streets, from the waterfront **Malecón 9 de Octubre** to **García Moreno,** form the grid that is "downtown" Babahoyo. Perpendicular to the waterfront, Avenida Montalvo to the east and Olmedo to the west mark the boundaries of the safer, busier center of town. **Plaza Central,** bounded in part by **Sucre** and **Gen-**

The Watery Child of Death and Destruction

There are some things on this earth that cannot be controlled, things that cannot be understood, things that leave us helpless and dumbfounded with their awesome power to destroy. The devastating **El Niño** is one of those things. A warm water current born off the Pacific coast of Panamá, it brings the rainy season to Ecuador's coastal region and Galápagos Islands. Because the current arrives annually around the time of Christmas, it has been given the deceptively diminutive name El Niño (The Child). Most years this restless child stays well-behaved, arriving in December and leaving on cue in late April or early May. However, in those fateful years when the child decides to act up, havoc ensues. The warm waters stick around longer than usual, continued rainfall causes floods in the lowlands, and tidal waves formed offshore race inland, destroying everything in their path. Many aquatic plants and animals can't take the abnormal heat; it's as if Mother Nature forgot to regulate properly the temperature in her giant aquarium. The last misbehaved child arrived in 1982, and when it finally receded in 1983, a crippled and broken Ecuador was left in its wake. Babahoyo and the rest of the lowlands were devastated by torrents of muddy floodwaters. One need only look at Babahoyo's disintegrating flood walls with their twisted, rusting steel reinforcements to understand the power of the temper tantrum. On the coast, fisherman returned with empty nets, and the national economy suffered. A certain species of green algae in the Galápagos was killed off, and an endemic marine iguana population dependant on that algae was decimated.

eral Barona, is a block from the **Río Babahoyo,** a block in the opposite direction from the buses, and directly adjacent to the government building and the church.

Change cash dollars (but not traveler's checks) for sucres at **Filanbanco,** on the corner of Eloy Alfaro and Barona (open Mon.-Fri. 9am-4pm). Most **bus lines** have offices and stops around Av. 5 de Junio and García Moreno, near Sucre. The busiest station is the **Flota Babahoyo Interprovincial (FBI),** with buses to Guayaquil (every 10min., 4:30am-9pm, s/900). Ticket office open daily 6am-9pm. **Transportes 22 de Julio,** on García Moreno near Rocafuerte (tel. 732-190), go to Ambato at 4:30, 6:30, 10am, and 2pm. (4hr., s/13,000). **Taxis** are common, and a ride across the downtown area should cost s/4,000 or less. There's a friendly self-service **laundromat** on Olmedo between Av. 5 de Junio and Moreno (tel. 734-212; open 6:30am-8pm; s/3,000 to wash or dry). There are several hospitals; the most convenient is the **Hospital Provincial de los Ríos,** at Barona and 27 de Mayo (tel.730-540), near the waterfront. Limited ambulance service to larger hospitals in Guayaquil. As usual, there are at least two pharmacies on every block. **Farmacia Apolo,** 1009 García Moreno near Icaza, is open 24 hours when the doctor is not on vacation. Five blocks down from the Plaza Central, the **police station,** Olmedo and Barona (tel. 730-020), is open 24 hours. The **post office,** at Barona between Sucre and Bolívar, in the government building, has a Lista de Correos (open Mon.-Fri. 8am-7pm, Sat. 8am-2pm). **EMETEL** phone offices are located in several spots, including Av. 5 de Junio and Rocafuerte (2 blocks down from Sucre), General Barona near Flores (a block up from the police station), and across from the FBI bus stop on Bolívar (open daily 8am-10pm). **Phone code:** 07.

Accommodations and Food You'll find a handful of hotel choices in Babahoyo: the dirt-cheap ones are a strain on the senses, and the more comfortable ones are a strain on the wallet. Most are on the blocks between Sucre and Pedro Carbo. **Mesón Popular,** Sucre and Av. 5 de Junio (tel. 730-068), across from the church. The cells, complete with fan, dented mattress, internal bar lock on the door, and three bathrooms down the hall (wear your shower shoes at all times), will set you back only s/15,000 per person, assuming your belongings remain intact. More in the mood for semi-luxury? Try **Hotel Capitol 2,** Av. 10 de Agosto and Martín Icaza (tel. 733-138), a notch up in terms of comfort (with A/C and TV) and price (double with fan s/50,000, with A/C s/70,000). **Hotel Cacharí,** Bolívar and Barona (tel. 731-205), is right off the plaza next to the government building. Private baths, TV, and some rooms with A/C and phone. 24-hour guard adds to the hotel's otherwise mediocre sense of security (singles s/21,000-s/40,000; doubles s/50,000-80,000).

Comedores are the cheapest options, and those with rotisserie chicken may provide the best meal deals. From there the prices rise. **Pizza Restaurante,** Av. 10 de Agosto and Rocafuerte (tel. 732-998), is two blocks down from Sucre. First, try to get over the incongruity—a pizza joint surrounded by Ecuadorian rice paddies and banana plantations? Delivery service, too? Of course. S/25,000 for a medium cheese pizza, s/10,000 for a heaping pile of spaghetti (open Mon.-Thurs. 4-10pm, Fri.-Sun. noon-10pm). **Típico Esmeraldeño,** Av. 5 de Junio between Icaza and Flores (tel. 733-646), is about three blocks from Sucre. An about-face from the pizza-and-burger alternative, Esmeraldeño fills the belly with typical Ecuadorian dishes from chicken to specialty seafood. Most dishes under s/20,000 (open daily 9am-10pm). **El Chifa Atlántico,** Barona between Av. 27 de Mayo and Calderón (no tel.), about three blocks from Sucre, serves savory Chinese food in the fresh Babahoyo (s/7,000; open daily 9am-8:30pm).

Sights and Entertainment At night, smooching couples haunt the **waterfront.** If you're in a voyeuristic mood, watch them; or if you're in a romantic mood, join them, but keep your eye on any valuables you'd like to keep. Otherwise, come during the day to see the **floating houses** (*casas flotandas*) on the banks of the Babahoyo. Built atop virtual rafts, these homes are still functional and ready to rise with the next flood. The first-ever *casa flotanda,* still inhabited by its original owner, has its own set of stairs leading to the bank, named in his honor. Other floating houses are reputed now to be part of the sex trade.

The **church** on the plaza houses a huge interior behind a mural of the Madonna and child. Surprisingly grand for such a gritty town, the building apparently doesn't get much respect from the locals. Ironically, hot and heavy couples use the dark corners and even the confession booth to make out. On the weekends, Babahoyo's many *discotecas* crank up the volume, turn down the lights, and pour techno into the streets. **Genesis,** in the Hotel Cacharí at Bolívar and Malecón, is a safe second-floor dance club that looks onto the plaza. Several blocks up from this area are **La Noche es Mía,** at Av. 5 de Junio and Av. 27 de Mayo, and **D' Cache,** at Av. 10 de Agosto and Av. 27 de Mayo. The action starts around 8pm and the clubs close around 2am. No cover. Popular **shopping areas** are around Av. 10 de Agosto and Av. 27 de Mayo, and along Calderón near Av. 5 de Junio.

▓ Quevedo

Going from Quito to Guayaquil? Santo Domingo to Babahoyo? The coast to the Sierra? There's a good chance you'll pass through Quevedo. Don't expect a fascinating historical journey, a mosaic of artistic possibilities, or a lively night on the town, but you will be able to buy anything from a bed frame with flowered plush velour insets to Tommy Hilfiger jeans in this bustling commercial center of banana country. Before and after its October 7, 1943 canonization, this agricultural hub has plowed ahead, growing with the practical and not-so-practical needs of an expanding Ecuadorian economy. The *centro,* a cluster of four-story buildings lining the Río Quevedo, does not cater specifically to tourists but is not unwelcoming. As with any non-tourist town, your uniqueness in Quevedo is a reason for caution, but do take the time to visit the market along the river and stroll through the *centro*'s streets.

Orientation and Practical Information "Downtown" Quevedo is a narrow few blocks between the river and the roughly parallel hill. The more the streets slope, the more strange looks you'll get, so stay close to the three principle streets: **Malecón Eloy Alfaro** along **Río Quevedo, Simon Bolívar,** and **7 de Octubre.** The perpendicular streets are conveniently labeled in ascending order from **Calle Primero** (1st), at the **Plaza de la Madre,** to **Calle Decima Quarta;** you'll most likely cross it if coming from Babahoyo. This triangular intersection is where the buses board and let off (look for—what else—the statue of the mother), and not coincidentally, it's also known for its thievery. This slightly run-down central plaza, between Quinta and Sexta, contains the only real greenery in the city.

Banco Internacional, Av. 7 de Octubre and Quarta (tel. 751-910), and **Filanbanco,** a block away at Bolívar and Quarta (tel. 755-344), exchange cash dollars and traveler's checks (open Mon.-Fri. 9am-3pm). **Buses** in this transportation hub are generally located near or in the Plaza de la Madre. **Transportes Interprovincial Asouado (TIA),** Av. 7 de Octubre and Tercera (tel. 750-565), has buses to **Guayaquil** (every 30min., 4:30am-6:30pm, s/8,000). **Transportes Valencia,** Bolívar and Segunda (tel. 750-177), serves **Babahoyo** and **Guayaquil** (every 20min., 3:15am-6:30pm, s/4,500 to Babahoyo, s/8,000 to Guayaquil). **Transportes Macuchi,** Bolívar and Primera (tel. 750-820), transports to **Quito** via **Santo Domingo** (every 30min., 2am-6pm, s/5,000 to Santo Domingo, s/13,000 to Quito). **Cooperativa Transportes Ambato,** Bolívar and Primera (tel. 750-134 or 753-085), goes to **Ambato** (8:30, 10, 11:30am, 1, and 5pm; s/14,000). **COTUR Taxis** (tel. 750-328), generally charges s/2,500 and up to get around town. Meet your worldly pharmaceutical needs at **Botica International,** Av. 7 de Octubre and Novena (tel. 750-480; open 7:30am-10:00pm). **Hospital Centro de Salud de Quevedo,** Av. Guayaranes 400 (tel. 750-373), is slightly east of *el centro*, with limited ambulance service. The **police** are on Novena near Progreso (tel. 750-361). For **emergencies,** (tel. 101). The **post office,** Decima Segunda between Av. 7 de Octubre and Bolívar (tel. 751-888), is tucked inside the Sindicato de Transportes building (open Mon.-Fri. 8am-6pm). The **IETEL office,** Av. 7 de Octubre and Decima Tercera (tel. 754-223), offers telephone and telegram services (open daily 8am-10pm), but you can only make international calls if you pay for them there. A 3-minute call within Ecuador costs s/3,000-5,000. **Phone code:** 05.

Accommodations and Food Hotels in Quevedo are nothing to write home about, but they certainly suffice. Most are in the *centro*. **Hotel Imperial,** Malecón and Septima (tel. 751-654), overlooks the market. Rooms provide low-end private baths, sexy high-powered fans, and concave beds. All but the ones overlooking the river have both windows and a balcony. The chatty patriarch downstairs speaks some English and will eagerly smooth over any problems (s/15,000 per person, s/25,000 for two). **Hotel Continental,** Av. 7 de Octubre between Septima and Octava (tel. 750-080), second floor, half a block east of the market, occupies a prime, though noisy, location along the busy strip. All rooms have private baths with locker-room style showers (spigot on the wall, no curtain), color TV, and fans. No hot water or phones (s/15,000, regardless of how many you cram into the cubicles). **Hotel Central,** 925 Bolívar (tel.757-579), is cleaner and lighter than most. Double rooms with private bath (no hot water), color TV, and fans go for s/50,000. Phone calls in the lobby are cheap: s/2,000 for a national call, s/1,000 local.

The sizeable Chinese community in Quevedo dominates a whole chunk of the restaurant selection. *Chifas* are frequent, cheap, and generally dependable, as well as being some of the only full-fledged restaurants in town with actual menus. **Chifa China,** Av. 7 de Octubre and Decima Quarta (tel. 751-343), next to IETEL at the end of the main strip, is one of the best and is even air-conditioned. Meals are about s/9,000 and you can get a multi-course meal for four (s/72,000), though maybe not the best service in town (open daily 11:30am-8pm). Most *comida típica* is taken in local *comedores*. **Restaurant Columbus,** Av. 7 de Octubre and Decima Segunda (no tel.), is a quality *comedor* with dedicated staff. *Desayuno* s/5,000, *almuerzo,* and *merienda* s/4,000 (open 8am-5pm). **El Fruital Soda Bar,** Av. 7 de Octubre between Decima and Decima Primera (tel. 756-332), is so cheap that it may cause you to double-take, serving favorites like hamburgers s/2,500, chicken sandwiches s/2,500, and smoothie-like yogurt and fruit blends s/2,000-3,500 (open daily 9am-11pm).

■ Santo Domingo de los Colorados

Before the roads and the buildings, Santo Domingo was home to the *indígenas* who give the city the second part of its name—the Colorados. The scant clothing and punch-red bowl cuts of this tribe are commonly exploited on postcards, and statues in traffic circles commemorate the days when they really looked that way. Now, only a costly cab ride and a tourist's eager bribe can buy a glimpse of the tribe's customary *traje* before the juggernaut of Westernization overtook them.

Getting to Santo Domingo is half the fun—the bus winds through the foothills of the Andes, culminating in a final downhill rush along vine-encrusted cliffs (don't look over the edge). The city itself, with a climate in-between that of hot, sticky Guayaquil and chilly Quito, caters to mainly Ecuadorian tourists seeking a vacation from Quito's smog. Downtown Santo Domingo, with its mud, litter, and assorted debris, is bustling but not particularly attractive—most of the better-off vacationers have houses slightly outside of town.

Orientation and Practical Information Santo Domingo is laid out in a rather irregular pattern. The grid form exists in a small area along the busiest three downtown streets, the parallel **Avenidas 29 de Mayo, 3 de Julio,** and **Quito.** The center, bounded by **Yambo** on the east and **Quininde** on the west, is the busiest section: the blocks near **Ambato, Latacunga,** and **Cuenca** are packed with booths that make up the market. From the eastern end of the *centro,* the **Avenida Tsachila** takes off to the north, past the post office, to the **terminal terrestre** about 2km north of town. **3 de Julio** and **29 de Mayo** head west and Quito leads east to less crowded terrain and some more upscale hotels. No CETUR here, but information on the area can be found in the bus terminal. **Banco Internacional,** Av. Quito and Río Blanco (tel. 750-503 or 750-603), changes cash US$ to sucres. **The Santo Domingo Casa de Cambio,** 29 de Mayo and Av. Tsachila (tel. or fax 760-729), sometimes has a better rate, and offers the added service of sending and receiving international faxes (s/30,000 to send a 3min. fax, s/3,000 per page to receive; open daily 8:30am-7pm). Across the street and up some, **Produbanco,** Av. Quito and Chorrera del Napa (tel. 751-616), exchanges traveler's checks (Mon.-Fri. 9am-3pm). **Filanbanco** (tel.750-092), also changes traveler's checks (Mon.-Fri. 8:45am-2pm). Santo Domingo is a busy bus transport hub between the coast and the Sierra. The *terminal terrestre* is out on Tsachila. There is a bus marked "Terminal Terrestre" that runs north on Tsachila. The wall of the *terminal terrestre* is lined with bus transport companies—take your pick. Buses leave from Santo Domingo to: **Quito** (every 20min., 4am-9:30pm, 3hr., s/8,000); **Esmeraldas** (every 15 min., 4am-6pm, 1½hr., s/8,000); **Guayaquil** (every 30min., 4am-6:30pm, 5hr., s/30,000). **Taxis** within the city run from s/3,000-4,000; one dispatch is the **14 de Febrero** company (tel. 751-218). A trip from the *terminal terrestre* to the center of town should cost s/4,000. **Local buses** run along major streets for s/250. The fresh-smelling **public market** bustles between Av. 29 de Mayo and Av. 3 de Julio, near Ambato and Cuenca (open daily 8:30am-6pm). Pharmacies line **3 de Julio** in the center of town. One of the best stocked is underneath the **Clínica de Santa Maria,** 29 de Mayo at Tulcán (open daily 9am-8pm). **Hospital Santo Domingo** (tel. 750-336), is off Av. Quito on a short street, past the traffic circle and across from Banco de Pichincha. The **police** (tel. 750-225), are headquartered on Tsachila next to the traffic circle, across from the terminal. In **emergencies,** call 101. The **post office,** Av. Tsachila and Clemencia de Mora (tel. 750-303), about a 10-minute walk from Av. 29 de Mayo on Tsachila, has a Lista de Correos (open Mon.-Fri. 8am-9pm). Make phone calls or send telegrams from **IETEL** on the second floor of the San Francisco de Asis building at Av. Quito and Río Toachi (tel. 750-083; open daily 8am-10pm). Expect to pay about s/ 1,000 for a collect or credit-card call. **Phone code**: 02.

Accommodations and Food Hotels are densely packed in the downtown blocks, especially near Av. 29 de Mayo. Most are of the "you-get-what-you-pay-for" variety. For those looking for rock-bottom prices (s/10,000-15,000 for a room with private bath, depending on how long you bargain), try the **Residencial San José #2,** 3 de Julio near Latacunga, **Hostal Las Brisas,** Quito and Cocaniguas (tel.750-560), **Hotel Unicornio,** Av. 29 de Mayo and Ambato (tel. 760-147), near the movie theater, or **Hotel Amambay,** Av. 29 de Mayo and Ambato (tel. 750-696). A few extra sucres make all the difference at **Hotel La Siesta,** Av. Quito 606 and Pallatanga (tel. 751-013 or 751-860). For s/66,000 you can have a spacious, clean double with phone, private bath with hot water, TV, and Mickey Mouse trash cans outside. Doubles without bath s/45,000; singles s/28,000, s/40,000 with bath. The shocking size of the rooms at **Hotel Jennifer,** Latacunga and 29 de Mayo (tel. 750-577), is also worth the extra sucres. An enormous, spotless room with two double beds, TV, and hot water in the private bath is s/60.000. **Restaurante La Siesta,** Av. Quito 606 (tel. 751-013 or 751-860), has the same aesthetic charm as the attached hotel, and doesn't snooze in its efforts to prepare savory food for all meals. *Desayuno* (s/7,000), steak (s/13,000), and chicken (s/10,000) are served. English menu translations suggest that foreign visitors aren't strangers here (open daily 7am-8:30pm). **Pizzeria Orégano's,** Av. Quito (tel. 759-729), 1.5km from *el centro,* next to Banco del Pacífico, provides combos of ham, salami, ground beef, olives, pineapples, onions, peppers, and veggie pizzas to those who crave Italian fare (small s/13,500, medium s/20,000, large s/25,000; open Tues.-Sun. noon-midnight). **Fruti Deli,** Av. 29 de Mayo and Julian (tel. 755-622), downtown offers fresh, mainstream hamburgers (s/3,000), juices, and a cheap *desayuno* (s/5,000; open daily 6:30am-8pm). Av. Quito near Tulcán offers a variety of *pollerías.* The rotisserie chicken at **Mr. Pollo, Pollo Lista,** and **Rico Pollo** will cost you s/22,000-s/23,000 for a whole chicken. The well-stocked **Itipermarket,** on the east end of Av. Quito, about a 10 minute walk from the center, rounds out the food options (open daily 10am-9pm).

Sights and Entertainment The market here is popular, safe, and ripe for the browsing during the day. Beware at night—almost everything closes by 9pm and the locals will most likely warn you to go home before you get robbed. There are also some movie theaters, including the **Cine Ambato** (no tel.), at Ambato and Av. 29 de Mayo, for not-so-recent Hollywood movies (s/3,000). For the more daring, **The Jungle Cervecería y Salsateca,** Av. Quito near the Siesta Hotel, stays open until 2am nightly; people in the know arrive at 9-10pm.

The nearby **Colorados** draw many visitors to Santo Domingo. In the nearby village of **Chihuilpe,** members of the Tsachila tribe don their postcard apparel for a price, letting salivating camera shutters snap them up. To witness the Santo Domingo traveler's rite of passage, head south on Av. Quevedo to the "km 7" mark, then take a left on a dirt road. Taxis charge a heavy s/30,000 or so for the trip. Another option is to take any bus marked "Via Quevedo" to "km 8" and walk 30 minutes.

If you're down for a raging party, the fiesta celebrating the **canonization of Santo Domingo** on July 3 draws enormous crowds. The usual extensive, lively, and bargain-crazy markets become even crazier, and the cock-fighting coliseum right outside the city puts on a grand show of killer poultry.

■ Near Santo Domingo: Río Palenque Science Center

The Centro Científico Río Palenque not only preserves dying breeds, it is one. The last tropical wet rainforest reserve in the western Ecuadorian lowlands, this terrain doesn't contain just the same old flora and fauna found in the Oriente. Researchers travel to the reserve to study what can be seen only here, including the 100 plant species first discovered within the reserve's boundaries. More than 3km of trails meander through the home of 360 species of birds, 350 different butterflies, and over 1100 catalogued plant species. Of these, more than 30 species of flowering plants claim their last remaining home in these tiny 200 hectares. Don't expect to see herds of animals swarming the forest here, but you may see one of the park's few *tigrillos* or growing population of monkeys if you are out early in the morning. Though the pressure of deforestation around the sanctuary virtually wiped out the extensive mammal population, the managers are making a strong effort to bring back the moving, breathing inhabitants of this *selva*. But the reserve does offer a number of trails that meander through the sanctuary of humid, thriving plant and insect diversity, and an enthusiastic host who will help make the less-than-luxurious accommodations more comfortable. First organized 12 years ago by a group of American scientists, the tiny forest sanctuary then consisted of 200 hectares (around 500 acres), a little less than it is today. For a while, the center was run by the University of Miami, but the university eventually pulled out, leaving the research facility to its handful of owners. Presently the whole reserve is owned by Dr. Carl Dodson, who has had to cultivate 100 hectares in order to fund the endeavor. Dr. Dodson has been involved with the reserve from the beginning and now lives in a house on the far edge of the land. The Science Center, a research-hotel facility for scientists and visitors, is 1km away.

To get here, take a bus from either Santo Domingo or Quevedo to the entrance along the highway. Coming from Quevedo, the entrance is at turn 58, past a farm called Tío Coco. From Santo Domingo, the entrance is 47km south, 2.5km past a town called Patricia Pilar. Be sure to let your bus driver know that you want to stop here ahead of time. To get back, just wave a bus down as it passes on the highway.

The **Center-Hotel** is a true hike from the bus drop-off on the highway. Head up the path, take a left at the fork, and expect to walk a good 25 minutes. One night's lodging costs US$15 if you bring your own food to cook in the kitchen facilities, US$50 with meals included. A day's hiking fee without staying over is s/9,000. Overnight guests should arrive before 9pm (a nighttime hike is not advisable anyway). Bring repellant—creepy-crawlers are everywhere, especially at night (after all, that's the whole purpose of the reserve). Although the place rarely fills up, it's a smart move to call ahead to the Center's office in Santo Domingo just in case (tel. 561-646; fax 225-468). For visitation requests or other information, write to: Río Palenque Science Center, Santo Domingo de los Colorados, Ecuador.

The Pacific Coast

Ecuador's convoluted Pacific coast, composed of a motley combination of beaches, mangroves, estuaries, and rocky shores, winds its way almost 3000km—from the town of San Lorenzo in the northern province of Esmeraldas near the Colombian border to the Peruvian border town of Huaquillas in Ecuador's southern seaside province of El Oro. While weather patterns are quite similar down the length of the coast, with a rainy season from December to April caused by warm water currents offshore, the finer details of life vary somewhat with latitude. The African-influenced northern reaches of the coast mellow more to the beats of the *marimba*. The unpretentious resort center of Atacames sits on Esmeraldas's shores with an abundance of beachside discos pumping late-night weekend jams to eclectic crowds of native Ecuadorians and foreigners alike. South of Atacames lie ever-so-sleepy Súa and almost-as-mellow Muisne, towns that do more of nothing than anything else. Venturing south from here takes you past miles of lonely beaches and forgotten fishing towns, to the Metroplex of San Vicente and Bahía de Caráquez, towns which sit opposite each other across the gaping mouth of the Río Chone. Bahía sets the stage for the urban coastal cities that start to pop up more frequently to the south of it, including Manta and the ritzy resort town of Salinas. Sprinkled along the sands north of Salinas are the gems of the coast, sparsely populated beaches with recreation ranging from surfing the echoing barrels of Montañita to testing the hammocks at the isolated resort Alandaluz. The nearby friendly town of Puerto López makes a good base for explorations of Ecuador's only coastal park, Parque National Machalilla. Wherever you decide to visit on the coast, bring your bathing suit and a healthy appetite for fresh fruit or seafood, because…it's what's for dinner.

▓ San Lorenzo

Surrounded by beautiful tropical forest and mangrove river areas, it is actually quite impressive that San Lorenzo has managed to maintain such a foul reputation as a dangerous travelers' hub. A steady and dependable supply of tourists flows to San Lorenzo because of the spectacular train ride from Ibarra, and locals have adapted to this intrusion by taking a strong interest in the lives of their visitors. The walk from the train station promises questions on your marital status, your travel plans, and perhaps your dancing ability. Most people stay only one night in San Lorenzo, then move on to other places. While it is most common to move along to Esmeraldas through La Tola en route to Atacames as a final destination, there are some more rugged, less well-traveled jungle areas that can be explored from San Lorenzo; inquire at SAEC or Safari in Quito for recommendations.

Orientation and Practical Information From the train station, **10 de Agosto** runs straight into the center of San Lorenzo. If for some bizarre reason you choose to travel by bus from Ibarra, you will probably be let off by the park near the dock area. **Cooperativo de Espejo,** 10 de Agosto (tel. 780-202), alongside the Park, goes to Ibarra (daily 6, 8am, noon, and 2:30pm). The boat dock has a few companies offering rides on old but reliable covered wooden boats. **Cooperativo San Lorenzo del Pailon** has boats to: **La Tola** (every 2hr., 5:30am-dusk, 2hr., s/13,400) where you can catch a bus to Esmeraldas (2:30pm, 4hr., s/10,000); **Limones** (every hr., s/10,200) or the **Colombian border** (7am and 2pm, s/10,400). San Lorenzo's **police station** (tel. 780-801), next to Coop. de Espejo by the park, has recently acquired the ability to deal with border crossing, offering immigration services such as stamping passports (open 24hr.). The **EMETEL** is located on the street across the playground from 10 de Agosto, toward the train station. The **hospital,** Ibina Providencia, is a small trek outside town; head down 10 de Agosto toward the train station, and veer right after the shops (open 24hr.). Money can be exchanged at the *almacén* **Su Econo-**

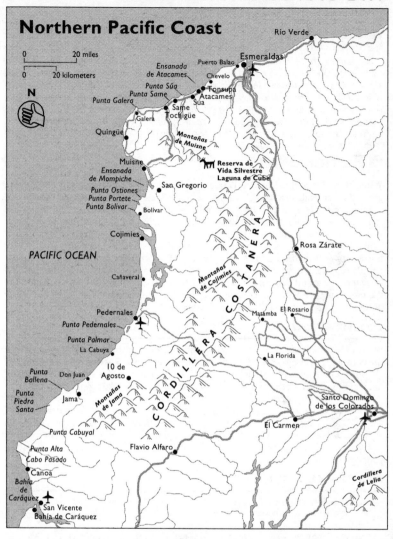

Northern Pacific Coast

0 — 20 miles
0 — 20 kilometers

N

Río Verde
Esmeraldas
Puerto Balao
Ensanada de Atacames
Chevelo
Punta Súa
Tonsupá
Punta Same
Atacames
Punta Galera
Súa
Same
Galera
Tochigüe
Quingüe
Montañas de Muisne
Reserva de Vida Silvestre Laguna de Cube
Muisne
Ensanada de Mompiche
San Gregorio
Punta Ostiones
Punta Portete
Punta Bolívar
Bolívar
Rosa Zárate
Cojimies
PACIFIC OCEAN
Cañaveral
Montañas de Cojimies
CORDILLERA COSTANERA
Pedernales
Matamba
El Rosario
Punta Pedernales
Punta Palmar
La Cabuya
La Florida
10 de Agosto
Punta Ballena
Don Juan
CORDILLERA
Santo Domingo de los Colorados
Punta Piedra Santa
Jama
Montañas de Jama
Punta Cabuyal
El Carmen
Punta Alta
Cabo Pasado
Flavio Alfaro
Canoa
Bahía de Caráquez
Cordillera de Lelia
San Vicente
Bahía de Caráquez

mia—if Patricio is there, you can also exchange traveler's checks at a not-so-good rate (on 10 de Agosto across from EMETEL). There is a **pharmacy** under the Hotel Imperial on Calle Imbabura. To find the **post office,** turn right on Calle Imbabura from 10 de Agosto, then turn right again on the last crossroad you come to on this track.

Accommodations and Food There are several passable places to stay in San Lorenzo. **Hotel San Lorenzo** and **Hotel Imperial,** Calle Imbabura and 10 de Agosto (tel. 780-242), function as two halves of the same building. The San Lorenzo side has decent rooms without private baths for s/10,000 per person. The Imperial side has high-quality rooms with hot water private *baños,* TVs, and refrigerators (singles s/ 20,000; doubles s/35,000; triples s/50,000). Another (expensive) possibility is **Hotel Continental,** 10 de Agosto, on your left as you walk from the train station. Simple, secure rooms with hot water and private bath for s/20,000 per person. The cheaper **Residencial Ibarra,** on the street going right from the Park as you come from the train station, has stuffy rooms and adequate shared bath for s/10,000 per person.

San Lorenzo has plenty of small, pre-prepared meal spots. **Ballet Azul** (tel. 780-241) offers seafood (*ceviche de conchas* s/10,000), chicken dishes, and sandwiches (s/ 1,500-3,000) prepared at a leisurely pace. They will prepare a vegetarian rice/beans/ onion dish upon request if they have ingredients on hand (s/6,500; open daily 7am until the crowds go home). **Restaurant Conchita,** 10 de Agosto, near the park, has friendly service, *desayunos* (s/5,000), and *almuerzos* with soup, salad, rice, meat or seafood, and juice (s/8,000; open daily 6am-11pm).

■ Esmeraldas

When they first arrived on the Ecuadorian coast, the Spanish conquistadors were greeted by emerald-clad *indígenas* and wrongly concluded that the land overflowed with that rare green gem. Despite the folly of its origin, the ensuing name stuck, and today the people of Esmeraldas regard it as a compliment to the beauty of their city and culture. Not quite a tourist town, Esmeraldas is an active hub of the fishing, banana, and oil industries, whose unseemly and malodorous by-products can sometimes detract from the waterfront experience. The bona fide gems of the city are the people of Esmeraldas, illuminating what would be a dingy port town with smiles and laughter, music and dancing. Every August 1st through 5th, the locals commemorate the city's independence and celebrate Esmeraldas's African ancestry with the music of the *marimba* and accompanying parading and dancing.

ORIENTATION

Buses from Quito usually drop off on **Avenida 10 de Agosto,** the northern border of the central plaza. **Bolívar** borders the park to the east, and **Sucre** to the west. Bolívar becomes **Libertad** north of Pichincha, and leads to Esmeraldas's beach community, **Las Palmas.** Buses from neighboring towns drop off along **Malecón,** which runs parallel to the **Río Esmeraldas** and leads to the port in the north. Esmeraldas is fairly spread out, and it is difficult to quickly discern where the hub of the city is. Most of the city's attractions are between Rocafuerte and Canizares, along the parallel streets of Olmedo, Sucre, and Bolívar. Beyond Montalvo is a bit more dangerous in terms of thieves; avoid being alone in this area. Ask around about safety before going out on your own at night in any area of the city.

PRACTICAL INFORMATION

Tourist Information: CETUR, Bolívar 2-29 and Mejia (tel. 714-528). Open Mon.-Fri. 8:30am-5pm. **Esmeraldas Tur,** Canizares 221 and Bolívar (tel./fax 726-875). Open Mon.-Fri. 8:30am-1pm and 3-7pm.

Money Exchange: Banco Pinchincha, Av. 9 de Octubre and Bolívar (tel. 728-743 or 728-748; tel./fax 728-745). Open Mon.-Fri. 8am-8pm, Sat. 8am-2pm. **Banco Popular,** Piedrahita and Bolívar (tel. 725-391). Open Mon.-Fri. 9am-6:30pm, Sat. 9am-2pm. Both change money and traveler's checks and have 24hr. ATMs.

Airlines: TAME, Bolívar and 9 de Octubre (tel. 726-863). Open Mon.-Fri. 8am-1pm and 3-6pm.

Buses: Trans Esmeraldas, Av. 10 de Agosto between Sucre and Bolívar. Buses to **Quito** (12 per day, 7:20am-12:30am, 5½hr.) come in 2 varieties: larger ones show movies and TV shows and have clean bathrooms (s/22,000), while smaller buses lack bathrooms and other luxuries (s/19,000). Buses to **Guayaquil** also come in degrees of luxury (11 per day, 7:45am-12:45am, 12hr., around s/22,000). **Coup La Costenita,** Malecón and Av. 10 de Agosto (tel. 721-381), has buses to: **Muisne and Salto** (every hr., 5am-8pm, 2hr., s/5,000); **La Tola** (every 2hr., 5:30am-10:30pm, 4hr., s/10,000); **Borbón** (6, 8am, every 2hr. noon-10pm, 4hr., s/10,000); **Atacames** (every 10min., 5am-10pm, 45min., s/2,000); **Súa** (every hr., 5am-10pm, 1hr., s/2,500); and **Same** (every hr., 5am-10pm, 1¾hr., s/2,900). **Del Pacífico,**

Malecón and Piedrahita (tel. 713-227), transports to **Muisne/Salto** (18 per day, 5:40am-7:20pm, 2hr., s/5,500); **Borbón** (every 2hr., 5am-7:15pm, 4hr., s/10,000); and **La Tola** (every 2hr., 4:30am-4:30pm, 4hr., s/10,000). Buses to **Atacames** (45min., s/2,000); **Súa** (1hr., s/2,500); and **Same** (1¾hr., s/3,000) leave at the same times as those to Muisne.

Taxis: Cooperativa de Automoviles 5 de Agosto, Av. 10 de Agosto and Bolívar (tel. 710-033), in the northern corner of the park. **Cooperativo Auto Taxi 2,** 9 de Octubre and Sucre (tel. 726-730 or 711-158), is also near the park.

Library: Bolívar and Av. 9 de Octubre (tel. 726-826), 1st fl., in back of the Municipal Building. Open Mon.-Fri. 8am-7pm, Sat. 9am-2pm.

Pharmacies: Farmacía Ortiz, Bolívar 2-00 and Salinas (open Mon.-Sat. 9am-6pm), and the **Farmacía Karina,** Sucre 806 and Piedrahita. Open daily 8am-1:30pm and 2-8pm. Ask for Dr. Fabio Dominguez.

Supermarket: Micromercado Imperial, Bolívar 2-40 and Mejia (open Mon.-Sat. 8:30am-1pm and 3-8:30pm).

Hospital: (emergency tel. 710-212), on the right side of Libertad as you head toward Las Palmas. Free 24hr. emergency treatment.

Police: Bolívar and Cañizares (emergency tel. 723-158 or 711-484). Open 24hr.

Post office: Montalvo and Malecón (tel. 726-831 or 726-834), 1st fl., in the same building as EMETEL. Open Mon.-Fri. 7:30am-7pm, Sat. 8am-1pm.

Telephones: EMETEL, Montalvo and Malecón (tel. 728-814), above the post office. Calls s/1,000 per 3min. Open Mon.-Sat. 8am-10pm.

Phone code: 06.

ACCOMMODATIONS

If arriving from Quito or any other Ecuadorian city with decent lodgings, prepare to be underwhelmed. After researching the options, you'll be fortunate if you've found two or three suitable budget destinations. Most charge around s/20,000 for musty, cramped rooms dying for new paint jobs. No hotels offer hot water, but you won't want it; Esmeraldas is very humid, and the cool water is refreshing.

Residencial Zulema, Olmedo (tel. 710-910, 711-789, or 712-424), between Cañizares and Piedrahita, in the southwest part of town. One of the few budget hotels in town that isn't downright depressing, thanks to the almost comical green paint job. Supple mattresses, ceiling fans, and friendly staff; common bathrooms could be cleaner. Rooms s/15,000 per person, with bath s/20,000.

Hostal Galeon, Piedrahita 3-30 and Olmedo (tel. 723-819; fax 714-839). Lobby adorned with paintings of sea adventures and a ship's wheel builds anticipation for ship-shape rooms, but sadly, you couldn't bounce a dime off these beds. Tiny showers more reminiscent of sailing conditions. Friendly staff makes up for any disappointment. Private baths in all quarters. Rooms s/25,000 per mate.

Hotel Roma, Olmedo 718 and Piedrahita (tel. 723-823), just north of the Galeon. Rooms fit for a prince or a pauper—it's all a matter of luck. At best, breezy rooms have color TVs, hardwood floors, and oak dressers. Not so ideally, some walls could use a paint job. All have private baths that may need new lightbulbs (make sure to check). Rooms s/27,500-38,500 per person, depending on fan or A/C.

Hotel Sandri, Libertad and Montalvo (tel. 726-861). Plain, sunny rooms. TV and private *baños* for all. This area of Esmeraldas is unsafe at night, but is convenient to EMETEL and the post office. Rooms s/25,000 per person.

FOOD

The major port town along the northern coast, Esmeraldas has lots of scrumptious seafood cuisine, served in both sit-down restaurants and tiny booths along the road. Typical regional dishes include *encocados* (seafood cooked in coconut milk), *tapaos* (meat or fish covered with plantains and wrapped in banana leaves), and *ceviche.* Av. Olmedo has an especially dense congregation of eateries with inexpensive sit-down meals. For those who don't like seafood, chicken is everywhere. For those who don't

PACIFIC COAST

eat any meat, the fruit is wondrous and fruit salads are easy to find. Otherwise practice your Spanish in requesting a meatless dish not listed on the menu.

Restaurant Las Vegas, Cañizares and Bolívar, 2 blocks south of the central plaza. No showgirls or slot machines here. Interior design looks like an immense double garage, but the food is mmmmtasty. *Salsa* music jams while ceiling fans provide a well-needed breeze. Gargantuan pasta dishes starting at s/5,000, shrimp dishes s/9,500, fried chicken s/7,000. Open Mon.-Sat. 7am-10pm.

Las Redes, Bolívar (tel. 711-739), facing the Parque Central. Bongo drums swing from fish-net ceilings over intimate fold-up picnic tables. Decorated with Nat King Cole albums and the Beatles's Abbey Road—they couldn't find a Yellow Submarine, so they settled for an Octopus's Garden. Seafood entrees right out of the nets (s/8,000-9,000), also serves chicken and rice dishes. Open Mon.-Sat. 7am-10pm.

Chifa China, Av. 9 de Octubre 3-20 and Olmedo (tel. 722-291). Providing much-needed variety, Chifa China breaks from typical regional cuisine. Slow service gives you time to learn the Chinese characters for men and women magic-markered over the restrooms. Ask the management to interpret. Massive rice dishes s/6,200-8,500, egg meals s/1,600-6,000. A reasonable lobster plate for s/18,000.

SIGHTS AND ENTERTAINMENT

Esmeraldas's **beaches** are less than picturesque, commonly cluttered with driftwood, stones, and a smattering of litter. The hard, smooth sand of the gray shore stretches for miles, the ultimate surface for the **soccer games** played here daily, but less than ideal for postcards and sunbathing tourists. The water temperature hovers around 21°C (70°F), perfect for a morning dip. At night, the beach becomes the center of the goings-on, with a few outdoor **bars** along Kennedy and a multitude of drinking and dining options down near the sand. **Keops,** one of the seven or eight *discotecas* along the seashore, rocks nightly to the rhythms of *salsa* and *merengue*. Both beer (s/4,000) and cover charge (s/10,000) are more or less standard (open daily 7pm-2am). For a more mellow night, there is the **Cine Bolívar,** Bolívar 5-09 and Piedrahita, which shows a wide variety of films, from American hits to hardcore pornographic films (ooh-la-la), so make sure to check the signs outside that indicate the night's feature presentation (screenings daily, 5:30pm, s/6,000).

■ Atacames

They're coming. If they're not here yet, just wait until Friday afternoon, when the buses start to arrive. Each weekend, Ecuadorian merrymakers and large groups of high school students infiltrate this small beach town, 30km southwest of Esmeraldas. In droves, they descend on its restaurants, *cabañas,* and bars, filling each to the brim. Groggy visitors wake every morning to the sounds of reggae and dance music flowing nonstop out of local bars from 9am until as late as 3am. Blenders whipping up *batidos* (fruit shakes) from coconuts, pineapples, guavas, and oranges can be spotted on every street corner and bar stand. During the week, Atacames slows down a little; the blenders go at half-speed, the music dies down around 1am, and the partiers rest up for the weekend. Arrive on a weekday to situate yourself before the hordes of hyperactive sun-seekers assault the sands of Atacames. Endless sun, swimming, volleyball, straw-roofed bars, music, and friendly (perhaps overly so) people boggle the mind. If you are alone, you will have no problem making friends here, but if you wish to be alone you may find it difficult.

Orientation and Practical Information The road from Esmeraldas runs through the center of town and continues on to Súa and Same. People refer to this road as **Principal,** but don't confuse it with the Principal that leads from the footbridge to the beach. Buses drop people anywhere along this main road, but it's best to get off at the center bus stop, recognizable by the long white bench in front of an *helado bar* and the sign that says *parada.* The road splitting to the right leads to the beach. To reach the center-of-beach action, walk along this road past the Nuevo Hotel and bear right as the road joins another. Cross the footbridge over the **Río Atacames** and take a right. The street that leads from the footbridge to the beach is **Calle Principal,** and the street that runs parallel to the beach is **Calle Malecón.** Malecón dominates Atacames, monopolizing most of the bars, *discotecas,* and budget hotels. **La Acacia** intersects the main road, Principal, a little farther south.

Banco del Pinchincha (tel. 731-029), on Principal just north of the central bus stop, changes cash or traveler's checks and has a 24-hour ATM (open Mon.-Fri. 8am-8pm, Sat.-Sun. 9am-2pm). Make national and international collect calls from **EMETEL** (tel. 731-104), one block south of the bank, opposite the park, first floor. The three booths cost s/600 per three minutes of usage for local calls (open daily 8am-10pm). Hire the **boats** scattered along the shore to take groups to: **Súa** (5-15min., s/5,000-15,000); **Same** (30-90min., s/20,000-120,000); and **Muisne** (2-4hr., s/100,000-300,000). **Buses** run through the town center from about 6am-10pm, going to: **Same** (30min., s/1,000); **Muisne** (2½hr., s/4,000); **Tonsupa** (10 min., s/1,000); and **Esmeraldas** (1hr., s/2,000). It is also possible to **walk to Súa** (1hr.), but only at low tide. At high tide, the water rises up against rocky cliffs, creating an insurmountable roadblock. **Taxis** are a scarce commodity in Atacames, since they are all based in Esmeraldas. You can get to Esmeraldas from Atacames for as low as s/5,000, but from Esmeraldas to Atacames bargaining starts at s/40,000. There are flocks of bicycles with benches on wheels that drive people all over Atacames. **Micro Mercado,** south of the bus stop but north of the basketball/soccer area, sells water, toilet paper, and other staples (open daily 6:30am-9pm). **Farmacía Popular,** La Acacia and Malecón, is on the south end of the beach (open daily 8am-noon and 1-10pm). **Farmacía** (tel. 731-253), on the corner by the basketball/soccer area, meets pharmaceutical needs, changes dollars, has a phone for international calls, and is connected to the **Centro Médico Quirojito** (cellular tel. 09-470-261), which has three doctors, including a surgeon and a pediatrician, to provide **emergency medical service** (open Mon.-Sat. 24hr., Sun. until 1pm). **Dr. Vinizio Díaz** (tel./fax 731-504), 40m north of the central bus stop, can also provide 24-hour emergency medical attention and laboratory/clinic services. The **police,** Acacia and Principal (tel. 731-275), near the beach, are south of town in a blue and white building. The **post office** is north of EMETEL, facing Banco del Pichincha (open Mon.-Fri. 8:30am-noon and 3-5pm).

Accommodations and Food Atacames is dripping with accommodations, but the riches are quickly devoured on weekends when the busloads of Ecuadorian beach-goers descend on the town. The sand-sprinkled Calle Malecón has the most places to stay, which range between s/20,000-30,000. The benefit of Malecón's beach proximity is negated by the noise from the street's assortment of bars, *discotecas,* and stereo-thumping automobiles. A cheap but quality escape from Malecón is **Residencial la Casa del Manglan** (tel. 731-464), to your left after you cross the foot bridge walking to the beach. Relax on their terrace or in the cheery, clean rooms—only a two-minute walk to the festivities (s/15,000 per person, with bath s/20,000). On the beach itself, **Hotel Galeria Atacames** (tel. 731-149), on the north side of Malecón, is just south of Hotel Tiburon. Climb two flights of stairs past the ocean view restaurant to reach rooms sporting sheet-metal ceilings, wood-plank floors, and mosquito screens on windows. Quarters can get a bit stuffy, but floors are well-swept and bathrooms well-kept. All rooms have private bath, and the hotel offers book swapping, money exchange, and a safety deposit box (s/20,000 per person). **Hotel Rodelu Cabañas,** Principal and Malecón (tel. 731-033 or 713-713; fax 714-714), is slightly removed from the action. *"Cabañas"* are really just hotel rooms that can hold hordes of people. Ceiling fans and tiny radio systems are provided for those who can't bear to leave the disco behind. Narrow beds with thin sheets and cold-water baths combine for an unexciting but adequate stay. Rooms hold four to eight; refrigerators s/3,000 extra (rooms start at s/20,000 per person—the more people, the cheaper). **Hotel Tiburon** (tel./fax 731-145), along Malecón, lies just north of Galeria Atacames. Simple, whitewashed rooms are concentrated toward the back to muffle the street sounds. Concrete floors and high-speed ceiling fans assure a chilly night's rest, as long as the fan works—be sure to check. All rooms have private baths and emit a reassuring cleaning-fluid odor. The second-story restaurant, festooned with seashells on strings, provides quality food and ocean views (meals s/5,000-25,000), while the cafe downstairs serves juicy hamburgers (s/5,000) and hotdog-with-fries plates (s/5,000). Rooms for up to 6 people (s/30,000 per person).

Most of Atacames's dining options are pressed from the same mold, serving a monotonous but enjoyable selection of rice dishes accompanied by seafood, beef, or chicken. Sidewalk chefs cook up beef shish kebobs and corn-on-the-cob at a number of cheap and savory pit stops along Malecón. **Marco's Restaurant** (tel. 731-541), on Malecón north of Hotel Tiburon, conforms to the popular tree house theme, perched just above the sidewalk on a foundation of second-story branches. Enjoy ocean views and ventilation while voraciously devouring various vitalizing victuals, including fried calamari (s/8,500), fresh fish dishes (s/8,500-11,000), and chicken plates (s/9,500-11,500). They can be persuaded to provide a simple meatless plate for s/5,000 (open daily 8am-10pm). **Paco Foco,** on the Calle Principal that leads to Malecón, just before the corner on your left, serves mountains of food, such as *camarones apanados* for s/10,000, or a meatless mountain for s/6,000. It's a popular place, and hard to find a seat at times (open daily 8:30am-10pm). At **Restaurant Karina,** on Malecón between Hotels Pelicano and Tiburon, big, plastic-covered picnic tables support monstrous servings of seafood and rice that more than make up for the lack of character. A color TV and stereo entertain from the corner. A feast of rice, shrimp, clams, oysters, and fried fish costs s/10,000. Breakfasts run around s/5,000, lunches around s/7,000. **Restaurante La Ramada** (tel. 731-207), on Malecón about 50m south of Principal, is set back from the sand and pleasantly removed from the *discoteca* music; the cluster of small picnic tables pleases intimate couples. They prepare shrimp delights (s/12,000), fish delicacies (s/10,000-12,000), and *desayunos* with fried *platanos* (instead of *pan*) s/6,000 (open daily 8am-10pm).

Sights and Entertainment

Lined with nearly 50 grass-hut bars, Atacames's well-maintained shore bursts with diversions. Though dull and gray, the beach is unsullied and soft, sprawling far enough for long walks in either direction. First-rate views of **Punta Esmeraldas** to the north and the jagged **Isla de Pájaros** to the south frame this enormous expanse. Though competing for the same prime beachfront space, sunbathers and soccer players coexist peacefully, while jet skis (s/100,000 per hour) and banana boats (s/5,000 per person), rentable on the south side of the beach, buzz by on the blue-green water. Though the beach is generally safe in the resort area, exercise caution if you decide to explore less populated stretches. Also be careful when swimming in the surf, as the undertow can be quite strong at times.

As the sun sets over the Pacific horizon, the grass-hut bars come alive with lights and activity. Packs of teenagers stroll down Malecón making eyes at each other. Adults with beers in hand attempt local moves on the sandy dance floors between the bars or disappear into the dance clubs. Older visitors catch their breath, sip margaritas, and enjoy the ocean views. The seaside bars, with their identical bamboo structures and woven thatched roofs, compete for the most complex tropical fruit arrangements. **Nagiba Bar,** just north of Principal along the sand, strives for individuality, with swings hanging from the ceiling around the bar rather than bar stools, and live marimba music Saturday nights. Just north of Nagiba Bar along Malecón, partiers of all ages cram into the **Scala Discoclub,** with neon orange and green lights to illuminate Latin and American dance beats (open daily 8pm-2am; cover s/5,000; Miller beer s/7,000). A darker, mellower choice is **d'Class,** a bit north of Scala. Same-priced cover and beer, same hours, different scene. Even late into the night, Malecón is well-lit, populated, and generally safe. The beach is more dangerous, and late-night walks are discouraged. Pool sharks leave the fanfare of Malecón for the mellow billiard hall, **El Gato Wilh,** on the street before the footbridge to the beach. Each of the three pool tables costs a low s/4,000 per hour (open Mon.-Sat. 10am-2am, Sun. 10am-10pm).

■ Near Atacames

TONSUPA

Following in Atacames's footsteps like an admiring younger brother, Tonsupa quietly mimics the boisterous performances of its elder sibling. *Más tranquilo* is how locals describe this little town. With beaches so relaxed the crabs dare to pop out of their holes to scurry across the sand, Tonsupa provides a chance to catch your breath after the wild flurry of activity in Atacames. Though there is a small bit of beach with grass hut bars and fruit salads, most of the sand is relatively quiet. There is no garbage littered along the shore, though where hotel/restaurant establishments meet the sand there may be some scruffy looking eye sores waiting for renovation.

While Tonsupa makes for a quick and painless daytrip escape from Atacames, few accommodations merit a night's stay. One commendable hotel is the still growing **Cabaña Turística Doña Emerita** (tel. 711-407), at the far south end of the beach. Situated on an empty stretch of sand, the *cabañas* enjoy a solitude unmatched in the area. Spotless white tile floors, whitewashed walls, and sophisticated floor fans add modernity to an otherwise traditional, grass-roofed, cracked-coconuts-in-the-courtyard establishment. All rooms have private baths and a few have balconies with an ocean view (quads s/80,000; for 6 people s/120,000). Smaller cabañas for two are being constructed and should be available soon. There are a couple of places to eat north of the *cabañas*, near the center of Tonsupa. The cheery, bright pink and blue **Hotel Miramac** (tel. 731-585), has ambrosial, affordable food despite its costly rooms. Two fans struggle to cool off customers as they down fish and shrimp *encocados* (s/8,500) and fruit salads (s/6,000). The accommodating staff prepares a vegetarian plate upon request (s/7,500; open daily 8am-10pm). The **Bar/Restaurant Los Corales,** 100m farther north along the beach, brightens up early mornings with breakfasts of eggs, juice, bread, and coffee (s/5,000). Lunch and dinner of the day go for s/6,000 and s/7,000 respectively (open daily 7am-2am). To get to Tonsupa from Atacames, take the **bus** (every 15 min., 10min., s/1,000) or **taxi** (s/5,000). The wide mouth of the Río Esmeraldas prevents walking between the two towns along the beach.

SÚA

A watered down, less energetic version of Atacames, Súa is visible from the crowded beaches of the larger town, shimmering with peace and tranquility. Though it is less intense, weekends still bring loads of beach-goers, and banana boats still frequent the lightly littered shoreline. Súa's surrounding green hillsides make hiking a popular and picturesque activity; there is a route that heads south of the bay along a dirt path up the side of the big green bluff. After a half hour of walking, a view of Súa/Atacames to the north and less developed coastline to the south will induce a frenzied attack of photo taking. One of Súa's big advantages over Atacames is quality accommodations at reasonably cheap prices. The **Hotel Chagra Ramos** (tel. 731-006 or 731-070), located on the far north side of beach, provides restful hillside villas (s/20,000 per person) and *cabañas* (s/15,000 per person). Set high upon the hillsides, the villas have private baths and patios with hammocks for reposing before scenic sunsets. The basic but blemish-free rooms boast screens on the windows to provide a cool, itch-free, and untroubled sleeping environment. The Chagra is also one the few quality places to eat in Súa. Relish the relaxing view of the bay under the shade of droopy palm trees as you feast upon…seafood! Surprise, surprise. Plates cost s/9,000-12,000. If you simply can't choke down another meal of *mariscos*, there is a s/4,000 salad, as well as American (s/4,500) and fried-fish (s/8,500) breakfasts (open daily 7:15am-9pm). The French-owned **Hotel Súa Café/Restaurant** (tel. 731-004), is 50m south of Chagra Ramos. Though few ne'er-do-wells wander into this hushed neighborhood, Hotel Súa takes safety seriously. Sturdy door locks and strongboxes for valuables are found in each room. Sleeping spaces are a little musty, with worn floorboards and old wooden dressers. Two rooms have patios facing the ocean, providing refreshing sea air. All quarters have clean, bright private baths (s/20,000 per person). The cosmopolitan restaurant downstairs serves French, Italian, and local cuisine. Menu is in French and Spanish, and prices are listed in francs and sucres. Daily specials like an *almuerzo* of fried fish, menestra, rice, and fried bananas from s/5,000. The seafood pasta is more reasonable (s/16,000; chocolate mousse s/6,000; open daily 7am-9:30pm). To get to Súa from Atacames take a **bus** (every 30min., s/1,000), a **taxi** (s/5,000), or walk south along the beach (1hr., only possible at low tide).

SAME

A honeymooner's paradise, the soft shore of Same waits each day to be deflowered by the first footprints to mark its untouched sands. Same's virtually uninhabited beach, 6km southwest of Súa, is trimmed with bountiful palm trees and tastefully commercialized with only a handful of low-key establishments. Though never more than 20m wide, the beach stretches to the south for a couple of miles. Its greenish surf is said to be the best in the Atacames area, and lingers at a refreshing 25°C (75°F) year-round. Same has many wealthy inhabitants, and its semi-resort status means prices are jacked up a bit more than at other local beaches. The **Cabaña Marinas,** just before the bridge to the beach, are less interesting than the beach front places, but more affordable. Each little wooden hut has a private bath, green painted floors, and bamboo walls (s/20,000 per person). The charming seafront *cabañas* of **La Terraza Quito** (tel. 544-507), are just to your left as you reach the beach from the main road. Built on stilts, each *cabaña* comes equipped with private bath, fan, and window screens (singles s/35,000; doubles s/70,000; quads s/100,000). Built around a tree trunk, La Terraza's **restaurant** is in touch with its natural side, adorned with giant turtle shells and deserted dugout canoes. Calamari spaghetti is s/12,800, lobster ceviche s/17,000, with tiramisu for dessert s/5,000 (open daily 9am-3:30pm and 7-9:30pm). **Restaurante Unicornio,** just before Cabañas Marinas on the road to the beach, is less expensive. A full *almuerzo* with seafood is s/8,000. Open daily 8am-9pm. Same can be reached by **bus** (s/12,000 from Atacames) or **boat** (s/20,000 from Atacames).

■ Muisne

Somehow escaping the epidemic of tourism that is sweeping the rest of the coast, the quiet island of Muisne, situated about 35km southwest of Atacames, remains ignorant of other beaches' touristy ways. Without cars and telephones, days on the island are as carefree as the inhabitants that walk barefoot through the streets. The lack of badgering tourist crowds allows the gregarious locals to take the time to befriend the visitors they do receive. A few days in Muisne and you'll probably know the names of all of the beach's restaurant owners. If you've got an affable disposition and a few words of Spanish under your belt, they may even remember your name. Sun, quietude, and hospitality unite here to create an experience of overwhelming leisure.

Orientation and Practical Information The bus stop is in the mainland town of **Salto,** just by the docks. It is a thrilling three-minute, s/500 trip across the 200m waterway that makes Muisne an island. On the docks of the island, boys on bicycles offer rides to the **beach** for s/2,000; otherwise, it is a 15-minute walk. The road directly perpendicular to the docks leads to the beach.

There are no official money-changing facilities here, but Paraíso will change dollars if you really need it. Transport to other destinations leaves from the mainland docks. **Buses** run to **Esmeraldas** (2hr., 5:30am-9:30pm, s/6,000) via **Same** (1hr.), **Súa** (1¼hr., s/3,000), and **Atacames** (2hr., s/4,000). **Boats** run to **Cojimíes** from the dock to the right of the main one (daily 7am-3pm, about every hr., depends how quickly they fill up, 1½hr., s/30,000). It pays to get there on time, and be ready to get wet (see **Near Muisne: Cojimíes,** p. 188). The **EMETEL** office and **hospital** are on the road from the docks to the beach, as is EMETEL (open Mon.-Sat. 8am-10pm, Sun. 8am-1pm and 7-10pm). The hospital (tel. 480-269), is open 24 hr. and offers free emergency care. **Farmacía Dolorosa,** 5 de Agosto, is on your right as you walk to the beach (open daily 7am-10:30pm). The **police** are in a blue and grey building on the street parallel to the main road, just before the Central Park, supposedly open 24 hr.

Accommodations While Muisne has few hotels, there's nearly always something available since so few tourists visit the island. All rooms come equipped with mosquito nets (an absolute must) and not-so-reliable cold water. Perhaps the biggest problem hotels here have is keeping wet sandy feet from creating indoor beaches. The pink **Hotel Plaza Paraíso** is at the far south side of the beach. Sherry, the Texan proprietor, treats every guest like family with her unbeatable tourist information. Soft cloth hammocks, reed mats, candled tables, board games, self-serve beer in the fridge…no wonder she called it paradise. Rooms share communal but well-scrubbed toilets and showers (s/15,000 per person). The **Cabañas San Cristóbal** (tel. 480-264) are at the far north end of the beach. Fancy tiled rooms available, but a better deal is one of the wooden huts that line the beach. Musty wooden floorboards whisper tales of bygone days, but fresh air flows through front and back windows. Doors open right onto the sand, equipped with good-sized locks to prevent unwanted visitors. All rooms have private baths. Showerheads curiously similar to toilet seats make for a peculiar bathroom experience (s/10,000 per person). On the sandy road that runs from Cabañas San Cristóbal into town, **Hotel Galápagos** takes the classic Muisne approach of relative isolation. It's more removed from beach life, plus the amicable management is conscientious about cleanliness, so no need to worry about sandy floors here. Immaculate, well-ventilated rooms sport pink-and-yellow mosquito nets, and all have private bath (s/20,000 per person). If you really want to treat yourself, the brand new **Mapara Hostel** (tel. 455-794), has elegant rooms, hot water, laundry, conference rooms, cafeteria, and tour options (US$15-22).

Food Dining on this coastal isle is an exercise in patience. The typical selection of seafood dishes is served up at an amazingly slow pace. But laid-back dining does have its advantages. Most restaurants sit right on the beach, and spending up to an hour or two napping, reading, chatting, or sipping a beer while you wait can be quite pleasant. **Restaurante Mi Delfin,** next door to Hotel Paraíso, fits the Muisne restaurant profile to a tee. Slow cooking has mouth-watering rewards here. Banana pancakes (s/3,000), loads of seafood dishes like fried shrimp (s/9,500), and a rare exciting vegetarian dish are all listed on the menu—noodles with vegetable puree (s/7,000; open daily 8am-10pm). **Comedor Rosita,** on the beach north of the main road, cooks an atypically quick breakfast, complete with bread, coffee, eggs with veggie bits, and assorted juices (s/5,000). Wash it down with a banana milkshake special. Rosita also serves assorted seafood dishes (s/9,000; open daily 8am-9pm). **Restaurant Tiburón,** on the north end of the beach, manages to flavor the same food you've been eating since you got to the coast in a new way that makes it a pleasure to dine. If even the rice and beans are this tasty, imagine what they can do to seafood (fried fish dish s/9,500; vegetarian plate s/5,000; open daily 8am-10pm).

Sights and Entertainment Muisne's shores are endowed with heaps of soft, unspoiled sand, strong surf, and gobs of solitude. The immense **beach** provides one and a half hours worth of walking room in either direction, and the difference between high and low tides can be as great as 70m. In an effort to realize their dreams of a palm-fringed beach, the locals have planted palm trees all along the beachfront, with fences to protect the tender young saplings. For the time being, straw-reed umbrellas and avocado branches provide shade until the trees reach maturity. The surf can be rough at times, especially since it is home to tiny stinging jellyfish. The stings can be healed immediately with a dab of vinegar; ask for some at the local *cevicherías*. Occasionally, small sea snakes get washed up on shore. Local children aren't afraid to kill them with rocks, but *Let's Go* recommends steering clear of these venomous creatures of the sea. While the beach is generally quite safe, at night it's best to stay near the lights of the hotels and restaurants. The **Habana Club,** about halfway between Hotel Paraíso and the main road to the beach, is a nice place to rest your weary traveling soul with a chilly beer (s/4,000) or a quick shot of rum (s/2,000). Huge selection of classic rock and reggae CDs, and amusing posters advocating the use of marijuana, including a never-before-seen version of the Mona Lisa chillin' with a spliff. Management is gregarious, and can provide tons of info on the destruction of the local mangrove forests (supposedly open all the time, but usually from 8pm-3am). Boating through the mangroves is possible and pleasurable though there are frequent blemishes in the green where the *camaroneras* (shrimp farms) have sprung up. These trips can aim for a destination, like Isla Bonita, with rolling green hills and rocky cliffs surrounding a sheltered beach, or they can be just boating for the sake of boating. Some people camp overnight on Isla Bonita or at Monpiche; others stay all day or just a few hours. If you plan to leave the sheltered area behind the island of Muisne, be prepared for rolling waves and a tottering boat. Boats with drivers can be found at the port for s/40,000 an hour, but it's better to ask around and settle a price suited to your plan. Having a driver wait for hours while you hunt for seashells at Isla Bonita can add up and get expensive. Sharing costs among a large group of tourists works best; to Monpiche can cost up to s/80,000. Mapara hostal plans to begin offering guides and tours of the Muisne area in late 1997.

■ Near Muisne: Cojimíes

For most, Cojimíes is little more than a necessary stop in a journey along the coast. The town itself isn't much of a beachy paradise due to the clutter of boats, shacks, and fishing gear covering the sand, but just south of Cojimíes there is a stretch of beach that is virtually empty (except for the *camioneta* traffic), exceedingly safe, clean, and beautiful, though a bit rocky in places. The most exciting thing about Cojimíes is getting there or away. The 1½-hour wet-and-wild **boat ride** between Muisne and Cojimíes is a motorized dugout climbing 7- to 10-foot swells as buckets of saltwater splash into the boat, inevitably soaking passengers to the bone. The boats that make the trip have a storage compartment for bags and other necessities that absolutely can't get wet, but they won't let people in there, so bring some kind of rain gear. Departures from Muisne are roughly scheduled between 7am and 3pm, every hour or as the boats fill up, and boats from Cojimíes leave also according to when they fill with passengers, between 7am and early afternoon. To ensure a seat, get to the docks early. **Camionetas** to Pedernales (1½hr., s/5,000) leave all day from the large plaza that doubles as a basketball court, near the dock, or along the main street. This ride is wild fun—racing along the beach in an old truck, over small rivers, through waves, around rocks, and past thick forests of palm trees.

Though there's little reason to spend much time here, if you need to make a phone call or require medical attention, Cojimíes does have an **EMETEL** on the principle street where the road from the docks intersects (open Mon.-Sat. 8am-10pm, Sun. 8am-7pm) and a **24-hour pharmacy/clinic** (ask for Dr. Jorge Cobos), just left of Calle Principal on the cross street after EMETEL. The **Farmacía Espíritu Santo** is open 24 hours (tel. 623-224 ext. 136). If somehow you get stuck in Cojimíes, you'll definitely save money on accommodations, but that is the only bright side of staying the night here. The **Residencial Manuelita,** with its cramped, dingy rooms and sturdy locks, is on the main street, a couple of blocks down from EMETEL (singles s/10,000). Farther down the main road is the **Residencial Popular,** which closes guests in with thick brick walls and wood-plank floors that don't quite fit together (s/10,000 per person, s/15,000 with a window). If these places are too depressing, **Residencial Cabañas del Atardecer** (tel. 623-224 ext. 127), at the end of Calle Principal on the beach has much nicer, more expensive rooms (s/25,000 per person). The dining options in Cojimíes are limited, but of a much higher quality than the lodgings. **Flabio Alfaro,** across the road from the basketball court by the port, serves *desayuno* s/5,000, *almuerzo* s/8,000, and seafood dishes like fried shrimp for s/7,000, or conch *ceviche* s/10,000. Alfaro's features outside seating in the shade (open daily 7am-8pm).

■ Pedernales

This tranquil seaport, approximately 70km north of San Vicente and 40km south of Cojimíes, takes advantage of its position in the center of things. Pedernales hosts the largest market on the northern coast, and serves as an important center for the shrimp industry. But while locals may consider Pedernales crucial, travelers searching for the perfect *playa* paradise normally look elsewhere. The town is only significant to coastal visitors as a crucial link in the coastline's chain of transport. The famous *camionetas* to Cojimíes travel north up the coast from here, and several bus companies link Pedernales with inland and southern coastal towns.

Orientation and Practical Information Pedernales's **central plaza** is on the corner of the town's two most important streets: **López Castillo** runs north-south and **Eloy Alfaro** runs east-west. The town's lackluster **beach** is at the west end of Alfaro. Due to free-wheeling cars and industrious fishing boats, the sand retains a grimy appearance and a potent, fishy aroma. The dirty-brown surf is solid, rolling in two- to five-foot waves—fine for swimming, but not much to look at. The town's **EMETEL,** Alfaro 5-10 (tel. 681-105), east of the plaza, cannot make international calls (open daily 8am-10pm). The town's **bus companies** are on López Castillo, south of the plaza. **Cooperativa Costa Norte,** López Castillo 5-28, and **Coactur Bus Company,** López Castillo 5-06, send buses to: **San Vicente** (3hr., s/10,000); **Portoviejo** (5hr., s/15,000); **Manta** (6hr., s/18,000); and **Guayaquil** (9hr., s/30,000), approximately every hour, 4am-11:30pm. **Cooperativa Trans Santo Domingo,** López Castillo 5-34 (tel. 681-260), goes to **Santo Domingo** (approximately every 30min., 4:30am-6:30pm, 3hr., s/10,000), where connections can be made to other inland destinations. **Camionetas** make the trip to Cojimíes (during low tide hours, 1½hr., s/5,000), leaving from the north side of the plaza. The trip begins on a dirt highway, but soon the trucks take to the sand and the joyride quickly becomes an off-roading adventure, filled with high-speed glimpses of the surrounding coastline and heart-pounding races to beat the rising water.

Accommodations and Food Given its transportation-hub status, Pedernales has a few suitable accommodations that don't exactly enchant with their ambience, but are decently-maintained and safe. If you arrive late at night, find a place in town rather than stumble around in the dark down by the beach. The **Hotel Pedernales,** Alfaro 6-18 (tel. 681-092), three blocks east of the plaza is clean, fresh, and friendly. Flowery bedsheets battle the drab forces of concrete walls and floors. Rooms have refrigerators and color TVs (s/15,000 per person, with bath s/25,000). **Aires Libre** (tel. 681-237), on the beach 200m south of Alfaro, supplies 23 rooms at spare-change rates. There is potential for supreme stuffiness, but opening a window allows for some *aires libres,* as the name suggests (communal bath without showers s/10,000 per person). If you're hungry, Pedernales bursts with bland eateries, both up in town and down on the sand. **Los Frailes** (tel. 681-212), on Alfaro by the beach, is named for the two rocks off Pedernales's jagged ocean cliffs. This place specializes in delicious *ceviche* dishes with fish (s/8,000) or shrimp (s/10,000). Turtle shells, flowering plants, and framed photos of the monolithic namesakes cheer patrons on as they down some of the town's fresh seafood (open Wed.-Mon. 8am-6pm). **El Rocio,** Alfaro 605 and Velasco Ibarra (tel. 681-337), east of the plaza, is across from Hotel Pedernales. Soft leather chairs give your legs and eyes a rest from the oft-repeated white-plastic-chair motif. Classy as well as comfortable, delicate Spanish guitar music and Coca-Cola from a gold rimmed silver cup and saucer soothe and cool along with multiple fans and a big doorish opening to catch breezes. Try their breakfasts of eggs, bread, juice, and coffee (s/6,000), or basic *almuerzos* and *meriendas* with soup, rice, entree, and juice (s/6,500-7,000; open daily 7am-9pm).

▓ Bahía de Caráquez

Glittering with clean white high rises and tastefully placed palm trees, the Miami-esque skyline of Bahía de Caráquez promises a city catering to the swanky elite. The trouble is, Ecuador doesn't have much of a swanky elite, and most of Bahía's locals live in metal shacks in the hills behind the city. The government pumps a portion of its mysteriously disappearing funds into making sure this home of ex-president Sixto Durán Ballen remains exactly as its opulent occupants like it. The immaculate streets battle trash with the ubiquitous, hypnotizing town slogan, *"Bahía no tiene una copia, cuidésela"* (roughly, "There's only one Bahía; take care of it"). Bahía's one insufficiency is in its want of beach space. Built on a rocky peninsula, neither the Río Chone nor the Pacific Ocean allow room for frolicking in the sand. The 10m of sludge-sand that appears at low tide is best used as a boat dock, not for tanning.

Orientation and Practical Information Boats from San Vicente drop visitors off along the muddy shore near the intersection of **Aguilera** and **Malecón** (also referred to as Alberto F. Santos), the main street in town. Malecón parallels the **Río Chone**, running north around the peninsula and south towards the bus station. The **Guacamayo Tourist Office**, Bolívar and Arenas (tel. 690-597), offers Bahía info and local tour options that become affordable as more people join in (open Mon.-Sat. 8am-7pm, Sun. 8am-2pm). Calls from **EMETEL**, Malecón and Arenas (tel. 690-020), cost s/2,000 per three minutes (open daily 8am-10pm). Change money and traveler's checks until 2pm, or just get some cash out of the 24-hour ATM at **Filanbanco**, Aguilar and Malecón (tel. 691-096, 691-102, or 691-053), next to the post office (open Mon.-Fri. 8:45am-4pm, Sat. 9am-2pm). **Coactur buses,** Malecón and Vineza (tel. 690-014), at the south end of the boardwalk, go to: **Portoviejo** (every 30min., 4am-7:45pm, 2hr., s/5,000); and **Manta** (3hr., s/7,000). Feeling ill? Go to **Farmacía San Gregorio,** Ascazubi and Montufar (open Mon.-Sat. 8:30am-1:30pm and 2:30-10pm). Feeling *really* ill? **Hospital Miguel H. Alcivar,** Rocafuerte and Cruzan (emergency tel. 690-002, 690-006, or 690-008; tel. 690-712 or 690-046), at the end of town, gives free treatment (open 24hr.). The **police** station, Sixto Durán Ballen and Av. 3 de Noviembre (tel. 690-484), is open 24 hours. Mail those postcards at the **post office,** Aguilera 108 and Malecón (tel. 691-177; open Mon.-Fri. 8am-4:30pm, Sat. 8am-noon).

Accommodations Just look around—Bahía wasn't built for the budget traveler. While blessed with numerous waterfront establishments suitable for *Lifestyles of the Rich and Famous,* Bahía doesn't brag about its cheaper hotels. The sketchier, shoddier low-rent accommodations are concentrated a couple blocks back from the beach, along Montufar between Ante and Riofrio. The frighteningly expensive accommodations begin to pop up farther north along the peninsula. Luckily, there are a few places that offer something in between these extremes, combining affordable prices with decently-kept premises. **Hotel Palma,** Bolívar 914 (tel. 690-467), between Arenas and Riofrio, around the corner from EMETEL, is just one block up from Malecón. Somehow managing to appear cheerful despite a lack of sunlight, rooms are heavily decorated, while "private bath" means a corner of the room set apart by a curtain. Most importantly, though the common baths could look better, the establishment is clean (s/10,000 per person, with bath s/15,000). **Hotel Bahía Bed and Breakfast Inn,** Ascazubi 316 and Morales (tel. 690-146), has neat, clean rooms with fans, a sunny dining room for breakfast, and a friendly English speaking owner. Prices vary through the year (singles s/20,000, with bath s/30,000; doubles s/30,000, with bath s/50,000). **Hotel Bahía,** Malecón (tel. 690-509; fax 693-833), near the bus stops is as whitewashed as the city's highrises. Secure rooms offer little excitement unless you happen to come when there's a rare live music performance. Bring a paperback and enjoy the quietude supplied by the immense hotel's thick walls. Tour info is available, and all rooms have private bath, scrubbed until sparkling (s/30,000 per person, with hot water and color TV s/35,000).

Food There are plenty of excellent dining opportunities in Bahía, with some cheaper places along the Río Chone. Expect to be inundated with typical coastal entrees—*ceviches*, fish plates, rice and seafood dishes—but along with the meal, enjoy views of the marina and bluffs of San Vicente. **Pablo's Restaurant,** Malecón 11-20 and Ascazubi (tel. 690-529), serves common seafood dishes with uncommonly efficient service. Impressive beer collection entertains while you await *almuerzo* (s/ 7,000 for soup, meat, rice, and salad), *ceviche* (s/10,000-12,000), or a specially requested vegetarian platter (s/4,000). Snack on *plátanos* sliced paper-thin (open daily 9am-10pm). Look to your left along Malecón as you step off the docks: **Muelle Uno,** on Malecón along the riverfront, is across from Banco Manabí. This newly renovated spot has been taken over by the swanky elite of Bahía, but still offers reasonable prices amidst the shaded tables and prime waterviews (fruit salad s/4,000, rice with pottage and meat s/8,000, chorizo sausages s/10,000). Cheaper, greasier food is sold at the street entrance (open Mon.-Sat. 9am-3am). **Restaurant Genesis,** on Malecón along the riverfront, is just south of Muelle Uno. A slightly more exciting menu and less expensive prices keep Genesis competitive. Choices range from pork and pineapple to crab, but prices always hover around s/19,000 (open daily 7:30am-9pm).

Sights and Entertainment The inhabitants of this sedate coastal city tend to be older, wealthier business-people who have done their darndest to keep Bahía clean and quiet. They've succeeded—the streets are reasonably safe, spotless, and supremely strollable. Signs remind inhabitants of the prohibitions against soccer-playing on the shore, sidewalk vending, and loud music. All of this gives Bahía a certain peaceful quietude, but its conservative creed also makes it a tad stuffy and boring. A walk along Malecón is a good way to get a feel for Bahía; it runs the length of the city and passes some of its more interesting attractions. As the road winds around the peninsula to the western side, the waves begin to crash violently against the rocky perimeters, catapulting water onto the streets and sidewalks above. On the western side, along Versillio Ratty, there is an excellent break for **surfing.** Although there isn't a beach, waves form so far out that surfers can get in good rides before they have to bail out to avoid a rocky conclusion. If you don't surf, it's almost as much of a rush to watch these talented daredevils challenge Mother Nature for quick thrills. **Cinema Bahía,** Bolívar 1418 and Pinveza (tel. 690-363), shows action movies in an air-conditioned (!) theater every day at 8pm (s/4000). It's worth the money even if you have no interest in the film, simply as an escape from the heat.

■ Near Bahía de Caráquez

CANOA

Canoa's beautiful, uncrowded beaches sit 17km north of San Vicente. Free from the tumult of tourist traffic and sedulous seafolk, only the sounds of the waves crashing against the cliffs to the north and the occasional crab scuttling across the sand upset Canoa's calm. The waves that swell the muddled green water bring a professional surfing competition here every February, but the waves are usually tame enough for more relaxed water fun, like late-night swimming in the bioluminescent plankton. Buses to San Vicente pass every half-hour (20min., s/1,000).

Somehow, this tiny town manages to have a 24-hour tourist information center, logically connected to a bar upstairs. **Blue and Green Tourist Information Center** is located 300m up the main road from the beach, ready to help with any tourism questions or problems. Next door is **La Posada de Daniel** (tel. 691-201 or 09-773-276), where you can stay in a newly built hillside cabin overlooking the ocean. Each cabin has a private bath, TV, comfy chair, and there is always a hammock nearby (s/25,000 per person). Guests can also stay in an older house with well-kept rooms, astoundingly high ceilings, and absolutely tiny private baths (s/20,000 per person). Soft leather couches and a scattering of paperbacks, magazines, and board games turn three breezy living rooms into chummy hangouts. Daniel will do his best to make sure his guests enjoy themselves; he offers daytrips to a series of caves hidden in the cliffs of Canoa, free to Posada guests, and may give tips or even a lesson in surfing. A cheap alternative to Daniel's Posada is to rent a hammock from **Hotel Bambu** (tel. 753-696), at the north end of the beach (s/10,000 per person). Don't put off eating dinner in Canoa—restaurants and any other place that may sell food tend to close up early. **Restaurante Costa Azul** (tel. 690-075), on the main road, is 10 steps from the sand. Azul amazes with decor and ocean views, not to mention its battered fish dish (s/7,000); they also serve breakfasts (s/6,000), *churrascos* (s/9,000), and *ceviches* (s/10,000; open daily 7am-8pm). **Arena Bar,** just left off the main road at the beach, serves *caipiriñas* (s/5,000) and lots of salsa music to whomever they can gather from among the few people in town (open daily whenever there are people around).

SAN VICENTE

San Vicente's site at the mouth of the Río Chone prevents it from developing into a beach community, but its sheltered marina is home to a healthy fishing industry. Across the river from Bahía de Caráquez, San Vicente cannot avoid constant comparison to its wealthier neighbor. Virtually every shop along the boardwalk faces Bahía, and boats leave every five minutes to cross the river. Visitors usually prefer to spend their time across the river, but those who need to pinch pennies often find themselves crawling back to San Vicente's cheap beds.

San Vicente is basically just one road, **Malecón,** which runs right along the waterfront. All of the bus companies have their offices at the northern end of this street, and go to: **Portoviejo** (every 2hr., 6am-8pm, 2¼hr., s/5,000), often continuing to **Manta** (3hr., s/8,800). **Cooperativa Costa Norte** also goes to: **Pedernales** (every hr., 6:45am-5:30pm, 3hr., s/10,000); and **Canoa** (every 20min., 7am-6pm, 20min., s/1,000). **Reina El Camino** (tel. 674-480), passes through Portoviejo on its way to **Jipijapa** (6:30 and 11am, 3hr., s/9,000). The blue-roofed **ferries** go to **Bahía de Caráquez** (every 5min., 6am-6pm, 10min., s/900 in the day, s/1,800 at night). At low tide, they leave from the sands just north of the car ferry dock, but at high tide (usually afternoon), they depart from the nearby pier. The **police** (tel. 674-202), are north of the boardwalk, where Malecón splits at the rotunda. **EMETEL** (tel. 647-821), is next to the police station (open daily 8am-9pm). **Farmacía Popular** is off Malecón on Carretera San Isidro, by the rotunda (open Mon.-Sat. 8am-8pm).

There are only a handful of places to stay in San Vicente, and the cheapest ones are clustered at the south end of the boardwalk. **Hotel San Vicente** (tel. 674-182), tries to sweep guests off their feet with crooked sinks, cracked headboards, and mildewy baths. Yet it is usually safe and some rooms have windows with an ocean view (s/7,000 per person, with bath s/15,000). The nearby **Hotel Narciso de Jesus** has attempted to decorate itself with movie posters and calendar pin-ups. Ceiling fans, mosquito nets, decaying walls, and communal baths complete the shoddy package (s/8,000 per person). San Vicente offers little in terms of dining options. There are a few unremarkable establishments near the bus stops, but you'll have to struggle to find one that's open due to an epidemic of quirky business hours. **Restaurant Yenni** (tel. 674-403), right by Hotel Narciso de Jesus, has simple atmosphere and food, but its location and surprisingly sane business hours make it quite a find. The bargains include *desayunos* (s/5,000), and *meriendas* (s/6,000; open daily 7am-9pm).

■ Manta

Dominated by its immense harbor, Manta has long been a hub of seafaring activities. Known as Jocay ("fish house" in Quechua) prior to Spanish intrusion, Manta was home to a hedonistic community distinguished for its maritime accomplishments. Voyaging the high seas in balsawood rafts and dugouts, the Jocay made frequent excursions to Panamá and Perú, and some zealous scholars of the ancient culture assert they navigated as far as Mexico and Chile. Visitors today might guess that they sailed so far to get away from the filth and urban squalor generated by Manta's beach-

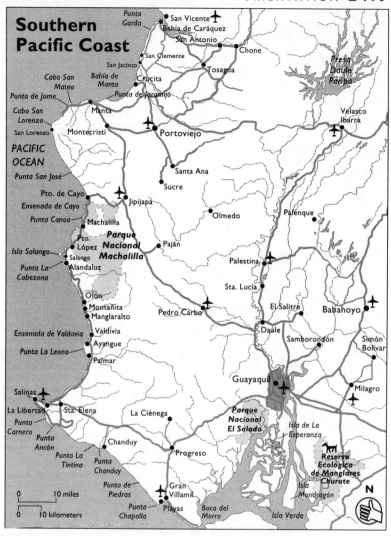

Southern Pacific Coast

Punta Gorda
San Vicente
Bahía de Caráquez
San Antonio
Chone
San Clemente
San Jacinto
Tosagua
Cabo San Mateo
Bahía de Manta
Crucita
Presa Daule Peripa
Punta de Jome
Punta de Jaramijó
Cabo San Lorenzo
Manta
Velasco Ibarra
San Lorenzo
Montecristi
Portoviejo

PACIFIC OCEAN

Punta San José
Santa Ana
Pto. de Cayo
Sucre
Ensenada de Cayo
Jipijapa
Olmedo
Palenque
Punta Canoa
Machalilla
Isla Salango
Parque Nacional Machalilla
Paján
Pto. López
Palestina
Salango
Alandaluz
Punta La Cabezona
Sta. Lucía
Olón
Montañita
Pedro Carbo
El Salitre
Babahoyo
Manglaralto
Daule
Ensenada de Valdavia
Valdivia
Samborondón
Simón Bolívar
Punta La Leona
Ayangue
Palmar
Guayaquil
Milagro
Salinas
La Libertad
Sta. Elena
La Ciénega
Parque Nacional El Salado
Isla de La Esperanza
Punta Carnero
Punta Ancón
Chanduy
Progreso
Reserva Ecológica de Manglares Churute
Punta La Tintina
Punta Chanduy
Punta de Piedras
Gran Villami
Isla Mondragón
Punta Chapolla
Playas
Boca del Morro
Isla Verde

0   10 miles
0   10 kilometers

N

going visitors and 200,000 inhabitants. The city's size and robust economy have left its beaches dirtier than those of nearby coastal towns, but they also make Manta the most convenient place in the region to exchange money, stock up on supplies, and move on to fairer lands.

ORIENTATION

Buses enter Manta by way of **Eloy Alfaro,** presenting fleeting glimpses of **Tarqui,** the southern beach, as they cross the inlet that separates it from Manta proper. The **terminal terrestre** is located just west of the harbor, not far from the bridge over the inlet. North of the bridge, Eloy Alfaro becomes **Malecón,** running parallel to the water as it passes east of town and leads north to Manta's **Murciélago** beach. In Manta *centro*, north-south streets are **Avenidas,** with numbers increasing as the streets get farther from the water. East-west streets are **Calles,** numbered beginning at the inlet. Calles and Avenidas in Tarqui begin with 101.

PRACTICAL INFORMATION

Tourist Information: CETUR, Av. 3 1034 and Calle 11 (tel. 622-944). Open Mon.-Fri. 8:30am-5pm. Provides maps of Manta and copious travel info.

Travel Agencies: Delgado Travel, Av. 2 and Calle 13 (tel. 620-046). Open Mon.-Sat. 8:30am-1pm and 3-6:30pm. This large travel complex also offers international phone service, car rental, and cash currency exchange. **Manatours,** Malecón and Calle 13 (tel. 621-020 or 621-026), in Edificio Vigía. Open Mon.-Fri. 8am-1pm and 2-7pm. **Metropolitan Touring,** Av. 4 1239-45 and Calle 13 (tel. 623-090 or 622-366; fax 611-277). Open Mon.-Fri. 9am-1pm and 3-7pm.

Buses: The **terminal terrestre** is along Av. 24 de Marzo just past Av. 4. **Coop Montecristi** goes to **Montecristi** (every 10min., 6am-7pm, 30min., s/2,000). **Coactur** (tel. 620-036), has buses to: **Guayaquil** (every hr., 4am-6pm, s/13,500); **Bahía de Caráquez** (every 30min. starting at 5am, 3hr., s/5,500); **Portoviejo** (every 10min., 4am-10pm, 1hr., s/2,500). **Reina del Camino** (tel. 620-963), goes to: **Quito** (12 per day, 4am-10:30pm, s/20,000); and **Guayaquil** (every hr., 2:30am-7:30pm, s/13,000). **Coop Manglaralto** travels to: **Jipijapa** (every 2hr., 4am-4pm, 1hr., s/2,000); **Puerto López** (every 2hr., 4am-4pm, s/5,000); **Salango** (every 2hr., 4am-4pm, s/5,000); **La Libertad** (every 2hr., 4am-4pm, 5hr., s/17,000). Two companies provide more luxurious night buses to Quito: **Flota Imbabura,** Malecón and Calle 8, has buses at 10 and 10:30pm (9hr., s/28,000). **Panamericana,** Av. 4 and Calle 12 (tel. 625-898), has cushy sleeping cars leaving at 10pm (s/42,000).

Taxis: Cooperación Ciudad de Manta (tel. 610-704), by the bus terminal.

Airport: A few km south of the *centro,* offers **avioneta** flights in the morning to Guayaquil (s/90,000) and Quito (s/150,000). Ask travel agencies in town for current schedules and bookings.

Pharmacies: Farmacía Rex, Av. 6 and Calle 12 (tel. 620-690). Open daily 8:30am-1pm and 3-6pm. **Farmacía,** Calle 7 and Av. 24 de Mayo (tel. 610-638), in municipal building. Open Mon.-Sat. 8am-7:30pm. Also many pharmacies adjacent to hospital.

Hospital: Hospital Rodriguez Zambrano de Manta, Av. San Mateo and Calle 12 (emergency tel. 611-849, 621-595, 625-603, or 625-610), Barrio Santa Martha. From the Malecón, head away from the water on Calle 12 and keep going. Free 24hr. emergency treatment.

Emergency: tel. 101.

Police: Av. 4 de Noviembre and Calle 104 (tel. 920-900). Open 24hr.

Post Office: Av. 4 and Calle 8. Open Mon.-Fri. 7:30am-6:30pm, Sat. 8am-1pm.

Telephones: EMETEL, Calle 11 and Malecón (tel. 622-700). Open daily 8am-10pm.

Telephone code: 05.

ACCOMMODATIONS

Although most of the action is found in downtown Manta, the hotels there tend to be geared toward businessmen or wealthy Ecuadorians. Budget lodgings capitalize on the lower property values of the less pleasant Tarquí. Don't dream of charming beachside villas—you're likely to find unimaginative concrete highrises. Malecón, Tarquí's beachfront avenue, monopolizes the accommodations market. A five-minute walk along its sandy sidewalk is an expeditious way to land yourself a comfortable room for the night. Make sure you've got a serious fan—Manta's muggy air is mosquito heaven.

Hotel Miami, Malecón and Calle 108 (tel. 611-743). Welcome to Museum Miami, where living quarters are included with the price of admittance. Artifacts from the indigenous cultures of Manta, Jipijapa, and Bahía de Caráquez clutter the walls and floors. Rooms haven't been preserved as well, but offer clean private baths and an occasional bamboo bed. Rooms s/20,000 per person; s/15,000 in large groups.

Hotel Mantamar, Malecón and Calle 103 (tel. 624-670). Floors are wet but policy is dry—absolutely no alcohol on the premises. Basic rehab-style cement cells have high-speed fans and toy-sized beds. All rooms have private bath, except the s/7,000 shoebox. Rooms s/10,000 per person, with ocean view and color TV s/15,000.

Panorama Inn, Av. 105 and Calle 103 (tel. 621-673; fax 611-552). Big windows in this spotless highrise give a panoramic view of the harbor. You have to pay for it though, as well as for the TVs, private baths, phones, and hotel pool. Singles with fan s/40,000; doubles s/70,000; about twice as much for A/C.

Hotel Pacífico, Av. 106 and Calle 101 (tel. 622-475 or 623-584). The name of this highrise is visible from almost anywhere in Manta. The nearby inlet's stench can be asphyxiating, but the small rooms smell oh-so-fresh, and fans cool you off after the hike up the stairs. All have private bath. Rooms s/30,000 per person.

Hostal Chimborazo, Av. 1 (tel. 612-290), between Calles 11 and 12, is right in the middle of Manta, which is fortunate since you may not want to spend time in your dark, dingy quarters. All have fans, some have TVs. Rooms s/20,000 per person.

FOOD

Believe it or not, most of the food in Manta once had gills. Options in Tarquí tend toward standard *comedores* and beach-side seafood joints. The main city has more in the way of restaurants.

Comedor Estrella del Mar, Malecón and Calle 106, Tarquí. A grass-hut restaurant in a deluge of grass-hut establishments, Estrella's bright yellow paint job and Pilsener propaganda are hard to miss. Prices conveniently absent in English menus. Fried seabass s/15,000, clam and rice dishes s/11,000. Open daily 7am-11pm.

Restaurante Carlos Escalante, Av. 6 8-16 and Calle 8 (tel. 612-722). Carlos never intended it to be a restaurant; he just let some locals in for lunch and suddenly his living room—which fits 6 tables at most—became one of the most popular diners in town. Enjoy a homecooked local dish in close company. Fish, rice, salad, and fried bananas s/7,000, *ceviche* s/5,000. Open Mon.-Fri. 8am-2pm, Sat. 8am-noon.

Topi Tu Pizza, Malecón and Calle 15 (tel. 621-180). The fine crust of the pizza is accentuated by the open view of the harbor. Equally diverting scenery inside, with a boundless beer display (*cerveza* s/4,000-6,000). Simple pepper-and-onion pizza costs s/15,000 for a large, and individual size pizza *especial* with the works is s/14,000. Open Mon.-Fri. noon-1am, Sat. 11am-2am, Sun. noon-midnight.

Restaurant Mar y Flor, Malecón and Calle 104 (tel. 611-529). The bamboo-lattice walls, TV, and sea air give this seafood specialist that informal Tarquí feel. Big, greasy helpings of *arroz con camarones* (s/13,000). Open daily 11am-9pm.

Chalet's or **El Paron,** Malecón and Calle 9 (tel. 610-566). You don't have to pay much more for an extra touch of class—tuxedoed waiters, complimentary bread with garlic butter, and *camarones* stenciled on the windows. Tangy *camaron al ajillo* will fill you up and keep vampires at bay. Open daily for lunch and dinner.

SIGHTS AND ENTERTAINMENT

There are two stretches of beach in Manta. **Murciélago** is located in Manta proper, while **Tarquí** includes the shores further south. A five-minute drive or 20-minute walk north of *el centro*, Murciélago clamors with the typical assortment of *cevicherías* and *peñas*. Cut short by a breakwater to the north, the beach has a good deal of soft sand, but is often spoiled by the presence of overturned garbage cans and scattered litter. Murciélago receives the Pacific's currents unfettered, and hence is inundated with signs warning of strong currents. The powerful currents also create fair-sized surf, active with three- to four-foot swells in wintertime.

Tarquí's beach, on the other hand, hibernates all summer, only to wake in winter, turn over its pillow, yawn, and go back to sleep. Placid as a lake at dawn, Tarquí's waters are a playground for pelicans and frigates, but offer little excitement for human folk. Still, the breakneck landing tactics of the sea birds are amusing. Scattered with its share of soft sand, Tarquí is smaller than Murciélago, cut short by a breakwater to the south and the by-products of the fishing industry to the north.

If you're tired of shaking the sand out of your clothes, you can always take a walk around **Manta's harbor.** The busiest port on the central coast, the harbor teems with

Old-World fishing vessels and gargantuan navy ships docked for refueling. Just over the bridge into Tarquí, across from Hotel Pacifico, is an oddly placed **statue of a Manabí fisherman.** It's hard to imagine how workers first erected the statue, since these days the stench is so pungent that it's impossible to stay in the area for more than five minutes. The **Museo del Banco Central,** Av. 4 and Av. 24 de Mayo, in back of the Banco Central, has a diminutive but worthwhile collection of indigenous artifacts accompanied by scores of information on culture and history. The black-and-white photographs of an earlier Manta show it less densely populated, but as dependent as ever on the sea (open Mon.-Fri. 8:30am-4:30pm). As befits an industrious city of this size, nights in Manta radiate with energy. **Escandalo,** Av. 5 and Calle 10 (tel. 623-653), screens the most recent films in town.

■ Near Manta

MONTECRISTI

Between the hurly-burly giants of Manta and Portoviejo lounges mellow Montecristi, patiently churning out its world-renowned and sadly-misnamed **Panama hats.** Though these high-grade hats have long been made in Montecristi, most of the ears that their woven brims shelter haven't heard the name. Montecristi's obscurity stems from the same reason Columbus thought he'd disembarked in India: gringo confusion (see **Panama Hats Are Not from Panamá,** below). *Montecristianos* do not appear overly obsessed with their industrial anonymity, though for obvious economic reasons, they'd probably endorse efforts to educate misinformed *sombrero*-seekers. Still, namelessness has its privileges. The town's streets are tranquil and uncommercialized, with only the light traffic of lethargic burros and wandering pigs.

Shopping in Montecristi is about as fast-paced as a ride atop one of the town's many donkeys, but (thankfully) a great deal smoother. **Avenida 9 de Julio,** Montecristi's principal street, presents four or five different *sombrero* shops, all selling similar items at comparable prices. Hats start at around s/25,000 and rise to s/150,000 and beyond. Prices drop steadily the more hats you promise to buy. *Superfinos,* the highest quality hat, are woven so finely that the best ones can be rolled tight enough to pass through a man's ring. Imagine the uses! Along with the famed Panamas, most of these shops sell collections of straw handbags, backpacks, and baskets. Wickerwork has also become a popular pastime in Montecristi, and shops selling items from baby cribs to baskets also lie along Av. 9 de Julio.

After shopping, pay a visit to Montecristi's impressive house of prayer, the church of **La Virgen de Montecristi.** Located on the corners of Sucre, Av. 23 de Octubre, and Av. 9 de Julio, this striking edifice is home to the venerated Virgin of Monserrat, said to have miraculously cured various sickly *montecristianos* on a number of occasions. Along with her medical practice, the Virgin is also known to be an avid walker, and legends describing her perambulatory jaunts around Montecristi circulate through the town. Apparently there's a shortage of quality hats in the hereafter.

Excellent hats *and* quality budget accommodations would be too much to expect from one town. Montecristi doesn't offer many places to eat either. **Pollos y Algo Más,** Av. 9 de Julio 404 and Olmedo, manages both quality fare and friendly local atmosphere. Typically provincial, Pollos is decorated with mounted Panama hats and wickerwork tablesettings. Lounge outside, adjust your newly-purchased, slightly stiff hat, and munch a s/6,500 serving of rice and fish (open Mon.-Fri. 8am-9pm, Sat.-Sun. 8am-11pm). A few road-side stands offer the cheap stuff along the central plaza.

Buses arriving in Montecristi drop passengers off along the highway just north of town. A walk up either Av. 9 de Julio or Av. Sucre leads to the town center, a **central plaza** bounded by those two streets and east-west Av. 23 de Octubre and San Andreas. This tiny, shade-filled park facing the adjacent church, is home to Montecristi's practical establishments. The **Banco del Pinchincha** (tel. 606-101 or 606-105), changes money, but doesn't exchange traveler's checks, nor does it have an ATM (open Mon.-Fri. 8am-8pm, Sat. 8am-2pm). The **EMETEL** office, on the central plaza at

Panama Hats Are **Not** from Panamá

Forget the name, forget your other misconceptions, **Panama hats are made in Ecuador.** Born of economic necessity, the Panama descended from the ancient straw hats of the pre-Columbians in the Manabí province. The industry got its start in the 1830s, when the poverty-stricken inhabitants of Cuenca were forced to make hats for a living. Exports got a major boost from a major monarch at the 1855 World Expo, when King Napoleon III (and subsequently the rest of Europe) fell in love with the hat. Fifty years later, the craze hit the States. During construction of the Panama Canal, American workers found the hats perfect protection from the scorching sun and dubbed them with the misnomer that stuck. Gangsters began wearing the hats in the 20s; to this day, a certain model is called the Capone. The industry reached its peak in 1946, when 5 million hat exports accounted for 20% of Ecuador's earnings. Presidents and Hollywood stars alike sported the stylish, exotic hat—an integral part of 30s and 40s American fashion.

Meanwhile, poor Ecuadorians worked for pennies, making hats that sold for a hefty profit in the States. The middlemen, processing factories, exporters, and retailers all took their share, leaving little for the actual artisans. These days, the hats are less popular and imitation paper hats have taken a substantial bite out of the market. The master artisans of Montecristi may soon cease to practice their art because it no longer supports them. So while you're in the neighborhood, help save a dying art, and pay your respects to the real creative geniuses; buy yourself an Ecuador Hat.

Av. 9 de Julio and Av. 23 de Octubre, has three booths for national calls only (open Mon.-Sat. 8am-1pm and 2-8pm, Sun. 8am-noon). The **post office** (open Mon.-Fri. 8am-noon and 1-6pm) and **police station** (open 24hr.) are in the same building at Sucre and Av. 23 de Octubre, directly opposite EMETEL.

This pleasant village is home to two small, free museums. **Museo Arqueológico Largacha Ceballos,** Calle 9 de Julio 436 (tel. 606-065), is a small private collection of artifacts from the Manabí, Valdivía, and Chorrere cultures. It's a bit cluttered, but the *dueña* will be happy to give you a tour (in Spanish). **Casa de Alfaro,** Eloy Alfaro and Rocafuerte, commemorates town hero and dead president Eloy Alfaro with a selection of historical objects and a library (open Mon.-Fri. 8am-noon and 2:30-5pm).

BAHÍA DE MANTA

On weekends, Manta residents drop their nets and head to the tiny fishing villages situated between their town and Bahía de Cáraquez. Collectively known as Bahía de Manta, these towns have beaches with sand that's no whiter or picturesque than the sands of Manta…there's just more of it. While beach space in Manta is limited, Bahía has endless, uninhabited sands under the feet of visitors looking for a more secluded escape. **Coactur** buses from Portoviejo go to San Clemente and San Jacinto, two larger Bahía villages (every 30min., 5am-9:45pm, 1hr., s/2,500). Coactur buses from Manta pass through Portoviejo and head to San Clemente (every hr., 2hr., s/3,000).

San Clemente, the northernmost of the two towns, lies roughly 30km north of Manta and 20km south of Bahía de Cáraquez. Buses stop on the highway, five minutes from the beach. The San Clemente beach has limited space, but as you walk south toward San Jacinto, the sands get wide and expansive. Aggressive tides keep the beach smooth, damp, dark, and firm—an excellent combination for games of pick-up soccer, but a terrible one for casual lounging. The beach is usually empty, so you won't have to worry about anyone stealing your sun. The waters are gentle and the mild current will have trouble storming even the most rudimentary sand castle. For a post-frolic meal, **Restaurant Gemita,** on the highway five minutes from the beach, serves s/5,000 fish plates over the sound of passing cars and buses. Scarf down enormous pieces of fish, rice, beans, and thinly-sliced banana chips, while keeping your eyes peeled for the bus back to Portoviejo. Scarf it down—they don't do doggy bags, and buses won't wait for you to clean your plate (open daily 6am-7pm).

A 15-minute walk along Av. Quito (also known as Malecón), leads to the beach at **San Jacinto,** 3km south of San Clemente. From Portoviejo, the bus will drop you off along the highway. Walk straight along what's referred to as "Calle Principal," which will reach Av. Quito in five minutes. Here, beach-going has become a spectator sport. Dark, damp, and solid sands often host a fascinating display of tuna fishing. Chains of seven or eight residents line the shore, holding ropes and playing tug-of-war with huge tuna nets. When the nets are finally dragged onshore, the people descend on the them, tossing the fish into the truck beds as quickly as possible, while seagulls and pelicans make kamikaze descents for scraps. Like a mediocre action movie, the performance is amusing and even somewhat educational at first, but ultimately the catching of the tuna makes for a disturbing beach experience, especially when San Jacinto's sands become a thoroughfare for vehicles loaded with dead sea life.

The beaches here are longer and wider than those of San Clemente, and the establishments near the sand seem less destitute. There are a number of food stands and restaurants along Av. Quito. The bar-restaurant **Copacabana,** wedged between a couple of other *comedores,* serves speedy seafood dishes to pacific ocean-watchers. There's more than just music and dancing at this Copacabana. There's also the cheapest *langostino* (jumbo shrimp) plate on the coast (s/15,000 for those battered exotica), as well as *ceviche* (s/5,000-7,000) and rice dishes (s/7,000). Start the morning off with a spartan *pan y leche* breakfast (s/2,000) or a shrimp omelette (s/3,500; open daily 7am-9pm). A few minutes north of Copacabana, along Av. Quito, the **Hotel San Jacinto,** does its duty decently. Located close to the sand, it's protected from the tides by a vision-obstructing slab of concrete, but who cares? Windowless rooms don't have views anyway. All rooms have private baths, but you'll need a shoe-horn to fit into them (s/20,000 per person, shoe-horn not included).

■ Portoviejo

Originally situated on the coast, Portoviejo (old port) moved 40km inland to its present land-locked locale due to continual pirate attacks. Now situated 95km southeast of Bahía, Portoviejo preserves its ironic appellation, but the distance from the coast has become cultural as well as geographic. While its maritime neighbors rock to the rhythms of the *marimba,* Portoviejo's population plods along to the drone of its serious-minded tasks—commerce, industry, and education. Although often regarded as the stiff-necked, straight-laced capital of an informal province, Portoviejo commands respect along the coast as a center of business and education.

ORIENTATION

Portoviejo seems oversized at times because everything is so spread out. Buses enter the city along **Avenida Universitaria,** making stops along Universitaria and the perpendicular **Pedro Gual.** The final bus stop, the **terminal terrestre,** is on Pedro Gual, on the western outskirts of town. The east-west Pedro Gual is one of the busiest and most important streets, possessing most of the banks and other necessary services. The other major street, Universitaria, becomes **Morales** south of *el centro.*

PRACTICAL INFORMATION

Tourist Information: CETUR, Pedro Gual 234 and Montalvo (tel. 630-877), 3 blocks east of Morales. Open Mon.-Fri. 8:30am-5pm.

Banks: Filanbanco, Pacheco and Pedro Gual (tel. 630-456), has a 24hr. ATM and exchanges dollars and traveler's checks. Open Mon.-Fri. 8:30am-4pm, Sat. 9:30am-1pm. **Banco del Pichincha,** Av. 9 de Octubre and Olmedo (tel. 630-800), doesn't change traveler's checks, but has the best hours in town. Exchanges cash and has 24hr. ATM. Open Mon.-Fri. 8am-8pm, Sat. 8am-2pm.

Buses: 3 bus companies transport to nearby coastal towns: **Carlos Aray** (tel. 932-269), **Reina del Camino** (tel. 932-377), and **Coactur** (tel. 931-069 or 931-287). They have the same prices, but Carlos Aray buses generally leave more frequently. Buses go to: **Quito** (5am-noon, every 1-2hr.; 8-11:30pm, every hr.; 8hr., s/22,000);

Manta (every 5min., 1hr., s/2,000); **Guayaquil** (every 30min., 2am-midnight, 3½hr., s/13,000); **Santo Domingo** (every 30min., 4:30am-10:45pm, 5hr., s/15,000); **San Vicente** (every hr., 4am-7:45pm, 2½hr., s/5,000); **Pedernales** (every hr., 4am-6pm, 6hr., s/15,000); **Jipijapa** (every 45min., 4am-9:30pm, 3hr., s/2,500); and **Bahía de Caráquez** (every hr., 5am-9pm, 2hr., s/5,000).

Western Union: The **DHL office,** Pedro Gual 621 and Ricuarte (tel. 565-059), is open Mon.-Fri. 8am-5pm.

Airline: TAME, Chile and America (tel. 632-429). Flights to Quito (Mon., Wed., and Fri. 5pm, 45min., US$40). Call ahead for weekend flights. Open Mon.,Wed., and Fri. 8am-6:30pm, Tues. and Thurs. 8am-12:30pm and 2:30-5pm.

Pharmacies: There are a ton, but the 2 most centrally located are **Farmacía Galeno,** Pedro Gual and Olmedo (tel. 639-748; open Mon.-Sat. 8:30am-7pm, Sun. 9am-1pm) and **Farmacía Portoviejo,** Av. 9 de Octubre and Ricuarte (tel. 652-344; open daily 8:30am-7pm).

Hospital: Regional Hospital de Portoviejo, Rocafuerte and Av. 12 de Marzo (emergency tel. 630-555, 630-087, or 636-520). Free 24hr. emergency treatment.

Police: (tel. 920-900; emergency tel. 101), 3km outside of town along Via Crocita.

Post Office: Correos del Ecuador, Ricuarte 217 and Sucre (tel. 634-151). Open Mon.-Fri. 7:30am-7:30pm, Sat. 8am-1pm.

Telephones: EMETEL, Av. 10 de Agosto and Pacheco. To make long-distance calls, buy a token, or *ficha para larga distancia* (s/1,000) from sidewalk vendors outside, and use it at one of the blue phones inside. Open daily 8am-9pm.

Phone Code: 05.

ACCOMMODATIONS

As in many other coastal cities, visitors have to search long and hard to find a place that balances quality and economy. Most of the prize budget establishments are situated in the eastern half of the city along Universitaria/Morales. The more expensive places are located along Pedro Gual, especially toward the western end of the city.

Hotel Paris, Sucre and Olmedo (tel. 652-727). This townhouse has collected some dust over the years, but still sparkles with antique architecture and charming family management. Immense rooms attempt ventilation with fan and walls that don't quite reach the ceiling. All have private baths with patchy tile work and mildew. Stay in shape on the family weight bench. Rooms s/15,000 per person.

Hotel Pacheco, Av. 9 de Octubre and Universitaria (tel. 637-695). This enormous maze of halls and rooms has at least 70 stark sleeping chambers. Mirrors decorate the rooms; tiny skylights battle the darkness. A losing battle for luminosity, victory will likely go to deep slumber. Rooms s/15,000 per person, with bath s/20,000.

Hotel Portoviejo Plaza, Morales 304 and Pedro Gual (tel. 634-442). Apart from an occasional crooked mirror or political sticker, the walls are silent and unadorned. Rooms are well-swept, bathrooms well-kept. Pipes sticking out at random angles pass for shower heads. Singles s/10,000, with bath s/15,000; doubles with bath s/25,000, with window and bath s/30,000.

FOOD

The cuisine of Portoviejo is slightly different from that of its more maritime neighbors. Though Portoviejo's *comedores* still offer many of the typical fish dishes, they concentrate more on beef entrees like *carne asada* or fowl plates like *seco de gallina.* Yogurt has become a wildly popular snack food, and the demand for the sweet bacteria has placed a late-night quasi-fast-food yogurt shop on every corner.

July's, Sucre 8-17 and Av. 18 de Octubre. A local favorite, July's delivers heaping portions, but not hefty prices. Mickey Mouse mirror says that *seco de chivo* (s/5,000) is the house specialty, but a breaded cod dish (s/7,000) begs to differ. Vegetarian dish (s/5,000) available upon request. Noisy fan is actually pleasant as it reminds you that something is being done about the heat. Open daily 10am-10:30pm.

Restaurant Palatino, Av. 10 de Agosto and Chile, 2 blocks east of EMETEL. Serving the business community, Palatino attempts to imitate them with efficient service and neatness. Fans powerful enough to keep the tie-choked clientele from fidgeting. They do not serve *desayuno*. Shrimp (s/15,000), heaping rice dishes (S/7,000) could feed the whole office. Open Mon.-Sat. 8:30am-10:30pm.

Fuente de Soda "Pollo Rico," Rocafuerte and Pedro Gual. Greasy treats done dirt cheap until the wee hours. Loiterers tempted inside with banana yogurt shakes (s/1,500). One whiff of the mayonnaise-heaped fries and chicken (s/4,000) and you'll be salivating up a storm. Open daily 10am-1am.

SIGHTS AND ENTERTAINMENT

For a capital city, Portoviejo has a sad scarcity of stuff to see and do. The **Casa de Cultura** (tel./fax 631-753), on the left side of Calle Sucre just past García Moreno, is a culture-enhancing excursion, offering occasional theater, dance, music performances, art expositions, and conferences. Events occur three or four times per month, with special festivities on August 9th and the week of October 9-18 (open Mon.-Fri. 8am-noon and 3-6pm). *Fútbol* fanatics might want to catch a live **soccer** match while in town. The local professional team, **Liga de Portoviejo Universitaria,** is competitive within Ecuador's premier league, drawing large, vivacious crowds (admission s/8,000). Games are scheduled throughout the week, so check the paper. The **Estadio Reales Tamarindos** is located on the right-hand side of Universitaria as you head north, about 0.5km outside of town. Also, two *coliseos* host live sports events. **Coliseos California and Eloy Alfaro** are on Av. la Juela. Look in newspapers or stop by to find out game schedules and buy tickets.

■ Jipijapa

Most of the fun associated with Jipijapa ("heepy-hoppa"), 60km south of Manta, comes from its bouncy, fun-to-say name. Otherwise, this 60,000 person city only offers a few useful amenities and a plethora of Panama hats. Shopping here is as bountiful as in Montecristi, but far less concentrated, with hat shops scattered throughout town. Situated between Manta and the southern coast's primary beaches, Jipijapa's chief function (outside of hat-making) has been shuttling eager sun-seekers and anxious surfers to the sandy shores of communities like Puerto López, Salango, and Montañita. Most travelers stay only long enough to get their shoes polished in the shade of Parque Simon Bolívar. Shiny-shoed, beach-bound travelers, be warned: there are very few, if any, places to change money or cash traveler's checks between Jipijapa and La Libertad. Stock up on sucres in Jipijapa while you can.

Orientation and Practical Information Much of what you'll need while you're in Jipijapa is located near its central plaza. The plaza consists of **Parque Simon Bolívar** and a concrete area adorned with an anonymous female statue. East-west streets **Sucre** and **Bolívar,** and the north-south **Colón** and **9 de Octubre** border the central plaza. **Coop de Transportes Turismo de Manta y Jipijapa (CTMS)** buses, arriving from the north, drop off along Av. 10 de Agosto near Santistevan, one block north and one block east of the plaza. **Cooperativa de Manglaralto (CITM)** buses, arriving from the south, let their passengers out along Sucre near Av. 9 de Octubre, a half-block east of the central plaza.

Banco del Pinchincha, Sucre 503 and Av. 9 de Octubre (tel. 600-472; fax 600-800), changes money, but doesn't accept traveler's checks (open Mon.-Fri. 8:30am-8pm, Sat. 8:30am-2pm). **Filanbanco** (tel. 600-345 or 601-620; fax 600-455), at Bolívar and Av. 9 de Octubre, takes traveler's checks but not cash, and has a 24-hour ATM (open Mon.-Sat. 8am-4pm). The **EMETEL** office, at Bolívar and Av. 9 de Octubre, across from Filanbanco, has two phonds, neither of which can make international calls (open daily 8am-10pm). The primary bus companies in town are located near the central plaza. **Cooperativa de Transportes Turismo de Manta and Jipijapa,** at Av. 10 de Agosto and Colón, sends buses to **Puerto López** (every hr., 4:30am-5:30pm, 1¼hr., s/4,000) and **Manta** (every 15min., 5am-9pm, 1¼hr., s/3,500). **Cooperativa Manglaralto,** Sucre 604 and Av. 9 de Octubre (tel. 601-000), runs to **Manta** (every

2hr., 5:15am-5:15pm, 1hr., s/3,500) and **La Libertad** (7 per day, 7:45am-7:45pm, 4hr., s/11,000) via **Puerto López**. The principal pharmacy is **Farmacía Corazón de Jesus,** Bolívar 301 and Santistevan (tel. 601-648; open daily 7am-9:30pm). If you're still aching, **Hospital Cantonal Jipijapa,** at Espejo and Av. 12 de Octubre (tel. 600-377), is open 24 hours for emergency treatment, but only Monday through Friday. The **emergency** telephone number is 101. The **police station** (tel. 600-444), is several blocks east of the plaza on Bolívar at Antepara. Jipijapa's **phone code** is 05.

Accommodations and Food   Should you inexplicably find yourself staying in Jipijapa, you have a few options for accommodation and food. The dungeonesque **Hostel Mejía,** Mejía 324 and Colón (tel. 600-387), endowed with poorly-lit hallways and low concrete ceilings, plunges you back in time to the Middle Ages. A bare, solitary bulb in each room reveals adequate concrete cells equipped with metal beds, naked walls, and well-swept floors. Bathrooms are clean enough, but crowded toilet, shower, and sink squeeze out into the bedroom (s/10,000 per person, with bath s/15,000). **Hostal Jipijapa** (tel. 601-365 or 600-522; fax 600-783), at Santistevan and Eloy Alfaro, provides a considerably more modern experience about 10 minutes away from the plaza. The smallest rooms with fans start at s/20,000 per person. Immaculate rooms with TV, A/C, and private bath cost more (singles s/38,000; doubles s/66,000). Happy dancers hop to the hip disco here on Friday and Saturday nights. A couple of unremarkable restaurants adorn Av. 9 de Octubre near the plaza. **Comedor La Rochelle,** Av. 9 de Octubre and Sucre, serves adequate *ceviches* for s/5,000. Benches may leave you walking funny, but not before you've been able to devour an *almuerzo* for s/6,000 (open daily 7am-11pm).

NEAR JIPIJAPA: PUERTO DE CAYO

Puerto de Cayo, 28km southwest of Jipijapa, is much like the other myriad beach towns up and down the coast, except everything here seems just a little richer. The houses along the beach aren't cinderblock fishing shacks, but real vacation homes. The beach is long, the sand is white, and the density of trash seems significantly lower than in resort towns like Playas or Manta. It's not an exciting place, but with Puerto López only 30 minutes to the south by bus (every 20min., s/2,000), this sleepy town is a possible base for Parque Machalilla excursions. The **Hostal los Frailes** (tel. 601-365; same management as Hostal Jipijapa, above), on the Malecón, can arrange tours to the various parts of the park for around s/120,000, and provides very clean and comfortable rooms with A/C, private bath, and TV for s/48,000 per person. Back in budget land, **Hostal Zavala's** (tel. 620-624 for the EMETEL cabin next door), also on a prime Malecón spot, has airy rooms with firm beds, private baths, and fans. Some have hot water and tantalizing ocean views (s/16,500 per person, with TV s/7,000). Both hostels have reasonable restaurants right on the beach.

▓ Puerto López

Blessed with tranquil waters and picturesque, looming bluffs, Puerto López is a fisherman's paradise. Resting their weary wooden hulls after a grueling day of pounding the waves, high-seas fishing rigs saturate the harbor, neatly anchored as if posing for cameras. The fish may have brought the boats, but it's the nearby Machalilla National Park and its famed Isla de la Plata that reel in travelers from around the world. Puerto López is the most convenient place to launch a trip into that worthy park; consequently, its restaurants and bars are convenient places for meeting other travelers.

Orientation and Practical Information   Machalilla, the principal road in town, runs north to Jipijapa and south to La Libertad. Buses stop here on the corner of Calle Cordoba. **Malecón,** the street closest to the sand, runs parallel to Machalilla two or three blocks to the west. The **Machalilla National Park Headquarters,** at Eloy Alfaro and Machalilla, back 50m from EMETEL and on the left, has info, t-shirts (s/

25,000), and a park museum (open daily 7am-noon and 2-5pm). There are no **banks** in Puerto López, so load up on sucres before you arrive. The **Hotel Pacífico** occasionally gives sucres in return for traveler's checks, but only in rare, desperate situations. **EMETEL,** at Machalilla and Atahualpa, only makes national calls (open Mon.-Sat. 8am-noon, 2-5pm, and 7-9pm). The **bus stop** is located at the southern end of town, at Machalilla and Cordoba. North-bound buses go to **Manta** (every 30min., 4:45am-6pm, 2hr., s/8,000) via **Jipijapa** (1¼hr., s/4,000). Buses going south run through town (every 20min., 4:45am-6pm), then continue to: **Salango** (10min., s/1,000); **Alandaluz** (15min., s/1,500); **Montañita** (45min., s/3,500); and **Manglaralto** (50min., s/4,000). Puerto López's favorite pharmacy, **Farmacía Edicita,** Av. Machalilla and Atahualpa (tel. 604-600), is across the street from the post office in the center of town (open daily 7:30am-8:30pm). And its most helpful hospital, **Centro de Salud de Puerto López,** is at the end of Machalilla, seven or eight blocks north of *el centro.* There is a sign, but it only faces north (open Mon.-Fri. 24hr.). The **police** (tel. 604-101), are at Machalilla and Atahualpa, next to EMETEL (open 24hr.). Around the corner stands the old reliable **post office,** at Atahualpa and Machalilla (open Mon.-Fri. 9am-noon and 3-5:30pm, Sat. 9am-noon). Puerto López's **phone code** is 05.

Accommodations and Food There aren't too many places to stay in Puerto López; the constant influx of tourists means it is a good idea to call ahead to reserve a spot. **Villa Colombia** is on the first right off Calle Cordoba after Machalilla when heading away from the beach; it's on the left. Weary visitors are welcomed with hot coffee and clean, friendly surroundings. Modest, multi-media rooms are constructed in a hodgepodge of concrete, wood planks, and bamboo (s/15,000 per person, with bath s/20,000; nicer "matrimonial" room s/25,000). **Hostel Tuzco,** Cordoba and García Moreno (tel. 604-132), is two and a half blocks east of Machalilla. Bright wall paintings of whales and funeral urns set the right mood for park forays, and the spacious rooms and baths make sure you've had adequate rest. The bright color scheme gives some aesthetic relief from the abundant use of concrete. Quarters fit up to six, all with private bath, but the single fan might have trouble keeping everybody cool (s/15,000 per person). The one beachfront lodging, **Hotel Pacífico,** Suarez and Malecón (tel. 604-147), is only 50m from the sand at the northern end of Malecón. Lush courtyard is laden with hammocks that swing from sun-fighting palms. *Cabañas* have dusty floorboards and ample beds with woolen blankets. Impeccable common baths flow with invigoratingly frigid water (s/25,000 per person). Fancy hotel rooms at Pacífico provide pristine tile in place of wooden floorboard, and transform your communal ice bath into a warm private shower for only double the price (s/50,000 per person).

Puerto López has plenty of seafood to go around. Various restaurants scattered throughout town cook up the traditional coastal dishes: *ceviche,* fried seafood, and battered seafood, invariably accompanied by a portion of rice. Due to the strange dearth of sidewalk vendors, most dining occurs in formal restaurants. If you want seconds, be economical about it and visit the **indoor food market,** diagonally across from the bus stop at Machalilla and Cordoba. **Spondyllus Bar and Restaurant,** Malecón and Cordoba (tel. 604-128 or 604-108), dishes outstanding eats in an international Latin milieu. Burlap ceiling, brimming with coffee beans, looks like it was just shipped in from Colombia. Owner plays anything from bootlegged Bob Marley to sauntering *salsa.* Munch on *ceviche de spondyllus* (s/13,000), *langostinos al ajillo* (s/25,000), or a nice vegetarian tortilla (s/10,000), all washed down with *jugo de mora* or a crisp Pilsener (s/3,000; open daily 10am-10pm, though sometimes until 4am). **Restaurant "Flipper"** (tel. 604-221), on Cordoba toward Malecón, doesn't have the fastest service in Ecuador, but offers possibly the tastiest *arroz con marinero* (s/15,000), as well as all manner of the ocean's gifts, plus spaghetti (s/7,000; open daily 11am-3pm and 6-10pm). **Viña del Mar,** Malecón 123 and Julio Izurieta (tel. 604-206), is the source of those smells wafting next door to Machalilla Tour. Grab something to eat so you'll be nice and full for the long whale-watching trip. Cozy outside seating provides ocean views and liberation from indoor wooden benches; full breakfast (eggs, bread, juice, coffee) s/6,000, and shrimp *ceviche* s/10,000 (open daily 6:30am-4:30pm).

Sights and Entertainment Puerto López is an ideal port from which to explore the marvels of **Parque Nacional Machalilla** (see p. 204). Multiple tour companies battle for tourists' bucks with bigger and better bargains, especially with **whale watching** tour packages to **Isla de la Plata,** situated 40km off of Puerto López. The boat ride out takes two solid hours and the high sea swells are tremendous, so anyone even slightly susceptible to seasickness should take precautionary measures. Before you fully realize that the waves are bigger than the boat, numerous humpback whale sightings attest that *everything* in the sea dwarfs your tiny craft. **Machalilla Tour Agency,** Malecón 119 and Julio Izurieza (tel. 604-206), offers whale-watching and Isla de la Plata tours (open daily 7am-6:30pm). **Mantaraya,** on Malecón (tel. 604-233), north of Machalilla Tour Agency, has similar packages, and rents scuba equipment as well (open daily 7am-6:30pm). Either the Isla de la Plata tour or a five-hour whale-watching trip costs about s/110,000, which includes a light lunch and guide (in Spanish) but not the s/40,000 park entrance fee. If you'd rather keep your feet on solid ground, Puerto López's own **beach** meets the challenge with brown, rather dirty sand. Not the best place for sandcastles, but the waters are tranquil and the pickup soccer games are intense.

■ Near Puerto López

SALANGO

Situated 5km south of Puerto López, Salango sits patiently, like an old man with a story to tell. Salango's tale comes whispering up from beneath its sands, which are home to a massive collection of **archaeological artifacts.** Dating back almost 5000 years, six different pre-Colombian communities thrived here, leaving behind scatterings of everyday life as well as jewelry and artwork. Many of the pieces have been excavated and now fill Salango's archeological museum, but a large number remain trapped in the silence of the sand, buried beneath Salango's fish factory. Or, at least, the factory *used* be Salango's. After a strike over low wages in 1989, the plant's foreign management fired its Salangan workforce and employed people from more impoverished neighboring towns. Salango has been hit hard by the lay-offs, and most locals have returned to unpredictable, and often unprofitable, fishing careers.

Only 10 minutes and a s/1,000 bus ride separate Salango from Puerto López. This quick trip can take you back 5000 years at the **Museo del Mar del Sur,** a well-preserved and informative collection which chronicles the six cultures found at the site. Valdavian culture is the oldest, subsisting from 3000-2000 BC, followed by the Machalilla (2000-1500 BC), Chorrera and Foriguroy (1500-500 BC), Guangala/Bahían (500 BC-AD 500), and Manteño (AD 500). For more information, see **The Earliest Ecuadorians,** p. 38. Each culture has separate glass encasements labeled with Spanish descriptions, which present various artifacts from religious, artistic, and daily life found at the site. Knowledgeable museum guides will show you around, answering any questions. The museum also has artists who create reasonably priced replicas of the artifacts (open daily 9am-5pm; admission s/5,000, children s/2,000).

Salango lacks accommodations, but it does support a couple of restaurants. The oft-praised **Delfín Mágico,** roughly 200m south of the museum, looks rather nondescript, with the usual bamboo motif and white plastic furniture, but just wait for the remarkable food. Deliciously affordable jumbo shrimp dishes (s/25,000), fresh shrimp and fish *ceviches* (s/8,000-12,000; open Mon.-Fri. 9am-8:30pm, Sat.-Sun. 8:30am-11pm).

The striking **Isla Salango** lies 2km off-shore; daytrips sometimes come here from Puerto López. Waves get uppity in this sheltered cove during *temporada* (Dec.-April). The beach's other sour note is the murmuring **fish factory,** at the south end of the shore. Incongruous with Salango's natural beauty, this drab, gray processing plant puffs miasmic wisps of smoke into the sea breezes. It is a five-minute walk south along the beach, and worth taking a look at, even if only to cheer on the frigate birds and pelicans as they snatch bits and pieces of the factory's profits. Salango's beach has calm water, picturesque fishing boats, and an attractive set of cliffs on both sides, but near the town the sands are covered with trash, vultures, and mangy dogs.

PARQUE NACIONAL MACHALILLA

Parque Nacional Machalilla's 55,000 hectares preserve archeological riches, one of the most untouched cloud forests in Ecuador, and the only substantial stretch of virgin dry tropical forest left in the country. Dry tropical forests may not be the most beautiful ecosystem around, but the park's beaches are some of the most stunning and cleanest in the country. To make things even better, Isla de la Plata summarizes the Galápagos experience—elegant sea birds, jovial sea lions, sea sickness—for only a fraction of the cost; hence the nickname "a poor person's Galápagos."

From the main gate, a dirt road winds 5km to the diminutive hamlet of **Aguablanca.** A languid, dusty one-hour trail through the lowland dry forest allows for careful study of the varied flora. Figs, laurels, and Kapok trees are scattered loosely, while the lush beanstalks of the pea-like, perennially-verdant *algarrobos* pierce the dry wasteland. Those dry-climate staples, cacti, abound in the arid terrain. The tall spindly cactus, the prickly pear, and the *pitahaya* (which sprouts a delectable red fruit Feb.-March), are well-represented among the spines. Aguablanca provides an interlude to the wilderness education, with both an archaeological museum and the ruins of the **Manteño,** an indigenous group who resided here from the 6th century AD until the Spanish conquest. The museum brims with Manteño artifacts, including art, jewelry, pottery, religious pieces, and miniature replicas of their **balsa rafts.** For a faint idea of what a labored task it must have been to build the real things, try one of the do-it-yourself raft replica kits for sale. The park does not allow visitors to hike to the sites on their own, due to the complexity of paths and dangerous surroundings, but instead offers affordable guided tours. The giant **pottery urns** on the way to the ruins were used as tombs for Manteño dead. Claustrophobes and the faint of heart beware—many of the skeletons have been left in the urns, crouched in the fetal position, strewn with ceramic offerings from loved ones. A half-hour walk uphill, the anticlimactic **ruins** themselves are only the basic foundations of the Manteño's homes and places of worship. Rumor has it that a dip in the **sulfur pond** on the way back to town does wonders for illness, soreness, and clogged nasal passages, but common sense maintains that these murky waters may cause your skin to take on a raw-sewage stench and emit a strange green glow. The entire two-and-a-half-hour guided package tour runs s/5,000 per person (museum admission s/3,000).

To explore the cloud forests of **San Sebastian,** visitors must hire a guide for the five- to six-hour round-trip trek (s/50,000-80,000). During the course of the hike there, the vegetation makes a striking transition from dry to cloud forest. San Sebastian sports many exotic animal species, including tarantulas, giant centipedes, scorpions, coral snakes, armadillos, howler monkeys, *guantas* (agoutis), anteaters, and numerous bird species. This trip generally requires two days. Tours on horse-back allow you to get further into the forest; the tour agencies in Puerto López can make arrangements, although you might find a willing guide in Agua Blanca.

For still more environmental contrast, the secluded shores of **Los Frailes,** 2km north of the Aguablanca gate, include three beaches: La Playita, La Tortuguita, and the star of the sand-show, Los Frailes. **Buses** from Puerto López make the 9km trip to the Los Frailes gate (s/1,000). About 100m past the gate, the road bends left at a *cabañita*, while a smaller dirt path leads to the right. You can buy your ticket for the park entrance at the *cabañita*. The two trails are the different ends of the same 3760m trail. The trail on the left leads through dry forest to Los Frailes (30min.). On the right, the tiny rock cove of **La Playita,** a 25-minute walk from the *cabañita*, is layered with black sands and lapped by calm waters perfect for waders and young children. Walk five minutes farther and reach a cove festooned with curious rock configurations, **La Tortuguita.** Though its ankle-deep, soft, whitish sand won't harm a soul, the chaotic swirling waterway, caused by two swells breaking toward each other, can be a danger. Despite its tremulous waters, La Tortuguita is a popular snorkeling spot, especially just off the rocks that separate its two sand plots. Swimming is not advised at the second beach, as there is a low line of rocks where the waters break. Two paths lead from here to Los Frailes: the easy lower road, and the overgrown high road. The high road leads to a wooden platform with a spectacular view of the beaches and ocean. The immense, almost perfectly symmetrical, rocky cove of **Los Frailes** rewards you at the end of your hike. Uninhabited except for a lining of greenery, the beach stretches in a golden arc of pure, solitary sand facing tranquil waters, perfect for sun-worship and cool dips.

In the Olympics of booby watching, the Galápagos Islands take the gold, but Isla de la Plata is happy with silver. The "Plata" in the name refers to the legendary lost pirate treasure of Sir Francis Drake, absconded from the Spanish galleons and hidden on the island. The boobies in question include the outlaw masked booby, the nurturing blue-footed booby, and the small but abundant red-footed booby. This 3500-hectare island, known as the "poor person's Galápagos," lies just 40km off the shore of Puerto López (2hr. by boat). In addition to the boobies, La Plata is home to the largest colony of frigate birds in the world. From April to November, the rare **waved albatrosses** wing in for fly-by-night mating season affairs. The boobies and the other birds aren't the only wildlives of this island party. A small off-shore colony of generally elusive **sea lions** is occasionally spotted sun bathing, and from July to September, the waters teem with **humpback whales**. Like the albatross, the whales prefer big love on the run, migrating here from the Antarctic to mate in the warmer waters. These amorous aquatics are best seen during the rollicking boat rides from Puerto López to the island. The only park office is at **Bahía Drake,** the island's only inlet and the docking point for mainland boats. Snorkeling and diving are possible here, but equipment rentals must be arranged in Puerto López and waters tend to be murky. From Bahía Drake, a 3km and a 5km trail head up hill, over dale, and through nesting sites. Bring your own food, water, hiking shoes and lots of sunscreen. Camping is strictly prohibited. In truth, Isla de la Plata does not offer the biological distinctiveness or the terrestrial treats of the real Galápagos—it is more of an extension of the mainland than a world in itself. But the mainland that it extends—the dry tropical forests of Parque Machalilla—is quite distinctive in its own right.

For more info on Machalilla National Park, visit the **headquarters** in Puerto López, at Eloy Alfaro and Machalilla, 50m from the EMETEL office. In addition to pamphlets, maps, and English brochures, the office has a museum featuring stuffed versions of park wildlife and a map of the park, great for orienting yourself before an expedition (open daily 8am-6pm). The **main entrance** to the National Park sits 7km north of Puerto López, off the coastal highway to Jipijapa. **Buses** leave Puerto López every half-hour; tell the driver to let you off at the main entrance at Aguablanca (s/1,000). Park **admission,** good for five days, is s/40,000 (s/4,000 for travelers with visas). Admission tickets are available at the Aguablanca main gate at the southern end of the park, the western gate at the shores of Los Frailes, the park's headquarters in Puerto López, and in the various tourist agencies of Puerto López. Services within the park are extremely limited. There is a primitive campground in San Sebastian with no facilities (s/5,000 per person). Before heading into the park, be sure to purchase bottled water and food, as they are almost impossible to find inside the park.

ALANDALUZ ECOLOGICAL TOURIST CENTER

Travel in Ecuador can be stressful for environmentalists. You ride in buses without emissions controls, you drink water out of plastic bottles that will never be recycled, and your tourist dollars encourage people to move into fragile ecosystems. The **Pueblo Ecológico Alandaluz,** however, puts such anxieties to rest. Arranged like a garden-filled village next door to neighboring Puerto Rico, Alandaluz is a gorgeous beach resort just off the road between Puerto López and Montañita. Constructed wholly of rapidly-growing, easily replenishable materials, Alandaluz is a temple of bio-friendliness, making daily offerings to an afflicted environmental goddess. Comically, visitors can make their contribution by frequenting the bathroom, where waste is mixed with sawdust and dried leaves to speed up the decomposition process.

Alandaluz's beach has impeccable and uninhabited sands fingered with palm-thatched umbrellas. The surf is monstrous, so a swim amounts to a salty pummeling. But if you have a surfboard, and you know how to use it, the water is ideal. Generally slow-breaking, crumbling waves, with six- to seven-foot faces in the summer and 10- to 12-foot faces in the winter, break in both directions. Alandaluz doesn't always have the echoing barrels of Montañita, but it also doesn't have the crowds.

The resort itself is set up like a tiny village. In addition to the two main buildings with regular rooms, there are several cabins right by the sand, complete with bamboo patio-decks and ocean views. All of the pristine bamboo quarters are festooned with cheerful, multi-colored curtains and mosquito nets, and equipped with bamboo bed frames and mounted bamboo water bottle holders for your complimentary bottles of Guitig water. The one exception is the *Cabaña del Arbol,* the honeymoon suite. Built into a live tree, you can feel the tree sway as you climb the tree-branch ladder into your lofty love nest. So luxurious, it even includes a private bath.

The complex boasts plentiful amenities. Relax at a cozy bamboo **bar,** furnished with cushioned straw couches and an outdoor furnace (open daily 8:30am-midnight). Alongside the bar, a first class **restaurant** specializes in vegetable and seafood dishes. The chef uses an oven constructed of hardened fecal matter to create his pride and joy, the *vivado de pasado* (an enormous serving of baked shellfish served inside a bamboo cane, s/17,000), *desayuno* s/7,000, *almuerzo,* and *cena* both s/15,000 (open daily 8:30am-9pm). Eco-conscious extravagance has its price, though. You can either camp (s/13,000), or use their tent or hammock (s/15,000). Impeccably-maintained common bathrooms scattered around the grounds have both hot and cold water. From there, the prices climb. (Cabins: singles s/45,000, with bath s/70,000; doubles s/65,000, with bath s/78,000; triples s/78,000, with bath s/100,000; quads s/91,000, with bath s/140,000. Luxurious rooms in the main building: singles s/105,000; doubles s/150,000; triples s/180,000; quads s/210,000.)

Alandaluz is 6km south of Salango, a 15-minute, s/1,500 **bus** ride from Puerto López. It is practically impossible to miss on the west side of the road. Even if you don't have time to spend the night, a 10-minute walk through the well-kept gardens along stone paths provides an excellent feel for this unique place, and its beaches are certainly worth a visit. For reservations, recommended in the July and August high season, call 505-084 or Quito tel. 604-103.

Alandaluz is within convenient striking distance of Parque Nacional Machalilla, and an on-site travel agency lets visitors take advantage of this. **Pacarina Travel** (tel. 601-203), in the main house, offers tours by land or sea into the park. Prices are determined by the size of your group, but it is reportedly easy to find other visitors at the resort interested in the same trip—yet another reason to hang out at the bar. Prices tend to be higher than in Puerto López, but with a large group you might come out ahead. If the numbers don't work out for a tour, you could still sleep in the eco-tranquility of Alandaluz and try your luck in nearby Puerto López. Pacarina can also arrange tours to **Cantulapiedra,** Alandaluz's organic farm, 90 minutes away in the forest, but not within the park.

■ Montañita

Situated 45 minutes south of Alandaluz, and a solid 65km north of La Libertad, Montañita is undoubtedly the most popular surfing spot in Ecuador. Hopping with surfers from all over Latin America, the streets of Montañita are a barefoot parade, flowing with bronzed, unclad torsos, long hair, and surfboards. The beach is mobbed during the temporada (Dec.-April), when it may be difficult to find some sand of your own. The town calms down considerably in the low season when the waves themselves are quiet, but a band of die-hard surfers stay there year-round, maintaining the mellow, almost hippy atmosphere that makes Montañita an excellent place to chill. The surfing life consists of early morning (pre-breakfast) surf sessions, mid-afternoon ses-

sions, and a possible dusk session, ending just as the sun dips below the Pacific horizon. It's a grueling regimen, often followed by nights of beach parties, bonfires,
cocktails, and general debauchery by the sea. Legends of revelry in Montañita that are
too intriguing to ignore permeate much of Latin America, and hundreds of non-surf-
ers also wind their way to Ecuador's all-around party town.

Orientation and Practical Information There are two separate and quite
distinct sectors separated by a kilometer of parallel beach and highway. The **pueblo**
to the south houses all of Montañita's practical resources, as well as its small population of Ecuadorian inhabitants. Here, **Calle Rocafuerte** runs from the highway to the
sand, while **Avenida 15 de Mayo,** perpendicular to Rocafuerte, is the last street
before the sand. **La punta,** the other sector to the north, is named for the rocky bluffs
that loom over its famous barreling brake, and has most of the hotels and some nice
restaurants. Surfers and sunbathers spend their lazy days here, visiting the *pueblo*
only for practical purposes. Although most of the area's practical resources (including the post office, hospital, and police station) are in the nearby town of Manglaralto,
Montañita does have a **pharmacy,** at Av. 15 de Mayo 836 and Rocafuerte. The **Casa
Communal,** on Calle Cheribogo, has local phone service (open Mon.-Sat. 8am-noon,
2-5pm, and 7-9pm, Sun. 8am-noon and 7-9pm).

Accommodations Loaded with cheap places to stay, Montañita is an easy town
to settle into. An alternative to hotels, beach houses often offer rooms for rent. The
pueblo has a few budget rooms, but most establishments are concentrated near *la
punta.* **Rincón del Amigo,** at the end of La Punta Road, is the epicenter of the surfer
and backpacker scene. Exotic quarters in this palm-thatched hotel come with all the
tropical necessities: bamboo ceilings, mosquito nets, and rickety homemade beds,
adorned with sea shells and coral (s/7,000 per person, with bath s/15,000). The
groovy restaurant-bar downstairs has billiards and foosball (open daily 9:30am-10pm).
Rincón also offers bike rental for daytrips to the Machalilla National Park (s/10,000
per hr.). **La Casa del Sol** (tel. 901-103; email casasol@pro.ec), the three-story building
just off La Punta Road, offers more services than the *pueblo.* It boasts fans, mosquito
nets, laundry service, phone service, firm beds, hammocks, surfboard rental (s/
15,000 per day), restaurant (spaghetti *vegetariano* s/9000), blues bar, and security
box; and you can pay for it all with dollars, sucres, traveler's checks, or credit cards.
You don't have to pay much, either (singles s/15,000, with bath s/30,000; s/25,000
per additional person). The **Cabañas de Tres Palmas** (tel. 755-717), between La
Punta Road and the beach, have the best deals for groups of 2-3 people. Rooms have
a clean, well-designed look, all with fans, mosquito nets, and private baths with hot
water. The conscientious management speaks English, Spanish, Portuguese, and
French (s/40,000 per *cabaña,* up to s/80,000 in high season). Away from the surf
crowd in the *pueblo,* **Hostal de Lucho,** Rocafuerte 830 and Av. 15 de Mayo, could
not get more basic without becoming a campsite, but where are you going to camp
for s/5,000 per person (s/10,000 Dec.-May)? Rooms have musty floorboards and
square foam blocks for pillows, with a scruffy-looking communal toilet and mildewy
shower, but prices are unbeatable. Lucho's kitchen is open to all, a 24-hour diner
equipped with stove and refrigerator.

Food Montañita makes sure to replenish all those calories lost in the waves. Occasionally, you'll stumble upon beach bonfires cooking up fresh oysters and fish, but
not as often as you might like. The *pueblo* has a number of restaurants plus a brilliant
collection of juice bars. In *la punta,* the restaurants at **El Pelicano, El Rincón del
Amigo,** and **La Casa del Sol** all serve up hearty breakfasts (s/6,000-9,000) and filling
meals. The most recommended place in town is the Tex-Mex restaurant at **Tres Palmas** (tel. 755-717). David, the owner, is from San Antonio, so he knows how an
enchilada is supposed to taste (s/6000; veggie burrito s/10,000). The kitchen is spotless and all the vegetables are disinfected to gringo standards. The Mahi-Mahi is
expensive, but highly recommended (s/40,000; open daily noon-10pm, closed 3-6pm

in low season). **Restaurant El Chivo,** Calle Chiribogo and Rocafuerte, offers cheap eats, town gossip, and a dose of surf videos on the immense color TV. Marvel at haphazard surfboards and the wall mural depicting a dreamy, flowered vision of Montañita. Mouth-watering rice and seafood dishes go for around s/8,000, and vegetarian entrees for around s/10,000. Chivo also sells and fixes surfboards (open daily 7am-midnight).

Sights and Entertainment Visitors flock to Montañita for one reason: the **surf.** The beach stretches endlessly south, but looming, jagged cliffs with peculiar rock formations contain it to the north. These cliffs are responsible for the consistent four- to five-foot swells with echoing barrels that always break right, away from the point. During the off-season, the waves struggle a bit, offering two- to three-foot apologies whose barrels whisper like the inside of a seashell. At low tide you can walk around the point for fantastic surf-spray views. Aside from the surfing, Montañita is a well-known party spot, where **beachside bars** open at around 6pm and don't close until the crowds stumble home. Though the area is overrun with surfers, you don't necessarily have to be a card-carrying member of the surf-party to enjoy yourself here. Montañita's nighttime party scene is dark and spirited, with bonfires, sandy dance floors, and tropical drinks to provide strength, social courage, and merriment for all.

■ Near Montañita

MANGLARALTO

Five minutes by bus south of Montañita and 60km north of La Libertad, an adequate surf taps the beach of Manglaralto. Manglaralto has a few more practical resources than the surf haven to the north, but it lacks the accommodations and drunken revelry. Quieter and gentler than Montañita, Manglaralto grows shady, sweet-smelling, orange-blossoming trees that add to the tranquility.

The main entrance to Manglaralto is along **El Oro,** marked by a liquor store on the south side and a small shop with a billiards table on the north. El Oro runs east-west, and the entrance is four blocks from the sand. **EMETEL,** Los Ríos and Av. 24 de Mayo, can theoretically make international calls, although they might not let you (open Mon.-Sat. 8am-9pm, Sun. 8am-4pm). A 24-hour **pharmacy** (tel. 901-172), sits at Malecón and Azuay. **Hospital al Manglaralto,** Av. 24 de Mayo and Av. 10 de Agosto (emergency tel. 901-192), provides free 24-hour treatment at the south end of town.

Alegre Calimar, along Constitución at the northern end of town, is an acceptable hotel/restaurant, decorated with a poster of the Last Supper and a creative arrangement of painted tuna, octopi, squids, and lobsters. Unfortunately, the food selection is less exotic: fried fish s/8,000, shrimp s/9,000, or calamari with rice (open daily 7am-8pm). Basic rooms have scruffy green-marble floors, but well-polished oak beds and desks. Common bath is clean enough (singles s/15,000; doubles s/25,000).

VALDIVIA AND AYANGUE

Just south of Montañita and Manglaralto, these two pint-sized fishing villages eagerly pursue the ones that don't get away. **Valdivia** is farther north, 50km from La Libertad, just over an hour from Puerto López. The Valdivians were the area's oldest culture, living here from 3000-2000BC. The **Museo Valdivia** displays a few originals and replicas of the culture's artifacts. The museum is off the main road—turn at the Pinguino. Closed in 1997 for remodeling, it should be open in 1998 with a cafe, gift shop, and possibly rooms for rent (open daily 9am-6pm; admission s/2000). From the town's main entrance a few minutes further along the highway, the road heads straight towards a sizeable statue of an anonymous woman and child, then continues to the sand. While the calm waters make for easier swimming than at other nearby beaches, the main occupants of Valdivia's beach are vultures picking through the garbage.

Although **Ayangue** is only 5km south of Valdivia, only mountain goats ever manage the walk. With a monstrous rocky point separating the two towns, motor-endowed vehicles provide the only reasonable inter-village transport, dropping passengers off along the highway near a cluttering of "Welcome to Ayangue" signs. The paved road heading west leads into town, a five-minute drive or a half-hour walk. This road leads directly to Ayangue's beach, a small, protected cove full of sand, dogs, and fishing families. The currents can get strong, but when the water is calm it's a beautiful spot for a swim. The dusty road to the beach houses vendors hawking gigantic pieces of coral and sizeable sea shells, and a caged howler monkey named Rocky will shake your hand, then steal anything in it. Rocky is the resident monkey of **Pension 5 Hermanos** (tel. 916-029), which has unmatching sheet covers and your usual mushy mattresses and no fans, but a breezy open-air feel and some nice sea views (s/15,000 per person). On the beach parallel to the street, **Hostal Un Millón de Amigos** (tel 916-014), provides clean rooms with fans and some private baths (s/30,000 per person). You're unlikely to find anywhere near a million friends in this sleepy town, but fortunately the rooms have some posters of naked people. A few simple *comedores* lie right on the beach. **Comedor Jenny Maria** is a prime spot to munch *corvinu frita* (s/ 6,000) and watch the dogs play in the surf (open daily 11am-9pm).

■ Salinas

In the hedonistic city of Salinas, BMWs cruise the streets, yachts rip across the harbor, and night greets the morning with the pounding sounds of the *discoteca*. Charged with affluence, the town is home to (that is, second or third home to) many of South America's wealthiest folks. At the westernmost tip of the Santa Elena Peninsula, 150km west of Guayaquil, the white high-rise skyline towers over the rubble of La Libertad. With well-to-dos from Chile, Colombia, Perú, and of course, Ecuador attracted to its streets and sands, Salinas cannot help but adopt a cosmopolitan air. Yet somehow it has ended up less sophisticated than it could have been. Rather than theater or ballet, Salinas presents discos and banana boats. But let's be realistic. Given the choice, who wouldn't pick a banana boat?

ORIENTATION

The beach cuts across the northern end of town, separated into two sections by the outcroppng of land holding the Salinas Yacht Club. The area around the eastern beach holds most of the town's services, restaurants, and lodgings. The only straight-forward street names belong to the roads running north-south, perpendicular to the water; these *calles* are numbered in order from lowest to highest, from west to east. The east-west streets, however, are a complete mess. Most have two names—the one on the street sign and the one most people use. **Malecón,** the closest parallel road to the water, offers most of the dining, nightlife, and expensive lodgings. Buses from La Libertad enter Salinas along Av. 3 (Tercera), parallel to the beach, three blocks inland. At about Calle 26, Av. 3 becomes Av. 7; catch a bus here for La Libertad.

PRACTICAL INFORMATION

Tour Agency: Pescatour, Malecón 577 and Rumiñahui (tel. 772-391; fax 443-142), leads 9½hr. deep-sea fishing adventures for 1-6 people (US$335). Lunch can be arranged for around US$10 per person. Open daily 8am-noon and 2-6pm.

Banks: Filanbanco, Enriquez Gallo and Las Palmeras (tel. 773-640 or 773-431), has a 24hr. ATM and changes traveler's checks, but not cash. Open Wed.-Sun. 8:45am-4pm. **Banco La Previsara,** Enriquez Gallo and Leonardo Avilles (tel. 773-092), has a 24hr. ATM, and changes cash, but not traveler's checks.

Buses: The town of **La Libertad,** a few kilometers to the east, is the peninsula's transportation hub. Buses from Salinas to La Libertad leave every few minutes 'round the clock (s/1,000), or take a taxi or *camioneta* (s/3,000-5,000) from Av. 3.

Library: Biblioteca Municipal, Los Almendros and Eloy Alfaro. Open Tues.-Fri. 8:30am-12:30pm and 1-4:30pm, Sat. 8:30am-2pm.

Pharmacy: Farmacía Central, Malecón 331 and Calle 23. Open daily 9:30am-1pm and 2:30-10pm. **Farmacía Adreita,** Av. 7 and Calle 18 (tel. 774-194). Open daily 8:30am-9pm.

Hospital: Hospital Jose Gaurez (tel. 776-017), 3 blocks south of Espinoza, past the police station in Ciudadela Frank Vargas Pazoz. Emergency room open 24hr.

Police: Espinoza and Calle 57 (tel. 778-699), on the east end of town.

Post Office: Las Palmeras and Enriquez Gallo, diagonally across from Filanbanco. Open Mon.-Fri. 8am-noon and 2-5pm, Sat. 9am-noon.

Telephones: EMETEL, Rumiñahui/Calle 23 and Enriquez Gallo. Buy s/700 *fichas* (tokens) from the police station next door to make international calls. You have to keep plugging tokens in just to keep the line alive, even after you're connected with an operator. Open daily 8am-10pm. Most of the **ritzy hotels** in town have public pay phones that accept calling cards.

Telephone Code: 04.

ACCOMMODATIONS

Salinas's budget accommodations are few but not far-between. Most congregate between Calle 22 and Calle 27, on the parallel roads south of Malecón. You won't find anything lower than s/15,000 per person, but almost all rooms are well-maintained and have private bathrooms.

Hostal Las Rocas, Calle 22 and Enriquez Gallo (tel. 774-219), 2 blocks from the beach, with white stucco and blue trim. Second-story rooms have lounge chairs and a breezy patio. Tidy curtains in immaculate rooms match exterior trim. Well-scrubbed private baths and fans, necessary when Salinas's mosquito population is on the prowl. English-speaking management provides helpful info and serves hot cups of complimentary Colombian coffee all day. Rooms s/25,000 per person.

Hotel Oro del Mar, Av. Segunda and Calle 23 (La Libertad tel. 783-110). Time-worn curtains redeemed by sizeable windows and ocean views. Spacious rooms seem sterilized with chlorine; lipstick kisses adorn otherwise stark walls. Brown tile in private baths masks the spots not hit by the chlorine. Rooms s/25,000 per person.

Hotel Albita, Av. 7 and Calle 23 (tel. 773-211), around the corner from Las Rocas. You can sit on the firm mattress within your recently repainted room, blow the fan on your face and ponder: which is better, octopus or squid *ceviche?* You can ponder this further in the extra-clean bathroom. Rooms s/20,000 per person.

Hotel Florida, Malecón and Calle 2 (tel./fax 772-780), offers a more tranquil experience just off the western beach. All rooms have fans, private baths, and cleanliness. There is a restaurant downstairs, which is fortunate because the hotel is about 10-15min. away from the dining action of the eastern beach. Rooms s/35,000.

FOOD

Salinas's seafood is excellent, but not necessarily good enough to justify these prices. Even sidewalk booths are on the expensive side. If you like *ceviche,* however, you've come to the right place. **Cevichelandia,** at Luz de Serrano and Las Palmeras, may be your wildest fantasy come true—a plaza containing 15 separate outdoor *cevicherías,* all fresh, all delicious. *Ceviche*-land continues along Enriquez Gallo, beginning at Las Palmeras and running until Calle 18, where another plaza of outdoor *cevicherías* awaits. Malecón is loaded with places to eat, but like the beachfront hotels, restaurants tend to be spendy.

Cevichería Carmenita, Isabel, and Genesis, Las Palmeras and Luz de Serrano, in *Cevichelandia.* The closest thing to fast food in Salinas, but easier on your arteries. Open-air sidewalk stands serve up *ceviche* (s/12,000) and frothy *batidos* (s/3,000). If one doesn't have the ceviche you want, go to the one next door. Genesis has the best juice selection in town. Open daily 7am-5pm.

Restaurant Herminia, Malecón and Calle 29. One of the few relaxed joints along the waterfront, Herminia's decor seems to have accrued over time. An empty box from a Miller 24-pack shares the wall with a painting of a sneering Barcelona bull, mascot of Guayaquil's popular *fútbol* club. Admire the harbor from the hammock while awaiting a plate of fried fish and rice (s/6,000) or a *churrasco* feast (s/10,000). Open Sun.-Thurs. 9am-midnight, Fri.-Sat. 9am-1 or 2am.

Restaurante Los Helechos, Malecón and Calle 28 (tel. 773-984). *Los helechos* (the ferns) hang everywhere in this simple, breezy diner, strewn with fishing nets and wood carvings. A feast of the senses; feel the scattered pebbles and seashells that rustle and chime as you step over them. Admire the various fish tanks as you enjoy *arroz con pollo* (s/15,000), battered trout (s/8,000), or a plate of steak, rice, and potatoes (s/8,000). Open daily from 8am, until late, depending on clientele.

Restaurant Vera Mar, Malecón between Calle 25 and 26. Authentic Spanish cuisine and intimate tables looking out on the water. Divine *paella* (s/14,000) almost makes you skip the hearty *tortilla española* (s/4,000). Open for lunch and dinner.

SIGHTS AND ENTERTAINMENT

Salinas has two beaches, divided by a small peninsula that houses the **Salinas Yacht Club.** Salinas's main beach covers the stretch of sand to the east of the Yacht Club. Palm-laden and relatively unlittered, the sands are packed to capacity with sun worshippers. The water is even more congested, teeming with every kind of watercraft imaginable: expensive yachts, luxurious sailboats, time-worn fishing dugouts, banana boats, paddle boats, and jetskis. Shallow water is safe for children and timid swimmers; the surface only stirs when a boat motors through. Join in the water diversions, like a **banana boat** ride for s/5,000. **Paddle boats** fit up to four (s/10,000 per hr.). The chronically lazy can rent junior **motor boats** to go around the harbor (s/100,000 per hr.). If you don't want to lift a finger, **tour boats** cruise the harbor as well (s/4,000 per person for 30min.). Never fear, high-speed enthusiasts, the sea's the limit on **jet skis** (s/100,000 per hr.), and boats can take you **waterskiing** (s/120,000 per hr.). The less-crowded beach on the western side of the Yacht Club doesn't offer any of the aforementioned diversions, but it does offer peace and quiet on its tranquil, protected shorebreak. Although this beach manages to avoid the crowds and the carnival-like atmosphere, the tacky white high-rises still loom inescapably in the background. If your appetite for inane diversion is still not sated, **Golfito Salinas,** Calle 24 and Enriques Gallo, provides mini-golf for s/3,000 per person.

When the sun goes down, Salinas's sandy carnival moves inside, infiltrating the city's bars and *discotecas.* Nightlife in Salinas means bar-hopping; just follow the teeth-rattling *discoteca* music. Frenzied dance action is restricted to the weekends during the dry season, but in the *temporada* the city gyrates with visitors almost every night. **Flintstone's Rockabar,** Enriquez Gallo and Rafael de la Cuadra (tel. 774-144), combines American cinema, a sports bar, and a *discoteca* in a tribute to pop culture. The DJed dance floor is covered with a strange collection of James Dean, Marilyn Monroe, and American football posters. Clumsy folk can rest on tree stumps covered with faux dinosaur hide, and watch cutting-edge sports on the TVs above. Billiards-and-foosball saloon upstairs provides a good dance floor scoping spot. Beer s/5,000-7,000, whiskey s/10,000 (open Thurs.-Sat. 9pm-4am; cover s/10,000). **El Patio,** Calle 27 and Enriquez Gallo, in Hotel Salinas Costa Azul, is another popular dance bar that really gets going after 10pm. You could lose yourself in the soft velvety couches, especially with lighting this dim. A disco ball rotates while the DJ spins *merengue, salsa,* and dance-hall hits (open Thurs.-Sun. 8pm-around 4am; cover s/10,000). **El Tobaco,** Malecón and Suastegur, has inside and outside dance floors under palm-thatched roofs, and enthralls an older crowd with the usual toe-tapping Latin and foreign hits (open Fri.-Sun. 9pm-late; cover s/10,000).

■ La Libertad

La Libertad is like a smaller version of Guayaquil: it's big (at pop. 50,000 it's the largest town in the area), it bustles with business and shipping, and there's no pressing reason for tourists to visit. But, as with Guayaquil, tourists wind up passing through because it's the regional transportation hub. Buses running between Guayaquil and Salinas pass through Av. 9 de Octubre, the main drag in town, one block inland from the Malecón and waterfront. The other main street is Calle Guayaquil, which runs perpendicular to Av. 9 de Octubre and houses a busy series of street-stands hawking all sorts of wares. Most of the bus-lines run on 9 de Octubre and stop along the Calles which intersect it. **Coop Libertad Peninsular** (tel. 785-850 or 786-433), **Coop Trans Esmeraldas** (tel. 786-670), and **Coop Intercantonal Costa Azul,** are all at Av. 9 de Octubre and Calle Guerra Barreiro. Libertad and Costa Azul go to **Guayaquil** (every 15min., 3:30am-8:10pm, 2hr., s/6,500) via **Progreso** (1hr., s/3,000), and Esmeraldas goes to **Quito** (8 and 9pm, 9hr., s/25,000).

Should you find yourself stuck in La Libertad, or if you just like busy commercial centers, the town has a few accommodation options. **Hotel Viña del Mar,** Calle Guayaquil and Av. 3 (tel 785-979), offers scrupulously clean rooms with fans, balconies, and private baths (s/30,000 per person). A less luxurious option is **Residencial Libertad,** Guerro Barriero and Diagonal 2 (tel 783-716), which offers cramped, windowless quarters for s/10,000 per person. All rooms have fans though, and some have funky painting. As long as the rooms are this cheap you'd might as well splurge on dinner at **Parilla Don Ciro,** Av. 9 de Octubre, which offers big steaks (s/30,000) and more affordable pizza (s/6,000-8,000). The s/50,000 *Parillada Doble* is about right for a family of four bull mastifs. For diversion, there's a park off of Av. 9 de Octubre, and the Malecón offers pleasing views of big boats and the high-rises of Salinas. A **cinema** on Av. 9 de Octubre shows double features for s/3,000.

NEAR LA LIBERTAD

Chanduy

The tiny fishing village of Chanduy is home to the **Complejo Cultural Real Alto** (tel. 772-699), an archeological museum detailing the history of Ecuador from the perspective of the ancient communities who lived in the Chanduy area. It's a nice introduction to area archeology, but it is a bit small and hard to get to (open Tues.-Sun. 10am-5pm; admission s/7,000). Buses come here from Libertad (1hr., s/3,000) or alternatively, you can take a taxi (30min., s/5,000).

Baños de San Vicente

Situated 20km east of La Libertad, the Baños de San Vicente offer a filthy good time. A miracle of nature, San Vicente's muddied volcanic crater is a natural panacea for such ailments as arthritis and rheumatism. Sufferers of these afflictions, as well as health-conscious pleasure-seekers, flock to San Vicente to experience this alternative physical therapy and enjoy extras like massages, steam baths, and health food.

General admission to the park (s/6,000, children under 6 s/3,000) includes access to the **mud bath,** where you can wallow the day away, as well as the three indoor pools, one of which is a natural hot spring. **Massages** using mud or *savila,* a natural aloe, relieve about s/15,000 of tension, while **hydra-massages**—20 minutes of high-powered jacuzzi jets—soak you for s/10,000. The jets bombard bathers with surges of water that activate the surface of the skin, relaxing muscles while improving circulation. The park also offers **internal purification,** which involves sweating away the evil build-up of everyday life in the s/10,000 steam bath (park open daily 7am-7pm).

After indulging in pleasures of the flesh, healthful gastronomic therapy awaits at the park's **restaurant,** which has sandwiches (s/3,000) and all-natural juices (s/2,500-3,000). Or, if you're tired of all this health crap, you can get something fried at a *comedore* outside of the park. **Hotel Florida** (tel. 785-020), a two-minute walk from the park, offers rooms with private baths and metal frame-beds. The top-notch **restaurant** downstairs serves full meals (s/60,000 per person, includes 3 meals).

Buses on the Guayaquil-Salinas route pass by the road to San Vicente between Progresso and La Libertad. Ask the driver to drop you off at Los Baños de San Vicente. From the highway, it's a 7km walk to the park.

■ Playas

As the closest beach resort to Guayaquil, Playas inevitably receives masses of *guayaq-uileños* during the sweltering weekends. And because it's cheaper than the other major beach resort at Salinas, Playas is the sunbathing spot of choice for most of the southern Sierra. The weekend invasions by fervent tourists have left Playas somewhat in disrepair. The beach is strewn with litter, evidence of the comings and goings of visitors who knew they wouldn't be around to clean up on Monday. But as an afford-able and almost effortless escape from the city, Playas will more than suffice.

ORIENTATION

Buses from Guayaquil enter from the north along **Pedro Hernandez Gilbert**, and exit Playas for Guayaquil out **Calle Paquisha**, parallel to Gilbert. Passengers are dropped off along east-west **Avenida 15 de Agosto,** Playas's main street. All of the town's prac-tical facilities are along this street, as is the **central plaza. Calle 9** runs south from the central plaza to east-west **Calle Malecón,** Playas's shoreline drive. **Avenida 2,** also called **Calle Jaime Roldos Aguilera,** runs parallel to Malecón, one street north.

PRACTICAL INFORMATION

Currency Exchange: Multibanco de Guayaquil, Av. 15 de Agosto and Gilbert (tel. 760-040), exchanges traveler's checks only. Open Mon.-Fri. 9am-6pm, Sat 9:30am-1:30pm. ATM accepts Visa.

Buses: Coop Transportes Villamil, Pedro Menendez Gilbert and Av. 15 de Agosto, goes to **Guayaquil** (every 20min. 4am-7pm, 2hr., s/6,200) via **Progreso** (30min., s/2,000). Wait at the station or at the **bus stop** at Paquisha and Av. 15 de Agosto.

Pharmacy: Farmacía Villamil, Av. 15 de Agosto between Gilbert and Paquisha (tel. 760-159). Open daily 8am-10pm.

Hospital: Hospital General Villamil Playas, Av. 15 de Agosto (emergency tel. 660-238), 1km east of town. Free 24hr. emergency treatment.

Police: Calle Asiselo Garay and Av. 15 de Agosto (tel. 764-145), on the right hand side of the street as you head north.

Post Office: Calle Asiselo Garay and Av. 15 de Agosto, next to the police station. Open Mon.-Fri. 9am-1pm and 2:30-6pm, Sat. 9am-1pm.

Telephone: EMETEL, Aguilera (tel. 660-104 or 660-105), 800m west of town, is the place for international calls. To talk to an operator from AT&T, Sprint, or MCI, s/5,000. Open daily 8am-10pm.

Phone Code: 04.

ACCOMMODATIONS

Most establishments in Playas have been around a while and show visible signs of their age. Many less expensive options congregate in the western end of town, along Malecón and Av. 2, but there are a few others dispersed along Av. 15 de Agosto. Note that Playas has a healthy mosquito contingent—fans or netting are essential.

Hotel Playas, Malecón and Jaime Roldos Aguilera (tel. 760-121 or 760-611). Across-from-the-sand location gives this hotel an edge over its competitors. Rooms are a bit bug-heavy, but all have good fans and private bath. Rooms s/20,000 per person.

Hotel Brisas Marinas, Av. 2 and 24 de Diciembre (tel 760-324). Like the pharmacy out front, this hotel is clean, subdued, and convenient. Rooms are plain but com-fortable. All with fans, private bath, and mosquito nets; s/30,000 per person.

Hotel Acapulco, Av. 2 and Calle 9 (tel. 760-343). Unusually sparse atmosphere, with ample but empty quarters except for the bed and solitary lightbulb. Mysteri-ous stains on the scruffy walls and creaky wooden floors. Common baths are clean but a bit decrepit. Rooms s/20,000 per person.

FOOD

For seaside views, a series of nondescript seafood establishments sits on the sand with standard coastal dishes and prices. The best food is found along Paquisha near Aguilera, where a collection of *cevicherías* use the freshest of shellfish the sea offers.

Cevichería Doña Gladys, Paquisha and Aguilera. Part of the *ceviche* streetside mall, complete with palm-thatched roof and Coca-Cola billboard. Various exotica laid out for appraisal: conches, oysters, and clams all begging to become your *ceviche* dinner. Shrimp *ceviche* s/13,000, basic plate of fried fish, rice, and plantains s/6,000. Open daily 7am-9pm.

Comedor Sabor Criollo, Jaime Roldos Aguilera and Calle 9, diagonally across from Hotel Acapulco, a couple blocks from the beach. The "Criollo" comes from the smiling owner's last name and the secret spices that give the food a New Orleans twang. *Churrasco* s/7,000, fried filet s/6,000, *corvina* with rice, plantains, and salad s/7,000. Open Mon.-Fri. 8am-8pm, Sat.-Sun. 8am-noon.

La Cabaña Típica, Malecón and Jaime Roldos Aguilera (tel. 760-464), on the beachfront, across from Hotel Playas. Tree-branch seats ground the bamboo surroundings. Ugly metal bars on the windows don't stop the cool breezes. Monstrous plate of rice and calamari, shrimp, conch, and fish s/10,000. Open daily 9am-8pm.

SIGHTS AND ENTERTAINMENT

The name says it all: people come for the **playas.** Most visitors spend the weekend either sweating in the sun or sprinting to the ocean in a quest for relief. Far from picturesque, the vast, treeless, litter-sprinkled sands of Playas are popular because there is room for everyone. While Playas Beach *(Playa Playas)* offers no shade, many sunbathers bring immense canvases to create tents over the sand. The surf is weak and perfect for wading and dog-paddling. When facing the ocean, turn right and head down a ways until you run into the local fleet of balsa fishing rafts—an interesting reminder of the days before industrial fishing. If you continue along the beach, you'll reach a deserted rocky section, full of tidal pools where the fancy holiday houses of Guayaquil's rich rise. If the sun's getting to be too much, duck inside Playas's **cinema,** Av. 15 de Agosto and Asiselo Garay. Films screened in English and Spanish; ask the ticket seller the language of the night (adult films featured Thurs.-Fri., Hollywood hits Sun.-Mon.; 9:30pm; tickets s/2,000). Alternatively, head to the hottest discos in town, **Mr. Frog** and **Coco Beach,** both rocking Malecón on the weekends.

Oriente

THE NORTHERN ORIENTE

The northern Oriente is Ecuador's last, but fast disappearing, frontier. It stretches from its easternmost urban outposts, Coca and Lago Agrio, for more than 100km, past thousands of acres of nationally-protected lands, to its remote borders with Perú and Colombia. This jungle, much of which consists of primary growth, is home to an immense diversity of fauna and flora. Countless plant and insect species thrive here, as do larger, rarer animals, like jaguars, sloths, monkeys, and *cocodrilos* (crocodiles).

The human history of the northern Oriente bears a striking resemblance to those of many other former frontier lands in this part of the world. For centuries, even after the arrival of the Spanish, the *indígenas* lived here in isolation, save for the occasional wandering missionaries. Only at the beginning of this century did colonists from the highlands descend upon the jungle and begin to clear plots of farmland, hunting the wildlife and intruding upon the *indígenas* who were already living there, including the Huaorani, Secoya, Siona, and Shuar peoples. The industrial growth surrounding the discovery of oil in the 1970s poses the greatest threat to these pristine natural areas and indigenous communities. The oil companies continue to cut roads deeper into the jungle, not only destroying the forest as they go, but opening it up for colonization and consequent deforestation and habitat destruction. Like the biodiversity, the indigenous communities are threatened by encroaching modern civilization.

■ Puyo

In Puyo, modern civilization is still negotiating its lease. At the eastern foothills of the Andes, a two-hour ride from the verdant valley of Baños, the Río Puyo passes through the town that bears its name and the sweeping Amazon rainforest materializes. While wilderness has the earliest and strongest claim on Puyo, human beings go back pretty far as well. Archaeological evidence indicates that people lived in the area as long ago as 4000-3500 BC. By the time the Spanish arrived, local tribes had united into a group called the Náparos. But in the years that followed, diseases decimated the Náparos to one-seventh of their previous population. Originally a missionary site, this present-day capital of the Pastaza province now has a population of over 15,000, a large part of which is Quechua. Now, whether out of heartfelt pride or simply as fuel for tourism, Puyo nurtures its jungle-town image. River scenes adorn the walls of virtually every hotel and restaurant, while most shops sell wood-carved parrots and postcards of exotic jungle fauna almost exclusively. Puyo itself is no more than a cluster of urban blocks that surrenders quickly to the surrounding wilderness; a very real, untamed rainforest canopy stretches east from town.

ORIENTATION

The road from Baños, **Ceslao Marín,** flows in from the west, past the high-class Hotel Turungia, past the **terminal terrestre** (a bit south of the highway), and smack into the **main plaza.** Just west of *el centro,* **Atahualpa** diverges from Marín at a slight angle and becomes another principal east-west thoroughfare. Hotels, *comedores,* and various shops cluster in the area of **Avenida 9 de Octubre** and Atahualpa. Most streets have no signs; get the map from CETUR to find your way around.

PRACTICAL INFORMATION

Tourist Office: At the northwest corner of the plaza, the underused and overstaffed **CETUR** office provides info on tourist facilities throughout the Oriente, and a decent map of town. Open Mon.-Sat. 8am-noon and 2-6pm.

Currency Exchange: Banks in town may exchange dollars, but **Casa de Cambios Puyo,** Atahualpa and Av. 9 de Octubre (tel. 883-064), changes traveler's checks and cash at very competitive rates. Open Mon.-Sat. 8:30am-9pm.

Buses: The **terminal terrestre** (tel. 885-480), is a 20min. walk or a s/2,500 cab ride west of *el centro.* Take Av. 9 de Octubre south past the market to the traffic circle with a bronze bust. Take a right on Alberto Nambrano and follow it about 1km. Serves arrivals and departures until 6pm, after which buses drop people off downtown. Evening and night trips leave from **Transportes Touris San Francisco,** on Marín about 10m west of where Atahualpa joins it. Due to construction, the Baños-Puyo road is only open on Sun.-Mon., so many take a much longer road Tues.-Sat. Most buses going west, therefore, pass through Baños Sun.-Mon., and go through Tena Tues.-Sat. Buses to: **Ambato** (Sun.-Mon., every hr., 6am-6pm, 4hr, s/8,000; Tues.-Sat., 9pm, 10hr., s/25,000); **Quito** (Sun.-Mon., 2, 9, 10am, 3, and 5:45pm, 6hr., s/15,000; Tues.-Sat., 7, 8:15am, noon, 3:30, 9, and 11pm, 8hr., s/18,000); **Coca** via Tena (daily, 8pm, 8hr., s/25,000); **Tena** (daily, approx. every hour, 7am-6pm, 2½hr., s/6,000); **Guayaquil** (Sun.-Mon., 9 and 11pm, 8hr., s/21,000); **Macas** (daily, 3, 8, 10am, 12:45, 2, 5:45, 6, and 8pm; 5hr., s/14,000); **Palera** (noon and 3:30pm, 2hr., s/4,000). **Local buses** to **Shell** leave from the south end of Av. 27 de Febrero, near Av. 24 de Mayo (every 15min., 5:45am-8:45pm, s/800).

Taxis: They can be scarce; try calling **Cooperativa 12 de Mayo** (tel. 885-185).

Laundromat: Clean your smellies at **Lavandería Mágica,** Av. 9 de Octubre and Av. 24 de Mayo (tel. 885-242). Drop clothes off in the morning, pick up in the afternoon (s/600-4,000 per piece). Open Mon.-Sat. 7am-8pm.

Library: Biblioteca Municipal (tel. 885-245) on Orellana near Av. 27 de Febrero, 2nd fl., Municipal Building. Open Mon.-Fri. 8am-noon and 2-6:30pm.

Red Cross: Sucre 1540 (tel. 885-214).

Pharmacy: Farmacía Atahualpa, Atahualpa and Av. 27 de Febrero (tel. 885-544), is part of the *de turno* system. Open 9am-1pm and 3-10pm.

Hospital: Hospital de la Brigada 17, Alfaro and Pino (tel. 883-131 or 885-541). In nearby Shell, **Hospital Vozandes,** Asunción (tel. 795-172), has American doctors.

Police: Av. 9 de Octubre (tel. 883-101).

Post Office: Av. 27 de Febrero and Atahualpa (tel. 885-332). Check the Lista de Correos here. Open Mon.-Fri. 8am-6pm.

Telephone: Call home from **EMETEL,** Orellana and General Billamil (tel. 883-104), 1 block west of the market. Open daily 8am-1pm and 1:15-10pm.

Telephone Code: 03.

ACCOMMODATIONS

Hotel Americano, Marín 576 and Alagualpa (tel. 885-227). The management tries awfully hard for that jungle lodge atmosphere, but the buses passing outside keep reminding you that you're in Puyo for the night. Clean, secure, electric hot water— an excellent deal at s/10,000 per person, with private bath s/15,000.

Hotel Europa Internacional, Av. 9 de Octubre (tel. 885-220 or 885-228; fax 885-120), between Atahualpa and Orellana. This trustworthy hotel rents rooms with private (hot water) baths. Restaurant downstairs. Rooms s/15,000 per person.

Hotel Granada, Av. 27 de Febrero and Orellana (tel. 885-578), 2 blocks south of Atahualpa next to the market. A no-frills low-cost option. Bare, reasonably clean rooms, cold water bathrooms. Rooms s/7,000 per person, with bath s/15,000.

FOOD

Mesón Europeo, Nambrano (tel. 883-919), east of the *terminal terrestre.* This open-aired *hacienda* restaurant sports fancy aesthetics; the cost is included in the price of the meal. Bow-tied waiters complete the picture. *Almuerzo* s/12,000, fried chicken s/12,000, banana split s/5,000. Open daily 11am-10pm.

Chifa Oriental, Marín and Av. 27 de Febrero (tel 885-113). Chomp cheap Chinese cuisine as you ponder a peculiar poster of tough toddler on a Harley. Beef dishes s/6,500-8,500, rice entrees s/5,500-9,000. Open daily 11am-3pm and 6pm-midnight.

Cha-Cha-Cha Pollo a la Braya (tel. 885-208), on Marín just past the Hotel Turungia. Say it out loud, and feel the rhythm… *Cha-Cha-Cha Pollo a la Braya.* Enjoy pizza,

Northern Oriente

PERÚ

N

COLOMBIA

Cantagallo
Tiphisca
Palma
Roja
Pto. El Carmen
de Putumayo
Pto. Bolívar
Río Putumayo
Reserva
Vida Selvestre
Lagartococha
Sta. María de
Huiririma
Tiputini

Pto. Colón
Gral. Farfán
Río San Miguel
Dureno
Pacayacu
Tarapoa
Cuyabeno
Reserva Producción
Faunística Cuyabeno
Río Cuyabeno
Shushufindi
San Roque
Pañacocha
Cap. Augusto
Rivadeneira
Nuevo Rocafuerte

Lago Agrio
(Nueva Loja)
Sevilla
Río Aguarico
El Eno
San Pedro
de los Cofanes
Enokanqui
La Joya de los Sachas
Limoncocha
Pompeya
Tafacoa
Río Aguarico
Reserva
Biológica
Limoncocha
Río Napo
Parque Nacional Yasuní
Río Rumiyacu
Río Yasuní
Río Nashiño
Río Cononaco

Río Coca
El Reventador
El Raphael
San Raphael
El Chaco
Sta. Rosa
Linares
Río Coca
San Sebastián
del Coca
Coca
(Puerto Francisco
de Orellana)
Loreto
Sumaco
Reserva
Biológica
Sumaco
Sumaco
(3732m)
Tiputani
Dayuma
Valle de
los Acuas
Folclor del
Oriente
Pto. Murialdo
Chontapunta
Río Tiputini
Río Tivacuno
Río Tyacunu

Pto. Libre
Reserva Ecológica
Cayambe-Coca
Reventador
(3562m)
Cayambe
(5790m)
San Fco.
de Borja
Baeza
Sardinas
Cosanga
Cuyuja
Reserva
Ecológica
Antisana
Archidona
Tena
Pto. Misahuallí
Ahuano
Río Napo
Sta. Clara

Otavalo
Quito
Papallacta
Parque
Nacional
Cotopaxi
Cotopaxi
(5897m)
Area Nacional
de Recreación
Boliche
Latacunga
Ambato
Cotundo
Cueva de Jumandi
Puerto Napo
Tnte. Hugo Ortiz
Reserva
Biológica
Llanganates
Veracruz
Puyo
Mera
Baños
10 de Agosto

30 miles
30 kilometers
0
0

chicken, and sparkling, welcoming smiles. *Merienda* with rotisserie chicken s/ 7,000. Open daily 10am-10pm.

Restaurant Hostelería Turungia, Ceslao Marín 294 (tel. 885-180), on the western edge of town. While the exorbitant rooms are out of most budget travelers' reach (s/50,000, *ouch!*), come as a spectator and visit the hotel's garden, pool, pet snake, and gourmet food. Polish up your hiking boots—this is the fanciest place in town. *Almuerzos* and *meriendas* are tasty and filling (open daily 7am-9pm).

SIGHTS AND ENTERTAINMENT

A good place to catch up on that novel you've been carrying, Puyo isn't exactly the amusement capital of the world. The **Parque Pedagógico Etno-Botánico Omaere** (tel. 883-001), north up Av. 9 de Octubre, is one worthwhile walk (or s/3,500 cab ride). Locals can point the way if you stray, but it is mostly straight ahead, along bumpier streets through a residential neighborhood (the map from the CETUR office makes things easier). The Parque itself lies on the Río Puyo, across a roped foot-bridge. Indigenous guides lead visitors through the park's grounds, identifying plants and explaining their uses (s/10,000). A number of traditional *indígena* homes are scattered throughout the forest. While the park has been financed by foreigners, it serves mostly Ecuadorian schoolchildren—Spanish-speaking guides only. Locals have recently set up a similar reserve about 20km out of town, administered by **Fundación Hola Vida,** which provides a no-frills version of the Omaere experience. In addition to jungle walks, the reserve offers cheap and basic accommodations (s/10,000) and meals. The best way to reach Hola Vida is by taxi (s/10,000 each way).

■ Tena

Just 197km southeast of Quito, Tena sits at the fast-flowing union of the Ríos Tena and Napo, part of the headwaters of the Amazon. East of Tena spans the jungle, and its western panorama is dominated by the jagged silhouette of the mighty Cordillera de los Llanganates. Tena's auspicious location has always been apparent; even the Spanish realized the geographic potential when they founded the city in 1560 as an ambitious reach into the Oriente. Today this provincial capital stands above the other towns in the Napo Province, developing quickly and eagerly to become the real, live tourist center that its location facilitates. What was once a Spanish reach into the jungle has become a gringo one, and a budding industry of tourist possibilities has risen up to meet the traveler traffic. Tena's entrepreneurs have developed a jungle playground here, with bamboo *cabañas,* cave spelunking, white-water rafting, kayaking, and any other adventure a weary urbanite could hope for. But as more established tourist destinations like Baños attest, Tena still has a ways to go. Hotel and restaurant choices are sadly limited, and menus have yet to include English translations.

ORIENTATION

If the mountains to the east are visible, use them for navigation. The most important parts of Tena are on either side of the area where the Ríos Napo and Tena merge. To the west, Tena *centro* spreads as an irregular grid, from **García Moreno,** on the river-front, to **Montalvo,** two blocks west, and from the **Main Plaza** along **Mera** to **Bolívar,** four blocks farther north. A pedestrian bridge crosses the river from Mera. East-west **Olmedo** becomes a vehicle bridge that takes a right on the opposite bank and becomes **Avenida 15 de Noviembre.** This strip houses the best hotel and restaurant selections, as well as the **terminal terrestre,** about 1km south of the bridge.

PRACTICAL INFORMATION

Tourist Information: CETUR, Bolívar (tel. 886-418), near Amazonas in *el centro.* Not well-known by the locals, and usually not too busy. Brochures on Ecuador and the Oriente in various languages. Open Mon.-Fri. 8:30am-5pm.

Currency Exchange: Banco del Austro, Av. 15 de Noviembre (tel. 886-446), between the bridges. Exchanges cash, traveler's checks, Visa advances. Open Mon.-Fri. 8am-6pm, Sat. 9am-1:30pm. In an emergency, ask around—several stores also offer exchange services, though not at very favorable rates.

Airport: Airstrip is 3 blocks uphill from Olmedo behind Bolívar, and offers flights to Coca or Puyo-Pastaza. The problem is frequency and price: to **Coca** (Wed., 9-10am, 30min., s/42,000). While severe, it beats the bumpy 7hr. bus ride. The flight to **Puyo** is less reliable since it depends upon demand for flights back from Coca.

Buses: The **terminal terrestre** can blend in with the buildings around it; look closely along the west side of Av. 15 de Noviembre, 1km south of the bridges. Plenty of destinations; some affected by road closure between Puyo and Baños. To: **Quito** (20 per day, 5½hr., s/16,000) via **Baeza** (3hr., s/8,000); **Puyo** (Tues.-Sat., every hr., 5am-9pm, 2½hr., s/8,000; Sun.-Mon., every hr., 5am-midnight); **Ambato** (Sun.-Mon., every hr., 5am-midnight, 6hr., s/16,000); **Riobamba** (Sun.-Mon., 2, 3, 4, 9am, 3, and 6pm, 6hr., s/12,000); **Coca** (4 per day, 4:30am-midnight, 7hr., s/20,000). Beware of the bad road to Coca. Buses to **Misahuallí** leave from Amazonas and the road adjacent to the airstrip, 1 block from Bolívar (every 45min., 6am-5:30pm, 1hr., s/2,500). From Amazonas and Olmedo, buses go to: **Archidona** (6am-7pm, every 15min., s/1,000); and **Ahuano/La Punta** via **Puerto Napo** and **Jatún Sacha** (every hr., 6:30am-5:30pm, 1½hr., s/4,000) making several stops along Av. 15 de Noviembre on the way.

Taxis: Taxis in this part of the jungle are not the familiar yellow boxes, but rather brawny white pick-up trucks. They're all over, and prices are comparable.

Public Market: One of the biggest is at Amazonas and Bolívar. Open daily 6am-6pm.

Pharmacy: Farmacía Amazonas, Amazonas and Calderón (tel. 886-495), in *el centro*. Part of the *de turno* network. Open daily 8am-9pm.

Hospital: Dr. Llamuca at the **Clínica Amazonas** (tel. 886-482), on Av. 15 de Diciembre 200m down from the terminal, has a solid reputation. Clinic open 24hr. **Hospital José María Velasco Ibarra** (tel. 886-302 through 305), on Av. 15 de Noviembre outside of town.

Police: (tel 886-425), on García Moreno next to Main Playa.

Post Office: Av. Olmedo and Amazonas (tel. 886-418), with a Lista de Correos. Open Mon.-Fri. 8am-6pm, Sat. 8am-4pm.

Telephones: EMETEL, Olmedo and Montalvo (tel. 886-105). Open Mon.-Sat. 8am-10pm, Sun. 8-11am, 2-5pm, and 7-9pm.

Phone Code: 06.

ACCOMMODATIONS

In Tena, and most of the Oriente, your room will be musty—this is not a sign of poor upkeep. If you hang around this damp place for long enough, you'll be covered in mildew, too. If you can get past the mustiness, however, there is no lack of decent reasonably-priced accommodations.

Hostal Traveller's Lodging, Av. 15 de Noviembre 438 (tel. 886-372), next to the footbridge landing. Welcome to gringo-central. Attached to a restaurant and tour agency, this reputable complex has private baths, electric hot water, fans, and back-friendly beds in all rooms. *Dueño* Don Mario has recently put in a row of new so-called luxury rooms, and has big plans to turn the hotel into Tena's in-town entertainment complex—stay tuned. Rooms s/20,000 per person.

Residencial Alemana, Dias de Pineda and Av. 15 de Noviembre (tel. 386-409), next to the vehicle bridge. A quiet sanctuary across from the Traveller's Lodge, Alemana is worn but friendly. All have private (cold water) bath. Singles s/27,500; *matrimonial* (2 people, 1 bed) s/38,500; doubles s/44,000.

Hotel Amazonas, Mera and Montalvo (tel. 886-439), just off main plaza. Breezy, open-aired rooms. The best choice when short on sucres: s/10,000 per person.

Hotel Turismo Amazónio, Amazonas and Calderón (tel. 886-508). Throw in the word "Turismo" and prices go up, as do the amenities. All have telephone, TV, fridge, and private bath (room-temperature water). Rooms s/35,000 per person.

FOOD

Fruit stands and *panaderías* line Av. 15 de Noviembre between the terminal and the footbridge. An important landmark for gringo palates is the aptly-named **Nutripan,** 100m down from the terminal. It is one of the few places in town that keeps the pork fat content of its bread to a minimum (open daily 7am-7pm).

Chuquitos, on Montalvo near Calderon, 3 blocks up from the footbridge. Doesn't look like much—if you don't watch carefully, you may miss the rickety flight of wooden stairs leading up to this popular little eatery. *Tilapía al jugo* (a local fish served in a savory tomato sauce) with fried plantains and rice, s/12,000; decidedly non-*típico* curried chicken, s/12,000. Open daily 7am-9pm.

Restaurant Cositas Ricas, Av. 15 de Noviembre (tel. 886-372), next to the footbridge. The alimentary sequel to Hostal Traveller's Lodge, this open-aired hangout often crowds to capacity with tourists. Lots of American-sounding dishes that all seem to come out a lot like *platos típicos,* but hey, it still tastes good. Veggie spaghetti s/12,000, choice-beef cheeseburger s/5,000. Open daily 7am-10pm.

Restaurante Servi-Pan, Diaz de Pineda and Av. 15 de Noviembre, under Residencial Napoli. A tranquil place to enjoy breakfast (s/4,500), lunch (s/6,000), or dinner. The baked goods are delicious; add jelly and you won't be able to control yourself (croissants *increíbles* s/800). Open daily 6:30am-9pm.

SIGHTS

Tena is the jungle gym of the Ecuadorian playground. Visitors swing from adventure to adventure, reveling in the junglescape. While some of Tena's attractions may exist Oriente-wide, others can be found nowhere else. Probably the biggest adrenaline-rush in Tena—and maybe all of Ecuador—comes from its killer **whitewater rafting.** Barely discovered by the world's whitewater enthusiasts, the region around Tena in the western Oriente is a truly amazing find. These rivers are the headwaters of the Amazon, rushing through canyons, over waterfalls and past rocky banks. While downstream piranha-filled currents run muddy and slow, near Tena the water flows fresh from the heights of the Andes mountains. The density of whitewater rapids is higher here than almost anywhere else in the world—and what's even cooler, it's always high season. East of the Andes, the whitewater rapids churn year-round.

Ríos Ecuador (tel. 887-438), from their new office across from Cositas Ricas, runs trips out of Tena, under the watchful eye of its owner, Gynner, a 25-year old kayaking and rafting pro with five years of guiding experience on rivers around the world. The congenial entrepreneur is a native Ecuadorian, but he speaks better English than most Americans. Using professional guides and equipment from the U.S., the company leads knowledgeable, energetic, and safety-conscious trips for travelers eager to feel the cold spray of whitewater in their faces. A one-day rafting trip is US$50 per person for Class II and III rivers (novice/moderate skill level), US$60 for the more challenging trips. Kayaking trips are also available for a day at US$60 per person. These prices include transportation from Tena, the guide's services, and a beachfront picnic along the way. Kayak rentals are US$15 per day, US$80 per week, or US$30 and US$160 with all equipment included. Ríos Ecuador also offers a five-day kayaking course, including all the funky maneuvers, for US$300. Reservations can be made through their Quito office (tel. 553-727).

For a more tranquil wilderness experience, spend some time at one of the many *cabaña* complexes scattered along the rivers. **Michael Porter** and his family have some of the best *cabañas;* they make a living through sustainable jungle agriculture, and taking in tourists lucky enough to find them. Sadly, as of this writing the Porters intended to leave the jungle at the end of 1997 and pass on their farm to someone who will continue their operation (hopefully, they will leave their cookbook of jungle cuisine). Quite possibly, indigenous neighbors will help the new owners with tours of the nearby **jungle, petroglyphs, raging whitewater,** and trips to **Mama Rosa's farm.** Ask at Rios Ecuador about the current status of the Porter farm. A night at the farm is US$35. Another first-rate jungle lodge is run by the **Mamallacta family,** through their **Fundación Izu Mangallpa Urcu.** The goals of the foundation are to pre-

The Tailbone Terror

Why, one might wonder, does a 130km (82mi.) bus jaunt take nearly seven hours? Your backside, your tailbone, and in fact your whole body will know the answer soon after the experience. The "road" to Coca from Tena is a tribute to linguistic flexibility. It is hard to call something a road when at times it's a stream, at times a waterfall crossing, and usually just a trail of rocks and potholes. With all of its darting and weaving, the drive seems like a video game with the most advanced virtual reality sensations in the world. Sooner or later (though probably later), after trundling through the towns of Archidona, Cotundo, Guamaní, and Loreto, after cramming more and more bodies and boxes inside, after the driver stops to grab a meal while the patient passengers hungrily guard their seats, the bus really will arrive in Coca.

serve Quichua traditions and to protect and document the biodiversity of the area. They've also constructed a few *cabañas* to house tourists. In addition to the usual jungle walks, sons Elias or Benjamin can take you through the **lava chutes** that crisscross the family's properties. These caves, extending for many kilometers underground, contain a few fast-running underground rivers, and some spectacular **limestone formations.** More sedate travelers can learn all forms of **artesanía** from the old and wise **Mama Mamallacta.** A vacation in paradise doesn't come cheap—staying at the **Fundación** costs US$35 per day, including all tours and 3 glorious meals per day, using ingredients from the family's farm. Contact the Mamallacta at tel. 887-487, or ask about them at Ríos Ecuador.

The best known *cabañas,* **Amorangachi Tours,** operates out of the Hostal Traveller's Lodging. While they also offer a quality jungle experience, rumors suggest that the menu consists almost entirely of yucca and/or plantains at most meals (US$30 per day, all-inclusive). Other lesser-known *cabañas* are often just as knowledgeable, and even a little quieter. Several hide behind trees along the whitewater routes, and a brief stop or night's stay may even be incorporated into a day on the rapids. For more info, contact Gynner at Ríos Ecuador or ask at Safari Tours in Quito.

You don't even have to roll the dice to get to the **Cuevas de Jumandi,** huge caves that lie between Archidona and Cotundo, north of Tena. A resort has recently been established here making it a convenient base for daytripping tourists who wish to explore the natural formations. Don't come looking for wilderness or isolation—the area is quite built up (the waterslide out of the mouth of the cave is lots of fun). Take a bus to Archidona from Amazonas and Olmedo (every 15min., 6am-7pm, 20min., s/ 1000), then catch the bus from Archidona to Cotundo and ask to be let off at *las cuevas,* about 10 minutes from Archidona. More a safari than a daytrip, With patience and persistence, you may be able to spot the peak of the strangely misplaced **Volcán Sumaco** which rises out of the damp, densely-vegetated hills northeast of Tena. With even more persistence, you might be able to reach the mountain itself, though guides and machetes are a must. For more leads, ask around in Tena or head to the town of Loreto, about three hours away by bus along the Tena-Coca road.

One of the most impressive municipal parks in the county, the **Parque Amazónico La Isla** occupies 2200 hectares between Ríos Tena and Napo. It connects to Tena via a bamboo bridge about 50m upriver from the main footbridge behind the Hostal Traveller's Lodge. Monkeys and birds live freely in the park's sprawling forest, which merges with the greater jungle in the distance. Closed-in pools and cages house animals recuperating from injuries, including alligators, capybaras, tortoises, and boas. Various swimming areas dot the bordering rivers, and a look-out tower provides a panorama of Tena (open daily 10am-5pm; admission s/6,000, nationals s/1,000).

ENTERTAINMENT

On Friday, Saturday, and Sunday nights, Tena goes disco. Travelers who haven't had all their energy sucked by the myriad jungle activities are welcome to take part. Join the visiting U.S. soldiers as they let loose at **La Gallera,** a well-lit bar and dance club playing Latin tunes and techno favorites. Follow Av. 15 de Noviembre to the vehicle bridge, then veer right to the waterfront—if it's after 10pm on the weekend, you'll hear it. **Tattoo's** overlooks the water on the opposite side of the river, between the vehicle and foot bridges. Its stilt-supported bamboo structure has a bar and a second floor loft, all open-aired and cozy. A popular dance club called **El Rodeo,** opposite La Gallera on the river, plays similar toe-tapping tunes.

■ Misahuallí

The jungle port of Misahuallí is the only town downriver from Tena known for its tourism. But tourism here is on the wane, and the cause, indirectly, is tourism itself. Years ago, when the town first started growing on the north bank of the Río Napo, its claims of sandy beaches attracted jungle-hungry tourists. These outsiders were most fascinated by the **Huaorani,** whose exotic, elaborate traditional body jewelry and clothing provided perfect gawking material. Eventually the Huaorani developed a resentment for the ubiquitous, camera-toting visitors and the local guides who exploited their native villages. As the Huaorani's passive welcomes were worn thin and their open statements of resistance went ignored, they escaped the uncomfortable situation by moving farther east into the Oriente, away from the tourist industry that had thrived off their presence. Today Misahuallí is still a hub for guided tours and the gringos who experience them. The town, for better or worse, grew around its heyday of tourism, and the mark left on this compact Oriente community is definitely permanent. Everybody and his mother runs hotels and gives tours into the *selva.* With the absence of the significant indigenous population, these tours have transformed into canoe cruises to *cabaña* complexes built to fill the Huaorani's void.

Orientation and Practical Information The road heads into town from the west, where a sign welcomes you to Misahuallí. Some hotels, restaurants (more like acceptable *comedores*), and shops congregate around the plaza. The best advice for **changing money** in Misahuallí: do it somewhere else. If in need, though, the general store **Don Alonzo Guevara,** close to the beach at the corner of the plaza, changes cash and traveler's checks at sad rates (open daily 7am-9pm). The only phones in town are at **EMETEL** (tel. 584-964 or 584-965), down the Panuno road about three blocks on the left. The town secretary at EMETEL answers the town's only two phone numbers (open daily 11am-1pm, 3-6pm, and 7-9pm). **Buses** go to **Tena** from the central plaza (approx. every hr., 5am-5:30pm, 1hr., s/3,000). You can also come and go from Misahuallí by **motorized dug-out canoe.** Because the options aren't dependable or affordable, bus travel is more common. Prices and frequency depend on demand; be careful you're not getting ripped off. Approximate per person costs are s/9,000 to **Ahuano,** s/50,000 to **Coca.** If you're lucky, you may happen upon one of the passenger boats that go to and from Ahuano for around s/5,000. The blue-and-white Registro Curl office houses vestiges of a **police** force and a **mail-drop box,** but don't count on anything mailed from here ever arriving. Around the corner in the same building, the **Centro de Salud** functions somewhat erratically. **Doctora Mercedes Alcivar,** at the dead-end of the Tena road, has permanent hours and runs **Farmacía Misahuallí,** half a block before the plaza (open Mon.-Sat. 8am-8pm).

Accommodations and Food The two most professional, comfortable budget accommodations emerge on the right just before entering town. First looms the **Hotel Albergue Español,** P.O. Box 15-01-254, Tena (tel. 02-221-626 or 553-857 in Quito). This "jungle lodge" has spacious, spotless rooms that include private bath with the elusive, rarely found jungle species, *agua caliente.* Lobby decor includes a huge black dog that looks like Marmaduke. (Here boy. Roll over. Speak. *Rrruff.* Sit, Ubu, sit. Good dog.) Rooms cost s/25,000 per person. The **restaurant** here specializes in high-class dining. But hey, who doubled all the prices? (Spanish omelette s/12,000; vegetable plate, s/10,000.) These folks sure know how to settle gringo anxieties—a sign assures that all water is boiled before use. **Hotel Dayuma,** Casilla 220 in

Tena, is camouflaged 50m down the road, in a four-story building. Immaculate rooms have stained-wood furniture, hurricane-powered fans, mini-bar fridges, pay-as-you-go snacks, and kick-ass comforters. A quality set-up, but try to negotiate the s/20,000 per person price tag. Down the street near the plaza, some slightly less glamorous options await. Below the s/15,000 mark, **Hotel El Paisano,** a block down the road to Panuno from the plaza, on the left, aims to please penny pinchers. Dwellings are more rustic, sheets more worn, but baths still private. If you're looking to chill, head to the hammocks outside ($4 per person). The **restaurant** in front cooks gargantuan Ecuadorian *platos;* US$3 for most plates.

Sights There's really only one reason to go to Misahuallí: the jammin' jungle tours. Tours down the river can last from a day to a week, and include two people or twenty. Packages are flexible, but the important part is getting a satisfactory guide. Key guide qualities include language ability (if you don't want a tour in Spanish) and wilderness experience. While a good number of the guides in Misahuallí have the experience under their belts, their language range is usually limited. If you've accepted this, along with the reality of the not-so-pristine jungle just east of Misahuallí, there are a few reliable tour agencies to pick through.

Cruceros y Expediciones Dayuma, out of the Dayuma Hotel, is one of the biggest tour agencies in Misahuallí, operated by Marena and Douglas Clarke, along with an army of tour guides. Dayuma has three- to six-day expedition packages, custom-designed to your needs. The trips zoom you downriver in motorized canoes to thatch-roofed jungle *cabañas.* Meals are cooked using *yuca* and other native foods; exploratory hikes pass oodles of waterfalls, squadrons of birds, and a few indigenous jungle-dwellers. Hopefully they'll be glad to see you. If the itineraries originate and end in Quito, they also throw in excursions to Baños and the hot pools near Baeza (for 1-8 people, US$35 per person per day for 3-5 days; for 8 or more, US$30). Some guides speak some English, but this is *not* a given. **Ecoselva,** across the street from Dayuma, leads similar trips into the jungle. Pepe Tapia González, who runs the place, speaks English, as his recent rainforest talks in British public schools indicate. Tours include cascades, lagoons, hopefully some alligators and piranha, and other assorted jungle stuff. Other guides work for him, but if possible, try to snag the man himself (for 5-15 people, US$25 per person per day for 1-3 days). **Sacha Tours,** very visibly next to the beach, is owned by Hector Fiallos. Hector has been around awhile and speaks some English. Again, try to get the man himself. Their mailing address is Casilla 225, Tena.

Entertainment Go play with the big black dog that looks like Marmaduke at the Albergue Español. *Rrruff.*

■ Near Misahuallí

JATÚN SACHA

Big forest. That's what you'll find at the Jatún Sacha Biological Station, and coinciden-tally, that's the Quichua meaning of the name. Located 8km east of Misahuallí, right off the south bank road of the Napo River, this 1437-hectare (3300-acre) tropical wet forest reserve is still 70% primary growth. Refreshingly enough, Jatún Sacha is com-pletely Ecuadorian owned and run, and in 1993 was named the world's second Inter-national Children's Rainforest. It also has tons of medicinal plants, a canopy of hillside trees, plenty of reptiles, and an alien empire in the form of insects galore. Founded in 1986, Jatún Sacha's aims both to conserve the incredible biodiversity of the land and to provide a window to it for researchers, especially Ecuadorian ones. Thus, as **Ale-jandro Suárez,** the long-haired, English-speaking administrator and co-founder will readily tell you, tourists are not invited to spend the night or even the day if they arrive in large herds. The forest is first and foremost for scientific study. Casual visitors can also benefit from the facilities—well marked paths meander through the forest past an incredible variety of carefully documented flora. The birds seem to love this peaceful place as well—to get a better view of Jatan Sacha's winged visitors, ask to be allowed up the station's 100 ft. bird observation tower. The facilities can accommodate 35 visitors and 13 long-term residents at once. A new part of the complex, the dining hall offers three safe *and* tasty meals each day. Bunk beds in screened *cabañas,* with nearby latrines, showers, and a supply of rainwater for hand-washing round out the amenities. **Buses** running between Tena and Ahuano can drop visitors off right in front of Jatún Sacha (from Tena, 1¼hr., s/3,500). The **entrance fee** is US$6 for foreigners and s/10,000 for nationals. Meals cost s/8,000 for everyone. One night's stay, including three meals and the reserve entry fee, is US$20 for foreigners, and s/25,000 for nationals. To contact the reserve or make research reservations, the **Quito address** is: Fundación Jatún Sacha, Casilla 17-12-867 (tel./fax 441-592; email dneill@isacha.ecx.ec). The **Tena address** is: Casilla 15-01-218. Crafts and t-shirts sold on-site support the reserve. But there's more than one way to support the biological station. Rejected non-"scientists" and travelers seeking more comfortable accommodations can head to the downright luxurious **Cabañas Alinahui,** 3km down the road to the east of Jatún Sacha (follow the signs; 1hr. walk). With an office in Quito, Río Coca 1734 and Isla Fernandina (tel. 253-267; fax 253-266), the *cabañas* help fund the reserve. The eight spacious cabins, raised on stilts above a hammock-blessed patio, each have two rooms that share a bath (one has hot water). Conference room, bar, and library are all in the package, but the price is certainly beyond budget—US$45 per person, including 3 meals per day; plus 20% in taxes; 10% discount for nationals.

LA PUNTA AND AHUANO

In mathematics, a point is a location that contains nothing at all. The Ecuadorian equivalent, **La Punta,** lies on the southern bank of the Río Napo about 10km east of Jatún Sacha, along the same dirt road. The tranquil *pueblito* of **Ahuano,** down the river and around the bend, can be accessed from here by motorized canoe for about s/3,000. Boat drivers often ask more from gringos, but hold out for the fair price.

With neither road access nor tour industries, there is actually little reason to visit Ahuano itself—it's the nearby resorts that really attract visitors. **Hotel Anaconda** and **Hotel Jaguar,** two moderate options upstream, feed on the reputations of the least common and most exotic animals of the Oriente. But Ahuano's most conspicuous specimen is **Hostería La Casa del Suizo.** You'll catch your first jaw-dropping glimpse when your canoe rounds the bend to Ahuano. There, on a bluff overlooking the Amazon, rests the decadent splendor of this wealthy traveler's paradise. Use of the topaz-blue pool, polished bamboo doors, and winding wooden staircases costs over US$70 per night. The well-monied can make reservations in Quito, at Reina Victoria 1235 and Lizardo García; post address Casilla 17-21-1608 (tel. 509-115 or 508-871; fax 508-872). Visitors rarely stay in Ahuano, but **accommodations** are there for the taking. **La Posada de Mama Aida** is on the road adjacent to the spot where the boats from La Punta pull up. The namesake is an endearingly protective old woman who has four immaculate beds upstairs, above the family's *comedor.* For a bed and three meals Mama Aida asks about s/40,000, but negotiation is possible. **Lojanito,** two doors inland, offers beds in much darker, cell-like rooms for about s/15,000 per person.

▓ Coca

The easternmost urban outpost of the Napo province, Coca (also known as Puerto Francisco de Orellana) has two histories that add up to one identity crisis. The first settlement was a tranquil jungle town seated 260m above sea level, where the Ríos Napo, Payamino, and Coca come together. This original Coca developed in the early 20th century, when its pioneer residents built a hospital, schools, and churches, and grew to a whopping population of 300. Then it happened. In the pivotal year of 1969, foreigners from the north found a wealth of bubbling ooze underground. With an eye for the black gold, oil tycoons decided not to sip but to chug this Texas tea.

Within a few years, Coca's population doubled and its landscape changed forever. Roads tore into the jungle and newly-erected pumps drained the land, filling the pockets of oil entrepreneurs. Whether you call them exploiters or sound economists, outsiders have transformed Coca into a gritty, dirty, riverside pit. Recently, the unmarked streets have been muddy disasters—the soggy, sticky result of an over-ambitious water-purification project. Regardless of the city's aesthetic, Coca is significant for travelers because tours often begin and end at this Oriente outpost.

ORIENTATION

The roughly gridded city has no street names or helpful vantage points, so orientation is a challenge. From the bus terminal in the north, **Calle Napo,** the principal mud-laden tourist drag, extends eight blocks to the **Río Napo,** the town's southern boundary. Another important road perpendicular to the riverfront is **Amazonas,** which dead-ends at the dock a block east of Calle Napo. The parallel **Tena-Lago Agrio Road** enters the town from the north, curves around, and eventually straightens out one block east of Amazonas. It then crosses the river to the **military camp. Hotel El Aura,** north along Calle Napo, six blocks south of the bus terminal, is a helpful landmark.

PRACTICAL INFORMATION

Tourist Office: Coca doesn't have a CETUR, but it does have an **INEFAN,** or *Instituto Ecuatoriano Forestal de Areas Naturales* (tel. 880-171), at the northern end of Amazonas bordering the airfield. Helpful info on nearby parts of the jungle, in Spanish only. Open Mon.-Fri. 8am-12:30pm and 1:30-5pm.

Currency Exchange: Hotel El Aura exchanges cash, but traveler's checks are a trickier matter. Ask around, but don't hold your breath.

Airport: The airstrip is on the highway, about 1km north of the river. It is also accessible by walking across the runway from behind the municipal building on Napo, 7 blocks from the river. Taxis from the center cost s/5,000. **AEROGAL** offers flights to **Quito** (Mon.-Fri. 11:30am, US$53), with **Guayaquil** connections from there. **Air Force planes** (FAE) take civilian passengers to Tena (Wed. 12:30pm, s/42,000).

Buses: The **terminal terrestre** is on Calle Napo, 8 blocks north of the river. **Transportes Jumandi** heads to **Tena** (8, 10am, noon, 6, and 10pm, 6hr., s/20,000). **Transportes Baños** (tel. 880-182), runs 2 routes to **Quito:** one goes north (7, 10:15am, 2, and 6pm, 12hr., s/30,000) through **Lago Agrio** (2hr., s/6,000); the other goes south (9am, 7, 8, 9, 9:30, and 10pm, 10hr., s/30,000) through **Loreto** (2hr., s/6,000). Buy a ticket beforehand for the trip to Quito only. **Transportes Petrolera Shushufindi** (tel. 839-310), goes back and forth to **Lago Agrio** (7, 8, 10am, 1:30, and 2:30pm, 3hr., s/8,000). Less comfortable open-air *rancheras* (farm vehicles) leave for Lago Agrio about every half hour. **Trans Esmeraldas** (tel. 881-309), goes to **Quito** (8:20 and 9:15pm, 10hr., s/30,000) via **Loreto** (2hr., s/7,000) and **Baeza** (7hr., s/20,000); ticket necessary only for Quito. **Transportes Zaracay** (tel. 881-191), goes to **Guayaquil** (3:30pm, 15hr., s/45,000) via **Santo Domingo** (10hr., s/30,000) and **Quevedo** (12hr., s/39,000).

Boats: Also known as the marina of Puerto Francisco de Orellana, Coca sees its share of boat traffic. Most tourist traffic on the river comes from organized tours, so travelers don't have to worry about prices or times. All boats on the river, whether coming or going, must record the names and passport numbers of all foreign passengers at the **Capitañia,** a government office right on the water at the end of Amazonas. Motorized canoes head downriver on Mon. and Thurs. at 8am, and return on Sun. and Wed. Destinations are **Hacienda Primavera** (s/17,600), **Pompeya** and **Limoncocha** (s/24,000), and **Panacocha** (s/49,500). Schedules may change due to variation in demand and water conditions. You can always hire a boat yourself, but this won't be affordable unless you're putting together a group.

Taxis: White jungle trucks, rather than normal taxis, reign supreme, but they are difficult to get late at night (about s/3,000 between any two points in the *centro*).

Library: (tel. 880-148 or 880-445), on the 4th floor terrace of the municipal building, 7 blocks north of the river on Napo. Open 8am-noon and 2-6pm.

Pharmacies: Farmacía Oriental, on Espejo between Amazonas and Napo, is a block from the waterfront. Open daily 7am-8pm. **Farmacía Bristol** (tel. 881-260), is next to Hotel El Aura on Napo. Open 8am-1pm and 2-10:30pm.

Clinic: Clínica Sinai, Napo and Morena (tel. 880-401). Costly, but the only reliable source of health care in Coca. Open 24hr. Lab open daily 11am-8pm.

Emergency: (tel. 880-101).

Police: Policía Nacional, Napo and Rocafuerte (tel. 880-525 or 880-101).

Post Office: At the southern end of Av. 9 de Octubre, by the river, 3 blocks west of Napo. Open sporadically Wed.-Fri. 8am-4pm.

Telephones: EMETEL (tel. 880-104), 1 block south and 3 blocks west of Hotel El Cluca, is under the big tower. No long-distance service, even with toll-free access numbers. Open Mon.-Sat. 8-11am, 1-5pm, and 6-9pm, Sun. 8-11am and 6-9pm.

Telephone Code: 06.

ACCOMMODATIONS

A few respectable hotels cluster on Calle Napo around the Hotel El Aura. Dank, simple cheapies hover close to the waterfront. The only other frequented tourist area of the city is just down the tiny street, Malecón, that veers off to the left before the bridge, where the **Hotel Oasis** and **Hostería La Misión** set up their quarters.

Hotel Oasis (tel. 880-164; fax 880-206), on Malecón on the river, 50m down the narrow left branch before the bridge. Climb up to the 2nd story of this getaway to escape the muddy quicksand of the rest of the city. Beds are fluffed, floors swept spotless, and private baths (in all rooms) well-scrubbed. Fans in all rooms. Often houses pre-packaged tour groups from Quito. A bargain at s/15,000 per person.

Hotel El Aura, Av. Napo and García Moreno (tel. 880-127), 6 blocks south of the *terminal.* A married couple runs this commune of red-roofed bungalows. Spider monkeys and parrots inhabit the garden courtyard with excellent Spanish accents. While it's *the* place for backpacking budget travelers to gather in the morning to form tour groups, El Aura refreshingly does not run its own tour operation. *Cabañas* vary in size; all have private baths. Singles s/35,000; doubles s/60,000.

FOOD

El Escondite, on Napo near Autica. Owned by a friendly Torontonian, *El Escondite* serves *típicos,* but in a form that tourists will find satisfyingly familiar and safe. *Almuerzos* and *meriendas* s/10,000. A *very* Canadian pancake breakfast (including bacon, of course) s/8,000. Open daily 7am-9pm.

Cevichería Macarena, on Alfaro between Quito and Av. 9 de Octubre. Their *encebollade* (fish soup with onions, s/7,000) is the favored hangover remedy for many locals, but it's fantastic any time—make sure to use the traditional fixin's (plantains, lime, hot sauce). The *ceviche* may be a little riskier. Open daily 7am-5pm.

Gran Chaparal, on Espejo, between Quito and Av. 9 de Octubre. Full of foreigners, but no tourists, this meat and rice joint is a favorite hang-out of imported oil workers. Dish of meat, rice, and beans, with cola, s/10,000. Open daily 3pm-midnight.

Restaurant Dayuma, in Hotel El Aura, invites anyone to grab a sound portion of *comida típica.* Slightly inflated prices and brusque service reflect its mainstream tourist status. American breakfast s/7,000, shrimp cocktail s/15,000, *arroz con legumbres* s/12,000. Open daily 6:30am-10pm, closed midday on Sun.

JUNGLE TOURS FROM COCA

Coca's location, farther *al oriente* than Tena or Misahuallí, makes it a good base for trips to the more isolated parks, reserves, and deep-jungle communities of the indigenous **Huaorani.** The still-untamed region east of Coca is home to some of the most remote indigenous communities and densest biodiversity in the world, but in an ironic misfortune, it's also home to Ecuador's most lucrative natural resource in the technological age—oil. Both the *indígenas* and the wildlife thrive in isolation, but exploitation of the oil reserves inevitably puts an end to this confinement. In addition to the toxic waste spills into the region's waterways, oil companies are responsible for most of the road construction that opens the land up to further development.

Industry and nature have always been quarrelsome neighbors, and the tourist industry is no exception. Despite universal claims of ecologically responsible tourism, the tours that stream into the jungle and down rivers and industry-made roads have had ill effects on the area (see **Environmentally Responsible Tourism,** p. 35). True, eco-tourism is an important part of sustaining the jungle, as it allows the local populations to earn a living without destroying the forest. Similarly, if you plan to visit some of the local Huaorani villages, avoid disrupting their community by making sure your guide has received permission to enter from the tribe.

While it is possible in theory to make excursions from Coca without a guide, this is probably not a good idea as it will take far longer to get around, and you will be unlikely to find any of the wildlife that you came all this way to see. A handful of villages and natural areas down the Río Napo are favorite tour destinations from Coca. A relatively short distance downstream, the **Reserva Biológica Limoncocha** and the mission towns of **Pompeya** and **Limoncocha** often make their way onto tour groups' itineraries. These days you don't even have to float to get there, courtesy of the road that the oil industry has cut past Limoncocha into "pristine oil country." **Pañacocha,** another nature reserve on the Río Napo, about halfway between Coca and Nueva Rocafuerte, is a popular tour destination. *Cocha* is Quechua for lagoon, and *paña* means piranha; that should give you an idea of what's there. The sprawling swamp has enough plant and animal species to make any biologist's millennium. Canoes wind their way through murky waterways and hikers wind their way through murky trails. **Cabañas Pañacocha** offers housing for tours; entrance is s/40,000, standard for all nature reserves in the area. Even farther downriver, rumored to be accessible to tourists by 1998, lurks the immense, isolated **Yasuní National Park** (p. 228). To the south of Coca, the village of **Tiputini,** on the Río Tiputini, is one of the closest Huaorani communities to Coca and consequently one of the most touristed.

Tours offered from Coca vary greatly in price and quality. Part of the expense is the s/40,000 **entrance fee** for each protected natural reserve on the tour. Some guides calculate their prices with this amount included, while others clearly state that it is additional. Either way, the INEFAN office in Coca strongly suggests that at least one person from your group accompany the guide to INEFAN to pay the required amount. It's a jungle out there, and INEFAN can't easily know how many people enter each area. By fudging the numbers, guides have been known to embezzle sucres meant for the reserves and parks. Check out a number of tour companies and make sure you find one that seems reputable. Recommended guides include: **Randy Smith,** a Canadian who has lived and worked with the Huaorani for years and can be found at **Amazon Jungle Adventures** (below); **Luis García,** who works out of Coca but may be contacted through **Emerald Forest Expeditions** in Quito (tel. (02) 526-403); and **Juan Medina,** who may be contacted through Baños's **Vasca Tour Travel Agency** (tel. (03) 740-147). Among the locals, indigenous guide **Ernesto Juanalea** and his son **Patricio** are good, and may be found through the Hotel Auca.

If camping out in the jungle sounds a little too intimidating, try visiting one of the wilderness lodges that sit a few hours downriver from Coca. The **Yuturi Lodge,** which operates out of Hotel Oasis (or can be reached in Quito, at Amazonas 1324 and Colón; tel. (02) 504-037), comes highly recommended for its five-day, four-night tours; all inclusive packages start at the not-so-low price of US$200 (US$290 including round-trip airfare from Quito).

Selva Tour (tel. 880-336 or Quito tel. 659-311). Easily contacted through Hotel El Aura, experienced director Whymper Jones leads his own tours to Pañacocha, Limoncocha, Yasuní, and wherever else. Groups of 5-10 people, 2+ days. US$45 per person per day, including food and transportation.

Ejarsytur (tel. 880-251), across from the Hotel Oasis near the bridge. In Quito at Jorge Washington and Amazonas (tel. (02) 569-852; fax 223-245). Julio Jarrín and his team of guides bring groups to Pañacocha, Yasuní, Tiputini, Cuyabeno, and other locations, depending on duration of the trip. Boat transport, cabins, food (vegetarian possible), and hikes included in the hefty US$80 per person per day.

Yuturi Jungle Adventure operates out of Hotel Oasis (in Quito, Amazonas 1324 and Colón; tel./fax 504-037, 503-225, or 544-166). Organizes 4- to 5-day jungle tours that leave from Quito. Recommended for tasty food, comfy lodging, and guiding expertise. Price varies by season (Dec., July-Aug. are busiest), group size, and duration. A 5-day, 4-night tour for 7-10 people, peak season, runs US$290 per person.

Amazon Jungle Adventures (tel. 880-606; fax 880-451). Operated out of Pappa Dan's bar on the waterfront, this English-speaking agency has built up experience in Pañacocha and other parts of the Oriente near Coca. One of the North American owners, Michael Muzzo, is the son of Pappa Dan himself. Half- or full-day, appropriate meals always included. Mailing address: P.O. Box 17-21-841, Quito.

■ Near Coca: Parque Nacional Yasuní

Coca is the push-off point to mainland Ecuador's largest national park, the 982,000-hectare Parque Nacional Yasuní. This is **Amazon River** country, with the Tiputini, Nashiño, Cononaco, Yasuní, and other tributaries coursing through the park's enormous expanse. Yasuní has three major habitats: dry land, sometimes-flooded land, and always-flooded land. While the rainforest is understandably wet year-round, the region's seasons still alternate between dry (Dec.-March), rainy (April-July), and unstable (Aug.-Nov.). Founded in 1979, Yasuní includes the greatest biodiversity in the country. The **Huaorani tribe** is as natural a part of the park as the wildlife; hunting and living off the land, they call this protected tropical jungle home. They are not alone; boa constrictors, alligators, jaguars, eels, parrots, toucans, piranhas, capybaras, monkeys, and sloths are just a few of the animals that share Yasuní. In spite of this biodiversity and the park's legally-protected status, the government has chosen to ignore the recent proliferation of a newly introduced species, *Oilus maximus,* which flattens paths across pristine jungle, before plunging its trunk-like mouth deep into the earth, sucking petroleum pools dry.

INEFAN has yet to organize a management system for the Parque Nacional Yasuní; it's simply too massive. A force of only 10 rangers controls activity within the sprawling park. Because of this ridiculously inadequate situation, INEFAN recently closed Yasuní to tourists temporarily—not in an attempt to discourage visitation, but to prepare the park for more orderly tourist traffic. This state of affairs has continued for a couple of years now, despite INEFAN's promises of its imminent reopening. To find out if tourists are permitted in the park, contact Parque Nacional Yasuní's **INEFAN** office in Coca (tel. 880-171), on the north end of Amazonas, next to the airport.

▓ Lago Agrio

A young city with a story, Lago Agrio is testament to exactly what is in a name. Way up north in Texas, an American city is named with its English translation, Sour Lake. That spot brought the Texaco conglomerate its first oil fortune, so it was only fitting that in the 1960s, when Texaco struck the jackpot at this location in Ecuador, they named it Lago Agrio. Though a community of Loja pioneers existed here prior to the oil pipes, Lago Agrio was very little before it was an oil town, and not surprisingly, the name has stuck. Ask locals nowadays, and many will claim that the source of the title is a nearby lake with green waters like a bitter lemon. This type of mix-up epitomizes the confusion of an Ecuadorian city developed by outsiders for foreign reasons, foreign buyers, and foreign motivations. Since 1989, Lago Agrio has been the capital of the Sucumbíos province, an area that was home to the Confane, Siona, Secoya, and Shuar *indígenas* long before Texaco, or any other oil interest, claimed a stake here. But despite the city's history of indigenous influences, oil transformed Lago Agrio into what it is today—strips of three-story banks, hotels, restaurants, and grocery stores, not to mention plenty of tour agencies and services. Close to the Colombian border and Parque Nacional Cuyabeno, Lago Agrio is more often a base for jungle tours or a destination en route than anything else.

ORIENTATION

Lago Agrio's main road is the east-west **Avenida Quito,** which runs from the **airstrip,** 5km to the east, and forks at the market, forming the southern branch of **Avenida Río Amazonas.** The **market** is a triangular area formed by the fork of Quito and Amazonas, and the north-south **Avenida 12 de Febrero,** one block west. **Francisco de Orellana** is parallel to and one block west of Av. 12 de Febrero. In the absence of a bus terminal, most bus *cooperativos* line up on Quito, to the east of the market; this is the most bustling area in town and has all you'll need for your (hopefully) short stay.

PRACTICAL INFORMATION

Tourist Information: INEFAN, Manabí and Av. 10 de Agosto (tel. 830-129). Open Mon.-Fri. 8am-noon and 2-6pm.

Immigration Office: Av. Quito and Manabí, in police station, across from market.

Colombian Consulate: Av. Quito 441 (tel. 830-084). Along with the immigration office, the consulate has info concerning the dangerous Colombian border crossing 20km north of Lago Agrio. Most Ecuadorians warn against crossing the border there, communicating the danger with a hand gesture across the throat.

Currency Exchange: Banco de Prestamos, Av. Quito (tel. 830-582), 100m east of the fork, changes cash or traveler's checks. OK rates. Open Mon.-Fri. 9:30am-3pm.

Airport: Located 5km east of the city center (s/5,000 taxi ride). TAME has flights to **Quito** (Mon.-Sat. 12:30pm, 30min., US$53). Flights from Quito to Lago Agrio (every Mon.-Sat. 11:30am). Book ahead, especially Mon.—these flights are often filled with package-tour groups. For more info, the **TAME office** is at Av. 9 de Octubre and Manabí (tel. 830-113).

Buses: All buses have their offices within a block of the Hotel D'Mario. For some reason, long-distance buses from Lago Agrio are more luxurious than others in the country, and companies are sometimes reluctant to sell tickets for intermediate spots en route to the final destination, so even if you don't plan to ride a bus to its last stop, be prepared to pay for the entire distance. **Transportes Esmeraldas** (tel. 830-161), has luxury buses with bathroom, TV, videos, and snacks to **Quito** (1:35 and 9:30pm, 8hr., s/30,000) via **Baeza** (s/20,000). **Transportes Occidental** (tel. 830-736), goes to: **Quito** (10pm, 8hr., s/30,000); **Guayaquil** (8pm, 16hr., s/45,000) via **Santo Domingo** (10hr., s/35,000); **Quevedo** (12hr., s/38,000); and **Babahoyo** (13hr., s/40,000). **Transportes Baños** (tel. 830-330), serves **Coca** (5, 11am, 3, 6, 7:30, and 8pm, 2hr., s/8,000). **Transportes Putumayo** (tel. 830-034), in the deep garage at Av. 12 de Febrero, also goes to **Quito** (6, 8:30, 10am, 7:15, 8:15, 9, 9:30, and 10:30pm, s/30,000). **Transportes Zaracay** runs to **Guayaquil** (14hr., s/32,000) and **Santo Domingo** (4:30pm, 11hr., s/35,000) via **Quito** (8hr., s/30,000). **Cooperativa Loja** heads to: **Loja** (1pm, 24hr., s/75,000); **Guayaquil** (4 and 7pm, 18hr., s/45,000); and **Quito** (10:45pm, s/30,000). *Rancheras* leave approx. every 30min. for **Coca** (s/8,000); they also make occasional trips toward the *parque;* ask at any of the bus companies for more info.

Taxis: Cabs take the form of yellow trucks and congregate at the fork.

Library: Casa de la Cultura, Av. 12 de Febrero and Jorge Añasco (tel. 830-624), 1 block from Av. Quito, hiding behind a fence. Open Mon.-Fri. 8am-5pm.

Pharmacy: Attached to Clinic Gonzales, **Farmacía International,** Av. Quito (tel. 830-038), near Av. 12 de Febrero. Open daily 7:30am-10pm. Part of the *de turno* system, so there is always a pharmacy in town that is open late.

Hospital: Hospital Lago Agrio, Av. Quito (tel. 830-198), about 500m west of the market, but local residents don't trust the local hospital. Those with enough cash and concern for their own well-being should try the **Clínica Gonzales,** Av. Quito (tel. 830-133), near Av. 12 de Febrero. Open 24hr.

Police: Av. Quito and Manabí (tel. 830-101), across from the market. Considered to be more competent than many of their counterparts elsewhere in Ecuador because of the high and serious crime rate they are forced to deal with.

Post office: Rocafuerte (tel. 830-115), just off Av. 12 de Febrero. Has a Lista de Correos. Open Mon.-Fri. 8am-noon and 1-6pm, but not always punctual.

Telephone: EMETEL, Av. Quito and Orellana (tel. 830-104 or 830-040). Open Mon.-Sat. 8am-10pm, Sun. 8am-noon and 8-10pm.

Phone code: 06.

ACCOMMODATIONS

Hotel Guacamago, Av. Quito, about 100m east of the fork. No matter what your price range, the Guacamago will find a room for you, ranging from one with 4 white walls and a bed (s/15,000 per person) to the decadent rooms with A/C, TV, phone, private bath, and big beds (s/30,000 per person).

Hotel D'Mario, Av. Quito 175 (tel. 830-172; fax 830-456), about 50m east of the fork. The street-level restaurant makes this hotel a tourist hive. Rooms are all refreshingly clean and well-cared for, with private baths and fans. Call for reservations, as it sometimes fills up. Usually very secure, and that means something here. Singles s/28,000; doubles s/40,000, with A/C, TV, and an extra-big bed s/45,000.

Hotel Oro Negro, Av. Quito (tel. 830-174), across the street from D'Mario. Named for the town's crude sustenance, this hotel houses mainly tourists, not drillers. Beds draped lavishly in grand mosquito nets; each floor fitted with communal bath, with toilets and shower stalls galore. Rooms s/15,000 per person.

Hotel Secoya, Av. Quito 222 and Amazonas (tel. 830-451), at the fork. Head up a vertiginous spiral staircase, then re-orient yourself on the 2nd fl. landing with patio, TV area, and 2 rows of spacious, fan-equipped rooms. Singles s/20,000, with bath s/25,000, with TV s/30,000. It's worth bargaining.

FOOD

Pizza Restaurant D'Mario, Av. Quito (tel. 830-172), in the eponymous hotel. This sidewalk restaurant feeds most of the gringos in town. White and sanitary decor reflects the food quality. Curried rice, s/11,000, fried chicken s/12,000. *Desayuno, almuerzo, merienda* each s/8,000. Open daily 7am-11pm.

Cevicheria Delfin, Añasco and Pasaje Gonzabana, around the corner from D'Mario. Don't worry, the only *delfin* at this popular *cevichería* is on the sign out front. Ever-changing variety of *ceviches* and *enceballados* (s/12,000) rumored to be the best in town. Open Mon.-Sat. 7am-5pm.

Restaurante Alexander, Av. Quito (tel. 831-468), near Av. 12 de Febrero. A bit dim, this spacious a la carte restaurant also cooks up *desayunos, almuerzos,* and *meriendas* for s/8,000 each. *Arroz con pollo* s/15,000. Open daily 6am-midnight.

Araza Hotel Restaurant, Av. Quito and Guayaquil (tel. 830-223). These overpriced dishes are probably the best in town, considering the extravagant clients tossing money to and fro. Most *platos* s/24,000. Open daily 7am-9pm.

JUNGLE TOURS FROM LAGO AGRIO

For most foreigners, Lago Agrio's charm lies not in its black, sticky oil, but in its mind-boggling natural surroundings. To the east of town, vast expanses of jungle resonate with the cries of monkeys, calls of birds, and chirps of so many insects that their diversity leaves the most ardent bug enthusiasts speechless. Rivers flow silently throughout the rainforest, swallowing the ripples left by alligators and monkey-munching anacondas. The area around Lago Agrio sees little hunting, despite the fact that several native and still-traditional tribes (like the colorful Cofanes and the formerly head-shrinking Shuars) continue to make a natural living off the jungle. Some of the tours that leave from Lago Agrio visit these native communities; as in other parts of the Oriente, each tourist must make the difficult decision whether or not to take part in this interesting but unavoidably invasive practice. Jungle tours often cruise the **Río Aguarico,** which runs near the city, and on to more remote areas, passing some indigenous villages along the way. The lagoons of **Lagartacocha** (alligator lagoon), **Limoncocha,** and **Pañacocha** please visitors particularly interested in experiencing oodles of wildlife; the last two are also accessible from Coca. The **Reserva de Produción Faunística Cuyabeno,** the mother of all wildlife areas in the Ecuadorian Oriente, lies two and a half hours east of Lago Agrio by truck (see below).

The most dependable way to plunge into the jungle east of Lago Agrio is to hire a tour guide from a reputable agency in Baños or Quito. This expensive proposition often disheartens budget travelers. Many cheaper tour operations are based in Lago Agrio; some are unlicensed or unqualified (and technically illegal). INEFAN officials have been known to check for credentials when tour groups enter nationally protected areas, and in these cases, unapproved tours are routinely turned away. Even if you make it into the park, a second-rate guide won't be of much use. Check the list of the INEFAN-approved agencies in the **Appendix** (p. 320). The current favorite in trips to Cuyabeno is **Native Life Tours,** Pinta 446 and Amazonas (tel. (02) 550-836), in Quito. Guide owned and operated, they run 5- to 8-day trips into the park. The popular 5-day trip costs US$260 per person, with a 10% discount for SAEC members. Recent Native Life clients rave about the piranha-fishing and monkey-watching experiences, but complain that the group size of 12 is a little too big for wandering in the jungle. For advice on a tour agency, SAEC members can consult trip reports in Quito for jungle tours in the Sucumbíos province. For the most up-to-date info and additional questions, INEFAN has offices in Lago Agrio (see **Practical Information,** p. 229), in Tarapoa en route to Cuyabeno, and at the bridge entrance to Cuyabeno.

■ Near Lago Agrio: Reserva de Producción Faunística Cuyabeno

When God created the animals of the earth, He must have stopped for a picnic in Cuyabeno. He looked at what He had made—giant armadillos, boa constrictors, electric eels, alligators, freshwater dolphins, spiders, monkeys, tapirs, land tortoises, piranhas—and it was good. Far to the east, past the Limoncocha mission and the Pañacocha lagoon, this 603,400-hectare wildlife reserve claims a proliferant chunk of the Sucumbíos province. The reserve was established in order to give Mother Nature some living space. Cuyabeno's organic orchestra perpetually plays a screeching symphony; howling monkeys and buzzing bugs replace dog barks and engine roars. The flora blooms and thrives as well, from joltingly colorful fruits and splashy flowers to enormous green leaves and fronds. A network of tributaries stems from **Río Aguarico** and **Río Cuyabeno,** and parades of wildlife follow the rivers as they flow into the reserve's **14 lagoons.** The park also encloses the homelands of indigenous communities, such as the **Siona, Secoya,** and **Shuar.** The *other* human presence in the reserve has come as a consequence of the oil industry. Over the last 30 years, oil companies have been having their way with the land despite its protected status. The damage here is reportedly less severe than in Parque Nacional Yasuní to the south.

There are several ways to approach the park from Lago Agrio. The drive by truck or bus through Tarapoa to Puenta Cuyabeno is a rough and dusty two and a half hours. This method is often used to access the popular lagoons deep in the bush. Other tours launch into the Río Aguarico, then travel by water through the upper or lower regions of the reserve. Sun block and bug repellant are necessities; exchange leather hiking boots for the big, tough, goofy, yellow boots supplied by many guides. If traveling by river, it's a good idea to do part of the tour by paddle canoe, since motors chopping through the rivers seem like little earthquakes to animals up ahead. For information on arranging a tour, see **Jungle Tours from Lago Agrio,** p. 230.

▓ Baeza

Officially a part of the Oriente, Baeza puts on the convincing facade of a Sierra hamlet. The quiet village lounges in a cushion of green mountains at the junction of three roads, known as the **Y de Baeza.** One road leads west to Quito, one south to Tena, and the other east to Lago Agrio. Though it elicits objections from red, blue, and yellow, green is the primary color here; green hills and mountains dominate even the concrete main highways. The town itself sits along a snaking segment of the Tena road, so those traveling between Quito and Lago Agrio don't even see Baeza itself. Not far from Quito and a step up (in altitude) from the jungle, Baeza is a pleasant stop on the way to or from the Oriente. Here, away from crowds, there's nothing to do but enjoy the coolness and scenery of the mountains. A major source of local entertainment is volleyball, but there are also trails leading through the forests with animals ranging in stature from awe-inspiring bears to delicate and fascinating butterflies. One recommended trail takes off from the end of the first road heading right as you come from the Y in Old Baeza. Follow this road up and up until it turns into a path up the mountain.

Orientation and Practical Information Heading southeast on the Tena road from the Y, **Baeza Vieja** (Old Baeza) appears first. Two roads head off to the right from the main Tena one, leading through some old buildings to a plaza in front of a small church. The main road twists over a river and leads to **Baeza Nueva** (New Baeza) as it becomes **Avenida de Los Quijos,** which runs straight through the length of New Baeza. **EMETEL,** Av. de los Quijos and Av. 17 de Enero (tel. 580-651), on the north end of Baeza Nueva, has the only phone number in town, but is fully equipped to make international calls (open Mon.-Sat. 8am-noon, 2-4, and 6-8pm, Sun. 6-8pm). Getting to and from Baeza is a cinch; just head to the Y, about 25 minutes downhill from the new town, and flag down a **bus** heading in the right direction. Traffic is fairly constant from 7am-midnight, with early buses to **Quito** (3hr.) passing through at 3 and 5am. Buses pass about every half-hour, but keep in mind that they may be full and simply pass you by. To **Tena** (2hr.), and **Lago Agrio** (6hr.). The **Hospital Estatal Baeza** (tel. 671-324), about 30m east down the street crossing Avenida de los Quijos by Hotel Samay and the *colegio,* is always open for emergencies. The **pharmacy** is next door (open daily 7:30am-noon and 1-4:30pm). The **police** are at the Y, and are supposedly always on call, though they may step out from time to time. Baeza does not have a **post office.**

Accommodations and Food Places to sleep and eat in Baeza are not overwhelming, but they're pleasant and safe along with the rest of the town. **Hostal San Rafael,** at the south end of New Baeza's Av. de los Quijos on the right as you come from the Y, has a clean, energetic atmosphere with tiled floors, colorful beds, and a woody living room. With communal bath and meals cooked to order on request, shared rooms cost s/15,000 per person. Slightly less expensive, **Hotel Samay,** in the New Baeza strip, on the right side on the road towards Tena, has wooden rooms that creak just a bit. Not much there, but not much to object to either. Communal baths are adequate, hot shower available downstairs (s/10,000 per person). Across the way in Baeza Vieja, **Hostal El Nogal de Jumandy,** above the Tena road, the second right if you're coming from the Y, is a bit run-down, but has a cool jungle house feel with great views from wooden balconies. Communal bath (hot showers s/1,000; rooms s/10,000 per person). **El Restaurante Gina,** the choice dining spot in Baeza, is on the same street as Hostal Jumandy. Run by the people from the Mesón, the savory and elegant *desayunos, almuerzos,* and *meriendas* are all s/5,000, and noodles with vegetables are s/8,000 (open daily 7am-10pm). In New Baeza, **Restaurante El Viejo,** Av. 17 de Enero off Av. de los Quijos, gives special attention to travelers. Glowing wicker lamps illuminate the slightly Polynesian setting. The three daily staples each cost s/5,000, *churrasco* s/10,000.

■ Near Baeza

VOLCÁN REVENTADOR

As Ecuadorian peaks go, Volcán Reventador is a baby giant. While more dormant volcanoes long ago settled into their habitat grooves, this hybrid of highland and jungle experienced some maturing eruptions in the late 1970s. The burst of magma shook the mountain so hard that it broke open, leaving slick beds of hardened lava on the floor of the wet, muddy jungle that lines its slopes. The 3562m green cone rises symmetrically between two mountain ridges, visible from Baeza, 50km to the southwest.

Like its jungle companion, the isolated Volcán Sumaco, Volcán Reventador guarantees a strenuous, messy climb through thick vegetation and slippery dried lava. Just finding the trailhead is confusing. The climb begins along the Baeza-Lago Agrio road, about two hours northeast of Baeza or four hours west of Lago Agrio by bus, just to the east of the **Río Reventador bridge.** Usually hidden by clouds and nasty weather, the volcano lies to the north of the road. If the bus driver doesn't know where the **oil pipeline** that crosses the street is, it's best to just get off the bus at the bridge and walk east up the road for 10 to 15 minutes until you reach it. You should be able to see the lower piping section from the bridge. Walk to the pipeline and follow it left for 20 to 30 minutes, up to a set of worn out **wooden steps** that cross the pipeline. There is not much of a trail to this point—just follow the pipeline and use a stick to get rid of all the spider webs you'll walk through. After the steps, keep on the path to the left until it reaches a hut; from there, go around to the right. Where it looks like there are two possible trails to choose from, take the left one. This fairly obvious trail leads through wet mossy forest, past a few lava slides (it may be a bit tough to pick up the trail again at these; just cross and you should find the trail starting again), and continues to the **refuge,** about a three and a half-hour walk. The refuge has no mattress, satellite dish, or Internet hook-up. From the refuge, find the **river** and follow it upstream for about a minute; this is another hard path to find. Look for a faint trail heading toward the forest. The angry volcano seems eager to keep the **crater** to itself. After all, it takes a six-hour hike on this trail to reach it.

The journey to the summit of Reventador is a non-technical climb that takes two to four days. Bring lots of water—at least four liters per person. Boots, machetes, and raingear are key, and a sleeping bag if you plan to spend the night near the top. Despite the fumaroles, it gets frigid up there. The **South American Explorer's Club** can supply current info about the experiences of members who have scaled the peak. The man who works at San Rafael Falls is willing to guide hikers between the 7th and 22nd of every month. Call Juan Velasquez (tel. 544-600) to inquire.

SAN RAFAEL FALLS

The **Cascadas de San Rafael** (San Rafael Falls) are another impressive display of natural beauty on the Baeza-Lago Agrio road. The falls dive down about 1km west of the starting point of the Río Reventador, about two hours east of Baeza or four hours west of Lago Agrio. Bus drivers generally know where to let you off if you ask for *las cascadas;* there is a sign and a little hut at the start of the road down. The trail descends from there, continuing past a bridge over a small waterfall and a little house where you pay to enter (adults s/10,000, children s/5,000). The attendant may not be there, so you might try to find him to pay (in order to further encourage wildlife conservation). The trail continues on to a group of *casitas* to rent (s/25,000). More expensive package deals with transportation included are available through Via Natura, Av. de los Shyris and Rep. de El Salvador (tel. 469-846 or 224-961). Camping is also an option (s/5,000). The hike to the waterfall cuts through thick jungle, with brilliant colored birds, armadillos, butterflies, *cabro de monte,* and other exotic species. The waterfall itself provides an incredible and worthwhile hike.

■ Papallacta

It's been exhausting and messy wherever you've been; dirt-smeared and drained, you're ready for Papallacta. The baby-Baños of Ecuador, this steaming sanctuary hides away in a spectacular Andean valley, one hour west of Baeza and two hours east of Quito. The cloud forest greenery, water piping industry, and especially the blue pools of steamy hot water make up just about all of Papallacta. The town itself is not much to look at—the piping industry sheet metal buildings have a tough time competing with the surrounding Andean mountains for attention. But Papallactans have no trouble luring visitors from all over with their surreal bathing facilities. At the base of the town itself, piping hot **blue pools** beckon through the few run-down buildings (admission s/5,000). Changing stalls, mandatory hot-water showers, and baskets for your belongings are provided (open daily 6am-6pm). One might think nothing could be more perfect, but if they were to hike the 1km up to the **Termas de Papallacta,** the genuine hot springs, they would see their error. The road to these *piscinas* veers

> ### Ribbit!
>
> Posterchildren of the fight to save the South American jungle, Amazonian tree frogs are doted on throughout the world for their surreal and bright coloring. In the Amazon itself, animals and humans alike have learned to keep their distance from these cute little fellows—their skin contains a poisonous chemical that acts as a metabolic suppressant, slowing down the bodily functions of whatever creature has been fool enough to meddle with it. Over the years, the indigenous people of the Oriente have learned to take advantage of this powerful toxin for hunting purposes. Darts dipped in a concoction made with "frog skin juice" are launched through a long tubular blow gun with a carefully timed puff of air. The blowguns are about seven feet long, and weigh a ton, yet hunters often hold them up for hours, waiting for the perfect opportunity to strike. The jungle's beautiful tree *ranas* don't all contain this potent drug, but it's best to leave them all alone, for your own safety as well as theirs.

off the main highway to the left as you enter the town from the west. There is a big sign for it, but in case you somehow miss it, walk about 100m west from Hotel Quito and go right, then up the hill at the sign and restaurants. The first half of this 1km hike is very uphill, but it flattens out a bit for the second half, and you will almost be glad for the extra work when you reach the hot springs—not only is it continually breathtaking, it will heighten your appreciation of such pleasurable relaxation. These pools have a completely different aura than the downtown Papallactan ones. With a resort-like feel, bathing suit-clad locals and tourists run from pool to pool testing the different temperatures, which range from very warm to painfully scalding. A nicer restaurant, changing rooms, more natural pools, and an unblemished scenic view makes for an enchanting but more expensive experience (open daily 5am-10pm, admission s/10,000). The same company that runs Las Termas offers horse riding (s/10,000 for 30min.) and has trails through the mountains' cloud forests.

Papallacta itself is a handful of small buildings including a **police station** (the gray and blue checkpoint on your right as you walk east from Hotel Quito) on the main road that is open 24 hours. The **centro de salud** is at the bottom of the town, to the right of the pools as you face them from the road (it has a pinkish roof). This small health center offers general medical and dental services, with a nurse and assistant always on duty (open daily 8am-4pm). Friendly and helpful, but obviously not the most equipped resource. There are neither phones nor a post office in Papallacta. Getting to and from Papallacta means catching a bus in the right direction—either to Quito or Baeza. Buses leave Quito towards Papallacta at least every hour, and buses heading to Quito through Papallacta come about as frequently. In front of the police station by the stop sign is a good place to flag a bus out of Papallacta towards Baeza, and at the bottom of the road to Las Termas, catch one to Quito.

The **Hotel Quito**, on your right as you enter Papallacta from Quito, is the best budget choice if you stay for the night. The unexciting rooms are generally clean and safe (s/12,000). The shared baths vary in quality—those downstairs have hot showers. Top floor rooms with fireplaces and amazing view are s/25,000. If you have money to spend, stay at **Hostal de Montaña**, by Las Termas. The cheapest room is s/36,000; this place is fancy and secure. There are several hot pools if you don't feel like walking the 45 seconds to Las Termas, a fireplace in the common room, a patio, and a shared bathroom in this deal; with a private bathroom and heater s/50,400. Ask about group rates at their office in Quito, Foch 635 and Reina Victoria #4A (tel. 548-521). **Residencial El Viajero** is your least expensive choice in Papallacta (rooms s/10,000). Small, clean rooms with great vistas and adequate shared bathrooms. **La Quiteña** (in Hotel Quito) offers meals (*almuerzo* s/6,000; open daily 5am-11pm). **Café Canela**, at Las Termas, is more expensive, at s/9,000 for a continental breakfast or s/16,000 for steak, potatoes, rice, and veggies, but offers less pricey foods as well (*empanadas* s/4,000, *llapingachos* s/6,000). **La Alicia**, at El Viajero is stark but cheap—s/4,500 for a hearty *almuerzo*. Snack bars dot Papallacta and the road to Las Termas.

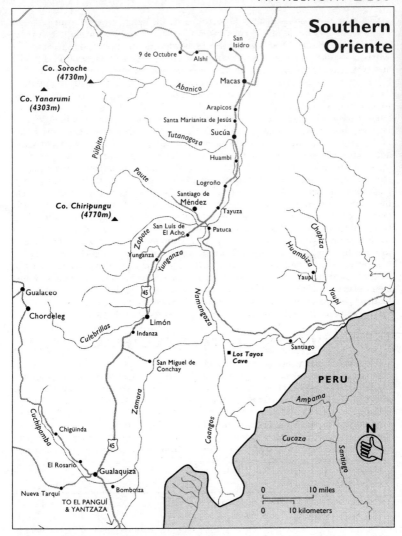

Southern Oriente

THE SOUTHERN ORIENTE

In the shadow of the sharply sloping eastern edge of the southern Andes, leafy palms hide the hot, humid clusters of flat concrete buildings and tin shacks that make up the tiny and hauntingly exotic villages of the Southern Oriente. As Ecuador's frontier has moved eastward, many of these towns have only recently popped up—and utility has governed their architecture. One road connects all: the single treacherous "highway" of the Southern Oriente traverses the land at approximately 1000m, linking the working-class jungle communities with the rural charm that embeds them. These cities and hamlets dot a region blessed by lush primary tropical rain forest and all the glorious wildlife that goes with it. Unfortunately, the land has been equally "blessed" with a swath of gold deposits which have in recent years brought on the destruction of some of its most precious natural treasures. The struggle between miners and conservationists takes on its bleakest incarnations on the battlefields of Parque Nacional Podocarpus and the mining areas near Zamora and Nambija. Meanwhile, a more international conflict broods in the nearby borderland of eastern Morona-Santiago, where a 50-year-old border dispute culminated in a 1995 skirmish between Ecuador and Perú. The turmoil cost Ecuador few lives but much pride.

Meanwhile, connected to the rest of civilization by little more than deep bush trails, the Shuar tribe, former headhunters and headshrinkers, must now content themselves merely to keep alive a liminal form of their distinct version of polytheistic animism. The Shuar still live in traditional log huts deep in the jungle, with little more than bamboo reeds for shelter and dugout canoes for locomotion. Lightweight aircraft carry some of the Southern Oriente's few tourists into Shuar villages from Macas and Sucúa for a glimpse at lives that have remained essentially untouched by technology for the past 500 years. But it does not take an airplane for the observant gringo to glimpse the essence of this hinterland. A good look at the rural highway-stop towns of Gualaquiza, Limón, and Mendez reveals a lifestyle which is perhaps most foreign to the tourist for its friendliness to the outsiders they see so few of: you will not walk past a rugged local without being stared at, but you will then be greeted politely—for God's sake, say "Buenos días" back! If you're willing to endure grueling bus trips over roads more rugged than any terrain on 4WD commercials, in a 1970s school bus, a more penetrating glimpse into the land and people of Ecuador will not be found.

Be aware that during the rainy season, from June to August or so, landslides and their ilk torment the narrow, bumpy, and unpaved roads of the southern Oriente. Don't plan too tight a schedule for yourself; buses are sometimes forced to stop and let their passengers walk a few kilometers to firmer ground. In rare cases, you may end up stranded in a town for a couple days, waiting out torrential rains.

▓ Entering the Southern Oriente

While the well-maintained (mostly) paved Panamerican Highway ferries most tourists north from Loja to Cuenca and beyond, the road from Zamora through Gualaquiza to Macas is more obstacle course than highway. It's occasionally cobblestoned, but usually muddy when it rains, dusty when it doesn't. Should you tire of the drive (as restful as it is), there are a few pleasant, uneventful small towns to wander around in. Stopping in **Yantzaza** and **El Panguí** eases you into the Oriente road system by breaking the trip into two hour segments. And if you miss a direct north-bound bus, it's easy to hop from town to town in smaller, open-air bench-seat buses run by **Transportes Nambija** and other provincial carriers.

YANTZAZA

Yantzaza comes alive for the Sunday market (a rambling collection of food and knick-knack vendors on the southern blocks of Riofrío), but is a typically quiet, small cobblestone-street town the rest of the week. It's flat and not particularly scenic, but offers a variety of services, hotels, and pleasant restaurants. The streets, except for **Juan Riofrío** (the main drag) are unnamed. The environmentalist and nationalist slogans illustrated with student paintings on the walls of the school on the north end of Riofrío offer a glimpse into the ideological side of Ecuadorian education.

EMETEL sets the tone by allowing collect and credit card calls, though the **Banco de Loja** on the corner of the park does not take the hint and won't change dollars or traveler's checks. **Farmacía Rex,** next door to the 24-hour **Policlínico** on the corner of the park, occasionally obliges by changing cash (open daily 8am-7pm). Buses lumber down Riofrío heading north and south, but if you like to plan ahead, the **Pullman Viajaros** and **Transportes Loja** offices on the edge of the park, as well as **Union Yantzaza** further north on Riofrío have schedules to answer your questions.

The restaurants, though uninventive in their cuisine, are better than the hotels in Yantzaza. **Viña de Mar** does not, despite its name and fish-pantry decor, specialize in seafood. In fact, they are frequently out of *corvina* and *camarones*. Soup and meat dish *almuerzos* are s/5,000, while a la carte items hover in the s/9,000-12,000 range (open daily 9am-8pm). **Restaurant Union Yantzaza,** north of Riofrío near the school, offers similar Ecuadorian specialties at identical prices (*almuerzo* s/5,000). The visual atmosphere isn't as stimulating as the oversize shrimp on Viña del Mar's walls, but the olfactory aspects fulfill the nostril's requirements. **El Emperador,** at the corner of the park on Riofrío, roasts chickens for your carnivorous visual satisfaction (s/7,000 for ¼ chicken with all side dishes). From the tools in the courtyard to the tin covering the central patio, **Hotel Amazonas** offers a unique version of the jungle. Small, dark rooms surround the scruffy courtyard, while cold-water common baths are rudimentary and toilet seat-less (s/7,000 per person). **Hotel Central** also suffers from cold-water common baths, but a few rooms have private bathing chambers without curtains. The small rooms have windows to let in light, but the door locks look less than sturdy (s/11,000 per person, with bath s/15,000). **Hotel Inca** (tel. 301-126), has conquered the competition with its color TVs, fans, and clean sheets. The empire crumbles, however, when one notices the scruffy rugs and lack of exterior windows in all rooms with private bath (s/20,000 per person, with bath s/30,000).

EL PANGUÍ

If there weren't so many potholes, El Panguí would be a blip in the banana-plant scenery of the Southern Oriente. But the buses are not exactly speedy, and often stop in this small town. Even more than Yantzaza, tourist-usable services cluster on the main road and more specifically, near the **Union Yantzaza, Cooperativa Nambija,** and **Transportes Loja** bus offices. The **Restaurante Coralito,** across the street from the bus station serves an *almuerzo* (s/5,000) with no surprises. It's *bistec* or *pollo* again, but it's sanitary, smells good, and is appreciated by the locals.

■ Gualaquiza

Hibernating deep in the heart of the southern Oriente, the forgotten jungle town of Gualaquiza lies buried in a den of dramatic tropical hills. As one of the largest towns in the area, it has its share of hotels and restaurants, but as a town off the tourist track, Gualaquiza sees few foreigners walking down its cobblestone streets. The idea that people might come just to enjoy the tranquility and nearby attractions—like the explorable caves at **Nuevo Tarqui,** a **Salesian mission** in Bomboiza, and undisturbed **Inca ruins** at Aguacate—makes people laugh. Curious stares bombard the occasional deviant tourist who braves the Oriente "highway" to reach this hidden city. Although die-hard off-road travelers are attracted to Gualaquiza's remoteness in any season, the town's stunning setting is at its best during May-June and September-October, when the seasons are changing. The October-April summer tends to be swelteringly hot and humid, while June-September tends to be rainy and sometimes cool.

Orientation and Practical Information It doesn't take long to get a feel for Gualaquiza; within an hour or so, you'll know its layout by heart. The main plaza, overseen by the tall white spires of the church, is uncharacteristically not the center of town, but is still a good place to visit and in a town this small, the hotels and restaurants are not far off. **Avenida 24 de Mayo** and **Domingo Comín** run the length of the park on either side, and **Pesantez** and **Ciudad de Cuenca** run uphill along the other edges. Parallel to Comín are **García Moreno, Alfaro,** and **Atahualpa.**

Make credit card and collect calls from **EMETEL,** Ciudad de Cuenca and García Moreno, one block from the park (open Mon.-Sat. 8-11am, 2-5pm, and 7-9pm, Sun. 8-11am and 7-8pm). **Buses** leave from the **terminal terrestre,** Pesantez and 12 de Febrero, three blocks from the plaza. Some run north to **Macas** (2, 6, and 7pm, 8hr., s/20,000), stopping in **Limón** (4hr., s/12,500), **Méndez** (6hr., s/14,300), and **Sucúa** (7hr., s/16,500). Buses go directly to **Cuenca** (7am, 8, and 9pm, 8hr., s/12,000). Buses head south to: **Loja** (2:30, 3, 4, 6am, 12:15, 9, and 10pm, 7hr., s/15,300) via **El Panguí** (1½hr., s/4,000), **Yantzaza** (3½hr., s/7,000), and **Zamora** (5hr., s/10,000).

The **16 de Agosto** company has daily trips to nearby small towns like Nuevo Tarqui, Valle de Quine, and Proveeduna up the river. Be forewarned that the Gualaquiza-Limón ride travels over roads that are horrible in some stretches—not for the weak-stomached. The **Farmacía Central** (tel. 780-203), is on Pesantez and Alfaro (open Mon.-Sat. 8am-10pm, Sun. 8am-1pm). The **hospital** (tel. 780-106), is up toward the church, near the school (open Mon.-Fri. 7am-noon and 2-5pm, 24hr. emergency service). The **police** (tel. 780-101), are located on Pesantez and 12 de Febrero near the **terminal terrestre.** Only extremely unimportant parcels should be mailed from the **post office,** Ciudad de Cuenca and Atahualpa (tel. 780-119), five blocks away from the park (open Mon.-Fri. 8am-noon and 2-5pm). **Jota Be Travel,** Av. 24 de Mayo 08-08 (tel. 780-236), at the main plaza, also sends letters and packages to the United States (letters s/5,000, packages s/17,000 per kg; open Mon.-Sat. 9-11:30am and 2:30-5:30pm, Sun. 9-11am). The **telephone code** is 07.

Accommodations and Food Just so you don't get your hopes up, accept it now: no hotel in Gualaquiza has hot water. **Hostal Guadelupe,** Pesantez and García Moreno (tel. 780-277), is the best-equipped hotel in town. Revel in the fans and private baths, which even include toilet seats, but no shower curtain. Somewhat clean, basic rooms have a mysterious, slightly unpleasant odor (s/10,000 per person, with bath s/12,000). **Residencial Amazonas** has cleaner, airy rooms, but suffers from communal bathrooms with less-than-pristine showers and toilet seat deficiency. The spartan white-walled rooms have windows but lack fans (s/7,000 per person).

At mealtime, head to **Cabaña Los Helechos,** Av. 12 de Febrero and Orellana. Though there's no beach in sight, the bamboo walls and palm-thatched awning over the bar bring the oceanside atmosphere inland (*almuerzo* or *merienda* s/3,500; open daily 8am-10pm). Up the hill on Domingo Comín, the **Bar/Restaurant Oro Verde** offers similar meals, similar views, and similar prices (around s/5,000). When it comes to ambience, you can't lose; choose a pleasant, polished room or the sidewalk (open daily 8am-10pm). The **Restaurant Sabor Latina** (tel. 780-113), serves traditional Latin food in the same building as Hotel Guadeloupe. Locals laud the *almuerzos* and *meriendas* (s/5,000), as well as a la carte entrees (open daily 5am-11pm).

Sights and Entertainment Admire Gualaquiza, but don't expect it to satisfy much more than your eyes. Moderately interesting both culturally and architecturally, the local **church** stands one block up from the main plaza. Diversions by night are sparse unless there's a street *fiesta* or school celebration in town. Overlooking the plaza next to the school, the **Teatro 16 de Agosto** houses occasional movies and events. **Memo's Bar/Cafeteria,** on Pesantez at the plaza, is a late-night hangout where the food and beer (s/3,000) glow in the aura of a huge 30-inch Sony TV, which blazes nightly until the place closes at 10 or 11pm.

But why sit around inside when there are nearby hills to be explored? Don't get lost in the **deserted caves of Nuevo Tarqui,** 15km west of Gualaquiza. A taxi, *camioneta,* or 16 de Agosto bus (s/2,000) can take you to Nuevo Tarqui from Gualaquiza, or you can lace up your walking shoes and make the long jaunt by foot. It's easier to find knowledgeable people in Nuevo Tarqui than Gualaquiza, but if you can't find anyone to give you advice, just head up the hill toward the black holes. Visit the **Salesian Mission of Bomboiza,** a bastion of New World civilization that holds its own against the jungle. This easy-to-reach daytrip lies just off the highway to Zamora. Buses traveling this road can drop you off and often stop to pick passengers up. The tiny village of Proveedoria, ideal for travelers who want to go where few have gone before without overexerting themselves, is just up the river from Bomoiza and can be reached via 16 de Agosto bus (s/2,000). Become the new Indiana Jones for a day with one last crusade, the relatively unexplored **Inca ruins** in the nearby town of **Aguacate.** The adventure starts in Gualaquiza, where you should ask at the bus station, library (near the main plaza), and possibly several *farmacías* to get vague directions on getting there. You'll have a half-day walk there unless you are lucky enough to find one of a rare breed of taxis. But you're guaranteed to be one of the few visitors there.

■ The Road from Gualaquiza to Macas

LIMÓN

Just north of where the road from Cuenca comes in from the west, Limón serves as a common rest-stop for trucks and buses running from Cuenca, Loja, and Zamora north to Macas. Also known as General Leonidas Plaza Gutiérrez, this tiny town has more playing children than running cars in its streets. Removed from the typical tourist track, the sleepy jungle town doesn't have many amenities like private baths, museums, or guided tours, but its quiet, friendly (and curious) attitude toward visitors is an intriguing glimpse into small-town life. The walk along the river is the most scenic part of town, but the architecture looks very postcard-esque too: tiny, tin-roofed houses stick up through the palms and tropical flowers, and precariously balconied houses pile over the river's bank. The houses along cobblestoned **Calle Quito,** the town's main street, are a creative mix of barn wood and cement.

The two streets of importance in Limón, **Quito** and **Avenida 28 de Mayo,** both run parallel to the river. **Avenida 12 de Diciembre** and the **highway** are across the river. **EMETEL** (tel. 770-104), on Quito next to Residencial Limón, uncharacteristically will allow calling-card or collect calls (open Mon.-Sat. 8-11am, 2-4pm, and 8-9pm, Sun. 8-11am). Most buses pass through the center of town via Av. Ejercito and Quito, but if you still feel the need for organized pick-ups, head down Av. Ejercito across the bridge and to your right until you reach the **terminal terrestre** and *salchipapa* vendors. Buses rumble by daily, heading north to **Méndez, Sucúa,** and **Macas,** and most frequently head south to **Gualaquiza, Zamora,** and **Loja,** and west to **Cuenca** (more overnight buses). Most of the buses pass by in the late afternoon and night—the earliest north-bound bus comes through at 11am. You can ask any shopkeeper along Av. Quito the schedule. Back in town, the small but pleasant **library** on Av. Quito has a TV and a small-scale model of the Parque Central across the street (open Mon.-Fri. 8am-noon and 2-5:30pm). **Farmacía Limón** is on Av. 28 de Mayo (open daily 7am-9pm). The **hospital** (tel. 770-738), to the right of the main bridge if you're facing the river, can give 24-hour treatment, but only in emergencies (open Mon.-Fri. 7:30am-12:30pm and 1:30-4:30pm; the emergency entrance is on Tut. Hugo Ortiz). Across the river, the **police** are occasionally found in a guardhouse building on Av. 12 de Diciembre, near the highway next to the bus stop. The **post office** is on 28 de Mayo near the corner of the park (open Mon.-Fri. 8am-noon and 2-6pm, Sat. 9am-1pm). **Jota Be Travel,** on Quito near Cordero, has a more reliable package shipping service (open Mon.-Fri. 8am-noon and 1-6pm).

Far better than the competition, the **Residencial Limón,** on Quito, surrounds its garden courtyard with spotless rooms sporting soft, spacious beds. Although they usually perform admirably, shared bathrooms sometimes lose running water and the water's never hot (s/10,000 per person). More basic hotels in town, the **Dominguez** and the **Santo Domingo** offer a little peeling paint and fewer toilet seats for s/6,000 per person. An attractive restaurant with well-washed wooden tables, **Chifa Rincón de Taiwan** is on Quito, near Bolívar. Chinese food like no other, but at least it smells good (entrees s/7,000-10,000; open daily 11am-9pm). The *almuerzo/merienda* pit-stops along Quito and Av. 28 de Mayo may be cheaper, but their sanitary standards aren't as reliable. **Catilis's Restaurant,** on Quito, whips up *almuerzos* and *meriendas* (s/4,000), as well as a la carte dishes like *trucha* (trout; s/7,000) or *chaulafan* (fried rice; s/7,000; open Mon.-Fri. 8am-9pm, Sat. 9am-4pm, Sun. 9am-2pm). **Soda Bar Stephanie,** on Quito at the corner of the park, has juices and sandwiches only, but it's a good place to watch the teenagers prowl (open nightly until 10-11pm).

MÉNDEZ

Méndez, another rarely visited pit-stop along the highway, is even more *tranquilo* than its southern neighbor Limón, worthy of a visit only if you're charmed by a place that hasn't seen a tourist in months; catering to gringos is as foreign a concept as a hot shower. As in the rest of the Oriente, the roads that tenuously connect Méndez with the rest of the world probably couldn't be much worse. Hard on the tailbone, they sometimes completely wash out during the rainiest months (June-Aug.). The view from behind the bus station captures Méndez perfectly: an industrial village amid tropical jungle hills, drinking from the banks of the muddy **Río Paute.** Legend has it that a treasure of gold lies in a cave in the nearby hills but—as luck would have it—access is impossible due to swarms of bats.

Everything of interest in this town predictably centers around the verdant, picturesque **main plaza.** Adjacent to the plaza on **Calle Cuenca,** the church is modern and strikingly angular. One major road, **Domingo Comín,** is on the left if you're standing in the park facing the church. **Guayaquil** runs parallel to Comín on the other side of the plaza, and the river runs parallel to Cuenca two blocks away. The **bus station** is at the **Turismo Oriental** office, Cuenca and Guayaquil (tel. 760-126), on the corner of the plaza. Buses head north to: **Macas** (8, 10pm, and 1am, 3hr., s/10,000) via **Sucúa** (2hr., s/7,000); and **Cuenca** (1:30 and 9:30pm, 6hr., s/15,000) via **Limón** (2hr., s/7,000). If buses aren't running, **camionetas** can make the same journeys (about s/90,000). **Farmacía Botica Méndez** is on the same corner of the plaza as the bus station (open daily 8am-6pm). All municipal offices, such as the **post office** and **library,** are on Comín at the plaza. In general, it is worthwhile to take care of things in the more "metropolitan" towns of Sucúa and Macas.

If you decide to spend the night in town, **Hostal Los Cerbos** (tel. 770-133), is a first-rate choice. Chock full of homey atmosphere, rooms have clean sheets and ceiling fans to boot. Shared, cold-water bathrooms are as spotless and painless as that deadly combination can get. The upstairs terrace's lovely view of Méndez makes a perfect place to while away those lonely southern Oriente afternoons (s/16,000 per person). More primitive pensions line Cuenca, a block or so from the plaza. Eating in Méndez is easy (chew, savor, swallow…chew, savor, swallow), but don't expect the savoring to be the highlight of the experience. **Turismo Oriental** is a well populated, blue-table-clothed exception, as well as a bus stop and an office. You wouldn't know its non-culinary alter-egos from the delicious *almuerzos* and *meriendas* (each s/6000), or their *pollo frito* (s/8000). Color TV and ice-cold beverages also help brighten any traveler's day (open daily 7am-10pm).

SUCÚA

The central office of the **Shuar Federation** is Sucúa's claim to fame, but the placid satellite of Macas (1hr. south) does not exactly appear to be an indigenous cultural center. An aboriginal group of the central and southern Oriente, the **Shuar** lived in relative isolation until the beginning of this century. Long considered a "savage" people because of their head-hunting and head-shrinking habits, the Shuar no longer practice these legendary acts. As missionaries, colonists, and oil companies moved in, the Shuar were forced to make the abrupt transition to life in the modern world, or risk losing their land and culture all together. As a result, Sucúa looks more like a strip mall for auto mechanics, with a few restaurants, hotels, and *panaderías* scattered among the machinery vendors. The Shuar Federation building itself is more an administrative office than a cultural center—ironically, the best place (outside of the Shuar villages) to learn about the culture is in Quito's museums. For more information on the Shuar and their Federation, see **Indigenous Identity,** p. 47.

Sucúa's main street is the dusty **Domingo Comín,** along which lies the small **Parque Central.** Other buildings of importance, as well as most of Sucúa's accommodations, lie along the Macao (north) end of Comín. When you're this close to Macao, you might as well spend the night there—but if you're stuck in Sucúa, the **Hostal Riviera Oriental** is the least unpleasant of the dismal selection of cold-water common bath hotels (s/11,000 per person). The *chifa* downstairs has the most varied menu in town. Buses cruise up and down Comín, running to **Macas** (every 30min., 1hr.) and, slightly less frequently, to Oriente towns to the south. Sucúa's **terminal terrestre,** a 10-minute walk down Comín (take a right at the fork), seems to get little action, since all buses go through town. Buses go to: **Morona** (10am, 5, and 6:45pm, 8hr.);

Gualaquiza (1:45 and 4:30pm, 8hr.); **Cuenca** (8 per day, 6:30am-10:30pm, 8hr.); and **Puyo** (8, 9, 10, and 11pm, 5hr.) sometimes continuing to **Ambato** and/or **Quito**, depending on the status of the Puyo-Baños road.

$2,000 for a Shrunken Head?!

In the not-so-distant past, head shrinking was practiced by many indigenous tribes in the depths of the Ecuadorian Amazon. While many of these groups continue to live in isolation from the modern world, shrunken heads are now thankfully out of fashion, and also illegal. If that doesn't deter you, here's an easy-to-follow guide to how it's done: (1) Obtain a head, preferably from someone over whom you would like to gain power; (2) Crush it, being sure to break all the bones inside; (3) Remove bones; (4) Smoke remaining skin and cartilage over an open fire; (5) Treat with "secret chemicals" to preserve for a lifetime of use.

In the *Casa de Cultura* in Quito (see p. 75), there is a speared and shrunken head from the *Huatingui* tribe; the Shuar people of the *Pastaza* area were famed head hunters in the past as well. It has been out of practice so long, though, that the rarity of owning such a treasure is so great that heads are rumored to fetch as much as US$2,000 on the black market.

■ Macas

As the cosmopolitan capital of the rural Morona-Santiago province, Macas outpaces other booming townships in the southern Oriente, which isn't saying much. With visions of jungle-resort grandeur, Macas makes a concerted effort to become a tourist destination in itself: lined with small CETUR-sponsored information booths, the town's main street, Domingo Comín, aspires to become a *paseo turístico*. Macas counts a huge bus terminal, a number of tour operators, and even a semi-high rise hotel among its worldly assets. Nevertheless, this growth is fighting Macas's more natural niche as a jungle tour launch pad. Unfortunately for Macas's city planners, however, the city's best assets lie far beyond its borders: although Macas is the closest city to the cavernous Cueva de los Tayos, traditional Shuar villages, and pristine stretches of Amazonian jungle, it's more than a day's travel to these areas. Apart from a small recreational park/botanical garden with a replica of a Shuar hut, there is little to see—culturally or environmentally—in Macas itself. The current mode of growth only deprives Macas of its quaint beauty—travelers seeking a glimpse of rural Ecuador might be better off in riverside Limón or Gualaquiza to the south.

ORIENTATION

The **airstrip** forms the western boundary of the town. Macas's main north-south road, **Amazonas**, runs one block east of it. The **terminal terrestre** is just west of Amazonas, on the east-west **Avenida 10 de Agosto**. North of Av. 10 de Agosto run the east-west streets **Comín, Bolívar, Sucre**, and **Cuenca**, in that order. East of Amazonas run the north-south **Soastri, Avenida 24 de Mayo**, and **Avenida 9 de Octubre**. The **main plaza** is between Comín and Bolívar, east of Av. 24 de Mayo, but the real center of activity is actually around the intersection of Amazonas and Comín.

PRACTICAL INFORMATION

Tourist Information: Check out the **CETUR**-sponsored info booths, on Domingo Comínin. **Tuntiale** (tel. 700-082), in the bus terminal, **Ikiaam** (tel. 700-457), across the street, and **Tsunka Tours**, on Domingo Comínin near Amazonas. Open daily 9am-noon and 2-6pm, when guides are in town. They also arrange tours (see **Jungle Tours from Macas**, p. 243). **INEFAN**, on Av. 29 de Mayo, has info on Parque Nacional Sangay and other areas. Open Mon.-Fri. 9am-noon and 2-6pm.

Airport: TAME, Amazonas and Cuenca (tel. 700-162), at the airport, has flights to and from **Quito** (Mon., Wed., and Fri., from Quito at 2pm, from Macas at 3:05pm, 30min., US$52 for foreigners). Open Mon.-Fri. 8am-noon and 2-5pm.

Buses: Macas's **terminal terrestre** is on Av. 10 de Agosto just west of Amazonas. Buses to: **Cuenca** (10am, 5:30, 6:30, 8, 8:30, 9, and 9:30pm, 10hr., s/30,000); **Morona** (9am, 4, 5:45, and 7:30pm, 9hr., s/16,000); **Gualaquiza** (12:45, 2, 3:30, and 5pm, 9hr.); and **Puyo** (4, 6, 9, 11am, 3, and 5pm, 5hr., s/14,000). **San Francisco Tours** sends high-profile, long-distance buses to faraway places like **Quito** (4 per day, 3am-11pm, 18hr., s/37,000) and **Guayaquil** (6pm, 21hr.) via **Riobamba** (14hr.). The quickest route to Quito via the Puyo-Baños road is under construction and only open Mon. Buses travel via Tena/Baeza all other days.

Taxis: Coop. Taxis 24 de Mayo (tel. 700-056). Cabs hang out all over Macas.

Pharmacy: Farmacía Central, Amazonas near Comín (tel. 700-388). Open daily 8am-10pm.

Hospital: Emergency tel. 700-904. Otherwise, there are a number of private **medical clinics** on Amazonas near Comín and Dr. Mario Alvarez, at the **Centro Medico Macas,** 10 de Agosto 7-34, (tel. 700-083), offers 24hr. emergency service.

Police: Emergency tel. 700-101.

Post Office: Av. 9 de Octubre near Comín (tel. 700-060), 1 block from the central plaza. Relatively reliable Lista de Correos. **Fax** service: U.S. (s/22,200 per page); Europe (s/27,400 per page); Ecuador (s/4,000 per page). Open Mon.-Fri. 7:30am-6pm. **Delgado Travel,** Comín and Amazonas, has a package-sending service.

Telephone: EMETEL (tel. 700-104), on Av. 24 de Mayo between Cuenca and Sucre. Free collect, calling-card calls. Open Mon.-Fri. 8am-noon, 2-6pm, and 7-9pm, Sat. 8-11am and 7-9pm.

Telephone Code: 07.

ACCOMMODATIONS

Hotel Splendit, Soasti (tel. 700-734), between Comín and Bolívar. The new half of the hotel offers color TVs, shiny faux satin bedspreads, and reliable hot water (s/25,000 per person). The older rooms with electrically heated water, no TV, and musty smells are not quite as "splendit," but are only s/5,000 per person.

Hotel La Orquidea, Sucre and Av. 9 de Octubre (tel. 700-970). Crisp, clean rooms that entice with their value and simplicity. They're not orchidaceous, but quality doesn't need to make a fuss. Good private bathrooms and a rentable kitchen (s/5,000), always a plus. Rooms s/15,000 per person, with hot water s/18,000.

Hostal Esmerelda, Cuenca and Soasti (tel. 700-160), 1 block from the airport. Great values seem to be a trend here. Rooms come fully equipped with a nice TV, hot (electric) water in private baths, immaculate maintenance, and a pleasant rooftop courtyard. Rooms s/15,000 per person, with hot water s/18,000.

Hotel Peñon del Oriente, Amazonas and Comín. As the tallest building in Macas, it's a landmark. Rooms aren't the best values in town, but the rest is heavenly; especially given its proximity to the Christian radio station that broadcasts from the roof. Comfortable beds, good views on higher floors, black-and-white TVs, and plenty of religious propaganda—from booklets strewn across the room to biblical passages plastered on the walls. Singles s/25,000; doubles s/50,000.

FOOD

Macas's restaurants, while plentiful compared to the rest of the southern Oriente, are sparse compared to most provincial capitals. A fine seafood or Cuban meal provides a welcome break after weeks of *almuerzos,* but once you've had that, don't expect much more culinary depth to tempt your palate. The best deals in town are at the simple lunch stands in and across from the market, near Hotel Peñon del Oriente, where s/3,000 *almuerzos* are the norm.

Bar-Restaurant La Randimpa, Bolívar and Av. 24 de Mayo (tel. 700-696). Cool, any way you cut it. Cuban music and food (including Cuban pizza, s/8,000) are as mesmerizing as the modern art on the walls. Sit at a tasteful wood table and be chilled by the breeze *and* the atmosphere. Theoretically open daily 8am-3am.

Marisqueria La Marinika, on Soasti near Tarqui (tel. 700-734), has all fish, prepared all ways. The *Langostikos al Vapor* are better than the decor, and the staff is eager to please (s/12,000; s/18,000 for seaside delights). Open daily 10am-10pm.

Adonde Ivan, Amazonas and Av. 10 de Agosto (tel. 700-826). Where did they go? Probably to this delightful thatched-roof hut. Opened in 1996, this restaurant is very tropical and very different. Seafood eaters sit at wooden picnic tables, cheered on by 2 huge squawking parrots. *Almuerzo* (s/5,000), *ceviche de camarones* (s/ 9,000). Open Sun.-Fri. 8am-5pm. *Peña* open until 11pm on Fri. nights.

Ten's Chop, Bolívar 621 near Soasti, specializes in pub-style nightlife, complete with tap beer (s/10,000 pitcher), but runs a side business in Venezuelan food and exotic juices (like alfalfa and avocado) during the day. The big-screen TV is always flickering—music videos at night, sports on weekends, and occasionally movies in the afternoon. Open Mon.-Wed. 10am-midnight, Thurs.-Sat. 10am-2am.

JUNGLE TOURS FROM MACAS

Macas is the most developed and convenient town in the southern Oriente from which to begin a jungle jaunt. While the northern Oriente sees more tourists, the jungle east of Macas provides some unique opportunities. As in the north, hundreds of thousands of hectares remain undeveloped and large tracts of primary forest still grow intact. Some of the more staggeringly beautiful areas remain untouched with the help of government protection, like Parque Nacional Sangay's *zona baja*, the ecological reserve near Santa Rosa, and the caves at Cueva de los Tayos.

This area is also home to Ecuador's second-most-populous indigenous group, the **Shuar.** While many Shuar around Macas and Sucúa have changed their traditional ways, more isolated communities in the jungle east of Macas continue to live as they have for centuries. Many of the longer (4-6 day) tours from Macas visit these communities. While the Shuar have not expressed as much distaste for this kind of tourism as the Huaorani and other *indígenas* to the north, the visits cannot help but affect their traditional way of life. If you do decide to visit one of these communities, do so with a Shuar guide; you will not be well received if you wander into town alone—prepare yourself for culture shock. The Shuar are usually friendly, welcoming hosts when the proper introductions are made. Accommodations are basic, and food is traditional. That means rice, and lots of it. You may even be offered **Chicha de Yuca,** an alcoholic drink made from the yucca plant, fermented with the saliva of an older Shuar woman. Your hosts will have precious little experience with the amenities of modern life, something you could either find refreshing or a bit unsettling. Visitors must also be sensitive to issues of Shuar religion and customs. Although many of the community's rites and religious festivals are closed to outsiders, going to a shaman is like visiting a doctor: you can have your own private audiences. The ritual purifications in the **Cascadas Sagradas** (sacred waterfalls) and ayahuasca-laced ceremonies that many tour guides arrange for their clients are as "real" as the traditional community's events, but far less invasive than simply showing up on a Shuar holy day.

For a less people-oriented experience, try a trip to the **zona baja** at **Parque Nacional Sangay** (Macas entrance). One of the most jungle-intensive excursions around, its trails climb hills and weave through primary tropical rainforest. At one point in the journey, cable cars cross the otherwise impassable Ríos Sangay and Upano. At least one trail actually traverses the park, crossing over into the *zona alta* in the highlands near Baños and Riobamba (see **Parque Nacional Sangay,** p. 122). If all you're dreaming of is jungle, jungle, and nothing but jungle, a trip to Sangay could be the ideal excursion. While some praise this tour as fascinating, others warn that after a few days of nothing but green, and lots of it, the park can get a bit monotonous. Some tour companies also make excursions to an **ecological reserve** near the town of Santa Rosa, about two hours from Macas. Jungle adventurers sleep in cabins and explore by horseback and canoe, with stints of tubing and swimming.

Another commonly visited sight near Macas, **Cueva de los Tayos** is an enormous (85m deep), pitch-black cave that can only be explored with a guide. Its name comes from the large colonies of oilbirds *(tayos)* that reside in the cavern. These unusual birds have picked up some telltale habits from their neighbors in the darkness, the bats. Not only are they nocturnal fruit-eaters, they also use sonar to stake out their location in the pitch-black environs. Yet another underground source of oil in the

Oriente; these *tayos* used to be captured and boiled for the oil harvested from their fat-rich flesh. Many tours leaving from Macas pencil Cueva de los Tayos onto their itineraries, but it can also be explored from **Morona,** a village on the Peruvian border with neither restaurants nor accommodations (12hr. from Macas).

The many **tour companies** leading trips from Macas offer a wide variety of packages that include one or more of the above attractions. Tours are expensive (US$45-60 per day per person depending on duration and group size), but hard to avoid. The best sights are the farthest away and unless you have a pilot's license and private plane or army contacts, you won't get far beyond the missionary-dominated Sevilla Don Bosco Shuar satellite of Macas. The tours are usually all-inclusive (food, lodging, transport, advice, wisdom, medicinal plants, etc.), but it is possible to hire a guide and pay for everything a la carte if you insist hard enough. It's polite to bring small gifts for any Shuar villages you plan to visit—ask your guide for suggestions. Most tours are flexible—partly due to unpredictable weather—and can often be customized to accommodate individual interests. Another important consideration is transportation mode. Some companies use small (and sometimes nausea-inducing) planes to conveniently and quickly transport people to remote parts of the jungle. Others tours include horseback rides, canoe trips, and varying amounts of walking. Before you leave, make sure the mode of transport suits your needs and desires.

Ikiaam, (tel. 700-457), across from the *terminal terrestre.* Run by friendly, knowledgeable Shuar tour guides (*Ikiaam* means "jungle" in Shuar). Trips usually last 1-6 days. A popular 4- to 6-day trip includes a visit to the indigenous community of Yaupi, 2 days of rainforest trekking, a horseback ride to the Shuar community of Tsawantas, a canoe trip, fishing, and a visit to Cueva de los Tayos (US$130 per day for 2 people, US$45-50 per person for 3-4, down to $35 per person for 9). Other 2- to 4-day trips visit Parque National Sangay and the reserve near Santa Rosa (about US$40 per person per day). Also offers daytrips (around US$35 per person). Meals and equipment included on tours. Office hours are sporadic.

Tunkiaka, (tel. 700-082; fax 700-110), in a building that is part of the *terminal terrestre.* Associated with Huasca Agencia de Viajes, this company is also Shuar-run. Offers similar trips to Ikiaam's at similar prices (see above), including canoe trips, horseback rides, piranha fishing, and visits to Shuar villages.

Adventures Tsunki, (tel. 700-464), across from Hotel Peñon del Oriente, builds its business on the talents of Shuar guide Marcelo Cajecai and English-speaking ecologist partner Sara. It offers same range of trips at similar prices, but can also help plan longer (2-30 day) excursions. Their office in Quito's Hotel Marsella, Los Rios 2035 (tel. 515-884, ask for David), helps you plan ahead.

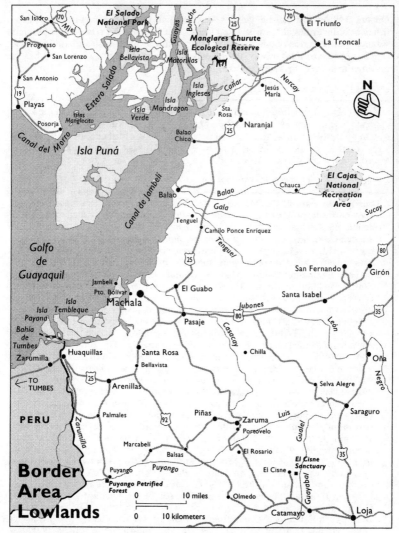

Border Area Lowlands

■ Machala

The self-proclaimed "banana capital of the world," the growing town of Machala (pop. 130,000) takes its peelable yellow fruit quite seriously. Located 200km south of Guayaquil, floating in a sea of banana trees, Machala greets entering visitors with a huge statue of **El Bananero,** a larger-than-life banana grower carrying an eight-foot bunch. Locals extol the sacred fruit with a **banana festival** during the third week in September; rather than work all night, they take this chance to kick back and take a drink of rum. The festivities include the selection of one lucky lady to receive the highest honor the city has to offer—the coveted title of Her Highness, the **Banana**

Queen. Far from just tallying bananas, Machala is also capital of the El Oro province. It has no conventional "tourist attractions," but its friendly, relatively safe atmosphere, good selection of budget hotels, and proximity to the fresh seafood and clean beaches of Puerto Bolívar and Jambelí make Machala an ideal place to stop before braving the border-crossing into Perú.

ORIENTATION

Streets in Machala use both a naming and a numbering system, but locals in the know generally use the names. **Avenida 9 de Mayo** is the main north-south thoroughfare, running past the **market,** and the **main plaza,** one block further south. The **church** stands on the west side of the plaza; its spire can make a useful landmark. There is no *terminal terrestre,* so buses arrive and leave from various places around town.

PRACTICAL INFORMATION

Tourist Information: CETUR, Av. 9 de Mayo and Pichincha, 2nd floor (tel. 932-106). Spanish-speaking staff answers questions and offers a booklet with helpful maps. Open somewhat erratically Mon.-Fri. 8:30am-4pm.

Peruvian Consulate: on Calle Bolívar near Colón, 2nd floor, room 102 (tel. 930-680; fax 937-040). Can supply visas, but most travelers who intend to spend less than 90 days in Perú don't need one. Open Mon.-Fri. 9am-5:30pm, Sat. 9am-noon.

Currency Exchange: Casa de Cambio Ullauizi, on Calle Páez between Av. 9 de Octubre and Rocafuerte (tel. 931-349); look for the men with guns. Open Mon.-Fri. 8am-noon and 2-6pm, Sat. 9-11am.

Airport: A few blocks west of *el centro* on Montalvo. Mainly served by TAME, with 1 flight to **Guayaquil** (Mon.-Fri. 11am, 30min., s/83,000) continuing to **Quito** (3hr., s/193,000). The **TAME office** (tel. 530-139), is on Calle Juan Montalvo between Bolívar and Pichincha, next to the post office (open Mon.-Fri. 9am-5pm).

Buses: CIFA, at the corner of Bolívar and Guayas, across from the Rizzo Hotel, has buses to the Peruvian border at **Huaquillas** every 30min. (6:30am-6:30pm, 1hr., s/5,000). You may be able to persuade the driver to stop in the intermediate towns of **Arenillas** (25min.) and **Santa Rosa** (40min.) for a lesser charge. There are routine passport checks en route to Huaquillas. To make these as painless as possible, have your passport ready and carry minimal luggage. Various bus companies serve **Guayaquil,** leaving from Av. 9 de Octubre around Tarqui (every 30min., 3am-10:30pm, 3hr., s/12,000-13,000). **Ecuatoriana,** on the corner of Colón and Av. 9 de Octubre, has air-conditioned "executive service" to Guayaquil (every 30min. from 4am-8pm, s/13,000). A few *cooperativos* on Colón between Bolívar and Rocafuerte leave every hr. (5am-7pm) to **Piñas** (1½hr., s/3,000), **Portovelo** (2hr., s/4,000), and **Zaruma** (3hr., s/7,500). **Coop Pullman Azuay,** on Calle Sucre between Junín and Tarqui (tel. 930-370), has buses constantly departing for **Cuenca** (43 per day, 1am-10:45pm, 4hr., s/10,000). Buses to **Quito** (via **Santo Domingo** or **Pallatanga**) depart from the **Panamerica** headquarters, on the corner of Bolívar and Colón (tel. 930-141; every 2hr., 8:30am-10:30pm, 10hr., s/27,000, s/22,000 to Sto. Domingo, s/20,000 to Pallatanga).

Pharmacies: Pharmacies are almost as common as armed guards in Machala. Coincidence? We think not. **Farmacía San Jose,** conveniently across from the hospital (no tel.); **24hr. Farmacía**, next door to TAME (tel. 939-035). Neither is huge, but both are open 24hr.

Hospital: Hospital Teofilo Pavila, at Buenavista and Boyaca (emergency tel. 937-581), in front of the Parque Colón (open 24hr.). **Policlinico**, next to TAME on Montalvo, is closer to the center of town (tel. 939-035); open 24hr. for emergencies.

Police: at Av. 9 de Mayo and Manual Serrano (tel. 930-449, 933-391, or 933-392; fax 933-911), about 3 blocks past CETUR (open 24hr.).

Post Office: at Bolívar and Calle Juan Montalvo (tel. 930-675; fax 931-908). Open Mon.-Fri. 8:30am-6:30pm.

Telephone: EMETEL, on Av. 9 de Octubre between Calle Velez and Anda de las Palmeras (tel. 931-515; fax 922-666). Open daily 8am-10pm.

Telephone Code: 07.

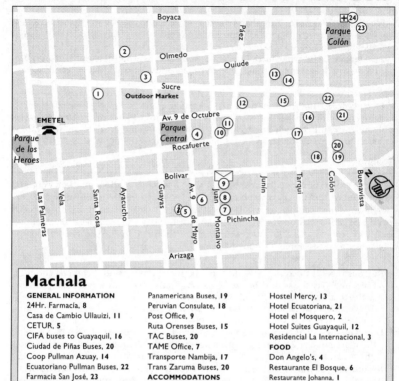

Machala

GENERAL INFORMATION
24Hr. Farmacía, 8
Casa de Cambio Ullauizi, 11
CETUR, 5
CIFA buses to Guayaquil, 16
Ciudad de Piñas Buses, 20
Coop Pullman Azuay, 14
Ecuatoriano Pullman Buses, 22
Farmacia San José, 23
Hospital Teofilo Davila, 24

Panamericana Buses, 19
Peruvian Consulate, 18
Post Office, 9
Ruta Orenses Buses, 15
TAC Buses, 20
TAME Office, 7
Transporte Nambija, 17
Trans Zaruma Buses, 20
ACCOMMODATIONS
Gran Hotel Machala, 10

Hostel Mercy, 13
Hotel Ecuatoriana, 21
Hotel el Mosquero, 2
Hotel Suites Guayaquil, 12
Residencial La Internacional, 3
FOOD
Don Angelo's, 4
Restaurante El Bosque, 6
Restaurante Johanna, 1

ACCOMMODATIONS

Because of the large number of tourists spending the night in Machala after shedding the shackles of Huaquillas, budget accommodations abound. Anyone staying overnight in Machala should check for window screens or mosquito nets during the hot, wet months. Hotels closer to the center of town, while usually noisier, tend to be safer than those on the outskirts.

Gran Hotel Machala, Montalvo at Rocafuerte (tel. 930-530). At first this centrally located hotel seems almost as boxlike as the town's forced street plan, but bedspreads peppered with flowers and cherubs keep the place cheerful. Most rooms have windows, and some even have balconies. An impressive iron gate and 24hr. security guard increase safety. Rooms for 1-6 people s/10,000 per person, with bath and fan s/20,000, with A/C and cold-water bath s/25,000.

Hotel Ecuatoriana, Av. 9 de Octubre and Colón (tel. 930-197), above the Ecuatoriana Pullman bus station. Though above the bus station, this hotel isn't any noisier than other places, unless you count the friendly receptionists. Try to get a room with windows; the interior ones are less pleasant. Rooms with fan s/16,000, with A/C s/22,000; all rooms have private bath and TV.

Hotel El Mosquero, Olmedo between Ayacucho and Guayas (tel. 931-752; fax 930-390). Staff is friendly, and shining but basic rooms all have private bathrooms. Some have TVs, a good distraction given the 2-tone chartreuse-and-white walls, which give the feeling of being submerged in a bowl of pea soup. Rooms with fan s/40,000, with A/C s/54,000.

Hotel San Francisco, Tarqui and Sucre (tel. 922-395), has clean, almost business-class rooms with phone, TV, and private (cold water) bath. Rooms with fan s/ 30,000, with A/C s/40,000.

Residencial La Internacional, Guayas between Olmedo and Sucre (tel. 930-244). Diligent young sweeper ensures simple rooms and communal baths are dust-free. Nearby outdoor market makes this place noisier than others, but sturdy screens block brutal mosquitoes and fans keep a-whirrin' (s/10,000 per person).

Hostal Mercy, Junín between Ouinde and Sucre (tel. 920-116). Tall plants thrive in the courtyard, well-tended by the sweet, grandparent-like owners. *Merciful heavens!* They sure do their best to make visitors feel at home. No-frills, spotless rooms with private baths and fans for 1-3 people, with fan s/13,000, with A/C s/17,000.

FOOD

Those in search of native flavor should head to Machala's **outdoor market,** centered around Sucre between Guayas and Montalvo. Fresh fruits and meats can be found at nearly any hour. The pricier restaurants at the nicer hotels are good for those special occasions. If it's seafood you're craving, join the locals at **Puerto Bolívar** (see below), only a five-minute cab ride away. Whatever you choose, don't be surprised if bananas constitute a considerable portion of the meal.

Restaurante El Bosque, Av. 9 de Mayo between Bolívar and Pichincha (no tel.). Famished? Try the walloping *carne asado y patacones* (meat and fried plantains with steaming rice, beans, and tomato s/8,000) or delicious *ceviche* (s/8,000). Afterwards, relax among the tropical plants beneath the bamboo awning, with a frothy glass of *jugo de mora* (blackberry juice, s/2,500).

Don Angelo's, on the corner of Av. 9 de Mayo and Rocafuerte (tel. 932-784). One of the most popular 24hr. restaurants surrounding the Parque Central, Don Angelo's offers a large-screen TV to accompany your *comida típica* (s/10,000-16,000).

Restaurant Johanna, at Sucre and Sta. Rosa (no tel.), fills the air with cheerful music and the smell of their delicious *empanadas* (s/1,500). Wide selection of fruit juices (s/2,500). Open daily 8am-11pm.

■ Near Machala

PUERTO BOLÍVAR

So here's land-locked Machala, absolutely bursting with bountiful bunches of bananas, with no way to ship them out before they start rotting in the hot equatorial sun. Not to worry. Almost before the town could grasp the magnitude of its problem, the international port at Bolívar, 6km west of Machala, was born. Though little more than Machala's cargo zone, Puerto Bolívar's waterfront doubles as a savory spot where savvy locals come for **scrumptious seafood.**

Compared to the polluted harbor and inland streets, Puerto Bolívar's restaurants are refreshingly clean. Each tries to outdo its competition with a stronger superlative, but when multiple restaurants claim to make "the best *ceviche* in the world," it's hard to know where to turn. Actually, it doesn't much matter; seafood here is universally delicious, and meals everywhere usually run between s/10,000-20,000. The *ceviche de camarones* (shrimp *ceviche*) is especially popular. The **Restaurant Warkiki** (no tel.) and **Pepe's** (also no tel.), both within sight of the dock, offer some of the best selections of seafood to be found in town. Pepe's *Orgia de Mariscos* (s/14,000) is one of the more scrumptious deals to be found. Puerto Bolívar's **police** (tel. 929-684) are located on the water, at the corner of Malecón and Municipalidad, in front of the piers (open 24hr.). The **EMETEL** office is next door (open daily 8am-10pm). Puerto Bolívar is not a safe place at night. Given the dreary selection of accommodations and the town's proximity to Machala, passing a night in Puerto Bolívar should be avoided at all costs. If you have to travel here after dark, by all means take a **taxi.** To get here, hop the #1 bus from Machala's Parque Central or anywhere on Av. 9 de Octubre, and

The Banana Wars

Who would imagine that the innocent banana, so beloved the world over, could be the source of controversy, intrigue, and even bloodshed in the "banana republics" where they are grown? But in Ecuador, this tasty yellow fruit is big business, generating more than US$600 million in export revenue annually. With all that money coming in, you'd think there would be enough to go around. However, as economists have long claimed, and multinational corporations long proved, human greed knows no bounds. The latest controversy involves a fight between foreign fruit companies and their local suppliers, over what constitutes a fair price for a box of bananas. The exporters pay growers s/7,000-9,000 per box, which workers complain is unjust, since the "going price" is US$4.20. In June 1997, negotiations broke down; banana workers took to the streets, blocking highways and generally wreaking havoc. The subsequent strike was said to be costing the country US$12-16 million per week. Government mediation will no doubt get the two sides back to work yet again, but it is only a matter of time before the next battle in the Ecuador's banana wars is ignited.

get off when you see the large street sign for Avenida Bolívar Madero Vargas (7min., s/500). The waterfront is one block to your right. Cabs cost around s/6,000.

JAMBELÍ

Though the Galápagos are prized for their endemic wildlife, it barely exists on the small island of Jambelí, 20 minutes by boat from Puerto Bolívar. Come here for the lively atmosphere, not looking for blue-footed boobies; Jambelí's wildlife consists almost completely of Ecuadorian day-trippers and vacationers with a few knowledgable tourists mixed in. Jambelí's palm-covered food stands and bell-ringing ice cream vendors congregate around the miniature tropical equivalent of Atlantic City's boardwalk, a cement and Spanish tile street that runs through the center of this small town. While music, swaying palms, and spirited volleyball matches give Jambelí a constant "spring break" feel, the atmosphere changes dramatically with the seasons. Hot summer months bring mosquitoes, so bring insect repellant and check hotel windows for screens. Tourists come in droves from August to October and during holidays (such as February's *carnavales*), causing prices to rise to even three times the normal rates.

Not all visitors are day-trippers, and Jambelí has several options for those looking for a place to hang their beach hats. Despite its fun-in-the-sun atmosphere, accommodations here—while pleasant—are by no means Club Med. The popular **Las Cabañas de Pescador** (Machala tel. 937-710) offers doubles for s/25,000, but is often full. Next door, the older **Hotel María Sol** (Machala tel. 937-461) has basic rooms with private baths (s/20,000 per person; discounts for larger groups). The largest rooms are at the pricier **Cabañas del Mar** (tel. 937-007, leave a message at the EMETEL office). Plan to share a shower with the adjacent room. Doubles s/65,000. Scrumptious seafood is almost always the specialty of the day in Jambelí. Restaurants **El Niño Turista** and **El Penguino,** next door to each other on the boardwalk, both serve fantastic, fishy, and frugal meals running between s/7,000-12,000. After supper, grab a cool drink and watch the sunset from the bamboo hammocks in front of El Penguino.

To get to Jambelí during the week, take a **boat** from Puerto Bolívar (Mon.-Fri. 7, 10am, 1, and 4pm; 20min.). The same boats also return from Jambelí (Mon.-Fri., 8:15am, noon, 3, and 5pm). On weekends, boats leave whenever they're full, though the wait usually isn't very long (round-trip s/10,000). Be prepared to pay the s/500 entrance fee on your way into town. Weekend or holiday travelers should find out when the last boat leaves, as some drivers like to start their own holidays early.

PUYANGO PETRIFIED FOREST

The Puyango Petrified Forest, near Ecuador's border with Perú, celebrates both the living and the dead. The park's few visitors roam under the towering palms and creep through the giant ferns that grow alongside Puyango's 100-million-year-old **Arcadia trees.** These stone-cold stumps have some of the largest fossilized trunks in the world, measuring 11m (36 ft.) in length and over 1.6m (5 ft.) in diameter. Though they'd be hard-pressed to nest in the Arcadias, over 130 bird species live in this small park. To fully appreciate and identify them, check out Dierdre Platt's *Puyango Bird Guide* (s/5,000), available from the park administration. The trail through the towering trunks is toilsome in places, with some tough terrain and river crossings. Gold panning and river rafting may also be possible—ask the park administration for more details. Larger groups have a better chance of arranging excursions. Making this a daytrip is hard, but the price of an overnight stay—US$20 per person camping, s/60,000 for a bed in a dorm-style lodge—is even harder. There is a relatively expensive (s/10,000 and up) restaurant on the premises. One of the few deals the park has to offer is that friendly local guides cost s/5,000 (admission for foreigners US$10).

Puyango is a worthwhile site for those with plenty of time or genuine interest. Other travelers might find that the extended travel time outweighs Puyango's pleasures. No buses go to the small city of Puyango (pop. about 200), but **Cooperativa de Loja,** corner of Tarquí and Bolívar, gets you pretty close. From Machala, take the 9am or 4pm bus to Alamor (s/5,000) and ask the driver to let you off at the second security checkpoint at the entrance of the park. If you miss the 9am bus, a more complicated route is to take a CIFA bus to Avenillas (every 10min., Mon.-Fri., 4:50am-7:45pm, every 30min., Sat.-Sun., 7am-6pm, s/5,000) and catch a collective taxi or local bus from there to the park. No matter how you get to the park's entrance, you'll still have to stroll with the butterflies for 3km from the security checkpoint to the park offices. Guides can be found at the park offices. Buses back to Machala or Loja pass by at frequent though uncertain times. Ask about return times when buying your morning bus ticket. Finding information about the park is difficult, but you can try calling the Puyango Adminstration Commission in Machala (tel. 930-012; fax 937-655).

▨ Zaruma

Founded in 1536, just after the arrival of the Spanish conquistadors, the mountainous, gold-mining town of Zaruma (pop. 7000) wears its age well. Most mines were believed to have been combed clean long ago, and the only sign of the international mining giants today is the surprising amount of golden hair among the local population. Nevertheless, the conspicuous number of *"Compro Oro"* ("I buy gold") signs still found around town do have a target audience: small scale miners inject cash into the local economy, and, unfortunately, mercury and gold waste into the local streams. Yes, several active gold mines are located just outside of town, and with a little research and persistence, it is even possible to visit one of them. Despite the gold, Zaruma is not a rich town and its narrow streets are still lined with aging but beautiful wooden buildings from the turn of the century. One of the town's biggest festivals, the yearly **Expo-Zaruma,** is held during the second week of July.

Practical Information Zaruma is easily accessible by bus either from Machala or Piñas. **TAC** (tel. 972-156) and **Ciudad de Piñas** share an office on Av. Honorado Márquez. Buses to: **Quito** (5:45 and 6:30pm, 12hr., s/34,000); **Guayaquil** (midnight, 2, 4 and 8:45am, 6hr., s/18,000); **Cuenca** (12:30am, 6hr., s/20,000); **Loja** (4 and 8am, 4½hr., s/13,000); and **Machala** (every hr., 3am-7pm, 2½hr., s/7,500) via **Portovelo** and **Piñas. Coop de Azuay,** down Márquez, has two additional buses to **Cuenca** (1:30 and 7:30am, 6hr., s/19,000). Most services are clustered near the town plaza: the **post office,** on the corner of 9 de Octubre and Rocafuerte, is down the street from the **police** station (tel. 972-198), on 9 de Octubre and 10 de Agosto. Pharmacies line 10 de Agosto—unfortunately none are open 24 hours. Those who want alternative medicine can try the **Centro Naturista,** on Bolívar behind the town plaza. Dr. Hugo Fernandez, on Cesino, has consultation hours Mon.-Sat. 8am-noon and 2:30-5pm—far more helpful than the **EMETEL** office next door.

Accommodations and Food On the main road into town, **Hotel Rolando** (tel. 972-800), sits just above the gold mine. All rooms have private bath, hot water, and TV; most have splendid views of the mountain valley, but latecomers might have to suffer views more reminiscent of a mineshaft. Pleasant, airy upstairs cafe serves breakfast (s/5-8,000; singles s/30,000; doubles s/35,000, with 2 beds s/40,000). The **Hotel Municipal,** Calle El Cesino (tel. 972-176), is near the mountain ridge. Though you might grumble your way through the hike up, the view is without a doubt the best thing about this place. All rooms have private baths and warm water. Make sure your *cabaña* isn't musty, and test your toilet's flushing action (s/20,000 per person with bath, *cabañas*—with better views—s/22,000 per person). Zarumans eat well, if dangerously. Small restaurants, most serving artery-clogging cheesy and rice-based dishes, line Sucre and extend down along Honorado Marquez. Near the top of the hill, the **Cafeteria I** is a cool local joint. The big thing here is *tigrillo* (*plátanos,* cheese, and eggs all scrambled up together; with drink, s/4,500). **Rico Pan,** across the street, may be better for your health (open daily 8am-10pm). **Mimos,** on Sucre near Bolívar, isn't afraid to experiment. Try their banana leaf-wrapped cuisine, like the *quimbolito* (a sweet cake with raisins, s/900) and *umitas* (ground corn, sugar, and cheese, s/700). **Picantería Mila,** on Honorado Marquez down the hill, specializes in seafood and spectacular scenery: the back porch, suspended over the valley below, is worth paying for even before the food comes (*arroz con camarones* s/8,000).

Sights Grab a pick-axe and hard hat, cross your fingers, and hope to strike it rich. Just outside of town, a number of active **gold mines** inspire dreams of the sweet life. Those wishing to visit or learn more about the mines should inquire at the Municipio (tel. 972-121; fax 972-194), or the radio station Radio Trebol (tel. 972-065, ask for manager Pepe Valdiviezo Leroux). **Compañía Bira** (tel. 972-766), a gold mining outpost on the road into town, has given tours in the past, but you have to be persistent and have a clear mission. Those overcome with gold-plated, greedy thoughts may want to absolve themselves of the deadly sin with a hasty retreat to the stunning **Iglesia de Zaruma** in the center of town (daily services 6:30am, more on Sun.). Started in 1912, this intricate chapel took over 18 years to build, and the decorating still isn't finished. Two surprisingly life-like series of paintings have recently been added to its ceiling. The first begins with the creation of Adam and Eve, the second chronicles the life of Christ. Both murals end above the two-story altar that gleams with a thin layer of the very best Zaruma's mines have to offer. The walls of shrine-like sarcophagi at the cemetery, on the edge of town along Honorado Marquez, are worth a visit; it is also the playground of the living for huge tree-dwelling spiders and butterflies.

∎ Near Zaruma: Piñas

In 1825, Spanish geologist Juan José Luis was given a large land grant for his work in the Ecuadorian gold mines near what is now the town of Zaruma. Eager to honor his homeland, the miner called his new ranch **Piñas** after his former home in Spain's pineapple region. Eventually, Piñas-the-big-ranch became Piñas-the-little-village, with a current population of about 10,000. Never ones to live in the shadow of a group of Spanish pineapple-growers, the people of Piñas happily spend their time cultivating coffee and bananas in the surrounding blue-green mountains. If you talk to anyone in Piñas about their home, the word *tranquilo* will doubtlessly come up, as it is the town's universally agreed-upon adjective. And as far as living in the shadows goes, the Virgen del Cisne and an accompanying pantheon of saints have far more presence than any of Juan's kinfolk. From the cross on top of the hill, to the electric candle-lit pictures of Madonna and child at roadside shrines, Piñas's piety is promiscuously displayed. Even for the less devout, the hilltop cross is worth a visit for the view. Countless mountains fade from deep green to even darker blue. Taxis in town will take you there for s/5000, otherwise the path is clearly visible from town.

The hardest part of maneuvering through Piñas streets is walking up and down the 45° hills. **Loja** and **Sucre,** which merge on the Machala end of town, are the most active streets, and the park, while attractive, has no relationship with the center of town. The unhelpful **EMETEL,** Ruminahui and Suarez (tel. 976-105; fax 976-990), called "Central Telefonica," does not allow collect or calling card calls. At least s/ 10,000 per minute, cash only, if you absolutely need to make international calls (open daily 8:30am-10pm). The two **bus** companies, **Ciudad de Piñas** (tel. 976-167) and **TAC** (tel. 976-151), share an office on Sucre between Moreno and Mera. Between the two companies, there are buses to: **Machala** (2hr., s/5,000), **Portovelo** (30min., s/2,500), and **Zaruma** (30min., s/2,500), every hour 4am-7pm, also 7:15, 7:45am, and 6:15pm; **Loja** (6am, 5hr., s/14,000), **Cuenca** (1:30am, 5hr., s/16,000), and **Quito** (6:45 and 7:30pm, 11hr., s/30,000) via Santo Domingo; **Guayaquil** (3am, 9:45am, s/ 15,000). There is also daily **local bus** service to the **nearby villages** of Balsas, Marca-belí, Paccha, La Bocana, Moromoro, and Palosalo. **Policlínico Reina del Cisne** (tel. 976-689), on Loja near Olmedo, is a 24-hour clinic, as is **Policlínico Los Angeles** across the street from Residencial Dumari. There are more *farmacías* than anything else in Piñas, but if you are looking for a natural alternative, Los Olivos (tel. 976-292), on Sucre near the park, has various mysterious looking herbs.

The **Residencial Dumari** (tel. 976-118), Loja at 9 de Diciembre, on top of the hill, has the most comfortable beds and cleanest sheets in Piñas. Impeccable bathrooms, color TVs, and terrace rooms with shockingly beautiful views (s/15,000 per person, with bath s/25,000). **Hotel Las Orquideas** (tel. 976-355), on the corner of Calderón and Montalvo, in the lower end of town, has windows and not much else—rooms are basic and furniture is minimal. All rooms have private bath and hot water; TV extra s/ 5,000 (s/20,000 per person, s/15,000 per additional person). It's easy to find a chicken—alive or roasted—or a plate of meat in Piñas, but harder to find other food. Vegetarians will want to stick to the numerous *panaderías*. The orchidaceous **Orquideas Restaurant,** on Sucre near Montalvo, has slightly more varied (but still chicken-based) *comida típica* (entrees s/4,500). If you really do want chicken or *bistec,* the spacious, sunny **Mundo Real,** on the corner of Mera and Sucre, second floor, serves meat with some satisfyingly greasy *papas fritas* (s/10,000 for a ¼ chicken with all the trappings). The **Soda Bar,** on the corner of Calderon and Mera, has sandwiches and juice for the less carnivorous (open daily 10am-10pm).

▓ Huaquillas

On Ecuador's border with Perú, the small town of Huaquillas enjoys a fame that is strictly geographic. Unlike many of Ecuador's beautiful small towns, Huaquillas isn't a place where anyone uses up a whole roll of film, except perhaps for the obligatory "Welcome to Perú" shot. In fact, when it comes to aesthetic value, Huaquillas's dusty streets simply disappoint. Because prices in Ecuador are lower than those in Perú, the main road becomes a virtual street market, swarming with Peruvian day shoppers, money changers, and ubiquitous mosquitoes. Travelers often swap horror stories about Huaquillas; mosquitoes certainly aren't the only thing to watch out for, as thieves lurk in the shadows and money changers are quick with their fixed calcula-tors. The border crossing is usually a painless affair, and most travelers opt to keep moving rather than loiter in Huaquillas.

Orientation and Practical Information Everything of any importance, including the bus stop, border, and immigration office, is along one of Huaquillas's three main dusty thoroughfares: **Av. Machala, Av. de la República** (also called Av. Central), and **Teniente Cordovez. EMETEL** phones are located on the main road across from Ecuadorian Immigration (open daily 8am-10pm). The bus *cooperativo* **CIFA** (tel. 907-370), two blocks from the immigration office just off the main road, goes to **Machala** (every 30min., 6am-7pm, 1¼hr., s/5,000). **Ecuatoriano Pullman** (tel. 907-025), a few blocks past the immigration office, has buses to **Guayaquil** (13 per day, 2am-6pm, 4½hr., s/14,000). **Panamericana** (tel. 907-695), at the corner of Cordovez and Santa Rosa, goes to **Quito** (10 per day, 6:30am-8pm, 11hr., s/35,000) via **Santo Domingo** (9hr., s/28,000) or **Ambato** (9hr., s/23,000). **Pullman Azuay,**

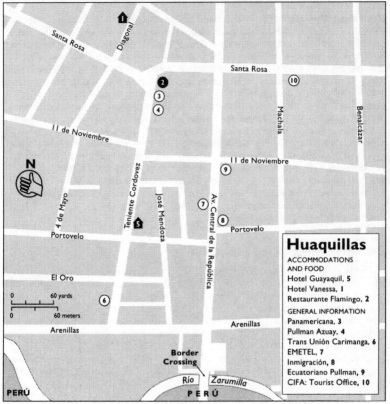

Huaquillas

ACCOMMODATIONS AND FOOD
Hotel Guayaquil, 5
Hotel Vanessa, 1
Restaurante Flamingo, 2

GENERAL INFORMATION
Panamericana, 3
Pullman Azuay, 4
Trans Unión Carimanga, 6
EMETEL, 7
Inmigración, 8
Ecuatoriano Pullman, 9
CIFA: Tourist Office, 10

next to **Panamericana,** has buses to **Cuenca** (6 per day, 3:30am-6:30pm, 5hr., s/ 16,000). **Trans Unión Carimanga,** two blocks away from the main road at the immigration office and one block to the left, goes to **Loja** (11:30am, 5½hr., s/15,000). **Police** are ready 24 hours at their station on Av. de la República near the park (tel. 907-341). Huaquillas's **telephone code** is 07.

Accommodations and Food Huaquillas is not a place where most budget travelers want to hang out, and incoming tourists often immediately catch an outgoing bus to Quito, Machala, Guayaquil, or Cuenca. Although spending the night here is not highly recommended, and is considered dangerous by some, travelers arriving late in the evening may find it more convenient to check into one of Huaquillas's several hotels, though those near the center of town can be noisy. The main selling point of **Hotel Guayaquil,** on Av. de la República (tel. 907-303), is its proximity to the immigration office next door. Basic *habitaciones* s/20,000 with private bath, s/10,000 without. **Hotel Vanessa,** Av. 1 de Mayo 323 y Hualtaco (tel. 907-263), is slightly off the main drag but easily accessible. The extra sucres are worth it—it's one of the best guarantees in town for spotlessness, safety, and pleasant smells. Rooms have private bath, TV, phones, and fridges; singles s/44,000, doubles s/66,000.

For some sit-down budget grub, several of the larger restaurants in town also contain smaller, cheaper cafes. Locals recommend **Restaurante Flamingo,** Calle Santa Rosa (tel. 907-876), next to the Panamerican Bus Company. A sweeping selection of seafood, chicken, and rice meals (s/5,000-16,000; open daily 11am-12pm).

Crossing the Border Ecuador and Perú are separated by the Río Zarumilla, which is crossed by an international bridge. In general, crossing the border in either direction is only a small headache. Everyone leaving Ecuador must pass through the **Ecuadorian Immigration Office** *(Oficina de Migraciones)*, on the left side of Av. de la República, about 200m before the Peruvian border (tel. 907-755). It's a good idea to get there early as the lines get longer throughout the day (open daily 8am-noon and 2-6pm). All persons crossing the border in either direction must have a tourist **T3 card**, available at both Ecuadorian and Peruvian immigration offices, and a **valid passport**. Tourist can spend **90 days** in Ecuador within a one-year period. Anyone who wishes to stay longer must get a visa (see **Entrance Requirements**, p. 9) Citizens of a number of Middle Eastern countries, Cuba, Asia (except for Korea and Taiwan), and all African countries except South Africa need a visa simply to enter Perú. All visas can be obtained at the Peruvian consulate in Machala (see **Practical Information**, p. 246). Occasionally immigrations officials ask for a **return ticket** out of the country or for **proof of sufficient funds** for each day travelers expect to spend there, but this is rather uncommon. Customs prohibits bringing bananas, oranges, used cars, or large quantities of clothing for resale into Perú.

■ Tumbes

In Tumbes, the sun shines. And shines. And shines some more. It shone on Pizarro when he sacked the then-Inca city (and missed out on the gold that neighboring tribes had just carried away during the Inca civil war). It shone on the oil prospectors who discovered South America's first oil here in 1862. It shone on the Ecuadorians who ruled the city for the first part of this century, and continued to shine on the Peruvians who took it back during the Border War of 1941. Tumbes is a sun-lover's paradise and a heat-hater's hell. The nearby beaches, unspoiled by hordes of oil-smeared bathers, are some of the finest in South America, and the surrounding mangrove swamps, tropical rainforest, and warm mineral mud baths offer more climate diversity than most other areas of Perú. On the other hand, Tumbes' streets tend to be dry, dusty, and scorching; the temperature in some unairconditioned budget hotel could cook your *ceviche*.

ORIENTATION AND PRACTICAL INFORMATION

The **Plaza de Armas,** on the southern edge of town, is the center of activity in Tumbes. Just south of the plaza's beautifully tiled walkways, the **Malecón Lishner** offers a shady walk along the **Río Tumbes.** On the cathedral end of the plaza, **Avenida Tumbes** (formerly Teniente Vasquez) and **Calle Bolívar** are the two main north-bound streets. Artisans and fruit-sellers hawk their wares at the **market** on Mariscal Castilla near the corner of Av. Ugarte. The center of town, near the Plaza de Armas, is much safer and better-maintained than the market area and eastern end of the Malecón.

Tourist Information: The Centro Civico, on the Plaza de Armas, offers various leaflets and local information for tourists. Open Mon.-Fri. 8am-4pm. Also ask for information at **Tumbes Tours,** 341 Av. Tumbes (tel. 52-6086; fax 52-2481). Open Mon.-Sat. 8am-6pm, Sun. 8am-noon.

Currency Exchange: For information on the **Peruvian exchange rate** and currency, see **Lima, Practical Information, p. 260. Money-changers** are far more common and flexible than banks near the Plaza de Armas. They generally quote good exchange rates, but beware of fixed calculators. If you simply cannot do without armed guards and long lines, **Banco de Crédito,** behind the cathedral on the Plaza de Armas, changes traveler's checks, dollars, and sucres to nuevos soles. Open Mon.-Fri. 9:15am-1:15pm and 4-6:30pm, Sat. 4:30-11pm.

Flights: Most of the airlines also have offices along Av. Tumbes, but a travel agency such as **Tumbes Tours** (see above), will be able to navigate you through the fare

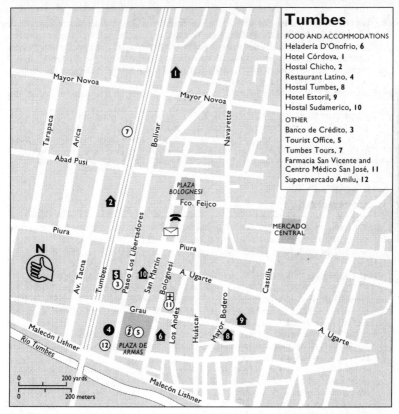

Tumbes

FOOD AND ACCOMMODATIONS
Heladería D'Onofrio, **6**
Hotel Córdova, **1**
Hostal Chicho, **2**
Restaurant Latino, **4**
Hostal Tumbes, **8**
Hotel Estoril, **9**
Hostal Sudamerico, **10**

OTHER
Banco de Crédito, **3**
Tourist Office, **5**
Tumbes Tours, **7**
Farmacia San Vicente and
Centro Médico San José, **11**
Supermercado Amilu, **12**

wars between Taucett, AeroPeru, and AeroContinente for flights to Lima (2½ hr., US$65-110), Trujillo (US$50-70), or Piura (US$15-18).

Buses: Most of the buses come in and go out along Av. Tumbes. **Civa,** 530 Tumbes (tel. 52-5120), has buses to **Lima** (5pm, 17hr., s/35, with bathroom, TV, and complimentary newspaper and snack) and **Trujillo** (5pm, 9hr., s/25, same amenities). There is a discount (s/10) for round-trip tickets. **Oltur S.A.,** 554 Bolívar (tel. 52-3355), has the only "bus-*cama*" trips to Lima (2:30pm, 17hr., with A/C, VCR, and bathrooms, s/50). That same bus stops in Trujillo (s/35). Oltur's "Servicio Economico," which is merely a seat in a bathroomless, hot, moving box is one of the cheapest ways to go south (s/35 to Lima, s/17 to Trujillo, s/12 to Chiclayo, 1:30pm). Other companies along Av. Bolívar offer similar low-priced, no-frills service. Local travel is generally done by **mototaxi,** s/2 - s/3 for a spin about town. Buses heading for the **playas** south of Tumbes pass by the bridge on Av. Tumbes' south end. To get to the **airport** north of Tumbes, take a *colectivo* (s/1) from the market on the corner of Ugarte and Av. Mariscal Castilla to the turn-off on Panamericana Norte or ask for one of the travel agencies to arrange a shuttle.

Taxis: Real taxis, other than in-town mototaxis, are difficult to find, but a few congregate in the market area.

Laundromat: Lavandería Flash, 1006 Av. Piura (tel. 52-3231), charges s/10 for 4 kilos of filthy clothes.

Pharmacies: As is so common in almost any town in South America, Tumbes has a *farmacía* on every corner. The **Farmacía San Vicente** on Jirón just off the plaza, is one of the best-stocked. Open Mon.-Sat. 9am-2pm and 4-9:30pm.

Hospitals/Clinics: The **Centro Médico San Jose** (tel. 52-3660), next door to Farmacía San Vicente, caters to tourists and locals (open daily 8am-8pm). For emergencies at odd hours, call the 24hr. emergency room/ambulance service at the **Hospital de Apoyo,** Av. Bolívar (tel. 52-2222).

Police: There are 3 different kinds of police in Tumbes, but unless you want to ask for a speeding ticket or sell Ecuadorian secrets to the army, the **Guardia Civil** at the San Jose Delegación (tel. 52-2331), north of town on the Panamericana Norte is your best bet as a 24hr. resource.

Post office: Calle San Martín 208 (open Mon.-Fri. 8am-6pm, Sat. 9am-1pm, with sporadic lunch breaks).

Telephone Services: Make local, national, and international calls from any **Telefónica de Perú** phone—dialing the international operator is a free call and other calls can be paid for with s/1 coins or the phone cards that are available in most *farmacías* and *bodegas*. If you have excessively complex phone needs, try Telefónica de Perú on the 6th block of Av. Piura below the tiled arch (open 8am-11pm daily).

Telephone code: 074.

ACCOMMODATIONS

Most of Tumbes' budget hotels (called "two-star" hostels or hotels) are within several blocks of the Plaza de Armas. All post their rates at the front desk, but most hotel owners will bargain for a *descuento* of up to s/5.

Hotel Córdova (tel. 52-3901), on Bolívar, and **Hotel Kiko's,** Bolívar 362 (tel. 52-3777), offer clean, basic rooms with windows and private (cold water) bathrooms. **Hotel Tumbes,** Grau 614 (tel. 52-2203) and **Hotel Estoril,** Huascar 317 (tel. 52-4906), are slightly farther away from the Plaza de Armas and therefore quieter. Singles s/17-20; doubles s/25-28; triples s/32-35.

Hostal Sudamerico, 126 San Martín (tel. 52-3415), has the cheapest rooms in town, but has only common bathrooms and rooms are less likely to have windows. Singles s/5; doubles s/10; triples s/12.

Hostal Chicho, Tumbes 327 (tel. 52-2282), offers the most amenities: hot water, radio/cassette player, TV, and fan. It also sports a convenient location near the bus terminals. Singles s/29; doubles s/35; triples s/41; room for 5-6 people s/70.

Hostal Casa Grillo, Panamericana Norte km 1236.5 (tel. 52-5207), south of Tumbes, is a pared-down, shared-bath version of a beach resort with a cheap (s/8-10) restaurant, rooms right on the beach, and laundry facilities. US$6 per person. Accessible via *colectivo* (s/1) from the corner of Piura and Av. Tumbes.

FOOD

You'll have no trouble finding *comida típica* in Tumbes. The *conchas negras* (black clams for which the region is famous), *ceviche,* and other seafood is universally fresh and well-prepared. **Panaderías** abound, with a particularly good one on the corner of Grau and Huascar, which offers fresh, warm rolls for pennies (multigrain *pan* s/.10; open Mon.-Sat. 8am-8pm, Sun. 9am-12pm and 6-9pm).

Restaurant Latino (tel. 52-3198) and **Restaurant Curich** (tel. 52-3201), neighbors on Calle Bolívar on the Plaza de Armas, have pleasant outdoor cafes and huge meals for s/10-15. (Latino open Mon.-Sat. 8am-12pm. Curich open daily 8am-10pm.)

Heladería D'Onofrio, across the plaza from Restaurant Latino, caters to the sweet tooth in all of us (s/2.50 for 6 bonbons; open daily 11am-11pm).

Supermercado Amilu, on the Plaza de Armas, serves to stock those backpacks well (open Mon.-Sat. 8:30am-9:30pm, Sun. 9am-1pm).

SIGHTS AND ENTERTAINMENT

The area surrounding Tumbes covers four completely different ecological zones, all easily accessible from Tumbes. First, there are the *playas*—all 100km of them. Take a *colectivo* south from Av. Tumbes near Piura (s/1-s/2), and take your pick of any spot on the white sand beaches that stretch out to the right of the Panamericana Norte. The villages of **Zorritos** (35min. south) and **Mancora** (1½hr. south) are popular destinations with a few small seafood restaurants, but you can ask the driver to drop you off at any point you want. To get back, flag down a north-bound *colectivo*. The second ecological zone, the *manglares* (mangroves) begins north of Tumbes at Puerto Pizarro. **Tumbes Tours** (see **Practical Information** above) has several excursions to the mangrove forests for US$15-20 per person, depending on group size. If you're in a more independent mood, take a *colectivo* north to Puerto Pizarro and ask one of the local fishermen to take you up the River Tumbes (about s/10 per person).

The *hervideros* (hot springs) in Bocapán, 35 km south of Tumbes off the Panamericana Norte, will drown your dermatological and spiritual woes in a sea of warm mineralized mud. The hot springs are just beginning to be developed as a tourist attraction and are still hard to reach without a car or tour from Tumbes Tours (US$10-15 per person), but are well worth the price. Two hours northeast of Tumbes await the orchids, butterflies, and savage beasts of the **Bosque Nacional de Tumbes.** Any of the travel agencies along Av. Tumbes can arrange tours for you, but Tumbes Tours is one of the best bargains at US$15 per person (less for larger groups) for a 12-hour tour including transportation, meals, and an informative guide.

Local residents emphasize that Tumbes is *muy tranquilo*. That translates into safety and cleanliness, but also into a sleepy nightlife. The *discotecas* near the Plaza de Armas are only lively on weekend nights and even then most empty out by 1 am. The **Restaurant Latino,** on the Plaza de Armas, has a large dance floor and salsa music on weekends. Smaller *discotecas* along the **Paseo de la Concordia,** off the Plaza de Armas, tend to play the latest "techno-hits" from 8pm-2am (no cover charge). The **Cine Teatro Tumbes,** on Av. Bolivar near Piura, shows one movie daily (s/2).

Lima, Perú

US$1 = 2.66 soles	1 sol = US$0.38
CDN$1 = 1.92 soles	1 sol = CDN$0.52
UK£1 = 4.25 soles	1 sol = UK£0.24
IR£1 = 3.81 soles	1 sol = IR£0.26
AUS$1 = 1.96 soles	1 sol = AUS$0.51
NZ$1 = 1.70 soles	1 sol = NZ$0.59
SARand = 0.57 soles	1 sol = SARand$1.76

The city of Lima began as a quietly prosperous Inca city on the banks of the Río Rímac; it was not the center of the empire, but had its share of gold, silver, and impressive architectural masterpieces. When the Spanish conquered Lima, they stripped the gold and destroyed most Inca buildings. The next cycle of Lima's history began as the Spanish built their city on top of the Inca ruins. The Spanish cathedral arose on top of the Inca temple, the Palacio de Gobierno took root on the Inca king's house, and so on. The city became the commercial and administrative center of the Spanish empire in South America—Chinese silks, fine furniture, and exotic spices flowed through the city's rich markets, and *criollos* spent fortunes on palatial mansions. South America's first university, the University of San Marcos, was founded in Lima in 1551 and the continent's first printing press went into action in 1594. Lima was the headquarters of the Spanish conquistadores in Perú for a generation or so—beginning when Francisco Pizarro founded the city in 1535—during which time the conquistadors accumulated a sizeable stash of human bones (now in the catacombs of the San Franciscan monastery). Lima prospered for quite some time, until an earthquake in 1746 reduced the city to 20 houses and killed 10% of the population.

The next cycle in Lima's history took place in the end of the 18th century under Viceroy Amat. The governor took advantage of the rubble to rebuild the city as he saw fit: as ornate as many a baroque European city. Lima's wide streets, old houses with elaborately carved balconies, and immense plazas are Amat's legacy. As the 19th century rolled on, and Lima became accustomed to its great post-independence economic stature, the city rose toward prosperity as the main port in mineral-rich Perú.

The good times didn't last forever, though; in the last half of this century, Lima has suffered political and economic crises, rising poverty, and rapid urbanization. Although the decline has not been as dramatic as the Spanish takeover or the 1746 earthquake, the problems of overpopulation—the proliferation of smog-emission, strained public utilities, and the struggle for scarce jobs—took their toll on Lima. In the past decade, generally considered the nadir of recent history, Lima has been pounded by terrorist bombs, shamed by a hostage crisis in the Japanese Embassy, impoverished by the severe hyperinflation of the late 1980s, overwhelmed by immigrants from Perú's interior provinces, and beset by an epidemic of cholera. The results of these events—aggressive street vendors, highly visible poverty, frequent petty crime, and unsafe lettuce, all combined with Lima's notoriously unpleasant cloudy weather—carved the city a reputation as a necessary evil: a gateway to Perú, but not a great place to visit.

The last decade, however, is in the past. Lima's fortunes are once again on the rise: the historic center is being restored, parks have been replanted, terrorist activity has been nearly eradicated, police vigilance has increased, and the cholera has retreated. The city's rich history, cosmopolitan atmosphere, and beautiful seaside parks are ready to redefine Lima as a destination city rather than a grimy portal into Perú.

▓ Orientation

Lima is huge—if you spend any time here, it's well worth your *soles* to buy a map. The main tourist districts are **Lima Centro, San Isidro, Miraflores,** and **Barranco.**

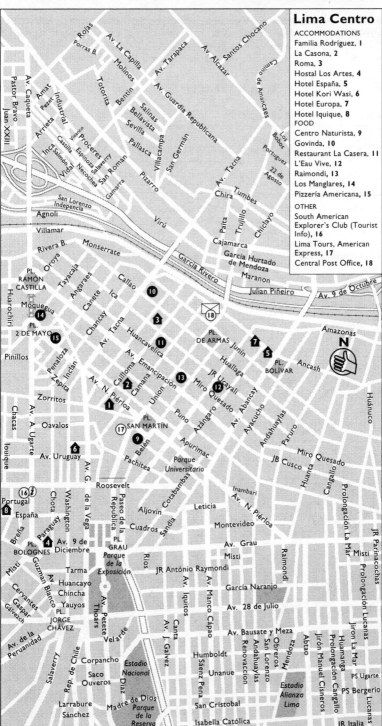

Lima Centro

ACCOMMODATIONS
Familia Rodríguez, 1
La Casona, 2
Roma, 3
Hostal Los Artes, 4
Hotel España, 5
Hotel Kori Wasi, 6
Hotel Europa, 7
Hotel Iquique, 8
FOOD
Centro Naturista, 9
Govinda, 10
Restaurant La Casera, 11
L'Eau Vive, 12
Raimondi, 13
Los Manglares, 14
Pizzería Americana, 15

OTHER
South American
Explorer's Club (Tourist
Info), 16
Lima Tours, American
Express, 17
Central Post Office, 18

LIMA, PERÚ

Avenida Arequipa connects the center to the southern suburbs of San Isidro and Miraflores. **Avenida Larco** runs into **El Libertador** to connect Miraflores to Barranco. The **Via Extoresa,** parallel to the slower **Paseo de la República,** runs north-south to provide a quick, direct route from Lima Centro to the southern suburbs.

■ Practical Information

USEFUL ORGANIZATIONS

Tourist Office: PROMPERU, on the 14th floor of the Ministerio de Industria building, Calle 1 (tel. 224-3125 or 224-3279), Corpac, San Isidro, has a binder full of tourist info, a few glossy maps and brochures, and a lot of posters. Open Mon.-Fri. 9am-6pm. The tourist office near the Plaza de San Martín, on Jirón Belén 1066, has a few booklets on walking tours of Lima. Open Mon.-Fri. 9am-4pm, Sat. 10am-1pm. The **Biblioteca Nacional** in the same building has more in-depth info (in Spanish) on Lima's history. Open Mon.-Fri. 9am-4pm. You must leave some form of I.D. to enter the PROMPERU office and the Biblioteca. Private tourist resources, such as the South American Explorer's Club (see below) or travel agencies are generally better-stocked. While the free tourist maps are helpful for the center of the city, anyone staying in Lima will want to buy a more complete map. **Guía 2000,** about s/40 in any bookstore, is detailed, laminated, and easy to carry.

Tourist Resource: The **South American Explorer's Club,** Av. República de Portugal 146 (tel. 425-0142; email montagne@amauta.vcp.net.pe), off Alfonse Ugarte near the 13th block, is by far the best tourist resource in Lima. Their clubhouse is a hub of gringo activity in Perú, and friendly English-speaking staff members will offer advice on all things Peruvian and South American—from reliable dentists to tips on trekking, useful info abounds in their library, up-to-date info binders, and trip report files. Message boards, a book exchange, equipment storage, mail, phone, fax, and email service, flight confirmations, and complimentary tea round

The Tupac Amaru Hostage Crisis

On December 17, 1996, during an elaborate soiree at the Japanese ambassador's residence in Lima, a group of Tupac Amaru guerillas blew a hole in the back of the ambassador's home and crashed the party. Once inside, they set off explosives and took hundreds of hostages, initiating what would turn into an interminable stand-off between the rebels and Peruvian President **Alberto Fujimori.** The rebels demanded the release of their jailed comrades, captured earlier in the year. In spite of the fact that his mother and younger brother were among the hostages, Fujimori took a characteristically hard line, refusing outright to free any Tupac Amaru prisoners. In the first few weeks, the rebels let many of the hostages go, but negotiations failed to bring about a solution. While the crisis initially attracted international attention, the affair dragged on, and even many Peruvians started to lose interest. The Tupac Amaru movement, which was founded in 1984 to defend the rights of Perú's indigenous underclass, found little sympathy even among those it claimed to be fighting for—after years of civil war, Perú's poor were tired of fighting and bloodshed.

In March, 1997, the hostage-taking found its way back into the headlines, with rumors that the Peruvian military was digging a tunnel under the residence in preparation for a rescue attempt, a claim that was vigorously denied by Fujimori. The rumors turned out to be true—on April 22, with a negotiated settlement apparently near, a team of Israeli-trained Peruvian commandos stormed the building, freeing the hostages and killing the rebels.

In the immediate aftermath, Fujimori was hailed around the world as a hero—the only hostage that died during the operation had succumbed to a heart attack, rather than shrapnel or gunfire. Only days later, stories of surrendering rebels being executed by the rescue team began to appear in the press, bringing Fujimori's record on human rights into the spotlight again.

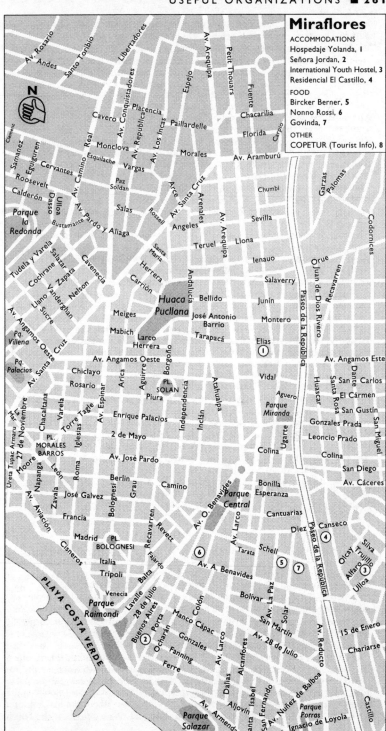

Miraflores

ACCOMMODATIONS
Hospedaje Yolanda, 1
Señora Jordan, 2
International Youth Hostel, 3
Residencial El Castillo, 4
FOOD
Bircker Berner, 5
Nonno Rossi, 6
Govinda, 7
OTHER
COPETUR (Tourist Info), 8

LIMA, PERU

out the list of SAEC amenities. But nothing is free in this world: membership costs US$40, US$20 per additional member. Open Mon.-Fri. 9am-5pm.

Travel Agencies: Lima Tours, Jr. Belén 1040 (tel. 432-1765), sets the standard for *agencias de viaje* with its wide selection of city and department tours and comprehensive travel services. Open Mon.-Fri. 9:15am-4:45pm. **COPETUR,** Schell 120 #25 (tel. 446-3083 or 444-8680), near Miraflores Parque Kennedy, offers impeccably organized trips all over Perú at good prices. One of the highest densities of travel agencies is on Larco near the Ovalo of Miraflores—beware of unbelievably cheap packages. If your tour guide does abandon you in the middle of the Andes, call 224-7888 (24hr.) for the Tourist Bureau of Complaints.

Embassies: Canada, Av. Federico Gerdes 130 (tel. 444-4015); **France,** Av. Arequipa 3415 (tel. 221-0273 or 221-7837); **Germany,** Av. Arequipa 4210 (tel. 422-4919); **Sweden,** Camino Real 348 (tel. 421-3400); **Switzerland,** Av. Salaverry 3240 (tel. 264-0305); **United Kingdom,** Natalio Sánchez 125 (tel. 431-5314 or 431-6395); **United States,** Av. Arenales 855 (tel. 330-8557).

Immigration Office: Dirección General de Migraciones, Av. España and Av. Huaraz (tel. 330-4114 or 330-4030), can extend your visa and issue new tourist cards.

Cultural Centers: Find home country newspapers, film screenings, and cultural events at the **Alliance Française,** Av. Arequipa 4595 (tel. 241-7014), **Centro Boliviano,** Av. Valles del Sur 350 (tel. 438-2334), **Centro de Estudios Brasileños,** Av. Grau 270 (tel. 241-0655), the **Instituto Cultural Pemano-Nortecamericano,** Av. Arequipa 4798 (tel. 446-0381), **Goethe Instituto,** Jirón Nazca 722 (tel. 433-3180), and the **British Cultural Association,** Av. Arequipa 3495 (tel. 470-5577).

Currency Exchange: There are *casas de cambios* and street money-changers all over the city, but the best place to do your banking is Miraflores, where most banks have offices on Av. Larco (blocks 5-8). The money changers are regulated, and you are less likely to be robbed. Five of Perú's largest bank chains: **Banco de Crédito, Banco Wiese, Interbank, Banco Continental,** and **Banco Latino** change traveler's checks and cash Mon.-Fri. 9:15am-6pm, Sat. 9:30am-12:30pm. Banco de Crédito, Av. Larco 1099, Miraflores, has ATMs that will allow you to withdraw money with PIN-enabled VISAs; Banco Wiese and Banco Latino will let you withdraw cash with a MasterCard after you've stood in a long line. Cirrus service does not work in Perú, but Plus cards work in Banco de Crédito's Unicard machines at Jr. Lampa 499 and Av. Larco 1099 (Miraflores).

American Express: In the Lima Tours office, Jr. Belén 1040 (tel. 424-6410).

Post Office: The postal system has recently been privatized and is supposedly more reliable. You can mail letters from **Wong** and **Santa Isabel** supermarkets (see **Supermarkets** below) and from the **Central Post Office** (tel. 427-5592), Pasaje Piura near Plaza de Armas (open Mon.-Sat. 8am-8pm, Sun. 8am-2pm; Lista de Correos). It's safer to send packages via **DHL,** Los Castaños 225 (tel. 954-4345), San Isidro; **EMS** (tel. 432-3950), next door to the Central Post Office, or **Federal Express,** Jorge Chávez 475 (tel. 242-2280), Miraflores, open Mon.-Fri. 8:30am-6pm. The **South American Explorer's Club** is one of the best places to receive mail in Lima if you are a member.

Emergency: Police 105, Fire 116.

Police: In **Miraflores:** tel. 445-6583, 445-4216, or 445-3537; **San Isidro:** tel. 442-4610; **Barranco:** tel. 477-0088; **Breña:** tel. 431-1425.

Internet Access: In addition to the South American Explorer's Club, **Café Internet Amarelo,** Av. Jorge Basadre 395 (tel. 442-0791) and **Interaxis Café,** Calle Tarata 277, have internet access and email daily for s/10 per hr. 10am-4pm, and s/12 per 30min. 4pm-midnight.

Telephone Service: You can dial the MCI (107) and AT&T (0800-50000) operators from most Telefónica del Perú phones, found on every street corner. The call is usually free, but occasionally costs s/0.30. Paying in Perú is more expensive than using a calling card or calling collect, but if you have to, Telefónica del Perú offers international service, as do many hotel receptionists. Dial 108 to reach an international operator, 109 to make long-distance national calls. Local calls can be made from any of the numerous pay phones. It is often easier to buy a Telefónica del Perú or Telepoint card from any *botica* or street vendor rather than looking for a phone that accepts coins. **Faxes:** You can send and receive faxes at the South

American Explorer's Club (fax 425-0142), or any Telefónica del Perú office such as the one on Av. Bolivia 347 near Ugarte, Av. Arequipa 1155 (tel. 470-1616) or Javier Prado Este 2392 (tel. 224-3030; s/8-10 per page). Open daily 7am-11pm.
Telephone Code: Peru: 51; Lima: 1.

TRANSPORTATION

Airport: **Aeropuerto Internacional Jorge Chávez** is located north of Lima on Av. Faucett in Callao. It is a relatively unsafe area; taxis are recommended (s/15-20 is a fair price between the airport and Miraflores). Several of the *colectivos* (s/1) that run along Av. Benavides and Brasil go to the outside gate of the airport, and unreliable buses (s/7-10) run along Av. Abancay.

Airlines: **Copa,** Av. Dos de Mayo 775 (tel. 444-7815 or 444-7816), **Iberia,** Camino Real 390 (tel. 421-4616), and **Lan Chile,** Av. José Pardo 805 (tel. 241-5522) have frequent flights to other Latin American countries. **Continental** (tel. 22-4340), **United Airlines,** Camino Real 390 (tel. 421-3334), and **American Airlines,** Juan de Arona 830 (tel. 442-8555), serve the U.S. and Europe, but usually have higher prices for flights within Latin America. **Aero Continente,** Av. José Pardo 651 (tel. 242-4260), **Faucett,** Av. Faucett 367 (tel. 451-6040), **Americana,** Av. Larco 345 (tel. 445-8089 or 445-5758), and **Aeroperu,** Centro Comercial Molicentro (tel. 368-0420), La Molina, are the principal domestic carriers.

Local Buses: Buses and *colectivos* (s/0.80-1) are cheapest to get around the city between 6am-1am. They are easy to use—all have their routes posted on the sides and will stop upon request (just say *"bajo aquí"*). The main *colectivo* routes are: Arequipa/Tacna/Wilson from Miraflores to San Isidro to Lima Centro; and Brasil/La Marina/Faucett from Miraflores to the market along La Marina and then to the airport. Any bus marked Chorrillos/Barranco will go to the southern nightlife district via Av. Larco and sometimes Arequipa. Many *colectivos* run east and west along Javier Prado from La Molina to San Isidro and Magdalena del Mar. The chaotic mix of *colectivos* and buses can be confusing at first, but the best thing to do is relate your destination to one of the major bus routes above, then look for your street name.

Long-Distance Buses: There is no *terminal terrestre,* so you'll have to go to the individual bus terminals. **Cruz del Sur,** Jr. Quilca 531 (tel. 432-1570), goes to **Arequipa** (17hr., s/35); **Chiclayo** (11-12hr., s/25-40); **Chimbote** (5½hr., s/15-25); **Chincha** (32hr., s/65); **Huancayo** (6½-7hr., s/20-23); **Huaraz** (7½hr., s/25); **Ica** (4hr., s/15); **Ilo** (4hr., s/15); **Juliaca** (36hr., s/55); **Nazca** (6-8hr., s/15); **Piura** (15hr., s/35-50); **Puno** (36hr., s/55); **Sullana** (15hr., s/35-55); **Tacna** (23hr., s/40-70); **Trujillo** (9hr., s/20-35); and **Tumbes** (20hr., s/40-65). **Ormeño,** Av. Javier Prado Este 1059 (tel. 472-1710), and Av. Carlos Zavala (tel. 427-5679), has buses to **Arequipa** (14-16hr., s/37-60); **Cañete** (3hr., s/4); **Chiclayo** (s/32); **Chincha** (3-½hr., s/5-20); **Casco** (36hr., s/72); **Huaraz** (7-½hr., s/22); **Ica** (4hr., s/10-40); **Juliaca** (36hr., s/67); **Nazca** (6-8hr., s/15); **Pisco** (4hr., s/8-25); **Puno** (36hr., s/67); **Sullana** (15hr., s/37); **Tacna** (23hr., s/45-70); **Trujillo** (7hr., s/40); and **Tumbes** (23hr., s/45-60). **Rodriguez,** Av. Roosevelt 354 (tel. 428-0506), specializes in trips to **Huaraz** (8hr., s/15) and the smaller towns near it: **Caraz** (9hr., s/15); **Carhuaz** (9hr., s/16); and **Chimbote** (8hr., s/15).

Taxis: The cheapest taxis in Lima are VW bugs and small Ticos with flourescent stickers, but these can be dangerous. If you do take a VW/Tico taxi, bargain with the driver—a ride from Lima Center to Miraflores should cost s/4-5; within the Miraflores/San Isidro/Barranco area s/3-4. The official taxi services are generally safer, but much more expensive (s/7 within Miraflores) and unwilling to bargain: **Eco Taxi** (tel. 446-6776), **City Taxi** (tel. 326-1885), **EconoTaxi** (tel. 421-7570), **Happy Taxi** (tel. 740-6979), **Taxi Mundo** (tel. 261-3022), **Taxi Real** (tel. 470-6263), and **Taxi Seguro** (tel. 438-7210).

Car Rental: Avis (tel. 452-4774), **Budget** (tel. 452-8706), **Dollar** (tel. 452-6741), **Hertz** (tel. 451-8189), and **National** (tel. 452-3426) all have offices at the airport. Rates change frequently, but expect to pay US$40-50 per day for a compact car.

Bookstores: Most of the English bookstores are in Miraflores near the Ovalo/Parque Kennedy. **Mosca Azul,** Malecón Armendariz 713 (tel. 445-6264), has used non-Spanish books. Open Mon.-Sat. 10am-8pm, Sun. 3-8pm. The **Instituto Geográfico Nacional,** Av. Aramburu 1190 (tel. 475-3085), near the 9th block of Rep. de Panamá sells maps, as does the South American Explorer's Club; their **book exchange** is the best place to find new reading material.

OTHER PRACTICAL INFORMATION

Shopping: The glitziest shopping is at the Centro Camino Real on Camino Real in San Isidro and along Av. Larco in Miraflores. The prices are far from bargains, but the people-watching is interesting. In the center of Lima, the 5th block of Jr. Unión has been converted into an outdoor mall that seems to specialize in shoes. The much cheaper and "Peruvian" artisan markets are along Av. La Marina around blocks 800-900. The quality of the sweaters, wall hangings, and bags varies, but you can find crafts and clothes from all over Perú. There are also more expensive artisan markets in Miraflores' Parque Kennedy or on the 6th block of La Paz.

Camping Gear: Alpamayo, Av. Larco 345 (tel. 445-1671), **Todo Camping,** Av. Angamos Oeste 350 (tel. 445-1696), and **Altamira,** Arica 800 (tel. 445-1286), have high quality, though very expensive, camping gear.

Supermarkets: Wong, at Ovalo Gutiérrez, and also Rep. de Panamá, and **Santa Isabel,** Av. Javier Prado Este 2030, Av. J. Pardo 707, and C.C. San Felipe Tolas 74-75, Jesus María, dominate the *supermercado* scene. All are open approx. 8am-9pm; Sta. Isabel's Av. Benavides 467 location is open 24hr. **Hipermercado Metro,** Venezuela and Alfonso Ugarte, Breña, is one of the few near Lima Center.

Laundry: Laverap, Schell 601 (tel. 241-0759), and **Lava Philip,** Av. Arica 448, have self-service washing and drying for s/5-7 (depending on load size), or do your laundry for you. **Lavacoin,** in Residencias San Felipe behind Sta. Isabel Market, has a TV and microwave popcorn to munch on while you wait (s/5 for washer or dryer).

Pharmacies: Abundant all over the city. **Morelti,** Av. Benavides 1741, Miraflores, and **Botica Fiorella,** Jr. Carhuaz 1199 (tel. 432-3829), Breña, have 24hr. service.

Clinics: The **Clínica Anglo-Americana** (tel. 221-3656), Av. Salazar San Isidro, has the best selection of vaccines (but no typhoid vaccine), while the **Clínica Adventist de Miraflores,** Malecón Balta 956 (tel. 445-5395), treats those illnesses you weren't vaccinated against. **Cruz Verde** (tel. 475-0446), San Isidro, **Auxilio Médico** (tel. 423-4236), Breña, and **Ambulancias San Cristóbal** (tel. 440-0200 or 441-9931), Lince, have ambulance service. Dr. Alejandro Bussalleu Rivera (tel. 471-2238), at the Instituto Médico Lince at León Velarde 221 speaks English and specializes in stomach troubles (s/100 for initial consultation).

▓ Accommodations

LIMA CENTRO

Casas antiguas are by far the most attractive and affordable options in the center of Lima. If you ignore the concave iron beds, uneven floor boards, and occasional errant paint chip, you can live like a *conquistador* in rooms with private balconies, elaborately painted ceilings (a la Sistine Chapel), and arched doorways. The rambling old mansions are usually filled with a young, international crowd and can be good places to meet other travelers. While staying in Lima Centro is more convenient for museums and will give you a better sense of Lima's colonial history than living in modern Miraflores, the area can be unsafe at night and noisy during the day.

Familia Rodríguez, 730 Nicolás de Piérola (tel. 423-6465), 2nd floor. Clean, pleasant family house with extra beds for 12 people, but only one bathroom. US$6 per person includes breakfast, phone, and fax access.

La Casona, Jirón Moquegua 289 (tel. 427-6273). Slightly decaying, but clean and plant-filled colonial house. Good restaurant in blue-tiled inner courtyard. All rooms have private baths. Singles US$8; doubles US$12; triples US$14.

Roma, Jr. Ica 326 (tel. 427-7576). One of the few hotels you'll find with your own skylight and angel paintings on the ceiling. Rooms vary in attractiveness—look before you pay. Rooms cost US$10, with hot water private bath US$20.

Hostal Los Artes, Jr. Chota 1454 (tel. 433-1454). Dutch-owned, cultured old house near the Museo de Arte and SAEC. Has small art gallery. Singles US$9; doubles with private bath US$12.

Hotel España, Azángaro 105 (tel. 428-5546). A rambling old mansion now echoing with the commotion of European, Israeli, and U.S. backpackers. Plants grow, birds fly, and traffic outside honks as international travelers meet, greet, and plan future adventure. Hot water (in theory), laundry, message board, good cafe, and locked storage facilities. Singles US$6; doubles US$10; triples US$12; dormitory US$3.

Hotel Kori Wasi, Washington 1139 (tel. 433-8127). Rooms are perpetually dark, but they are clean. A guard posted at the door ensures safety. Most rooms have windows; all have TV, fridge, and private bath. Singles US$8; doubles US$10.

Hotel Europa, Ancash 376 (tel. 427-3351). This *casa antigua* needs some more open windows, but otherwise it offers the same deluxe accommodations as its neighbor, Hotel España. No phones, only common bath, occasional carved wood paneling. Singles US$5; doubles US$8; triples US$10.

Hotel Iquique, Iquique 758 (tel. 433-4724). Nondescript, clean rooms; close to Museo de Arte and SAEC. Private baths (hot water). Singles US$10; doubles US$13.

SOUTH OF CENTER

Hotels get larger, more modern, and more expensive as you move from Lima Centro to the San Isidro/Miraflores area. The area is generally safer, quieter, cleaner, and more convenient for seaside nightlife—all advantages have a price. You'd have to pay US$150 per night to swim in a private pool in one of the Park Plaza hotels, but there are several more affordable options if you've left your Platinum card at home.

Near Center Lima

Hostal Renacimiento, Parque Hernán Velarde 52 (tel. 433-2806). A well-kept *casa antigua* in a quiet, tree-filled park near the first block of Arequipa. Simple, well-lit rooms, most with hot water and private bath. Convenient for buses to Chosica, Lurín, and other near-Lima excursions; also near main route (Av. Arequipa) to southern suburbs. Singles US$15; doubles US$30.

Hotel Mont Blanc, Jirón Emilio Fernández 640 (tel. 433-8055). All the amenities of a 3-star hotel: toilet paper folded into triangles, heavy ponderous furniture in the hallway, fans, TV, refrigerators in the rooms, private baths, and even room service. Airy old house with inner courtyard. Singles US$17; doubles US$29; triples US$32.

Hotel Columbus, Av. Arequipa 1421 (tel. 471-0129). Spotless rooms with tasteless floral bedspreads; most have private balcony and TV. Dim hallways with suspiciously threadbare carpets belie the light, airy rooms. Doubles US$24, 10% more with credit card payment, but frequent random discounts.

San Isidro/Miraflores

Youth Hostel Malka, Los Lirios 165 (tel. 442-0162), San Isidro. Given its low price and only 16 beds, this private houselike/*albergue juvenil* is almost always full. Quiet, safe neighborhood, good security, and stern *señora* to keep watch over everything. US$6 per person.

Hospedaje Yolanda, Domingo Elías 230 (tel. 445-7565), near Arequipa block 47. Small, spotless rooms in private house. Use of kitchen, small lounge with outdated English and French magazines. Hot water, too. Singles US$20; doubles US$30.

Señora Jordan, Porta 724 (tel. 445-9840), near Ovalo, Miraflores. Call ahead to see if the talkative *señora* has free rooms—her herd of nephews, grandchildren, and company often fill the house and crowd the common bathrooms. It's like home—if your home has trees with grapefruit-sized avocados in the courtyard. US$13 per person, with hearty breakfast US$15. Reservations essential.

Pensión Jose Luis, F. Paula Ugarriza 727 (tel. 444-1015), Miraflores. The low price of a hostel, but none of the institutional feel. Winding old house with plants, parakeets, and sunny patios. Cable TV (BBC, MTV...) and owner speaks fluent English. Small rooms, some kitchenettes. With breakfast US$12 per person. Must call ahead.

International Youth Hostel, Casimiro Ulloa 328 (tel. 446-5488). It's hard to turn an aristocratic old house into an institution, but neatly lined up bunkbeds and orange lockers have succeeded. It's the largest hostel in the area, with typical hostel amenities: kitchen, dining room, locker room-like bathrooms. Hot water. No phone. Single with private bath US$16; dormitory-style room US$10.

Residencial El Castillo, Diez Canseco 580 (tel. 446-9501). The family has adjusted well to the strangers living in their midst. Friendly, quiet house; all rooms with private bath, hot water. Use the kitchen upon (polite) request. Mostly doubles, some singles; US$12 per person.

■ Food

Peruvian food (at least as Lima interprets it) is heavy on the fish and rice. *Criollo* food, often the substance of the cheap lunchtime set *menús,* is usually a sauce-covered or stir-fried meat and potato dish with a side of rice. It's definitely worth a visit to one of the more expensive restaurants to sample true *criollo* food—the cheap menus tend to be indifferently prepared. *Chifas* (chinese food restaurants), are common, though not necessarily related to Chinese food elsewhere.

LIMA CENTRO

The lunchtime *menús* in Lima Centro offer the most calories per dollar, but are not always the best representatives of Peruvian cuisine. For US$2 you can buy a drink, soup, appetizer, and main course of *criollo* food in any small, street-side restaurant, but for a few *soles* more, you can dine in style and enjoy a whole new level of food.

Pizzería Americana, 520 Nicolás de Piérola, serves (you guessed it) American-style pizzas with delicious chewy crusts. The cool, dark interior is not far from a Pizzeria Uno. Pizzas s/8-14. Open daily 10am-midnight.

Centro Naturista, 958 Nicolas de Piérola, substitutes tofu for meat in its wide selection of *criollo* food, and will modify any of its dishes to suit particular dietary restrictions. Juices s/1-2, main dishes s/4-5. Open daily 9am-9pm.

Los Manglares, Jr. Moquegua 266 (tel. 427-6126), is a campy combination of a fish-tank and Tumbes-style fisherman's restaurant. It's a bit disconcerting to eat *cebiche* (s/10-15) under the watchful gaze of the larger-than-life sea creatures painted on the walls, but the restaurant is one of the less risky places to eat seafood in Lima Centro. Live *criollo* music daily 2-11pm. Open daily 8am-12:45am.

Restaurant La Casera, Huancavelica 244, near the Teatro Municipal, is one of the more popular places for a lunchtime *menú* (s/5). Open daily 8am-10pm.

L'Eau Vive, Ucayali 370 (tel. 427-5612). The s/8 lunch menu is one of the best bargains in central Lima—carefully prepared French delicacies served by friendly nuns can't be found for this price anywhere else. The old convent's quiet interior seems like heaven after the *ruido* (noise) outside. A la carte lunch s/10-20, dinner s/20-30. Open daily 12:30-3pm and 7:30-9:30pm.

Raimondi, 110 Miró Quesada. A favorite haunt of Lima's dark-suited businessman, it maintains its reasonable prices for the occasional scruffy tourist. The set lunch is s/10, but a la carte dinners get pricey at s/20 and up. Open daily 10am-9pm.

OUTSIDE LIMA CENTRO

Restaurants become more expensive as you move away from the tangled downtown area. With a few exceptions listed below, there are three types of restaurants in the San Isidro/Miraflores/Barranco area: cheap fast food; expensive cafes where the people are more beautiful than the food; and succulent, delicious, exquisite, and otherwise excellent, relatively expensive *criollo* restaurants and *cebicherías.* The latter, although detrimental to your budget, are definitely worth the extra *soles.*

Restaurant Pisces, 2700 Petit Tuouars (tel. 440-3880). The *aguadito de mero* (fisherman's stew) is a festival of fresh *mariscos* (s/13). The s/4.50 *menú,* usually featuring fried fish, puts all imposters to shame. Open daily 10am-9pm.

Bircker Berner, Schell 598 (tel. 444-4250). Slightly pretentious vegetarian restaurant (set lunch menu noon-1pm, s/8.50) in nutritional center. Consult trained nutritionists and buy miracle herbs in the Naturalix Store. Open Mon.-Sat. 8:30am-10:40pm.

Govinda, Schell 630, is a little less scientific when it comes to vegetarian nutrition, but the Hare Krishna's cuisine (s/8-15) demonstrates that religion can keep up with science any day. Open daily 9am-midnight.

Nonno Rossi, Porta 185a. *Criollo* food that is similar—except in price (*menú* s/6)—to food in Lima Centro. Sandwiches and snacks, too. Open Mon.-Sat. 10am-11pm.

Vrinda, Av. J. Prado Este 185. Cheapest vegetarian food south of Lima Centro. A bulletin board advertises trips to "ecological communities" for yoga and meditation. Whole food shop sells organic yogurt and other rarities. Open Mon.-Fri. 10am-7pm.

Punta Sal, Av. Conquistadores 948, San Isidro, is famous for its fresh *cebiche* (s/24-30). Think of the high price as insurance against sickness—after all, this is raw fish you're eating. Open daily 11am-5pm.

Cheap, Fast Food

The cheapest food options in Miraflores are the fast food *pollo a la brasa* and pizza places. **Subito** (pizza), **Bembo's** (burgers), and **Chifast** (Chinese food), across from the Sta. Isabel Supermarket on Benavides near Larco, will stuff you full of greasy Peruvian fast food for s/5-10 (open Sun.-Thurs. 11am-midnight, Fri.-Sat. 11am-2am). **Silvestre's,** in the same cluster on Benavides, has healthier fruit shakes and vegetarian sandwiches, but the *menú económico,* for s/10, is double the going rate in Lima Centro. Open daily 7am-midnight. **Super Rueda II,** Porta 133, is like Taco Bell with sandwiches (open Sun.-Thurs. 10am-midnight, Fri.-Sat. 10am-2am). **El Peruanito,** Angamos 391, near the Via Expresa, has some of the best sandwiches (s/5) in metropolitan Lima (open Mon.-Thurs. 8am-midnight, Fri.-Sat. 8am-2am).

Cafes

Feast your eyes, not your stomach in San Isidro and Miraflores' overpriced cafes. You'll spend more for a slice of tasteless quiche than for a full meal in Lima Centro in these gathering places of the beautiful ones, but the drinks are quite affordable.

Ovalo Gutiérrez, where Comandante Espinar, Conquistadores, and Av. Santa Cruz meet, Miraflores, has several overpriced, yuppy gathering places. **Mango's** charges s/22 for a sandwich and pisco sour and **Bohemia's** food, while well-prepared, will cost s/40 for dinner. Both open Sun.-Wed. 7am-1am, Thurs. 7am-4am, Fri.-Sat. 24hr.

Gelateria Laritza D., 845 Comandante Espinar, has some of the best ice cream in Lima (s/3.50 for two scoops). Open daily noon-12:30am.

Café Olé, Pancho Fierro 115, has a pleasant tree-enclosed patio on the corner in San Isidro's ritziest shopping district. Turns into a sea of dark suits and pearls at night. Sangria s/15 per ½L. Open daily 7:30am-2am.

Café Café, on Olaya just off Parque Kennedy. Good coffee drinks and ice cream; filled with chic 20-somethings. Open Sun.-Wed. 7am-2am, Thurs.-Sat. 7am-3am.

Fine Food

Manos Morenas, 409 Pedro de Osma Barranco (tel. 467-0421). *Criollo* food at its best, served in a 19th-century mansion near the ocean. Live *criollo* music shows often accompany dinner Wed.-Sat. Entrees s/20-25. Open Mon.-Sat. 12:30-4:30pm and 7:30-11:30pm, Sun. 12:30-4:30pm.

El Señorío de Sulco, Malecón Cisneros 1470 (tel. 445-6640). The Incas would have been obese if their food was anything like Señorío's. They use only traditional tools—like earthen pots—to prepare exquisite fish, meat, and vegetarian dishes (s/25-35). Open Mon.-Sat. 12:30-4:30pm and 7-11:30pm, Sun. 12:30-4:30pm.

Las Brujas de Cachiche, Av. Bolognesi 460 (tel. 444-5310), will bewitch you with their *tamales verdes* (s/15) and beguile you with fish from the sea. Have no illusions, however, the bill for the meal (s/40-45 per person) will not disappear. Open Mon.-Sat. noon-4:30pm and 7pm-1am, Sun. noon-4:30pm.

■ Sights

Most of Lima's historical sights—plazas, museums, and *casas antiguas*—are clustered in the complicated maze known as Lima Centro. This district of Lima, bounded roughly by **Avenida 28 de Julio** to the south, **Avenida Alfonso Ugarte** to the west, **Río Rimac** to the north, and **Avenida Abancay** to the east, was built on top of the old Incan capital and almost nothing remains of the pre-colonial Lima. One of the last visible reminders of the country's indigenous heritage, the crowds of *ambulantes* (street vendors) have been removed in the past year in an effort to renovate the aging, decrepit city center. The center has become much safer and cleaner and is maintained by hordes of orange-clad municipal sweepers and patrolled by mysterious men in blue, but it is still unadvisable to wander around aimlessly at night.

A small part of Lima's historical center spills over into **Rímac** to the north of the river, across the 17th-century **Puente de Piedra.** While the center shows what Lima was, the southern districts of **Miraflores** and **San Isidro** demonstrate what Lima might be in a few decades. The glittering, modern suburbs between the center and beach are the commercial heart of Lima as well as fashionable high-rent residential districts. **Barranco,** further south on the coast, was an outlying beach resort for colonial Lima, but modern transportation and urban sprawl have made it an easily accessible, popular nightlife district for young *limeños*.

PLAZAS

The **Plaza de Armas** is the pride of central Lima. Built squarely on top of an Inca temple dedicated to the Puma god, the last Inca king's palace, and an Incan envoy's mansion, the square now glorifies Spanish culture. An ornate fountain, beds of red and white flowers, and a larger-than-life statue of Francisco Pizarro on horseback dominate the square, while a large stone monument to the Inca king Tauri Chusko stands on a side street beside the Palacio Municipal. In **Palacio de Gobierno** to the north, a replication of Pizarro's original house is now home to a recreated baroque interior and some slightly mismatched colonial-style furniture (free guided tours from entrance on Jr. de la Union). A more impressive sight, the changing of the guard, takes place outside Monday through Saturday at 11:45am. The **Catedral** on the east side of the Plaza is resplendent in all of its gold, silver, and carved wood glory. The glass coffin in the sacristy contains some gory remains which may or may not be Pizarro. The attached **Museum of Religious Art and Treasures** contains more carved wood (choir stalls by Pedro Noguero) and a large collection of gilt-encrusted 17th- and 18th-century paintings. (Cathedral and museum open Mon.-Fri. 10am-1pm and 2-5pm, Sun. 10am-3:45pm. Admission to cathedral free, to museum s/5.) The **Palacio Municipal,** Jr. de la Union, on the west side of the Plaza, has a small Pancho Fierro art gallery which highlights the work of colonial Peruvian artists (open Mon.-Fri. 8:30am-1pm, bring a passport or other ID to leave at the door; free). The **Biblioteca Nacional** is in the same building as the tourist office. The **Correo Central,** Jirón Conde de Superunda, just off the plaza, is more of a stamp-collector's museum than an important mail center since the privatization of the postal system (museum open Mon.-Fri. 8am-noon and 1-4pm, Sat. 8am-1:30pm; free).

The **Plaza San Martín,** bounded by Av. Nicolas de Pierola, Jr. de la Union and Jirón Carabaya, is the lesser of Lima's city plazas: it's a big square with some erratically working fountains in the center. It is an attractive place to stroll or sit and tourists in search of a glimpse of Lima's city politics can often find some kind of demonstration here. Three smaller, very similar plazas (essentially traffic circles with statues in the center and well-maintained monochrome colonial style buildings on the outside)— **Dos de Mayo,** where Av. Colmena and Ugarte intersect, **Plaza Castilla,** where Av. Emancipación meets Oroya and Ugarte, and **Plaza Bolognesi,** where Av. Brasil meets Guzman Blanco and 9 de Diciembre—round out central Lima's collection of open spaces. **Plaza Gran,** at the end of Paseo de la República, offers little more, but the neighboring park between the Sheraton and Palacio de Justicia features more shrubs, flowers, and life-size animal statues. The **pedestrian mall** on Jirón de la Unión between the Plaza de Armas and Plaza de San Martín, has high concentrations of shoe and jewelry stores, as well as a thriving population of pickpockets.

RELIGIOUS SIGHTS

The Spanish quest to save Incan souls resulted in the construction of numerous visible reminders of God's glory, power, and wealth. Lima's churches are masterpieces and almost invariably filled with ornate wooden carvings, gold and silver covered altars, and soulful paintings. **La Merced,** Jr. de la Unión Cdra. 7, contains the massive, much-kissed silver cross of the Venerable Padre Uvraca. The church, on the site of the first mass said in Lima, has been destroyed twice by earthquakes and once by fire, but its original appearance has been carefully restored (open daily 6:30am-12:30pm and 4-9pm; free). The church of **Santo Domingo,** across from the Correo Central at 170 Camaná, houses sainted *limeños* such as the ever-virginal Sta. Rosa (see below) and San Martín de Porras. The tile mosaics of Sto. Domingo's life have been well-preserved and the cloisters offer a pleasant, dark retreat from the streets outside (open Mon.-Sat. 9:30am-12:30pm, Sun. 9am-1pm). The **Convento de San Francisco,** Jr. Ancash 471, has the unique distinction of being a mass graveyard as well as museum and church. While the Sevillian tilework upstairs is standard church fare, the pits full of bones in the catacombs downstairs are reminiscent of a B-grade horror movie—except that they are real. The catacombs are reportedly haunted by a mischievous ghost who likes to scare tourists that stray from their group (open daily 10am-1pm and 3-6pm). The **Santuario de Santa Rosa,** on the 1st block of Tacua, glorifies Sta. Rose's virginal and ascetic life. Visitors can see the small adobe meditation/prayer hut she built with her own hands, the tree trunk bed where she allowed herself two hours of sleep with a stone for a pillow, and the well where she threw the key to her chastity belt. There is also a small church on site (open daily 9:30am-1pm and 3-6pm; free). The **Convento de los Descalzos,** on Alameda de los Descalzos (Rimac), displays the only slightly more comfortable cells Franciscan friars lived and worked in. It also contains an art museum with examples of the Cusco, Quito, and Lima schools as well as a ponderous gold altar (open Wed.-Mon. 9:30am-1pm and 2-6pm). **Las Nazarenas,** on the corner of Huancavelica and Tacua, contains one of the oldest, some say miraculous, walls in Lima. While the original church crumbled in the 1655 earthquake, one wall with a large mural of Christ on the cross, painted by an ex-slave, survived (open daily 6-11:30am and 4:30-8:30pm; free). The church of **San Pedro,** Jr. Azángaro 451, has gilded altars with Moorish style balconies (open daily 8am-noon and 5-8pm; free). **San Agustin's,** Ica and Carmaná, is full of carved effigies (Death is in storage now) and *churriguerresque* carving (open Mon.-Fri. 9am-noon; free). **San Tomás's** unique circular cloister (now a school on Júnin at Audahuaylas) completes Lima's show of religious finery (admission by request to doorman on Audahuaylas; free).

MUSEUMS

The **Museo de Arte,** Paseo Colón 125 (tel. 423-4732), houses everything from Chavín ceramics and textiles to colonial silverware in a huge 19th-century palace. The collection spans 3000 years of Peruvian history and the paintings of Apocryphal Gospel scenes will re-educate anyone who has been brought up believing in the St. James Bible. The museum also shows films and has short-term art classes (open Tues.-Sun. 10am-5pm; admission s/6, students s/3, ½ price Wed. and Sun). There are smaller, more specific art museums scattered throughout the city: **Museo de Arte Italiano,** Cdra. 2 Paseó de la Republica (tel. 423-9932), houses early 20th-century European art in an imposing neoclassical building (open Mon.-Fri. 9am-4:30pm; admission s/1, students s/0.50); **Arte Popular de la PUC,** Jr. Camaná 459 (tel. 427-9275), shows more modern art (open Tues.-Sat. 10am-12:30pm and 2-7:30pm, Sun. 10am-1pm and 2-5pm; free); and **Museo Rafael Larco Henera,** Bolívar 155 (tel. 461-1312), displays ceramic pots depicting everything from ancient medicine to erotic sexual practices of pre-Columbian cultures (open Mon.-Sat. 9am-6pm, Sun. 9am-1pm; admission s/15, students s/7.50). **Museo Pedro de Osma,** 423 Av. Pecho de Osma (tel. 467-0141), Barranco, is much smaller and focuses on art, furniture, and artisanry from colonial Perú (limited to 10 visitors at one time, call for tours Tues.-Sun. 10am-6pm; admission s/10, students s/5). The **Museo de Oro del Perú y Armas del Mundo,** 1100 Alonso de

Molina (tel. 425-2562), off block 18 of Av. Primavera, Monterrico, displays gold and guns—what more could budding bank robbers ask for? The basement vault looks like the Federal Reserve, except that the gold has been used for ear plugs, jewelry, and ornate metal-plated capes. Upstairs the improbable shapes and ridiculous decorations in the world's largest collection of firearms will intrigue even the most peaceable people (open daily 10am-5pm; admission s/15, students s/7).

Small galleries seem to be a fashionable accessory for banks in Lima and it is worth calling to see what special collections the following banks are displaying: **Galería de Exposición del Banco Continental,** Av. Larco and Av. Tarata (tel. 444-0011; open Mon.-Sat. 10am-9pm); **Sala de Cultura del Banco Wiese,** Av. Larco 1101 (tel. 445-2390; open Mon.-Sat. 10am-8pm). The **Banco Central de Reserva del Perú,** Ucayali and Jr. Lampa (tel. 427-6250, ext. 2660), has a permanent collection of ceramics (open Tues.-Fri. 10am-4:30pm, Sat.-Sun. 10am-1pm; free), and the **Museo Numismático del Banco Weise,** 245 Cuzco (tel. 427-5060), is a coin collector's dream (open Mon.-Fri. 9:15am-12:45pm; free).

The **Museo de la Nación,** Javier Prado Oeste 2466 (tel. 437-7797), San Borja, offers an overview of Perú's archaeological heritage (open Tues.-Sat. 9am-5pm, Sun. 10am-5pm; admission s/10, students s/5), having robbed the **Museo Nacional de Antropología, Arqueología, e Historia** (tel. 463-5070), Plaza Bolívar, Pueblo Libre, of some of its best pieces (open Mon.-Fri. 9am-6pm, Sat. 9am-1pm; admission s/5, students s/2). The smaller **Museo Amano,** Retivo 160 (tel. 441-2909), Miraflores, specializes in Chancay culture (open on weekdays, call ahead for tours; free). The **Museo of Cultura Peruana,** Av. Alfonso Ugarte 650 (tel. 423-5892; open Tues.-Fri., 10am-4:30pm, Sat. 10am-2pm; admission s/2, students s/1), and **Museo de Arqueología "Josefina Ramos de Cox,"** Jr. de la Unión 554 (tel. 442-7678; open Tues.-Sat. 10am-noon and 2-8pm; admission s/1, students s/0.50), also offer smaller, cheaper archaeological collections. The gory **Museo de la Inquisición,** Junín 548 (tel. 428-7980; open Mon.-Fri. 9am-1pm and 2:30-5pm; free) and **Museo Taurino,** Plaza de Acho Hualgayoc 332, Rimac (tel. 482-3360; open Mon.-Sat. 8am-4pm; admission s/2, students s/1), exhibit Perú's bloodier history. The first displays torture instruments, the second bloody costumes from bull-gored matadors.

CASAS ANTIGUAS

While most of the old mansions in the center of Lima have been allowed to gradually rot away or have been converted into cheap *hostals,* some have been preserved in their original grandeur. **Casa Aliaga,** Jirón de la Union 445, is one of the oldest, but Lima Tours (see **Practical Information,** p. 260) has a monopoly on access to it and charges US$24 for a half-day tour that includes the Alioga mansion. The **Torre Tagle palace,** Ucayali 363, is only slightly more accessible: you can enter the building on Saturday when its usual residents, the Foreign Ministry Offices, are not working. The **Casa de las Trece Moredas,** Jr. Ancash 536, **Casa de Oquendo,** Conde de Superunda 298, and **Casa de Riva Agüero,** Jr. Camaná 457, are a few more impressive *casas antiguas,* but getting into them can be difficult.

The **Huaca Huallamarca,** on El Rosario at Nicolás de Riviera in San Isidro, and **Huaca Juliana,** on the 4th block of Angamos in Miraflores, are *casas* more *antiguas* than the Spanish mansions. These Inca ruins are minor compared to Maccho Picchu in the mountains above, but admission is cheap (s/1) and they are in metro Lima (open Wed-Mon. 9am-3pm).

OUTSIDE LIMA CENTRO

San Isidro's biggest attraction is its mall, **Centro Camino Real** on Camino Real. International mall rats won't want to miss the fountains, piped-in music, or overhyped international boutiques. The district also has a few discos and overpriced cafes, but they are scattered and not as pleasant as those in Miraflores or Barranco.

Miraflores fills the space between San Isidro and the beach with modern high-rises, glittering casinos, and well-kept oceanside parks. The **Ovalo Miraflores,** at the end of

Arequipa, flanked by **Parque Kennedy** and **Parque Central,** is the focal point of the people-watching and nightlife, although you'll have to go farther south along **Avenida Larco** to lose your money in a casino. The park at the southern end of Larco offers breathtaking views of the cliffs and ocean below. St. Valentine would have a field day with the **Parque del Amor's** enormous statue of lovers embracing, love poem-inscribed mosaics, and population of real life kissing couples; but he would be a bit disturbed by the way the floodlights shine up the stone woman's skirt at night.

It's an easy *colectivo* (take any marked "Chorrillos" or "Barranco") from the Ovalo of Miraflores to the nightlife district of **Barranco.** The old mansions and seaside promenades that fan out from the **Parque Municipal** on Av. Grau and Pedro de Osma are pleasant for walks during the day, but the crowds really come out at night to drink, dance, see, and be seen. During the day, the walk along the beach from Miraflores to Barranco is about 15 minutes, but at night the area below the cliffs—except for the luxurious **La Rosa Náutica** restaurant on the pier—is dangerous and deserted.

The string of parks continues west to the middle class suburbs of **Magdalena del Mar, Pueblo Libre,** and **San Miguel.** Lima's zoo, the **Parque de Las Leyendas,** is in San Miguel on Av. La Marina (take the *colectivos* marked "La Maria" that run along Benavides or Javier Prado; zoo open daily 9am-5pm, admission s/4, students s/2).

■ Entertainment

Lima is a veritable haven for all forms of entertainment, from thrilling soccer matches to the raging nightlife for which the southern suburbs are famous. **El Comercio's** Friday supplement, **Visto y Bueno,** has excellent listings of concerts, sporting events, plays, movies, and other diversions.

SPORTS AND RECREATION

Soccer (*fútbol*) is more than a sport in Perú; it is a religion with the power to empty the streets, halt traffic, and drag even policemen away from their work. The **Estadio Nacional,** off blocks 7-9 of Paseo de la República, hosts most of the important matches (for national matches, seats are s/25-45) but you can also listen to the games in *colectivos,* parks, and any other public venue with a loudspeaker. **Volleyball,** also played in the Estadio Nacional, comes in a distant second.

When you've tired of watching humans play, turn to the animals: **bullfighting, cockfighting** (*pelea de gallos),* and **horse racing** are all popular spectator events. The Plaza de Acho, Hualgayoc 332 (tel. 481-1467), Rimac, hosts matadors during Fiesta Patrias in the last week of July, as well as during October and December. The chickens do battle to death in **La Chacra,** end of Av. Tomás Marsano, Surco and **Coliseo El Rosedal,** near the Plaza de Armas (s/10 for national championships). Watch horses and jockeys run in circles at the **Hipódromo de Monterrico** (tel. 436-5677), on Javier Prado Oeste at the Panamericana Sur.

MOVIES

High budget, flashy Hollywood films with Spanish subtitles are easy to find and generally cheap (s/4-6). The **Cine Pacífico** (tel. 445-6990), in Miraflores on the Parque Kennedy, **Cine Orrantia,** on the corner of Javier Prado and Av. Arequipa, **Cine Bijou,** Jr. Union 446 (tel. 428-2163), and **Cine Plaza** (tel. 428-6042), Plaza San Martín, have cleaner seats and better sound quality than most other locations. The **Cine Club de la Católica,** Av. Camino Real 1075 (tel. 422-3305), San Isidro, **Cine Club Miraflores,** 770 Larco (tel. 446-2649), **El Cinematógrafo,** Pérez Roca 196 (tel. 477-1961), and the **Museo de Arte,** Av. 9 de Diciembre (tel. 423-4732), show artsier movies.

THEATER

The **Teatro Municipal,** Ica 300 (tel. 428-2303), and **Teatro Segura,** Huancavelica 261 (tel. 427-7427), host most of the big name, professional, expensive operas, ballets, and plays. Call ahead for sometimes-available student discounts. Smaller plays with local actors can be found at the **Teatro Montecarlo,** Elías Aguirie 479 (tel. 445-5037), Miraflores, **Teatro Real,** Av. Belaúnde 180 (tel. 421-4689), San Isidro, and the **Centro Cultural de PUC,** Av. Camino Real 1075 (tel. 422-3305), San Isidro.

NIGHTLIFE

Lima comes alive at night—and stays that way until 5 or 6am. The parks, large and small, fill with families, cruising teenagers, strolling couples, and attentive snack sellers; the clubs blare all varieties of music, and the energetic salsa away while the sedentary imbibe. While you can find "night life" and liveliness all over the city, it's safer to stick to the bars and clubs clustered in Miraflores and Barranco. Take a cab and know the club's address if you do go to a club in Lima Centro.

Lima Centro

Kong Restaurant y Espectáculos, 1223 Washington (tel. 330-1459), Breña. *Muy peligroso* (very dangerous) at night, but an ideal spot for diehard salsa fiends during the day. You can't miss the multi-colored facade or mirrored entrance of this megadisco. Dance floor is open, and occupied, all day.

Las Brisas del Titicaca, Jr. Wakulsky 168. A small, relatively cheap *peña* with enough pull to attract nationally known folk, Andean, and occasionally *criollo* acts. Fri. and Sat. shows usually s/20. Opens 10-10:30pm.

Peña Hatuchay, Jr. Lima 228, Rímac. Although the area can be risky at night, the Andean music here on weekends is worth the cab ride. Shows s/15-25.

Miraflores

Most of the trendiest places are within a few blocks of the Parque Kennedy. There are several nondescript, but usually active salsa clubs above the pizza cafes on the San Ramon walkway off Diagonal near the park. **El Latino** has particularly good sangria, tables to sit and rest, and no cover charge. **Media Naranja Brasileiro,** also near the park on Schell, plays the latest Latin-inspired techno music. Its outdoor cafe and small dancefloor are crammed with gyrating beautiful people (no cover). The larger, indoor *discotecas* **Bizarro,** Calle Lima 417, and **The Edge,** on Larco, have an unofficial bonus for foreigners: they often waive the s/20-25 cover charge. Thursday night is ladies' night at **Bizarro. The Edge,** despite its 80s era front, avidly displays 90s style affluence and glamour. **Brenchlay Arms,** Atahualpa 174, eschews dance fever in favor of dart playing and British pop. **Metropolis,** Av. 2 de Mayo 1545, in San Isidro offers drunken gringos and *limeños* a chance to make their own music via karaoke. At the bottom of Miraflores cliffs (not a good place to walk around after dark), the **Muelle Uno Club** (tel. 444-1800), **Playa Puerta Roquitas,** and the several other beachfront bar/cafes fill Lima's salsa requirement (live weekend shows s/15).

Barranco

The best way to choose where to go in Barranco is to stand in the middle of the Municipal Park and listen to the various strains of music and chatter. Follow your ears—to classical music, jazz, techno, folk (both Andean and Joan Baez-style), romantic whispers, or lively drunken chatter. **Ludwig Bar Beethoven,** Av. Grau 687, a cul-de-sac of culture among the younger indiscriminate partiers, specializes in classical music. **El Ekeko,** Av. Grau 266 (tel. 477-5823), on the park, **La Estación,** Pedro de Osma 112 (tel. 247-0344), and **La Casona de Barranco,** Av. Grau 329, have high quality shows from all parts of Perú—Andina, Costeña, and Tropical (varied cover charge). El Ekeko is the most likely to have shows on weekdays and often branches out into jazz. **Los Duros,** Av. Bolognesi 348, will impress the hard-core black leather wearers with its metal concerts, while **Sargento Pimienta,** Av. Bolognesi 755 (tel. 477-7720), showcases Peruvianized classic rock and reggae.

If you're looking for a place to sit and drink, the loudest places tend to be on Sánchez Carrión off Bolognesi: **La Noche,** on the corner of Bolognesi and Sánchez Carrión diffuses the excited chatter through three floors, while **Delirium,** closer to the Parque Municipal, drowns voices in darkness and loud music. **Las Terrazas de Barranco,** on the park, offers a much more civilized, tree-screened, candlelit meeting place for the young elite. **Juanitos,** Av. Grau 687, takes pride in romantic atmosphere—and avoids interrupting its ambience with pop music of any sort. **La Posada del Angel,** Pedro de Osmas 164 (tel. 247-0341), has photos on the wall and a tranquil, softly chattering crowd which recreate Barranco as it was before the partying hordes (no cover, but s/3.50 drink min.; live music Wed.-Sat., cover s/3).

Barranco's walkway to the ocean and **Puente del Suspiros**—named for the love-lorn who sigh *(suspiran)* as they gaze at twinkling lights and waves below—are behind the parkside church and down the stone steps. Pounding surf replaces disco, salsa, and all other music. The bars near this seaside lookout are more romantic, thus more expensive, than other bars in the area. The late night revelers can always find a sandwich (s/5) and a *jugo* (s/3) in the shops along Pierola's first and second blocks.

NEAR LIMA

There are three main escape routes from Lima's honking horns, constant fog, and urban bustle: north to the tiny coastal towns of Chancay, Churín, Ancón, and the Lomas de Lachay wildlife reserve; inland (and uphill) to Chosica and the Marcahuasi ruins; or south to the Pachacamac ruins and surfing beaches along the coast to Paracas. Travel inland and south is much easier than going north—these areas have more tourist facilities—but the northern coast is worth a visit if you have access to a car.

■ North of Lima

The **Panamericana Norte** heads north to the seaside town of Ancón (about 40km). Weathered wooden houses interspersed with box-like modern apartments testify to the town's past fame as an exclusive resort village for upperclass *limeños*. Most of today's visitors are less affluent daytrippers seeking a spot on the beach and a cheap seafood meal. The beaches are relatively clean, but check the ratings posted on large signs by the beach—avoid the *"muy malo"* water. Because of Ancón's accessibility via *colectivo* from Plaza Dos de Mayo (45min., s/2), you will usually have to share your sand. Numerous pre-Inca ruins lie in the Chillón valley near Ancón, but they have not been developed for inquisitive tourists and it's best to ask around in Ancón for a guide to visit the three pyramids of the **Templo El Paraíso.**

Further north of Lima along the Panamericana, the **Chancay Valley** harbors more rarely visited ruins. You can take a northbound bus from the Plaza de Acho in Rimac to Huaral, the valley's gateway town. In Huaral, ask around for guides to take you to the Añay ruins near Huayopampa, Rupac ruins near La Flonda, or Chiprac ruins near Huasloy. There is very little tourist-oriented infrastructure here, so don't expect to spend the night and try to start the trip early. The **Lomas de Lachay,** near Huacho, are a good excursion for the less adventurous. You can take an Empressa Huaral bus from 131 Av. Avancay (2½hr., s/7) or a *colectivo* (3hr.) to Huacho; the reserve's visitor's center is 3km out of town along a well-marked access road. A resting place for migrating birds and an oasis in the middle of the northern desert, the reserve is at its best during the spring flowering (Sept.-Oct.), but trees are green between June and December. The sight has a useful interpretive center (open daily 7am-7pm). **Canta,** inland to the north of Lima, offers another breath of fresh air and escape from Lima's smog. *Colectivos* (s/2.50) marked "Canta" leave along Lima's Av. Tupac Amaru. The best time to catch them is early in the morning from Plaza 2 de Mayo.

■ Inland and Uphill from Lima

It takes less than an hour to change seasons in Peru, exchanging Lima's clouds and winter cold for **Chosica's** sun and warmth. *Colectivos* run inland along Av. Grau from Plaza Bologuesi (5am-9:30pm), and return along the central highway. The bus trip from Lima provides an interesting glimpse of the city's industrial parks and poster neighborhoods before entering the more scenic foothills of the Andes. There are two small archeological sites along the way to Chosica: **Peruchuco,** an Inca chief's house, at 4.5km off the central highway is easily accessible and has a very informative site museum (open Tues.-Sun. 9am-5pm; s/1.50); **Cajamarquilla** is a partially restored Wari city about 5km off the central highway at 9km. Its adobe walls are not as impressive as the interlocked stones of Inca ruins, but they have managed to survive earthquakes and stormy weather for over 1000 years. The Caja marquilla zinc refinery, a hulking industrial building is an added—if unattractive—bonus.

The enigmatic **Marcahuasi** rock formations, 90km east of Lima, are a strenuous daytrip (or a more relaxing overnight camping trip). Nobody quite knows how the massive chunks of granite were transformed into a hippopotamus, human profile, a few llamas, and other identifiable shapes; die-hard scientists call it a "weathering process," sociologists point out the stylistic similarity to Egyptian and Chinese sculpture, and Marsophiles see it as yet one more proof of alien presence in pre-Inca Peru. Surprisingly, the area has not been developed for tourism; although the numbers of visitors have increased dramatically over the past decade (as have pollution levels and camping supply prices in San Pedro), you still need to walk to get there. You can take a bus from Chosica to San Pedro de Casta (2-3hr., s/5-7), but you'll need your feet or a mule to see the weathered rocks on the plateau. The trail begins in San Pedro and is well marked by the refuse of previous travelers. You can buy all necessary supplies in Chosica or San Pedro, but Lima is much cheaper—small town monopolists seem to have no qualms about squeezing dollars from tourists.

■ South of Lima

Limeños head south for one reason: the beaches. Tourists head south for two; the Pachacamac ruins and the beaches. The coast south of Lima is more developed than to the north—so it's easier for you to get to and easier for the rest of the world to follow you. The Pachacamac ruins are the site of a Wari shrine so sacred that even the Incas didn't tamper with it when they razed the rest of the Wari settlement in 1470. The site is only slightly less impressive now that it has been half-covered with sand drifts. The top of the partially restored Temple of the Sun (the Inca contribution) offers the best vantage point for viewing the sight and the nearby ocean and house-covered hills of Villa El Salvador. You can get to the ruins easily by taking one of the brown and white *colectivos* marked "Lurín" and "Pachacamac" from anywhere along Av. Grau. Ask for *las ruinas* to be dropped off at the small museum near the site's entry (open daily 7am-7pm; s/5). You can also get off in Villa El Salvador just before the ruins and hire a mototaxi to squire you around the Inca village (s/7). The southern part of Villa El Salvador is getting more dangerous, and it's right next door to the park; there have been reports of numerous rapes in the area. There are policemen scattered throughout the site, but not enough to be very effective—use caution.

Real *limeños,* however, bypass all of these tame attractions and head south to the pounding surf of Cañete, El Silencio, Caballeros, Punta Rocas, and the other southern beaches. **Playa San Pedro** (just beyond Pachacamac) provides waves for swimmers gone mad, while **El Silencio's** waters are, well, more silent. More food and drink options exist on this bayside beach. **Pico Alto,** visible from the Panamericana Sur, has been compared to Hawaii's Sunset Beach—the 8.25 ft. waves are better for surfers than swimmers. **Playa Norte,** near the village of Punta Hermosa, has one of the largest sun-bathing beaches; the site is far from secluded. **Pucusana,** 45 minutes south of Lima, is quieter than some of the closer beaches, while **Las Salinas,** slightly further south, has *baños medicinales* to soak your surf-inflicted injuries away.

Colectivos, marked "Pucusana," leave from Av. Montevideo and Ayacucho (8am-9pm, 1½hr.) and will drop you off anywhere along the way. You can take southbound *colectivos* from Pucusana to Chilca and Las Salinas.

If you're stuck for cash on your travels, don't panic. Western Union can transfer money in minutes. We've 37,000 outlets in over 140 countries. And our record of safety and reliability is second to none. Call Western Union: wherever you are, you're never far from home.

WESTERN UNION | MONEY TRANSFER ®

The fastest way to send money worldwide.

Get the MCI Card.
The Smart and Easy Card.

The MCI Card with WorldPhone Service is designed specifically to keep you in touch with people that matter the most to you. We make international calling as easy as possible.

The MCI Card with WorldPhone Service....

- Provides access to the US from over 125 countries and places worldwide.
- Country to country calling from over 70 countries
- Gives you customer service 24 hours a day
- Connects you to operators who speak your language
- Provides you with MCI's low rates with no sign-up or monthly fees
- Even if you don't have an MCI Card, you can still reach a WorldPhone Operator and place collect calls to the U.S. Simply dial the access code of the country you are calling from and hold for a WorldPhone operator.

For more information or to apply for a Card call:

1-800-444-1616

Outside the U.S., call MCI collect (reverse charge) at:

1-916-567-5151

Pick Up The Phone.
Pick Up The Miles.

You earn frequent flyer miles when you travel internationally, why not when you call internationally? Callers can earn frequent flyer miles with one of MCI's airline partners:

- American Airlines
- Continental Airlines
- Delta Airlines
- Hawaiian Airlines
- Midwest Express Airlines
- Northwest Airlines
- Southwest Airlines

Your MCI Worldphone Access Numbers

MCI

COUNTRY	WORLDPHONE TOLL-FREE ACCESS #
# South Africa (CC)	0800-99-0011
# Spain (CC)	900-99-0014
# Sri Lanka	440100
# St. Lucia ÷	(Outside of Colombo, dial 01 first)
# St. Vincent (CC)	1-800-888-8000
# Sweden (CC) ♦	020-795-922
# Switzerland (CC) ♦	0800-89-0222
# Syria	0800
# Taiwan (CC) ♦	0080-13-4567
# Thailand ★	001-999-1-2001
# Trinidad & Tobago ÷	1-800-888-8000
# Turkey (CC) ♦	00-8001-1177
# Turks and Caicos ÷	1-800-888-8000
# Ukraine (CC) ÷	8★10-013
# United Arab Emirates ♦	800-111
# United Kingdom (CC) To call using BT ■	0800-89-0222
To call using MERCURY ■	0500-89-0222
# United States (CC)	1-800-888-8000
# Uruguay	000-412
# U.S. Virgin Islands (CC)	1-800-888-8000
# Vatican City (CC)	172-1022
# Venezuela (CC) ÷ ♦	800-1114-0
Vietnam ●	1201-1022
Yemen	008-00-102

Automation available from most locations.
(CC) Country-to-country calling available to/from most international locations.
÷ Limited availability.
▶ Wait for second dial tone.
◀ When calling from public phones, use phones marked LADATEL.
■ International communications carrier.
★ Not available from public pay phones.
♦ Public phones may require deposit of coin or phone card for dial tone.
● Local service fee in U.S. currency required to complete call.
▲ Regulation does not permit intra-Japan calls.
÷ Available from most major cities

And, it's simple to call home.

1. Dial the WorldPhone toll-free access number of the country you're calling from (listed inside).

2. Follow the voice instructions in your language of choice or hold for a WorldPhone operator.
   - Enter or give the operator your MCI Card number or call collect.

3. Enter or give the WorldPhone operator your home number.

4. Share your adventures with your family!

193

The MCI Card with WorldPhone Service... The easy way to call when traveling worldwide.

MCI — Calling Card
415 555 1234 2244
J.D. SMITH
WorldPhone

For more information or to apply for a Card call:
1-800-444-1616

Outside the U.S., call MCI collect (reverse charge) at:
1-916-567-5151

Please cut out and save this reference guide for convenient U.S. and worldwide calling with the MCI Card with WorldPhone Service.

COUNTRY	WORLDPHONE TOLL-FREE ACCESS #
#American Samoa	633-2MCI (633-2624)
#Antigua (Available from public card phones only)	#2
#Argentina (CC)	0800-5-1002
#Aruba ÷	800-888-8
#Australia (CC) ◆	
To call using OPTUS ■	1-800-551-111
To call using TELSTRA ■	1-800-881-100
#Austria (CC) ◆	022-903-012
#Bahamas	1-800-888-8000
#Bahrain	800-002
#Barbados	1-800-888-8000
#Belarus (CC) From Brest, Vitebsk, Grodno, Minsk	8-800-103
From Gomel and Mogilev regions	8-10-800-103
#Belgium (CC) ◆	0800-10012
#Belize From Hotels	557
From Payphones	815
#Bermuda ÷	1-800-888-8000
#Bolivia ◆	0-800-2222
#Brazil (CC)	000-8012
#British Virgin Islands ÷	1-800-888-8000
#Brunei	800-011
#Bulgaria	00800-0001
#Canada (CC)	1-800-888-8000
#Cayman Islands	1-800-207-300
#Chile (CC)	
To call using CTC ■	800-207-300
To call using ENTEL ■	800-360-180
#China ◇	108-12
(Available from most major cities)	108-17
#Colombia (CC) ◆	980-16-0001
Colombia IIC Access in Spanish	980-16-1000
For a Mandarin-speaking Operator	0800-012-2222
#Costa Rica ◆	0800-012-2222
#Cote D'Ivoire	1001
#Croatia (CC) ★	080-30000
#Cyprus ◆	00-800-22-0112
#Czech Republic (CC) ◆	00-42-000112
#Denmark (CC) ◆	8001-0022
#Dominica	1-800-888-8000
#Dominican Republic (CC) ÷	1-800-888-8000
Dominican Republic IIC Access in Spanish	1121
#Ecuador (CC) ÷	999-170
#Egypt ◆ (Outside of Cairo, dial 02 first)	355-5770
El Salvador ◆	800-1767
#Federated States of Micronesia	624

---- FOLD ----

COUNTRY	WORLDPHONE TOLL-FREE ACCESS #
#Fiji	004-890-1002
#Finland (CC) ◆	08001-102-80
#France (CC) ◆	0800-99-0019
#French Antilles (CC) (includes Martinique, Guadeloupe)	0800-99-0019
#French Guiana (CC)	0-800-99-0019
#Gabon	00-005
#Gambia	00-1-99
#Germany (CC)	0130-0012
#Greece (CC) ◆	00-800-1211
#Grenada ÷	1-800-888-8000
#Guam (CC)	950-102
#Guatemala (CC) ◆	99-99-189
#Guyana	177
#Haiti ÷	193
Haiti IIC Access in French/Creole	190
#Honduras ÷	122
#Hong Kong (CC)	800-96-1121
#Hungary (CC) ◆	00▼800-01411
#Iceland ◆	800-9002
#India (CC) ◆	000-127
(Available from most major cities)	000-127
#Indonesia (CC) ◆	001-801-11
#Iran ÷ (SPECIAL PHONES ONLY)	
#Ireland (CC)	1-800-55-1001
#Israel (CC) ◆	177-150-2727
#Italy (CC) ◆	172-1022
#Jamaica ÷	1-800-888-8000
(From Special Hotels only)	873
Jamaica IIC Access	#2-from public phones
#Japan (CC) ◆	
To call using KDD ■	0039-121
To call using IDC ■	0066-55-121
To call using ITJ ■	0044-11-121
#Jordan	18-800-001
#Kazakhstan (CC)	8-800-131-4321
#Kenya ÷ (Available from most major cities)	1001
#Korea (CC)	
To call using KT ■	00309-14
To call using DACOM ■	00309-12
Phone Booths÷ Press red button, 03, then ★	
Military Bases	550-2255
#Kuwait	800-MCI (800-624)
#Lebanon ÷	600-MCI (600-624)
#Liechtenstein (CC) ◆	0800-89-0222
#Luxembourg	0800-0112

---- FOLD ----

COUNTRY	WORLDPHONE TOLL-FREE ACCESS #
#Macao	0800-131
#Macedonia (CC)	99800-4266
#Malaysia (CC) ◆	800-0012
#Malta	0800-89-0120
#Marshall Islands	1-800-888-8000
#Mexico	
Avantel (CC)	01-800-021-8000
Telmex ▲	001-800-674-7000
Mexico IIC Access	91-800-021-1000
#Micronesia	624
#Monaco (CC) ◆	800-99-19
#Montserrat	1-800-888-8000
#Morocco	00-211-0012
#Netherlands (CC) ◆	0800-022-91-22
#Netherlands Antilles (CC) ÷	001-800-888-8000
#New Zealand (CC) ◆	000-912
#Nicaragua (CC) (Outside of Managua, dial 02 first)	166
Nicaragua IIC Access in Spanish *2 from any public payphone	
#Norway (CC) ◆	800-19912
#Pakistan	00-800-12-001
#Panama	108
#Papua New Guinea (CC) Military Bases	05-07-19140
#Paraguay ÷	008-11-800
#Peru	0-800-500-10
#Philippines (CC) ◆	105-14
To call using PHILCOM ■	1026-11
Philippines IIC via PLDT in Tagalog	105-15
Philippines IIC via PhilCom in Tagalog	1026-12
#Poland (CC) ÷	00-800-111-21-21
#Portugal (CC) ÷	05-017-1234
#Puerto Rico (CC)	1-800-888-8000
#Qatar ★	0800-012-77
#Romania (CC) ÷	01-800-1800
#Russia (CC) ◆ ÷	
(For Russian speaking operator)	747-3320
To call using ROSTELCOM ■	747-3322
To call using SOVINTEL ■	960-2222
#Saipan (CC) ÷	950-1022
#San Marino (CC) ◆	172-1022
#Saudi Arabia (CC)	1-800-11
#Singapore	8000-112-112
#Slovak Republic (CC)	00421-00112
#Slovenia	080-8808

The Galápagos Islands

The Galápagos Islands are like no other place on earth. The Galápagos tortoise, from which the Islands took their name, is perhaps the best example of this. It is bigger than any other tortoise, lives longer than anything but trees, has no fear of man, and can prosper for months without food or water. It is this type of biological distinctiveness, born of the unique conditions of the archipelago, that caused a young Charles Darwin to scratch his head, and that brings over 60,000 tourists here each year. But the tortoise is an apt emblem for the islands in another, darker way. Despite their powerful legs and impenetrable shell, their existence is fragile. Centuries of human predation nearly wiped them out before the archipelago was declared a National Park in 1959. Even with the protection of the government and concern of scientists and tourists worldwide, existence is still precarious, as new threats continue to arise from the feral goats and rats that continue to overrun the islands.

Although there are undeniable problems, the Galápagos is still one of the shining stars of ecotourism in the world. From the amazing amiability of the animals to the tranquil beauty of the landscape, the Galápagos Islands appear nothing less than magical—evident in the common translation of the Islands' nickname of *Las Encantadas* as "The Enchanted Islands." But, as always with the Galápagos, there is another level; the original meaning of *Encantadas* was "bewitched," an epithet bestowed on the Islands by sailors who disdained the powerful currents and lack of freshwater. As with their nickname, the Islands present multiple levels for appreciation and understanding and a unique chance to gain insight into the inner workings of nature, and humanity's place within it.

ESSENTIALS

■ Budget Travel in the Galápagos: Fact or Fiction?

The Galápagos is not a cheap destination. Aside from all the expenses involved in getting to Quito or Guayaquil, you still need to pay a US$400 cover charge of airline tickets, park fees, and municipal taxes just to enter the islands. Once there, tourist oriented prices and expensive tours could easily push a two-week vacation over US$2000. But don't give up hope; the key to inexpensively enjoying the Galápagos is realizing that the animals and natural attractions—the really remarkable aspects of the archipelago—are the same for the lowliest budget traveler and that guy on the US$300-a-day cruise ship. All you'll need is a little savvy, negotiation, and patience, and you can have an incredible two-week adventure for around US$1000. You could live on that for two months in the mainland, but waved albatrosses don't nest there.

There are basically two ways to budget travel the Galápagos: the inexpensive tour, and independent travel. The ideal cheap trip would combine both, but if you have to choose, go with a tour boat. There are three reasons for this recommendation: there are islands, so you need a boat to go between them; non-tour transportation is very limited and inefficient; and you need to have a licensed guide with you to visit most of the Galápagos visitor's sites. It's unlikely that you'll find a better way to get a guide to a site than to travel on the boat they guide. **Tour boats** come in three classes: economy, touristic, and luxury. Economy boats tend to be small, with limited facilities, mediocre food, and mediocre guides. Many of these boats are okay but some are downright primitive. It's probably a good idea to see the boat and guide in person before you pay for one of these. Touristic boats tend to be a little bigger (averaging 16 passengers), with private baths, palatable food, better guides, and can handle longer itineraries. Unlike with paintbrushes, the size of the boat really does matter. Bigger boats won't rock so much in the waves, they'll have more

TO ISLA DARWIN (CULPEPPER)
& ISLA TEODORO WOLF (WENMEN)

Isla Pinta
(Abigdon)

PACIFIC OCEAN

Punta Albemarle

**Volcán
Wolf
(1660m)**

Cabo Berkeley

EQUATOR (0°)

Punta Vicente Roca

Banks
Bay

Isla Santiago
*(San Salvador,
James)*

Isla Albany

⑰

**Volcán Darwin
(1330m)**

James
Bay ⑱

**Cerro
Cowan
(920m)**

Sulivan
Bay

Punta Tortuga

Punta García

⑲

Isla Bartolomé

Punta Espinosa

Puerto
Egas ㉑ ⑳

*Isla Sombrero
Chino*

㉒

㉓

Urvina
Bay

Isla Rábida

**Volcán
La Cumbre**

**Volcán
Alcedo
(1125m)**

Isla Beagle

*Isla Fernandina
(Narborough)*

Isla Guy Fawkes

Isla Edén

*Isla Isabela
(Albemarle)*

Cartago
Bay

⑮

Isla Mariela

*Isla Pinzón
(Duncan)*

Elizabeth Bay

Punta Moreno

Punta Ballena

**Volcán Sierra Negra
(Santo Tomás)
(1490m)**

Santo
Tomás

Punta Cristóbal

⑤

㉕

Cerro
Azul

㉖

㉔

Punta Essex

Puerto Villamil

N

0   25 miles

0   25 kilometers

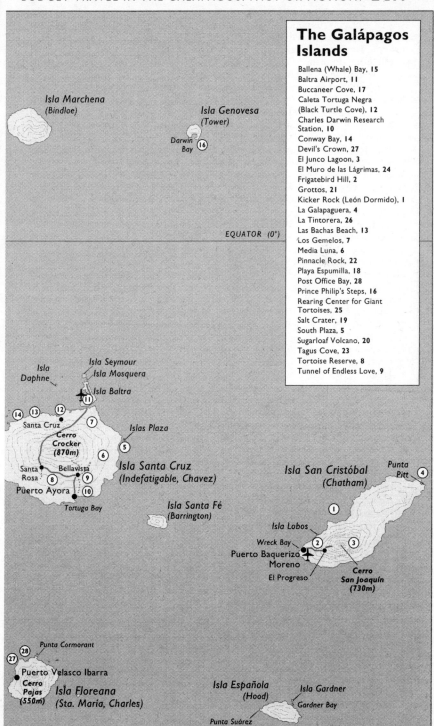

The Galápagos Islands

Ballena (Whale) Bay, 15
Baltra Airport, 11
Buccaneer Cove, 17
Caleta Tortuga Negra
(Black Turtle Cove), 12
Charles Darwin Research
Station, 10
Conway Bay, 14
Devil's Crown, 27
El Junco Lagoon, 3
El Muro de las Lágrimas, 24
Frigatebird Hill, 2
Grottos, 21
Kicker Rock (León Dormido), 1
La Galapaguera, 4
La Tintorera, 26
Las Bachas Beach, 13
Los Gemelos, 7
Media Luna, 6
Pinnacle Rock, 22
Playa Espumilla, 18
Post Office Bay, 28
Prince Philip's Steps, 16
Rearing Center for Giant
Tortoises, 25
Salt Crater, 19
South Plaza, 5
Sugarloaf Volcano, 20
Tagus Cove, 23
Tortoise Reserve, 8
Tunnel of Endless Love, 9

space for privacy (important if you're at sea for a week), and they can handle longer voyages, which enables them to reach some of the fantastic outer Islands like Genovesa and Fernandina. The quality of the guides is important too (although their size doesn't seem to matter). There are three classes of guide: Naturalist I theoretically know English and some biology, but really just keep you on the trails; Naturalist II have completed some biological degree; and Naturalist III can speak three languages, and have substantial training in natural history. A great guide can really make your trip, but a bad one doesn't have to ruin it. If you study your Galápagos natural history before you go, you can counteract a bad guide and ask more pertinent questions of a good one.

In finding a tour, remember this principle: the price of the tour goes down the closer you are to the boat when you book it and the closer it is to the time. Thus, someone booking a June 14 tour from the U.S. in April may pay twice as much as someone who signs up on June 13 in Puerto Ayora. The trade-off is uncertainty—those who wait run the risk of not finding a suitable boat. An alternative is to book through a tour agency in Quito or Guayaquil. These agencies can often arrange very cheap passage on boats which are set to leave in a few days but have some empty spaces. Agencies that directly represent their own boats will be able to negotiate a lower price. The cheapest option is to fly to Puerto Ayora and arrange your tour there. Although this option involves some uncertainty, it offers strong advantages. First, you get to see the boat before you decide on it, which is crucial for less expensive tours. Second, your bargaining power is at a maximum because by the time boats are here, the cost of bringing you on is low. Third, you can avoid the wasted day spent traveling to and from Baltra airport and exploring Puerto Ayora.

Once in Puerto Ayora, there are two ways of getting on a tour. The easiest is to look for an empty spot on a soon-departing boat. Visit all of the tourist agencies on Av. Darwin to see what they've got, or talk directly to the boat's captain. Note that the travel agents do not necessarily know what they're talking about, nor do they feel bound to be scrupulously honest. If one tells you something, try to check it out with the boat's captain, the guide, and if you can, another travel agent. The other option is to put together a group of travelers yourself and charter a boat. This usually doesn't take long, as travelers are constantly looking for this sort of deal, but it can be a hassle for you and doesn't necessarily save you money. Puerto Ayora prices for economy tours run around US$55 per day, touristic US$65-80, and luxury US$90+. These prices are probably at least 50% better than what you would have paid back home. In the low season you can often get on a higher class boat for the price of the class beneath it.

Your other option is independent travel, which isn't as good for wildlife observation and isn't even that cheap, but it allows you to explore the interiors of the big islands and gives you the chance to do your own thing. Note, however, that while doing your own thing you are still bound by the rules of the Park. The main problem with this type of travel is that the forms of public transportation—INGALA ferries and EMETEBE airplanes—are expensive (s/110,000 and US$50, one way) and follow inconvenient schedules. Add the cost of transportation, food, and housing, and your independent travel may cost more than a comparable economy tour. Check out the destination ahead of time to make sure it's worth it.

Tipping on Tour Boats

It is standard to tip the crew on a tour boat about US$25 to US$50 per week, depending on the quality of the service. Crew members work hard and aren't paid very well (particularly on economy boats), so this is probably not the best place to economize. The guide usually gets paid about twice as much as the crew. It is best to pool your money with the other passengers and then divide it up for the crew members yourselves, but if this is awkward you can give it to either the guide or the captain to divide as they see fit (although if you do this, someone might get screwed).

■ When to Go

The stability of the equatorial climate means that you can have a rewarding experience in the Galápagos any time of the year, but the two seasons have different attributes. Warm ocean currents cause hot, rainy weather from January through April, while the rest of the year is relatively dry and a bit cooler. Neither season is completely ideal—during the rainy months, the ocean water refreshes at a comfortable 75°F (24°C), but heavy rain showers often disturb the tropical tranquility. Likewise, while rain may fall rarely during the dry months, the sky is often overcast, the water a chilly 70°F (21°C) or lower, and the waves choppy from sporadic winds. The ideal visiting months are between seasons—March and April, when rain begins falling less frequently, and November and December, as the climate warms up. Note also that some animals are only around at certain times. If seeing a certain animal, such as the waved albatross, is important to you, check that they're there.

If you want to save money, go in the off-season. Tourist traffic is heaviest during vacation times—Easter week in the spring, late-June through August, and December and January. In fact, August and December can get so busy that finding a boat becomes challenging, bargaining is nearly impossible, prices rise significantly, and flights need to be booked well in advance. October is not a busy month, but precisely for this reason many boat owners choose to make repairs then, so many vehicles are out of commission. The best time to travel to the Galápagos is in May and June, when tourism is down, the climate is moderate, and the seas are still calm. July and August tend to be the worst times to go because tourism peaks and the seas are cold and rough—if you are subject to seasickness, this is not the time to travel. January to April are the hottest months; consider splurging on a boat with air conditioning.

■ Useful Organizations

Charles Darwin Foundation, Inc., 100 N. Washington St., Suite 311, Falls Church, VA 22046, USA; P.O. Box 17-01-3891, Quito, Ecuador. A non-profit membership organization which promotes conservation, education, and scientific research in the Galápagos. Publishes a newsletter, the *Galápagos Bulletin*, 3 times a year.

Corporación Ecuatoriana de Turismo (CETUR), Eloy Alfaro 1214 and Pasaje Carlos Tobar (tel. (02) 229-330; fax 507-560), Quito. A government-run tourist info agency with valuable facts about hotels and transportation. Provides maps and info as specific as animal mating seasons and the best sites to spot various types of wildlife. There are CETUR offices in all major cities in Ecuador, including one on Av. Charles Darwin in Puerto Ayora (tel. 526-179).

South American Explorers Club (SAEC), 126 Indian Creek Rd., Ithaca, NY 14850 (tel. (607) 277-0488; fax 277-6122; email explorer@samexplo.org; http://www.samexplo.org); J. Washington 311 and L. Plaza, Apartado 17-21-431, Eloy Alfaro, Quito, Ecuador (tel./fax (02) 225-228; email explorer@saec.org.ec). A non-profit organization with extensive info of all kinds on traveling, working, volunteering, and researching in Latin America. Their "Galapagos Packet" of practical info about the islands is updated every few months. SAEC has reports on the various boats operating in the Galápagos; it's a good idea to check them out.

■ Getting There and Back

TRAVEL BY PLANE

Ecuador's two national airlines, **TAME** and **SAN/SAETA,** provide the only available flights to the Galápagos. All flights originate in Quito, stop in Guayaquil one hour later, then take an additional 90 minutes to reach the islands. Both airlines have similar round-trip fares, but prices fluctuate depending on the season. During the high season (Dec.-Aug.), round-trip tickets run around US$375 from either Quito or Guayaquil; low-season fares dip to approximately US$280 from Quito and US$260 from Guayaquil. Passengers can pay for tickets either in dollars or sucres; compare the airline exchange rate and the street rate to determine which is the better bargain. Officially you need to book your flight a day in advance, but travelers have been known to buy tickets up to 10 minutes before the flight. Flights are routinely over-booked, so arrive at the airport at least an hour in advance to secure a seat and re-check return flight information a day or two before departing the islands.

TAME runs most flights to the Galápagos, departing Mon.-Sat. from Quito at 8:30am, and Guayaquil at 9:30am. Planes land on Isla Baltra, with easy access to Isla Santa Cruz and Puerto Ayora. Returning flights leave Baltra at 11:30am. TAME also offers a 15% discount to students with valid university ID and an international student ID. If you plan to arrange a tour in the Galápagos, your prospects are much better in Puerto Ayora than in Puerto Baquerico Moreno, so go with TAME.

SAN/SAETA flights take off every day except Thurs. and Sun., at 11am (Quito) or noon (Guayaquil). Arrives on Isla San Cristóbal, not especially convenient unless your tour leaves from that island. Most tours depart from Isla Santa Cruz; check your itinerary before making reservations with a particular airline.

TRAVEL BY BOAT

Although sea travel isn't necessarily any cheaper than an airplane, sailors-at-heart can opt for salty air, open waters, and leaving the land-lubbers behind. There are three ways to get to the Galápagos nautically. Voyage by **cargo ship** is the cheapest way to go. The three-day, two-night journey costs about US$150 each way, but cabin space is limited and are strictly Bring-Your-Own-Food. Arrange passage at the TRAMSFA office in Guayaquil (Av. Baquerizo Moreno 1119 and 9 de Octubre, 6th fl.), or ask for the *capitano* of the port along the Guayaquil *malecón*. It is rumored that some ships will take passengers for as low as US$65, but finding such a boat takes patience and luck. Some ships only leave once a month, so be ready to be flexible with departure dates. **Cruise ships** are the most comfortable option, but loungers definitely pay for that luxury, often over US$100 per day. Those with the money to spare should contact a travel agent; some ships include benefits such as spacious cabins and bilingual naturalist guides. **Military ships** used by the Ecuadorian Navy are another option, though they charge more (US$300) and take longer (11 days) than cargo ships.

ENTRANCE REQUIREMENTS

When arriving on Isla Baltra or Isla San Cristóbal, everyone must pay a US$80 park entrance fee in cash, whether in dollars or sucres (traveler's checks and credit cards not accepted). There is no getting around this charge, and it's a good idea to keep the receipt if you'll be traveling between islands. Visitors continuing onto Isla Santa Cruz must pay an additional s/33,000 entrance tax. Those entering San Cristóbal must pay US$30. If it ain't cash, they don't want it. A passport is required to enter the island.

■ Getting Around

PACKAGE TOURS AND CRUISES

Tours come in many lengths, from daytrips to three-week cruises. The most common are four-, five-, and eight-day trips. Each island is unique, and your appreciation tends to increase the more you see—if you can afford it, go for at least a full week. SAEC recommends the following tour companies, all based in Quito:

Angermeyers Enchanted Excursions, Foch 768 and Amazonas (tel. (02) 569-960; fax 569-956).
Andes Discoveries, Amazonas and Davalos (tel. (02) 228-591; fax 550-952).
Galasam, Pinto 523 (tel. (02) 561-470 or 567-662).

INTER-ISLAND TRAVEL

Instituto Nacional Galápagos (INGALA) (tel. 526-199), the government-run public transportation system, offers shuttle boats between the archipelago's three most populated islands in various exciting combinations:

San Cristóbal to Santa Cruz	Mon. and Wed., 10am-2pm
Santa Cruz to San Cristóbal	Tues. and Sat., 8am-12pm
Santa Cruz to Floreana to Isabela	Thurs., 8am to 12pm to 4pm
Isabela to Santa Cruz	Fri., 10am-2pm

While INGALA is the most reliable means of inter-island travel, it gives preference to residents and charges *extranjeros* inflated rates (s/110,000 each way, under 12 s/ 55,000). Ticket-purchasing policies differ among towns, but it is generally a good idea to get your ticket as early as possible—you may be able to get a ticket on board, but the boat may well be full. **Private boats** also transport adventurers for about the same cost. Some run on schedules as regular as the ferries; the *Estrella de Mar* always leaves at 10:30am, traveling from Isabela to Santa Cruz on Tuesday and returning to Isabela Wednesday. Just track down Captain Juan Mendoza at Hotel Salinas in Puerto Ayora on Tuesday evening to buy a ticket (passage takes about 6hr.). Other private boat owners run daytrips from Puerto Ayora or Puerto Baquerizo Moreno to some of the closer islands: South Plaza, Bartolomé, Seymour, and Santa Fé. Daytrips generally include transportation to and from the dock, breakfast, lunch, and a guide, and cost around US$45. Just make sure that you and your guide speak a common language. Visit **Coltur** (tel. 526-177) in Puerto Ayora for a list of boats and owners, as well as info about which are available and where they can be found.

There is also an inter-island airplane service, EMETEBE, that flies between Puerto Ayora, Puerto Baquerizo Moreno, and Puerto Villamil about three times per week. The planes carry six passengers, the tickets cost around US$50, and the flights take less than a half hour. This only costs a little more than INGALA and it's much faster; if you want to go directly between Isabela and San Cristóbal, call tel. 526-279; in San Cristóbal tel. 520-339; and in Isabela tel. 529-209.

RENTALS

Sailboats are difficult to find, but some rentals are available. They only carry about five passengers (US$65-80 per person per day) and travel more slowly than larger boats, but you can feel like a pirate, arrr! Keel-hauling discouraged. **Bicycle** and **horse** rentals are also available on the larger islands; ask at hotels for who's renting.

■ Practical Information

MONEY AND BARGAINING

Ecuadorian sucres are the common currency, but U.S. dollars are often accepted. However, prices listed in dollars are aimed at rich gringos and are probably higher than prices listed in sucres. Prices are often negotiable, particularly in low season. Locals routinely overcharge tourists; be prepared to ask the price beforehand and bargain it down. There are few places to **exchange money,** and rates tend to be exploitative. It makes sense to change money ahead of time in Quito or Guayaquil; the islands tend to be safe, so carrying lots of cash is less of a concern than on the mainland. Currently, Banco del Pacifico, located in Puerto Ayora and Puerto Baquerizo Moreno, is the best place to change money (ATM does not accept Visa).

THE GALÁPAGOS ISLANDS

TIME DIFFERENCE

The Galápagos Islands are one hour behind the Ecuadorian mainland, or six hours behind Greenwich Mean Time. As on the mainland, the Galápagos do not observe Daylight Savings Time.

WHAT TO BRING

The stores in the Galápagos tend to be small, expensive, and oriented towards t-shirts and souvenirs; buy everything you'll need beforehand, either at home or in Quito or Guayaquil. Footwear is an important part of a trip to the Galápagos. **Hiking boots** or **sturdy shoes** are a must for craggy lava fields, and **waterproof sandals** or **flip flops** are just the thing for those wet landings. Insect bites can bring you down, so bring along some **insect repellant.** Even if it's the rainy season, the sun's rays can still be killer, so stock up on **sunscreen** and bring a **rimmed hat.** Likewise, it gets nippy in the evenings no matter what the season, so keep cozy with a **sweatshirt** and a pair of **pants.** It's best to prepare for any kind of weather with a couple of **t-shirts,** a pair of **shorts,** and a **light raincoat.** The latter is an absolute necessity during the rainy months (Jan.-April). Finally, if you plan to do any snorkeling or scuba diving (which we recommend), bring your own gear if you've got it. Most tour boats have a supply of masks on board, and if not you can rent masks and snorkels for about US$3 per day in Puerto Ayora. A **short-sleeved wetsuit** is a good idea if you plan to spend much time in the water during the chilly dry season. All towns in the Galápagos shut off power during the night, so a **flashlight** is recommended.

SCUBA DIVING

Scuba diving in the Galápagos is about as exciting as submerging yourself into fast-moving currents full of sharks, rays, and sea lions. Actually, it's exactly that exciting. The fish and coral are pretty but relatively unremarkable; the reason why divers from all over the world come here is the unparalleled chance to swim with the playful sea lions, the lightning-fast schools of hammerhead, and even the elusive whale shark. Strong currents make diving here relatively difficult, so evaluate the situation before you decide to jump in. The most established diving outfit in town is **Galápagos Sub-Aqua,** Av. Charles Darwin (tel. 526-350; fax 526-350, international fax 593-4-314-510; email sub_aqua@ga.pro.ec; http://www.galapagos_sub_aqua.com.ec), 800m from the Darwin Center. Diveleader Fernando Zambrano is a consummate professional and a friendly teacher; he is licensed as a Naturalist Guide and speaks English. Daytrips for beginners to divemasters are offered ranging from US$75-110 (including all gear, tanks for two dives, and a divemaster guide). Sub-Aqua also offers "all-inclusive dive packages" (US$135 per day, up to 8 days), which includes accommodations, three meals, and diving, as well as introductory scuba courses for non-certified divers. Full certification courses are also available, but take seven days. Sub-Aqua gives a 10% discount when you pay in cash. Also nearby is **Galápagos Scuba Iguana** (tel. 526-330; fax 934-564; email jgallar@ga.pro.ec; http://www.scuba-iguana.com), located at the Hotel Galápagos. Daytrips span three to eight hours and prices range between US$75-110 (trip price includes dive gear, tanks for two dives, a divemaster guide, and a box lunch). Divemaster Mathias Espinosa is a certified divemaster/instructor and naturalist guide who speaks Spanish, English, and German. Scuba Iguana also offers a 5% discount when you pay in cash. Both give discounts if you bring your own gear.

THE GALÁPAGOS: AN INTRODUCTION

■ History

All the flora and fauna on the Galápagos mysteriously crossed nearly 1000km of ocean to reach the islands, and the first human inhabitants arrived with the help of auspicious waves as well. Pottery shards found on various islands suggest that pre-Inca *indígenas* spent some time on Santiago, Santa Cruz, and Floreana, likely the result of their balsa rafts floating astray. But the first Galápagos tour to be recorded in the annals of history set sail around 1485, when the Inca prince Tupac Inca Yupanqui sent his army on an exploratory expedition of the islands. Like all Galápagos visitors, they returned loaded with souvenirs; though souvenirs like the gold treasure, bronze seat, and horse's skin and jaw they brought back aren't sold in any of Puerto Ayora's gift shops today.

The first Europeans on the islands were also accidental tourists. At the time, Fray Tomás de Berlanga, the archbishop of Panamá, and his Peruvian-bound ship didn't think it too propitious when a week-long storm and a six-day drift carried their boat so far off-course. Berlanga was a bit put-off by the remoteness of these arid islands, although he was struck by the tameness of the animals. This 1535 voyage is considered the official "discovery" of the Galápagos. When the islands were first included on maps 35 years later, they were given the name Galápagos (Spanish for "tortoise") after the enormous shelled specimen that Berlanga described.

For the next few centuries, pirates used the islands (most notably Isla Santiago's Buccaneer Cove and James Bay) as hideaways and launching pads for surprise sea attacks. Raiding and pillaging can be hard work, and when hungry pirates discovered that the Galápagos tortoises could survive for months with little food or water, they began storing them in their ships to use as a fresh meat source on voyages. When this trend caught on, the tortoises began dwindling at astonishing rates; at the time of Charles Darwin's 1855 visit, he reported the ships would take as many as 700 tortoises with them. In subsequent years, hunters continued to harvest the animals for their meat and the fine oil that can be prepared from their fat.

Darwin only stayed in the Galápagos for five weeks, but his visit would ultimately determine the historical path of the archipelago and its badly endangered tortoises. Darwin's writings about the islands and their purported impact on his theory of evolution eventually gave the archipelago a high profile worldwide. Ecuador had claimed the islands only a few years before Darwin arrived, and used them as a penal colony at first. But due to the Galápagos's fame and importance in the scientific and ecological world, a few areas were declared wildlife reserves in 1934, and in 1959 all non-colonized areas officially became the Parque Nacional Galápagos. In the following decades, tourism steadily increased. In 1994, the islands hosted 54,000 visitors, 76% of whom were foreigners. It appears that many of the tortoise populations will continue to survive, despite their difficulties, because of a selective advantage that Darwin could not have foreseen: people like them.

■ Geology

The first Galápagos island was formed over 4 million years ago, and new islands have been forming ever since. The islands were never part of the mainland, but instead were formed by underwater volcanoes that spit out lava, building themselves higher and higher until they finally broke the surface of the ocean. Volcanically active islands like Fernandina have continued to add new territory even within the last decade.

Tectonic theory proposes that the surface of the earth is made up of a number of **tectonic plates** that are suspended on the **magma** (molten rock) that lies below them. These tectonic plates are constantly moving, each one being pushed and pulled by the plates around it. The Galápagos are located on the **Nazca plate,** which

A Fistful of Finches

The natural history of this archipelago is very remarkable: it seems to be a little world within itself; the greater number of its inhabitants, both vegetable and animal being found nowhere else.
—Charles Darwin, *Voyage of the Beagle*

In 1831, Darwin was a 22-year-old medical school dropout and mediocre theology student. Young Charles looked forward to a simple life as a country person in which he'd have the chance to indulge his true passion—natural history. One of Darwin's professors, John Stevens Henslow, recognized that the bright young man was more interested in worms than in the Edict of Worms, so he hooked him up with a job as ship's naturalist on the H.M.S. Beagle and as "gentleman companion" to the captain, Robert Fitzroy.

The Beagle set off on a five-year, around-the-world voyage exploring and demonstrating British superiority. Darwin's observations and collections of the flora and fauna of South America, the Pacific Islands, and Australia made him something of a scientific celebrity by the time he returned to England. But young Charles had done more than observe and collect. After examining multiple, disparate ecosystems, Darwin began to see a certain set of patterns. An eager reader of Charles Lyell's *Principles of Geology,* Darwin was willing to see the natural world as a product of constant change. Evolution was not a new idea—geologists had developed the fossil record sufficiently by the 18th century to see convincing evidence for change. What Darwin provided was a mechanism. His idea that the brutal competition to survive and reproduce writes its story in the offspring of the victor—the survival of the fittest—was as insidiously persuasive as it was an anathema to conventional views of natural history and man's place in the universe. Upon the 1859 publication of *The Origin of Species,* scientific and social firestorm broke out across the literate world, and biology and philosophy were never again the same. His notebooks later revealed these cryptic words: "In July opened first book on 'transmutation of species'—Had been greatly struck from about one month of previous March—On character of South American fossils—and species on Galápagos Archipelago—These facts (especially latter) origin of all my views."

is being pushed towards the southeast by plates to the north and west of it. The volcanoes that formed and continue to form the Galápagos are the result of a "hot spot," a stationary area beneath the Nazca plate that is hot enough to melt the plate above it. This causes magma to be released onto the surface of the earth, usually in the form of a volcano. Other famous hot spots are responsible for the Hawaiian Islands and the geothermal activity of Yellowstone National Park in the U.S. While the Galápagos hot spot remains stationary, the Nazca plate is moving to the southeast, taking the older islands with it and leaving the hot spot to form new islands to the northwest. Thus Isla Española in the southeast is the oldest island in the archipelago, while Fernandina and Isabela to the northwest are the youngest and most volcanically active.

While most people come to the Galápagos to see the unique wildlife, the geology is some of the most interesting in the world. Very young geologic formations abound, since the islands themselves are so young (four million years is a blink of the eye, geologically speaking). The volcanoes of the Galápagos were formed by basaltic lava, which has a relatively fluid consistency. For this reason, the Galápagos volcanoes are more inclined to vent their fury in the form of lava flows than enormous explosions, which is why they tend to look more like domes than the perfectly shaped, conical volcanoes most people know and love.

There are many volcanic phenomena you might come across during your travels through the hot, smoking Galápagos. On the island of Santa Cruz, you can lose yourself in the **lava tunnels** of love (p. 297). These were formed by lava flows that hardened on the outside but remained liquid and continued to flow on the inside, eventually forming a rocky hollow tube. On Isabela, visit one of the largest **calderas** in the world (10km in diameter) on the summit of Volcán Sierra Negra (p. 308). Also on Isabela, witness the steamy, vaporous emissions of the **fumaroles** of Volcán Alcedo (p. 307). The 6.5km-wide and 900m-deep *caldera* of Volcán La Cumbre is the fiery heart and soul of Isla Fernandina (p. 309). The island grows larger and larger with every eruption; a 1975 eruption caused the uplift that formed Punta Espinosa to the northeast, and an eruption in February 1995 caused a lava flow that resulted in the formation of a new cape on the island's southwest end. While this recent flow is not yet open to visitors, many slightly older lava flows are, including the beautifully sensual *pahoehoe* flows at Sullivan Bay on the island of Santiago (p. 311).

■ Fauna and Flora

One fine day around 4.5 million years ago, some bacteria carried by wind and water happened upon a steaming clump of volcanic rock, just emerged from the sea. These microorganisms, simple but resourceful, settled on that rock to do what bacteria do: process minerals and sunlight into energy creating more bacteria to do the same. Thus, the first life-forms on the primordial Galápagos were hardly elegant—prokaryotes rarely are—but they were essential to all life on the archipelago. These bacteria did two important things: they broke down the hard volcanic rock and they left the remains of their bodies (minerals and organic compounds); the result was that a substance began to accumulate on the rocky surface that a wandering seed might consider soil. These seeds, brought from great distances by the wind, the currents of the sea, or perhaps a passing seabird, found their way to little crevices in the rocks where they could sprout. These hardy plants, capable of living with little water or nutrients, further broke up the rock and added to the organic mass of the islands, allowing larger plants to survive. Birds and insects, blown to the islands by strong winds, found that the plants could provide food and shelter. Animals arrived by flying, swimming, or rafting, and either found a way to live on the barren islands or died. It is probable that for every creature that made it on the islands, hundreds or thousands died a hot or salty death. The ones who made it found a large area with lots of land and fish, and little competition. Isolated from the mainland by about 1000km and isolated from each other by up to 200km, the islands of the archipelago provided the perfect environment for rapid speciation. Darwin could not have found a better laboratory to demonstrate the geographical distinction of species due to varying selective pressures. The time scale was sufficient that the changes from the mainland ancestors were obvious, yet not so great that the connections were not readily apparent.

The lifeforms that arrived had a few traits in common. They had to be able to make the voyage in the first place; therefore, the sea lion had a chance while the llama did not. Once on the island, they had to be able to survive the vigors of the sea and extreme deprivation of fresh water; water-efficient reptiles thrived while wasteful mammals hardly stood a chance. With the advent of boats, however, the mammals have been popping up with greater frequency, inflicting massive, rapid change to the islands' ecosystems. Humans and our retinue of goats, horses, cats, dogs, and rats have upset the ecological balance considerably, both by consuming the food of the aboriginal animals and the animals themselves. Humans have done their share too, feeding on the large, meaty, helpless tortoises that inhabit many of the islands.

Ecological awareness and a very active park service, however, have largely stopped the contamination of the ecosystems (although humans continue to arrive). The purity that remains is unique and extraordinary. The biological distinction of the islands is apparent upon first observation, and continued examinations reveal complex interconnections, remarkable adaptations, and fascinating communal behaviors. Perhaps more pleasing to the visitor is the unbelievable amiability of the animal life. They are sometimes described as tame, but this is inaccurate: they are wild animals who are entirely unafraid of humans, a phenomenon which provides some of the most exhilarating natural observations and photography on earth.

RESPONSIBLE ECOTOURISM

The islands' ecosystems are fragile. The regulations of the National Park Service are designed to protect those areas for future generations and in that spirit should be followed: stay on the trails, don't molest the wildlife, don't take or leave anything, and if your guide tells you not to do something, don't do it. This admonition extends to your purchases: don't buy souvenirs made of animal parts (particularly black coral) and if lobster is overfished, as in recent years, think twice about ordering it. At the most basic level, the mere presence of tourists on the islands contributes to their contamination; recognize that these islands are a unique natural treasure as well as that they can provide the adventure of a lifetime (for more info, see **Ecotourism,** p. 58).

BIRDS

The Galápagos are well-known for their birds, the most prominent and diverse type of animal on the islands. The different species of birds found in the Galápagos are presented here grouped by habitat, the first group being birds of the **sea.** Undeniably a seabird, the endemic **Galápagos penguin** is an aberrant member of its cold-water family. These shy birds (long-lost relatives of the penguins of southern Chile and Antarctica) live mainly around the Bolívar Channel between the western coast of Isabela and Fernandina. They are also found in various places near the Isla de Santiago. Some of the most well-known birds in the Galápagos are the **boobies,** of which there are three types: the blue-footed, red-footed, and masked. The boobies, like the frigates and cormorants, are related to the pelican, members of the order *Pelicaniformes.* They use their large and sometimes colorful feet to incubate their eggs and to swim through the water after a dive-bombing fishing foray. Red-footed boobies are the most common in the islands, with the highest concentration of birds on Genovesa. They are the only boobies that nest in trees or bushes. Blue-footed and masked boobies nest on the ground, surrounding their territory with a circle of *ejecta* (bodily waste). The identity of masked boobies is given away by the black mask that contrasts with their otherwise white bodies. Another famous endemic seabird, the **flightless cormorant** is found only on the westernmost islands of Fernandina and Isabela. These cormorants were originally a flying species, but the lack of predators or food on land meant that big wings were a waste of time; instead, selective pressures favored the strongest divers, those with webbed feet, powerful legs, and small wings. They nest in small colonies on sheltered shorelands. Some of the largest and most notable birds on the islands are the black **frigatebirds.** Both humble species (the Great and the Magnificent) are **cleptoparasites,** which means that they make a living by stealing the food of other birds, usually harassing them in midair, and forcing them to give up their catch. Since they spend so much time in the air, their wingspans grow up to 2.3m—they have the highest wingspan to weight ratio of any bird. Their cleptoparasitic ways have pre-empted the need to get their feathers wet, and they have consequently lost the ability to produce the oily secretions that protect the feathers of other seafaring birds. One of the most outstanding features of the frigates is their enormous red pouch beneath the beak that males inflate when courting. To witness this sensual display, visit the colonies on San Cristóbal and Genovesa during the mating season (March and April), or North Seymour Island anytime. Perhaps the rarest bird in the Galápagos, the **waved albatross** is endemic specifically to Isla Española. The largest birds in the archipelago, weighing over 4kg with a wingspan of 2.5m, they only stay on the island from April to December; they spend the rest of the year in various places around the South Pacific. Other seabirds include five kinds of **petrel** and two endemic **gulls,** the swallowtail, the lava gull, and the ever-present brown pelican.

Of the **shorebirds,** the **flamingos** are by far the most well-known. These guys are fairly rare, inhabiting only a few lagoons around the islands. They feed on small animals living in the silt and shallow water, and build nests of mud on shore. They can be seen on Isla Rábida, in lagoons near Puerto Villamil on Isabela, at Punta Cormorant on Floreana, and at Espumilla beach on Santiago. A much more common shorebird is the **heron,** of which there are three types in the Galápagos: the great blue, lava, and night heron. These long-legged waders feed on all kinds of small animals, from beach creatures to lagoon-dwellers. A more specialized shorebird is the **oystercatcher.** The size of your average heron, this bird is not as common due to its particular habits. It is mostly brown, with a black head and red eye ring and feeds primarily on shellfish, like abalone and sea urchins. Other shorebirds include **egrets, gallinules, turnstones, stilts,** and **whimbrels.**

The **landbirds** of the Galápagos, because of their isolation from other landbird populations, include the greatest percentage of endemic species (76%). Most famous are **Darwin's finches,** of which there are 13 types. Tiny sparrow-sized birds, they all look extremely similar and can only be differentiated by beak morphology and feeding habits; Darwin himself didn't recognize them as distinct species until after he'd left the archipelago. While some live simply on seeds or fruits, the carpenter finch uses a stick to dig insects out of trees, and the "blood-sucking" finch of Wolf Island actually uses its sharp beak to suck the blood of red-footed and masked boobies. There are also several endemic species of **mockingbird,** all of which are descended from a species native to mainland Ecuador. These brown and white birds are carnivorous, eating insects, lizards, and even small finches. Extremely social and territorial, they are often seen in large numbers and are not afraid of humans. Other notable endemic landbirds include the Galápagos **hawk** (the largest land predator on the islands), the Galápagos **dove,** the Galápagos **martin,** and the Galápagos **rail.** Some of the more striking land birds are non-endemic. The **vermillion flycatcher,** a red and black bird found in the humid highland forests of the central islands, is a favorite, as is the nearly universal **yellow warbler.** Lastly, as surprising as it may be, some pioneering, adventurous owls must have made the trip from the mainland long ago; the islands are now populated by two subspecies of **barn owl** and **short-eared owl.**

REPTILES

The namesake of the islands, the undisputed king of the Galápagos reptiles, is the **giant tortoise.** These are the animals that really set the islands apart (only one other island in the world has a tortoise population). How the tortoises first came to inhabit the islands is to this day a mystery. Their closest relative is a species of tortoise native to Argentina; it is possible that the big guys (up to 250kg) got stuck on some floating vegetation that carried them out to sea and eventually to the Galápagos. Whatever their origin, the anomalous giant tortoises have been appreciated for centuries. Back in the day, whalers and pirates cruising the Pacific used to visit the islands to stock up on these defenseless but hardy animals, piling them in their holds for months at a time to use as a fresh meat supply. As a result, the tortoises aren't as plentiful as they once were. Three of the original 14 sub-species are now extinct, and introduced animals such as rats and dogs continue to threaten the populations. While each animal can live to be over 150-years-old, they do not reproduce very often, and when they do, it is not guaranteed that the vulnerable hatchlings will ever reach maturity. The Galápagos National Park and the Darwin Research Center are doing what they can to prevent predation and boost the population by harvesting eggs, raising the hatchlings to four years of age, and then releasing them in their original habitat. The largest tortoise population is found on Isabela, concentrated around the crater of Volcán Alcedo. Other islands where wild tortoises can be observed are the Tortoise Reserves on Santa Cruz and Española. Captive tortoises can be observed at the Darwin Research Center on Santa Cruz, and the Rearing Center for Giant Tortoises on Isabela.

Back in the sea and on the beaches, **marine turtles** are also commonly found. These animals float easily on the water's surface and can therefore travel great distances across the seas with the greatest of ease. Four of the eight species of marine turtle have been seen on the Galápagos, and none of them are endemic (given their great mobility). The black turtle, a sub-species of the Pacific green turtle, is the most common. They lay their eggs in nests on the beach, burying them to incubate in the hot sun. While they can lay their eggs year-round, it is most common from January to June. For a day or two after the eggs are laid, visitors may observe tracks leading from the sea to the nest and back again. Night visitors may even catch a turtle in the process of laying eggs. In these cases, it is fine to watch quietly, but do not disturb the animals, especially not with the beam of your flashlight.

One of the most bizarre and unique reptiles of the Galápagos is the **marine iguana,** the only aquatic iguana in the world. Related to the land iguanas of the American mainland, marine iguanas have evolved to eat green algae that grows underwater. For this purpose they have developed the ability to swim a depth of 20m, the capacity to stay under the water for up to one hour at a time, the tendency to shoot excess absorbed salt out of their unusually square noses at great speed, and a tail tailored for efficient swimming. The largest marine iguanas (on Isabela) can grow up to 1m long. Like other reptiles, these strange creatures are ectothermic, meaning that their body temperature is determined by the temperature of their environment. As a consequence, they can often be seen sunning their big, black, spiny bodies on the rocks, piled on top of each other in big groups. Darwin called it "a hideous-looking creature, of a dirty black colour, stupid and sluggish in its movements," but some people think they're cute. Two species of **land iguanas** also inhabit the islands; while their genus is endemic to the Galápagos, they are not quite as unusual as their marine counterparts. They can also reach up to 1m in length, but their noses are more characteristically pointed. Their diet varies depending on their particular habitat. They eat insects and scavenge for other meaty meals, but also love to eat grasses, cacti, fruits, and flowers, particularly the big yellow blossoms of the **opuntia** cactus.

Long ago, through some heroic feat of seamanship, **snakes** also reached the islands. On land, the non-poisonous Galápagos **land snake** slithers hither and yon in search of small prey that it can crush with its 1m length of constricting power. Found on all but the northernmost islands, these brown or gray snakes have yellow stripes or spots. On a smaller scale, seven species of **lava lizard** are also endemic to the islands. Reaching up to 25cm, they feed primarily on plants, with the occasional insect thrown in for good measure. They are gray, and females typically have eye-catching red-orange throats. While they are very territorial, most confrontation takes the form of bouncing up and down on the forelegs; fights are seldom serious.

MAMMALS

The most prominent and strangest mammals of the Galápagos inhabit the islands of Santa Cruz, San Cristóbal, Isabela, and Floreana, though some may be found on other islands from time to time. Social animals, they live in big groups, primarily by the ocean, but also in more fertile and moist regions of the islands. Their bodies are quite strange in form, and vary greatly in size. At night they usually gather around unknown sources of strange rhythmic sound, and consume various quantities of liquid that alters their behavior dramatically, causing some of them to make more noise and others to regurgitate and eventually lie prone, presumably in a state of dormancy. While these **Homo sapiens** have arrived only recently on the islands, they have had a great impact on the ecology. The number of individuals in the population fluctuates regularly, but continues to rise steadily. It is unclear whether the population can continue to grow at this rate without damaging the islands beyond repair. Humans have also increased the mammal contingent of the islands by introducing several dogs, cats, goats, and rats, which have multiplied faster than their primate companions.

A less disturbing large mammal found in astonishing abundance in the Galápagos is the endemic **Galápagos sea lion.** Relatives of the sea lions of California and Perú, they live in colonies on the beaches of most of the islands. Males are much larger than females and can reach up to 250kg. They are very territorial, holding territories for about a month at a time, defending them from any kind of intruder (usually from other males). Mating occurs in the ocean, but females give birth on land. Pups are suckled for up to three years before being weaned. The animals are playful and are commonly seen surfing or showing off for tourists. Another related but quite distinct species found in the Galápagos is the **fur sea lion.** The endemic Galápagos subspecies is the only non-antarctic fur sea lion. They were once on the brink of extinction due to hunting by fur traders. They can be easily differentiated from other sea lions by their thicker coat, smaller size, pointed nose, and proportionally thicker head.

The only other mammals on the islands that were not introduced by man are the **rats** and the **bats.** Two species of bats comb the islands of Santa Cruz, Floreana, Isabela, and San Cristóbal for insects, while two species of brown rice rat scurry across the islands in search of vegetation. Lately, the rat population has been decreasing due to the introduction of the black rat, which competes with the rice rat for food. Before the black rat's arrival on the island, there were seven species of endemic rice rat.

MARINE LIFE

The waters of the Galápagos are truly tropical, teeming with just about every kind of marine life. The islands are fed by three nutritious currents: the Humboldt, the Cromwell, and El Niño, which bring a bounteous supply of species and nutrients from all over the Pacific. Sixteen species of **whales** and seven species of **dolphins** have been sighted around the Galápagos, with a particularly high concentration of sightings off the west coast of Isabela where the Cromwell current brings plankton and other delectable organisms to the surface. Whale species include sperm, humpback, blue, and killer whales. The most prevalent species of dolphins are the common and bottlenosed dolphins. Twelve species of **shark** also inhabit these waters. By far the most common is the white-tipped reef shark, but black-tipped reef sharks, hammerheads, Galápagos sharks, and tiger sharks are common as well. Also sharing these waters are five species of **rays,** including stingrays, eagle rays, and manta rays. Hundreds of species of smaller fish make their home in the open water, the **coral reefs,** and isolated coral heads near several of the islands. Lobster, crab, squid, octopus, starfish, sea cucumber, and shellfish of all kinds add to the submarine extravaganza. Because of this great diversity, the waters in and around the Galápagos, an area of 70,000 square km, are part of a marine reserve established in 1986. Snorkeling and scuba diving are possible at numerous sights throughout the islands. If you want to go snorkeling, just let your boat captain know. Scuba diving requires a bit more preparation and planning (see **Scuba Diving,** p. 282). While the area is protected, regulated commercial fishing of certain species is still permitted. But before snagging a salt-water snack for yourself, consult the locals or your trusty tour guide. Some boats' crews have been known to harvest some of these aqueous treats for their passengers' dinner. Fishing in the area is quite controversial. Several species, in particular sea cucumbers, have been overfished. If fish populations are depleted, the seabirds and sea lions will inevitably feel the effect, perhaps with disastrous consequences. In past years relations between the park service and local and international fishermen have been strained.

FLORA

The Galápagos have seven vegetation zones that are home to over 600 species of plants, approximately 170 of which are endemic. The zones range from dry and low to high and moist. The area right on the coast is the **littoral zone** and is dominated by plants that have adapted to the presence of salt, such as **mangroves.** The **arid zone** is the driest region and comes just above the littoral in altitude. Generally on the side of the island opposite the prevailing winds, this region is dominated by cacti and other dry-weather plants. The **opuntia cactus** with the yellow flowers is the only endemic species of cactus and also happens to be the most common. It often grows like a shrub, except on islands where it is threatened by herbivorous animals; there these cacti can grow trunks up to 5m tall. The **Palo Santo** tree is also native to this zone. Producing only small leaves during the wet season, the branches of these stark gray trees are often burned for their incense-like odor. The next highest zone, which is also more humid, is the **transition zone.** The most common inhabitants are the Palo Santos again and the **pega pega** (which translates literally as "it sticks, it sticks"), that has spread-out branches and a short trunk. When those damn leaves stick to your clothes, you'll understand the name. The next zone is very humid and has been called the **scalesia zone** for the endemic scalesia trees that are so common here. In addition to scalesia trees which can grow up to 10m, there are many mosses, ferns, and grasses. The scalesia forest of the Santa Cruz highlands is the best place to see this kind of vegetation. The three remaining zones are the **brown, miconia,** and **pampa zones.** The brown is named for the prominent **brown liverwort mosses** found here. The miconia zone gets its name from the endemic and shrubby **miconia plants** that look somewhat like a flowering cacao plant. The highest and wettest vegetation zone is the **pampa,** dominated by mosses, ferns and grasses; very few trees or shrubs grow in this hyper-humid region.

ISLA SANTA CRUZ

Known also by its English name of Indefatigable, Isla Santa Cruz's never-ending diversity—its myriad of wildlife, radically varied geology, and scores of international visitors—is indeed tireless. As Santa Cruz lies geographically near the center of the archipelago, tourism in the Galápagos revolves around this hub. Nearly every visitor stops here, whether to schmooze with the tortoises or just to stock up on supplies. After all, **Puerto Ayora** is the largest and most developed town on the islands, and Santa Cruz is a conveniently close first stop if you arrive at nearby **Baltra Airport.**

The scenic trip from the airport to Puerto Ayora serves as the perfect introduction to the islands. Baltra looms barren and powerful, and the entire landscape is covered with lava rock, cacti, and wind-blown trees. After a short boat ride across shimmering turquoise waters, visitors enter the central highlands of Santa Cruz, where the bus jostles its way through vegetation that seems all the greener in comparison to the desertscape before it. From there the bus descends to the cool, relaxed port town.

Good news for landlubbers—Santa Cruz is one of the few islands in the Galápagos where you don't need a boat to see all the sights. The intellectually curious should make for the **Charles Darwin Research Station** just outside of Puerto Ayora. At the station, visitors can get up close and personal with the undisputed star of the island, the giant Galápagos tortoise. Those with more time on their hands can journey into the lush scalesia forests of **Santa Cruz's highland region,** where you can rent horses or hike into the **Galápagos Tortoise Reserve** to interact with these friendly giants in their natural habitat. After exploring the island, rest your bones on the white sands of **Tortuga Bay,** a relaxing 3km walk from town.

■ Puerto Ayora

The Galápagos Islands prove that Mother Nature has a unique ability to roll with the punches. Over the years, the plants and animals of the archipelago have managed to adapt to fill virtually every unexplored niche. The wings of the flightless cormorants on Isabela have gradually grown short and stumpy because the lack of predatory animals renders flying pointless; the previously arctic penguins on Bartolomé and Fernandina (like so many Floridians) have happily given up their frigid ways to adapt to life under the hot equatorial sun. Not to be outdone by other Galápagos phenomena, the seaside settlement of Puerto Ayora eagerly rises to the archipelago's call for a "developed port town."

The constant influx of tortoise-happy tourists has given the town a vaguely cosmopolitan air, a high standard of living, and a happy-go-lucky attitude. However, this has made Puerto Ayora far more expensive than mainland Ecuador, and has converted part of it into a string of souvenir shops and bars. A local custom illustrates the hospitality of the town: shop owners will often collect small piles of coconuts from nearby trees. If you get a hankering for one of these island treats, don't try to buy one—the town's juicy supply of coconuts comes from the mainland, making it a commodity most islanders refuse to sell. If there is an extra 'nut lying around it will, of course, be free—a gift from both the island and the islanders.

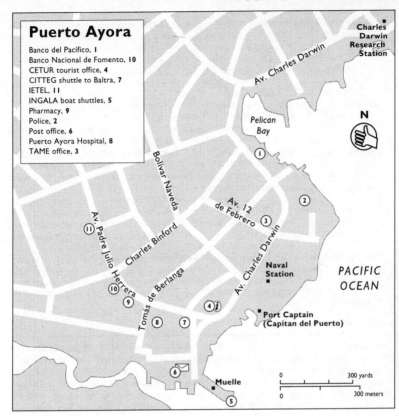

Puerto Ayora

Banco del Pacífico, **1**
Banco Nacional de Fomento, **10**
CETUR tourist office, **4**
CITTEG shuttle to Baltra, **7**
IETEL, **11**
INGALA boat shuttles, **5**
Pharmacy, **9**
Police, **2**
Post office, **6**
Puerto Ayora Hospital, **8**
TAME office, **3**

ORIENTATION AND PRACTICAL INFORMATION

While nearly all of the islands in the Galápagos archipelago have three or four names, many of the streets in Puerto Ayora have yet to receive even one. Don't fret, though. Virtually everything of importance is located on the city's one major street, **Avenida Charles Darwin** (what else?). The other busy street is Avenida Padre Julio Herrera, full of restaurants, hotels, and shops.

Tourist Information: For all those pesky questions regarding everything from hotels to heron-mating seasons, visit the **CETUR information office,** Av. Darwin (tel. 526-179), next to the Geminis 2 souvenir shop. Answers always up-to-date and always *en español.* Also provides informative (albeit blurry) town maps of Puerto Ayora, Puerto Baquerizo Moreno, and Puerto Villamil, and info about INGALA, the Galápagos' public transportation system (see **Inter-Island Travel,** p. 281).

Travel Agencies: Several travel agencies in town arrange boat tours, daytrips, and inland excursions. Two helpful, English-speaking agencies are **Moonrise** (tel. 526-403; fax 564-636), and **Encanturs** (tel./fax 526-581), both on Av. Darwin.

Bank: Banco del Pacífico (tel. 526-282 or 526-365), on Av. Darwin just beside Hotel Sol y Mar, changes traveler's checks and cash for more *sucres* than other restaurants and shops around town. ATM accepts Cirrus, Next, and Mastercard. Open Mon.-Fri. 8am-3:30pm, Sat. 9:30am-2:30pm.

Airport: Getting to Puerto Ayora from the **Isla Baltra airport** is easy enough. Buy the requisite 2 tickets at the airport (the first for the shuttle boat, 15 min., s/8,000; the second for the 50min. bus ride to Puerto Ayora, s/7,000). The **shuttle** back to the airport leaves from the center of town in front of the CITTEG sign at 8 and 8:30am (get there early). Buy the ticket to Baltra at the **CITTEG office** and the second ticket to the airport (s/6,000) at the **TAME office**, Av. Darwin (tel. 526-527). Open Mon.-Fri. 7am-noon and 1-4pm.

Market: Proinsular, Av. Darwin (tel. 526-104), across from the dock, is as close as it gets to a real supermarket. Best prices and selection in town. Open Mon.-Sat. 8:30am-8pm, Sun. 8:30am-12pm.

Restrooms: Public restrooms are located on Av. Darwin near the park.

Laundromat: The **Pelegrina B&B,** Av. Darwin, runs a *lavandería* (s/4,000 per kg). They have a dryer, so your clothes can be ready in a few hours if you're lucky. The shop beneath the New Hotel Elizabeth also does laundry, but they charge more.

Pharmacies: Farmacía Edith (tel. 526-487). Open daily 8am-11pm. **Farmacía Vanessa** (tel. 526-392). Open daily 8am-10pm. Both can be seen from the hospital.

Hospital: Puerto Ayora Hospital (24hr. emergency tel. 526-103), near the corner of Av. Padre Julio Herrera and Pelicano Rd.

Police: (tel. 526-101), by the water off Av. 12 de Febrero, at their headquarters beside the Estrella del Mar. On duty daily 8am-6pm.

Post Office: The **Correo Central** (tel. 526-575), in the Proinsular shopping center on Av. Darwin, near the dock. Postcards and stamps are available here; mail to the U.S. may arrive in about 2 weeks. Open Mon.-Fri. 8am-noon and 2-6pm.

Telephone Service: EMETEL, Central Telefónica de Puerto Ayora, Av. Herrera (tel. 999-170). International phone calls, faxes, and telegrams. Open daily 7am-9pm. Only 1 line calls outside of the islands; be prepared to wait. Banco del Pacifico also allows international calls and faxes (expensive; cash or credit card).

Telephone Code: 05.

ACCOMMODATIONS

The selective forces of the fertile coastal environment have led to the development of several hotels, although the large price discrepancies leave visitors wondering if they really could have evolved from a common ancestor. Accommodations in Puerto Ayora change hands often, so always ask to see a room before sleeping in it. Besides doing a quick cleanliness check, look for netting or window screens to keep out mosquitoes—while not usually a problem, they can be murder during the wet season. In general, you pay for luxury, leaving budget travelers more likely to hear the sounds of the local disco than waves gently lapping outside their door. Some gems, however, are still hidden alongside Puerto Ayora's increasingly busy streets.

Bed and Breakfast Peregrina (tel. 526-323), off Av. Darwin, just behind Pippos Restaurant. The best deal in town: the beds aren't terribly comfortable, you share your room with friendly local spiders, and it's strictly BYOT (towels and toilet paper), but free breakfast (bread, jam, eggs, fruit, juice, and coffee/tea) at nearby **Kathy's Kitchen** nearly justifies the price by itself. Laundry service (s/3,000 per kg). Secure rooms fit up to 4, have fans, and cost s/15,000; some have a private bath.

Estrella del Mar, Av. 12 de Febrero (tel. 526-427), right next to the ocean, just off of Av. Darwin. One of the prettiest hotels in town, this *estrella* twinkles with airy rooms, extra clean baths, and fantastic ocean views from the balconies. Hot water in cold weather. Singles s/30,000; doubles s/60,000; triples s/80,000.

Residencial Los Amigos, Darwin and Av. 12 de Febrero. The island's answer to the youth hostel, with communal bathrooms and large dorm-type rooms that are shared when it's crowded. The college atmosphere often spills like an overflowing beer into the courtyard, where people gather to discuss animal encounters, swap scuba gear, or just to play cards. Rooms start at s/15,000 per person.

Hotel Lirio del Mar, Tomás de Berlanga and Bolívar Naveda (tel. 526-196). 3 stories high with 2 breathtaking terraces that overlook Pelican Bay, the harbor, and the restaurant/bar below. Sparkling, safe rooms; owners as accommodating as the weather. All rooms have private baths and fans. Singles s/30,000; doubles s/45,000.

Hotel Darwin, Av. Herrera (tel. 526-193), 1 block from the ocean. The cheapest group-rate in town and the hammocks of the mellow frond-covered patio out front have helped the Hotel Darwin survive the natural selection of Puerto Ayora's hotels, but its bathroom fixtures and thin mattresses betray their years, despite their cleanliness. Singles s/15,000; s/12,000 per additional person.

Hotel Palmeras, Bolivar Nevada and Tomás de Berlanga (tel. 526-139), just past Lirio del Mar. Big, bright rooms, unusually firm beds and tasteful interior design, complemented by a jacuzzi on the terrace. *Comedor* provides all 3 meals (*desayuno* s/ 7,000). Singles s/40,000; doubles s/50,000; *especial* rooms s/10,000 more.

Hotel Lobo de Mar, Av. 12 de Febrero (tel. 526-188; fax 526-569), just off Av. Darwin. Unfortunately, no sea lions, but the balconies, fans, and pleasing mattresses do what they can. Clean, colorless rooms; TV lounge and restaurant help liven things up. Doubles s/35,000.

New Hotel Elizabeth, Av. Darwin (tel. 526-178). Run by the friendly couple Vilma and Victor. Rooms all have private bath, but some lack shower curtains. Flashers may enjoy the suite with an all-glass door. Singles s/20,000; doubles s/30,000.

Hotel Sol y Mar, Av. Darwin (tel. 526-281; fax 471-701), overlooking Pelican Bay. A bit pricier, but you get what you pay for. Generally clean, safe rooms; dining with sun-soaked iguanas on oceanfront patio; private baths with hot water; and the priceless company of owner Jimmy Pérez. Doubles US$25; quads s/60,000.

Residencial Flamingo, Tomás de Berlanga and Bolívar Naveda (tel. 526-526), behind the skeleton of a larger hotel. Budget travelers flock here like long-legged pink birds, settling in the sunny, overflowing floral courtyard. Don't squawk too loud— the doors (and mattresses), are stick-thin. All have private baths. Rooms s/15,000.

FOOD

The two most common sights on Av. Darwin are the diving pelicans and the seaside restaurants. The eateries on the first few blocks of this main drag are moderately priced; a bare-bones meal goes for s/6,000-12,000. Perhaps because these places tend to attract the timid tourists fresh off the boat, the patio furniture has become a great spot to meet other visitors and arrange boat tours. Farther down towards Darwin Station, more expensive restaurants cater to money-bearing tourists. Travelers looking for more endemic fare should check out the Av. Charles Binford just off of Av. Herrera, where locals get cheap, fresh meals from small wooden shacks.

Restaurante El Sabrosán, Calle Julio Herrera (tel. 526-262), across from Mini Bodega Santa Cruz. Cooperative chefs and good food on a bamboo-covered patio. Watch super-friendly Ramón make *chuzos* (steak, onions, and peppers on a stick, s/7,000) over an open fire. Conch and shrimp *chuzos* on days when there's a good catch. All meals served with beans and rice. Open for lunch and dinner.

Cuatro Linternas, on Av. Darwin after the turn towards the Darwin Station, is the place to take that special someone. Four lanterns throw soft lighting on authentic Italian cuisine. The pizzas (s/17,000-24,000) are big though a little bland, and the pastas (s/15,000-25,000) are rich and al dente. This is one of the few restaurants that has been around for more than 3 years—romance pays.

El Pirata, Av. Herrera (tel. 526-213), just up from El Sabrosán. A big place by Puerto Ayora standards, its 6 plastic tables are often full of locals and tourists in the know. Heaping portions of excellent local food served daily for breakfast, lunch, and dinner. *Almuerzo* (beef stew, fried fish, rice, salad, and juice) for s/6,000.

Nameless Restaurant/La Dolce Vita, on Av. Darwin just before the turn to the Darwin Station. This restaurant/bar/open-air pool hall/strange mini-golf-type place has understandable difficulty finding a name, but the food is good (big T-bone steak s/ 18,000), the atmosphere is easygoing, and the drinks keep flowing.

Playa Sol y Mar, on Av. Darwin across from the park. The big, shady trees are just right for enjoying that *cerveza* or papaya juice. Food may take a while if you don't order the special. Traditional breakfast, lunch, or dinner s/6,000. Menu items, which include pasta, cost around s/15,000.

Kathy's Kitchen, Av. Herrera (tel. 526-323), just off Av. Darwin, is almost too charming with its wooden tables, open-air atmosphere, and tasteful garden. But when the beer mugs are so cold that ice forms in your Pilsener (s/7,000), you have to forgive that excess charm. Great juices and hearty food (lasagne s/9,000).

El Rincón del Alma (tel. 526-196), facing the park on the waterfront, with both indoor and patio seating. Open bar reveals eclectic decorations. Great place to meet other travelers on the street. Entrees s/15,000; so big they're hard to finish. *Menú del día* s/5,000.

Media Luna Pizza, on Av. Darwin past Hotel Sol y Mar. Homemade pizzas *a la Galápagos,* with fresh toppings such as shrimp and blue crab. Sandwiches like the top-notch avocado sub, plus a fun, easy-going crowd. Pizzas s/13,000-22,000, sandwiches s/9,000-12,000. Open for lunch and dinner.

La Panera, Herrera (tel. 526-176), past the hospital. A bakery whose bread rises with the sun. Grab a bite here before an early morning boat trip. Breads and pastries are as tasty as they are cheap. Open daily at 6am.

ENTERTAINMENT

The constant influx of happy-go-lucky tourists and the high standard of living in Puerto Ayora have combined to make this port town an exciting place once the sun is down. On almost any night of the week you can find visitors or locals ready to party. Follow the loud music to the best bar in town, **Galapason,** Av. Darwin and Floreana. The pool table, slide, foosball table, and oh-so-tropical decor try a little too hard to be the perfect Galápagos bar, but the people keep coming anyway. An older, more intimate place is **El Bar de Frank,** where the *caipiriñas* (s/7,000) keep flowing as long as the electricity does, usually until around midnight. The crowd is usually sunburnt and very friendly. **Panga,** a *discoteca* at Av. Darwin and Tomás de Berlanga, attracts both endemic and migratory Galápagos residents and is the standard late-night dance spot. Another option is the **La Fraguta,** just down Av. Darwin. Both discos sell cold drinks, have pool tables, and stay open into the wee hours of the mornin'. For more sedentary entertainment, the **Cine Santa Cruz** screens porn flicks and soccer. Occasionally it has children's movies in the afternoons.

■ Near Puerto Ayora

Instead of drinking that cold pineapple juice in the shade of Puerto Ayora's busy streets, get it to go and head down Av. Darwin to the **Charles Darwin Research Station,** 20 minutes from town on an easy trail, just past Hotel Galápagos. The trail leads past both a national park info center and the park's administrative headquarters (tel. 526-189; fax 526-190). Info on the islands' natural history, and Darwin Station education and conservation programs, is found in the nearby **Van Straelen Exhibit Hall.** The station is run by a small but enthusiastic staff. Feel free to poke around the other buildings if no one is there to answer your questions. An explanatory film is supposedly shown twice daily, but because of uncertain visitor numbers it rarely runs.

Just beyond Van Straelen is the station's **tortoise rearing center.** A shady path leads past pens containing baby giant tortoises, fresh from the egg to a couple of years old. To get a good look at the cute little *galapaquitos,* visit between 9am and 4pm on a weekday so the covers of their pens will be open. The big boys are just around the corner and their pen is open to all. For many, this is the only chance to see a Galápagos tortoise. The animals in this area were originally kept by islanders as pets, so they really do like people and very rarely retreat into their shells like the wild ones do. Some even stretch out their necks in hopes of getting a nice scratching; even tortoises have those "hard-to-reach" places. While in the tortoise pens, however, be careful not to walk across or stand on the tortoise feeding platform, as this may contaminate their food with harmful organisms. For more info about the Galápagos, the Darwin Station, and its projects, visit the station's **library** in the area behind the Exhibit Hall (open Mon.-Fri. 7am-noon and 1-4pm). If you have a specific interest or question, this is a good place to find Gail Davis, an extremely helpful staff member who came to the islands years ago on a research project and never left.

If it is leisure and not enlightenment that you seek, head to **Tortuga Bay.** Considered by many to be the most beautiful beach in the Galápagos, the picturesque white sand beach is accessible to anyone anytime. The beach gets its name from the large number of sea turtles that come to lay their eggs. Sharks and marine iguanas have also called Tortuga Bay home. When swimming, be careful of the unusually strong currents, and if snorkeling, bring a buddy; there's no lifeguard on duty to save yo' booty. If you turn right at the beach and walk its length, you'll come to a rocky, iguana-filled coast on your left, a cactus forest straight ahead, and gentle lagoon to your right. Pelicans, flamingos, and other folk roost high in the mangroves on the water's edge.

To get to the beach from the town park, walk past the hospital to Calle Charles Binford, turn left, and follow the dirt road out of town for about 200m. Beyond the interesting assortment of island houses stands a sign welcoming visitors to the **Galápagos National Park.** Check out the observation tower standing high on a sheer rock cliff; Tortuga Bay is a pleasant 2½km stroll from the tower. The path is good for birdwatching and meeting other travelers. A closer swimming spot is Las Grietas, a placid grotto on the far side of the water from Puerto Ayora's dock. Ask a *panga* to take you to the other side, then follow the signs. The private beach of the Hotel Delfín is nearby.

If you've always wanted to walk on water but were never sure that you were ready, here's your chance. The Bote con Fondo de Vidrio—**Glass-Bottomed-Boat**—gives views straight down into Academy Bay and surrounding waters. The boat leaves from the Municipal dock at 8:30, 11:30am, and 2:30pm, and costs US$25 per person.

Lonesome George

Lonesome George is a large tortoise who lives at the Charles Darwin Research Center...but George isn't like all the other tortoises. He isn't like any other tortoise anywhere—George is a sad tortoise, the last of a dying race.

Found in 1971, George was the first **Pinta tortoise** (*Geochetone elephantopus abingdoni*) seen in 65 years. Tragically, the story of George's race is all too reminiscent of other tales of endangered species the world over. When pirates and whalers discovered that the tortoises could survive long periods of time without food or water, they rushed to store the animals on their ships as a fresh meat source. The dwindling tortoise population of Pinta suffered another blow when goats drastically affected the island's habitat, further contributing to the demise of George's tragedy-stricken race.

Some think he should live out the remainder of his days on his home island of Pinta, now goat-free. Currently, George remains at the research center, comfortably housed with two lovely lady tortoises from Isabela, genetically his closest relatives. But sadly, it appears that George is far too depressed to think about sex; the females just don't arouse his interest. Researchers are offering a US$10,000 reward to anyone who can supply a female Pinta tortoise, so keep an eye out. Unfortunately, the Pinta is not the only tortoise species in danger. Of the 14 species that originally inhabited the Galápagos Archipelago, five others are in danger and may soon join the three species that are already extinct.

▓ The Highlands of Santa Cruz

For those who haven't quite gotten their sea legs, never fear—the interior of Santa Cruz offers a plethora of land-based outings. One of the best things about these day-trips is that many of them can be visited independently of tour groups or guides. The towns of **Bellavista** (about 6km north of Puerto Ayora) and **Santa Rosa** (8km northwest of Bellavista), though without hotels and almost everything else, do allow camping and are ideal departure spots for nearby hikes. Two popular hiking peaks are **Media Luna,** a crescent-shaped volcanic cinder cone about 5km from Bellavista, and **Cerro Crocker,** about 3km beyond Media Luna. There is a hill near Santa Rosa known as **Mirador** which offers an impressive view of the south coastal area, although one side is blighted by a nearby mine.

Several travel agencies in town offer tours of the highlands which tend to be more convenient but more expensive than doing it independently. Trips usually last around four hours and cost US$15-25 per person. Some charge a flat rate for the car and guide, so if you put together a group and haggle a little it could be quite cheap. Definitely compare the deals between different agencies. The most stylin' way to see the highlands is atop your very own **horse.** Amalca Horse Trekking offers horse trips through a highland farm, up Cerro Crocker, and to Garrapatero, which cost US$15-25, but you need to get to their ranch in the first place; about s/40,000 by round-trip taxi. Contact the Moonrise Travel Agency in Puerto Ayora to arrange a trip.

Buses serve the highlands from Puerto Ayora; the bus stop is on Charles Binford Road (from Parque Central, walk 4 blocks away from the ocean). Tickets may be purchased onboard (6:30am, 12:30, and 4:30pm; s/2,000). Buses follow a circular route, traveling to Bellavista, on to Santa Rosa, then returning to Puerto Ayora via Bellavista once again. Passengers may get on and off at any point on the route. Travelers can also take the CITTEG shuttle to Baltra, which goes all the way across the highlands (8, 8:15, and 8:30am; s/7,000). These buses return full of new arrivals at around noon, depending on where you are in the highlands. Though *Let's Go* does not recommend hitchhiking, it is not unusual for trucks to stop and pick up passengers for a fee similar to that charged by the buses. It is a good idea to head out early in order to ensure catching a ride back into town before dark. While there are no hotels or hostels in the highlands, **camping** is available in Bellavista and at the Tortoise Reserve near Santa Rosa. To camp in Bellavista, contact Spanish-speaking Eddie Gallardo (tel. 526-532), or fax his English-speaking brother, Marcello, at the same number. To arrange camping in the tortoise reserve, contact the National Park system (tel. 526-189).

■ The Tortoise Reserve

Chillin' with the *tortugas* at the Darwin Station is fun, but it can't match the visceral satisfaction of meeting these guys on their own turf. These reptiles are as wild as 250kg tortoises can get, which you can tell by their trails—although slow, they're quite powerful and leave behind a bulldozer-type effect of flattened vegetation and fences. Larger tour groups, fearing the mighty beasts, rarely come here. Because the reserve isn't in a regulated section of the park, visitors are not required to be accompanied by a guide, but a knowledgeable one can greatly enrich the experience. Tortoise sightings, for instance, cannot be guaranteed, but a good guide will know where to look. The tortoises tend to move around according to weather conditions, and at the wrong time and place you could spend all day without that wild tortoise sighting. The trails also can be confusing and many lone tourists have lost their way.

Luscious but lengthy, the (1½-2hr.) hike to the reserve can be a challenge through all the dense, low-growing vegetation. Highland tortoises have gradually developed large dome-shaped shells that enable them to burrow through Santa Rosa's plant growth. Mario Ramón outfits visitors with guides and horses (ask for his house at the Santa Rosa bus stop); each costs s/25,000. Riding to the reserve also provides better views of the surrounding landscape. If you decide to use a guide, you'll have to rent a horse for him or her as well.

The reserve itself offers a feast of sensation. Depending on the time of your visit, the reserve may be a celebration of blooming flora, bursting with bright hibiscus. Red, yellow, and orange *pajaritos* (little birds) dart to and fro, dive-bombing unsuspecting tortoises and occasionally perching on the heads of tourists. No festival would be complete without food, so appropriately the reserve bears many fruits as well: bananas, coconuts, Galápagos oranges, passionfruit for the wild-at-heart, and more exotic fruit. *Guayabanas* are yellow with a pink fleshy inside, about the consistency of a fig; *maracuyas* are yellowish-orange, and filled with a tasty green pulp.

At the end of a day at the Tortoise Reserve, hungry hikers may direct their noses towards one of the two restaurants back in Santa Rosa. **Jolita's** serves up native cuisine in a thatched-roof bamboo hut for only s/5,000 a meal.

■ Los Gemelos

These "twins" are a pair of craters, each approximately 30m deep, on either side of the road to Baltra, just outside of Santa Rosa. Their origin remains mysterious; the holes may have been caused by a volcanic explosion, or they may simply be caved-in magma chambers. But the craters themselves are not the only attraction; the walk through the mist-enshrouded forest can be rewarding on its own. Bird life abounds; witness species such as the vermilion flycatcher, yellow warbler, cattle egret, and the occasional short-eared owl. Yet while birds may be easy to spot, the trail to Los Gemelos from the road is not, especially during the rainy season, when vegetation begins to grow over the path. To ensure your very own encounter with these concave beauties, consider hiring a guide, or get very detailed directions from someone who knows what they're talking about (try Jolita's in Santa Rosa).

Most day-tours of the highlands come here. The quickest way to see the craters is to glimpse them from the bus to Baltra. You can ask the driver to drop you off there, although this is not recommended if you have a plane to catch.

■ The Lava Tunnels

The island of Santa Cruz is riddled with **lava tubes** *(los tunneles)*, the remains of ancient magma flows that helped form the Galápagos Islands. The outer crust of these molten streams hardened as it cooled, but the liquid magma within continued flowing. When it ceased, these empty tubes were left behind.

There are several tunnels around the island, but the most frequently visited is Bellavista's **"Tunnel of Endless Love,"** named not for the Casanova-type guides but rather for the heart-shaped hole in the roof. Though the tunnel is only 800m long, it does begin to seem endless the further you explore. The entrance to the tunnel is a gaping black hole, in sharp contrast to the lush growth around it. A rickety banister provides support, but visitors may choose to take their chances or to hold onto the nearest tree for support. The pathway inside is generally smooth, except for the occasional pile of rubble. The exit, in the spirit of romance, is draped with leaf-covered vines that filter the rays of the sun and the idyllic singing of the birds outside.

The number of tubes and caves open to the public varies. To get there, follow the Carretera al Cascajo out of town for 1km to a large sign announcing the tunnels (the caves are always open; admission s/6,000). If you need a flashlight, Sr. Antonio Gallardo in Bellavista (tel. 526-532), rents them for s/6,000 and provides guides (though none is needed) for s/15,000. Another set of lava pathways are Furio's Tunnels, which are farther from the towns and more often visited by tour groups. These tunnels are shorter but well lit and divided into three levels, connected by slime-coated ladders (admission US$3). There is a pretty but expensive restaurant at the mouth of the tunnels (lunch US$15).

■ Other Sites on Santa Cruz

The far northwest side of Santa Cruz boasts beauteous bays and beaches that can be reached by boat. In the past, daytrips to these areas left from Puerto Ayora, but now most people visit them as part of larger multi-day boat tours and scheduled daytrips are no longer offered. Special day tours, however, can be arranged for groups.

The best of the sights is **Caleta Tortuga Negra** (Black Turtle Cove) on the northern side of the island. Visitors float in *pangas* or kayaks through silent mangrove inlets (all three mangrove types are found here) and experience Galápagos nature at its best. Gradually, dark circular shapes start swimming under the boat—the first glimpse at the Galápagos green sea turtle. Yes, the turtles really are green, not black, as the name of the location and the view under the water imply. Turtle encounters are especially frequent during breeding season (Sept.-Feb.). Visitors watch turtles mating, and some see intense, multiple-hour underwater turtle embraces. The elegant sharks and rays darting around in the water also make Black Turtle Cove an excellent introduction to the Galápagos animal kingdom.

Not far from this site, **Las Bachas Beach,** near the Baltra Airport, makes for a refreshing swim. Bring repellent, though, as the beach is home to stinging flies. **Conway Bay** and **Ballena Bay** (Whale Bay) lie on Santa Cruz's west coast, though neither is often visited. Conway is a good place to see sea lions. **Cerro Dragón,** on the northwest coast between Las Bachas and Conway Bay, is a recently opened visitors' site that doesn't get many visitors. The name comes from the imposing hill, which resembles a very green and hillish dragon. Its summit is reachable by about a 2km hike. The more commonly used trail winds through scrubby vegetation and reveals dragons of another sort—monstrous, cactus-eating land iguanas.

■ Islas Plazas

Of the tiny twin islands, only **South Plaza** (a mere 13 sq. km) is open to visitors. **North Plaza** remains off limits due to mysterious scientific research. While one can only guess what goes on over on the north island, the flat, desert-like interior of South Plaza can be viewed from the rocky trail that circumscribes the island. Reddish vegetation carpets the ground and overgrown **prickly pear cacti** dominate the landscape. The colossal cacti soar over 8m tall—much larger than those found elsewhere in the world. The Galápagos have no large native trees; over the years the prickly pears have grown unchecked, assuming the domineering role usually reserved for water-guzzling hardwoods. Gargantuan land iguanas often lurk beneath these cacti. The iguanas and the cactus fruit bear the same bright yellow hue, and the two share a scintillating tale of evolutionary intrigue. Centuries ago, these reptilian culprits voraciously devoured low-growing flowers. The only cacti able to reproduce were the taller, tree-like plants with large trunks that the chubby iguanas weren't able to climb. Now the skyscraping prickly pears prevail, and the shrunken dragons must wait for their succulent treats to fall to the ground.

On the south side of South Plaza, a set of **cliffs** towers over the ocean waves. These sheer rock palisades provide a bird's eye view of seagulls returning to their nests after a hard day of fishing. Blue-footed and masked boobies, frigatebirds, and lava gulls reside here as well. Keep a lookout for the rare swallowtail gull, with its striking white-and-gray body and large orange eyes. Glance over the cliff to see how easy it is for diving birds to spot schools of fish in the water; sometimes even sharks and eagle rays lurk below. Don't get too close to the edge—even the best boots don't grab limestone the way boobies do. The cliffs are also home to the only colony of bachelor seals on the islands; the old bulls are exhausted after years of courting females, so now they wrestle, tumble, and swim all day. Come nightfall, the slippery animals scale the steep rock wall to reach their refuge above the sea.

When you land on the beach, expect a warm welcome from the unofficial greeting squad of female sea lions and pups that crowd the shores, basking in the sun and frolicking in the surf. Galápagos sea lions bear little resemblance to their docile cousins often seen in zoos; these gregarious animals become visibly excited when human guests arrive. As if to keep the exuberantly immodest females in check, the colony's dominant male, a mammoth bull named Charlie, keeps an eye on his brood from the visitor's dock. Most sea lions love to interact with humans, but large bulls such as Charlie, like most jealous husbands, are best left alone. In fact, sea lions bite several tourists each year, making them statistically more dangerous than sharks. If Charlie doesn't seem particularly excited about letting your group pass through, a few loud hand claps will generally persuade him to move away. Let your guide handle it.

By all means bring a snorkel and mask to South Plaza—few animals make more exciting swimming partners than sea lions. It is easy to lose oneself in the sea lion experience, so bathers should swim with a human buddy too. The furry torpedoes literally surround bathers and swim straight toward them at full speed, only to spiral downward in a series of somersaults at the last second. Because of their location on the equator, sea lions notice none of the changes in seasons and breed year-round; playful pups always pack the waters. If you encounter Charlie underwater, don't be alarmed—he's only patrolling his territory. Give him room by swimming *away* from the island; ignore the impulse to make a quick dash for land. Disposable underwater cameras are now cheap and universally available—consider bringing one along.

■ Isla Santa Fé

Isla Santa Fé doesn't believe in ostentation; she keeps her treasures well-hidden. Like many of the islands, this one teems with life both above and below sea level. Though the sprightly sea lion colony couldn't be discreet if it tried, the elusive Galápagos hawks and snakes, as well as the endemic land iguanas and rice rats, don't often advertise their presence (watch out for spiders).

One of the more concealed island creatures, the crested *Conolophus pallidus* subspecies of **land iguana** is found nowhere in the world but here on Santa Fé. A mere visit to the island, however, doesn't guarantee a sighting. Hide-and-seek champions with a little patience and time to spare stand the best chance of spotting one. The prickly pear iguanas found on South Plaza also call Santa Fé home, but here they are a richer golden color than those on other islands. These gargantuan reptiles commonly measure over three feet long, and some giants even break the four foot mark.

To experience Santa Fé to the fullest, take one of the two easy hiking trails. There is a short 300m path and a longer 1.5km trail that extends into the highland region. Both are somewhat rocky but accessible to most visitors. The longer trail offers a better chance of spotting the iguanas, and it passes the Galápagos' largest prickly pear trees, which at a towering height of 10m couldn't hide even if they wanted to. The trail is also an excellent place to birdwatch and to look for the **Galápagos snake** and **rice rat.** Large **Galápagos hawks** frequent the area, as well as curious **Galápagos mockingbirds** who have been known to land on startled visitors' hats.

One of Santa Fé's best features is the beautiful, sheltered **cove** in its northeast bay. Snorkeling here is no more difficult than hiking, though to be safe you should bring a friend for both. Some groups make sightings before they enter the water—keep an eye out for schools of **eagle rays,** often seen "flying" in perfect synchronization just under the water's surface. **Hawksbill** and **green sea turtles** also hang out in these parts. The latter is endangered in much of the world, but abundant in the Galápagos.

■ Isla Seymour Norte

North Seymour is the thrifty corner store in the midst of the glitzy outdoor bazaars that make up the Galápagos. Convenient and dependable, it delivers the basic wildlife staples—frigatebirds and boobies, sea lions and iguanas—without much fuss or flash. And it's certainly no secret around town—Seymour's central location makes it easily accessible to daytrippers from Santa Cruz. Its proximity to Baltra (which used to be called *South* Seymour) makes it a favorite last stop for boat tours as well.

After making a somewhat slippery dry landing on a set of natural steps, visitors are greeted by hordes of sea lions and swallow-tailed gulls, who love to watch the activity surrounding the landing site. Once on shore, take the red, sandy 2km trail that loops around the island to Seymour Norte's nesting colonies of blue-footed boobies and frigatebirds. The **boobies** strut their stuff across the rocky path, making every effort to draw attention to their technicolor feet. The only sight more amusing than the booby mating dance is that of less-coordinated humans imitating them.

The inflated red pouch of the **frigatebird** is a common sight on most islands, but Seymour Norte is one of the few places where these sleek black birds form large colonies, and one of the only spots where both fabulous subspecies (the Magnificent Frigate and the smaller Great Frigate) nest side-by-side. At first glance it's almost impossible to tell these two birds apart, and after a quick look at a bird manual it's still tough (see **Fauna and Flora,** p. 285). Like many magnificent or great humans in history, the tyrannical frigates prove that they can bully the smaller and weaker. Because their feathers aren't waterproof, frigates don't dive down into the sea to collect fish. Instead, they harass smaller diving birds as they return from the sea; when a startled booby or gull drops its fish, the speedy frigates zoom down and scoop it up. Nesting mothers are also favorite targets—frigates will wait for the birds to begin feeding their wide-mouthed babies, and then swoop down and stick their large beaks right into the booby's mouth to snatch a regurgitated fish.

THE GALÁPAGOS ISLANDS

■ Isla Mosquera

So small that it is often referred to by the diminutive "islet," Mosquera hides quietly between Isla Baltra and Seymour Norte. However, its prime location and proximity to Baltra Airport cause Mosquera to lose any potential anonymity. The first island excited visitors see as they arrive, Mosquera is a common starting point for departing boat tours. Reached via a wet landing, the island contains no visitor trails, so many tourists simply soak in the warm water with the sea lions. Others sprawl across Mosquera's shimmering white sand beach. While the attention-starved sea lions would never admit it, Mosquera really does have more marine life to offer—just take a look at its many tidal pools, each a separate world of activity.

ISLA SAN CRISTÓBAL

Isla San Cristóbal, the second largest island in population and the fifth largest in size, is perpetually a distant second to Santa Cruz as headquarters for Galápagos tourism, despite its airport, location closest to the mainland, and status as the administrative capital of the islands. Although its attractions are only mediocre by Galápagos standards, it's one of the islands you can adequately explore without being on a tour boat. The oldest of the islands, San Cristóbal was formed by the towering volcano **Cerro San Joaquín** (over 896m high) and low-lying lava flows that filled out the southern regions of the island. The northern part of the island is dry and rather barren, but the lowlands are kept moist by humid winds from the south. The island's first settlers founded the towns of **Puerto Baquerizo Moreno** and **El Progreso** to take advantage of the fertile soil and favorable climate. Today the island boasts a naval base and the islands' only radio station. Puerto Baquerizo Moreno has plenty of comfortable places to stay, and an unusual number of sites can be reached by foot and without a guide. There are also a number of interesting daytrips that can be made by *panga* to **Isla Lobos, Leon Dormido,** and the easternmost point in the Galápagos, **Punta Pitt.**

■ Puerto Baquerizo Moreno

Far fewer tourists stay in Puerto Baquerizo Moreno than in Puerto Ayora. But then, San Cristóbal has always had to work just a little bit harder to attract people—its first residents were convicts who revolted and killed their overseer, and it's always hard to correct a bad first impression. The island is more peaceful today—the violence of the first settlers would be unthinkable, as well as far too strenuous, for the nearly 3000 laid-back residents of Puerto Baquerizo Moreno who pride themselves on their town's small size, safety, and peaceful disposition.

Puerto Baquerizo Moreno is the political capital of the Galápagos, but that certainly is not readily apparent. Instead, having a drink has become an art form and failing to take an afternoon siesta is tantamount to breaking the law. You can't beat them, so you might as well join them for conversation and a cold one while overlooking **Wreck Bay,** a smooth harbor with a rough name. Note: the power goes off at midnight, so have your flashlight ready.

PRACTICAL INFORMATION

Tourist Information: CETUR, on Av. Charles Darwin at the center of town—look for the unmistakable pink box topped by the life-sized smiling gray whale: like the whale, this office is more cute than useful. Open Mon.-Fri. 8am-noon and 1-5pm.

Bank: El Banco del Pacífico, Av. Charles Darwin near Av. Jose de Villamil (tel. 520-365; fax 520-368), next to the ocean between the police station and post office. Changes dollars and traveler's checks, higher rates than the mainland. ATM does not accept VISA. Open Mon.-Fri. 8am-3:30pm, Sat. 9:30am-12:30pm.

Airline: SAN/SAETA office, Av. Darwin and Av. Teodoro Wolf (tel. 520-156), in the string of shops on the left. SAN offers flights to Quito via Guayaquil (Mon.-Sat., to Guayaquil s/166,500, to Quito s/188,500).

Buses: All buses leave from the *muelle* at the end of Av. Darwin. **Airport** buses depart several times a day (ask at the SAN office for details). Several buses travel to **El Progreso** in the highlands, daily at 6:30, 7am, 12, and 6pm (s/2,000).

Shuttle Boats: INGALA travels to Puerto Ayora (every Mon. and Wed., 10am); arrive at the *muelle* at least 30min. early. Buy tickets early that day to ensure a seat. Ticket counter moves so ask around; they go on sale at around 7:30am.

Pharmacies: Farmacía Tabavi, Av. 12 de Febrero (tel. 520-235). Open 8am-8 or 9pm). **Farmacía San Cristóbal,** Jose de Villamil, 1½ blocks from El Banco Pacífico. Open daily until 10pm.

Hospital: Hospital Oskar Jandl, Quito and Alsacio Northia (24hr. emergency tel. 520-118), next to the Catedral and museum, is the place to go for tortoise-bite first aid. Open daily 7:30am-noon and 1-4:30pm. A doctor and one or more nurses are on duty 24hr., some English spoken.

Police: Policía National, Av. Darwin and Española (24hr. emergency tel. 520-101 or 520-129). Blue and grey building just before the naval base. One can't help but wonder why such a small town needs such a big police building. Open 24hr.

Post Office: (tel. 520-373; fax 520-373), at the end of Av. Darwin, in the string of shops just past the police headquarters. All mail comes through this office since Puerto Baquerizo Moreno is the provincial capital of the islands—the safest bet for your postcards. Fax service. Open Mon.-Fri. 8am-noon and 2-6pm.

Telephone: Central Telefónica San Cristóbal (EMETEL), Av. Quito (tel./fax 520-104), 4 blocks past Darwin. If you're not wearing shades, put them on and look for the building with blaring blue windows. Fax service. Open daily 7am-9pm.

Phone Code: 05.

ACCOMMODATIONS

Although foreign tourists rarely take advantage of them, Puerto Baquerizo's hotels offer a decent alternative to cramped ship's quarters. **Camping** is sometimes permitted on the beaches surrounding Puerto Baquerizo Moreno and in the highlands at El Junco Lagoon. Natives assure that no permission is necessary, but truly law-abiding campers should inquire at the CETUR office or the Park Information Site, just out of town on Av. Alsacio Northia towards the Grand Hotel.

Hotel Mar Azul (tel. 520-139 or 520-107), head away from the waterfront and turn right on Av. Alsacio Northia; it's on the right. All rooms have ceiling fans and private baths with hot water, but some lack toilet seats. Two shady courtyards filled with large, old trees. Singles s/20,000; doubles s/30,000.

Cabañas de Don Jorge (tel. 520-208; fax 520-100), on Av. Alsacio Northia on the east side of town; turn left at the CETUR office and take Av. Darwin towards the edge of town. Walk up a large set of white stairs, turn left at the flamingo statue, and follow Av. Alsacio Northia as it veers to the left out of town. After the 5min. walk, Las Cabañas are a sight for sore eyes. Each cabin is different and surrounded by palms, cacti, and hibiscus-draped seating areas. Private bathrooms have hot water. One cabin even has a kitchen (breakfast s/8,000). Singles US$10; roughly US$6 for each additional person. Longer stays encouraged. Call for reservations.

Hotel San Francisco, Av. Darwin (tel. 520-304), just across from El Banco del Pacífico. One of the best cheap places to stay, Hotel San Francisco has a rambling indoor courtyard filled with murals, plants, and staircases somewhat reminiscent of the set of Sesame Street. Rooms with fans, black and white TVs, and clean private bathrooms are just s/15,000 per person. There is an in-house *lavandería*.

Hostal Northía, Alsacio Northía and 12 de Febrero (tel./fax 520-041), offers clean rooms as plain as the building's gray exterior. All rooms have fans, hot water, balconies, and firm mattresses, and 4 rooms have TVs. The ground floor houses a restaurant and TV lounge. Singles s/40,000; doubles s/50,000; triples s/60,000.

FOOD

Puerto Baquerizo Moreno may suffer from a lack of many things, but it has good food in abundance. Seafood lovers can sample *ceviche* from just about any restaurant. Juicy morsels abound in the many fresh fruit stands scattered across town.

La Zayapa, Av. 12 de Febrero, one block up from the *muelle.* A bit pricey, but considered by most to be the best restaurant in town. Enormous portions of fish, shrimp, and chicken (s/25,000; lobster s/40,000) served beneath gently rustling palm fronds in the romantic yellow glow of insect-repelling lights. Feel free to grab an after-dinner nap in the hammock. Open daily until 9pm.

Genoa, near the end of Av. Darwin across from the *muelle;* just follow the music and colored lights. Highly recommended, this tin-roofed comfort zone is a great place for *comida típica,* and also sports an exotic assortment of fresh juices.

Soda Bar de Nathalí, on Hernán Melville just off of Alsacio Northía. Yield to your inner carnivore at this shack-like barbecue joint. Wash down that heaping plate of chicken, rice, and beans (s/14,000) with a frothy *batido* (s/5,000).

Restaurante Rosita, Villamil and Ignacio de Hernandez (tel. 520-106). Approaching near cult status in town, Rosita is famous for her fantastic fish. Big *almuerzo* s/ 9,000. Vegetarians can opt for the *arroz con vegetales* (rice and vegetables; not on menu—made to order). Dine indoors or outside under the palm-frond awning.

Galapan, Av. Darwin and Av. 12 de Febrero (tel. 520-292). One of the town bakeries, come for the bready, doughy goodness. Great cookies too. Run by the owner and her 3 daughters, all named María. Open Mon.-Sat. 9am-1pm and 3-8pm.

SIGHTS AND ENTERTAINMENT

A cold drink under a palm tree is all most tourists experience of this small town. You might consider getting your drink to go and taking a walk up to the **Museum of Natural History,** on Alsacio Northia next to the cathedral, for a look at poorly preserved Galápagos wildlife. Compared with the live goods outside, these animals are just depressing but the admission price (s/3,000) also lets you chill with tour mascot Pepe the Tortoise (open Mon.-Sat. 8:30am-noon and 3:30-5:30pm). An **interpretative center,** which will present the wildlife of the islands, is scheduled to be open for summer 1998 on a spot on Alsacio Northía past the Cabañas de Don Jorge.

The best disco in town is the **Blue Bay** near the center of town. Blue Bay cranks out a loud Latin/techno beat every night except Sunday, though groovesters with any pride wait until after Wednesday to bust their moves. Friday and Saturday nights are

---

El Progreso's Progress

The first settlement on Isla San Cristóbal, El Progreso was founded in the 1880s by **Manuel J. Cobos.** Cobos imported a group of convicts to serve as laborers on his sugar plantation, halfway between the highlands and the current capital of Puerto Baquerizo Moreno. His ruthless overseeing practices and slave-labor policies quickly incited an infamous mass-mutiny in which rebellious workers took his life. These days the memory of Cobos lives on, immortalized by the numerous street signs around the island that bear his name.

The small agricultural town he founded also survives, easily accessible by hike or taxi from Puerto Baquerizo Moreno. El Progreso boasts one of the best highland restaurants around, **Quita d'Cristhi.** Never a dull moment, come to enjoy great meat and chicken, stroll through the forest, or nap in a hammock beneath the orange blossoms. Particularly active on weekends, Quita d'Cristhi usually has soccer games, arm-wrestling matches, and particularly heated card games. For a Tarzan-esque sleeping experience, try **La Casa del Ceiba** (tel. 520-248), a large bamboo cabin built 12m off the ground in a gigantic *ceiba* tree. Visitors enter via a hanging bridge made of vine-covered bamboo. The two-story house is completely furnished with two beds, a bathroom, hot water, music, television, a refrigerator, and a complete bar. US$10 a night, tours US$1.

best, and with a little Club beer (s/5,000), things can get pretty wild. The nearby **Neptunus,** next to the *muelle* in the large white house, attracts an older, more touristy crowd. But they still know how to get down (perhaps helped by the slightly more expensive selection of American and European brews). **Terruza Yolita,** on the waterfront next to the lagoon, brings in the younger funksters.

■ Near Puerto Baquerizo Moreno

Most of the sites on San Cristóbal can only be reached by boat, but the few listed below are accessible by foot or by a short truck ride from Puerto Baquerizo Moreno, and can be visited without a guide. Ask at CETUR or your hotel about trucks. For more serious daytrips by boat, talk to Bolívar at **La Zuyapa** or Gustavo at **Rosita's.**

FRIGATEBIRD HILL

Breathe in the fresh air, lace up those hiking boots, and head on up to Frigatebird Hill. The hike up the hill is by no means easy—the trail misleadingly begins with a pleasant walk along a shady, pebble-lined path, and by the end visitors scramble over large boulders in the hot equatorial sun. The view from the top is breathtaking (literally and figuratively)—the red roofs of Puerto Baquerizo Moreno stretch out to one side, with beautiful views of bright white sand and lava rock beaches on the other. Both narcissistically-named species of **Frigatebird** nest here: the Magnificent Frigate and Great Frigate. With wingspans of about 2.3m and bright red, inflatable pouches, they actually do live up to their names. Since these birds only frequent the hill at certain times of year and certain hours of the day, there's no guarantee you'll spot one; consult a guide before leaving town. While hiking, also watch out for the endemic **Chatham Mockingbird,** the only type of mockingbird on San Cristóbal.

To get to Frigatebird Hill, start at the Grand Hotel and continue along the same dirt road for five to seven minutes. The trail head is at the end of the road. A series of rocks on both sides of the trail make it relatively easy to follow, but it is rocky and in places overgrown. Although only 3.5km long, allow two hours for the challenging hike. Be sure to wear good hiking shoes and bring plenty of water.

LA LOBERÍA

Located just outside of Puerto Baquerizo Moreno, this rocky beach abounds with the sounds of the oodles of sea lions. Those who choose to linger until sunset can watch the water darken from crystal clear to bright blue to deep purple; make sure you've got a flashlight for the trip home. La Lobería isn't on any tour company's "must see" list and snooty cruise ships don't come here. To get here, follow directions to Hotel Mar Azul, then take the road out of town (about a 30min. walk). Keep towards the right and don't take the sharp right turn into the Naval Base. When you reach the beach, turn left at the Galápagos park sign. When returning to town, use the same road and walk toward the airport signal tower. Taxis from town cost about s/20,000.

EL JUNCO LAGOON

Earth, wind, fire, and water came together to form the elemental extravaganza that is know as Junco Lagoon. A road winds up the verdant sides of an extinct volcano, reaching at the summit a beautiful lagoon formed by hundreds of years of rain water collecting in the caldera. Frigate birds use the lake as a bathtub, gliding through the mist and cleaning themselves in the fresh water.

A narrow trail winds its way around the perimeter of the rim, past numerous land and sea birds, and overlooks nearly all of San Cristóbal (including León Dormido to the north and Punta Pitt to the northeast). A small portion of the coastline is obstructed, however, by the looming **Cerro San Joaquín** (at nearly 900m, the highest mountain on San Cristóbal). Despite rumors to the contrary, visitors do *not* need to be part of a tour group to visit the highlands. While tours can be arranged in town (ask at Restaurant Rosita or any hotel), the highlands can also be reached by foot or by hiring a truck in town (prices are bargainable, but it should never cost more than US$20). To reach the lagoon, first head 8km east of Puerto Baquerizo Moreno to the town of **El Progreso.** From here, it is 10km farther to El Junco.

■ Other Sites on San Cristóbal

The most popular excursion is to the islands of **Isla Lobos** and **León Dormido** (also called **Kicker Rock**) off San Cristóbal's western shore. These nearby sites are accessible by boat, either as daytrips from Puerto Baquerizo Moreno or as longer tours from other islands. Lobos, the first of the two islands, is about one hour northeast of Puerto Baquerizo Moreno. Separated from San Cristóbal's shore by a small channel, the tiny, rocky island has a white sand beach where blue-footed boobies nest and sea lions sunbathe. Humans, however, only observe the habitat from the 300m trail that cuts across it from east to west. León Dormido, another hour northeast of Lobos, gets its name from its resemblance to a sleeping lion. But whoever named it must've had one mighty imagination; it looks more like a monstrous rock sticking straight up out of the ocean, with a gigantic splinter to one side. Unlike in Aesop's fable, you don't need to remove the splinter to tame this lion and its waters; adventurous captains smoothly sail through the small channel between the sliver and the mother rock. Scuba diving here is prime, but watch for dangerous currents.

The easternmost point in the archipelago, **Punta Pitt,** is another of San Cristóbal's notable sites. Located on the far northeast corner of the island, it takes quite a while to reach from Baquerizo Moreno. But booby fanatics won't think twice about making the trip; red-footed, blue-footed, and masked boobies all call Punta Pitt home. After the landing in a sandy cove, a trail leads up into the mountainous terrain, weaving through swinging booby territory and providing lofty views of the rocky shore below and the sea beyond. One final site in the mountains of San Cristóbal, **La Galapaguera** is just down the shore from Punta Pitt. Giant land tortoises roam free at this site, which is very similar to the Tortoise Reserve on Isla Santa Cruz, but not nearly as easy to reach. As with the Tortoise Reserve, the site is large, trails are badly marked, and tortoises may be hard to come by. An experienced guide is a must.

ISLA ISABELA

Though Isabela is the largest of the Galápagos Islands, making up over 58% of the archipelago's entire land mass, it is one of the most rarely visited. Its lack of a true airport or developed town makes it an unlikely base for tour boats, and the inconvenient location of most of the visitor's sites on the distant western shore renders it logistically infeasible for all the boats except for fast ones or those on extended (10+ days) tours. For those who surmount these obstacles, however, Isabella presents unique wildlife-viewing opportunities and extraordinary geological phenomena. One of the most volcanically active islands, it was once six separate volcanic isles, but lava flows united them into one landmass. Few of these volcanos have lost their steam; eruptions have occurred on **Volcán Wolf, Cerro Azul,** and **Sierra Negra** in the past 20 years, and in 1991 earthquakes shook **Volcán Alcedo.** The towering shield volcanos are truly mastodonic, dominating Isabela's skyline. Those sailing to the western side of the island pass through the narrow **Bolívar Channel** separating Fernandina from Isabela; steaming volcanic fumaroles sometimes flare up, and sometimes groups see dolphins and whales pop out of the water.

■ Puerto Villamil

As of yet, the southern-tip town of Puerto Villamil (pop. 1500) is untouched by commercialization. There is no tourist office, no phone book, and in lieu of a newspaper, people make announcements from a loudspeaker in the center of town. Prickly pears substitute for fence posts and disco lights struggle to compete with the stars above.

Like many small towns, Villamil gossips and gawks. Don't be surprised if an islander invites you in for a bit of conversation; everyone's got a story to tell. Life here is not complicated; all you need to live is four walls, a roof, and a spot on a fishing boat. A stroll at sunset along the Puerto Villamil's coconut-lined beaches makes the exploitative T-shirt shop scene of Puerto Ayora seem a world away.

Practical Information There is no formal tourist office, but the hotel proprietors can generally help you with any question. Town info books are available at the Hotel Ballena Azul and at various shops in Puerto Ayora (s/10,000) but are only really useful for their maps, which you can get for free at the CETUR office in Puerto Ayora. Make calls from the **EMETEL** office, on Calle Las Escalecias, three blocks away from the beach (head towards the big orange antennae). **Buses** leave from the Municipio for the highlands (7am and 2pm, s/3,000-5,000; return trips 7:30am and 2:30pm). **INGALA** (tel. 529-157) travels to Puerto Ayora (every other Fri., 10am, s/110,000). Tickets can be bought after 2pm on Thursday at the INGALA office, 200m past Hotel Ballena Azul on the right. Captain Juan Mendoza takes passengers to Puerto Ayora each Tuesday morning on the municipally-owned **Estrella Del Mar** for s/90,000. Purchase tickets in the municipal offices on Mondays. If you have to get back quickly, or don't like boats, **EMETEBE** flies to Puerto Ayora on Tuesday, Thursday, and Saturday mornings for about US$45. To buy tickets, ask for EMETEBE agent Emma Ramón at the Hotel Ballena Azul. There is no hospital on Isabela, but Puerto Villamil does boast a **health center** (open daily 8am-noon and 2-5pm), on Av. 16 de Marzo, across from El Municipio. In case of an emergency after hours, try calling Dr. Bazan's **private practice** (tel. 529-165), or go to her house in the INGALA compound, 200m past Hotel Ballena Azul. The **Capitania** (tel. 529-101), in the center of town across from El Municipio, knows when boats are leaving and is supposedly open 24 hours. The **Policía** office is next door, but is rarely occupied. Coconut theft has not become a problem.

Accommodations Lodging in Villamil is good, verging on excellent. **Hotel Ballena Azul** and the adjacent **Cabañas Isabela del Mar** (tel./fax 529-125 for both), on Calle Conocarpus at the edge of town, are easily two of the best places to stay in the Galápagos. The large, rustic rooms of Hotel Ballena Azul, with hot water baths, wooden walls, mosquito netting, and ocean views, would have made Hemingway's old man content to simply *look* at the sea (s/12,000 per person, with bath s/20,000). The Cabañas Isabela del Mar are spacious and spotless. Each private cabin fits two or three people, with a ceiling fan to ward off mosquitoes and a private (hot water) bath. Dora, the Swiss mistress of the house, loves to sit down and chat (in English, Spanish, French, or German; s/22,000 per person, singles s/30,000). Ballena Azula has an inexpensive laundry service. The nearby **Hotel Terro Real** (tel. 529-106), is conveniently located on Calle Terro Real—look for the red roofs. Two-story, triangle-shaped bungalows with refrigerators and private baths house four to five people each. Friendly management included in the s/20,000 per person cost. **Hotel San Vicente,** Calle Los Cormoranes and Calle Pinzon Artesano (tel. 529-140 or 529-180), offers basic, clean rooms with private bath for s/12,000 per person. They also allow free **camping.**

Food If you aren't invited to eat in someone's house, the restaurant at the **Hotel Ballena Azul** is the next best thing. Join Antonio and Dora for great local and international food that borders on gourmet. Breakfast of fresh fruit, bread, homemade jam, and coffee s/6,000, with eggs s/7,000. Lunch and dinner (rice, meat, salad, and vegetables) go for s/12,000 (dessert s/2,000 extra). For smoother sailing, let your hosts know in advance if you plan to have lunch or dinner. For the reptilian beachfront feel, try the **Restaurant Iguana,** between the disco and the ocean. This informal nightlife center serves up tasty treats in an atmosphere that can't be beat. Pull up a chair beside the Bob Marley poster and try the tuna pizza (s/13,000). For local food, try one of the restaurants near the Municipio. Many recommend **Ruta,** which serves hot food and ice-encrusted drinks (meals s/7,000), but there's usually only one choice of entree. For a little more selection, head to the nearby **Costa Azul**. Meal of the day costs s/7,000, just like Ruta. A la carte items cost a bit more (mixed *ceviche* s/15,000), but the food is good, and yes, the purple tentacles are octopus.

Entertainment Come weekend, *villamileños* love to drink and dance with the best of 'em. To accommodate these passions, they've built a lagoon-shaped dance floor, complete with driftwood column, right on the beach next to Restaurant Iguana. The men arrive early and nurse their buzzes until the *chicas* arrive. Some guys sip exotic drinks at the bar, but many more go across the street to the **Iguana Bar** (the after dark alter-ego of Restaurant Iguana) for a cold beer. There, fluorescent animal figures lounge outside while a school of pufferfish lights swim over patrons' heads on waves of music and MTV videos. Try a cold Pilsener and watch the sleepy town wake up for the weekend. The town's power shuts down at 11pm, but the Iguana's prized generator keeps its school of pufferfish lights up and swimming until midnight. The disco stays open as long as the scene is still hoppin'.

■ Near Puerto Villamil

The marine site **La Tintorera** is about a five-minute *panga* ride from Puerto Villamil. Ask in town to see who's going, or walk past Hotel Ballena Azul to the docks and bargain with one of the *panga* owners (a group should not cost more than s/40,000). After a short walk, the rocky black lava trail approaches a large channel beside a lagoon. Small fish swim around the narrow channel entrance, but farther up lurks a bigger catch—white-tipped reef sharks. Bilingual marine experts will know that these sharks give the site its name. Far from aggressive, these docile creatures glide in and out of the channel in groups. Only 2 ft. from the trail, cliques of 30 or more bask in the shallows. Some daredevils jump in with the sharks; while this is not dangerous for the humans, it is for the sharks. They scare easily, sometimes cutting themselves on the sharp lava rocks in their attempt to avoid running into clumsy tourists. Best to take a dip in the adjacent lagoon, where sharks swim among smoother rocks. If you're lucky, you could also spot a sea turtle or spotted eagle ray.

For more crazy tortoise action, the **Rearing Center for Giant Tortoises** (tel. 529-178), run in conjunction with the National Park Service, provides up-close looks at Galápagos tortoises in all degrees of giantness (open daily until 4pm). The center focuses on the rearing of two breeds of Isabelan tortoises from eggs to adulthood. To get there, follow Av. Antonio Gil past the health center to the edge of town, where a sign points to the station, another 1km past the stadium on the right.

One last visitor's site near Villamil, **El Muro de Las Lágrimas (The Wall of Tears)** commemorates Isabela's past as a penal colony. In June 1946, then-President José María Velasco Ibarra decided to move 300 prisoners and 30 guards from Guayaquil to the base of "La Orchilla," about 5km outside of Puerto Villamil. With no other means of employing the prisoners, the chief of the penal colony decided to begin construction of a jail with the only substance available—lava rocks. Because of the lack of building materials, the wall was constructed without cement, by simply piling the rocks on top of each other. The extreme variety in the shapes of the rocks prevented efficient stacking. The result was a long pile of rocks, 2-3m high with sloping sides. The grueling hours in the hot sun and back-breaking labor also broke many men's spirits, stealing away their will to live. Over time, it came to be known as the place "where the cowards died and the brave wept." Construction of this "wall of tears" ceased when the sadistic chief was transferred and the colony moved to the highland agricultural area, where it was later abolished in 1959.

To get there, follow Av. Antonio Gil past the health center to the outskirts of town. From there, signs guide the way. The walk takes about two hours and there are several nice lagoons and beaches along the way (including the particularly secluded and aptly named **Playa de Amor**). **Horses** can be rented in town.

ELIZABETH BAY

Elizabeth Bay is a marine visitor site on the western side of Isabela, rife with marine and bird activity. There are no landing sites, so get out those binoculars and hope for a clear day. To the north of the bay lie the **Mariela Islets.** A landscape of rugged cliffs and gnarled trees, these islands are frequented by penguins and *pangas* alike. Be quiet when observing the penguins; despite their formal attire, these birds are quite shy and will turn their backs if startled. Like ostriches who stick their heads in sand, penguins seem to think if they can't see you, you won't be able to see them. Be especially careful during molting season; their feathers are not yet waterproof and they really don't enjoy getting wet, so try not to scare them into the water.

At the other end of the bay, a labyrinth of channels and lagoons snake in and out of an aquatic **mangrove forest.** Clear blue water provides contrast to the sinister-looking roots of the red mangrove. The devious mangroves serve as breeding grounds for several types of fish and green sea turtles. Rays and white-tip reef sharks often make rounds in search of a quick meal. Some tours provide kayaks that make for a more personal mangrove experience; ask about it when you book your tour.

PUNTA MORENO

On the western side of Isabela, Punta Moreno can be one of the most memorable sites of an entire tour. The juxtaposition of craggy lava rocks and small, idyllic lagoons scattered across the landscape is home to varieties of birds—including blue herons and flamingos—who flock to these watering holes. These amazingly sleek birds are mesmerizing in flight. If you visit around mating season, the coloration of the flamingos is particularly vivid, with some birds sporting an uncharacteristic dark red color. The journey to the watering holes from the landing site traverses fields of jagged lava rocks. The black rocks reflect heat and the air is often very dry. Bring plenty of water and sturdy hiking shoes; sandals definitely won't do for this one.

Near Punta Moreno some groups might visit a series of coastal pools, one of which is known as **Derek's Cove.** While it is illegal to go ashore, these pools are an excellent place to observe sea lions and large numbers of sea turtles.

URVINA BAY

Urvina is one of the most surreal sites in the Galápagos. After a wet landing on an otherwise normal-looking beach, a trail leads a short ways to a bizarre, unnatural dreamscape. Coral heads seem to sprout from the sand, and where fish should be swimming, cormorants and iguanas make their homes. This entire area used to be underwater, but was completely uplifted due to volcanic activity by the nearby giant, **Volcán Alcedo,** in 1954. Though no one was present at the time, skeletons of marine turtles, sharks, and even entire schools of fish were found here when a crew of Disney filmmakers arrived on the scene a few days later. The fast-moving animals didn't even have time to escape, testimony to how quickly the uplift occurred.

VOLCÁN ALCEDO

For many years, Volcán Alcedo had been the height of Galápagos adventure for mountain-climbing visitors. The 10km climb led to fantastic views and a 7km *caldera* housing the largest population of tortoises on the islands (5 species, 4,000 individuals). That strength was tested by a recent invasion of voracious goats, driven onto the volcano by Isabela's packs of savage dogs. The dogs have been eliminated but the goats, at home on the scrubby, mountainous terrain, keep breeding. Their exploding population has taken a toll on Volcán Alcedo's vegetation, depriving the tortoises of food and shelter from the sun. The national park has closed the site while its team of expert goat assassins brings the shaggy horde down to size. With limited funds and inhospitable terrain, the eradication program may take years. The volcano cannot be re-opened to visitors until the ecosystem is stabilized. Unless you're a biologist with an uncanny skill at shooting goats, you'll have to put off Alcedo until your next trip.

PUNTA GARCÍA

One of the few sites located on Isabela's eastern side, Punta García used to be one of the best places to see flightless cormorants without traveling to Isabela's western side. Now...well, judge for yourself. Lately the birds have become rarer and rarer, and the number of visitors has declined along with the cormorants. The site also has a small mangrove forest, and lava herons have been spotted from time to time. The terrain is primarily sharp lava rocks, so good shoes are a necessity.

PUNTA ALBEMARLE

Punta Albemarle stands guard over the remote northern tip of Isabela. Passing sailors can see the abandoned water towers of a defunct United States radar base from World War II. Because of the rough sea here, few boats go ashore. Wildlife on Punta Albemarle includes flightless cormorants, fur sea lions, and the largest colony of marine iguana on all the islands.

PUNTA TORTUGA AND TAGUS COVE

A young visitor's site on the northwestern side of Isabela, **Punta Tortuga** is the result of volcanic uplift that occured in 1975 at the base of Volcán Darwin. Like the goddess Venus, this natural beauty was borne from the sea. The mangroves that surround the swimming area here are home to the tool-using mangrove finch. Endemic to Isabela and Fernandina, these talented birds explore tree bark using sticks or cactus spines held in their beaks. After some digging, they usually score a tasty grub or two. When they find a particularly good tool, they stash it away for later use.

South of Punta Tortuga, **Tagus Cove** bears the unmistakable mark of man, like Post Office Bay and so many other Galápagos sites. The "historical graffiti" here dates back to the turn of the century, when sailors scratched their ships' names on the cave walls. Current travelers are encouraged *not* to add their own mark. Instead, follow the trail to the nearby **Darwin Lake,** a saltwater-filled crater. Due to volcanic uplift, the lake lies above sea level. Later, enjoy a *panga* ride along the cliffs of Tagus Cove past flightless cormorants, penguins, and blue-footed boobies.

VOLCÁN SIERRA NEGRA (SANTO TOMÁS)

After two hours of pounding your butt against a tough little *caballo*, the mist parts, your jaw drops, and you tell your butt that it was worth it. The dark, ominous caldera extends in all directions, refusing to fit in even the widest angle lens. Volcan Sierra Negra is the oldest and largest of Isabela's six volcanoes; with a diameter of 10km, it is the second-largest volcanic crater in the world.

A bus from Puerto Villamil stops about 10-20 minutes away from the **crater rim.** The crater itself is often filled with mist and can be rainy during the wet season. For better views and less chance of rain, there's another trail leading around the crater rim to **Volcán Chico,** on the north side of Sierra Negra. Just about a two-hour horse-back ride from the bus stop, it offers excellent views of the crater and impressive panoramas of the rest of the island. One vista reveals Isla Fernandina, Volcán Alcédo, and Isla Santiago simultaneously. Adventurous travelers follow the trail westward along the crater rim to the **sulphur mines.** Just inside the crater, three levels of sulphur formations bubble and steam. Over the years, the geothermal activity has created a landscape of strange formations. Is it just fumes, or really sulphur castles and flowers? Keep an eye out for a hole full of boiling mud that gurgles by onlookers' feet.

Visitors should be in good physical condition, with some riding or hiking experience. Be forewarned: the horses are small and bony and the "saddles" do little more than protect you from horse sweat. It's a great, scenic ride, but because of the distance (2hr. by horse) you may be rushed to make it back in time for the bus (see below). A more leisurely option is to hire private cars (about s/120,000). A cheaper and more hard-core option is camping at the crater rim, which allows unlimited time to see all the sites. Before camping, it's a good idea to talk to the park officials in

Puerto Villamil (tel. 529-178), on Av. Antonio Gil. Remember, fires are not permitted and trash must be carried out. Tents can be rented from Hotel Ballena Azul, though other items (including rain gear) should be brought along.

To get to Sierra Negra independently, take the bus to the highlands that leaves from the Municipio (daily 7am). On Saturday and Sunday, trucks also leave at 6 and 8am. The cost varies (s/3,000-5,000). Catch the bus home between 2:30 and 3pm. A semi-autonomous option is to arrange for a guide and horses to meet you at the bus stop by radioing ahead from one of the hotels in Villamil (try Ballena Azul). The bigger your group, the cheaper the service, but you should be able to hire a guide with horses for around s/25,000-30,000, or you can join an already existing tour group. Tours leave town about three times per week. The ride up the mountain exposes you to sun, rain, and overgrown bushes; long pants, long sleeves, and a rain coat are recommended.

OTHER ISLANDS

▓ Isla Fernandina

An island of superlatives, Fernandina is the newest island in the archipelago, the westernmost link in the Galápagos chain, and the most volcanically active. The last eruption was in January 1995, and experts say **Volcán La Cumbre** could perform again anytime. Perhaps most impressive is Fernandina's lack of non-native plants and animals, a distinction that prompts many to award it the sought-after title of "the most pristine island in the world." In light of the colonization of the other islands by goats, rats, and dogs, Fernandina's purity is surprising. Evidence that some fishermen have been using Fernandina as a campsite has biologists biting their rat-fearing nails. Visitors must be careful not to accidentally transport plants, seeds, or nasty flesh-eating microorganisms onto the island. You may be asked to strip down and stand naked before high pressure water jets in the decontamination tank before stepping into the *panga*. In most cases, you will just be asked to wash your feet.

Fernandina has only one visitor's site, **Punta Espinosa,** a geologic baby formed by tectonic uplift in 1975. The dock here is an outcropping of lava that only allows dry landings during high tide, so be prepared for wet shoes. Snorkelers and scuba divers can explore underwater, and some tours go sea kayaking around the *punta* to a lagoon surrounded by jagged black lava spires and green mangroves. The lagoon is frequented by white-tipped sharks, rays, turtles, and schools of glimmering fish.

On land, the visitor's trail branches in two directions. To the left, the path winds its way over dry fields of *pahoehoe* and *aa* lava, which take their names from similar flows in the Hawaiian islands. Although this walk takes longer, it passes through more interesting and recent lava formations, which guides can often discuss in great detail. Be careful of the *aa* flows, however, as these formations are *very* sharp—wear sturdy, closed-toed shoes.

If your time is limited, try taking the road *more* traveled, on the right. Make your way past all the barking sea lions onto a narrow sandy trail. Afternoon trekkers will likely encounter hoards of **marine iguanas** basking in the sun after a lunchtime feed. Marine iguanas are voracious eaters—after gorging themselves on a meal of seaweed and algae, these social animals stretch out next to (if not on top of) their neighbors to dry out, warm up, and digest their food. These reptiles are excellent swimmers; if forced, they can stay underwater for over an hour. Darwin's "Imps of Darkness" have one more trick up their scaly sleeves. They have evolved a unique way to excrete the salt they unavoidably consume from their seaweed main courses—they blow it out of their noses in a sneezing action. Years ago, pirates thought this "poisonous spit" was an acid; even though it's only salt water, it can pack quite a punch—the excreted salt often shoots three or four feet.

The iguana nests lie on either side of a very narrow sandy path, where blue herons, Galápagos hawks, and other predatory birds look to make a quick meal of their hatchlings. Be careful—any visitor that strays from this path can kill the iguanas before the birds even get a chance. Nesting sites are well concealed and quite fragile; the weight of a human being could easily crush an entire nest. Not too many visitors seem to have strayed from the straight and narrow, though, as just beyond this trail hundreds of iguanas are often dozing in the sun. This prodigious outpouring of animals is due to reptilian hormones plus Fernandina's lack of introduced predators—this is what all the islands must have been like years ago.

Punta Espinosa also offers the opportunity to see the rare **flightless cormorant.** This strange-looking subspecies is only found in the Galápagos; one of the rarest birds in the world, only about 800 pairs exist. For centuries, the birds have had no predators on the islands and thus no need to fly, so while most cormorant wings are large and impressive, those of the flightless cormorants have grown short and stubby. The birds instead rely on their powerful legs for swimming and catching fish. The cormorants have odd nest-building habits, too: every time a bird returns to the nest, it brings some new sort of decoration. By the time the chicks are grown, the nests are eclectic masses of seaweed, stones, and shells. Before returning to the boat, stroll past the mangrove forest just beyond the shore. This shaded area sometimes serves as a nursery for sea lion pups while their mothers fish.

▦ Isla Santiago (James, San Salvador)

To put it bluntly, Santiago rocks. In the face of catastrophe, this resilient island has triumphed time and again over the destructive forces of volcanic activity and mankind's influence. Its volcanic cones, beach-front lava spires, gentle *pahoehoe* lava flows, and black sand beaches are reminders of the island's explosive past. The first humans to inhabit the island were 16th-century pirates who used the island's canopied coves as hideouts. But it wasn't until the 1880s that the most irreparable damage was done, when four rather amorous goats were abandoned on the island. The goat population soon ballooned to over 100,000 and the gluttons ate everything in sight. Since then, environmentalists with voracious appetites for conservation (and goat stew) have managed to keep the population in check. Many a tour boat is rumored to still serve Chiva de Santiago. The island was further sullied in the 1920s and 60s by two commercial salt mines that unsuccessfully attempted to profit from the island's salt-lined crater. Several rusty buildings built during these periods still stand near the western shore; tearing them down would cause more damage to the island than letting them stand. Despite its turbulent past, there is much to see and do on Santiago. Its central location makes it easily accessible, and its four visitor sights are among the best in the Galápagos. The island is a destination on nearly all tour itineraries.

■ Puerto Egas

Over the years, wind and currents have carved unique sand formations in the black sand beach of Puerto Egas in Santiago's **James Bay.** Apertures, crevices, and natural bridges form a masterpiece at the island's most impressive visitor sight. The alcoves are perfect nesting spots for sea lions seeking refuge from the glaring equatorial sun.

A short trail from the beach leads to one of the best tide pool areas in the Galápagos. Gleaming sandy beaches contrast with black lava towers, basins, and craters, filled with crystal-clear sea water. Scattered over the coastline, each pool is its own universe, teeming with numerous schools of tiny fish, sea anemone, oysters, and hermit crabs. Lucky groups might even see large Galápagos eels and beautifully colored octopi. Sea birds also abound; lava herons, ruddy turnstones, oyster catchers, terns, and other birds often gorge enthusiastically near the tide pools. Look under warm rocks for the small Galápagos scorpion. These little fellows aren't really a threat, but the slippery lava rock along the tidal area is, so be very careful when walking.

Past the tide pools visitors come to what, for many, is the highlight of a trip to Isla Santiago: the **grottoes.** These pools, formed by the island's numerous lava flows, are constantly filled and refilled by the open sea. One pool, appropriately dubbed **Dar-**

win's Toilet, fills with a particularly noisy flushing force. Clear, gently circulating waters surrounds swimmers, while lava arches and natural bridges tower overhead. Fish, seals, and sea lions swim in and around these pools.

Snorkeling and scuba diving are popular activities around these parts, but check with your guide before taking a dip, as a swim in the grottoes at the wrong time is less than idyllic. Currents and tides rush through quickly, and unlucky swimmers may find themselves at the mercy of the sea. If the tide is changing, it's best to watch from the side and let the seal and sea lion experts do their thing. The ocean teems with turtles, tropical fish, eels, and even sharks, rays, and **Galápagos fur seals.** Technically fur seals are not seals at all, but rather a species of smaller sea lion with pointed ears and more fur. The rich pelt of these animals was once very much desired and hunted by humans; one boat in the Galápagos killed 50,000 in a period of three months.

NEAR PUERTO EGAS

A 2km path from Puerto Egas leads to the summit of San Salvador's **Sugarloaf Volcano (Pan de Azúcar).** Because of the challenging rocky terrain and the heat absorbed by the black lava, this short distance can be an exhausting two- to four-hour hike. Water and sturdy shoes are a must. At the 395m summit, views of James Bay and the two tuff cones at Sullivan Bay simply stun. A less strenuous 3km trail leads to the **salt crater.** There is a good view from the top, but the walk there is not as aesthetically pleasing as the hike up Sugarloaf. Remnants of human presence are juxtaposed with the otherwise pristine area. Houses and leftover equipment from salt mines mar the landscape. Cats, pigs, rats, and goats have also caused obvious damage. The thin gray branches of the gnarled *palo santo* (holy stick) trees are often used as incense in Ecuadorian churches. Sniff the sap to experience wholly the tree's divine aroma.

At the north end of James Bay, visitors have the chance to see a slightly different type of wildlife—ducks and flamingos at **Playa Espumilla.** The site is accessible via a wet landing on a sandy beach. Be careful where you step, as sea turtles often lay their eggs here. A 2km bird-watching trail into the interior passes one of the island's inland lagoons. These lagoons bustle with activity; be quiet and you might come across a few flamingos. They aren't hard to spot—Galápagos flamingos are among the most colorful in the world because of the keratin in the bright pink shrimp they eat.

■ On Isla Santiago

BUCCANEER COVE

An impressive reminder of the renegade pirates that used to dwell here, **Buccaneer Cove** is located at the northwest end of Isla Santiago. After climbing volcanoes, swimming with sharks, and hiking across lava fields, a visit to Buccaneer Cove is a pleasant change of pace. The site's landscape and sheer cliff walls are most impressive from the sea, but true sea dogs will jump ship or brigand snorkeling.

Pirates frequented this cove in the 1600s and early 1700s, later followed by visiting whalers. Today it is populated by feral goats that do as much damage to the landscape as the pirates did on the high seas. Plant and animal diversity is not Buccaneer Cove's strongest attraction, but the cliffs themselves are amazing. Apparently, sailors watched the passing pinnacles and rock formations with the same imagination people use when looking at clouds. Watch out for "The Monk" and "Elephant Rock."

SULLIVAN BAY

Santiago's final visitor's site is the unique **Sullivan Bay,** on the east coast of Isla Santiago. The most interesting part of this bay is not the water itself, though snorkeling is decent. Rather, its "beach" is completely unlike the typical sandy specimens lining most shores. Sullivan Bay's solid black fields were formed by a *pahoehoe* lava flow, and there's not a grain of sand in sight. This flow is only about 100-years-young (new by geological standards), and a walk across it can be a sizzling experience, especially for those interested in volcanos and island formation. Pockets of water and gases trapped under the lava, known as *hornitos,* exploded to form the wrinkles breaking up the smooth black span. If you look closely, you can find the pioneer plants taking a foothold in cracks in the land. The actions of these hardy specimens and their successors will eventually break the lava into inhabitable soil. Be sure to notice the "islands within the island": two tuff cones that were once their own autonomous rocky isles—before the sudden attack from all sides by Santiago's quick-flowing lava. The one- to one-and-a-half-hour trail loops around the bay. As with all lava walks, proper footwear is necessary, as are water and sunscreen.

▓ Isla Bartolomé

You know that picture of the Galápagos in which a wind-sculpted spear of rock juts defiantly over a blue sea with a white-crescent beach underneath? That's Bartolomé. Although only 1.2 square km, the island's striking geology makes it one of the most stunning to visit—deep reds, blues, and shimmering blacks mingle and shift over each other, creating a kaleidoscopic landscape. Dominated by an ancient volcano of stark and imposing beauty, this barren island consists of ash and porous lava rock on which colonizing plants are just beginning to grow. The *isla* boasts two visitor sites: the **summit** of the volcanic cone and the **twin crescent beaches,** with the only colony of Galápagos penguins this side of Isabela (a wet landing site).

The easy trail to Bartolomé's summit begins as a set of natural stairs that are a sunbathing spot for marine iguanas. Further along the trail, lava lizards dart back and forth, rarely stopping long enough to allow spectators to get a good look. On a clear day, the view from the summit enables climbers to grasp the immensity and uniqueness of the archipelago. North Seymour, Daphne Major and Minor, Santa Cruz, Sombrero Chino, Isla Sin Nombre, and Santiago are visible from here; some appear truly mastodonic, while others are tiny knolls sticking out of the water. From here it is easy to understand why Bartolomé is compared to the surface of the moon—unearthly craters coated with black ash surround the volcano and fill the shallow beaches.

On the way down, take time to notice colonizing plants growing on the island. The **lava cactus** (*Brachycereus nesioticas*) has developed a unique method of forming its own soil. These spiny banana-shaped plants grow bright green arms from a central stalk, and as old growth decays, it falls to the side, generating its own natural fertilizer. A less inspiring sight is the erosion on either side of the trail. This gradual destruction is the result of the large number of boat-tours and daytrippers who visit the island each year. If it continues, it will eventually seriously damage the fragile landscape. For your own safety and that of Bartolomé, it is imperative to stay on the path.

Bartolomé's **twin beaches,** lying on either side of the island, double your pleasure. Before landing at the beach, it is advisable to change out of hiking boots into something more beach-and-seaworthy; some brave souls try to go barefoot, but are quickly discouraged when they hit the hot island sand. Swimming is only permitted on the North Beach. Powerful tides and currents, wandering sharks, and stingrays make the South Beach worse for swimming, but top-notch for nature-watching. Look for nesting sea turtles from late December to early March, and great blue herons year-round.

On the North Beach, the massive **Pinnacle Rock** (the one in the pictures) points majestically to the sky. This "rock" is made up of tightly packed sand shaped by the wind and sea. As with everything in the Galápagos, Pinnacle Rock is still changing; the Swiss cheese holes caused by the wear-and-tear of the elements will eventually cause the Rock to crumble into the sea. The oceanside base is a popular place to try to spot the Galápagos penguin *(Spheniscus mendiculus),* an endemic bird markedly smaller than its Antarctic cousin. Though shy when it comes to nesting, the birds will let people get quite close in water; snorkelers in the bay get quite a sight of these slippery sun worshippers swimming by.

▓ Isla Rábida

As if embarrassed of its English name "Jervis," the sheepishly small island of Rábida constantly blushes, its beaches glowing with maroon and deep scarlet hues. Just south of Santiago, Rábida is near the exact center of the Galápagos archipelago. After a wet landing, visitors usually encounter a number of animals resting in the shade of nearby caves or under mangrove trees. Here's a shocker—sea lions top the list of beach bums. Past the mangroves lies a small lagoon where flamingos occasionally dwell. This is also one of the island's few nesting sites for the brown pelican, among the largest birds in the Galápagos. Travelers may want to lace up some sturdy shoes and continue along the walking trail to a small cliff overlooking the inlet; sharks and manta rays are sometimes sighted.

▓ Isla Española (Hood)

Española brings out the birdwatcher in all of us. The southernmost island in the archipelago, Española's distance from the rest of the chain may well be its greatest asset, as it has induced a number of the archipelago's avian inhabitants to settle down and raise some chicks. The secluded wildlife has gone to evolutionary lengths never imagined—most people couldn't come up with such wild coloration and species diversity in their dreams. On most of the Galápagos, visitors have to climb mountains, scale cliffs, or snorkel their way into the heart of it all, but Española presents nature at its in-your-face best. Don't let Española's distance deter, as a visit to this remote island is the highlight of many an island tour. Not all boats go here though, especially not those departing from Santa Cruz, so travelers should take special care to make sure Española is on their itineraries. Upon landing at **Punta Suárez,** visitors are besieged by barking sea lions hungry for attention (as if the spoiled suckers don't get enough).

PUNTA SUÁREZ

Boats reach Española via one of the more exciting soaking-wet landings, on Punta Suárez, a visitor's site covering the island's western tip. They anchor rather far out, so you'll have to take a *panga* to the island, riding waves and dodging large rocks (not to mention those increasingly annoying sea lions). When disembarking a *panga,* especially on Española, grab your guide hand-to-elbow. This grip gives a stable hold—*pangas* tend to jostle and a mere hand clasp just doesn't cut it.

One of the trails from Punta Suarez provides a prime view of the island's famous **blowhole.** A seaside cliff on the south end of the trail provides the perfect vantage point to watch wave-powered spray soar over 25m into the air. Incoming waves rush through a lava tube and get forced out of narrow volcanic fissures at the end, producing a geyser effect powerful enough to make the folks at Yellowstone nervous. The unstoppable force of the ocean meets the volcanic shore in a fantastic face-off.

Perhaps alerted by the squabbling sea lions, the endemic **Española Mockingbird** curiously observes most groups. Slightly larger than its relatives on other islands, the Española subspecies also has a longer, curved beak. A communal bird, it travels in small tribes called "family groups." This is the only known occurrence of communal behavior in mockingbirds. Don't be surprised if these tricksters land on your head or shoulder and try get a look at the contents of your knapsack. A short ways down the visitor's path, proudly strutting **blue-footed boobies** have claimed the trail for themselves. These grayish, duck-shaped birds caress the rocks with their sensuous blue feet, honking and whistling. The newly renovated Punta Suárez trail winds its way into one of the archipelago's primary booby nesting grounds. These birds normally raise two eggs annually; parents take turns standing over them for incubation, encircling each egg with bright blue, webbed blankets. Males and females look quite similar but there are ways to tell them apart. Female boobies have larger eyes and voice their opinions by honking, while beady-eyed males answer with an unmistakable whistle. Sex distinction becomes crucially important when watching the boobies' mating dance, which not surprisingly focuses on those unforgettably sexy feet.

However, the most famous wildlife spot on the island is the nesting area of the **waved albatross,** the only one on the planet. They breed here between mid-April and mid-December. This striking bird, who has made guest appearances in Disney flicks like *The Rescuers Down Under* and *The Little Mermaid,* combines elements of grace and ungainliness in a way only the albatross can. The stately bird is a creamy blend of brilliant white and yellow, with gray wings spanning up to 2.5m. However adept in flight, these birds have a hard time getting it together enough to land. Be patient as the albatrosses glide to the cliff's edge, put their feet down, and stumble to a halt. Albatrosses mate for life but romantically renew their vows each year, re-performing their complex mating dance, a five-day spectacle involving strutting, stumbling, honking, and a good deal of beak-fencing. They say it's better than dating.

GARDNER BAY

White sand, white sand, and more white sand. Though that's the majority of what you'll find here, the beach is far from humdrum. Waves crash and sea lions dance themselves into a frenzy in desperate competition for an audience. Divided into two sections by an outcropping of lava rock, the long, open shoreline is one of the few places in the Galápagos that is completely safe to explore without a guide. Visitors planning to walk the entire length of the beach should bring sturdy shoes. This type of independent, Darwinesque exploration is often the most rewarding—look for an endangered species, or maybe even discover a new one. Snorkeling is possible in Gardner Bay, but is usually more rewarding nearby at the aptly named **Turtle Rock.** You might also spot white-tipped sharks and colorful parrotfish cruising the shallows.

■ Isla Floreana

The Galápagos islands have their own set of rules and nothing, least of all the animals, behaves conventionally. Separated from the motherland by nearly 1000km of open ocean, the islands provide a holistic separation that allows arrivals here to carve out unique ways of life. Española received the extraordinary mating habits of the waved albatross; Isabela became home to the anomalous behavior of the Galápagos penguin; Floreana got strange people.

The town of **Puerto Velasco Ibarra** is sometimes visited by tourist ships, like the Tip Top 11, owned and operated by Rolf Wittmer, one of the first natives of Floreana. Rolf's mother, Margret (see **Murder in the Galápagos,** below), runs the small **Pensión Wittmer** (tel. 520-150, in Guayaquil 04-244-506), the only place to stay on Floreana. Rooms with private baths, hot water, and an ocean view go for s/20,000 (breakfast s/ 10,000; lunch or dinner s/15,000). Pensión Wittmer also sells autographed copies of Margret's book, *Floreana,* and stamped letters for the post office barrel.

POST OFFICE BAY

Sometime in the 18th century, a British whaling captain erected a post office barrel on the quiet bay of an uninhabited island. The island was later named Floreana, and for a long time its barrel was the only postal facility for hundreds of miles. Whaling ships from around the world left their letters in the barrel and picked up those addressed to their next destination. Although the first post-barrel is now long gone, the tradition is kept up by the island's many visitors every year.

Today's visitors get to the post-barrel via a wet landing at a brown beach on Floreana's northern shore. From there, the barrel is not far away. Today's barrel is quite different from the original, bare-bones one left by the British whaler so long ago. No longer content with simply leaving letters, numerous visitors have added signs, pictures, and other wooden messages to this growing piece of public art. Drop off a postcard or two and see if any are addressed to an area near you. When you get home, drop it in the mail, or if possible, deliver it personally. Who knows, maybe it could lead to a sordid romance in the spirit of Floreana.

Murder in the Galápagos

Isla Floreana received its first residents in 1929, and hasn't been the same since. **Friedrich Ritter,** a German doctor and devoted follower of Nietzsche, retreated from society with **Dora Strauch,** his patient and lover. Their goal: to create an untainted community of two, dedicated to the healing powers of the mind. Before coming to the island, Ritter insisted that both he and Dora have all their teeth removed and **stainless steel dentures** made; one pair was soon lost, so the couple had to share. Over the next five years, more and more goofy Germans moved to the isolated isle. The temperamental **Baroness** von Wagner de Bosquet blew into Floreana like a hurricane, dressed in riding pants and tall leather boots, with a revolver in one hand and a **whip** in the other (presumably to keep her own two lovers in line). Of course, she could have used it to crack the tension in the air when she proclaimed herself **"Empress of Floreana,"** a declaration that went over big with Ritter and his dreams of intellectual isolation. But in 1934, the baroness suddenly disappeared with one of her lovers, and the mutilated body of the other was found on the beach of a distant island, mummified by the sun. Moreover, Dr. Ritter, a vegetarian, mysteriously died from poisoned chicken. Onlookers say he cursed Dora with his dying breath; she lived only long enough to write the book *Satan Came to Eden* before falling victim to that curse. Today, one of the less eccentric of Floreana's original residents, **Margret Wittmer,** still lives on the island. Nobody ever proved any foul play, but ask Margret if she ever picked up on any fishy smells during the whole sordid mess.

PUNTA CORMORANT

Floreana's colorful history is notorious around these parts, full of wacky stories about meat-eating vegetarians and communal dentures (see **Murder in the Galápagos,** above), but Punta Cormorant takes on more conventional hues—red mangroves, gray hillsides, pink flamingos, white sands, blue waters, and glistening green stones. Visitors arrive at this sight via a wet landing at the northern end of the island, on a beach littered with thousands of small, green beads. This unique crystal, known as olivine, was formed centuries ago as a volcanic by-product. A short walk through several different regions of vegetation leads to one of the few colorless sites at Punta Cormorant—a dark, murky, mangrove-encircled lagoon. Flashy, filter-feeding, fluorescent-feathered flamingos add life to these dusky waters. While captive flamingos are fed a mixture of shrimp and red dye to achieve their characteristic color, the coloration of the **Galápagos flamingos** is naturally maintained by their diet of bright pink shrimp. The graceful flamingos stand in sharp contrast to the gnarled, gray *palo santo* trees on the hillsides surrounding the lagoon.

Another site at Punta Cormorant, **Flour Beach,** may have the softest, cleanest sand ever to grace the human foot. Visitors who fail to take off their shoes might never forgive themselves. Shadowy, gray ghost crabs and green sea turtles frequent this beach. The latter come at night to lay eggs, but only one out of 100 survive as frigates, sharks, and other predators anxiously await the turtles' birth. Finally, keep an eye on the shallow waters of Flour Beach's quiet cove; large numbers of sting rays come here to feed. If you enter the water when the rays are around, shuffle your feet as you enter to give these barbed creatures ample time to squirm away. Snorkeling and swimming here are pretty good, but if possible, don't miss a chance to snorkel at Devil's Crown.

DEVIL'S CROWN

At one time, this underwater visitor's site just off the coast of Punta Cormorant was a submerged volcano. Subsequent eruptions and the powerful ocean eroded the cone into a jagged ring of black lava spires rising from the sea floor. Yield to your temptations to descend into this dark world of devilishly good underwater delights. Devil's Crown offers some of the best snorkeling in the islands, thanks to currents that bring

THE GALÁPAGOS ISLANDS

in tons of fish and coral. Snorkelers should be cautious; these same currents can be dangerous if ignored. Listen to the guide's instructions and use common sense.

The island's morbid history often prompts potential swimmers to joke about the odds of a close encounter with a shark. The chance of seeing these elegant creatures is actually very real—both white-tipped reef sharks and hammerheads frequent the area. Despite their incredible speed and fierce appearance, these animals are not aggressive; the skittish hammerhead rarely approaches if snorkelers are in the area. For the best odds of seeing a shark, remain calm, quiet, and close to your guide. Enjoy the lava rocks and fish below, but keep an eye on deeper waters, where groups of sharks sometimes cruise past. While the chance of seeing something big gets the adrenaline flowing, the often-ignored world of the small is amazing as well. Starfish, sea cucumbers, sea urchins, and eels also lurk in Devil's Crown.

■ The Northern Islands

The distant northern islands (**Pinta, Marchena,** and **Genovesa**) are rarely visited by one-week touring boats, as the sail here takes about eight to 10 hours and the seas are usually rough. Many residents and guides list secluded Genovesa as their favorite island. A visit to Genovesa Island (often known as **Tower Island**) is particularly rewarding for those salty enough to make the trip—attempt to go if you have the time. Genovesa has two visitor sites, both accessible via **Darwin Bay** on the east end of the island. At the wet landing site, the bright coral of **Darwin Beach** contrasts sharply with the bay's deep green color. After passing a tidal pool section, the trail enters a wooded area of salt-bushes and mangroves where a red-footed booby colony builds its nests (the only Galápagos species to nest in trees). In addition to boobies, visitors to this island often see frigatebirds, Galápagos doves, and the beautiful red-billed tropic bird. Genovesa's other visitor site, **Prince Phillip's Steps,** is also an excellent birdwatching area. The rocky trail winds its way through several colonies of nesting sea birds to a wooded area (keep an eye out for short-eared owls and red-footed boobies), continues to a large lava field where hundreds of storm petrels dwell, and finally ends at the cliff's edge. Don't think that all life on Genovesa is avian. A look from the cliffs into the bay might offer a glimpse of another animal often spotted here: the hammerhead shark. Marchena Island offers excellent scuba diving, but has no land visitor sites and is therefore only visited by diving tours. Pinta, with its collapsed volcano, is closed to the public as well.

APPENDIX

HOLIDAYS AND FESTIVALS

Consult the **South American Explorer's Club (SAEC),** (tel. (607) 277-0488; fax 277-6122; http://www.samexplo.org; email explorer@samexplo.org. In Quito, Ecuador; tel./fax (593) 2-225-228; email explorer@saec.org.ec), or the tourist office **CETUR,** (tel. 514-044 or 507-555), for the dates of art exhibitions, theater and music festivals, and sporting events. CETUR offices around Ecuador can provide specific information. Where possible, *Let's Go* lists specific 1998 dates in individual cities. Be aware of them, as banks, restaurants, stores, and museums may all close, potentially leaving you broke and hungry.

Date	Festival	English
		National Holidays
January 1-6	El Año Nuevo	New Year's Day, with festivals throughout the week
January 6	Festividades de los Reyes Magos	Festival of the Three Kings (Epiphany)
late Feb.-early Mar.	Carnaval	Carnival
April 9	Jueves Santo	Holy Thursday
April 10	Viernes Santo	Good Friday
April 12	El Día de Pasqua	Easter
May 1	Día de Trabajador	Labor Day
May 24	Fiesta Cívica Nacional	Battle of Pichincha (Independence Day)
July 24	Napalece de Simón Bolívar	Birth of Simón Bolívar
August 10	Aniversario de la Independencia de Quito	Independence of Quito
October 9	Aniversario de la Independencia de Guayaquil	Independence of Guayaquil
October 12	Aniversario del Descubrimiento de las Americas	Discovery of America
November 1	Día de los Santos	All Saints Day
November 2	Día de los Difuntos	All Soul's Day
November 3	Aniversario de la Independencia de Cuenca	Independence of Cuenca
December 6	Aniversario de la Fundación Española San Francisco de Quito	Foundation of San Francisco de Quito
December 25	La Navidad	Christmas Day
		Regional and Folkloric Holidays
February 12	Aniversario del Descubrimiento de los Ríos Amazonas	Discovery of the Amazon River
February 27	Recordación de la Batalla de Tarqui, Día del Civismo y la Unidad Nacional	Commemoration of the Battle of Tarqui, National Unity Day
May 4-10	Fiesta del Durazno	Peach Festival (Gualaceo)
April 19-21	Feria Agrícola, Ganadera, Artesanal, e Industrial.	Farming, Cattle, Handicraft, and Industrial Fair (Riobamba)

APPENDIX

May 2-3	Fiesta de la Cruz	Festival of the Cross
May 11-14	Feria Agrícola e Industrial de la Amazonía	Agricultural and Industrial Festival of the Amazon
June (59-61 days after Easter)	Corpus Christi	Corpus Christi
June 24	Fiesta de San Juan	Saint John the Baptist's Day
	Fiesta del Maiz y del Turismo	Corn and Tourism Festivals (Sangoloqui)
	Gallo Compadre, Vacas Loca, Castillo, y Chamiza	Rodeo Day (Calpi)
June 29	Festividad de San Pedro y San Pablo	Saint Peter's and Saint Paul's Day
July 16	Celebración de la Virgen del Carmen	Celebration of the Virgin of Carmen (Ibarra)
July 22	Aniversario de Catonización	Canonization Anniversary in Pelileo
July 23-25	Aniversario de Fundación de la Cuidad de Guayaquil	Anniversary of the Foundation of Guayaquil
July 29-August 3	Santo Domingo de los Colorados	Celebration of Saint Domingo of the Colorados (Calpi)
August 3-5	Independencia de la Cuidad de Esmeraldas	Esmeraldas's Independence Day
August 10	Festividades de San Lorenzo	San Lorenzo Festivities (Pillaro)
	Fiesta de San Jacinto	San Jacinto Festivities (Yaguachi)
September 2-15	Fiesta de Yamor	Festival of Yamor (Otavalo)
September 6-14	Fiesta de Jora	Festival of Jora (Cotacachi)
September 20-26	Feria Mundial del Banana	Banana's World Fair (Machala)
September 24-28	Fiesta de los Lagos	Festival of the Lakes (Ibarra)
November 4-11	Aniversario de la Independencia de Latacunga	Independence of Latacunga
December 28	Los Santos Inocentes	All Fool's Day
December 31	Incineración del Año Viejo	New Year's Eve

CLIMATE

The following chart gives the average high and low temperatures in degrees centigrade (Celsius) and the average yearly rainfall in centimeters during four months of the year. The Galápagos are 1000km off the Pacific coast, Guayaquil is on the Pacific coast, and Quito is in the northern Andes.

Temp in °C	January		April		July		October	
Rain in cm	Temp	Rain	Temp	Rain	Temp	Rain	Temp	Rain
Seymour Island, Galápagos	30/22	2.0	31/24	1.8	27/21	0.0	27/19	0.0
Guayaquil	31/21	23.9	32/22	11.7	29/19	0.5	30/20	0.8
Quito	22/8	9.9	21/8	17.5	22/7	2.0	22/8	11.2

To convert from °C to °F, multiply by 1.8 and add 32. For an approximation, double the Celsius and add 25. To convert from °F to °C, subtract 32 and multiply by 0.55.

°C	-5	0	5	10	15	20	25	30	35	40
°F	23	32	41	50	59	68	77	86	95	104

TELEPHONE CODES

Ambato	03	Guayaquil	04	Portoviejo	05
Azogues	07	Latacunga	03	Puyo	03
Babahoyo	05	Lima	1	Quito	02
Cotopaxi	03	Loja	07	Riobamba	03
Cuenca	07	Macas	07	Tena	06
Esmeraldas	06	Machala	07	Tulcán	06
Galápagos	05	Otavalo	06	Zamora	07

Ecuador	593
Perú	51

TIME ZONES

The Ecuadorian mainland is five hours behind Greenwich Mean Time, equivalent to North American Eastern Standard Time. The Galápagos Islands are an additional hour behind. There is no change for Daylight Savings, as the days and nights are always the same length due to Ecuador's location on the equator.

MEASUREMENTS

The metric system is used almost universally throughout Ecuador. For help with the conversion:

1 inch = 25 millimeter (mm)	1mm = 0.04 inch (in.)
1 foot (ft.) = 0.30 meter (m)	1m = 3.33 foot (ft.)
1 yard (yd.) = 0.91m	1m = 1.1 yard (yd.)
1 mile = 1.61kilometer (km)	1km = 0.62 mile (mi.)
1 ounce = 25 gram (g)	1g = 0.04 ounce (oz.)
1 pound (lb.) = 0.45 kilogram (kg)	1kg = 2.22 pound (lb.)
1 quart = 0.94 liter (L)	1 liter = 1.06 quart (qt.)

Comparative Values of Measurement

1 foot	= 12 inches	1 cup	= 8 ounces (volume)
1 yard	= 3 feet	1 pint	= 2 cups
1 mile	= 5280 feet	1 quart	= 2 pints
1 pound	= 16 ounces (weight)	1 gallon	= 4 quarts

Electrical Current

110 volts. 60 cycles. AC is the standard voltage in Ecuador. This is the same as in North America, but is not compatible with Europe and Australia. Ask first, though, as some places might have alarm-clock-melting 220 volt outlets. If you're planning to rely heavily on electricity, bring ample adapters and converters, including one for converting three prongs to fit two-pronged outlets. Many hotel rooms won't have outlets, or will have only one (which is taken up by the fan).

INEFAN-APPROVED TOUR COMPANIES

INEFAN, the government's National Park Administration, has approved the following tour companies for these protected areas. Once agencies are approved, they tend to maintain that status. To check whether a company is still approved, or whether a company not listed has since been approved, contact Edgar Rivera at the INEFAN office in Quito (tel./fax (02) 506-337; open Mon.-Fri. 8am-4:30pm) or try one of INE-FAN's general information numbers (tel. 541-988, 541-955, 507-630, 548-924, or 563-816; fax 564-037).

Reserva Faunística Cuyabeno: Jungaltur, Kempery Tours, Turisamazonas Turismon, Transturi , Native Life Travels, Nomadtreck, Selvanieve Expediciones, Crucero Fluvial Harpia, Rainforestur, Etnotur.
Parque Nacional Cotopaxi: Exploratur, Agencia de Viajes Surtrek, Etnotur, Cretertur, Pamir Adventure Travels, Aventura Flying Duthcman, Expediciones Andinas.
Parque Nacional Machalilla: Agencia de Viajes Pacarina, Agencia de Viajes Surtreck, Señor Elpidio Parrales Caiche
Parque Nacional Sangay: Expediciones Andinas, Exploratur
Reserva Faunística Chimborazo: Expediciones Andinas, Exploratur

LANGUAGE

Even if you speak no Spanish, a few basics will help you along. Any attempts at Spanish are appreciated and encouraged, and you'll find that many people in larger cities understand some English. Learn the vocabulary of courtesy as well; you'll be treated more kindly if you are polite to those around you (see **Customs and Manners**, p. 50). Those who already know Iberian Spanish will find that many common nouns and expressions are different in Ecuador. You are likely to hear *indígena* languages in addition to Spanish.

Pronunciation is very regular. Vowels are always pronounced the same way: *a* ("ah" in father); *e* ("eh" in escapade); *i* ("ee" in eat); *o* ("oh" oat); *u* ("oo" in boot); *y*, by itself, is pronounced like i. Most consonants are the same as English. Important exceptions are: *j* ("h" in "hello"); *ll* ("y" in "yes"); *ñ* ("gn" in "cognac"); *rr*, (trilled "r"); *h* is always silent; *x* has a bewildering variety of pronunciations.

Let's Go provides phonetic approximations for particularly tough town names. Stress in Spanish words falls on the second to last syllable, except for words ending in "r," "l," and "z," in which it falls on the last syllable. All exceptions to these rules require a written accent on the stressed syllable.

PHRASEBOOK

English	Spanish	English	Spanish
			Phrases
Hello	Hola	**Good-bye**	Adiós/Hasta Luego
Yes/no	Sí/No	**How are you?**	¿Cómo está?
Sorry/Forgive me	Lo Siento	**No problem**	No/ningún problema
Please	Por favor	**Thank you**	Gracias
Excuse me	Con permiso, disculpa	**You're Welcome**	De nada
Good Morning/Afternoon	Buenos días/tardes	**Good Evening/Night**	Buenas noches

When?	¿Cuándo?	**What?**	¿Qué?
O.K.	O.K./Está bien	**Where is...?**	¿Dónde está?
Who?	¿Quién?	**Why?**	¿Por qué?
My name is...	Yo me llamo....	**I am from...**	Soy de....
What is your name?	¿Cómo se llama?	**It's a pleasure to meet you**	Mucho gusto de conocerlo/la
What's up?	¿Qué pasa?	**Pardon/me**	Perdón/perdóneme
How much does this cost?	¿Cuánto cuesta?	**Is (Joanna) available?**	¿Está (Joanna)?
Go away/Leave me alone	¡Déjame (en paz)!	**Stop/enough**	Basta
I don't understand	No entiendo	**Could you please repeat that?**	¿Podría repetirlo, por favor?/Otra vez, por favor
Please speak slowly	¿Podría hablar más despacio, por favor?	**Could you tell me?**	¿Podría decirme?
Could you help me?	¿Podría ayudarme?	**What time is it?**	¿Qué hora es?
Good Appetite	Buen provecho	**Help!**	¡Socorro!

Directions

(to the) right	a la derecha	**(to the) left**	a la izquierda
next to	al lado de	**across from**	enfrente de
straight ahead	todo derecho	**(to) turn**	dobla
near	cerca	**far**	lejos
above	arriba	**below**	abajo
traffic light	semáforo	**corner**	esquina
street	calle	**block**	cuadra
How do I get to...?	¿Cómo voy a...?	**How far is...?**	¿Qué tan lejos está?
Where is...street?	¿Dónde está la calle...?	**What bus line goes to...?**	¿Qué línea de buses tiene servicio a...?
When does the bus leave?	¿Cuándo sale el autobús?	**Where does the bus leave from?**	¿De dónde sale el autobús?

Numbers

one	uno	**two**	dos
three	tres	**four**	cuatro
five	cinco	**six**	seis
seven	siete	**eight**	ocho
nine	nueve	**ten**	diez
eleven	once	**twelve**	doce
fifteen	quince	**twenty**	veinte
twenty-five	veinticinco	**thirty**	treinta
forty	cuarenta	**fifty**	cincuenta
one hundred	cien/ciento	**one thousand**	mil

Food

breakfast	desayuno	**lunch**	almuerzo
dinner	cena/comida	**dessert**	postre
drink	bebida	**water (purified)**	agua (purificada)
bread	pan	**rice**	arroz
vegetables	legumbres/vegetales	**chicken**	pollo
meat	carne	**milk**	leche

APPENDIX

eggs	huevos	coffee	café
juice	jugo	tea	té
wine	vino	beer	cerveza
ice cream	helado	fruit	fruta
cheese	queso	vegetarian	vegetariano
soup	sopa or caldo	main course	segundo or plato fuerte
fork	tenedor	knife	cuchillo
spoon	cuchara	cup	una copa, taza
napkin	servilleta	the check, please	la cuenta, por favor

Times and Hours

morning	mañana	afternoon	tarde
evening	tarde, noche	night	noche
today	hoy	yesterday	ayer
tomorrow	mañana	week	semana
month	mes	year	año
midday	mediodía	midnight	medianoche
early	temprano	late	tarde
open	abierto	closed	cerrado
What time is it?	¿Qué hora es?	When is it open?	¿A qué horas está abierto?

Other Helpful Words

embassy	embajada	consulate	consulado
post office	correo	hospital	el hospital
alone	solo(a)	friend	amigo(a)
good	bueno(a)	bad	malo (a)
happy	feliz, contento(a)	sad	triste
hot	caliente	cold	frío
I am hot/cold	Tengo calor/frío	It's hot/cold out	Hace calor/frío
How do you say...?	¿Cómo se dice...?	I'm lost	Estoy perdido(a)
How old are you?	¿Cuántos años tienes?	Where do you live?	¿Dónde vives?
Are there rooms?	¿Hay espacio?	Are there student discounts?	¿Hay descuentos estudiantiles/para estudiantes?
No poking	No empujar	I like Shakira	Me gusta Shakira

GLOSSARY

A **abanico**   fan

aduana   customs

aguadito de mero   fisherman's stew

agencias de viaje   travel agency

aguardiente   very strong liquor

aguas termales   hot springs

aire acondicionado   air-conditioned (A/C)

ají   red Peruvian chili used in criollo cooking

albergue (juvenil)   (youth) hostel

alcaldía   mayoral district or headquarters

almacén   (grocery) store

	almuerzo	lunch, midday meal
	amigo/a	friend
	arroz	rice
	arroz con mariscos	rice with seafood
	arroz con menestras	rice with lentils or beans
	artesanía	arts and crafts
	avenida	avenue
	ayllu	a kinship-based Inca clan (see p. 39)
B	**bahía**	bay
	baño	bathroom or natural spa
	barato/a	cheap
	batido	n: a shake (fruit and milk); adj.: whipped or beaten
	biblioteca	library
	bistek	beefsteak
	bodega/tienda	convenience store
	borracho/a	drunk
	barrio	neighborhood
	bocaditos	appetizers, at a bar
	botica	drugstore
	boletería	ticket counter
C	**caballo**	horse
	cabañas	cabins
	cabildos abiertos	town councils during the colonial era (see p. 40)
	cabina	cabin, often just used to refer to a hotel room
	cachos	croissants
	cajeros	cashiers
	caldera	coffee or tea pot
	caldo	soup, broth, or stew
	caldo de balgre	catfish soup
	caldo de pata	hoof soup
	calle	street
	camarones	shrimp
	cambio	change
	camino	path or track
	camioneta	small, pickup-sized truck
	campamento	campground
	campesino/a	person from a rural area, peasant
	caneliza	a drink made from boiling water, aguardiente, cinnamon and lemon juice (see p. 53)
	canta de monte	Andean tapir
	cantina	drinking establishment, usually male dominated
	carne asada	roast meat
	carne a la plancha	grilled beef
	caro/a	expensive
	carretera	highway
	carro	car, or sometimes a train car
	casa de cambio	currency exchange establishment

APPENDIX

casado/a	married
casas antiguas	mansions
caseríos	hamlet/small village, often unregulated by govt.
caseta de larga distancia	long-distance phone booth
catarata	waterfall
cena	dinner, a light meal usually served after 8pm.
centro	city center
cerca	nearby
cerros	hills
cerveza	beer
ceviche/cebiche	raw fish marinated in lemon juice, herbs, veggies
chica/o	girl/boy
chicha	a liquor from the Oriente made from fermented yucca plant and human saliva (see p. 53)
chifa	Chinese restaurant
chuleta de chancho	pork chop
chompas	sweaters
churrasco	steak
churriguerresco	rococo (in the style of the 18th century Spanish architect Churriguerra)
coche	car
colectivo	municipal transit bus
coliseo	coliseum
colonia	neighborhood in a large city
comedor	small local restaurant (Ecu.); dining room (Peru)
comida corrida	multi-course *á la carte* meal
concha	shell
consulado	consulate
correo	post office
cordillera	mountain range
Cordillera de los Andes	Andes mountain range
corvina (fried)	sea bass (fried)
criollos	people of European descent born in the New World (see p. 40)
cruz roja	Red Cross
cuadra	street block
cuarto con dos camas	a room with 2 beds; **con una cama:** with 1 bed
curandero	healer
D desayuno	breakfast
descompuesto	broken, out of order; or spoiled/rotten food
de turno	a 24-hour rotating schedule for pharmacies
discoteca	dance club
E embajada	embassy
emergencia	emergency
encebollado	stew flavored with onions
encocados	seafood cooked in coconut milk
encomiendas	estates granted to Span. settlers in L. Amer. (p. 39)
estrella	star

	extranjeros	foreigners
F	farmacía	pharmacy
	ferrocarril	train
	ficha para larga distancia	calling coin/card which makes long-distance calls
	fiesta	party, holiday
	finca	a plantation-like agricultural enterprise or a ranch
	frontera	border
	fumaroles	hole in a volcanic region which emits hot vapors
	fútbol	soccer
G	ganga	bargain
	gorra	cap
	gorro	hat
	guatita	grilled stomach
	guayaquileño/a	a native of Guayaquil
H	habitación	a room
	hacienda	ranch
	hackney, ryan	tortoise-food
	hervido/a	boiled
I	iglesia (**Católica**)	(Catholic) church
	impuestos	taxes
	indígena	indigenous, refers to the native population
J	jugo	juice
K	kilo	kilogram
	kuraka	the chieftan of an Inca clan (see p. 39)
L	ladrón	thief
	lago/ laguna	lake
	langostino	jumbo shrimp
	larga distancia	long distance
	lavandería	laundromat
	lejos	far
	limeños	natives/residents of Lima
	lista de correos	the general delivery system in most of Ecuador
	llapingachos	potato and cheese pancakes
	loma	hill
	lomo	sirloin steak
M	malecón	pier or seaside thoroughfare
	maneje despacio	drive slowly
	menú del día	fixed daily meal often offered for a bargain price
	mercado	market
	merienda	late afternoon snack
	mirador	an observatory or look-out point
	mita	a system of forced labor imposed upon indigenous communities by the colonial Spaniards (see p. 39)
	mitayos	workers under a system of forced labor
	mordida	literally "little bite," bribe
	muelle	wharf
O	obraje	primitive textile workshops

	oficina de turismo	office of tourism
P	panadería	bakery
	panga	motorboat
	parada	a stop (on a bus or train)
	páramo	highland plain
	parilla	various cuts of meat, grilled
	parque nacional	national park
	parroquia	parish
	paseo turístico	tour covering a series of sites
	payaso	clown
	peligroso/a	dangerous
	peña	folkloric music club
	picante	spicy
	piropo	jibe, verbal wolf-whistle, or flirtatious remark
	pisco	a traditional Peruvian liquor made from grapes
	plátanos	banana; plaintain
	playa	beach
	policía	police
	pollo a la brasa	roasted chicken
	pueblito	small town
Q	quiteño/a	a native/resident of Quito
R	rana	frog
	reloj	watch, clock
	riobambeño/a	a native/resident of Riobamba
	ropa	clothes
	rosero	a thickened fruit beverage (see p. 145)
S	sala	living room
	salchipapa	french fries with fried pieces of sausage
	salida	exit
	salsa	sauce (can be of many varieties)
	salsa/merengue	Latin dances
	seco de cordero	pieces of lamb in a flavorful sauce
	seco de gallina	pieces of chicken in a flavorful sauce
	seguro/a	noun: lock, insurance; adj.: safe
	semana	week
	Semana Santa	Holy Week
	SIDA	the Spanish acronym for AIDS
	solo carril	one-lane road or bridge
	supermercado	supermarket
T	tapaos/tapados	meat/fish covered with plaintain and wrapped in
	tapetes	carpets
	tarifa	fee
	terminal terrestre	bus station
	tienda	store
	tipo de cambio	exchange rate
	trucha	trout

Index

Numerics

INDEX

INDEX

★Let's Go 1998 Reader Questionnaire★

Please fill this out and return it to **Let's Go, St. Martin's Press,** 175 Fifth Ave., New York, NY 10010-7848. All respondents will receive a free subscription to *The Yellowjacket,* the **Let's Go Newsletter**.

Name: _____

Address: _____

City: _____ **State:** _____ **Zip/Postal Code:** _____

Email: _____ **Which book(s) did you use?**_____

How old are you? under 19   19-24   25-34   35-44   45-54   55 or over

Are you (circle one)   in high school   in college   in graduate school   employed   retired   between jobs

Have you used Let's Go before? yes no **Would you use it again?** yes no

How did you first hear about Let's Go? friend   store clerk   television   bookstore display   advertisement/promotion   review   other

Why did you choose Let's Go (circle up to two)? reputation budget focus   price   writing style   annual updating   other: _____

Which other guides have you used, if any?   Frommer's $-a-day   Fodor's   Rough Guides   Lonely Planet   Berkeley   Rick Steves   other: _____

Is Let's Go the best guidebook? yes no

If not, which do you prefer? _____

Please rank each of the following parts of Let's Go 1 to 5 (1=needs improvement, 5=perfect). packaging/cover   practical information   accommodations   food   cultural introduction   sights   practical introduction ("Essentials")   directions   entertainment   gay/lesbian information   maps   other: _____

How would you like to see the books improved? (continue on separate page, if necessary)_____
_____

How long was your trip? one week   two weeks   three weeks   one month   two months or more

Which countries did you visit? _____

What was your average daily budget, not including flights? _____

Have you traveled extensively before? yes no

Do you buy a separate map when you visit a foreign city? yes no

Have you seen the Let's Go Map Guides? yes no

Have you used a Let's Go Map Guide? yes no

If you have, would you recommend them to others? yes no

Did you use the Internet to plan your trip? yes no

Would you use a Let's Go: recreational (e.g. skiing) guide gay/lesbian guide   adventure/trekking guide   phrasebook   general travel information guide

Which of the following destinations do you hope to visit in the next three to five years (circle one)? South Africa   China   South America   Russia   Caribbean   Scandinavia   other: _____

Where did you buy your guidebook? Internet   chain bookstore   independent bookstore   college bookstore   travel store   other: _____